THE
Bassler Family
in Focus Through Photos,
Diaries and Letters

SUSAN BASSLER PICKFORD

ISBN-10: 1508954372

ISBN-13: 978-1508954378

Library of Congress Control Number: 2015909842

CreateSpace Independent Publishing Platform, North Charleston, SC

CONTENTS

DEDICATED

To

Our ancestors who had the courage
to leave the old and familiar
and strike out for the new and unknown
willing to work hard and accept difficult challenges

And to

The United States of America
the adopted homeland that provided the
stability of government,
the protection of laws, the separation of church and state
and the economic opportunities
to succeed.

INTRODUCTION

This is the genealogy of Honorable William G. Bassler and his sister, Susan Bassler Pickford. It is our family story and it is a typical American story. What may not be typical is the extraordinary amount of primary source materials that have been preserved.

I began this genealogy while in high school on a large piece of brown cardboard. The technology changed as I continued working, on and off, for the next fifty years. The internet opened many portals from the comfort of my desk, but actually putting foot down on family sites and visiting graveyards added a depth of feeling I had not expected.

It is not a definitive study but merely a jumping off point. I hope it speaks to future genealogists and historians in the family to fill in the gaps and correct errors as they come to light and more information becomes available, as it most surely will.

I was fortunate to have many published records including a *History of Mercer County*, PA.; *A History of the Town of Chazy*, Clinton County, NY; *A History of Alburgh*, VT; *The Annals of Henry County*, Vol I 1885-1900 Compiled by Kathleen White Miles; *Benson Hubbardton and Sudbury Cemetery Inscriptions*, Rutland County Vermont Recorded April and May 1993 by Margaret R. Jenks; *Tennessee Records of McMinn County, McMinn County Tombstone Inscriptions* Vol. 3; *History of the General Synod of the Evangelical Lutheran Church* 1748-1845-1904 by Rev. Ellis B Burgess, Published by authority of the Synod by the Lutheran Publication Society Philadelphia 1904; journals; diaries; lists; obituaries, newspaper clippings; notes and family stories to help me with this task. My cousins, Patricia Kerr Pavlic, Doreen Kerr Heitzer, Carl Sherman, Jr., Don Sherman, Shari Sherman Mayer, Waneta Wallace Smith and Connie Smith contributed valuable information and photographs. I traveled to the Adams Historical Society in Gettysburg, PA; to the Vermont Historical Society in Barre, VT; to the Benson Museum in VT; to the Henry County Museum in Clinton, MO and to various places in Virginia following Pastor Bassler's <u>Diary of a Journey to Virginia</u>. I wrote to historical societies, I used Ancestry.com and of course I "surfed" the web. This quest has taught me the importance of oral tradition and the importance of grandparents as trustees of family lore. I have been able to document many stories remembered from my childhood and only time and energy prevent me from validating the existence of others, but I do not doubt their truth.

There are quiet heroes and patriotic heroes but few public heroes in this story. Some have achieved modest fame but most have been content to work hard, raise their families and hope for a better future. So we are typical. As far as I know, all strands originated in Europe from France, Germany, England, Ireland and Scandinavian countries..

I begin the story with my mother, Ethel Marion Kerr and her parents – James Chauncy Kerr and Roxanna Jaxtheimer, and then continue with my father, Sherman Gilbert Bassler and his parents – Julia Elizabeth Sherman and William Gottlieb Bassler.

CHAPTER 1

THE KERRS

Roxanna Jaxtheimer   *James Chauncy Kerr*

Ethel Marion Kerr was born 22 December 1908 in Greenville, Pennsylvania. She was the second child and only daughter of Roxanna Jaxtheimer and James Chauncey Kerr

James Chauncy Kerr was born 14 July 1873 in Greenville, Pennsylvania to James Kerr (1 August 1839) and Mary O'Riley both born in Ireland and married in Pennsylvania in 1863. Mary died in 1902. James was born in County Tyrone, a second son to Patrick Kerr from County Armagh and Ann Hallagan from County Tyrone. Patrick died in NY City in 1865. James came to the United States in 1860 on a sailing vessel 31 days in crossing. In 1862 he went to Corey, PA where he worked on the Atlantic and Great Western Railroad helping to grade and lay the rails on that great thoroughfare. Later he was made section foreman and afterwards removed to Greenville. After the Great Western was merged into the Erie Railroad system he still remained foreman. He served on the Erie Railroad from 1877 to 1902. His sister Ann Kerr had been the first to emigrate to the United States. (*History of Mercer County p.489*)

If Ann was typical, then she found work as a domestic.

James and Mary had six children live to adulthood: five boys and one girl. John, residing in Meadville, PA was an engineer on the Erie railway. He married and had two children. Patrick lost his life by accident on the Erie railroad while running his locomotive. He was an engineer though only twenty-two years of age. James Chauncy was an engineer for the Bessemer & Lake Erie Railway. Brothers Harry residing at Greenville, was an assistant store-keeper working for the Bessemer & Lake Erie Railway, and Charles E. of Greenville, an engineer on the Bessemer & Lake Erie Railway. One daughter Annie never married

James Chauncy Kerr's parents died before he married. He always said his mother would have liked Roxy. It was also said that James did not get along with his mother and left home when he was sixteen. He did not graduate from high school. A poignant story told by his daughter recounted that he held up one spoon and said: "This is all I have from my family."

James Chauncy came from a family of nine but three died in infancy. Tragically his little sister was hit by a train while his father was supposed to be minding her. The child ran onto the tracks behind the house and was struck and killed

Many years later, Ethel, his daughter, recounted that after James left home he began working as a fireman shoveling coal for the Buffalo and Erie RR. After four years with that corporation he resigned his position to become the stationary engineer for the Buffalo Electric Light Company of Buffalo, New York but a desk job wasn't for him. He missed the open road. So after a year he returned to railroad work with the Pittsburgh, Bessemer and Lake Erie Railroad and Ohio Company. In 1895 when James was twenty-five he worked as a brakeman on the Pittsburgh, Shenango and Lake Erie railroad. An unidentified newspaper cutting saved in his wife's Bible recounts an interesting anecdote about Jimmie Kerr in the 50 Year's Ago section.

> Jimmie Kerr "the handsome young brakeman of the P.S. & L.E" was a busy fellow. Recently Kerr officiated as a peace maker but won the ill will of a chap who wouldn't pay his fare, a Regular Army soldier home on furlough. One night later the soldier and four of his friends were at the Shermansville station armed with bludgeons and as soon as the train stopped rushed up the steps to the attack. It seems that Kerr had in pickle a shillalah that his great grandfather had used at Donnybrook and this he laid over the heads of the wild men from Shermansville as they reached the platform. It required 30 stitches to repair the leader of the attacking force.

What is amazing is that his granddaughter Doreen Kerr Heitzer inherited the shillelagh from her father, Marvin. She found the old newspaper clipping in her Grandmother Roxy's bible.

James belonged to the Brotherhood of Locomotive Engineers, No 282, to the Benevolent and Protective Order of Elks, No. 145 and was a member of the Meadville-Taylor Hose Company for fifteen years. He was allowed to work through World War II and didn't retire until he was seventy.

James Kerr in his railroad uniform.

James Kerr most likely met Roxanna at a dance and was smitten with her beauty as she was with his good looks. Their daughter, Ethel, recalled that the handsome couple often led the promenade around the dance floor in the custom of the time. They had a brief formal courtship and although Roxanna had some misgivings, she married James Chauncy on 15 October 1902 in St. Michaels's Roman Catholic Church, Greenville, Pennsylvania. She was twenty-five and James was twenty-nine.

After they married, they lived in a small cottage on the Jaxtheimer property. It was close enough that Roxy's father could hear James yelling and reportedly said: "What's the matter with that fellow. I gave him my best girl." They soon saved enough money to build a house in Greenville. James gave up smoking cigars at this time to help in the effort. They started a family. Robert Edward was born on 15 March 1906 and Ethel Marion was born 22 December 1908. Marvin J was born 5 October 1909.

During her childhood Ethel recalled her mother falling so ill that Roxy's sister came down from Greenville to stay with the family. Ethel remembered going next door to have her hair combed by a neighbor. It is not fair to speculate what might have caused this illness. Roxy had three young children close in age and her family was 55 miles away by train. She may have suffered from post-partum depression, a condition not understood at that time or any number of ailments. Or simply suffered disillusionment over her marriage to a difficult man.

Roxy and Ethel 1909

Ethel related the following story about her father: he was standing outside a drinking establishment in town when his brother happened by and said: "What are you doing here, boyo?" The family saw themselves as lace curtain Irish and frowned upon the stereotype of the drunken Irishman. However, James did like the theater and theater people. I was told that Ethel was named for the actress Ethel Barrymore.

Tragedy befell the Kerrs more than once. As mentioned, Patrick , a beloved son and brother died while operating his engine. Years later James Chauncy would accidentally kill a little girl who had run onto the tracks when he was an engineer. He kept a picture of this child on his bureau. There may have been another child who was run over by him because engines could not stop on a dime. Any infractions were punished by lay-offs without pay,

225 N. Elm St., Butler, Pa
The Kerr home for over sixty years.

so Roxy and Jim always had to have savings just in case of such an event.

When Ethel was three or four her parents sold the home that they had built in Greenville and moved to 225 N. Elm Street, Butler, Pennsylvania. James, now an engineer on the Baltimore and Ohio Railroad, found it was easier for him to be situated in Butler and Roxy enjoyed being able to walk to Church and the stores. The family was registered with St. Paul's Catholic Church and the children attended the elementary school run by the Sisters of Mercy. In later years Roxy would walk to St. Peter's church catering to German worshippers because it was closer and James would continue to worship at St. Paul's which catered to Irish worshippers.

Roxy enjoyed playing the piano for her own pleasure. *Rustles of Spring* by Christian Sinding was one of her favorites, but James only remembered one recital piece that he would play from memory when pressured by his grandchildren. Ethel was given piano lessons. Both of her parents had taken piano lessons from the same teacher when they were youngsters in Greenville and even performed in the same recital; although they did

First Grade St. Paul's Elementary School, Butler, PA
Ethel about 6 years old; 3rd row up 2nd from right

not know each other then. Music was always an important part of family life. They had a piano and they had a Victrola and many records including the Irish tenor, John McCormack. Ethel's brother Robert played the saxophone in a band. They often practiced in the living room. Roxy wanted to give Marvin singing lessons but he declined. Marvin was a star basketball player winning a college scholarship to Allegheny College. He unfortunately lost that and attended Slippery Rock College but did not graduate.

Because the family pronounced their name "Kerr" to rhyme with "cur," unlike the actress Deborah Kerr who pronounced her name to rhyme with "car," Ethel's brothers would came to her defense when boys inevitably taunted her with "cur dog." All the children attended Butler Public High School. Ethel loved high school so much so that she wanted to do a fifth year but instead went to Pittsburgh Musical Institute (PMI) which had been one of America's most prestigious music schools for forty-eight years. Two thousand

8th Grade graduation St. Paul's Elementary School Butler, PA
Ethel front row fourth from left

students were enrolled when Ethel attended. For the first year she lived with her maternal, Aunt Mame, in Pittsburgh but later roomed with fellow students. This was a happy time.

When Ethel looked at this graduation picture, she pointed herself out and said: "All the girls in the front row have their ankles crossed but look at my feet, I'm ready to bolt!"

Ethel was a sensitive child who was very close to her mother and afraid of her father because of his volatile temper. James traveled a lot and was absent for days on end. Ethel and the rest of the family were fine with those absences. Ethel suffered from hearing loss due to ear infections. She also hated math drills. Not usually found in the modern classroom, drills could cause terror for some as the questions went up and down the aisle and you had to be ready. Sr. Bertha struck Ethel during a math drill for not paying attention. Roxy went down to the school and told the nun she wasn't to hit her daughter again because

her hearing was impaired due to the ear infections. Ethel never liked math or the sisters, although she did take piano lessons from a nun for some years until her mother seeing her talent sent her to a woman in town. Ethel played at many recitals, but she did not allow her mother to attend any of them and Roxy deferred to her daughter's shyness. Ethel hated to leave Butler Public High School but loved PMI and the city of Pittsburgh when she got there.

Ethel remembered her father fix-

Ethel's long tresses

"the bob"

Ethel (1925) and Marvin (1926) Butler High School portraits.

ing her breakfast and brushing off her coat before she took the train down to Pittsburgh. The family set great store on appearances. They also kept a close watch on Ethel's social life. However, Roxy fought hard for her daughter's right to date. Something she and James argued heatedly about. James' sister, Annie, never married because according to Roxy she was too well chaperoned, a fate she did not want for her daughter. So Ethel was free to date in Pittsburgh but there were limits. Ethel told of dating a suave older man in Pittsburgh who said: "I don't want to be the one to give you your first alcoholic drink." The family put a quick stop to her dating another man when they found out he was married. Nor was she allowed to string along more than one gentleman at a time. Those were her mother's rules.

As mentioned, during her first year away from home, Ethel lived with her mother's sister, Mary, nicknamed "Mame." Mame had married John LaSalle, a banker, and lived in Pittsburgh. They had no children but kindly took in a baby, Ethel (Bunny) following the death of Mame and Roxy's sister, Hannah Keane, who died after childbirth. Hannah's children were John, Katherine, Jeanette, Ethel, Philip, Rita and Edward. Hannah died three days after giving birth to Edward (Sonny) who was raised by his paternal grandparents, the Keanes. James and Roxy took in Jeanette. Ethel saw her as a little sister and later she was her maid of honor.

Ethel spent happy times as a child visiting her Aunt Mame in the summer and later as a young woman. Her aunt lived a more cosmopolitan lifestyle than her mom did in Butler. She treated Ethel to white gloved lunches at posh hotels and arranged swim dates at the Judge's pool next door. Aunt Mame was affluent enough to have a cook and a maid. There were always fresh flowers on the table and finger bowls. Ethel did say that her mother's cooking was better and that even the services of a cook didn't guarantee a gourmet dish without input from the lady of the house. But Ethel developed a taste for the good life and refined sensibilities.

Ethel Kerr early 20's

Roxanna was a skilled seamstress and made her husband's dress shirts but stopped when she felt her labors weren't appreciated. She made Ethel's complete wedding trousseau. She was active in the Rosary Altar Society and made altar linens for the parish. She was adept at figuring out directions and would help her neighbor, Till, decipher complicated knitting instructions. She learned how to quilt from her German grandmother, Katherine Wiand and made beautiful hand stitched quilts. Her bedroom held a large wooden frame that her son Robert made. It took her a year to finish a quilt which she would work on during the winter months listening to the radio. Roxy went to great lengths to treat everyone fairly. Every child and grandchild was given one of these precious works of art. Jeanette Keane returned home when her father remarried but didn't like the situation and asked to return to the Kerr's. This says a lot about the family. Roxanna and James welcomed her back. Roxy was devoted to her children and grandchildren despite unhappiness in her marriage.

Ethel said James liked Roxy's family and was happy when they came to visit. On Saturdays Roxy baked bread for the week. She cooked and always had cookies ready for after school snacks. At Christmas the grandchildren received homemade sweaters and mittens. She taught her granddaughters how to play the piano and how to cut quilt squares and began to teach knitting and crocheting to me while I lived in their home. Ethel, Bill and I lived with them for five years. Both grandparents remained supportive of the family and never spoke a word of rebuke to us or badmouthed our father in any way. In retrospect I see this as heroic. Roxy and Jim, however, continued to have their personal tiffs and loud voices and slammed doors were common.

Roxy took great pride in her family and was content to live comfortably middle class all her life. She was sad to see her sister, Mame, have to contend with adjusting to a lower standard of living after her husband lost his job at the bank in the wake of the 1929 crash and refused to take work that he felt was beneath him. There was a family lesson here and Ethel understood it. Years later when Mame was diagnosed with cancer, she would take the train to Butler to sit with her older sister, Roxy, on the Kerr's front porch. It was where she wanted to be.

Roxy announced in 1952 and again in 1956 that she voted for Adlai Stevenson II because he was family. This I was eventually able to prove. We are distant cousins through Roxy's grandmother, Hannah Fell Jaxtheimer. (Appendix 1 Stevenson Connection)

Robert (15 March 1904-10 July 1987) was James and Roxy's first born. He married Frieda Cubbison (16 Dec 1903-11 April 1970) in December 1925. Their first child, Robert James was born at 225 N. Elm Street.. He worked for Armco Steel Corporation (now AL Steel) as an electrician. This is similar to his maternal grandfather, William Jaxtheimer's career. When laid off during the Depression he learned the upholstery trade and worked at that until rehired by Armco where he worked until retirement. As mentioned, he was an accomplished saxophone player and traveled with a band until his son William was born.

He and Frieda had four children:

> **Robert James** "Bobby Jim" (3 December 1926 – 15 May 1996) married Catherine "Binky" George (11 April 1924-04 Feb 2002)
>> **Dennis Richard** (10 March 1948)
>> **Linda (** 2 Aug 1950, m. George Patten II 21 Aug. 1971 **)**
>> **Bruce (**10 Feb 1953, m. Charlene Andre 17 Sept. 1955)

> **William** Leroy (28 May 1930 – 12 May 1989) never married

> **Patricia Ann Kathleen** (6 April 1937) married Eugene Pavlic (29 Aug 1933) on (13 July 1957)
>> **Eugene Francis Paul Pavlic**(15 July1958-16 Oct 2013)married Lorna Lee McEwan (29 Oct 1984)
>> **Angela Thoune** (08 Feb 1975) adopted
>>> **Tiana** (06 Jan 1998)
>> **Danielle Nicole** (25-June 1985)
>> **Amanda Jean** (20-Aug 1990)
>>> **Mya Jones** (15 Aug 2008)

> **Thomas Richard** (16 June 1944-24 Feb 1994) married Eileen Young (26 Oct.1944)
>> **Timothy** adopted
>> **Kevin** (6 July 1976) adopted
>> **Mark** (21 March 1982)

Bill, Bobby Jim, Tommy, Bob, Patty Kerr at Robert Kerr's home 2nd Ave, Butler,PA

Robert and Marvin Kerr

Marvin & Henrietta Fogel

Doreen Kerr Heitzer

Julie & Catie Hertz

Marvin Kerr enlisted 23 July 1942 in Pittsburgh, Pennsylvania as a Private 302 Base Unit Air Force. From the National Archives:

> … he was born 1910 had 3 years of college and was married, civilian occupation – unskilled routeman. Enlistment for the duration of the War or other emergency plus 6 months only at the discretion of the President or otherwise according to law.

Bill Kerr with Ethel's children William Bassler holding Susan's hand, Patty Kerr 225 Elm St. Butler, PA 1940s

When he finished basic training in Washington, DC his brother Bob drove the whole family in their father's Buick to celebrate Marvin's achievement. Ethel said it was a memorable trip and her father was in a good mood and generous. The family visited the White House and Bob's young son Bobby Jim sat in the President's chair.

According to the 1940 U.S. Census, Marvin was 29 and living with his parents. Henrietta Fogel was 26 and also living with her parents, Bertha and Constant Fogel, and Henrietta's 6 year old daughter Renelle.

Marvin Kerr with Bob's children Patty, Bily, Tommy, Bobby Jim   Kerr's back porch

Marvin courted Henrietta, a woman whose parents had emigrated from Alsace-Lorraine region of France. He married Henrietta and adopted Renelle. Together they had a son, Stephen, who died as an infant and then a daughter named Doreen and another baby boy who did not live. Doreen Kerr graduated from Slippery Rock College and worked as a school librarian until retirement. She married Raymond Heitzer. Their daughter Julie married Chris Hertz and they have a daughter, Catie. Doreen continues to live in Butler.

James Chauncy Kerr was a hard-working, non-drinking man who cared about his family. He brought his paycheck home and there was never any talk of his being unfaithful to Roxanna. He was first generation Irish. The couple saved for their children's education; although none of them completed higher education. My brother, Bill, recalls that after Grandpa retired he read two newspapers every day, plus magazines like *Colliers*, *Reader's Digest*, and *Saturday Evening Post*. He loved jury duty. He went to

Sherman Bassler with brothers-in-law Marvin Kerr, Robert Kerr 225 N.Elm St. Butler, PA

church every Sunday and practiced the works of mercy. Roxy called him "Jim" but my father would refer to him as "J.C." The unspoken joke being those were Jesus Christ's initials as well.

His daughter, Ethel, remembered that when hungry men came to the back door, James would fix them breakfast and take it out to the porch. It is possible hobos along the rail line were made aware of his kindness. This was before welfare and food stamps. James' father and grandfather were born in Ireland at the cusp of the Great Famine that devastated the country from 1845-1852 when over a million people starved to death. James Chauncy would not have turned a hungry man away from his doorstep.

Grandma & Grandpa Kerr's 1955 visit to Long Branch, NJ

My brother Bill and I have fond memories of Grandpa. Bill recalls going to the train station to watch the elephants disembark and parade to the circus grounds with the calliope playing. I remember Grandpa walking me to Church to see the crèche at Christmas and to have my throat blessed on the Feast of St. Blaise in February. His home was always open to any family member who needed a roof over their heads. As mentioned, he took in his wife's niece, Jeanette. Then Robert and his wife lived at 225 N. Elm St. until they got on their feet. Frieda had their first born there. My mother, Bill and I lived with them for five years. When we finally moved to New Jersey, James Chauncy assured all of us as we said our good-byes that we always had a home with them.

His temper was not a lasting concern for his eldest son, Robert, who years later disagreed with Ethel about the trauma it caused. She, however, remembered one violent struggle that took place in the kitchen. Robert wanted to borrow the car to go to a music gig where the band would be performing for pay during a school night. James felt his son was out too much; not appreciating that Bob was actually working. He wrestled his son for the car keys and had his pinkie broken in the tussle. Ethel said her father recalled the story not in anger but with some pride in his eldest son. It was a rite of passage for the two of them, but my mother never saw it that way.

James Chauncy attended his youngest son's basketball games but according to Ethel would get angry if Marvin didn't score. It is not known when Marvin began drinking but it was a life-long struggle and he probably lost his basketball scholarship bcause of it. Years later, when inebriated, he would go to his elderly father's bedroom and yell at him over unresolved issues. His relationship with his wife Henrietta and daughter Doreen also suffered because of his addiction. The last twelve years of his life Marvin stopped drinking and took loving care of his father. My mother told me that when James was in extremis Marvin called in the family and they said the prayers for the dying at the bedside. Roxy told Marvin he was welcome to move back home as long as he was sober. He complied and then took care of his mother for three years until she died. Marvin then moved into an apartment nearby and Henrietta would occasionally invite him to have dinner with her. Doreen said that she had only four years to get acquainted with her dad before he died.

James' temper caused his daughter great anxiety. She recalled one phone call after she was married where he asked her to come to the house because Roxy was lying on the floor. Ethel responded but wondered forever after if her father had struck her mother. Of course, Roxy might have fainted or suffered a transichemic attack since she died of heart problems years later. Ethel was also annoyed that he did not provide a private room at the hospital after Roxy broke her hip. Roxy, living far from her sisters and family, had unfortunately confided in her daughter about the difficulties of living with James. Using her only daughter as a confidante, while understandable, was not a good thing to do.

James Chauncy sadly remarked that he had outlived all of his family. In his mid- 80s he began to suffer memory loss and perhaps had alzhiemers since he would walk to get his paper in his pajamas or nothing at all until even the basement door needed to be locked. Before I knew this, I thought he had vascular dementia. In high school while sitting on the Kerr's front porch swing, Grandpa asked me: "What town was this?" I said: "Butler, Grandpa." A little while later, he said annoyed: "I knew that."

At her father's wake Ethel did not understand how her mother could look so lovingly at her deceased husband. James Chauncy Kerr is buried in Mount Calvary Cemetery, Butler, Pennsylvania next to his wife, Roxanna and son, Marvin and near his eldest son Robert Kerr and his wife Frieda.

James Chauncy Kerr's thirty- year service medal. He would also receive a gold watch and a diamond pin for fifty years of service that hopefully remain in the family.

CHAPTER 2

THE JAXTHEIMERS

William F. Jaxtheimer and Katherine Wiand
Married 27 December 1876

Roxanna Jaxtheimer always called " Roxy" by her family, was born 18 August 1877 in West Salem Township, Pennsylvania to William F. Jaxtheimer and Katherine Wiand. Her paternal grandmother could trace her lineage back to 16th century England; while her mother, Katherine Wiand, was first generation German.   Roxy was a product of the settlers of the new territory that opened in western Pennsylvania after the Native Peoples moved on pressured either by treaty or war.

While the Jaxtheimers and Fells on her father's side had been homesteading for some time, Roxy's mother came from newer stock. Yet the Wiands were included in the *History of Mercer County 1888* on page 428.

John and Katherine Wiand, both natives of Germany and parents of eight children of whom six still survive. John Wiand came to Pennsylvania and settled in Hickory township, Mercer county, where he mined coal for a number of years. He later purchased a farm which he tilled up to the time of his death. He and his family were members of the Roman Catholic church and in politics, he was a Republican.

Young Roxy spent happy times with her Grandmother Wiand on the farm learning how to quilt and drive a pony and cart. She told me these stories while teaching me how to cut quilt squares. She once expressed regret at not learning to speak German with her grandmother also named Kathryn. Her grandmother did share a family story of why the Wiands came to America. We have this note on an undated, yellowed slip of paper in her own hand:

> Kathryn Wiand's father came from Germany because his father gambled money. His father lived in a home like Washington's and had servants. It was like a castle with homes around it. These people were employees of the family. This boy went into the looms room to make fine linen, had education and background. He met grandmother, married in Germany and when the oldest boy was about two came over to the United States.

Future family genealogists can research ship and marriage records to find out more. Roxy said there was a strong prohibition of card playing and gambling in the family. Nonetheless, Roxy liked to play Canasta and 500 for fun.

William F. Jaxtheimer's parents were William Jaxtheimer and Hannah Fell. William Jaxtheimer's parents were Amos Jaxtheimer and Uta (Judith) Christman. The Jaxtheimer name has variant spellings. Roxanna pronounced her name "jacks timer."

William F.'s grandfather, Amos Jaxtheimer was one of the pioneers in West Salem Township. His picture was found on the web and under it the word "mercenary." We have no family story that would explain why he should be identified as a paid soldier for hire. Perhaps he was an Indian fighter.

Amos Jaxtheimer (1806-1871)

The History of Mercer County gives an account of the Jaxtheimer family on page 427.

> William Jaxtheimer (1831-1922) was born in eastern Pennsylvania and went west to Mercer county with his parents when a small boy. His father, Amos, was one of the pioneers in West Salem township. William was a blacksmith and farmer and retired in 1901. Politically he voted the Democratic ticket.

His son (Roxy's father):

William F. Jaxtheimer (1856-1932)

> William F. Jaxtheimer was educated at the public schools and at the International Correspondence school of Scranton, Pennsylvania where he was instructed technically in electric engineering, mill-wright work, mechanical science, etc. having had some previous experience in 1890, he worked as an engineer and had charge of P.L. Kimberley's plant at Sharon, Pennsylvania. He next was called to take full charge of the Carnegie Steel plant at Greenville, which position he held up to 15 July 1905, when he was given charge of A.D. Gillespie's electric Light, Heat and Power plant which responsible position he still holds. He is a member of the Knights of Pythias

Order, Custer Lodge No. 469. Politically, he is a supporter of the chief principles of the Republican party. *History of Mercer County*

William F. Jaxtheimer's mother, Hannah Fell, (Roxy's grandmother) was born in West Salem township. Her people were also among the early settlers of Salem township. Her father was William Fell, (Roxy's great- grandfather) the son of John and Elizabeth (Hartley) Fell (2 April 1756 – 1828).

Hannah's father, William Fell, married Agnes Anderson (15 February 1761). He was an accomplished weaver in the summer months and taught school during the winter. One of his double sided blankets was passed down to the fifth generation. The following is taken from *the History of Mercer County, 1888,* p.1176

William Fell was a son of John and Elizabeth (Hartley) Fell, and was born in Bucks County, Penn., 2 April 1756, removing to Westmoreland County, Penn., after reaching manhood. He married Agnes Anderson, born 15 February 1761. He followed weaving in summer, and teaching school in the winter. In the fall of 1796 he and his son, George W., came to Mercer County, and selected a piece of land in what is now the southern part of West Salem Township. In the spring of 1797 they came back to the land, built a log cabin, and commenced a settlement in the dense forest. Mr. Fell returned to Westmoreland County early in July, leaving his son, George W., then a boy thirteen years old, to continue the settlement, and he remained seven weeks longer before joining his father in Westmoreland County. Mr. Fell moved his family to Mercer County in the spring of 1798, and lived upon the same farm through all the hardships and privations of pioneer days, up to his death, July 16, 1841. His wife had died twenty-one years before, 8 August 1820. They reared a family of five children:

Mary wife of Timothy Dumars;
*George W. Fell (Hannah's father and Roxy's great- grandfather)
Miriam, who became the wife of James Stevenson
Jonas
Agnes, wife of William McKnight.

Each left numerous descendants.

Again the *History of Mercer County* p.427 recounts:

In the autumn of 1796 he (William) and his son George W. came to Mercer county, Pennsylvania and selected a piece of land in what is now known as the southern part of West Salem township. In the spring of 1797 they returned to this land and built a log cabin and commenced making an improvement in the dense forest. In July of that year, he went back to Westmoreland county and moved his family to Mercer county in the spring of 1798. He spent the remainder of his days there being the first Fell to locate in West Salem township.

George W. Fell, eldest son of William and Agnes Fell, was born in Westmoreland County, Penn., 31 August 1784, and came with his father to Mercer County in the fall of 1796. They made a permanent settlement in the spring of 1797, and the whole family removed there the following year. He was married 14 April 1806, to Nancy Ann Dumars and located on a portion of the old homestead. She was born in April, 1787, and reared eight children:

Mary, who still resides upon the old homestead in her eighty-second year;
Sarah, who married Frank Merry;
William G., by profession a civil engineer;
 Jonas, a physician of Lexington, Ill.;
Amos D., a surveyor of Trumbull County, Ohio;
 Fannie, wife of Aaron M. Clark;
*__Hannah,__ wife of William Jaxtheimer, of West Salem Township, and residing upon the old homestead (Roxy's grandparents)
 Roxanna, deceased.

Mr. George W Fell was appointed justice of the peace in 1822, and served in that office for eighteen years, consecutively. He followed farming all his life, and died 15 August 1849, upon the farm which he settled in 1797. Nancy, his widow lived until 21 September 1871. Both were members of the Methodist Episcopal Church, and politically Mr. Fell was a Democrat and belonged to the Masonic fraternity. He lived through all the early settlement of Mercer County, and endured the hardships and trials incident to pioneer life.

Roxy wrote this note about her ancestors but John Fell was actually her great-great grandfather.

> *John Fell - Great-grandfather Fell was a lawyer who came from England. Left their property there and came to the United States. Settled in West Salem Township in Pennsylvania. Great- grandfather came over and settled the land. After he got the farm settled he went over to England and left the boy in charge of the farm to keep the claim. Later the father brought the family over to the United States. He had a farm then gave each child 100 acres when they left home.*

John Fell's parents were Benjamin Fell (1703) and Hannah Scarborough (1704-1742). Hannah Scarborough can trace her family back to 16th century London. Her father, John, was born about 1667 in London and died 27 January 1726 in Buck's County, Pennsylvania. Her mother was Mary Pierson. John's father and grandfather both named John were born in London. William Scarborough was born about 1598 and his father, Isaac Scarborough, was born about 1560 in London. Benjamin Fell's parents were Joseph Fell (1703-1758) and Bridget Wilson.

The old families of Jaxtheimer and Fell were joined together with the newer family of Wiands when William Jaxtheimer and Kathryn Wiand were married on 27 December 1876. This family left farm life behind and eventually moved to the city of Greenville, Pennsylvania.

They had seven children:

*Roxanna 18 August 1877 married James Chauncy Kerr
John M
William R
Mary (Mame) wife of John LaSalle
Hannah wife of Leo Keane
Katherine wife of William Reagle
Elvira wife of John (Jock) Brown

Roxanna seemed in no rush to marry even though she was the eldest and had many responsibilities at home. She had fun with her sisters who also loved dances. If one sister needed a ball dress for a dance, the others would cut and sew the dress and have it ready in time for the evening affair. Roxy didn't finish high school. Instead she began working for a hat maker in town. In those days women wore large hats adorned with feathers. The story goes that a man offered her a good job, but it would take her "on the road." Her father said "No" to that. According to her daughter, Roxy had seven proposals of marriage. One proposal came from a man who later was made the president of the railroad that employed her husband. Reportedly, James Chauncy even showed her the newspaper clipping of the man's promotion.

When first married Roxy and James lived in a cottage on the Jaxtheimer property until they had saved enough to build a house on the outskirts of town. Ethel told me that she didn't understand how her mother could bear to sell that house and move to Butler. It had built in cupboards under the stairs, and two parlors and Ethel still had a memory of her own bedroom. As mentioned, Roxy preferred the convenience of in-town living and didn't regret their decision to move.

As mentioned before, the couple did not agree on how their daughter should be raised. Ethel would not end up an old maid like her Aunt Mary if Roxy had anything to do with it. Ethel's introduction to her future husband was through a friend.

Ethel Kerr had a best friend Hannah Larden whose parents owned a jewelry store in Butler. Hannah was also a pianist who studied during the summer at Chautauga where

Ethel's first and last horseback ride

Ethel accompanied her friend one summer. Hannah had a brother, Dan Larden, in the Pennsylvania State Police who knew Sherman Bassler, a radio operator at the barracks and he introduced Sherman to Ethel. But when I asked how my parents met they replied: " In a crackerjack box." The couple dated for four or five years before marrying on 23 October 1934. Ethel enjoyed her long courtship with Sherman. They went with friends to the beach at Lake Erie and even went horseback riding. In a letter to Ethel, Sherman refers to being sore and draws a picture of a horse at the bottom of the page. (Appendix 27) Sherman would often meet her in Pittsburgh after her music courses were finished. When she returned home to 225 N. Elm St. she would put the flowers her beau gave her in water with an aspirin. She recalled that this effort to prolong the life of

Sherman's homemade Valentine to Ethel

the flowers annoyed her dad to no end. James Chauncy called him "that fella." Sherman recalled a Pittsburgh policeman tapping on the window of his car because he and Ethel were kissing and the window was all steamy. Roxanna didn't believe in long engagements. She knew her daughter had fallen head over heels in love.

Ethel M. Kerr & Sherman G. Bassler
Wedding portrait taken in Kerr's backyard
23 October 1934

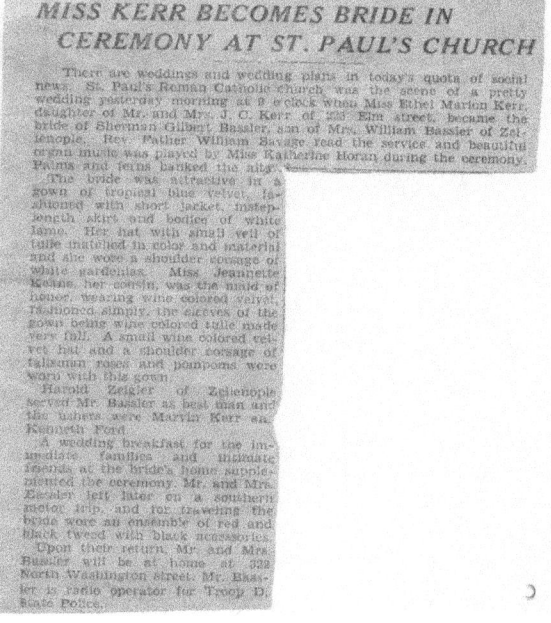

Wedding announcement in the Butler Eagle

Ethel insisted that Sherman convert to Catholicism, a decision she later regretted. She did not want to be married in the rectory where mixed marriages took place. It's safe to say that she was placating her Catholic parents as well. The marriage banns and announcement appeared in the *Butler Eagle*:

Front row: Sherman & Ethel Bassler; Harold Ziegler, Jeanette Keane,
unknown women, Kneeling: Bobby Jim Kerr
Back row: James C. & Roxy Kerr; Frieda & Robert Kerr; Sara & Elmer Gross,
Julia Bassler; Marvin Kerr

CHAPTER 3

THE SHERMANS

William Gottlieb Bassler   *Julia Elizabeth Sherman*

Sherman Gilbert Bassler was born on 8 November 1907 to Julia Elizabeth Sherman and William Gottlieb Bassler at 302 E. New Castle St., Zelienople, Pennsylvania. He was an only child.

Julia, had traveled by train from Clinton, Missouri to Pittsburgh, Pennsylvania to marry William. An entry in Julia's Diary reads: "Feb 13, 1903 1 year since I left home." Five months after her arrival in Pittsburgh, Julia was married 16 July 1902 in the Hotel Boyer by Rev. Robert R. Durst. Julia was 27 and William was 47 years old.

After the wedding the couple returned to 302 East New Castle Street to live with Will's aging mother, Elizabeth Catherine Gilbert Bassler called Eliza. Julia would take care of her for five years until Eliza's death in 1907– the same year Julia gave birth to her son, Sherman. There was no wedding reception in Pittsburgh or festivities in Zelienople by willing friends because as remembered by Ethel, Julia's daughter-in-law, Will explained they would not be able to reciprocate. We have no photo of the newly married couple.

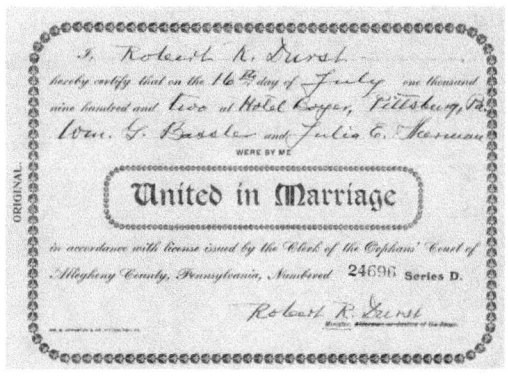

Marriage certificate of Julia Sherman and Willam G. Bassler

Bassler family home for over 70 years
302 East New Castle St. Zelienople,PA
Julia on porch and Sherman in yard about 1910

Julia was born in Clinton, Missouri on 9 March 1877 to Laura Buckingham and Albert G. Sherman[2] the home of her maternal grandparents, John L. Buckingham and Susannah Margaret Gilbert. Julia was the third in a family of nine. She and her mother were the only red heads until her youngest sister, Clara, was born.

Julia traveled east in 1902 against her family's wishes to marry a man who was her first cousin once removed and twenty years her senior to begin a new life in Zelienople, Pennsylvania Forty years earlier her father, Albert Gallatin Sherman, had traveled west to make his fortune. He kept a <u>Pocket Diary</u> in 1864 which gives a day to day account of a seventeen year old in Vermont at the end of the Civil War. (Appendix 3)

Julia Elizabeth Sherman- age four
The family had a painting done from this photo 1881

Julia at 15 years old

Julia in her 20's

"Go west, young man!" is credited to Horace Greeley who supposedly advised young men to head across the country in the late 1800's. Thousands did and Albert was one of them.

(The Shermans continue after The Honsingers)

CHAPTER 4

THE HONSINGERS

Margaret Honsinger & Albert Gallatin Sherman,Sr. (tint type)

Albert Gallatin Sherman[2] was born 23 January 1847 in Chazy, New York to Albert Gallatin Sherman,[1] (1814-1885) and Margaret (Deuel) Honsinger (1814-1899). Albert and Margaret married 14 February 1839 at the bride's hometown in Alburg, Vermont. It deserves comment that less than 40 years after hostilities ended with Great Britain, Margaret Honsinger, the granddaughter of a Tory soldier, married Albert G. Sherman, the grandson of a Patriot.

The Honsinger family was well known both in Alburg, Vermont and Chazy, New York. These towns are only nine miles apart. Margaret's parents were Philip(pus) (5 October 1749) and Lucretia Deuel Honsinger. Her tombstone in Benson reads: "Lucretia wife of Philip Honsinger August 23, 1779 to Dec 11, 1867." Census records show that she lived with Margaret and Albert and her unmarried daughter, Julia, until her death. The following information is taken from an *Unfinished Typescript for History of Alburgh, Vermont* Volume II by Allen L. Stratton.

> Variant spellings for Honsinger are: Hunsicker, Hunziker, Hunsinger and Honsaker. They were a Swiss Family from what is now Alsace. They left Switzerland because of religious persecution about the middle of the 17th century. (*The Mennonite Encyclopedia*, Vol.2, p.844) Note: a German custom was to name all boys "Johannes" and girls "Maria" and then use their second name.
>
> Joannes Honsinger, a Palatine, arrived on the ship *Robert and Alice* 11 Sep-

tember 1733 *(History of Pennsylvania German Pioneers,* Vol.1, p.212). The ship was English. They embarked from Rotterdam, Holland and landed at Philadelphia. The early Honsinger's took the oaths and repeated the Declaration by an Act of Parliament made in the 13th year of the reign of King George, the 2nd, entitled " An Act for Naturalizing such Foreign Protestants and others therein mentioned as are settled or shall settle in any of His Majesty's Colonies in America." This was witnessed by M.C. Krell, John Phafer, Laurens Van Boskereck on 25 April 1743 (NY. G&B Vol XCIV #3 Naturalization of Foreign Prostestants in the American Colonies p.31.)

Johannes had a son Johannes <u>Michael</u> who married Maria Christine Hilfen-stein. Discharge papers from the King's American Regiment of Foot declare that Michael has received " pay, arrears, cloathing and all other just demands from the time of my enlistment into the within mentioned Regiment unto this Day of my Discharge. 10 October 1783."

Michael was given title to settle on Caldwell Manor…at the annual Rent of four pence per Acre, the Spanish Dollar reckoned at five Shillings due and pay-able the 1st October…provided he has built a House and cleared Three Acres on said Lot in the course of Six Months from the Date hereof otherwise this Permit (which is not transferable) will be null and void. 25 October 1788 (signed) Pat Conroy.

Presumably Michael served in the British forces from Rhinebeck, N.Y. He was discharged at St. John's Harbour, Nova Scotia in 1783. Toward the latter part of the Revolutionary War estates of known Tories were confiscated by the Americans. A majority of the early settlers of the Town of Alburgh were Tories who fled from their homes in the States and settled in Alburgh, thinking they were in Canada and under the protections of the British. Michael Honsinger was one of them. When it turned out that his land was on United States soil the situation became complicated but eventually the title to his land was cleared.

Michael had a son Johann <u>Frederick</u> who married Rachel Walker. They had a son Philip(pus) who married Lucretia Deuel and became the parents of Margaret Honsinger who married Albert Gallatin Sherman.

Lucretia Deuel's parents are Michael Deuel and Elce Slocum. Michael's parents are Philip Deuel (Davol) and Elizabeth Sherman. Elce Slocum's parents were John Slocum and Deborah Almy. John Slocum's parents are Eleazer Slocum and Deborah Smith. Debo-rah Almy's parents are Job Almy and Lydia Tillinghost. It is through Lucretia Deuel (Davol) that the family can trace its line back to George Soule, a passenger on the May-flower according to the *Unfinished Typescript for History of Alburgh, Vermont* Vol. II by Allen L. Stratton. (Appendix 2)

Deuel is French in origin and has variant spellings. According to one story, the Quak-ers thought the pronunciation of "Davol" sounded like "devil" and so changed it to Deuel.

An interesting coincidence brought east and west Honsinger cousins together. The

Sherman sisters went to hear Welthy Honsinger Fisher speak about her book and travels at the General Conference of the Methodist Evangelical Church which met at Kansas City, Missouri. The eldest sister, Minnie, knowing her Vermont grandmother was a Honsinger thought they might be related and bought the book titled: *The Top of the World*. When Welthy became aware of the connection she wrote to Minnie Sherman.

Welthy Honsinger Fisher

Top of the World

Letter from Welthy to Minnie Sherman August, 1928

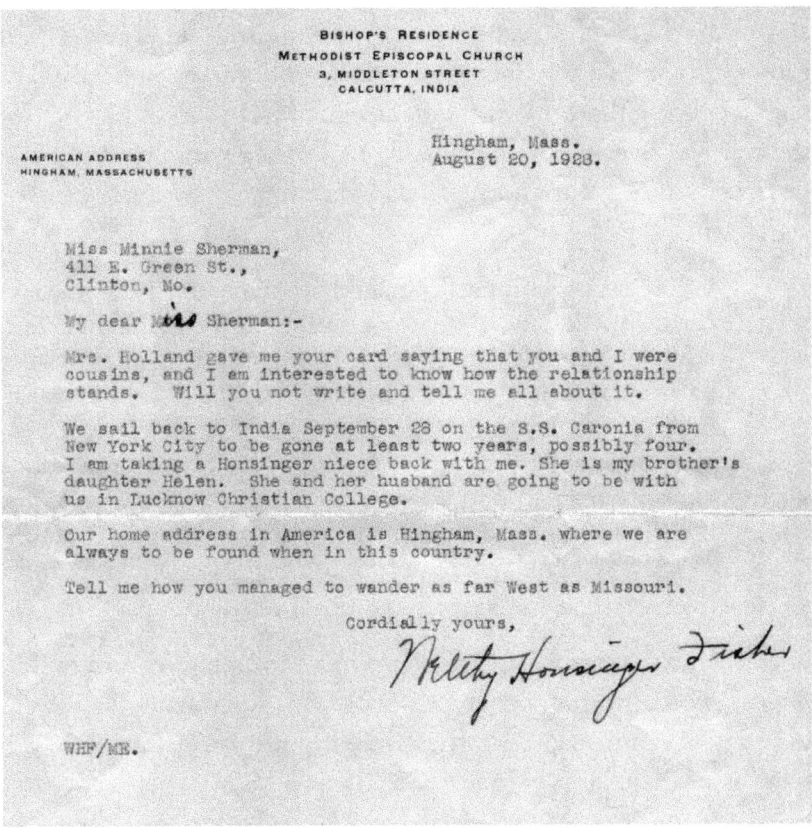

BISHOP'S RESIDENCE
METHODIST EPISCOPAL CHURCH
3, MIDDLETON STREET
CALCUTTA, INDIA

AMERICAN ADDRESS
HINGHAM, MASSACHUSETTS

Hingham, Mass.
August 20, 1928.

Miss Minnie Sherman,
411 E. Green St.,
Clinton, Mo.

My dear Miss Sherman:-

Mrs. Holland gave me your card saying that you and I were cousins, and I am interested to know how the relationship stands. Will you not write and tell me all about it.

We sail back to India September 28 on the S.S. Caronia from New York City to be gone at least two years, possibly four. I am taking a Honsinger niece back with me. She is my brother's daughter Helen. She and her husband are going to be with us in Lucknow Christian College.

Our home address in America is Hingham, Mass. where we are always to be found when in this country.

Tell me how you managed to wander as far West as Missouri.

Cordially yours,

Welthy Honsinger Fisher

WHF/MR.

Welthy is known for being an American Methodist educational missionary in China and being a literacy pioneer in India. Welthy and her fellow literacy pioneers started two non-profit organizations, World Education in 1951, which started as World Literacy and the World Literacy of Canada in 1955. Welthy was closely involved in both organizations for many years, either as President or as an advisor. The organizations are still functioning. Even in her nineties, she traveled throughout the world. Six weeks before Gandhi's death in 1947 he asked her to work for India's villages. Welthy made her final trip to India as a government guest in 1980, shortly before her death at the age of 101 in Connecticut. In a stunning example of synchronicity, Sharon Sherman Mayer, a Honsinger descendent, has also traveled to Tibet in humanitarian efforts.

(The Shermans, cont.)

We have no family stories shedding light on how Margaret Honsinger met Albert Gallatin Sherman who was a blacksmith. He was the son of Ebenezer Sherman born 4 July 1782 in Brimfield, Massachusetts. Ebenezer was also a blacksmith and served in the War of 1812 in Captain Fillmore's company, a member of the 42nd Brigade, 36th regiment, Clinton County, 28 October 1818 (*History of the Town of Chazy Clinton County, New York* by Nel Jane Barnett Sullivan and David Kendall Martin 1970.) His dates of service are so short I've thought perhaps it is a recording mistake. However, it seems the peace treaty took effect soon after Ebenezer enlisted. Abraham Alphonse Albert Gallatin was influential in securing the Treaty of Ghent signed in 1814. It may be that Ebenezer appreciating the war was over before he actually had to see battle named his son Albert Gallatin after this Swiss immigrant and American statesman. From the *History of the Town of Chazy* we also learn:

> Black smithing flourished in Chazy until the automobile. It was vital for farm life. The shoeing of horses and the making of wagons, carriages and sleighs were important but the smith also produced axe heads, gun barrels, bayonets, combat swords, chains, hoes, hay forks shovels, knives, butcher knives, door latches, hinges and flintlock parts. The blacksmith also made all his own tools as well as his horseshoes and nails. (p.114) Ebenezer Sherman had a fine blacksmith shop. It was a large stone building three quarters of a mile from the lower bridge in lot 186 of the Refugee Tract; it was built there before the road was opened on the east side of the river. He had the first trip hammer in town. (p.115)

Ebenezer was among 132 petitioners for a liquor license in Chazy. (p.273) Ebenezer Sherman built his hop on Tracy Brook which maintained a thriving business. (p207) During the 50th anniversary of the United States on 4 July 1826 Ebenezer volunteered this toast as recorded in *A History of the Town of Chazy:*

> Clinton County Rich in Soil, abundant in ore. May the bellows of her furnaces never blow the coals of sedition, her anvils & her hammers echo the voice of Industry.

Addie Shields the Clinton County Historian at Plattsburgh, NY in 1979 provided a cemetery record:

> *Riverview Cemetery, Chazy, NY*
>
> *Ebenezer Sherman, died 4 October 1867 Age 85–*
>
> *Betsey (Belding), his wife died 11 September 1850 age 64.*
>
> *Ebenezer was a member of Harmony Lodge #154, F.& A.M.*

Ebenezer's father was Thomas Sherman, a revolutionary soldier with National DAR #859335. Thomas was born in Brimfield, Massachusetts 10 August 1745. His services were as follows: Capt. Joseph Thompson's Co., Col Timothy Danielson's Regt. Enlist 1775 and Capts. Bardwell, Howard and Cols. Brewer and Wells. He and his brother both fought for independence. Thomas later moved to Windsor, Vermont and then to Chazy, New York.

Thomas and his wife Zeriah Lumbard (1749-1837) were married in Brimfield, Massachusetts 7 March 1771. They had ten children:

Daniel 10 August 1771 married Sally Dimmick
Mary 23 Sept 1772 married Thomas Burch
Thomas Burch 23 Dec 1774
Zerviah 23 Mar 1778
Asenath 14 May 1779 married Timothy Lawrence
Sarah 03 Aug 1780
Ebenezer 04 July 1782 (our ancestor) married Betsey Belding/Beldon
Lydia 01 June 1784
Joel 10 Oct 1786
Ruth June 1793

Thomas died 1 April 1829 and is buried in Weybridge, Addison Co. Vermont. I found the pension papers Zerviah submitted in Vermont after his death at the National Archives and Records Administration at Waltham, Massachusetts.

The New England Shermans by Roy V. Sherman (1974) traces our branch of the Sherman family back to Rev. John Sherman born 26 December 1613 in Dedham, Essex, England. Rev. John Sherman graduated Trinity College before emigrating to the colonies in the 1630's. He was ordained third Pastor of the Congregational Church at Watertown, Massachusetts and was a Fellow of Harvard College. The Reverend was celebrated for his writings. He was known as the "College Puritan" and began a long line of Shermans in the New World. This information comes from *The New England Shermans* which I was fortunate to find in the library of the Vermont Historical Society during a visit 16 October 2006. (Appendix 4) Rev. John Sherman is interred in the Old Burying Place, Watertown, Middlesex Co. MA. (Appendix 5 for inscription) Family Tree Sherman connects the genealogical dots from Rev. John Sherman to Thomas Sherman and to Albert Sherman[1].

Albert Sherman[1] was a member of the Chazy Lyceum debating society organized on 24 April 1847. Although in no formal sense schools, a vital part of the intellectual life of the town at the end of the 1840's was the debating society of which two were organized by the young men of Chazy Village. Albert[1]. belonged to the Lyceum that had twenty-seven members. Some of the questions that were raised for debate included:

"Has the United States had justifiable cause for war with Mexico?"

Decided in the negative.

"Could the immediate emancipation of the slaves in the Southern states be affected without colonization consistent with the welfare and safety of the Several States of the Union?"

This was decided seven negative and four affirmative.

"Ought Congress to prohibit slavery or involuntary servitude in the Territories belonging to or which may hereafter belong to the U. S?"

Decided eight affirmative and four negative.

(Taken from the *History of the Town of Chazy*)

It is interesting to note that Albert's son would move to Missouri where the ramifications of the slavery question would historically play out in the Missouri Compromise and finally in the Civil War.

Records show that Albert[1] voted Democratic in the Chazy election of 1844. *The History of the Town of Chazy* points out that his father, Ebenezer, chose Oscar Livingston, his son-in-law, to follow him in his blacksmithing shop not his son, Albert[1]. This seems unusual for the time and may indicate a falling out between father and son. Perhaps this caused Albert[1] to eventually relocate to Vermont. According to the census, Albert[1], Margaret, Elvira 10, Julia 8, Margaret 6 and Margaret's mother Lucretia Honsinger and her maiden sister, Julia Honsinger were still living in Chazy, New York in 1850.

However, by the 1860 census the family had moved to Benson, Vermont. I have speculated as to a rift between father and son as a possible reason for the move, but certainly other reasons may have caused the departure from Chazy. From the 1860 census we learn that Elvira 20 and Julia 18 were both teachers and had attended school within the year. Maggie, 16 also attended school. Albert, 12 did not attend school and Isaviah , 10 did go to school, also there was a baby, Eva Bell. A daughter, Ellen, died in infancy. By 1860 Lucretia Honsinger, Margaret's mother is no longer alive and Julia Honsinger, Margaret's maiden sister is now 49. One more son was born to the couple, Ebenezer, who later married but had no children. He lived out his days in Benson, Vermont

Albert[1] and Margaret had eight children, six lived to adulthood.

Elvira 1840 married Franklin Walker, son also named Franklin

Julia 1842

Margaret (Maggie) 1844 -1917 married Edwin Walker

Albert[2] 1848 – married Laura Buckingham   our ancestor

Isaviah (Isa) 1850-1934 married Maturin Wilcox, daughter LauRetta Wilcox

Ellen died as an infant

Eva 1860-1864

Ebenezer (Eben) 1862 married Maude

The picture of the blacksmith shop is courtesy of Genevieve Livingston Trutor and the Benson Museum, Benson, Vermont.

Sherman blacksmith shop, Benson, Vermont
(since torn down)

In 1875 a year before my grandmother, Julia Sherman, was born in Clinton, Missouri, her parents and sisters, Minnie and Laura, went to visit their grandparents in Benson, Vermont. Minnie kept track of the family in her notes in the Family Record (Appendix 10) that 9 June 1934 Isa Wilcox, Julia's paternal aunt, died in Benson, VT. Cousins Frank and Clara Sherman Walker and LauRetta Wilcox also visited the family in Missouri. Isa Wilcox, a voice teacher

and painter, sent her niece Julia a framed poem perhaps as a wedding gift that is hanging in my guestroom. Considering it is over 1,300 miles from Clinton, MO to Benson, VT and an incredibly arduous and costly trip by train and carriage, family ties were strong.

Charlotte McGeary granddaughter of Don Sherman & Nancy Hodina Sherman, and great-great-great-granddaughter of Albert[1] and Margaret visited the Sherman family plot in Benson, Vermont.

Julia's father, Albert[2], didn't follow in the blacksmithing trade of his father and grandfather although Albert's[2] Pocket Diary (Appendix 3) indicates that he helped his father in the shop on Saturdays and knew the trade. It is not yet known when or how he made the transition to stone work. The family in Clinton, Missouri saved the Pocket Diary kept by the 17 year old Albert[2] during his last year in school in Benson, Vermont in 1864. It is clear from his entries that he was working very hard and saving any extra money he earned. He shot four squirrels in one day and earned $1.00. Other times he worked mending fences and earned $1.00 for the day. He took care of his sheep and milked the family cow. He picked berries and walnuts. He made maple syrup. And he hauled, cut, and stacked wood endlessly.

Albert[2] left Benson, Vermont and headed west in 1865 at the end of the Civil War. A story told by both east and west spurs of the family recounts that the teenager walked across Pennsylvania herding sheep and doing other odd jobs. There is no reason to doubt that Albert[2] worked his way across the country first to Macon, Illinois where his sister Maggie was teaching and then to Clinton, Missouri, but I don't know how much time elapsed from the time he left home until he arrived at his chosen home town. His obituary mentions that he arrived in Clinton before the railroad was built.(Appendix 8). Minnie preserved letters sent to Albert[2] from his mother and sisters beginning in 1865 Letters from Vermont (Appendix 6)

On our trip to Clinton, Missouri in October, 2013 my brother and I visited the Maplewood Cemetery in Osage Township, Henry Co. to see an extraordinary headstone carved by our great-grandfather, Albert[2] for Richard Garland in 1905. It had been carried on a

Maplewood Cemetery, Osage Co. Missouri
Albert Sherman's work.

A. G. SHERMAN
—DEALER IN—
Granite and Marble Monuments
111 EAST JEFFERSON STREET

CLINTON, MO.

wagon pulled by horses to its resting place. Albert[2] set up his business in 1883 which he followed successfully all his life. A picture shows him standing proudly in front of his shop "A.G. Sherman's Marble Works" with two assistants. Julia saved her father's well-worn mallet that was part of his trade. It remains in the family.

Albert's obituary mentions the palsy he developed as a by-product of spending many hours chiseling marble headstones for the community. (Appendix 8)

No stories survive about how Albert G. Sherman[2] met his future bride Laura E. Buckingham but meet they did.

The Daily Democrat of Clinton, Missouri carried the wedding announcement:

Albert G. Sherman and Miss Laura E. Buckingham, both of Clinton, Missouri, were married by the Rev. J. W. Newcomb on the evening of December 8th at the residence of the bride's father in Clinton.

411 East Green Street, Clinton, Missouri
Sherman family home stood for over 140 years

Albert[2] and Laura raised their family at 411 Green St. They had nine children:

Mary Parsons (10 Nov. 1872-16 Dec. 1950), a schoolteacher who never wed;

Laura[2] Evans (21 April 1879-June 1901) + Padfield and died after giving birth to a son, Murhl;

Julia Elizabeth (10 March 1876-10 January 1975) + William G. Bassler, one son, Sherman; our ancestor

Albert[3] (Bert) Gilbert (6 Dec. 1868-16 June 1969) + Stella (1881-11 Sept. 1969), one daughter Margaret Eloise

John Larkin (25 November 1881-23 November 1902) Died of typhoid fever after a camping trip to Colorado.

Wilber (30 March 1885-30 May 1885) Wilber was the second person buried in the Englewood Cemetery.,

Eva Bell (20 July 1886-July 1974) + Padfield then Cowman, no children

Carl Buckingham (25 November 1889-18 January 1988) + Katherine Markley (7 Nov 1893-11 Oct 1988) m 22 Nov 1919, Carl[2] and Harold

Clara Wells (5 July1893-) + Floyd Wallace. They had:

Howard 18 January 1926 (who adopted a child)

Herschel Lee 7 November 1916; who had Roger and Alan

Waneta Ruth 2 February 1923; + Shobe Smith who had Connie, Lowell, Mark

Wayne Sherman 9 December 1932

(See Family Trees Sherman p. 439)

Albert[2] provided well for his family. All of the children completed high school except the youngest Clara. "Mother was simply just too tired to keep Clara at school when she didn't want to be there," quoted her daughter, Waneta, during our visit to Clinton, MO. Minnie graduated from the public school in 1886. Exercises held during the afternoon and evening in the Opera House located in the central part of the east side of the Square. It would have been the same for Julia five years later. Minnie became a schoolteacher and took a position in Arkansas City, Kansas in 1893. She accepted fifth grade work in the fall of 1896. When Julia was 25 she went to live with Minnie: "We kept house in rooms at Flora McDowell's home until November when mother and Clara came for a while." (Minnie <u>Family Record</u>. Appendix 10) Julia was unmarried at twenty-five and her family would have wanted her "settled." Perhaps by going to Arkansas City, Julia was trying to see if she would like to become a school teacher like her oldest sister, or perhaps she was leaving Clinton to try to widen her marital prospects. At that time women teachers could not marry.

No doubt Julia helped her mother in the care of the children and the endless work of the home. She was almost a surrogate mother for little Clara. They also needed outside help. Years later Julia told me that one time when she made a visit to Clinton from Zelienople, she was walking down the street with friends and a Negro woman (Grandma used the term "darky") who had worked at the Sherman home for many years, passed by on the street. Julia did not say hello or indicate that she recognized her. She had

Left to right: Carl, Minnie, Laura[1], John L. Bert, Albert, Julia, Laura[2] E., Eva, Clara

Clara age 4

Mary Parsons (Minnie) Sherman (Appendix 12 for her letter to Laura in 1899)

John (tint type)

snubbed her and this act of cowardice continued to shame Julia into her old age.

Sometime during Julia's toddlerhood her mother's first cousin from Zelienople came to visit. My mother told me that Julia sat on William G. Bassler's lap. He was probably in his early 20's at the time. His mother, Eliza, and Julia's grandmother, Susannah Margaret, were sisters. Whether Mr. Bassler made more than one visit to Missouri is not known, but what is known is that he would return when he was forty-seven. This time he made a proposal of matrimony to Julia when she was 26. She accepted.

Julia had an ear for music but was not given piano lessons. In her nineties, she could sit at a piano and play many songs and hymns by heart, *Sweet By and By* being one of her favorites. Another reason to assume the family enjoyed comfortable circumstances was the many family portraits and pictures and oil paintings done from photos that have survived. Everyone is dressed fashionably.

Julia kept the tint type picture of John and a postcard telling her that her beloved younger brother had contracted typhoid fever while on a camping trip with his brother, Bert, in Colorado.

The Sherman Family Studio Portrait
Front row: Julia, Laura[1] holding Clara, Eva, Albert holding Carl
Standing: John, Laura[2], Albert, Minnie

Minnie says that she and others in the house also became infected but survived. Sadly John succumbed in 1902 at 21 years of age. From <u>Minnie's Family Record</u>: "Bert and John went to Colorado for a short trip. John took sick with typhoid fever on July 14th and passed away November 23rd. Buried at Englewood Cemetery on the 25th (his birthday). (Appendix 10)

This picture of Laura[2] in front of the family home in Clinton, Mo standing beside a stone planter fashioned by her father, was identified by her niece, Waneta Wallace Smith in 2015. It is undated. Mr. Padfield married Laura's younger sister Eva and they raised Murhl. Eight months after Laura died, Julia left for Pittsburgh, PA

Laura[2] Evans Sherman

and married 16 July 1902. This had to have been a terrible time for their mother.

My grandmother, Julia, was nine when her three month old brother Wilbur died. She was ten when her sister Eva Bell was born; thirteen when Carl Buckingham was born and seventeen when the last baby, Clara Wells, came along. Julia was especially close to the red-headed baby Clara and they corresponded across many miles all their lives. When she was nineteen Julia's grandfather, J.L. Buckingham, died in 1895. Since one of Julia's siblings was named John Larkin it is most likely J.L.'s name as well. (For more Family Recollections from Waneta and her daughter Connie see Appendix 12)

Clara, Carl, Eva mid 1900s
Photo courtesy of Waneta Smith and
Kevin & Diane Diehl

Laura, Fay Johnson, Jennie Titus, Julia, Eva in the Sherman parlor

Albert [2] and Laura [1] holding granddaughter
Eloise (Bert and Stella's child)

CHAPTER 5

THE BUCKINGHAMS

John L. Buckingham
Susannah Margaret Gilbert

Julia's mother, Laura[1], was born to John L. Buckingham and Susannah Margaret Gilbert in Piqua, Ohio in 1850 where her parents resided for a time buying and selling property. The firstborn, Jesse, was born in Kentucky. Census records have them living in Illinois before finally settling down in Clinton, Missouri. They had married in Gettysburg, Pennsylvania 10 October 1837 but soon moved west – first to Ohio, then to Illinois and finally settling in Clinton, Missouri.

John L. Buckingham was born in Baltimore, Maryland on 23 July 1815 to parents who were also from Baltimore but nothing more is known about them at this time. How he met and married Susannah Margaret Gilbert in Gettysburg, PA on 10 October 1838 is anyone's guess. Some Gilberts were living in Maryland and perhaps that is how he was introduced to the family. Proper young women were almost always introduced to their future husbands through a trusted family member and at that time people were more apt to marry into the same ethnic-social background as their own. The Gilberts were a German family.

Laura[1] Buckingham

I conjecture that John L.'s surname may have originally been spelled "Buckingheim," which would suggest German origins rather than English. That might explain why researching John L.'s parents has been difficult. However, there is an extensive genealogy of an English Buckingham family on the internet but no conclusive proof that it is the family of origin for John L. except for a mention of someone named Larkin. As mentioned, Julia Sherman's brother was named John Larkin. This is only a clue and future research may solve the problem.

In the 1870 Missouri census, John L.Buckingham lists his occupation as wheelwright. He also claimed to be a carriage maker in the 1850 Ohio census and a hotel keeper in the 1869 Illinois census. He too felt the pull of the west where opportunities for success seemed abundant.

As mentioned, records in Ohio seem to suggest Laura's father was engaged in land speculation. We can identify eight children, four sons and four daughters.

> **Jesse Gilbert** (abt.1838) born in Kentucky, married Eliz A.Clark (1847) and then Susan Eliza Philip(1859);
>
> **Anna E.**(1836) married Zenus E. Condit;
>
> **Thomas Benton** (24 June 1844) second wife Rosa Ann Rosebaugh (07 January 1846);
>
> **William R.**(4 August1846);
>
> **Clara Jane** (6/1848) married William D. Kreamer (10/1847);
>
> **Laura E**[1]. (14 July 1850) married Albert Gallitan Sherman (23 January 1847) ancestor
>
> **Dillie** (1855) married F.B.Scott;
>
> **John F.** (1869) married Celia (1860).

Three of John L.'s sons served honorably as Union soldiers in the Civil War: William R., Thomas Benton, and Jesse G. Buckingham. A family story says " brother fought against brother" indicating that one brother fought on the side of the Confederates. I heard the story from my grandmother, Julia, and my brother heard the story from our father. In addition, Kevin Diehl a descendent of Thomas Benton Buckingham, also heard the same story. He suggests that perhaps the brothers engaged in heated arguments at the family table but not on the battlefield. John.L. Buckingham's obituary mentions nine children born to the couple, but we have recorded eight. This could simply be a reporting mistake or perhaps the missing sibling is the rebel soldier. Confederate records must be accessed state by state. Another mystery to solve.

William R. Buckingham was born at Piqua, Miami Co., Ohio 4 August 1846. He was 19 when he enlisted at Cincinnati, Ohio. Information from the Danville Branch, National Home for Disabled Volunteer Soldiers states that William R. Buckingham served in Co. I 60th Regiment Ohio Infantry. and served from 20 January 1865 to 28 July 1865 when he was honorably discharged at Columbus, Ohio. The official list of battles that occurred while he was enlisted were at Fort Steadman, VA 26 March 1865 and the Fall of Petersburg, VA 2, April 1865. It would seem he had enlisted for a six-month tour of duty. He lived in Texas for 50 years and worked as a painter. He never married. William R died in

1928 at 82 years of age and is buried in Englewood Cemetery, Clinton, Missouri.

Information from the National Archives 8 September 2002. affirmed that. Thomas Benton Buckingham served in Company E 98 Illinois Infantry –enlisted 5 August 1862 and discharged 6 July 1865. (The file on TBB is over 200 pages generated during the years when he was seeking a pension. Kevin Diehl has the file.)

He enlisted as "Ben" when he was eighteen and served in Company E 98 Illinois Infantry and later detailed as an orderly to Gen Wilder's Lightning Brigade, Renold's 3 Div 14 Army Corps. This position is attributed to his neat appearance and ability to read and write. " Ben" states that he was detailed at Murfreesboro, Tennessee after the Stone River fight. This occurred 31 December 1862 to 3 January 1863. Thomas had been married in Alabama where his wife died. He later married Rosa Rosebraugh from Zelienople, Pennsylvania. They had four children:

John Adam Buckingham born Texas, 17 April 1882
Margaret Elizabeth born 16 August 1884
Henry Kimble born March 1886 in Clinton, Mo. Henry was injured on
    the Frisco RR and died 21 December 1910.
Mamie Tellin Buckingham born May, 1889 Clinton, Mo. (Kevin Diehl's
    ancestor)

Thomas Benton died in Iola, Kansas at a home for Disabled Volunteer Soldiers when he was 93 years and 11 months. Among Thomas Benton's papers was an affidavit from another brother Jesse.G. Buckingham as to the identity of his brother "Ben." Jesse served in Company B 11th Ohio Volunteer Infantry. Jesse met up with his brother Thomas while they were in service at Carthage, Tennessee.

Julia Sherman Bassler had a photo in her belongings that is a mystery. It is a portrait of a distinguished looking older gentleman. The pin on his lapel suggests a Grand Army of the Republic pin from the Civil War. If so, he would have served in his forties.

EWB
Grandpa age 83, 1901
(This photo was in a memento box of
Julia Sherman Bassler)

Thomas Benton Buckingham
aka Uncle Ben
On the back is written "Molly
Cottontail"

Thomas Benton Buckingham
Son of J.L. Buckingham
perhaps related to EWB

On the back of the well preserved photo is the notation "EWB, Grandpa Age 83, 1901." So he would have been born in 1818. It is quite possible that EWB is John.L. Buckingham's brother. And the initials could perhaps be Edward William Buckingham. We hope in the future a family genealogist will find the answer.

I presented this problem to Kevin Diehl, a Buckingham family genealogist who said…"this is the strongest evidence to date that John L. Buckingham had a brother. Compare the picture to that of the photos of Thomas Benton Buckingham (J.L's son) the mystery grandpa has a fuller beard but the eyes and ears show a strong family resemblance to me."

My grandmother, Julia, spoke often about her mother's brother, Uncle Ben, and said he had a sense of humor and was fun. She also said he had served in the Civil War, a claim I was able to prove. At first I thought "Ben" was short for Benjamin. I sent for his military records and was surprised to receive a very large package. As mentioned he signed up as Ben Buckingham but later, when trying to secure a pension for war injuries, he had to explain and prove that his real name was Thomas Benton Buckingham. This was problem before Social Security numbers. A plethora of paperwork was created to and from compatriots, doctors, and anyone else who could testify to the identity of Uncle Ben, including his brother Jesse, as mentioned before. Even his son wrote to the Veterans Association explaining why his dad needed aid. It is a story in itself. Eventually he was awarded his due pension for injuries sustained during the Civil War. It seems he suffered from hemorrhoids caused by long hours on horseback that left him in pain and unable to pursue his livelihood as a house painter.

Thomas Benton Buckingham and Rosa Rosebraugh

Thomas Benton and his second wife Rosa Rosebraugh are buried in Englewood Cemetery, Clinton, MO

(Rosa Rosebraugh was born in Zelienople, Pennsylvania. This is another coincidence. Thomas, son of Susannah Margaret, was Eliza Bassler's nephew. Perhaps Eliza was a go-between Rosa and Thomas.)

Although we don't know much about the beginnings of John L. Buckingham from Baltimore, we do know much about the last years of his life recorded in the local Clinton newspaper.

Death of J.L. Buckingham

Wednesday afternoon John L. Buckingham's spirit passed to that world beyond, where sickness and sorrow cannot enter. The subject of this sketch was born in Baltimore, Maryland, 23 July 1814; came to this city to reside in 1867, and for the past 28 years has lived on the place where he died. Fifty-seven years ago he married Miss Margaret Gilbert, the loving and faithful wife who survives him, she now being in her 77th year and they were perhaps, the oldest married couple in this county. To celebrate this anniversary, they planned a trip through Kansas and other states, to see their children and friends, and on the 8th of October, started, in good health. The trip was enjoyed to its utmost until about the first of December, he took sick in Texas, and they returned home, but all that loving hands and skilled physicians could do was of no avail, and he passed away with quick consumption, and to-day Clinton mourns the loss of a noble pioneer citizen, with such a spirit so near akin to God, so God like in attribute that "live forever" seems an attribute of his Godliness. And he does live forever- his spirit, his example, his services, everlastingly survive him.

John.L. Buckingham's tombstone was most likely done by his son-in-law, Albert Gallatin Sherman, in 1904.

Nine children were born to them, eight of whom are living. Mrs. A.G. Sherman and T.B. Buckingham, this city; Jesse Buckingham, living at Dallas Texas; William Buckingham, Austin, Texas; Mrs. Anna Candit, Fredonia, Kansas; Mrs. Clara Kreamer, Arkansas City, Kansas; and Mrs. Dillie Scott, Stillwater, Oklahoma.

The funeral services were held at the residence at 2 P.M. yesterday, conducted by Rev. S. J. Heaton of the M.E. church after which his remains were followed to Englewood by a large procession of sorrowing relatives and friends.

Fifty seven years ago October 8th, he married Miss Margaret Gilbert, the loving and faithful wife who survives him, she being now in her 77th year and they were perhaps, the oldest married couple in this county. To celebrate this anniversary, they planned a trip through Kansas and other states, to see their children and friends, and on the 8th of October, started, in good health.

Laura's[1] mother, Susannah Margaret Gilbert Buckingham, was to live nine more years after the death of her husband. She died on 6 April 1904 at the age of 87 and was buried next to her husband in the Englewood Cemetery. Her obituary reads:

Clinton Missouri, Apr 9 1904 - Mrs. S. M. Buckingham, one of Clinton's pioneer mothers, died at the home of her daughter, Mrs. A. G. Sherman, on Wednesday morning in the 87th year of her age. She came to Clinton in 1867 and was loved by a large circle of acquaintances. She was a member of the M. E. Church. Her beloved husband preceded her to that better world a number of years ago. They had nine children, seven living: Ben Buckingham and Mrs. A. G. Sherman, Clinton; John F. Buckingham, Boonville; Mrs. Clara Kreamer, Arkansas City, Kansas; Mrs. Anna Condit,

Fredonia, Kas; William Buckingham, Austin, Texas and Mrs. F. B. Scott. Funeral services were held at the residence of A. G. Sherman, 411 East Green and burial was in Englewood

Albert's[2] mother Margaret had died five years earlier in Vermont in 1899 at age 85 in Benson, VT her obituary also appeared in the local Clinton, MO paper:

> The mother of our prominent marble yard man, A. G. Sherman, died October 16, aged 85, in Benson, Vt. Margaret Honsinger Sherman was born at Alburgh May 11, 1814 and at her death was the oldest person in Benson. There were nine children in her father's family; two brothers still living, Philip of Michigan and E. Baker Honsinger of Waterford, N.Y. She married Albert Sherman of Chazy, N.Y. on February 14, 1832 and they lived there until they came to Benson 42 years ago. Mother of 8 children, 5 still living. Her faculties were acute to the last and greeted the children, young and old, with a smile, always keeping in touch with them. Tho old in years, she seemed young; erect in figure, and her bright black eyes and dark glossy hair gave her a youthful look. She asked to go out on the piazza her last Sabbath morning and when there, she looked all around, and remarked on the beauty of the world and the glorious sunshine

(Margaret's letters to her son Albert can be read in Appendix 6 Family Letters from Vermont)

On 11 October 2013, my brother and I flew to Kansas City. We were met by a cousin, Sharon Sherman Mayer who drove us to Clinton, Missouri for the first family reunion of the east and west branches of the Sherman Family. Don and Nancy Sherman hosted the gathering at their home. In attendance were the above plus Waneta Wallace Smith and Carl Sherman, Jr., father of our host, Don. Waneta and Carl are the niece and nephew of Julia Sherman Bassler, our grandmother who left Clinton in 1902. Kevin and Diane Diehl and their three children: Nathan, Andrea and Alex also joined the group. As mentioned, Kevin has done extensive work on the Buckingham genealogy. He descends from Thomas Benton Buckingham's daughter, Mamie.

A landmark for three generations. Don, Carl[2] and Carl[1] in front of Sherman's Plumbing and Heating, Clinton, Missouri
Although no one followed Albert[2] into the monument business, his son, grandson and great grandson became successful business men in the town.

Front: Shari Mayer, Andrea, Alex, Kevin and Diane Diehl
Standing: Don Sherman, Nathan Diehll, William Bassler, Waneta Smith, Susan Pickford, Carl[2] Sherman, Nancy Sherman
Henry County Museum, Clinton, Missouri 12 October 2013

CHAPTER 6

THE GILBERTS

Susannah[2] Margaret Gilbert was born 8 February 1818. At nineteen years of age she married John L. Buckingham in Gettysburg on 10 October 1837. He was among other things a wheelwright from Baltimore, Maryland. It is not known how he knew the Gilbert family. Perhaps business brought him to Gettysburg or a member of the Gilbert family living in Maryland introduced him to Susannah Margaret. She was named after her mother also called Susannah[1], so the family always referred to her simply as Margaret. We have no family pictures of the Gilberts other than Susannah Margaret and her younger sister Elizabeth Catherine (Eliza.)

Margaret's mother came from a large well- established family in Gettysburg, Pennsylvania. Susannah[1] (1786-1863) married her first cousin Barnhard Gilbert (1786-1868) Susannah[1] and Barnhard had ten children:

> **Delilah** who married Rev. Edwin Atlee of Lancaster, PA;
> **Sarah Ann** who married Rev. Henry G. Dill of Gettysurg;
> **George** Ritter who married Sarah Jones;
> **Jacob** who married Elizabeth Sweigart;
> **Susannah[2] Margaret** who married J.L. Buckingham, (our ancestor)
> **Elizabeth Catherine** who married Rev. Gottlieb Bassler, (also our ancestor)
> **John Bernhard**;
> **Mary Ann Gilbert** who married Rev. George Parson;
> **Benjamin Franklin** who died at 3 months and
> **Edwin D. Gilbert** who married Nancy Jane Cox.

Our great-grandmother Elizabeth Catherine (Eliza) kept a <u>Family Record</u> (Appendix 14) wherein she chronicled the important events in the family. It suggests that she was in close contact with her family via letters although none have survived. These notes vary little from other Gilbert genealogies on the internet and is a testament to her pride in family and her prodigious memory.

Susannah's[1] father was Jacob Gilbert, a Revolutionary soldier and her husband Barnard's father was George Gilbert, who was also a Revolutionary soldier. George and Jacob were brothers. So Susannah and her husband were first cousins.

In 1924 Anna Rupley, a family genealogist, wanted to document that her great-grandfather George served in the Revolution so she submitted an application to the Daughters of the American Revolution (DAR) and was given a national number 146200.

> A Record Copy of the National Society of the Daughters of the American Revolution National Number 146200 submitted by Anna Rupley in October 1924 states: Penn Arch. Series 3 Vol 7 – page 56 for list of Fines rec'd by Hans Morrison Esq, 4th Batt. Verified by National Number 25547

Seventeen years later, in 1941 Mary Jane Gilbert established her connection to her revolutionary ancestor, Jacob Gilbert and was also given a national DAR number # 33701 for Jacob. But as the following reference indicates the DAR now required greater documentation since the complete muster rolls of Pennsylvania's Fourth Battalion hadn't been found and so an affidavit was submitted testifying that both George and Jacob Gilbert's names appear on the List of Fines received by Hans Morrison, Sub-Lieut of York County (April 1777 to March 1780)

> A Record Copy of the Daughters of the American Revolution National Number 337701 submitted by Mary Jane Gilbert in 1941 states: "The said, Jacob Gilbert of York County (Now Adams Co.,PA) is the ancestor who assisted in establishing American Independence while acting in the capacity of a soldier in the 4th Battalion, York county Militia Pennylvania Archives Vol 7, p. 56 of Series 3

Ancestor's Services

> A private in the 4th Battalion of the York County, Pa. Militia. The complete muster rolls of the Fourth Battalion have never been found but the list of Fines received by Hans Morrison, Sub-Lieut of York County (April 1777 to March 1780) has preserved the names of many otherwise not on record. See Pa.Arch.-Series 3. Vol.7-page 56.

> A certificate from the late George R. Prowell bearing on the above statement was given us to prove the service of George Gilbert, a brother of Jacob, and both names appearing on the same list applies to one equally as well as another. This certificate is on file with the records of National #146200.

Barnhard[2] Gilbert's (1786-1868) father was George Gilbert (1735-1803) and his mother was Elizabeth. George's father was Barnhard[1] Gilbert (1724-1802) and his mother was Catherine Bender.(1728-1805?) The father of Barnhard's wife Susannah was Jacob Gilbert (1756-1831) and her mother was Anne Margaret Fox (1769-1838). Jacob's father was Barnhard[1] and his mother was Catherine Bender. Since Barnhard[2] and Susannah were first cousins they share the same set of grandparents.

Barnhard has variant spellings: Barnhart, Barnhard, Bernhard and they were all used by the same gentleman in various documents. Understanding Eliza's <u>Family Notebook</u> was initially very confusing and relationships difficult to sort out before it was understood that Barnhard and his wife were first cousins.

My husband and I traveled to Gettysburgh, Pennsylvania on 26 June 2002 and visited the Adam's Historical Society on the grounds of the Lutheran seminary. My great-grandfather, Gottlieb W. Bassler, actually lived and studied in the same building as a seminarian. The cupolas of both the Lutheran Seminary and Pennsylvania College were used by General Lee during the battle of Gettysburg. The family has three large silver serving spoons that were buried during the Civil War at Gettysburg.

The Historical Society had a folder on the Gilbert family which included a *Lineage of a Pennsylvania Family* traced by Nancy B & Anna R. Rupley, Mercersburg, PA and George Rupley, Duluth, Minn. The following is copied directly from that material: *Part II Chronicles of a Gilbert Family Chapter l Bernhard[1] Gilbert:*

The Gilbert Family whose history is set forth in the following pages was founded, in America, by one Bernhard[1] Gilbert, our immigrant ancestor (1724-1802) who arrived in Philadelphia, Sept 30, 1743 on ship *Robert and Alice* from Rotterdam, last from Cowes. (*Author's note: You may recall that another ancestor Johannes Honsinger came over on the very same ship in 1733. The Robert and Alice operated as a virtual ferry across the Atlantic.*)

The following is a copy of the original record in the State Archives Department at Harrisburg.

(List 101C)
At the Courthouse at Philadelphia Sept 30, 1743

Present

The Honorable George Thomas, Esqr, Lieut Govr
Samuel Hassel
Abraham Taylor
Joshua Maddox
Benjamin Shoemaker Esqrs

The foreigners whose names are underwritten, imported on the ship <u>Phoenix</u>, William Wilson, Commander, and in the ship <u>Robert and Alice</u> Hartley Cusick, Commander, from Rotterdam, but last from Cowes, did this day take the foregoing Oaths or Qualifications to the Government, viz: (Names of the Phoenix male passengers or 16 years of age and upwards)

(List 102 C)

The names of those imported in the *Robert and Alice*, Martly Cusack, Commander (Names of the Robert and Alice male passengers of 16 years and upwards.)

Bernhart[1] Gilbert's name appears on this passenger list in his own hand. Thus:

The characters are English, though the formation of the letters shows a German influence. At that time all foreigners were required to take the Oath of Allegiance to Great Britain. The passengers of the *Robert and Alice* who took this oath, for the most part signed by "MARK" and the names of those so signing are in English, having been written by a clerk. The rest, those whose actual autographs appear are all wholly in German script save and except that of Bernhart Gilbert which shows a decided English influence which differentiates it from the other autographic signatures to the document.

His given or Christian Name has been variously spelled. Viz; Church record-Bernhart; enlistment certificate-Barnard; tax lists-Barnard, Barnabas, Barnet, Barney, and on his tombstone Barnhard.

A tradition persistent in several branches of the family is that Bernhart Gilbert came from Alsace. That his father or possibly a more remote ancestor had come from England into France as a soldier in one of the numerous French English wars, had been made a prisoner by the French and so kept until the end of the war, when having become wonted to the country and its people, he had elected to remain there permanently.

The province of Alsace, while under French domination from 1697 to 1872 was essentially German, in speech and habits, an Englishman interned there would in time become Germanized.

Bernhart Gilbert's age of 19 when he immigrated probably precludes the possibility of his being the internee. The probability is that it was his father or even his grandfather who was the interned British subject and that Bernhart was the offspring of a German marriage made in Alsace.

That he spoke German and affiliated with the Germans is undoubted. His wife, Catherine Bender, we know was German, his children and grandchildren spoke and read in that language equally as well as in English. York Co., PA where he settled was overwhelmingly German.

On July 14, 1746 Bernhard[1] Gilbert enlisted in the English Colonial Army as a private under the command of Samuel Perry. This is recorded in *the Pennsylvania Archives* Series 2 Vol. 2 p.419 5th Series Vol. 1 p.15. His company was one of four raised for an expedition into Canada. They went into winter quarters at Albany, N.Y. (1746-1747) and were finally discharged Oct. 31, 1747, the late intended expedition against Canada having been by his Majesty laid aside for the present. (Votes of Assembly Vol. 4 p.50 & 71;Vol. 6 p. 127 Colonial Records)

…we find our forebear settled in the County of York in the Twp of Straban, where he engaged in the occupation of farming. He arrived in the early 1770's accompanied by his wife Catherine and a little colony of their own: at least six of their children must have been included in that band:

Sophia born 1752

George born 1754 married Elizabeth Ritter Knouse (our ancestor)

Jacob born 1756 married Susanna Strine and then Margaret Fox (our ancestor)

John born 1758 married Christine Walter

Bernhard[2] born 1762 Married Catherine Clapsaddle and then Mrs. Mowry

Lenhard born 1765 married Elizabeth

Henry born 1772 married Elizabeth Boltz

Catherine born 1775 married George Clapsaddle Henry Hoffman

Elizabeth married Daniel Hoffman

Sophia Gilbert married Adam Walter

Christine married ?

We have found no active military service for Bernhard[1] most of the muster rolls of the Battalion covering that part of York Co. are lost, but as our ancestor was then beyond the draft age he probably was not enrolled. Barnabas Gilbert held the office of Township Constable during that period which shows he was a supporter of the Patriot cause. Three of his sons did however serve in the Revolution: George, Jacob and John.

The rest of the Rupley history discusses property and the investigation into the whereabouts of the old family homestead.

In a separate paper in the Gilbert file is a history of the <u>George Gilbert Line.</u>

George was the eldest son of Bernhard[1] Gilbert and Catherine Bender Gilbert. As mentioned, he served in the Revolution from 1777-1780 as a private in the 4th Battalion, York County Militia.

George's son Barnhart[3] married Susanna Gilbert. Barnhard[3] enlisted in the War of 1812 and served in the fortifications around Baltimore. Also in service with him was Simon Rupley, who married Barnhart's sister Sally in 1815, the grandmother of Anna R. Rupley, our hard driving family historian.

Barnhart[2] was licensed to keep a tavern in Gettysburg from 1814 through 1820 and again from 1824 through 1828.

This Barnhart[3] served on the organizing commission and Board of Directors of the Gettysburg National Bank; he was an unsuccessful candidate for the office of coroner in 1812; was a member of the Gettysburg Town Council in 1816, 1817 and 1818; was Sheriff of Adams County 1821-1824, was Prothonotary 1835-39, and county treasurer 1836-1837.

Barnhart[3] was a landowner, as indicated by his 1831 deed to Thaddeus Stevens of interests in three parcels...

His business fortunes took a down turn in the panic of 1837, which resulted in his moving to Tennessee. Barnhart and Susannah are buried in Cedar Grove Cemetery, Athens, Tennessee.

His and Susanna's[1] children are:

Elizabeth died as an infant

Jesse Gilbert (1807-1838) a physician, married Jane Sloan

Delilah Gilbert (1809-1885) married Rev. Edward Atlee

Sarah Ann (1811-1891) married Rev. Henry G. Dill

George (1814-) married Sarah Jane Jones

Jacob (1815-) married Elizabeth Swigart

Susannah Margaret (1818-) married John L. Buckingham (Julia Sherman Bassler's grandmother**)** ancestor

Elizabeth Catherine (1820-) married Rev. Gottlieb Bassler (William Gilbert Bassler's mother) ancestor

John Bernhart lived nine months 1823

MaryAnn (1824-) married Rev. George Parson died after childbirth

Benjamin Franklin lived 3 months 1826

Edwin (1828-) married Nancy Jane Cox

—— End of *Lineage of a Pennsylvania Family* ——

Eliza's family was large but comfortable. Her father was a banker and an involved citizen. She was educated at the Gettysburg Seminary for Women and could read and write Latin and Greek. Her uncle, Dr. David Gilbert taught at the Lutheran Seminary in Gettysburg. So most likely she was introduced to her future husband through that connection. This was probably also true for her sister, MaryAnn.

In 1837 there was a bank crash and the family was forced to sell their holdings and move with their two unmarried daughters to Tennessee where they had family. Her father became a shopkeeper. The two young ministers who met the sisters in Gettysburg continued to court them even after they moved to Tennessee.

When Barnhart[3] and his wife Susanna moved to Athens, Tennessee, MaryAnn was twenty and Eliza, was twenty two. We know of this early migration from an obituary notice in a local newspaper in Zelienople, PA. This was a reprint in part of a section "What Happened 50 Years Ago."

> The journey took three weeks in a carriage. They crossed the mountains at Waldron's Gap and drove over the Natural Bridge in Virginia. The vehicle forded the Roanoak River seven times. A double log cabin was the only hotel at which to stop overnight. Two years later. Eliza and MaryAnn were married in a double wedding ceremony October 31, 1844 by the Rev. Jim Kelly in Athens, Tennessee.

> After they were married the bride's father took the couples to Nashville where they boarded a steamboat. They journeyed down the Cumberland River and up the Ohio arriving at Beaver, Pennsylvania November 23rd after sixteen days of river travel. The couples parted when MaryAnn and George headed to Sudbury. He being from Muncy, PA and Eliza and Gottlieb continued on to Zelienople the next day. They arrived in time to

fill an appointment to preach to the newly organized English Lutheran congregation which at that time met in St. Paul's Lutheran Church.

Sadly MaryAnn Parson died 4 January 1846 only three months after giving birth to her first child, William Edwin Parson, on 18 October 1845.

Before the journey to Tennessee, Eliza was given an Album to keep as a Memory Book by her father. He signed "Presented to Miss Eliza C. Gilbert by her affectionate Father B. Gilbert." The album carries a 1835 publication date. It is brown with embossed

gold on front and back and is in remarkable condition considering it is 177 years old. Most of the writing is clear and readable.

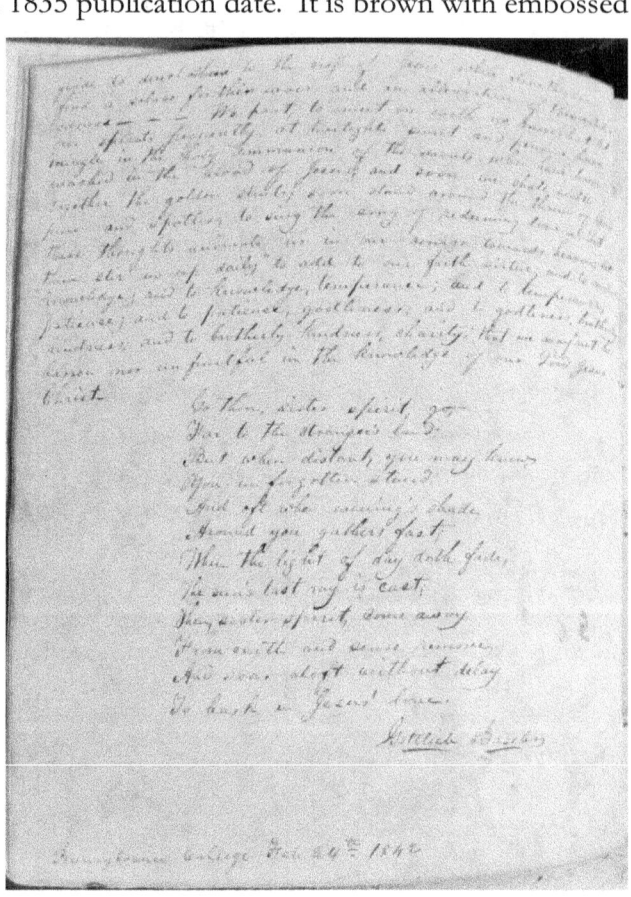

The dated entries indicate that the book was kept from 1838 to 1844. Her family, cousins, niece and future husband all wrote in it. There are pressed flowers still preserved along with the fine sentiments of her friends. Some entries are dated and signed in Athens, Tennessee; others from Cedar Springs, Tennessee. It looks like her Grandfather Jacob Gilbert also signed it. One entry was from Gottlieb Bassler signed Pennsylvania College 24 February 1842. This would have been two years before he and Eliza were married. Another is signed Seminary 27 July 1838 by a friend or family member, L. Lepley. The last entry is written by Eliza's future husband on the inside back cover:

Gottlieb Bassler's entry signed Pennsylvania College 20 Feb 1846

> *In memory leaves O may I share*
> *One lonely vacant spot*
> *Of all the names recorded there*
> *Let mine nere be forgot*

– *GWB*

This is the only example of Gottlieb using a middle initial and it probably stands for William. Since

Cover of Eliza's Album

Inside leaf, signed by her father, B Gilbert

Hon. William G. Bassler standing in front of his grandfather's birthplace Director's residence, Lutheran Orphanage, Zelienople, Pennsylvania

he named his son, William. It is interesting to note that Eliza's sister Delilah married Edwin Atlee and her cousin Sarah married his brother, William Atlee. Their names figure in the Memory Book and Eliza named her daughter Mary Atlee.

Eliza was a life-long reader. One of her books has survived. In it she signed her name, Eliza Catherine Gilbert, Gettysburg, Adams County, and the date 1833 on the front page. It is *The Poetical Works of Thomas Campbell*, published by S & D A Forbes New York 1830. She would have been ten years old. One of the two existing pictures we have of her shows Eliza reading in the upstairs bedroom of her home on New Castle St.

Eliza's husband had accepted the call of Bishop Schweitzerbarth to pastor the first English speaking Lutheran Church in Zelienople. At first the couple worked together in the ministry. The 1850 Census indicates that Eliza assisted in teaching at the orphanage. But those duties diminished as the family grew. Eliza had seven children but only one survived to adulthood.

Eliza and the Rev. Bassler lived in Zelienople for five years, then they moved to Middle Lancaster for the next five years. When they returned in 1849, Rev. Bassler took charge of the Orphan's home. They lived in a brick house on the grounds of the English Lutheran Orphanage. The building still stands. Our grandfather, William G., was born there.

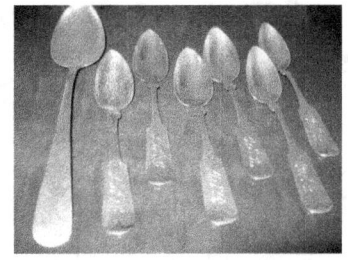

Large serving spoon buried during the Civil War in Gettysburg

Small spoons made from melted silver coins Gottlieb had them inscribed G & E

It is unlikely that Eliza ever visited her family in Gettysburg again. Certainly most of the entries in her Memory Book sound as if she is parting from her friends forever. Both the difficulty and expense of travel at that time, and the fact that she was pregnant with child every few years, would conspire against her traveling. The Civil War also prohibited visits for many years. Of course it is possible that some of her family visited her, but we have no record of it. The family surely would have sent letters, which as mentioned do not survive. What has survived are stories and spoons.

During the next fifteen years Gottlieb and Eliza gave birth to:

Susannah b.12 Sept 1846 d.12 March 1855. We have a copy of a composition she wrote at age 8. (Appendix 13)
Louisa Dill b. 9 April 1848. d. 21 March 1859 when she was 2 ½.
Francis Gilbert, named after his paternal grandfather. d 25 March 1854 at 3 ½.mos

Mary Atlee b. 24 November 1852 d 5 Dec 1868 named for Eliza's sister
Mary Ann who passed away in 1846.

William Gottlieb b. 6 December 1854. d 29 June 1934

Augustus Herman b. 28 September 1858 d, 11 April 1859 at six months
of age.

Anna Elizabeth born 16 April 1861 and died 26 February 1862 at ten
months

With the exception of Susannah, Mary and William, two children died as toddlers and
two as infants. An entry from William's <u>Diary</u> (Appendix 22) dated May 27, 1910 states: "...
then went out to Home cemetery to plant a couple of Geraniums on our graves…" Later
according to William's <u>Diary</u> two of the bodies were moved to Rev. Gottlieb's plot in the
English Lutheran Cemetery. He writes 8 Nov 1911: " In PM was out at the Home, Charlie
Goehring was removing the remains of Father and Sister Mary to the cemetery above
town." (Appendix 22) I presume the graves of the other children are on the grounds of
the Old Lutheran Farm School and Orphanage but I have been unable to document that.

Eliza came from a large family of twelve. It must have been a great heartache to
lose so many children. Three died in March, one in
April and another in February. No family story ex-
plains these deaths. We know Rev. Gottlieb died of
tuberculosis but we don't know when he contracted it and Eliza remained unaffected. Looking at the
time of year, the deaths may have been due to the
flu. Infant mortality was high and expected but one
wonders what took Susannah at eight and a half and
Mary at sixteen? Looking at other large families in
our genealogy there is noted the loss of one or two
infants. But no family suffered the calamitous tragic
losses of Eliza and Gottlieb.

Susanna A. Consort of Bernhart Gilbert
Formerly of Gettysburg
Cedar Grove Cemetery, Athens, Tennessee

Eliza and Pastor Bassler were celebrating the birth of a child as another perished
the following year. In what must have been a terrible year – 1854, Eliza gave birth to a
son and buried another in the same year! Only to be followed by yet another funeral for
daughter, Susannah in 1855. Even for people of great faith they must have felt sorely
tried. And on 21 July 1863 Eliza's mother, Susannah died 21 July 1863 at 77 years of age
and is buried in Cedar Grove Cemetery, Athens, Tennessee.

Eliza gave an engraved gold watch to her only surviving child, William
Gottlieb on his 21st birthday saying: "This is all that is left." Her grandson,
Sherman Gilbert Bassler gave it in turn to his son, William Gilbert Bassler.
It was purchased from Bailey Banks & Biddle, a jewelry store still doing
business in the Philadelphia area.

CHAPTER 7

THE BASSLERS

Gottlieb W. Bassler

Gottlieb Bassler was born 10 December 1813 in Longenthal, Canton Berne, Switzerland. He was four years old when he boarded ship in 1817 with his father, Franz, and his mother, Barbra Kafer. The story told is that mother and child died during the crossing. Perhaps Barbara died after giving birth. Barbra's parents were Johanas Kafer and Maria Melch. Franz was a cooper or barrel maker by trade. He settled in Harmony, Pennsylvania. At some point, Franz anglicized his name to Francis and became a citizen 9 June 1834. He died at age 88 on March 1847 and is buried at Harmony.

Marriage certificate of Frantz and Barbra Kafer Bassler

The citizenship papers for Francis (Franz) name Baden as place of origin. However, there is a Baden, Germany and a Baden, Switzerland. Baden, Switzerland is predominantely Catholic. A story retold is that when William G Bassler heard that Sherman would marry a Catholic he said. "Well, the family had been Catholic." The Alumni Record for Gottleib lists Longanthal, Switzerland as his birthplace and in another place Berne, Switzerland. Census records are no help because sometimes Germany is listed as place of origin and other times Switzerland. Perhaps the family left Germany and moved to Switzerland before emigrating to the United States. Yet another field for further research. After graduating law school my brother tried to research the family in Switzerland but was told that fire had destroyed the church and the records.

In any event, Francis and his son settled in Harmony. *The History of Butler County Pennsylvania 1895* Harmony Borough Chapter 28 mentions Francis Bassler among other coopers (barrel makers) " as the pioneers of 1816-1817" but it was Zelienople that was to become the home of the Bassler family for over one hundred and thirty years. Only in her 90's did Gottlieb's daughter-in-law, Julia move to New Jersey to live with her son, Sherman and daughter-in-law, Ethel.

9 June 1834 Citizenship papers of Francis (Franz) Bassler indicates "Badden" (misspelled) as place of origin. It is most likely Baden, Switzerland which is largely Catholic. A family story is that the Bassler family was originally Catholic.

Gottlieb Bassler's Indenture papers

On 10 September 1827 Gottlieb was apprenticed to Jacob Steck for five years and three months. Steck was a printer in Greensburg. Gottlieb was fourteen years old when he left home. His indenture papers said he was to receive six months night schooling and at the conclusion of his indenture, a new suit of clothing and freedom. The indenture was signed and sealed in Presence of Gottlieb Bofsler, Franz Bafsler, J. L. Steck, John Harper on 10 September 1827.

The young boy took full advantage of his schooling which was probably one night a week during the school year. After his indenture, Gottlieb actually worked as a journeyman printer first at Greensburg, Pennsylvania and then at Washington, D.C. We know from Benjamin Franklin who worked for his brother, a printer, that this apprenticeship was an excellent education in the printed word. Apprentices learned to read text upside down as they were setting it. They were exposed to contemporary writing as well as religious texts.

In 1831 a special conference of Lutheran pastors was held in Greensburg. Gottlieb was eighteen. The first President of the Pittsburgh Synod (1840-1845) was Rev. Michael John Steck who founded the Ohio Synod in 1818. Michael J could be the brother or eldest son of Jacob Steck to whom Gottlieb was apprenticed. It would explain how young Gottlieb was introduced to the Lutheran ministry and how they in turn were introduced to a serious and intelligent young man.

On 10 December 1832 Gottlieb turned nineteen. He had served his indenture and was a free man with a new suit of clothes. After a few years of working in the trade, Gottlieb became a private student of Bishop Schweitzerbarth of Zelienople. Gottlieb taught Latin and Greek at the Connoquenessing Academy. By 1836 at age 23 Gottlieb began studying at Gettysburg institutions and entered the freshman class of Pennsylvania College in Gettysburg. The minutes of the Phrenakosmian Society show that he was one of the most active members of his period. He attended the Lutheran Theological Seminary, Gettysburg from 1841-1842 and was licensed to preach in 1842. It would seem that the Lutheran community took Gottlieb under its wing and supported his education.

Rev. Gottlieb Bassler

In the Sixth Commencement of Pennsylvania College, Gettysburgh, PA Wednesday 16 September 1840 after a prayer by Rev A. Lochman followed by music, Gottlieb Bassler gave the Latin Salutatory address. His degree was conferred by President Krauth.

The Pennsylvania College book 1832-1882 E.S. Breidenbaugh, Editor published for the Alumni Association of Pennsylvania College Philadelphia Lutheran Publication Society 1882 contains a lengthy historical perspective and tribute to the legacy of Gottlieb Bassler.

The *Gettysburg Lutheran Theological Seminary Vol. Two Alumni Record* says: *Entered 1840*

> Bassler, Gottlieb, b. Berne, Switzerland, 1813; A.B. Gettysburg Col., 1840; grad Gbg Sem., 1842; lic. W. Pa. Syn., 1842; ord. Pb. Syn., 1845; pastor, Zelienople, Pa., 1842-1864; tutor Gbg. Col., 1841-42; dir. Zelienople Orphans' Home, 1854-68; one of founders of Pb. Syn.; pres. Reading convention, 1866; pres. G.C., 1867-68; m. Eliza Gilbert, Oct. 31, 1844; d. Oct. 3, 1868.

On 14 April 1841 Gottlieb at twenty-eight began a journey south to visit Lutheran communities in preparation for his consecration as a man of God. He kept a journal of his trip titled: <u>The Diary of a Journey to Virginia</u>. My husband, Richard, and I took the same journey over 150 years later, stopping at the towns he visited including the Luray caverns and Harper's Ferry. The following is a short excerpt from the <u>Diary of a Journey</u>. (Appendix 16)

> About 2 1/2 o'clock P.M. I started from Gettysburg and after a tolerably pleasant although fatiguing walk of 3 1/2 hours we arrived in Emmittsburgh. Brs. Bear and Gelweck accompanied me, (the latter of whom will stop here) I immediately went to Mr. Winter's and although I did not meet with that cordial and warm reception apparently which I had expected, my especial friend Miss Barbara having from home yet after this family recollected me again more distinctly I began to feel at home.
>
> It happened that a bible Class was held at the house of "mine host" in this evening by Rev. Fries, pastor of the German Reformed Church. I was tolerable pleased with a few exceptions which I will not mention here....

In 24 February 1842 Gottlieb wrote in Eliza's memory book and signed it- Pennsylvania College. His intentions were clear. He knew he wanted to share his lifetime journey with Eliza and even though she would move to Tennessee with her family he would travel there to marry her.

On 13 November 1842. Bishop John Scheizerbarth of St. Paul's, Zelienople called Pastor Bassler as his assistant to preach in English for young people who no longer conversed in German. Pastor Gottlieb Bassler answered the call and came to Zelienople. He was 29.

This was to lead to the founding of the English Lutheran Church in Zelienople. January, 1843. Gottlieb was 31 when he organized the English Lutheran Church in Zelienople. The following year on 31 October 1844 he married Elizabeth Gilbert. He was 32 and she was 24. Pastor Bassler's salary was less than $200.00 of which $100 came from the Zelienople Church and $50 came from the Butler Church. Parishoners held subscription books and Pastor Bassler went door to door to collect money for his salary. The salary was set by the Pennsylvania Ministerium of the Lutheran Church.

Pastor Bassler served four parishes: English Lutheran, Zelienople; Butler County Evangelical Lutheran; Zion Middle Lancaster Lutheran and Emmanual Lutheran at Prospect. For years the family had a leather pouch and one leather boot that was used by the Pastor when traveling by horseback. It was donated to the Harmony Museum. Pastors working to develop the Lutheran Church in western Pennsylvania saw the need for organization. This is recounted in the *History of the Pittsburgh Synod of the General synod of the Evangelical Lutheran Church:1748,1845,1904 (1904)* by Ellis Beaver Burgess.

The founders of the Pittsburgh Synod 1844-1845 were Rev. Michael John Steck,

George Ehrenfeld; Abraham Weills; David Earhart; Elihu Rathbun; William Passavant; Gottlieb Bassler; and Samuel Witt. William and Gottlieb went to Gettysburg Seminary together. The Synod records are at Thiel College.

> In 1850 ...Rev. Bassler was sent on a missionary tour to Canada. He found the Lutherans of the Province in great spiritual destitution. After spending several weeks with them, journeying from settlement to settlement, baptizing the children and conducting divine services in their churches and school-houses, he returned to Pennsylvania and published a full account of his journey in *The Missionary*. A large interest was created at once. P.78 *History of the Pittsburgh Synod*

From December 1853 to November 1854 Gottlieb was the supply pastor to St. Peter's Evangelical Church in Evans City, Pennsylvania. In 1854 Pastor Bassler gave up the Butler Church for the second time (I don't know when the first time occured). He was 41 and not in good health. Most likely he was already suffering from tuberculosis.

On 25 March 1854 Gottlieb's father died. Francis was buried in Harmony. His age as recorded in the Family Bible was eighty-eight. In 13 May 1861 Pastor Bassler again resigned. He was fifty-one. The church hired someone for a year and a half.

In 1867 Gottlieb was elected President of the General Council of the Pittsburg Synod. He had concern for the historic position of the Lutheran Church. Division threatened the unity of the synod. There were many issues. (See Appendix 17 for more information about the formation of the Pittsburg Synod.) In 1868 the Zelienople Church asked him to be Pastor again. In March they got Rev. Kunkleman. Kunkleman received $250 from Zelienople and $250 from Lancaster, the use of a house and a garden plot at the Orphan's Home and School.

In 3 October 1868 Gottlieb traveled to Atlantic City for treatment and relief of his worsening tuberculosis. He returned to the house of Dr. Krauth in West Philadelphia where he lingered for weeks. Finally he reached Pittsburgh where he died 3 October 1868 at the home of Dr. Passavant, his college friend and co-laborer in the ministry of the church. His last thoughts were of the Church and as the brethren on their way to Synod bade him farewell in his sickroom, his prayer was "God bless the Church. God bless the General Council, God bless the Pittsburgh Synod." According to Rev. Ellis Burgess:

> In addition to his pastoral work, he had to bear the heaviest burden of the Synodical Academy and his health was not strong enough to endure it. His love for the Synod was a passion; all her interests were his. ... He took a deep interest in the organization of the General Council and was elected President of the Reading Convention. The men of the General Synod very generally recognized and respected the sincerity of his Lutheran convictions, and admired even while they opposed him. P. 57 *History of the Pittsburgh Synod*

He was 55 years of age. He is buried in the English Lutheran Cemetery, Zelienople.

There is a large monument marking his grave. It receives perpetual care. The lettering was re-pointed by my brother and me in 2009. Two months after her father died Mary Atlee died 5 Dec 1868. She was sixteen. Her stone is to the right of her father's memorial. Her brother William was 14 on his birthday, the very next day, December 6th.

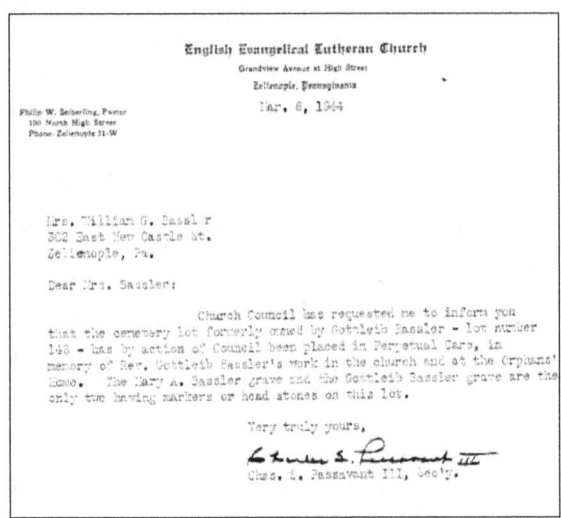

Perpetual care letter.

Eliza at age forty-eight and after seven pregnancies was left a widow with one son. In 1865 when William was eleven years old, Abraham Lincoln was assassinated April 15th. The funeral train of the slain president rode slowly back to Springfield, Illinois and young William watched it pass near Zelienople. He placed a coin on the tracks which rolled over and flattened it. It remained in the family.

William G. Bassler would have been fifty when he took this touching picture of his newborn son in the arms of his elderly mother, Eliza. She was to pass away in 1908. William had had a difficult childhood. Every new birth of a sibling to Eliza and Gottlieb brought joy and every journey to the cemetery brought grief to the dwindling family. When his sister, Mary, died at age 16, William at 14 found himself an only child with a widowed mother.

As the son of a Lutheran pastor, William would have been eligible to attend Thiel College. This school founded by Rev. William A. Passavant in 1866 began at Phillipsburg, now Monaca, and later moved to Greenville, Pennsylvania in 1870. Although tuition was free, room and board while cheap by today's standards would still have been a great burden to Eliza who now had no visible means of support. However, there must have been some source of income perhaps provided by insurance or a church fund or a modest inheritance; but if so, no one ever mentioned it. William was sent off to school and there is a record of

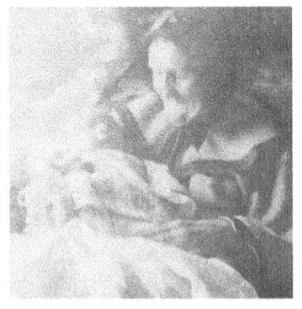

Eliza holding her grandson Sherman Gilbert Bassler 1907

his attending Thiel College during the year 1877 to 1878 but his name is listed under the Academic session which would have been equivalent to a preparatory high school. (Appendix 18) However, at the time of his attendance he would have been 23 years old. Where he was from the age of 17 or 18 at the normal end of high school until he is mentioned in the Thiel Catalogue in 1877 is unknown. He may have been working to save money for additional schooling or perhaps he traveled west to spend time with family in Missouri.

The family story relates that when Eliza became ill William was called home from school to attend to his mother. He never returned to Thiel. But the family story is silent about what this would have meant to young William. In September of 1876 when William was 22 years old he took a trip to the Centennial Exposition in Philadelphia and was quite taken with the latest machinery displayed there. He sent his mother a commemorative typed memento.

Sherman talked very little about his father. So we have to create a picture of him through the bits and pieces that we do know. It is tempting to look back at this family's tragic losses through the lens of modern psychoanalysis but Eliza and William soldiered on through sadness or depression relying on each other's inner strength and their Christian beliefs.

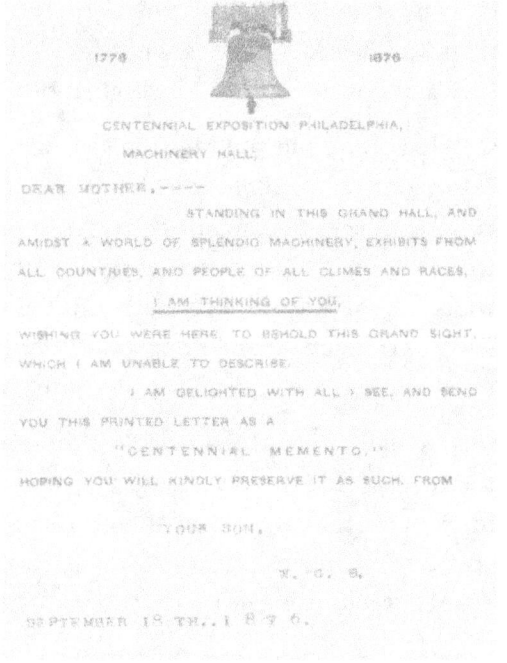

As already mentioned, William did take a trip to Clinton, Missouri to visit his mother's older sister, Susannah Margaret Gilbert, who married a Buckingham and his Aunt Laura Buckingham who married Albert Sherman. At this time, William met Julia, Laura's daughter. Perhaps, Eliza hoped he would meet a young woman and return to Zelienople with a bride. But that did not happen on this trip.

There is little known about what did happen during the next twenty plus years of this man's life. At some point he found a way to make a living. William G. Bassler took up photography. I don't know when or how this took place. His <u>Diary</u> (Appendix 22) attests to the frequent photographs he took of babies, farms, horses, pets, family and community gatherings. His glass plates lay on wooden shelves in a bedroom closet for years and years, but were broken when the shelves gave way and the plates shattered. We have been told that there are people in the community who still have some of those precious plates.

Eliza in her 80's surely wanted to have her son "settled" before she died. After all the loss in the family, she would not have wanted him to live the rest of his days alone. She must have exerted pressure on him to make another trip to Clinton, Missouri. We

William Gottlieb Bassler studio portrait

Probably a self-portrait of WGB

do know that William attended the 1893 Chicago World's Fair and it is reasonable to think while that far west, he would again visit his family in Missouri. This time his first cousin once removed, Julia, was now twenty-seven. She also had no prospects of marriage. Observers could easily say this was an arranged marriage of convenience. My mother, Ethel Bassler, certainly felt that her mother-in-law married into the job of caregiver, first and foremost. And while there is no denying that, both Julia from 1903-1904 and her husband, William from 1909-1911 kept diaries and these personal records of everyday life tell a different story. They tell about love and consideration. They tell about a child they created and cared for deeply.

Julia raised in the Methodist Episcopal Church became a Lutheran. (Years later Julia asserted to her daughter-in-law, Ethel, that her conversion to Lutheranism was in no way comparable to Sherman's conversion to Catholicism.) She was a dutiful daughter-in-law from the time she married in 1902 until the death of Eliza in 1908. She entered into the social life of the English Lutheran Church which included her neighbors. Their familiar names come up again and again in her Diary and years later many sign her Memorial Funeral book at the end of her long life. (Appendix 21)

A stamped address of the photographer and his Bell phone number 33J appears on the reverse side of the undated photo of the Lutheran Orphanage picnic. The young boy in front of Julia is not her son so this photo was probably taken sometime between 1902 and 1907. William's Diary (1909-1912) mentions taking local photos at least two or three times a week. It is fair to say he chronicled the life of this small town of Zelienople at the beginning of the 20th century. His Diary also indicates he was an agent for the German Mutual Insurance Co. based in Zelienople. (Appendix 22)

My father said he was embarrassed about the great age disparity between his parents. Teenagers are especially sensitive about such things. My dad even joked to his wife that his was a "virgin birth" and he was conceived after his parents had taken a walk in the rain. His wife, Ethel, also recounted that he was embarrassed to push his aging father downtown in a

Julia (left of center) sits in front row behind a child at the Lutheran Home's picnic

wheelchair. Then of course he felt guilty about being embarrassed. However, had he ever read his parent's diaries written in the early years of their married life, he might have felt differently.

With that said, we have no wedding picture of the couple in the Hotel Boyer in Pittsburgh. Julia wed without family or friends present. William as the sole surviving sibling had no family or friends present either. His ailing mother waited in Zelienople for the married couple to return from Pittsburgh. There was no party or reception to celebrate the occasion. Looking back at the Sherman family pictures in Missouri we see a lively and engaged group

THURS., JULY 2, 1964—BUTLER CO. NEWS-RECORD—15

Do You Remember?

SOCIAL CIRCLE—This photo of the Social Circle of the English Lutheran Church, Zelienople, was taken about 1910 and submitted by Mrs. Paul F. Davies of 102 N. Division St., Rev. George H. Schnur was pastor at the time. In the second row, second from the right, is Mrs. William G. Bassler, oldest present member of the church. In that same row, at the very left, is Mrs. Elizabeth White. Standing in the back row, fourth from the right, is Emma Gross, resident of the Lutheran Old Peoples Home. Seated in the center, wearing black, is Sister Catherine, then matron at the home. Behind her is Mrs. Davies. At Mrs. Davies' right is Emma Passavant; at her left is Mrs. Sidney Passavant. In the front row, from left, the first person is Mrs. Carl Hartmann who was then Edna Gross; third from the left is Eleanor Stout, Zelienople High School English teacher, and fifth from the left is Fred Zehner, manager of Penney's Hardware in Zelienople.

Julia sits to the left of Sister Catherine in black Probably taken by her husband, WGB circa 1910, Published 1964 in Butler Co. News Record

of people. However, Julia's new Bassler family would be as opposite a scenario as she could have imagined. William was Postmaster of Zelienople during the Republican terms of Theodore Roosevelt (1901-1909) and Howard Taft (1909-1913) The political job with its steady income ended with the Democratic election of Woodrow Wilson (1913-1921). Thereafter, William worked as a photographer earning meager wages.

Julia making bread

*Julia probably took this picture of her husband
"Sherman's little basket of acorns" circa 1909*

Julia's <u>Diary</u> (Appendix 19) and WGB's <u>Diary</u> (Appendix (22) can be accessed in full but I will choose a few entries to describe the daily, mundane married life William and Julia embarked on.

Julia begins:

Jan 7, 1903 Wednesday:

Weather cloudy snowed most of the day. Sophie washed, I baked pumpkin pie and mince then I made a shelf in the cellar way under steps. Got dinner and washed the dishes read some home papers Pa sent then wrote to Bert. Will came home a little early and fixed the doorbell, after supper I ironed some then went down town and got some meat and some muslin for pillowcase.

Jan 9 Friday

Cold all day, in A.M. I dressed M and cleaned her room was all done my work by 9. I read awhile then Will came brought me a letter from home. All was well. In P.M. Will came home early and took a sleep. I finished my pillowcase in evening. Will wrote to Minnie and sent her cap, about 9 I went to bed. Will was late this evening.

January 23 Friday Papa's Birthday 56 yr.

Weather gloomy in A.M. but cleared off in P.M., in A.M. I was busy cleaning and washing off flowers. I then baked an apple pie and made a dumpling for dinner. After dinner, I swept his Mothers room, hung some pictures up in her room. Finished my letter home. Then Mrs. Wright came over. I went upstairs and sewed some on a pillow case. Will went to the funeral of a Zeigler boy, after he came home he put some hooks in our new rooms. Got supper. I wrote to Miss Cornish, Miss Studibaker called. I put his M to bed then I read some.

William begins his <u>Diary</u> in 1909 after the birth of his son in 1907 and the death of his mother in 1908. Clearly baby Sherman brings joy to his life.

Oct 3 Sunday

We were all at Church in AM Sherman good boy. Rev Rex preached good sermon in PM, Julia, Sherman and I walked out past the Catholic church and gathered Sherman's little basket of acorns. Stopped to see Adam Endress, in evening we all went to church again but Sherman was restless and Julia brought him home. Weather pleasant.

Oct 19 Tuesday

Julia washed this AM I looked after Sherman and helped a little in PM down at office wrote up some insurance. Sherman opened a door turned the knob for the first time – the door to hall from dining room. I was hot all day. Old Stout took up flag stone in side walk and dug it down. Weather pleasant

Oct 29 Friday

Everybody feeling better today I was working in den most all day felt tough for awhile, in fact I was weak and tired all day about 4 or 5 PM gave S a long ride down WC Street to Railroad then up home on other street in evening Julia and I took S up to Dr. R who said he has whooping cough.

A little apprehensive, Sherman keeps his balance. But baby Sherman's patience is wearing thin as the photo session goes on a little too long and he is fighting back tears. William took many, many pictures of other people's babies but clearly his talent is revealed in these beautiful portraits of his toddler son.

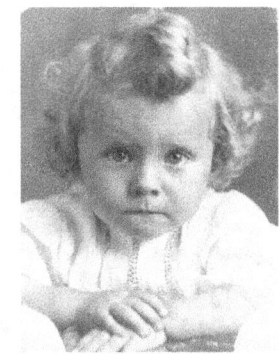

Sherman circa 1909.

Sherman was baptized on 22 December 1907. His name along with his parents are inscribed in a memento booklet "The Sacrament of Holy Baptism." His parents were the sponsors and the Pastor was L.J. Baker. His christening dress is preserved. When Sherman was thirteen he made his confirmation. We have the booklet commemorating the event, 28 March 1920. This certifies that:

> *Sherman Gilbert Bassler having professed faith in our Lord Jesus Christ and vowed obedience to his gospel as confessed by the Evangelican Lutheran Church was received into full communion with the English Lutheran Church of Zelienople, P.Ad. By the solemn rite of confirmation. Signed M.M. Allbeck, Pastor.*

There was very little money. But a copious photo album shows Sherman as an infant, toddler and young man surrounded by loving gifts from his mother and father and extended family in Missouri. Whatever discretionary money the family had went to Sherman. He is well-kept and well-dressed even at great sacrifice.

The family stayed in close touch through the years by letters. Julia's mother and sisters and nephew also made the long expensive trip from Missouri to visit her in Zelienople. The group posed on the rocks at the historic site of McConnell's Mills in Portersville in Lawrence County which is 11 miles north of Zelienople. It encompass-

Julia's Missouri family visiting McConnel's Mill
Forefront: Laura Sherman, Julia Bassler, Sherman

es 2,546 acres of the spectacular Slippery Rock Creek. William also took pictures of the visitors on the Bassler's front porch.

Julia was Sherman's friend and playmate trying to make up for the vast age difference between the child and his father. Years later in a letter to his mother on his birthday

Portrait of Julia & Sherman taken by WGBassler circa 1910

he mentions how they built a radio from scratch together and how much fun it was. (Appendix 34) He was understandably very close to his mother. But she could say "No." They lived in a small community and when Sherman wanted to get a dog, Julia wouldn't allow it because she feared it would cause trouble with the neighbors. She also gave good advice to her grandson, William, who recalls: "Grandma B would often say to me: 'If you can't say something good about some one, don't say anything at all.'"

Sherman went with his mother more than a few times to visit his extended family in Missouri. He always spoke kindly of his cousin, Hershel. The family in turn traveled to Zelienople. In 1910 Julia took her second visit home to Clinton, Missouri when Sherman was three years of age. Julia wrote a humorous letter to her husband.. (Appendix 23) After the visit Aunt Minnie wrote to her little nephew. (Appendix 11a) More Bassler photographs are in *Images of America-Zelienople for Zelienople Historical Society* by Tom Nesbitt.

As mentioned Sherman loved to make radios with his mother and with his best friend Henry (Henny) Ziegler. Sherman attended the Zelienople public schools. Julia saved his report cards. They show good grades through grammar school but achievement in Junior year of high school is spotty. In 1957 on his fiftieth birthday Sherman reminds his mother in a letter of their radio making days. (Appendix 34)

Clinton,Mo family visiting Zelienople,PA

Sherman at a Clinton, MO bog - sixth from right or left.

Eva, Julia,unidentified woman back porch Zelienople undated

Sherman,Julia & WGB back porch

Julia and Sherman visiting Clinton, MO 1910

3rd Grade, Sherman standing at end of 2nd row (Halloween essay writing in 1917 Appendix 25)

The family did not have the money to send Sherman to college, but Julia's sister, Minnie Sherman sent money and funded Sherman's two year post- secondary schooling at a technical school at Indiana, PA where Sherman learned Morse Code and earned a certificate to become a radio operator. On April 8, 1927 he was issued a license of Radio Operator, Commercial First Class from the US of A Department of Commerce #4292.

On 18 May 1931 he received a license 6889 Detroit, Michigan. Sherman's first job was as an operator on the Great Lakes. Other than a few trips to visit family in Missouri this exposure to life on the Great Lakes was an eye opener to the sheltered young man. We have a letter from Sherman from S/S Michigan Oct. 28th Lake Eire 10:30 AM.

He writes a very descriptive letter home. However only one page survived.

Dear Dad and All:

Friday morning and just entering the Detroit River bound up to Marquette again. We were at Ashtabula from ten in the morning till about ten thirty at night as there were two other large boats ahead of us, the Wm K Fields and the Joseph Frantz. Both are big boats and sure are floating palaces compared to this one. I never knew lake boats were so fine. So that gave us a little more time in port as they had to unload them first. They were nearly through the Fields but hadn't started on the Frantz. I was up town after

Sherman played the trumpet in the school band Written in his high school autograph book: "B sharp B natural but never B flat"

Studio portrait of Julia, Sherman and William undated circa 1920 perhaps Confirmation

Graduation picture 1925

Zelienople High School graduating class of 1925. Sherman sporting glasses and bowtie in 3rd row. He was president of his class.

20 yr old Sherman in Radio Operator Clute Studio, Zelienople, PA

Morse key

Proud to be on the S/S Michigan

dinner time and called mother up and got some envelopes at the PO. Not much doing in Ashtabula up street. Lots of activity at Ashtabula Harbor where the boats come in. It is about 15 min street car ride up to the town. Was tough luck to hear that you never got the 25 dollars I sent but guess I will know better next time. That was a big pay 36 dollars and came pretty nice as it is always easier it seems if the trips are long to save money. I thought this time we would go to F. William, Canada for grain but I guess if we go there we will get storage grain for Buffalo and lay up there. When they get storage grain they leave the grain in the boat all winter where it is layed up. I see all the boats that were layed up at Ashtabula are in operation again. There were a dozen big steamers layed up here.

I guess you can get a good idea of the Michigan from the pictures. I took one down in the hold as they were unloading coal but didn't give it enough time I guess so it was a dud. You can see the clam buckets and the rigs. They move the rigs along the dock to get to the various hatches. There are 30 12ft center hatches on this boat. And at the time of the picture she was unloading 10,000 tons of coal. The boat is 6934 gross tons. It takes 24 tons of coal to keep her going every day. How would you like to be a fireman?

One fireman shovels a ton and a half of coal every three hours. There are 6 fireman who work 5 hours and are off 6.

It is noteworthy that the letter is addressed to "Dad" and that he is sending money home. Something he would do for the rest of his life. It is also obvious that he likes his job and finds the whole business of shipping interesting. Port cities and "salty" sailors were quite an education for a sheltered young man from Zelienople. Later he would know ports like San Juan, Puerto Rico, Bremerhaven, Germany and exotic places like Basra in the Middle East.

Sherman worked from July, 1927 to May, 1929 on the Great Lakes and he loved it. He especially loved the science of the locks that allowed huge ships to be raised up or down to accommodate the level of the next body of water. Above is an aerial view of the locks at Sault St. Marie in Michigan- Soo Locks.

However, Sherman's mother called him home to help with his ailing father. (This is reminiscent of Eliza calling William home from school to aid her.) Julia had no family near to help her nor did she have money to hire help. William had long suffered stomach complaints which he mentions in his Diary in 1909. He may have been suffering from Chron's disease which in the future afflicted his great-grandaughter, Julia. By 1930 he needed an operation which took place on the kitchen table. It may have been a colectomy. At first the anesthesia, probably ether, caused dementia and although that cleared in time, William's overall health began to decline. In the 1930 census Julia lists her occupation as photographer. So she is now the breadwinner of the family. A document shows that Sherman returned to the Great Lakes receiving license # 6889 on 18 May 1931 Detroit, Michigan and he worked from 16 June 1929 to 23 March 1933 with a Satisfactory rating. Although the stock market crashed in 1929, it did not directly effect the families of

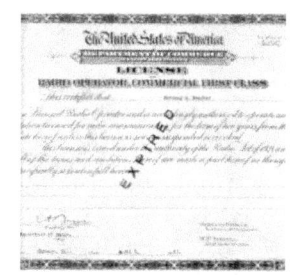

First License April 5, 1927

Sherman's first car

this genealogy because they owned no stock and had little discretionary money to begin with. All had jobs except Ethel's brother, Bob Kerr, who worked for an upholsterer to get by during the subsequent Depression He returned to the steel mill when a job became available and remained there until his retirement.

As mentioned, a friend, Dan Larden introduced Sherman to his sister Hannah's good friend Ethel Kerr. They hit it off right away. Being a radio operator on the Great Lakes was not conducive to maintaining a relationship so Sherman eventually got a job with the Pennsylvania Motor Police stationed at Butler. He and Ethel had a long engagement. Photos show a young and happy couple getting to know each other. Ethel was still attending Pittsburgh Musical Institute and Sherman would meet her on Fridays and drive her home.

The earliest letter we have from Sherman to Miss Ethel Kerr, 272 Bellefield St. Pittsburgh, PA is dated 12 January 1931.

> Dear Ethel:
>
> …Up bright and early Sunday morning (11AM) had dinner and walked up the hill to see Dan. Their little house had just burned down. That's one fire that H and I missed. After loading at the Filling Station all afternoon we walked up to the Lindseys in the evening. Taking a big breath I went up and pushed the bell. Mrs. Lindsey came out of the living room and went upstairs. She was smoking a cig in a long holder. Did she look hot. I think she thought it was the telephone and she must have had guests or at least one guest for she was answering it from upstairs. Then I gave the bell another of my determined pushes and got results. Isabelle wasn't in but I explained about the gloves and finally got them. You should have seen her try to hold the dog and that cig and hand me my gloves at the same time. She missed her calling. Ringling Bros is looking for an act like that. I thought plenty after seeing that woman. Well, I got my gloves and that was that. Went back to H's and listened to the radio then back up the hill again. In bed by 11 with an extra blanket and my overcoat on the bed. Was I cold. Had the chills and sure thought I was in for the Hoof and Mouth disease or something. But feel fine today. Not nutty though. Maybe that will come later on.
>
> I'll bet you thought that was a terrible date Friday night. I don't often feel like that so cheer up. It may not happen for a long time. But when I gets the blues I has em. Stand by for lunch. The Finger Print Operator just gave me a drop cake so if there are any crumbs in this letter you will know where they came from. It was pretty good and now I'll have to go and get a drink of water. You know me… Be seeing you. SB

Sherman received his Amateur Radio Station License in 1932. He kept up his interest in amateur radio and his license for the rest of his life. Amateur radio (ham radio) is the use of designated radio frequency spectrum for purposes of private recreation, non- commercial exchange of messages. Users can use Morse code or voice. It was a lifelong hobby. In 1934 he qualified for a license as Radio Telegraph Second Class in Buffalo, N.Y. and also Radio Telephone First Class. In the following letter to my mother, he is working at the State Police Barracks in Butler.

Butler, PA
Feb 3, 1931

Dear Ethel;

Nine am. Tuesday morning. Sun shining brightly thru the mist. At least its shining in Butler, I don't know about Pgh. Intended writing you yesterday but too much going on here in the office to get anything like that done. I have to be alone. The fingerprint Operator had 15 prisoners to fingerprint and photograph. They brought about 12 prisoners up from Beaver County. Three girls included in the cast. That's something unusual here. Quite a novelty around this bastille. In all the time I've been here I never saw such a collection of human derelicts. About every crime you could think of and some more besides was represented in that aggregation.

Well that's enough of that. How are you? That's good so am I. I really feel full of vim and vigor this morning. The air "feels" like spring even if it is still cold. You know that sounds funny after reading it over even if it is still cold. Oh well, you know what I mean and since this isn't for Aunt Gertie I can let my self ramble along. Just spent 20 minutes fixing the ribbon on this %*#@ typewriter. Noah had this one on the Ark. So you know how that dirty smudge got on the top of this sheet.

I wish we could have had a longer time to talk Sunday night. But that's the way it goes. Gee I'll bet its hard to get up and get the train in the morning. Monday morning are always so disillusioning. Getting some $ 40 words in but it seems to do the trick. I took a taxi up the hill as I didn't feel quite as well as I thought I did,. The more I thought of walking the more tired I felt. After an extended conversation with myself Yellow Cab went up a point.

Perhaps I think too much of the future but can't help it. Sure am planning on having a good time this summer with you. Maybe that will help make up for not being able to take you out this winter. We are not going abroad though so get that out of your mind. Was in Europe last summer and didn't have a good time. No fooling now. I never had a kindred soul that could understand all my crazy stuff like you do. There are some thoughts that just can't be expressed that way. You know though. A person would think the way I blah blah sometimes I could reel it off by the mile but no can do. You will just have to take my word for it. Say just look at all the "I's" that are in the above. How can you write and not get in so many I's?

H(Harold) was writing down all the places we want to go this summer. After he finished we de cided we would have to quit working so we could get every place we planned. Have been wanting to go to Cleveland together for some time but never made the grade. He had Erie I week,

Penn State 2 days and so on with the list. With a two weeks vacation we had quite a time getting everything in that two weeks.

Think I better sign off now. This letter isn't so hot I know but – oh well I would rather talk to you than write when I feel like this. Do you understand?

49, million, billion, always SB

In the following letter Sherman mentions his future mother-in-law, Roxy trying to dissuade Ethel from continuing the romance.

Feb 9, 1931

Dear Ethel,

Eleven o'clock and just back from the Hot Dog Shop with Dan. Spent the evening out at Lardin's practicing code with Daniel. This has been a rather busy day for me. Quite a bit of traffic and the static has been terrible for some reason. Guess the weather is so unsettled that it is making a fuss about it. …Thought of you this morning at 6:30 and wondered if you were on the Choo choo going to Pittsburg. Were you? And since 6:30 just one continuous thought about the same party, Happy thought ! oh what?

Air castles, dreams, plans, ambitions all went through my mind today. Sometimes I think life is too complicated. And that all the scramble after material things is just a waste of time and nervous energy. Feel like living on a desert island with nothing to distract and worry you. Know of any good islands that we could buy at a reasonable price. We'll pack up our fig leaves and sail tonight.

Say hon what did your mother mean Sun evening when she was talking about you broadcasting. She said something about getting – if you would get one thing or another out of your mind. Gee dear if your mother thinks I'm occupying too much of your time. Oh I suppose I'm imagining things again. If I could only get rid of some of my sensitive nature.

If I could only tell you things perhaps you would understand me better. I gave you an idea one night but that isn't the half of it. Anyhow this

Sherm and Ethel-courtship

airing your troubles isn't interesting and isn't polite so that's that... Suppose you are out tonight to grand opera. Finally got it spelled OK didn't know I was so ignorant. I have a diploma tho. So can prove I'm not. It says I'm a bright boy in great big type. This poor little "he" Cinderella is sitting here pounding away while you are at the ball... See those tear drops. Better get off the tear subject it makes me feel like kicking myself. That's awful. Please forget it. Just lost the wheel for a minute...

Eight days later Sherman is concerned that Ethel would be gone for the summer on vacation at a ranch out west. She never went on that vacation. Ethel with only one year to go, also didn't graduate from PMI.

Butler Pa Feb 17,1931

Hello thar Honey Chile:

Supper over and having my awfta dinnah cigarette. Doncha know. How's "Skippy" today? That's a good little girl. Been pretty good myself too. ...Do you think you will go out west on that ranch this summer. That would be a wonderful vacation for you, and a treat for the cowboys but how about me. Woof! ...well Hon I thought of you starting out in the bleak and lonely dawn Monday morning. Gee that must be tough. Five am. Unthinkable... Saw "Cimmaron" at the Capitol. Rather good show. ... Nothing exciting to write about...I could tell you that I love you like you said to do but that's no news

If I had my car I would come in and see you tonight. Rain or snow or what have you. But as it is I'll have to take it out in thinking of you. Not that I don't usually think of you, for if you don't know it, you are the one big thought. Say Honey how come you cried Saturday. You forgot to tell me what it was. Oh well perhaps you don't want to or you would have told me. Sometime we will get a chance to talk and talk. Alone. What sayeth thou.

I don't quite understand what your Mother means by saying we are too much alike. Its just as you say. That's the reason. You know Dear I've tried so often to tell you just how it is and can't do it so no use attempting it again. It means the world and all; to have your love. I can understand what you mean about religion. But don't know what to do about it. I love you and you love me. What is to be done about it is more than I can figure out. Why do problems like that always have to come up. Don't worry everything will come out OK. IT HAS TO.

Lots of love Sherman Gilbert

(Be seeing you Fri)

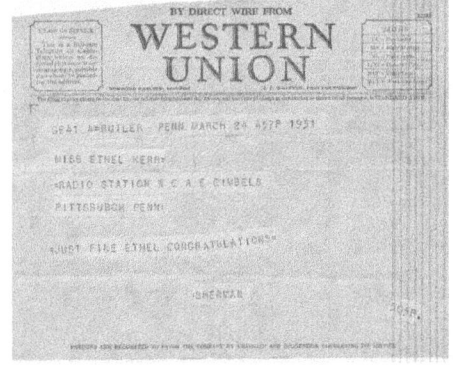

Telegram Sherman sent to Ethel after she performed on the radio.

Sherman was raised in the English Lutheran Evangelical Church founded by his grandfather, Rev. Gottlieb Bassler and Ethel was raised in the Roman Catholic faith. Sherman converted to Catholicism and promised to raise their children in the Catholic faith which he did.

> Zelienople, Pa March 30,1931
>
> Dearest:
>
> Its going to be rough for you trying to read my writing but hope you can put up with it for one time at least.
>
> Gee dear, I've been worried ever since I discovered I had tonsillitis for fer you would get it or rather did get it. Surely hope not. I'm feeling better this morning but still have spots on my throat. If I don't feel much better I'm going to stay home for a few days.
>
> Listening to my favorite station (WCAE) now. Will hear you tomorrow I suppose. Did you think of me last night. That was the first Sunday night we haven't seen each other for some time. Sorry I couldn't fone you Sunday afternoon but I was in bed and my throat was so sore I could hardly squeak …

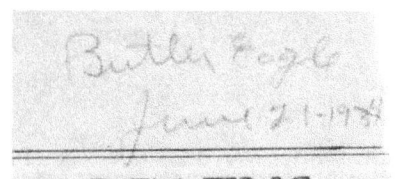

DEATHS

All obituary notices are given in eastern standard time unless otherwise noted.

William G. Bassler

William G. Bassler died last night at 11:40 o'clock after a lingering illness in his home at 302 New Castle street, Zelienople. He had been an invalid for ten years.

A member of a pioneer Zelienople family, Mr. Bassler was at one time postmaster there. His father was a Lutheran minister in Zelienople and he was a member of the Zelienople English Lutheran church.

Surviving are his widow, Mrs. Julia Sherman Bassler, and a son, Private Sherman G. Bassler of Troop D, headquarters of state police here.

Funeral services will be conducted tomorrow afternoon at 3:30 o'clock (D. S. T.) at the home in charge of the Rev. C. W. White, superintendent of the Lutheran Orphans' Home and Farm school, Zelienople. Burial will be in the Zelienople cemetery.

The couple had more than religious differences to cope with. Sherman's father was near death. Sherman had always supported his family and would need to do so in the future taking care of his soon to be widowed mother. Finances would always be an issue for the couple. Ethel was also very emotionally attached to her mother and had been Roxy's confidante throughout a difficult marriage. Ethel told me years later that she and dad were both too attached to their mothers. The couple was very much in love and continued enjoying their courtship that was fun, romantic and exciting to both of them.

The Sherman family in Missouri celebrated A.G. Sherman's 87th birthday and the get-together was noted in *The Clinton Eye.* Sherman accompanied his mother on this trip. (Appendix 7) However, in May of that year Julia's father, Albert, suffered a stroke and a month later her husband, William died.

Minnie records: "Clara and Wayne left for Julia's in Zelienople, Pa June 18th." (Appendix 10) because on 20 June 1934 Julia's husband, William Gottlieb Bassler, died and was buried June 22nd. He left a will leaving everything to Julia. (Appendix 9) Two months later on August 20th Julia's father, Albert Sherman died and was buried August 31 in Clinton. (Appendix 8) One can only imagine what these multiple losses meant to Julia Sherman Bassler who was now 58 years old. In less than two months her son would be married.

Back row: Eva, Carl, Bert
Sitting: Minnie, Julia, Clara Photo undated circa 1935

Julia remained close to her brothers and sisters and made the long and costly trip home as frequently as she was able. As mentioned, she and Minnie, Eva, and Clara were frequent letter writers. (Appendix 12) Julia's sisters almost always included a few dollars. (Appendix 41)

Sherman and Ethel were married 23 October 1934. They sent a letter to Julia on their honeymoon from Fitzgerald, Georgia (Appendix 28) and set up housekeeping on Washington Ave. in Butler, PA. Sherman worked long hours at the State Police station and Ethel continued with her music interests often performing in the homes of distinguished residents.(ironically playing at a mansion on Maine St., that was converted to a nursing facility many years later where her mother died less than two weeks after suffering a stroke.)

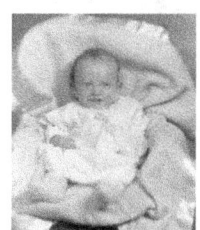

After a few years, Roxy Kerr wondered why there were no children. I doubt Ethel told her about their use of condoms that did not bother the couple's conscience at the time. Only years later during obsessive-compulsive periods did Ethel worry about the moral implications of her choices. It was, and still is, against Roman Catholic teachings. Finally, Ethel did conceive. She suffered severe morning sickness. Ethel expected to give birth at home as her sister-in-law Frieda did. But because of her high blood pressure the doctor recommended the hospital. She gave birth to a 5 lb 4 oz jaundiced baby boy on 6 March 1938 at the Butler Hospital. Everyone was happy.

Except Ethel. She most likely suffered from post-partum depression, a hormonal ailment. Even Hippocrates in 700 BC recognized women suffering from emotional difficulties after giving birth, but it wasn't until the 1850's that the problem was given a name and a hundred years later that drastic measures like electric shock were used to cure the "neurosis." Many women even today just suffer through the "baby blues." In the photo, Ethel has dark circles under her eyes and looks pensive.

This layman's diagnosis 75 years after the fact is based on

  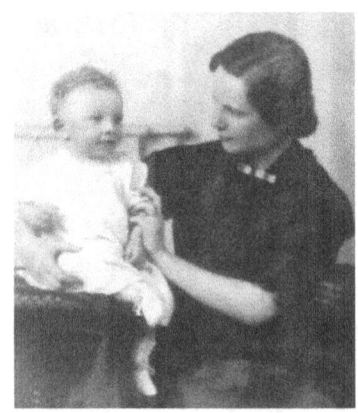

First Christmas 1938

two conversations I had with my parents. One was with my dad in the backyard, shortly before he died while Ethel gave piano lessons. Many topics were covered. Sherman recounted Ethel would leave dirty diapers on the hard wood floors in their apartment. This,

I submit, is a clear sign of depression. The other conversation with my mother occurred fifteen years after Sherman's death when she revealed a great secret that she had been carrying since the early days of her marriage.

Sitting side by side at the piano is a very composed picture which says a lot about how the newlyweds viewed themselves and how they wanted to be viewed - the Tree of Life wall hanging stitched by Ethel, the vase on the piano, Ethel poised and lovely sitting beside her handsome husband in his smoking jacket and pipe. Perfect. But it did not last.

Traveling photographer and Billy

Ethel and Susan Ann

Sherman was unfaithful. He had an affair with Hazel for over five years. They had a child in 1939. The 1940 U.S.Census lists Hazel and her one year old daughter Darlene living in Butler. I was unsuccessful in finding a birth certificate for Darlene. This news came as a terrible shock to the family. Years later Ethel told me that it was not all Sherman's fault. This might mean that while pregnant with her first born, Ethel suffered from depression and rejected amorous advances from her husband thus driving him into the arms of another woman. Ethel also confided that because her father had allowed himself angry outbursts whenever he wanted, Ethel thought that when she was in charge of her own home she too could let loose angry barrages whenever she felt like it.

Billy striking a Grandpa Kerr pose

The honeymoon was definitely over. The romantic courtship was over. The fantasy was over. The reality of a new baby and a changed life hit hard. The financial reality also hit hard. Sometimes the newly widowed Julia would call, and the couple would drive to Zelienople to deliver needed food. It was all too much for Sherman. What had happened to his fun loving and laughing fiance? What had happened to his "Skippy?" This of course can never excuse the terrible damage he did to his wife and family. It is given only as a possible explanation of his unfathomable behavior.

Brady St. Butler, PA

Sherman enrolled again in the State Police16 June 1939 as Private First Class Pennsylvania Motor Police stationed in the Butler Barracks as a radio operator. On 18 October 1941 Ethel gave birth to a daughter Susan Ann — me — who although only a few more ounces at birth than her brother, was not jaundiced but round and healthy looking.

Sherman, Ethel, Susan, Billy Brady St. Sherman is somber and noone is touching. The family would soon be broken circa 1944

The family was now living in a rented home on Brady St. It is at this time that Ethel learned of the affair. Eventually, of course, everyone that mattered to her knew of her disgrace- her parents and brothers, her Tuesday Musical Club, her bridge club, the society people she had entertained. Sherman moved out of the house, and Ethel sublet two upstairs rooms to single women. Finally, due to financial necessity, she took her family back to her parent's home on 225 Elm Street where they would live for the next five years. Grandma B had also offered her upstairs apartment to the family.

The next period in my dad's life was unsettled. He left the State Police with an Honorable Discharge and a small pension. Although World War II was still raging, I understood that he was ineligible for service due to his flat feet. However in a letter to my grandmother he states that he passed his physical. From May 1942 to June 1944 he worked part time for William Calters. From June to July 1944, he was unemployed. Then he took a job at Sperry Gyroscope Co. in Long Island, New York. Sperry was located at Lake Success in the Town of North Hempstead on northwest Long Island.(Appendix 29) If you were involved in the war effort your military service could be deferred.

Sherman saved receipts that indicate he was sending money to Hazel who was also living in Long Island. They were addressed to "Mrs. Bassler." They show that money was being sent to Hazel as late as 1947. Of course, she and her baby needed this money. But as the following letter from Sherman to Julia indicates, he was also sending his mother "cabbage." He was trying to support seven people on his paycheck. None of the parties could have received very much.

Dear Mom,   undated

Enclosed some cabbage. Hope your feeling well. I have been feeling pretty good, have lost my big belly, ha and am down to my slim? Self again. Will let you have my new address soon as I am sure of it.

Have been working hard and am beginning to enjoy it some now. Sure hard for old dog to learn new trix, ha but certainly has given me more confidence in myself. Quite some change from State Police, I'll tell you expecially since that was practically my whole working experience with exception of (Herb Bush) and Lakes.

Remember when Herb fired me for going to Pgh and getting suit.

Sorry I forgot Mrs. Rapes birthday. When you told me I thot now I will remember and get her a card but I forgot as usual.

By now you have no doubt received check. I would deposit it and use it as you see best put on house and better keep a little back. Makes a person feel good to have a little in bank for emergencies. Taxes came to a rather staggering total of $228 and some odd cents but they are all paid. So you won't have to worry about them. They are paid right up to date so you pay Lizzie Kettle and other things that have been annoying you and you can be a free citizen again, ha! Don't spend all on house. I sure am glad to have taxes paid. Maybe able later to pay that cemetary bill and also get a stone for Pops grave.

If anything should happen to me, you see that I am put up on the Zelienople Hill in the right place. Don't let above worry you as I feel swell even my bowels are working 150%. Brother have I walked. I'll bet I average 5 miles per day…

Have finally gotten some benefit from Capitol Eng Course I took (Didn't finish as usual) but it has helped me a lot. When I get new address I will have you send all my books as I need them. Don't know what job will be like after war but one day at a time. I never thot I would be at State Police for 15 yrs either At least there is no one like Crowley to make life miserable.

Haven't heard any more from draft board except I passed my physical exam OK. I checked to make sure they sent in my deferment here. Weather has cooled off and it is really pleasant. Have quite a time getting used to noise in plant after such a quiet peaceful place like S.P. Just between you and I, I can appreciate what a snap I had but would sure have gotten in a rut there. It's all right to stay in one place but not too long. Saw a fellow the other day that won $18,000 on a horse race. WOW….Girl at work today just had on shorts. Guess just way it is. You see women about 60 with a sunsuit on. Varicose veins. No fooling the rigs are sure something. No one pays any attention. Well have gabbed enough. The brownies were good but were all dried out and crumbly when I got em. Got a belly ache anyway don't know if it was from them or chicken? Croquettes I had at a Greek Lunchroom, ha! 73 for now. Write when I send new address.

Billy's letter

Puerto Rico San Juan, 1947
(Letter to "E and All from San Juan
see Appendix 30)

Roxy and Jim kept their daughter and grandchildren afloat during this difficult time.. Roxy encouraged Ethel to travel to Long Island in an attempt to bring her husband home. Ethel told me it turned out to be a humiliating disaster. They probably did not know that Hazel was also living in Long Island. Sherman wrote a three page letter to his mother at this time that Julia kept. But he doesn't mention Hazel or the baby. He has sent money "cabbage" and is explaining how he is adjusting to leaving the State Police and learning a new job at the Sperry Corporation. The Sperry Corporation was a "closed shop" which meant that Sherman would have to join a union as a condition of employment. Sherman declined. The company wrote a generic reference letter March 29, 1946. "His work indicates that he pos-

The smiles say it all. Susan, Grandma B & Billy " Zelie" PA

When visiting Grandma B the first stop was always - Isaly's. Courtesy of ZHS Historical Society

sesses a sound basic knowledge of a-c circuits. He is a thoughtful, conscientious worker" Sherman left Sperry Gyroscope Company and took a job with Pan Am in San Juan, Puerto Rico January 3, 1947 for a few months as a radio air controller. (Appendix 33)

Playing cards at Roxy's home with Susan Grandma B and Billy

Sherman resigned from PanAm March 1947. One reason he gives is that he could not find suitable housing for his family. Finally, in 1948 Sherman was hired by the Isthmian Steamship Co. in NY and sailed on the SS Citadel Victory as a radio operator. He returned to Butler on periodic visits. His trips took him to postwar Germany where he saw children rummaging in garbage pails. He was in Basra in the Persian Gulf and brought home unique gifts from the Kasbah. Once Ethel traveled to New York City to see him off. She described watching him climb up the side of the ship on a rope ladder. She returned to Butler having only an apple to eat and a dollar in her purse for the bus ride home to Butler.

When the contract with the Isthmian Co. expired, Sherman found work at WKIN radio station at Kittanning, PA. from December 1949 to June 1950. He worked, ate and slept on-site near the transformers. When he was diagnosed with multiple myeloma in his sixties, he thought that this rare bone marrow cancer might be due to exposure to radio waves at the station. Forty years after his death the cause of this disease is still unknown and still incurable. According to the Mayo Clinic; ...*almost all people with multiple myeloma have genetic abnormalities in their plasma cells ...but they haven't yet discovered the cause of these changes.* www.mayoclinic.com

Billy using dad's ham radio on the Kerr's back porch

My brother and I owe much to the love and protection of our grandparents during this difficult time. Our maternal grandparents opened their home to us in 1946 for five years. During the summer months Bill and I traveled to Zelienople to stay with our Grandma B. She provided an emotional safe haven and a great place to have fun.

Both of us exhibited signs of stress during our parents' troubles but this was in an era

before school psychologists and family counselors. Although always a good student, Billy got into some trouble due to hanging around with "street friends." Once he set a fire next to the house on Brady Street and another time he ran upstairs at 225 Elm Street before a policeman appeared at the door. He had pulled a knife on a kid. I also kept up my grades in school but remember recurring nightmares. I began biting my fingernails and wetting my pants and bed. Of course, it was not a good time for our mother either. In 1942 she enrolled in a home nursing course perhaps as part of the war effort or as a means of earning money in addition to teaching piano lessons. Bill and I attended St. Peter's Grammar School staffed by the Franciscan Sisters of Millvale. It has since been torn down.

Half a letter that Sherman wrote to his children has survived.

After school we played outside with friends, came in when it got dark, had supper and did our homework. We didn't have a TV. But had favorite radio programs like *The Lone Ranger*, *Lassie* and *The Green Hornet*. To earn spending money, Billy had a paper route and sometimes I tagged along.

Sherman's friends wanted him to come to his senses and return to his family. Ralph Oshe told him that the Signal Corps in New Jersey was hiring and he should apply. The application arrived but got "mislaid" for several years. Finally, Sherman secured the job at Fort Monmouth, bought a car, packed up his family and moved to New Jersey.

Thirteen years after her husband died. Ethel told me that she and Sherman never discussed the infidelity. Ever. The move to New Jersey was a new start for everyone. But what is truly amaz-

> BREMEN GERMANY
>
> SEPT 11, 1947
>
> DEAR BILL AND SUSAN
>
> I suppose by now both of you kiddies are going to school. Bill you ask Susan if she has been like Tome the cat or whether she forgot.
>
> Take good care of Susie crossing the streets Bill. The ship I am on brought over a load of wheat and is now loading army trucks for return to the states. I am sorry I didn't bring my camera and take some pictures
>
> It was a nice trip coming over with hardly any bad weather. You try and get a map and see where I went from Galveston texas we went through the strait of florida and up and across the north atlantic through the English channel into the north sea and up the Weber river to Bremen. See if you can find those places on a map, bill. If you were with me you wouldn't have any trouble seeing the stars. I can see them very distinctly at sea. The stars they used mostly for navigating coming over were Polaris which is the north star, Arcturus, vega, altair, Deneb,

Big brother and little sister
6th Ave. Long Branch, NJ

Star of the Sea Grammar School
staffed by the Sisters of Charity of
Convent Station, N.J.

ing is that no one in the family ever told my brother and me what had happened. Long after my dad had died when I was forty-five years old my mother finally revealed this

Photo Made Atop Empire State Building, New York   1250 feet 102 stories

William, Sherman & Grandpa Kerr 1950's

secret of betrayal.

The move to New Jersey was a sacrifice for everyone. The grandparents had to accept twice yearly visits at Christmas and summer. Sherman made a choice to leave Hazel and Darlene. He also gave up the love and lure of the sea for a nine to five government job at the Signal Corps, Fort Monmouth, New Jersey. Ethel gave up her family and friends as did Bill and I. We attended Star of the Sea Grammar School in Long Branch, N.J. run by the Sisters of Charity of Convent Station, N.J. The family lived in rented houses until a home in Red Bank was purchased on 5 William Street. I attended St. James Grammar School and Bill and I attended Red Bank Catholic High School, staffed by the Sisters of Mercy. The rest of my story is told in my memoir *Removing the Habit of God Sister Christine's Story 1959-1968*.

Sherman worked at the Signal Corps until retirement in 1967. He bought a sailboat and took pleasure in taking people out on the Navesink River. He and Ethel enjoyed European trips and cruises.

5 William St. Red Bank,NJ

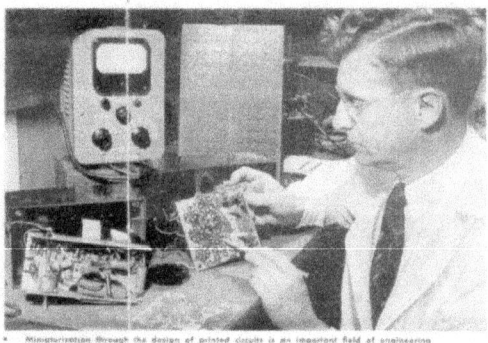

Sherman Bassler at Signal Corps labs

Sherman, William Susan & Ethel Bassler, Dorn's portrait 1959

Sherman & Ethel on Dinner cruise on the Seine R. Paris

He loved his children and he loved his grandchildren. After a four year struggle with cancer, he died 28 September 1973 at Riverview Hospital in Red Bank, NJ and is buried at Mount Olivet in Middletown, NJ. Sherman kept a <u>Desk Diary</u> from 1 January 1973 until 20 September 1973. (Appendix 38) Ethel continued to live in Red Bank and taught piano lessons for almost twenty years. She eventually sold the house on William Street and lived two years with me in Chelmsford, MA and two years with Bill in Fair Haven, NJ. She spent the last eight months of her life at King James Nursing home in Atlantic Highlands where she died on 19 October 1997 of congestive heart failure She was 88 years old. Ethel is buried next to her husband at Mount Olivet Cemetery, Middletown, NJ.

As mentioned, my brother and I attended Red Bank Catholic High School. We both studied diligently and enjoyed our new home and school. Bill joined the Forensics Club and became a top notch debater and public speaker winning many awards. He encouraged me to do the same.

Bassler tombstone at Mount Olivet Cemetery

After high school, my brother went to St. Charles College in Catonsville, Maryland to become a parish priest. After graduating from St. Charles he went to St. Mary's in Baltimore, Maryland but after a few months he left. He taught at Red Bank Catholic High School for a semester and then matriculated in Fordham University completing a year's work in one semester. He graduated 1960 and received a scholarship to Georgetown University Law School and graduated 10 June 1963. Following the traditional trip to Europe, he began clerking for Judge Mark Sullivan at the Superior Court Appellate Division, Newark, NJ. After that he worked at Parsons, Canzona, Blair and Warren.

King's Point, LI, New York

William courted and wed Eileen Schilling of Locust, Middletown, and they were married at St. Agnes Roman Catholic Church in Atlantic Highlands, NJ on 10 September 1966.

Sherman wrote a chatty letter telling his mother about the wedding gifts the couple received and what the mothers were wearing. (Appendix 38)

Red Bank Catholic Senior In Oratory Semi-Finals

RED BANK — Following a brilliant victory in the preliminaries of the N.Y. Journal-American's 14th Tournament of Orators, William Bassler, 18-year-old Red Bank Catholic High School senior is now eligible for the semi-finals at State Teachers College in Jersey City April 9.

But the crowning glory will come on May 7. If young Bassler is a successful semi-finalist, he becomes eligible for the finals, which will take place at the Metropolitan Opera House before a capacity audience of 4,500.

Bassler's victory came in the preliminary round in the Little Theater on the Seton Hall Campus at South Orange Monday. He got the news yesterday.

This phase of the tournament saw eight New Jersey sections represented by the cream of high school oratory. Bassler was judged winner over a field of seven preliminary contestants.

Should he emerge victoriously in the Met finals on May 7, he will have realized the victory he came close to winning in 1955. Bassler was a finalist in the Met last year, but an unsuccessful one.

He won his preliminaries with a 6-minute talk on "John Adams." All contestants spoke on the same subject. It was along the lines of a commemorative speech on any phase of Adams' life.

Bassler has been a member of the Forensic Club at Red Bank Catholic High School since his freshman year. The club is coached by Sister Mary Eleanor and Sister Mary Charitas, both of whom have produced winners consistently over the years.

Besides being the state oratory champ, Bassler was also a successful candidate in the State Declamation Contest in September. As the state champion, he represented New Jersey at the National Student Congress at San Jose, Cal. last summer, where he was chosen the outstanding speaker.

A victory in the Met finals would entitle Bassler to a $1,000 bond and a large trophy.

The tournament is sponsored by the N.Y. Journal-American. It offers a total of $25,000 in contest money for public speaking and has extended to more than 600 high schools in three states and 60 leading colleges and universities throughout the country.

WILLIAM BASSLER
In Semi-Finals of Contest

TO ADDRESS ELKS—William G. Bassler, 18-year-old Red Bank Catholic High School student, will be the speaker at today's Flag Day services on the lawn in front of the Asbury Park Elks Lodge, Eighth and Park Avenues. William received a $1,000 bond last month for winning the finals of the Eastern Oratorical Contest at the Metropolitan Opera House, New York.

Prepared Month For Winning Speech

To Study for Priesthood

Hearst Papers Classic:
City's Oratory Champs Win Eastern Title Too

(Photo in Picture Section)

By JIM MORTON

The Citadel's Ronald Weiss and William Bassler of Red Bank Catholic High School—top New York winners last week in the Hearst Newspapers' Tournament of Orators—once again were partners in victory today, taking the Eastern titles of the Coast-to-Coast classic.

May 7, 1956

is new Fair Haven mayor

By RILEY McCORMICK

Accepts Position

William G. Bassler received his bachelor of laws degree from Georgetown University Law Center, Washington, D.C., June 10. Mr. Bassler is the grandson of Mrs. W. G. Bassler of Zelienople, and Mrs. J. C. Kerr of 225 Elm St. He resides with his parents, Mr. and Mrs. Sherman G. Bassler of Red Bank, N.J.

A graduate of St. Charles College and Fordham University, Bassler was on the staff of the Georgetown Law Journal, president of the Butler Law Club, member of the Tutor Society and a resident counselor at Georgetown College. He is a member of Phi Delta Phi Legal Fraternity. Mr. Bassler will serve a legal clerkship with the Superior Court, Appellate Division, Newark, N.J.

RUE, BERRY & BASSLER ON TAXES

Rue Saves Fair Haven Taxpayers $15,000

In 1977, when many municipalities consulted expensive outsiders for the Master Plan required of them under the Municipal Land Use Act, Bill Rue gave the job to the Fair Haven Planning Board. The saving to the Boro, $15,000 by conservative estimates, or 3¢ to every dollar on the tax rate, is an example of how the Republican Team believes in careful spending and local ability.

William F. Rue

Rue Team Calls Licensing of Health Inspector Expensive Medicine for Taxpayers

It's not enough for the Democratic Majority in Trenton that for years Fair Haven has had a competent health inspector (remember, he contained the hepatitis outbreak?), now he has to be licensed. The diagnosis? We'll have to dig deeper into our pockets and come up with more money for the same kind of service. The Rue Team is not against spending money—it's against spending money unnecessarily.

William G. Bassler

Mayor Kiely and Rue Team Fear Prevailing Wage Act

Both the present mayor and the candidate for mayor agree that the prevailing wage act will cause a terrible impact on all public works contracts. Trenton now requires that Fair Haven pay the prevailing wage (based on union wages) plus 18% to 25% additional benefits. That's at least double the rate of local labor. In other words, with the prevailing wage act, inflation will prevail.

George L. Berry

The couple had four children:

Julia Elizabeth 28 July 1967 -13 June 1997
William Gilbert 22 September 1968- 10 August 1990
Roseann 30 April 1970 married Louis "Del" DalPra 2 August 2000
    William K. 12 February 2002
    August "Gus" D. 22 July 2004
    Henry "Hank" T. 30 July 2005
Elizabeth 23 June 1972 married Christopher J.
    Jannuzzi 19 October 2001
    Michael A. 18 August 2003
    Raymond J. 19 October 2005
    Julia M. 22 February 2008

After nine years in the convent, I left and returned to Red Bank, N. J. to teach at Red Bank Catholic High School for four years. In 1971 I met Richard S. Pickford and we wed the following year in St. James R.C. Church, 10 June 1972. We had two boys:

Agnes Schilling, Eileen Schilling Bassler, William G. Bassler, August Schilling

Richard Samuel 5 Nov. 1972
John Sherman 2 Nov. 1974 married Lisa Menard 29 August 2009
    Lucy Jane 21 April 2011
    Charles Christopher 17 January 2013

Richard Pickford, Sr., Mary Gaffney Pickford, Richard Pickford, Jr. Susan, Sherman Bassler, Ethel Kerr Bassler

Julia Sherman Bassler enjoyed a long life. All of her great-grandchildren were born in her lifetime. She lived in her own home in Zelienople for 64 years, and moved in with Sherman and Ethel in Red Bank in 1968. After Sherman was diagnosed with multiple myeloma, and after she was hospitalized with pneumonia, Julia moved into the King James' Nursing Home in Middletown and died 10 January 1974 two months shy of her ninety-ninth birthday.

The English Lutheran Church in Zelienople, Pennsylvania played an important role in the history of the Bassler family.

Even in her nineties, Julia enjoyed her family and enjoyed flying from Pittsburgh to Newark to visit them.

*Julia Bassler was also present at the ceremonial groundbreaking
for Bassler Hall, an addition to the church.*

After Julia Bassler's death, her body was returned to Zelienople. She was buried from the English Lutheran Church and laid to rest next to her husband. Her grandson, William, gave the eulogy.

In October 1975 my brother was invited to be a lay-preacher at a Sunday service

Bill continued to study - going first to New York University School of Law and receiving LL.M in 1969 and then the University of Virginia Law School receiving an LLM in Judicial Process in 1995. Since 1964 and until his first judicial appointment in 1988, he

*Clockwise: Sherman, Grandma B, Julia,(not seen Roseann) Eileen, William,
Susan, Ethel at the Basslers first home in Applebrook, Middletown, NJ 1970*

Julia is holding her great grandson William in Sherman and Ethel's home.

18-19, 1975— BUTLER COUNTY NEWS

English Lutheran Church hosts grandson of founding pastor

William G. Bassler, great grandson of the Rev. Gottlieb Bassler, founding pastor of the English Lutheran Church in Zelienople, will be the lay preacher Sunday, Oct. 19, at the 8:15 and 10:45 a.m. worship services at the church. He will speak on, "The Lay Apostolate: The Role of the Layman in the Church Today."

Bassler will preach from the pulpit from which he often heard sermons when his grandmother, Mrs. William Bassler, brought him to church as a small boy.

He followed his mother's faith and was brought up in the Catholic Church.

Following fours years of studies toward the priesthood, he changed his vocation to law, graduating from Georgetown University, Washington, D.C.

Bassler is a practicing attorney in Red Bank, N. J.

His interest in Christianity and the church continues and he is active in lay ministry duties in the Catholic Church.

Earlier this year, he took part in the funeral service of his grandmother, Julia Bassler, who died at 98, and was buried from the English Church.

Bassler and his wife, Eileen, are the parents of four children.

Mr. and Mrs. Bassler will be the house guests of the Rev. and Mrs. Douglas J. Toepel while in the area.

Honorable William G. Bassler

was an attorney in private practice at various New Jersey firms. He was appointed to the New Jersey Superior Court in 1988 and then to the federal bench by President George H.W. Bush on 14 June 1991. William retired from the bench on 31 August 2006. Since then he has been working as an independent mediator and arbitrator. Some of his achievements include: Lifetime Achievement Award, Essex County Bar Association 2008, Hon. William J. Brennan, Jr. Award, Association of the Federal Bar of New Jersey, 2006 and St. Thomas More Medal, Seton Hall Law School and the St. Thomas More Society, 1997 More information can be found at www.wgbddisputeresolution.com.

——— The Next Generation ———

Back:Elizabeth Jannuzzi, Christopher Jannuzzi, Eileen Bassler, Bill Bassler, Roseann DalPra, Del DalPra
Front: Raymond Jannuzzi, William DalPra, Hank DalPra, Julia Jannuzzi, August DalPra, Michael Jannuzzi

Clockwise: John Pickford holding Sam, Lisa Menard Pickford holding Charles, Susan holding Lucy Jane, Rich and Richard Pickford

ACKNOWLEDGEMENTS

Addie Shields, the Clinton County Historian at Plattsburgh, NY, Robert Kerr, Xerox copy of *The History of Mercer County*; Doreen Kerr Heitzer, newspaper clipping 50 Years Ago from Roxy's bible; Patricia Kerr Pavlic; Roxanna Jaxtheimer Kerr notes; newspaper clips from *The Butler Eagle*, Butler, Pennsylvania; Unfinished Typescript for *History of Alburgh Vermont Volume ll* by Allen L. Stratton; *History of the Town of Chazy* Clinton County, New York by Nell Jane Barnett Sullivan and David Kendall Martin 1970; *History of Butler County Pennsylvania* 1895: Zelienople Borough, Chap. 27, Harmony Borough Chap. 28; Vermont Historical Society, *The New England Shermans* by Roy V. Sherman, 1974; *Soldiers, Sailors, and Patriots of the Revolutionary War*, 1860, 1870, 1800 U.S. Census Records; Genevieve Livingston Trutor, The Benson Museum, Benson, Vermont; *Unfinished Typescript for History of Alburgh, Vermont Vol. II* by Allen L. Stratton; Brown Library, Maine Historical Library; *History of the Pennsylvania Synod of the General Synod of the Evangelical Lutheran Church*: 1748-1845 1904 by Ellis Beaver Gurgess, Albert G. Sherman's <u>Pocket Diary</u> and family letters courtesy of Don and Nancy Sherman, Clinton, Missouri; newspaper clipping from *The Daily Democrat* of Clinton, Missouri; Minnie Sherman's <u>Family Record</u>; National Archives information on Thomas Benton Buckingham, William R. Buckingham, Jesse Buckingham and Marvin Kerr; Buckingham information and photos from Kevin and Diane Diehl, Olathe, Kansas; <u>Family Recollections</u> from Connie Wallace Smith and Waneta Wallace Smith, Clinton, Missouri; Record Copy of the Daughters of the American Revolution for Thomas Sherman; Adam's Historical Society, Gettysburg, Pennsylvania folder on the Gilbert family; Sally Roth, Passavant Center, Thiel College, Greenville,PA; Tennessee Records of McMinn Co. McMinn Co. Tombstone inscriptions Vol.1; newspaper clipping *What Happened 50 Years Ago* and *Do You Remember? Butler Co News Record* 1964 Zelienople, Pennsylvania; 1934 death notice of William G. Bassler, *Butler Eagle*, Pennsylvania; Elizabeth Gilbert Bassler's Album; Elizabeth Gilbert Bassler's <u>Family Record</u>; William G. Bassler's <u>Diary</u>; Julia Sherman Bassler's Diary; Bassler documents and Family Bible courtesy of Honorable William G. Bassler; Pennsylvania College book 1832-1882 E.S. Breidenbaugh Editor; *The Gettysburg Lutheran Theological seminary Vol Two Alumni Record*; English Lutheran Memorial booklet, Zelienople, Pennsylvania; *Thiel College Catalogue* courtesy of Sally Roth, Passavant Center, Greenville, Pennsylvania; news clipping *The Monitor*, Trenton, NJ; 1973 death notice of Sherman G. Bassler, *Red Bank Register*; Sherman Records from Englewood Cemetery, Clinton, Missouri; Addie Shields, the Clinton County Historian at Plattsburgh, N.Y.; Vermont Historical Society; Zelienople Historical Society, Ruth Townsend Story, Editor; Elizabeth Jannuzzi, Hon. William G. Bassler

Special thanks to my brother for his continuing support.

Special thanks to my husband, Richard S. Pickford, Jr. (7 March 1938- 24 November 2015) who traveled with me and totally supported this project from start to finish.

Special thanks to Judy Wood of Wood and Company for the interior design and layout.

APPENDIX 1

Stevenson Connection

1. Joseph Fell + Bridget Wilson

   2. Benjamin Fell (1703-1758) + Hannah Scarborough (1704-1742)

   3. John Fell (1730) + Elizabeth Hartley

   4. William Fell (2 Ap 1756 -16 July 1841)+Agnes Anderson

   5. George W.Fell (31 Aug 1784-15 Aug 1849) + Nancy Dumars

   6. Hannah Fell (31 May 1832) +William Jaxtheimer

   7. William F Jaxtheimer (15 July 1856-1932 + K. Wiand

   8. Roxanna Jaxtheimer (1877-1965) + James Kerr

   9. Ethel Kerr (1908-1997) + Sherman.Bassler

   10. William Bassler (1938) + Eileen Schilling

   10. Susan Bassler (1941) + Richard Pickford

   4. Benjamin Fell (1739-1811) + Rebecca Castnert

   5. Jesse Fell (1777) + Rebecca Roman

   6. Jesse W.Fell (10 Nov 1808-25 Feb 1887) + Hester Brown

   7. Eliza B. Fell (1842-1900) + William Davis

   8. Helen Louise Davis (17 Sep 1869-16 Nov 1935) + Lewis Stevenson

   9.Adlai Stevenson II (5 Feb 1900 – 14 Jul 1965)

APPENDIX 2

Mayflower Connection

George Soule b. 9 Feb 1593 Worcestershire, England d. 22 Jan 1680 Duxbury, MA

  George Soule Jr. b. 1639 d.12 May 1704 Dartmouth, MA

    Mary Soule b. 1673 Dartmouth, MA   m. Capt Joseph Devol (1675-1726) d. 17 June 1729

      Joseph Deuel, Jr. b. 15 Dec 1703 d. 1782

        Philip Deuel 1727-1812 m. Elizabeth Sherman relocated to Duchess Co. NY (Beekman Patent) later the family moved to Alburg,VT

          Michael Deuel b.1750 Dartmouth, MA m. Elce Slocum (1753-1808) d.12 Jan. 1830 Alburg,VT

            Lucretia Deuel b.25 Aug 1778 m. Philip Honsinger d.14 Dec. 1867 Benson, VT

              Margaret Deuel Honsinger b.1814 Alburg,VT m. Albert G. Sherman 14 Feb 1839 (b. 24 May 1814 Chazy, NY d.7 Nov.1885 Benson,VT) d. 16 Oct 1889 Benson, VT

                Albert G. Sherman, Jr. b. 23 Jan.1847 Benson VT m. Laura E. Buckingham 8 Dec 1870 d. 20 Aug 1934 Clinton, MO

                  Julia Elizabeth Sherman b.10 March 1876 Clinton, MO m William G. Bassler 16 July 1902 d. 10 Jan. 1975 Middleton, NJ

                    Sherman G.Bassler b. 7 Nov. 1907 Zelienople, PA m. Ethel Kerr 23 Oct 1934 d. 28 Sept 1973 Red Bank, NJ

                      William G. Bassler b. 6 March 1938 Butler, PA m. Eileen Schilling 10 Sept 1966

                        Susan Bassler b.18 Oct 1941 Butler, PA m Richard Pickford 10 June 1972

APPENDIX 3

<u>Pocket Diary</u> of Albert G. Sherman, Jr.

B. 23 January 1847 in Benson, VT D. 20 August 1934 in Clinton, MO

The <u>Pocket Diary</u> **was** kept from 1 January 1864-31 December 1864. Introduction: This small notebook was kept by Albert Gallatin Sherman, Jr. in 1864 when he was 17 and in his last year of school in Benson, Vermont. It was preserved in Aunt Minnie Sherman's tin breadbox for 149 years and was loaned to Susan Bassler Pickford by Don & Nancy Sherman during a visit to Missouri October 13-15th 2013. Susan is the granddaughter of Albert's third daughter, Julia and Don is the grandson of Albert's youngest son Carl.

January Friday 1 1864.
>Happy New Year Benson, VT
>This has been a very unpleasant day it rained all the forenoon us
>Boys snowballed down st. & played in the old Church & this after
>we went over to Kellogg's home. Frank & Hart this eve.

Saturday, 2.
>School don't keep today it is the coldest day we have had this winter.
>I went up to Ben's this forenoon and we fixed his sled this after-
>noon I was down town helped Father some. The wind blows very
>hard & cold.

Sunday, 3.
>At Church today this afternoon I went over to Bemis little while. It
>is very cold tonight.

Monday, 4.
>At school today it is moderated down good   this eve a lot of us
>boys went down to the pond skating we skated on the river we
>played isfry in the bushes we had fun. Albert G. Sherman Jr….

Tuesday, 5.
>At school today it has snowed all day long and spoilt our skating. I
>have been a helping Isa in her Arithmetic this evening Mother wants
>words written in our Books before hand for Birthdays

Wednesday, 6.
>At School today it is very cold out & in the school house.

Thursday, 7.
>At school today this is the last week Henry so school anymore
>Albert G. Sherman Jr. Benson Vermont
>BeM was over here this evening
>This is the last day of school of Henry School, Benson Vermont

Saturday, 9. Friday, 8.

School don't keep today. I helped Father little this forenoon & this afternoon I did not do anything.

January Sunday, 10 1864.

At Church to both Churches today & this evening to.

Monday, 11.

I went to school today our new books commenced Young Smart is the fellow

Tuesday, 12.

I did not go to School today but helped Father in the shop worked on the shed H… Mils   I set 2 shoes on Y.M Walker horse.

January Wednesday, 13.

Not to school today but went up to Ladds mountain chopping, Smith helped with me we cut a pile of 12 ft wood.

Thursday,14.

I & 2 others went up Thurs chopping & had ex teams drawing home we got a big pile.

Friday, 15.

I worked some in the shop today. This evening Em Fassock & Frank Schrams was up here & spent the evening.

Saturday, 10.

I worked in the shop all day……bells & ….off a pair of (iron) shills this evening

Sunday, 17.

At Church today & this evening to it is quartermeeting. Mr. Hulbirt preached.

Monday, 8

I went to school all day & this evening us boys slid down the hill.

January Tuesday, 19.

At school today it is nice sliding in the road now up top. Best.

Wednesday, 20.

At school today I went up to Will's this evening. There is a party over to Al Gibb's this evening I did not go. Ben went

Thursday, 21.

At school today it is pleasant out now the moon shines bright.

Friday 22.

At school today this is the last day of Smart's teaching. He don't like it.

Saturday,23.

School don't keep today I went up to the mountains drawing wood this forenoon with Mr. Noble. It is my birthday I'm in the 18th year of my age. I had a cake as usual.

I am 17 years old.

Sunday, 24.

At Church today & this evening t. Albert G. Sherman Jr. Benson Vermont (followed by a drawn flourish)

Monday,25.

At school today to …new teacher Mr. Smith, Esq of Benson things One of my sheep kicked up today. I like him very well for the first day. Albert Sherman This noon I went up to the mountain with Mr. Nobles & Gabalard ? observed.

Tuesday, 26.

At school today. I pulled my sled high today & got 2 ½ lbs of wood. I cut some of my wood to night after school nearly ½ a cord. I shaved for the first time this evening all of our folks was gone but Eva, Isa & Eban

Wednesday, 27.

At school today. We slid down hill some this morning. I cut some more wood tonight, this evening Wall, Will, Ben & Al put a board … the road by strings where the boys were sliding.

Thursday, 28.

At school today. Us boys sled down the hill today some

Friday, 29.

At school today. Wall got excused this afternoon, he is taking down sick.

Saturday, 30.

 School today don't keep and I chopped all day. I have got a new ax & it goes well. I cut chopped 1 ¾ cord today.

Sunday, 31.

At Church today and this evening it snowed last night some.

February Monday,1

At School today. Wall is very sick.(practices writing Benson and his name)

Tuesday, 2.

At school today learn some & played some   Benson Vermont

Wednesday, 3

Went to school today. Father sent to get a ton of coal for Whitehall then Leittle got it.

Thursday, 4.

At school today us boys went in to see Wall this morning They don't think he will get well, he is very sick.…

Friday, 5.

At school today it is the last day for this winter for the upper school. We have had 3 three teachers this winter and they have all give out

Saturday, 6.

Wallace died this morning at 6 o'clock he came to himself before he died & he knew all that was in.

Ben Will and I went in to see the corpse this afternoon. I cut wood this forenoon. Father & I turned a dozen shoes today.

Sunday, 7.

At Church today and this evening too. The funeral is tomorrow in the afternoon at one o'clock.

Monday, 8.

I chopped wood this forenoon & this afternoon I went to the funeral it was at the house. Will, Ben Decator & I was pallbearers. They felt very bad.

I chopped some wood before dark.

Tuesday, 9.

I cut wood all day today. It is pleasant today.

Wednesday, 10.

I chopped wood today & have got good deal cut, Mr. Abels is very sick with the same complaint that Wallace had & isn't expected to live. Father has gone to Brandon today to a blacksmith convention.

Thursday, 11.

I did not cut my wood today, it was so cold & windy

Friday, 12.

I chopped & finished it today. Mr. Abels died at 7 o'clock this evening. The Ledger came tonight & I have been in reading to Father.

Saturday 13.

I piled up my wood today & have got 8 ½ cords cut in four foot ready to saw. This afternoon I went up north with Eugene after work. Decator was drawing too.   Albert G. S

Sunday, 14.

At Church today this afternoon was the funeral, good many there. I went this evening.

Monday, 15.

I sawed wood today. I cut 1 ¾ cord of soft- very hard wood.

I bought a new saw this morning price 75¢, I had Mr. Gibbs file it. I bought the file price 1 1/2¢

Tuesday, 16.

It is awful cold today. The wind blows very hard. I cut some hardwood & split it & piled it up in the shed most half of a day.   Albert Sherman

Wednesday, 17.

I split wood today. D & L changed works & sawed some too.

Thursday, 18.

I finished splittin what wood I had sawed today.

Albert G. Sherman, Jr. Benson, Vermont February 1864

Friday,19.

I worked at the wood today. The Ledger came tonight & I read it at the folks this evening. *Bert Sherman*

Saturday, 20.

Eban, Eva, Isa & Velna & I went down st this morning. Even, Isa had their pictures taken. they were very good but father went down with Eva & had hers taken over again. *Bert...*

Sunday, 21.

At Church today & this evening. Eva has taken down sick. I went after the Dr. about 10 O'clock. He thinks she has the same complaint as the others.

Monday, 22.

I went up on the mountain chopping wood today ...I rode down with Bayeth.

Tuesday, 23.

I went up to the mountain chopping wood alone. I got some cranberries. Eva is worse today ... bad. The snow has most gone off.

Wednesday, 24.

I worked at home on the wood a little today. We think Eva is a little better today but she is very sick. We sent a dispatch to Jarkier today & she did not get it until Thursday evening at 10:00.

Thursday, 25.

I worked at the wood a little today. Eva seems to be a little better this morning but it has been the hardest day she has had.

Friday, 26.

I did not do much today. I went up in Bascum's woods & see their sap syrup a while. Eva is a little better today.

I made me a new ax handle the first one in my life.

February Saturday, 27.

We just got up from the breakfast table this morning & what did we see. Julia a coming in She got a team of horses to bring her up. They came in about 1 ½ hour. I split & sawed wood today. Get my saw filed today.

Sunday, 28.

At church today & this evening too. Julia went this evening & Father Julia and I. Eva is a little better. The Doctor thinks but she is very sick indeed.

Monday, 29.

I worked at my wood today. I want to saw it up this week but I don't know.

March Tuesday, 1.

I cut wood today and split it, got a long ... wall. Eva is getting better.

Wednesday, 2.

I haven't went up to the mountain a chopping today. Old Howard & bee help me draw wood out to the road of J drew out – 2 cords.

Thursday, 3.

I sawed wood today. This evening the Sawer came off. I went & had great times had a good supper over to Strings block got home at 2.

March Friday, 4.

Ben, Will & I went down to the lake a food to a Horon Street good many then we rode back with Benjamin's father.

Saturday, 5.

I sawed a little wood this morning & then I went down to Griswolds sugar woods. Edger went with ... a gazing to ...his trees an help. I went down & cleaned out the buckets – 88 of them this afternoon, ...got 150 I think.

Sunday, 6.

At Church today & this evening. This afternoon I took a book up to Ben's & we read it and ... in the Barn & ...the woods.

March Monday, 7.

It snowed very hard last night – over a foot. I almost it off today I helped Father in the shop making *(unreadable)*

Tuesday, 8.

I worked in the shop this forenoon we made 16 *(unreadable)* in all. This afternoon I went over to Joes I cleaned out the kettles.

Wednesday,9.

I made some boils the first my sugar in today. Eva is worse this week.   Benson

Thursday,10.

I boiled again today. Ben & Will was … … with me last evening. We sugar off this evening. There was 10 lbs of it . I gathered most sap today.

Friday,11.

I boiled today & left it untended til morning. I took the old horse down & drew some wood.

Saturday, 12.

It rained last night some. I went down & finished tapping this fore-noon about 20. This afternoon I got Mrs. Walkers iron Kettle and Jim came up to get it and took it-to the woods I have got 3 at a large tub. I gathered this afternoon got …

Sunday, 13

At Church all day and this evening . Will, Dave & Frank sat with me this evening. It snowed slight this Eve but it has slowed off now. Eva is no worse.

Monday, 14

I was down to the woods to the bog and cleaned the kettles & got ready for boiling. We got them hung.

Tuesday Saturday 12

…boiled in my syrup today I have got a nice pl..? to boil with under a hill.

I gathered some syrup today.

Father bought an old horse today He paid 43 dollars for it

Wednesday, 16

I boiled again today Ben & Will was … me last evening. We syruped off this evening there was 10 lbs of it. I gathered more syrup today.

Thursday, 17

I bottled syrup today and left. It …to morning. I took the old horse down & drawn some wood.

Friday, 18

I boiled & gathered sugar in today We sugared off tonight had 10 lbs Just went back home as Eg says today. To Chester

The syrup run very good today. Leon Reed came down Sunday night

..

Saturday, 19

I boiled & gathered some today but it can't any syrup today. ...rained & snowed some last night

Sunday, 20

..At Church today & this evening. Let with Ben returned this afternoon …down that little bit & back 5 ..bs

The …. Was …today over to the Mrs. Church Daniel of Maggie S

Monday, 21

I had today & left it in the he.. It has froze up very hard & it is cold.

Tuesday, 22

I helped Father in the shop some today we ? some shoes & ? teeth…?

Wednesday,23

I helped Mr. Little this morning & then went down and boiled that down what was in the kettle it is so cold that it won't run

Thursday, 24

It run some today but not much. Father sold the old horse today got 100 lbs of sugar for it.

Friday, 25

I boiled all day & gathered 44 pails. It run very well.

Saturday, 26

I boiled again today & gathered.

Sunday, 27

At Church today & this evening. This afternoon Father & I went down to the woods. It seems some one gathered 15 pails.

Monday, 28

I boiled all day today & gathered 11 pails. We boiled that down this evening & had 25 lbs. It took up until 12 o'clock.

Isa came down this afternoon & Bill Clark came along to.

Tuesday, 29

I boiled & gathered 23 pails today. It is a drying up some. The tree don't run much.

Wednesday, 30

I boiled down the rest of the syrup that I had .It don't run any more. There was 4 pails of syrup very good. Langer? was with me.

Thursday, 31

I pulled one sheep today then fooled around. I sugared 2 today had 14 pounds.

April Friday, 1

I worked some in the shop today. We made 5 drug teeth & two plates for a wagon.

Saturday, 2

I went a hunting a spell today then Decator & I pitched grates a spell. I was down street this evening.

I have made 60 lbs of syrup for my part – 120 in all.

Sunday, 3

At Church today & this evening too. A…folks have made B a suit of clothes out of calico. Elvira gave him, he feels big with his family & such.

Monday, 4

I helped cover my trees today. Leny was with me. I got hurt this afternoon it is most serious.

Tuesday, 5

I boiled today and gathered some.

Wednesday, 6

I boiled & gathered again today it runs very well.

Thursday, 7

It is fast day & then is hot going down to the river hunting, fish. I boiled in what I had & then Leny & I went down to the river. Ben had my gun & shot em. Bill Chase and Decator came down and stayed with me all night. We sugared off 2 in the night.

Friday, 8

I boiled again today & gathered some. I did not feel much like work.

Saturday, 9

I went down this afternoon & gathered 10 pails & started up a fire. Bill C & Decator came down & staid until I boiled it- nine.

Sunday, 10

At Church today. It is the last Sunday that Mr. Bassett preached …?... for this year. I went this evening Mr. McBells preached … morn.

Monday, 11

It rained & snowed today. I piled up a little wood in the shed.

Tuesday, 12

This forenoon I worked in the shop, this afternoon I wheeled over those wagon wheels so be drilled Mr. Berns helped me over to Mr. Strings shop.

Wednesday, 13

I split wood today. Sap weather is most gone. EB (younger brother Ebenezer) is out with me all the time. I went down & emptied out the… so they…-of the pails & buckets.

Thursday, 14

This forenoon went down to gather 20 pails of sap & this afternoon Eb and I went up to Ben Berns & house it – rained some.

Friday, 15

I went down & boiled in that sap today & got home after dark. H. Hanley has hired me for six months & I have hired out to Mc. Omly ? for 6 months $100.00

Saturday, 16 *(at the left of the date is long division, 6 into $100.00 is 16.66 a month)*

I sawed wood all day & finished it after dark. Ben & Decatis was out there. D & B sawed & split some wood at his house this eve it was much lighter. I have made 200 lbs of sugar in all.

Sunday, 17

I stayed at home all day, Mr. Fassult has gone to Bonfrince.
Eva is sick yet it not much better. She has been sick 8 weeks.

Monday, 18

I finished splitting my wood this forenoon & this afternoon Baerme up helped me 2 ½ hours we wheeled in a big pile of wood.

Tuesday, 19

I went down & gathered my pails and buckets Mrs. G drew then up Lerts Dinner there then we cleaned them out.

Wednesday, 20

I helped father in the shop today we split out some iron for horse shoes.

Thursday, 21

I worked in the shop today.We turned 20 horseshoes. Signed Albert G. Sherman

Friday, 22

We made 5 drag teeth this morning then I came up & took the banking down in the West side. I made Eb a little cart today. (*Eb is Ebenezeer. Albert's little brother*)

Saturday, 23

This forenoon I went down to D & we played ball on the barn. This afternoon I D B & W went down to the river we fished and hunted & rode my strold canoe & played ball in the old bard down there when we came home Ben shot a Grevy we had a good time. This evening I & P bought a bunch of firecrackers & shot some off. It rained hard now.

Sunday, 24

I went to Church today this afternoon Eb & I went over the hill to see that tree we set on fire. D & Laniser came over then we dug a little well. I went to the Congo Church this evening.

Monday, 25

I started for Hanley's this morning commenced my 6 month labors. I went to sawing wood then we fixed fences the rest of the forenoon. Then after we went to picking up stones down in the meadow.

Tuesday, 26

I sawed wood a spell this morning then H & P went down to the meadow knocking manure - we came up to Din then I went back it rained most all of the afternoon. I foddered the sheep and came back. I killed a woodchuck in the barn with a fork.

Wednesday, 27

I split wood in the shed this forenoon & this afternoon H & I went a fixing fences. It rained this evening.

Thursday, 28

We repaired fences this afternoon, cut wood this forenoon. It is getting cold today. The wind blows.

Friday, 29

I helped repair fences this forenoon & then afternoon we tore down a strip & put it up new. Our folks put out word today that Eva was worse. I started & met Ben coming after me on horseback.

Saturday, 30

Didn't work today because we thought Eva was a going to die but she did not. Mrs. Paeled & Sarah came and stayed tonight. I did not

sleep much.
May Sunday, 1
George Gibbs died this morning about 12 ½ o'clock. I attended Church today. Eva is some better. Roana Lachelle is very sick. Mother & I went over to see her.

Monday, 2
I did not go to work today. Roana L died about 5 this morning. It is very pleasant today. D & I went over the hill this afternoon. Eb went with us. We played ball. This evening I helped P finish sawing his wood.

Tuesday,3
Mr. Gibbs funeral was today also Roana's. …? Benny Bascem, Decator Carter and I were pall bearers. The funeral was at the Church at 2 o'clock. It rained very hard.

Wednesday, 4
This forenoon I tagged and marked my sheep 5 ..? This afternoon I drove them down by the mill pond in Mr. Walkers pasture. I rode back with Amish Rabadeaux. I went out to Manley's tonight rode out with Jim String.

Thursday, 5
I worked all day planting potatoes out to the West farm.

Friday, 6
I worked today planted potatoes some and spread some manure.

Saturday, 7
I planted some potatoes & split wood the rest of the day. I came home this evening. Eva is no better but they say she is a little.

Sunday, 8
I went to Church for the first time he was good as could be. Eva is failing. I walked out to Hamby ? this evening. Ben & I went up in the woods & climb up to a hawk's nest.

Monday, 9
I worked today we were out meadows this forenoon, this afternoon I split wood. This evening Miss Beldem ?, Horace & I went down to the Carters.

Tuesday, 10
……………………………………series of dots 4 layers deep
I worked today. Cleaning out manure, it rained hard today. It thundered & lightened hard. I was a milking when it did.

May Wednesday, 11 1864
I was splitting wood this morning when Roy Carter came out after me. Eva was worse. I came home she did look bad. She lingered along until 3 ½ in the afternoon when she dropped away. She gasped 7 times and then died. It is Mother's birthday.

Thursday, 12
I stayed around the house today. I rode down to the mill with Mr. Leadel & looked at my sheep They were all right. Dan Southworth & wife waked here tonight & Liz an Patter Le Knipper ? last night

Friday, 13

I was down street since this forenoon & this afternoon at 1 0'clock was the funeral of Eva at the Church it was a nice day it did not rain. There was a good many there. The Bearers & Paul B was Jennie Gibbs Fannie King, Belle Benidrad & Leonisa Caster. Boys Jimmie King Vera Jones, Ralf Patter, John Fasselt.

Saturday, 14

Father hired Decator to help me plant potatoes that piece of Fathers down in Ronny Walkers, Frank Carvey, Dr. Fasselt, John f came down a hunting they all shot 6 times at a red then John Franks rifle & betched this first duck

Sunday ,15

At Church today & this afternoon to the other church I think I will go out there tonight after meeting. Mother is a sitting by the table a writing to the Girls.

Monday, 16

I worked today this forenoon I spread manure & this afternoon I planted potatoes.

Tuesday, 17

I worked today we planted beans and picked up stones today.

Wednesday, 18

I worked today we planted beans and potatoes today.

Thursday, 19

Worked today we planted corn this forenoon and beans this afternoon.

Friday,20

I worked today we sowed squash this forenoon and this afternoon I planted beans. It is a big price 425 hils in a ...?

Saturday, 21

Worked today churned this morning and this forenoon planted corn this afternoon, planted beans and finished them. I went home tonight H took me

Sunday, 22

I went to Church today and to the Congo this afternoon. I walked out to Mswinis ? tonight, as EB says

Monday, 23

I worked today I went and worked for Mr. H Gibbs they had a fusa? They was 15 then they ? will of his soveng? And planting corn.

Tuesday, 24

Worked today We washed sheep this forenoon it rained last night, when we got home Lenny Gibbs pushed me over into the ovest? All ? with my clothes on. Sproutat some put ? & sawed some wood.

Wednesday, 25

I worked today worked at the wood all day. I started for home to night and got a ride from Rlash Preachemns. ?

Thursday, 26

I worked today H & L planted beans this forenoon & I planted this afternoon alone 36 rows between the corn. Mr. & Mrs. Manly have gone to Brandon. I am sitting here by the table. Bradford bastrox the school teachers horse Sarah and I am here alone

Friday, 27

I worked. I planted beans alone today, I finished them this afternoon. All Gibbs came afternoon, Chris Addams tonight.

Saturday, 28.

Worked today. I churned this morning and sawed & split some the rest of the forenoon & this afternoon I split a big pile. The old folks came this afternoon. I went home tonight a foot and alone.

Sunday, 29

This morning I took some salt and went down where my sheep were Decator went with me. Ed and I went to 4 meeting today. They are having a great revival here. Brajett spoke today and a number of others.

Monday, 30

This forenoon we washed the rest of Sitis' sheep and this afternoon we fixed fences down by Sitis Lake road side. I walked home. I was tired.

Tuesday, 31

We went out to the East place today. We sowed potatoes this forenoon and this afternoon H and I went back to draw stones off the meadow. Mr. Brassilt was here for dinner today.

Wednesday, June 1

It rained some this forenoon & I split wood but this afternoon I worked in the barn and cleaning it up.

Thursday, 2

One man- HB- finished the bar out this forenoon and had some potatoes but it rained awful hard just noon this afternoon I split wood. However over yon West Haven it is two Smith Girls he got them. Mr. & Mrs. Ann Manley has gone away to be gone a week.

Friday, 3

I split wood this forenoon and this afternoon H & I went out to the East place and picked up stones and then we went out to the Village.

Saturday, 4

We worked on the road today until 4 then we went to a raising to Mr. M Barlour. Decator came out this evening and we went down to the lake a fishing. I caught one big snake. We got little after 11 ? with me. The rest of the crew have gone out to Fondeltzs ?

Sunday, 5

I milked and we walked out home. I went to church this forenoon and this afternoon Bruthus and I went down and looked my sheep up we found them all. I started for Manley's little after dinner for I had to do all of the chores, milk 6 cows and Harruse took shoes ? home tonight.

Monday, 6

We worked on the road today I went out to the ? this evening. It is quite chilly this evening.

Tuesday, 7

We worked on the road today. They got down on the East road.

Wednesday,8

I went out East and worked alone today, clearing up stones off of the meadow. I had old Tom. I have got a bad cold and sore throat. H & P went out this evening. The folks came home this night.

Thursday, 9

I started and did work on the road about an hour while it rained. I split wood the rest of the day. I feel as if I had been drowned thru a knot hole. They aint 13 ½ out of 20 that would worked the last 2 days if they felt as I do.

Friday, 10

We worked on the road today we finished up our side.

Saturday, 11

We hoed corn today. H & I alone this afternoon. I went home to-night.

Sunday, 12

Eb & I went to Church all day to both Churches. I walked out to Manley's this evening.

Monday, 13

Me, Mr. Manly & P hoed corn all day. H sheared sheep for Henley, I guess. Benson Vermont

I went down to the Leaki this & got me some hepos ? & Enould ? evening

Tuesday, 14

We hoed corn all day & finished it very good hoeing.

Wednesday, 15.

I planted corn potatoes & oats today alone. They sheared sheep.

Thursday, 16

I hoed in the garden & sawed wood & helped them some today. They finished shearing today.

Friday, 17

I fooled around & split wood today. I am writing to Maggie this week *(His sister Margaret was 3 yrs older)*

Saturday, 18

I split wood most of the day long towards night & I mowed the yard. I walked home tonight. I bought me a new suit of clothing this evening price $28.24

Sunday, 19

At Church all day Eb with me I wore my new suit. I walked out there this evening.

Monday, 20

We hoed potatoes out to the other place today. I went to the Leaki this evening to get me a bottle of ink.

Tuesday, 21

I rode out a horse-bench this morning & hoed this forenoon then

Mr. M came out we finished them. I wrote to Jenha

Wednesday, 22

I hoed the Garden this forenoon & this afternoon hoed corn. I went down to the Leakie this evening with the letters.

Thursday, 23

We hoed corn all day south of the house it was in green wood. Length. I have had the headache hard today.

Friday, 24

We hoed potatoes all day long and finished them. Mr M gave me a shirt. Tomorrow to pick 10 qrts of strawberries.

Saturday, 25 June

We went down after the machine this morning and cleaned it up. Then I went to sawing wood this afternoon. Mersch and I went a strawberrying we got 2 pails full. I walked home tonight. It has been awful hot today.

Sunday, 26

I went to Church all day and Eb with me. I went over to the store and got me a stick of licorice today

Monday, 27

Worked in the garden and split wood in the afternoon …blows away hard and is quite cold. I got a letter from Julia tonight. Albert ? brought it out.

Tuesday, 28

I ploughed corn this forenoon and they mowed down a small ? Then this afternoon me and P sawed wood this afternoon.

Wednesday,29

We hoed corn all day long this AM is very good. 7 weeks ago today Eva died at half past 3.

Thursday, 30

We finished the corn this forenoon and this afternoon we got up the hay. I split wood some wood. PM is a raining very hard this evening for the first time in 3 weeks ago today.

Friday, July 1

All of us hoed beans all day . It was tough hoeing and we cedy ?

Saturday, 2

I split wood and threw in and pidect ? all day. It rained all day hard. I walked home tonight. I saw Rivd down street this evening very glad to see me.

Sunday, 3

At Church all day. There was a lot joined and baptized to the other Church to day. The boys met in our yard this evening and chatted about going on about tomorrow. I walked out tonight

Monday, July 4

This morning the boys came along quite early for Whitehall. (Whitehall is in NY) We took the boat *United States* in the morning, we raced the village all day had a very good time., my headached, good we came back on *the America.* They had a number of fire engines there. The Plattsburg but ? them all with me. Decator staid.

Tuesday, 5

I hoed bean all day long. D ain't got back yet he came tonight.

Wednesday, 6 July

E, H, and I hoed beans all day got them most done all but 3 rows.

Thursday, 7

French and I went down and finished shurs ? beans and then some wood in the shed, this afternoon we shrin ? in 3 loads of hay.

Friday, 8

We mucked and got in all day, it quite warm.

Saturday, 9

I pitched and ? and tumbled and mowed the hay and raked and loaded and mow… today then walked home. I believe I have got done work for brothers in Emly and son. I can't stand it in haying no I shant by Grassiners, he owes me $6.65 cts

Sunday, 10

At Church today Dr. read a sermon. Dec and I went down to the river tonight. It was …? Us

Monday. 11

I went out and bid Mr. Manly good-by this forenoon and brought my chicks home this afternoon. I picked cherries at home.

Tuesday, 12

Picked cherries this forenoon. Afternoon helped Father in the shop.

Wednesday, 13

I worked in the shop all day helped father set 12 tires.

Thursday, 14

I worked for Bill Malory hoeing potatoes. Marlory & Decator worked too. I earned about $1.25

Friday, 15

I worked in the shop this forenoon. Afternoon mowed down over Renas Malkers, Evening went to a concert most of it was very good.

Saturday, 16

Mowed and spread in the forenoon, raked and got in a load, father helped me, we had Mr. Southwerth's team.

Sunday, 17 July

At Church today. It is quartermeeting day. Benson, VT Sherman, Jr.

Monday, 18

I am a going to work for Carter this week commenced today. We drew in hay for Bill this forenoon, this afternoon I polished in the shop. I work for 1.25 each day.

Tuesday, 19

I worked today in the shop polishing 2 big base, got it done most.

Wednesday, 20

I worked today in the shop polishing, Carter came home from Tie ? tonight.

Thursday, 21

I worked today. Decatur and I went up and mowed all day in Widow

Pslhur's lot. He has taken it on hellos ..?

Altho once Julia popped in about 12 this day, she woke us all up, she came to the lake. She has a vacation 6 weeks.

Friday, 22

We went up to mow this forenoon and finished it. We got it all in this afternoon 4 loads.

Saturday, 23

I polished this forenoon and helped carry timbers this afternoon, helped drag stones and timber for their barn. I have earned $7.1/2 this week.

Sunday, 24

At Church today with Eb, Mother, ...Julia and Lisa. Mr. Fesselt. I expect to work for Zramer this week for 1 ½ a day If I do I have got to walk down there this week   //// scribble...Benson.

Monday, 25

I mowed all this forenoon and some of the afternoon until it rained awful hard.

Tuesday, 26

It looked to rain this morning. I went home then the Bascom boys and Bill C and I went out to the lake a fishin lot of other boys to went out. We got some fish 3 pickerel and some others. I walked down there tonight.

Wednesday, 27

We worked all day got in some and mowed some and raked some and worked hard some.

Thursday, 28 July

We worked in the other meadow today.

Friday, 29

We worked in a bo lot we all eleurd...? it today 5 acres Benny Ladd died this morning, he is 86 yrs.

Saturday, 30

We did not work today. Larry is coming home and he is a going to ...? His machine up to the village and get it fixed. It went out I went over and mowed a little for father but it cut so hard I could not cut it.

Sunday, 31

Eb and I went to Church today to the funeral , they sent after Mr. Fasset to Saratoga he came. I went over the hill this afternoon, D was over there we got some black berries. I walked down to his bramons tonight after their meeting.

Monday,1 August

We worked hard all day and I went in swimming.

Tuesday , 2

We got in two loads of hay. It rained some then cleared off and we mowed the rest, down and then rained some more. I am a going haying after dinner. I got wet through and through. I have worked there 5 days $7.50

Wednesday, 3

It rained all night and all day today steady. I worked some in the shop. I went up to Ben's and got some ripe apples.

Thursday, 4

Turned some shoes in the shop this morning there for a skin and I went over and mowed down a piece of grass for Father an Walkers. I went over to finish it after dinner then worked in the shop some.

Friday, 5

We turned a few shoes and then I went over and spread that hay. Father and I racked it up and Nell Ladd drew it in.

Saturday, 6

Jo Bascom and I mowed down another piece he had his machine and racked it this afternoon and Father and I racked it this afternoon and Father and I racked it all up 46 sacks it has got today out over Sabbath.

Sunday, 7

At Church today. Dr. preached a sermon. Dec and I went down to the river tonight . It was need ? us.

Monday, 8 August

I worked in the shop today. We turned some shoes but this forenoon I got Will Clark and Mr. Kellog's team and Father and I all together got in 2 loads of hay.

Tuesday, 9

I worked in the shop today and went a berrying – got some.

Wednesday, 10

I worked in the shop some today we got out seven patterns and shoes.

Thursday, 11

I worked in the shop this forenoon and this afternoon I got D to go with me to W Ladd's a mowing. We cut some and gave it up, it was so stoney. We went to the river this evening.

Friday, 12

I ground ..? up and went down and mowed all the forenoon and this afternoon raked and mowed more all that was good enough. I had 21 tumbles. Fayette drew it in for me.

Saturday, 13

Decatur and I went berrying today , all evening went across our pasture and milked our cows and had berries and milk. Good we got 6 quarts.

Sunday, 14

At church today. Walked up street this evening.

Monday, 15

I worked in the shop today turning shoes.

Tuesday, 16

John Williams, Decatur and I went over the lake a berrying, lot went I got 12 quarts. I bought a new knife 39¢

Wednesday, 17

Worked in the shop today turning shoes. I made a fitter..? bow today. It rained all day.

Thursday, 18

Worked the shop today.

Friday, 19

Mackin boy, Tracy and Isa and I went a berrying over the lake. I picked 16 quarts. Isa 10, Julia 6, went with Woodard and ...? We all got a bushel.

Saturday, 20

I worked in the shop most all day. We have got most 100 shoes. I turned over 50 or about 50 made out of old ones.

Sunday, 21

At Church today. Eb and I went Ben and I went down to the river andwent in tonight. Mother has gone off north a visiting. Julia is a writing to her.

Monday, 22

I worked for Mr. Southworth today polishing marble. $1.00 a day and board myself not enough.

Tuesday, 23

I worked for Haley today. We went way up to A rwell a haying. I mowed only hay. 1.50 I shall ask.

Wednesday, 24

I worked for Southworth today. I am a going to ald of the week.

Thursday, 25

Worked in the shop today very hard. Got a letter from Mother tonight.

Friday, 26

Worked some in the shop today. Decator and ..? ran away going to Fair Haven and took the cars and went at all over the worked they thought.

Saturday, 27

Worked in the shop today. The boys came back today and they thought it hard in going away.

Sunday, 28

At Church today over to the Congo this afternoon. I walked ...west Will and Ben was there we got some apples.

Monday, 29

Worked in the shop today.

Tuesday, 30

Worked today and have got an awful cold.

Wednesday, 31

I worked in the shop today and most too hard for $1.00 a day.

Thursday 1 September

I worked in the shop this week. It is quite chilly this week.

Friday, 2

I worked today It makes 10 days. I have been there.

Saturday, 3

I did not work there today but helped Father turn 4 shoes and then went down to see my sheep 5 of them, one was lame. Then went over in Ladd's pasture and see my heifer went in swimming in evening.

Sunday, 4

I went to Church today, this afternoon too. The b..? after Dinner walked up to Wills and went over in the Orchard and got some apples.

Monday, 5

I started to make patterns in the shop today but the horses came in and we could not get out any more only 6. I went to the lake this afternoon with a load of the pays people for Leon Read. I got .50 for going

Tuesday, 6

I worked for Mr. Southerworth today. I guess I will work all the week. Gown Meeting is today. Daniel Crofer is Prothonotary of this town. Kellogg wanted to be.

Wednesday, 7

Worked in the shop today.

Thursday, 8

Worked in the shop today.

Friday, 9

Worked today. Will did not work today

Saturday, 10

Worked all day and was glad when it come night, then I came up and patched the house sen…? I have worked 15 days for Dan that will make $15.000,000,000.

Sunday, 11

At Church today at the Congo this afternoon. Eb with me in the forenoon. Mr. Smart preached a funeral sermon for a soldier Parch. Eb and I walked along up to Bens, we went up in the woods and Orchard. I think I will go to meeting this evening.

Monday, 12 September

I worked in the shop today we got out a lot of patterns out of old horseshoes.

Tuesday, 13

Worked in the shop today trimming horse shoes.

Wednesday, 14

Worked in the shop today.

Thursday, 15

Worked all day in the shop.

Friday, 16

Worked hard all day, we turned 37 shoes and drawed out 17 out of an old wagon tire.   *(tiny handwriting Miss Julia L ..)*

Saturday, 17

I worked this forenoon, we have got 110 shoes turned this afternoon. I went a hunting got 1 grey squirrel and caught one young one.

Sunday, 18

At Church all day, to the Congo this afternoon. Mell Grassoldt is here after meeting we all went out on the hill and cracked some buttermilks (butternuts) Then Eb and I went up to Bens. Ben and I went to milking this evening.

Monday, 19

*Drawing of man with a beard on left side of page…*is looking some like him

I commenced going to school today…his name is C P W Wheeler Esq. I like him very well there are over 20 scholars. I sold my sheep tonight, to Bill Brown for $3.00 a piece 5 of them for $15.00

Tuesday, 20

At school today like very much. I study Phonography (steno)

Wednesday, 21

At school today. I shot a grey squirrel tonight.

Thursday, 22

At school today. I helped Brother in the shop this evening making patterns, 14.

Friday, 23

At school today. Then worked this evening got out…?

Saturday, 24 September

School don't keep today. I worked in the shop this forenoon. We turned 22 horseshoes and drew out some steel… ?   I went a hunting this afternoon had Gibbs gone 2 .. I shot 4 greys and sold them to Malory .25

Sunday, 25

At Church this all day to the Congo this afternoon. Smart preached a funeral sermon of Robert Black. I went over to Mrs. G's after meeting. At meeting this evening and went home with Ethel Schinder.

Monday, 26

At school today we had a lot of scholars come today. There were 34 in all.

Tuesday, 27

At school today. This evening I went up to Bens, Earn Will, Pat Therefore Ben, Will and I husked corn.

Wednesday, 28

At school today. This evening us boys went up there to told stories had fun. Ben, P and I went a hunting awhile. Ben shot one and …?

Thursday, 29

At school today, home in the evening. Gheadon and I went a hunting little up hill tonight. I shot 3.

Friday, 30

At school today. Father and Eb went after Mr. Thir this afternoon. Thirty is a carillon in Brandon today but I can't go. Therefore I and P went hunting a little while. P shot 2

Saturday, October 1

Theadore and I went hunting this forenoon and P shot 5 grey squirrels had his gun. School don't keep today this afternoon Ben Will T and I went again and got 4 I one makes 17 so far this year.

Sunday, 2

At Church this forenoon at both Churches. This forenoon it rained so there wasn't any to curs…? I have been writing today this evening. I was over to Etherton awhile this evening.

Monday, 3

At school today, down street this evening.

Tuesday, 4

At school today went over the hill after school and shook a tree of walnuts but did not pick them up but came back and went to my photography class this evening.

Wednesday, 5 October

I got up before day light this morning and I went over the hill and picked up Tuesday's walnuts it was awful foggy. I came back to get ready to go to Whitehall with Father and Fayell. Boyd returned and some nailrods…barrel to Eban and pair of boots. I went to the Carousel and lot of animals of all kinds

(written upside down: I rode home with the Balkoms..I got me a Photosophy ? we had good times)

Thursday, 6

At school today. Down street this evening.

Friday, 7

At my school today and down street and got a letter from Maggie. She has commenced her school for 66 months. I studied this evening some. It rained awful hard tonight.

Saturday, 8

The first thing I done today I went down to Dec after a long fork he gave me lot of rope. (he said he did last night) then cleaned out my stable some went by to Bens went down to the shop…? And filed something on my boots, came up eat diner went up north and dug some potatoes for Mrs. Walker and then went a hunting…I got 1 grey that makes 18 this year, barrel of cider today.

Sunday, 9

At church today was over to Ryles father while tis afternoon, took them over a little cider, went to Church this evening Ben set with me.

I am up stairs writing ..the bed. It snowed little today

Monday, 10

At school today and evening down street.

Tuesday, 11

At school today.

Wednesday, 12

At school today. There is a fair in Fair Haven today and morrow. It rained some today. I am going tomorrow.

Thursday, 13

I started to go I rode down to Fair Haven today with Hen Little and rode back with Decator. It rained most all of a this time. Lot of the Benson folks was there. I got a good.... unreadable

Friday, 14

At school today. It rained most of the day.

Saturday, 15 October 1864

I helped Father in the shop today, we got out some patterns. Ret was over to our house most of the day.

Sunday, 16

I went to Church all day and Eben with me, after milking I went over to Mrs. Walkers and spin the...

Monday, 17

At school today, tonight I went down to Mr. Kelloggs and bought 6 traps and went over to the Beaver meadow and got ...came back and it was dark

Tuesday, 18

At school today this morning I went up and looked at my traps , got nothing. Set them again tonight, this evening going to Phonography class. (use of symbols for sounds: the use of symbols to represent speech sounds in writing ; shorthand with symbols for sounds: a method of writing in shorthand that uses symbols to represent speech sounds)

Wednesday, 19

At school today, got two rats (muskrat) feet in my traps this morning they eat their legs off. I set them again tonight.

Thursday, 20

I went to school today. Got nothing so > no more signs of it.

Friday, 21

I went to school today. Got a little hairs in my trap. I went to my Phonography this evening. Then lot of us boys played ” i-spy” in the sheds had good time then I came down and staid with Decator over night we had fun especially for a while.

Saturday, 22

School don’t keep today and I have been a digging potatoes Father got ...in what for they wet.

I did not set the traps tonight.

Sunday, 23

At Church today. D and I went out to set my traps again tonight. I went to macking this evening...am up in my room writing letters Eban ...?

Monday, 24

At school today worked in the shop this evening.

Tuesday, 25

At school today, this evening at my phonography class after it was out Mark and I came up to Potters, they had a husking bee , we did not go in. Mark, Dec, Pat and I got a lot of rotten eggs and went up by Mr. Bascoms… this fence and when he came asking we gave him Jisqu it ? was Me D we hit him how he did swear, he could not catch any of us

Wednesday, 26

At school today, this evening worked in the shop, we got out a number of patterns

Thursday, 27

At school today, worked in the shop, this evening getting out patterns for horseshoes. I blistered my hand.

Friday, 28

At school today, this evening to my shorthand writing, it is awful dark tonight.

Saturday, 29 October 1864

School don't keep today. Father and I turned ….shoes. Will Clark and I went to the river ahunting, we seen a lot of rats but did not get any, we got cash of grey squirrel - 3 makes 19 this year.

Sunday, 30

At Church today although he did not preach and general feeling had because his brother Dr. Faussett is dead. I went down to meeting this evening.

Monday, 31

At school today, this evening worked in the shop, we got out 28 patterns.
I went down to the river after school and shot at a muskrat but this gun hung? Fire and off

Tuesday, November 1

At school today, this evening to the school house. I am a learning a good deal in Phonography. *(drawing below this)*

Wednesday, 2

At school today but got excused and got in sowing potatoes, then D and I went down to the river but did not get anything.

Thursday, 3

At school today, worked in the shop this evening.

Friday, 4

At school today, this evening down to the school house.

Saturday, 5

Father and I turned …shoes today and got done by 1, then I went and banked up Mrs. Walkers house.

Sunday, 6

At Church today, this evening over to the other Church.

Monday, 7

At school today, after school was out, I went over to get my traps and …? And I went down to the river, we got nothing.

Tuesday, 8

At school today, this evening to the phonographic class.

Wednesday, 9

At school today this evening worked in the shop.

Thursday, 10

I helped Father set 4 tires this forenoon for Carver and this afternoon I banked the house Bill Clark and Plaski helped me, Bill and I
went over to set my traps tonight, then I came back and worked in
the shop awhile.

Friday, 11

Went to school today, down to the class again tonight, after that was
our went down street and a lot us us boys and Jumped and played.

Saturday, 12

Father and I turned 42 shoes today and got done at noon. Then I
helped him a little after dinner, then Will Clark and I went down to the
river, but got nothing. I went to Engenst ? little whirl this evening.

Sunday, 13

At church today, Fausselt preached a funeral sermon of Will
Beadons, shot in the army, over to the other Church this afternoon
and down to ours this evening. It snowed last night and most all day,
it is 5 or 6 inches. My heifers came.

Monday, 14 November

At school today, a few boys and girls went down in Mr. Barbers a
skating this evening for the first time, it was some rough.

Tuesday, 15

At school today, this evening helped Father in the shop, we got out
some taicorks ?. I sent after a time …? This money to N.Y.

Wednesday, 16

At school today.

Thursday, 17

At school today down street this evening.

Friday, 18

At school today this evening went down to the school..Phonography
class for the last time. I suppose. I received my Novel.

Saturday, 19

At school this forenoon and after lunch to the teachers examination.
The teachers were Nell Fassolt, Amelia Beseam, Jenny Adams, Fran
West Hears, Mary Grimell and Deal P ?

Sunday, 20

At Church today and this evening too. I read my novel today and ?
Wrp;egsd brought them, here for me to read.

Monday, 21

Mr. Bascoms folk killed two of their hogs and .. I went to school
this afternoon, this evening Father and I cut the hog and weighed it.
It weighed 330 Sebs, 30 lbs in 2 leafs ?

Tuesday, 22

At school today, tomorrow I suppose is the last day for this fall school. (in script and underneath each other are Benson, Rutland County Vermont

Wednesday, 23

It rained some today and worked a little in the shop and got my ax ground today, ready for tomorrow

Thursday 24

Lot of us boys went out on Carvers land a sketching today. It is Thurs 22 s given all day. We had a good time, this evening went down on Prentiss a shooting. We had spare rib for dinner.

Friday, 25

I banked this house a little and finished at and fixed the bard and hog pen and then went down to the river and I put on my skates and had a good skate …of the pond and I took my gun down and shot a duck

Saturday, 25

I helped Father some in the shop and sawed up some wood, then Dec and I went down to the Pond askating, it was nice we skated across it- it cracked. Decator broke in and hurt him bad, I went down an ….tonight.

Sunday, 27

At church today. Mr. Smert preached at our Church and Faussett over to the other.

Monday, 28

It has rained all day and our skating is done with

Tuesday, 29

It rained some today and I worked a little in the shop and got my AX ground today ready for tomorrow.

Wednesday, 30 November 1864

Will Clark and I started for the mountain and chopping. We worked hard all day put up 1 cord and Bill ¾ of a cord of hard wood, he gets $1.25 for hard wood and !.00 for *mihed*   *(mixed hardwood and softwood)*

Thursday,1 December

We went up today, shopping. Bill cut a cord and I one cord. We got home in little better season tonight.

Friday, 2

We went up again today , I chopped 1 ¼ cord and Will ¾ mihed wood. W.A. Ladd is chopping by us, And Heath and Herr Santhwerth is chopping south of us. I got me a pain of Back tonight as Father did, down to Reds.

Saturday, 3

I got up this morning and found lot of snow on the ground, first I went down to the Tailors and got measured for a pair of pants and then sawed wood the rest of the day.

Bills   A

3   1

4   1

1	1
½	½
4	1 ¼
2 ½	3 ¼

Sunday, 4

At Church today, this evening went over to the Church to a meeting.

Monday, 5

I went up to the mountain alone. I chopped 1 cord most hard wood and I ½ cord. It has frozen up hard. and came home.

Tuesday, 6

Albert went up a chopping today and put up his cord and came home.

Wednesday, 7

I sent after a Chinese novel today. It is rainy day. Bil Lark and I went a hunting all over after partridges but did not get any , we shot a mark. ...

Thursday, 8

Mr. Belchim and I went up to the mountain chopping , we cut for us, he chopped 1 ½ all soft wood. I did not cut only ½ of a cord because my hand was so sore.

Friday, 9

Mr. Makim went up with me today he cut 1 ¼ cord most hard wood and I ½ cord. It has frozen up hard. Albert 1 cords

    1
  01/2
  01/2

    3 cords   We have got 11 cords & !/2

Saturday, 10

I got up this morning and found some snow on the ground, it has spoiled skating. I sawed wood all day and was down street. I had on my new shoes tonight and I weighted 146 ½

Sunday, 11 December 1864

At Church today and this evening too.

Monday, 12.

I commenced going to school today. ....

Tuesday, 13

At school today, down street this evening. I enlisted into the Malislia (Militia). Will Clark put his name down too and lot of others. ...this evening and went 149 labor...?

Wednesday, 14

At school today and this evening went down street

Thursday, 15

At school today, down street this evening and saw a big dog fight. This afternoon us boys went down to the pond a skating, not good.

Friday, 16

At school today, down street this evening, all quiet.

Saturday, 17

At school today, my face is so bad, I can't go down street tonight.

Sunday,18

At Church today and this evening too.   (Signature) Albert

Monday, 19

At school today, down street this evening.

Tuesday, 20

At school today. I have been a reading this evening.

Wednesday, 21

Went to school today, this evening went down street, the wind blows hard and it snowed very hard. I called for Isa to Mr. Faussett this evening, we stayed late. The girls making things for Christmas table.

Thursday, 22

At school today, I'm a writing in school, boys have been a trying tricks in the school house. I expect to go down street and get a dime novel this evening but hardly think there will be a mail on account of the snow.

Friday, 23

At school today, this evening went down street. This morning I went down to Southworth shop & commenced a ring for Nell Faussett. I got my novel tonight or rather last night.

Saturday, 24

I worked down there all the forenoon and that & finished it. I was a going to hang it on the tree but won't now. This great ..Snwri versil ? came off this evening. I helped pass some things. I got a locket from Francis Rigel this eve, Isa cloth from Jessica. Eb got a ? on the tree.

Sunday, 25

All Church today, all hands of us, it is Christmas all day. We had a dinner of 2 roosters today. I have been a writing to Bia?

Monday, 26

Went to school today, it has been a raining almost all day. This evening went down street to a Corker ?meeting, so did Capt F? Fred Reed but afraid won't eat it tomorrow..

Tuesday, 27

Our boys all went over to Hartswill today to Elect the officers. Pitts is the …Fred Reed 1st lieut, D Haking, Isa Lisarnt, It rained all the way there and back. Lrodeourwith Hall, Benson

Wednesday, 28

Went to school today. We had a good time. Snow balling. Hattie V her folks was down here today. Not went to school, afternoon. I get a letter from C.W. Wheeler to night.

Thursday, 29

At school today, it has snowed some today and I think will freeze up some tonight. (Practices making written L's   L   L   L)

Friday, 30

Today Will Clark and I went a chopping for Bill up on Mr. J Grimell way beyond the Bull leap pond. I cut ¾ of a cord and Bill ½ We did not get through until late, we walked home. School did not keep today.

Saturday, 31

I went up chopping again today but I done a little better. I put up a cord and Bill ½ 1.25 a cord. Went down street this evening and Will Goodrich had a turkey for me. I came up with it and then went down to Decator, we played checkers until his Dad came.

Our folks have been up to W Ladds this afternoon. The whole lot of them were there, well it is the last day of the year and now will see where I will be a year from now. I am now in the house by the fire.

(On top of this entry is ¾ page full of division problems 3.50 .40 8 ¾ bus oats)

This ends the diary except for pages of lists with expenses/ tallies. . . . .

There is a list of novels Albert has read during the winter:

Hermit of the Colorado Hills
Rebel Friend
Robbers Terror
Bret Sternem or the Strong Hearted Scout
Rolicking Rangers
The Scout
Wild Scent of the Mountains
The Indian Slayer
Brothers Betrayed
On the Planes or the
Race for Life and Good
Light for the Scout
The Man eater

APPENDIX 4

Author's trip to Benson, Vermont October 18, 2006

Today my husband Richard and I returned from Benson, Vermont. We left Wadleigh Pond, Lyman Maine on Monday, October 16th and headed for Vermont. My grandmother, Julia Sherman Bassler had told me years ago that we had an ancestor who had fought in the Revolutionary War.(This would qualify us to become members of the Daughters of the American Revolution. I had written to Clara my grandaunt in Missouri about the subject) I was told a cousin in Vermont had the information. My Grandmother died in 1975. So for many years I have tried to verify this family story.

I purchased a publication from Chazy, NY-*A History of the Town of*

Chazy Clinton County, New York by Nell Jane Barnett Sullivan and David Kendall Martin. The copious information has been incorporated into the body of the Bassler Family History.

APPENDIX 5

REV. JOHN SHERMAN'S MEMORIAL INSCRIPTION
(taken from internet site findagrave.com)

Translation of the Latin inscription(sent to me by contributor Ruth I. Stude):

Sacred to the memory of John Sherman, a man distinguished for this piety, character and truth; a profound theologian; as a preacher a veritable Chrysostom; unsurpassed in his knowledge of the liberal arts, particularly mathematics; a faithful pastor of the church of Water Town in New England; an Overseer and Fellow of Harvard College. After a life of faithful service to Christ in the church for upwards of 45 years, in the fullness of time he passed away and received from Christ the palm of victory. In the 72nd year of his age, August 8, A.D. 1685.

- Epitaphs From The Old Burying Ground In Watertown, [Middlesex Co., MA] Collected by William Thaddeus Harris, L. L. B. With Notes by Edward Doubleday Harris, Boston, 1869 [Transcribed by Jane Devlin]
- Rev. John SHERMAN was b. in Dedham, Eng., 26 Dec 1613, graduated at Trinity College, and came to New England about 1635. He was ordained the third minister of Watertown about 1648; was twice married and left many descendants. His wife Mary d.9 Mar 1709-10.

APPENDIX 6

FAMILY LETTERS FROM VERMONT

A cache of letters written to Albert G. Sherman were preserved for over 150 years in Minnie Sherman's tin bread box in her home in Clinton, Missouri. Found when the homestead was sold, Nancy Sherman and Kevin Diehl lovingly sorted and placed them in archival plastic sleeves with the date and year printed on each sheet. In most cases the envelopes were also preserved. Albert G and Laura's marriage certificate of 8 December, 1870 was also preserved. Some letters are clearly legible others have nearly faded out. I have chosen some letters from the early years and some from the latter years, some from his mother and some from his sisters. The letters begin 23 June, 1864 and end in 11 March, 1889.

South Macon (Illinois),   **June 24rd, 1864**

Dear Brother Bert: *(from sister Maggie teaching in Illinois)*

I received your very welcome letter this morning before breakfast and it gave me an extra good appetite. I hasten to reply hoping it will get to you before you receive one from Julia – then you must keep your promise and 'like me best.' I was very glad to hear from you but wish you had a place where you would not have to work so hard. They cannot make the hired men milk out here. Mr. Sillinsen's people are shearing now – they have more than a thousand and it will take them all of the week to finish. It is very warm indeed and I almost melt going and coming from school. The school house is very warm – not a tree in sight but a large wheat field a <u>mile square</u>, which will make it much warmer when it turns, it will draw the sun so much more.

I believe I have suffered more from the heat this summer than I ever did before. I do not think it has been any warmer than it is in Vt. But country is so level with no trees near here to shade the least. This is a new country but I think in a few years from now it will be as thickly settled as the Eastern states. I am so glad that school is almost out- then I shall rest some – any way will not have much walking to do. I think I have done very well to teach nine months with only a few days vacation. I would really like to step into Mr. Manly's and see ? for while, but would not put myself out of the way much if I could get any where near home. I don't see how I am agoing to stay way out here so long. I have been a good deal homesick. How I will miss the little scholar when I get home. I had laid such plans for her to come and stay with me. I should like it if little Ella was lying by her side, it would not seem so lonely for us to see them both together. I would give anything if I was in a school as Elvira was in Miss. I would like it so much better than a district school. I don't see any chance for me elsewhere. What are you agoing to do the 4th? Going to Burlington again? How little I thought a year ago that this year I would abe far off West. There is a picnic in Decater, possible I may go but it is uncertain. Are you going to school this fall ? I thought you had some lambs last fall, have you kept them? Do you ever see Ed – now-a-days, I wonder if he wouldn't like my photograph to look at once & a while as I promised to send one to him when I sent you one. I wish you could have yours taken for me. Won't you when you get you $1.00 I will have mine taken after school is out. I wish I were down where Julia is, we could spend our vacation together. Do you ever see Agnes or home this fall but I must wait a year or two more before I leave the West. Ebbie will be a big Adelie P ? Are they at home, I suppose you do not have much chance to call at Mrs. Walkers now. Is James at home this summer? I am going to write to Ethelinda when I get all of the letters answered on hand. I ought to answer three this evening but I get sleepy before dark and then can hardly get up in the morning. I am getting tired of school and will be glad of a change. I wish I could go boy and Isa a young lady but no little Eva to change anymore.*(Eva died in 1864)* That little picture is quite natural. Wouldn't you like to send one of the little ones to Helen Day? I would send one if I had it. I haven't made quite so long a letter as you did but I would like to get a dozen like yours a week. Please give my love to Sarah and be a good boy and don't get the actions of that good boy if you can help it. Now please write soon and give my love to all, from your aff sister Meg

Dear Brother Albert, *(from sister Isa)* **July 2, 1863**

We received your loving expected letter last evening with one from Maggie, Father came in with them asked for his glasses and a light and opened them pretty quick and then I read them. Father thinks that he can have the pleasure to open them if not to read them.

I have been to meeting all day at our church this forenoon and the other church this afternoon. There were only 28 on account of it raining so hard this forenoon but a great many at the other church. Randelle Byron and his Mother joined the church and were baptized today. I sit out here in the hall where we use to have so many good sings and I wish you were here now.

I guess we would have another good one. Have you sung Retrospection, Dennis Church Grateful Tribute or any other of those good old pieces since you left home a year from next fall. Maybe I shall come out west if you and Maggie stay out there by that time I hope I shall have taught one or two seasons. The garden looks very nicely this summer. There are not any plums nor a great many cherries. I don't know who will pick the cherries this year. You have always seen to them. The heifer has got a little calf, she is quite a large cow. I have earned quite a little stock of money a selling berries this summer $1.25, sold some 25 to Mrs. Heath and some to father. Father got me a new calico dress last week. I wore it today. I am a trying to get enough to get me a new .... Dress. Well as the bell is ringing for five o'clock I will stop....not returned from meeting and now will write a little more. Mother got sick of *Eb (Ebenezer-youngest child)* yesterday and sent him down street but he didn't want to go so she told him to go down so he went and got her a black spool of thread (she didn't think that he would go but he did go) and get a spool just she might member. Tell Mag that I will write to her this week. Little Frankie grows...every day and so close Grampie Southworth. I will try and not forget so put in Wallis picture this time. Frank twice has been off to school and graduated. I haven't seen his diploma yet. Francis Rivet and Mr. Peirce Mr. Ramner, Mr Watts was a coming got to Baltimore fell off from the cars, hurt his head, broke two ribs. They think he will recover soon. Mattie Leaded says that her father is agoing to sell his horse and get her an Oregon but I guess that she will get one about as soon as I do. Mrs. Walker and family seem to be all quite smart. I was over there tonight. Mr. More Coldvester came in a little while. Eb and I would get some pictures taken but they cost so much. Where are you a going the fourth? I don't expect to go anywhere. Annlie sits here a telling me Just what to write. She wants you to know all that is agoing on. This is all that I can think of to write tonight. Write and soon. Good night. From your youngest sister, Isa. Write to me just soon as you get this. Tell Maggie that I guess that I will get some burs for her room. (Now don't get homesick) P.S. All what did you do

Dear Dear Albert   *(from mother Sept. 10, 1865)*

I have had a severe headache all day, it rained so I did not go to meeting, thought I could not write any today but since supper I feel better so thought I would write a short letter to you, we are all quite well but Ebbie I guess he is more cross than sick, he has been to meeting with the girls, Auntie is undressing him. He is crying to go with father after the cows, it has been very dry here lately we have had to fetch water from the Ladds to wash till they thought they could not spare any more.

Their house well is dry or it takes so much water to make a hartue ? Then we fetch from Mr. Gibbs or Mr. Carter's well to wash with some one informed Mr. Knap there used to be a well down there front of their house by the ditch and Mr. Steek filed it up so he got Tom Clark or they looked it up and dug it out and it is a nice good well. He has put in a pump so we get water from there now both pumps well are nearly dry but I guess we shall have water now it is raining now moderately.

Evening

Well Albert since supper we have had a surprise just before we lit the light, your Father was down to the gate and Kindle Ladd drove up with two ladies and you guess who they were, Aunt Vira and Lucy Ann, they come to Ladds yesterday at 8, we have just been to supper and then the girls have just gone to bed, we are all in the kitchen now, bubbie is crying with a sore foot, they don't fetch much news, there has been some deaths. Mrs. McCulof (that is not spelt right) Mr. John Aldridge barn was burnt last week with all his crops. LucyAnn is a big girl. Eddie is at home and Oscar with Amasa is going out west this fall to look him a place, to move. She says we look odd enough to see such a few in our family. She misses you very much, says give my love to Albert, tell him to be a good boy and come home or see her before she goes home.

Decater *(Albert's friend)* started yesterday for the west, he went to Castleton with a load for someone and got a boy to come back with the team, his Father was over to Fri did not know that he was going, but he has said so many times he was going to see Albert but I am sorry he is gone, they say they don't know where he got his money. Father says he would rather five dollars than have him go there for he is a miserable boy. I hope he will not plague you any. I would not work with him any way, he has been a bad boy this summer but I tell them I aint going to borrow any trouble, he was going with that fellow that lived to Page Balis, well I guess I must bid you good night, they have all gone to bed. I wish you and Mag wore both here to visit with Aunt Vira, write often tell me how your clothes are or who does your mending, I wish I could

Forget me not Albert

Mother

Good night

The Saloon just left yesterday Thursday eve

Dear Albert   (from Julia)   **Oct. 16, 1865**

I promised you I would write you a few lines this week and they will have to be few. I guess for I've only few minutes to write in. My eyes refuse to remain open so if I keep the line at will be Father is getting better slowly. He has sit up sometime today at several different times. His lungs are yet very weak but Dr. Prad, Dr. Cushmann came in to see him the other day. He decided then there are no bones broken and said his lungs would heal with great care. That gave us great encouragement. He says he shall be in the shop in two weeks but I doubt it. Isa wanted me to ask you and Laura to send her a lock of your hair quite a lock if you can spare it. She is going to make her a wreath and I want a little of Laura's in mine if she is willing. We were somewhat disappointed in not hearing from you tonight. My five minutes are up. Love from all Sister Julia

                              Benson Vermont   **Thursday July 1866**

Dear Brother Albert, *(from sisters Isa and Maggie)*

After eating my dinner this noon felt some tired and thought I would lie down and take a short map but the plagny ? flies bit me so that I couldn't take a minutes peace. I happened to think that I told you that I would write again this week so I hopped up went in the pantry and got the pen and ink, went in Mothers bed room and got her portfolio (as she calls it) came up stairs seated myself by the east window and went to writing. We are all well this warm day. Father had gone to Fair Haven after some iron. He went with the stage, I guess he will get some chairs. Mother and Julia are in papering the west room, we had to tear off every bit of the old paper because it showed through. Auntie is a doing the house work. Ebbie is down street, rode down with A R Ladd, he catches a number of rides (now and then) Father gives him a penny every day to get spearmints with them. "Abert comin home: he asks very often."

Well I guess that if I keep on at this rate I shant have any room to write the news if there is any. I believe I left off with Potter folks. Mr. Gibbs is to work over to the east first of the town, I don't know who for or what at. I don't see as Eddie has gone a bit since you went away. Jennie is growing very fast both in size and mind, her Ma thinks I might go with her just as much as with Ret and Ada but I don't see it. Fred Reed lives in the front part of their house, he keeps a boarder , his name is Scott, he works at the tire shop daytimes and sits in Mrs W. Walkers sitting room evenings two or three times a week. I am a little acquainted with him. He appears to be a fine gentleman. The school house is unoccupied at present and has been for almost four weeks. Mr. Hanley our preacher is a fine man and good preacher. He has three children, all girls, his wife is our cousin to Mr. L Barber so that makes them a little nicer you see. The M E Church comes next it is very dirty indeed, quarterly meeting is to be held there Saturday and Sunday. The two strongest cannot say much about only that Julia and I are a going over there tonight and get some white paint of them, Father and they are on good terms as ever. By Carter is in his store yet Bernie is his clerk. Carl Smith keeps hardware. Carrie Wittles works there. They seem to be very lonesome, at the Doc yet. They haven't a moment for the boys it is beautiful. Carters Store much trade is going on. Mr. Cephas Knapp works at the tin shop. Leon Reed keeps grocery, his father shoe shop a bore him. Mr and Mrs. Naramore boards at the hotel. Orpha Barber live there and takes music lessons of Mr. Ross. I guess I won't go over on the other street only to say the folks are all well. Will Kellogg and wife arrived week before last. The wheelwright shop is going on yet, I don't know what Henry Worton is doing now not anything I guess. You know that that was his disposition to as still as possible. John Adams still works in his shop. Frank is a going off a visiting next week. I don't know a thing about the Reynolds work. Mr. Dick is still alive.

Benson Vt   **Aug 7th 1866**

Dearest Brother   *(sister Julia)*

By going up stairs I have succeeded in getting some paper to write upon. Mag returned last eve and Libbie came home with her. She is grown almost a young lady, very pretty appearing indeed.

We have all been in the parlor playing and singing but Mother. I thought she was writing to you but I came out and found her serving entirely forgetful of you until I reminded her of it. The girls have gone to bed and I presume they will talk till most day. School goes on very well. We were very glad to get your expected letter last eve and wish heartily with you that you were at home. Mrs. Barrows is here. She was talking about you to Elvira the other day, said they liked you so much that they never had a man before who would go and milk when Mr. Haran gone. She thinks you will stay West till you have visited Mo. (Missouri) We have got the other room so newly fixed I think you would not recognize it. We wish we had your shirt here to make over – and is there nothing you want us to make for you and send by Mrs. Barrows if she would take them. Mother just said she wished she could get hold of your clothes, she would fix them up for I've no doubt they need it. Do you need any new every day ones. Mother says if she had anything to get them with she would not ask you if you needed them but if you want do to get them and make them and if that will be any help we shall be so glad to do it.

Did you not want to work for Mr. A longer or did he not want you. You spoke of his having another man. Where are you going now? I hope you will not have to pay for your board. If I could 2 arms to dolls in one or two weeks. I should be very well satisfied. If you should take that ….?…. you could come home this fall – could you Gather wishes you could be counted to have the trade. He thinks you would do well in time.

How does your corn look. Father says there is not going to be much here for the suckers those are little branches are growing so fast. Mag went to Chazy *(New York)* –they were all very well. Grandpa doesn't know much, growing old and childish every day. She went over the lake to Maria's, they are building a new house they need it don't they, went up to Mr. Imons and downed through the street to nearly every house. Dr. Fisks took dinner at Rus brothers. Mrs. Fisk sent them (Mrs. Moore and her) up to Jack McAnn her carriage and had a very nice visit. Went to Schuyler Falls *(New York)* and found so many new friends. She is tired but tonight and almost sick. Mr. B wants her to go home with her again. What would you say to have me go visit. I wish I could be near you don't you believe I would keep your things in repair. But I don't think of going, I wish I could. I guess I cannot write any more tonight my eyes give out sometimes. Eba is a very good boy now adays, shoots with his bow and arrow and takes good aim. He leaves Mother to make him arrows, tonight she did not take much pains and made them from an old stick, he grumbled some and wanted them made sharp, he came and shot the flies from the stove pipe or thereabouts, we have plenty of them. Little Will is a nice boy he and his mother were up tonight. He can't let father or Eb from his sight. Write every well- Good night, Sister Julia

Tell us when you intend to come home.

Benson VT   **Oct 13**th **1867**

Dear Brother Albert   *(sister Isa)*

We have just eaten dinner and it is now most five and I want to see how long I am in writing.

Julia and Auntie are washing the dishes, Father and Mag are reading. Grandma sits by me, she is not very well. She has some very bad spells and then she gets over them and is real smart again. Yesterday she had a very bad day but today she is some better. Mother and I are writing and Ebbi's has just come in from outdoors, he first asked ma who she was writing to and then asked me when I told him he said tell Albert if he ever goes a fishing now write it before you forget it he says. His school is out tomorrow, he likes to read very much every evening he gets his book and reads.

Julia has had a swelling under her right arm, she put on a tight dress today for the first time in two weeks. Old Mrs. Adams was buried yester-day, she had a cancer over her eye. She was 89 years old.

Helen Bascom and Ale Dick were married over to the other church a week a go tomorrow. They have gone out West on their wedding tour… Auntie and Mag went to Brandon two weeks ago and got over 200 yds of cotton cloth. Mr. Gibbs, Jennie and I went to Brandon to a fair last Wednesday. Had a nice time, a good many went from here.

Julia and I were going to the musical convention last week but she was sick so we couldn't go.

Mr. Hawley and Frank Foster went down to Hampton last night to the "troy praying band"

Do you ever hear from Nell Faussett. I have not this summer. Do you know how old she is. We had a dispute about her age this morning. Auntie thinks she is about 21 and I think about 22 or 23. Do you expect that we shall meet 1870 I hope so but am some fearful. I have had two letters from John this summer.

Father has bought 8 bushels of butternuts this fall. We had a crack yes-terday. Well the sun has just gone down and as I think of nothing more to write will leave the last page for someone else. Good night write soon to Isa

(on the back side of the sheet of paper another sibling continues to write to Albert)

Brother Alb

Isa has left a portion her sheet for someone to fill out and as I am under obligations to you for a letter I will partly return the favor by writ-ing a few lines. We are all ready for pray meeting but mother, she remains at home with Grandma. I received a letter from Elks last evening, he said you were doing well this summer, would make 4 or 5 hundred. He talks of Missouri too, of land being so cheap. Has Mr. Albert any idea of selling? I would like to go there next year. I am glad you're paying some attention to the ladies. All but for mercy's sake don't fall in love with any of them. Alb I sent my picture to Mrs. Allisin someone else with the promise to return if I do not forget it after meeting. Alb why didn't you write your favorite girls names "to now" Father has got the blues, doesn't take money enough to buy better his insurance as the payment of $28. Comes $25. Worth of coal. I would like to give him some but cannot. I fear he will have to give up tis place. He has a good many dollars owing him but money is very scarce. Oh? Albert –Grandfather died the 4th of this month, the letter did not get here until he was buried. Elvira and children are fine. Will talks of his Aunty. Says I see remember me to all inquiring friends As your sister Mag.

Thursday eve (no date)

Dear Albert,   *(from Julia)*

I promised you I would write you a few lines this week and they will have to be few. I guess for I've only few minutes to write in. My eyes refuse to remain open so if I keep the line it will be Father is getting better slowly. He has sit up sometime today at several different times. His lungs are yet very weak but Dr. Prad, Dr. Cushmann came in to see him the other day. He decided then there are no bones broken and said his lungs would heal with great care. That gave us great encouragement. He says he shall be in the shop in two weeks but I doubt it. Isa wanted me to ask you and Laura to send her a lock of your hair quite a lock if you can spare it. She is going to make her a wreath and I want a little of Laura's in min if she is willing. We were somewhat disappointed in not hearing from you tonight. My five minutes are up. Love from all Sister Julia

Benson   Sunday January 5, 1868

My Dear Albert son

The sun is setting and I have just took my pen in hand to talk with one so far off and so much loved by all at home but how much rather would I lay aside this pen and talk with you. We have all been to quarterly meeting today, the Elder was here, it stormed so hard yesterday we did not go none but Julia she came home Friday, she has a good school this winter. Mag enjoys her school this winter. Isa is not very well, sometimes I fear she is going in the consumption but we have to do everything to keep up her spirits, her appetite has been very poor but for a few days she has relished her food better, she was very much pleased with the little box and its contents. I think it is the most natural one you have sent some sometime if you see a pretty piece of music send it to her, she does not go to school, she has rode out to the seating once but the Dr. says she will come up again, it don't seem to her as if I could spare her, she enjoys herself better in religious things than anywhere else, praise the Lord for what he is doing for my childrens

Well Elvira has just come in, she has it hard cold, it is getting dark and I must adjourn till after meeting, we have just returned had a good meeting this is to be a week of prayer, the other Church is going to join us. The house was quite well filled. Well Albert how are you today. Have you been to meeting, how do you enjoy self this winter where were you Christmas and New Years. We had a tree in the other Church. Our folks joined them. Eb got some things on the tree, a little horse and wagon, a little Poof, he is not as much engaged in such things as Eva was, he don't learn very fast but reads in the second reader.

Well Albert have you decided to go further west. I hope not. Sometimes I have a presentiment sometimes that you are coming home this spring. Ebbie talks very much about Albert. Mr. Gleath was in here this 8 PM, he is lonesome, said he thought he saw you in the store the other night. Mag says you would know everyone and everyone would know you for we have no new folks, there has been but few changes since you left home, but a good many deaths. We are lonesome here, we miss Grandmother very much, she was so kind and good natured but she was so happy we cannot risk her stay in this troublesome world. We had a letter from Aunt Vira last week. They are afflicted again. Amasa Scott got a fall the other day, fell on the scales on Monday and lived till Friday. He was a great sufferer. He has quite a good property and a new house to four little children. Poor Maria she was born for a hard fortune, your Father went there when he went up to Alburgh (VT) He call in to see Maria Amasa was hurt the day before. Maria has been sick all summer. Oscar is yet in California. There comes up your father with another big rat. He caught them with your traps. We never was so trouble with them as we are now. Well Albert I suppose you think you are almost a man in years, do you realize you are most twenty-one years old. Your Father says he would like to send you a watch but the times are so hard, he can't, so you must take the will for the deed. I fear you will be disappointed in your box. Mrs. Ladd was in the other night, she spoke of sending your last box thinking it terminated when you was twenty-one. I told her she was mistaken. I was to make him a cake every year till he got married and then I was going to make his wife promise to do so or I should as long as I live. I suppose some think this is a foolish thing to keep up but you and I don't do, do we Albert? I think every year perhaps this may be the last but wouldn't we have sad remembrance of that day if either of us were gone, it seems to me as if I should have to make one if I had no Albert to send it to. I will make a little one so we can as usual have piece of your cake or eat it at the same time. I feel that my prayers have been answered in behalf of my children. I wish I could say something that would encourage you, you are now just merging into manhood. You will have more cares and more responsibilities and I am so thankful that you have chose Christ as your friend in the morning of life. You will never regret it if you live to be as old as grandma. She was most 89 in seventy years she had tried to follow Christ.

Page 2 *(Julia writes then Maggie and finally Mother finishes this birthday letter to Albert)*

Well Alb here I am at home sitting by the cooking stove toasting my feet and writing on my any hand. Mother says we must all write a few words. Do you believe Mr. Hawly has invited the other Church to join with us in our meetings through this week and they have accepted this invite-tonight two of their brethren stood and prayed. I suppose I should return to the moment – tomorrow it is so lonely here that I don't enjoy being at home as I used to. I wish you were at home tonight. How much longer are you going to be away. Write to me and direct to Chipman's Point, Orwell, VT and I will write you a long letter – Julia

Mother wants a specimen I all over hand writing and has handed the paper over to me. All we have all got it in our heads that you are coming home –I wish you could if you go to Missouri. I had a splendid offer of a school in Ill, Morris Grundy Co not far from Mo. It was an Academy – salary $800 for a year and board, wasn't that good. Father and I went down to Mr. Lurat's and asked for a dismissal, but he would not let me off – I would have given up half my months wages any way. I did want to go so much. I am almost sorry I did not go anyway. I shall go West somewhere in the Spring if I can get a situation. I have only 8 weeks more to teach here. Ebbie says tell Albert, father and I caught two large rats this evening. Awful big, down cellar, he wants to see you very much. Give my love to Mrs. Slkieoers – proper, If I was there I would go to Missouri with them. Write to me. Maggie

(written upside down in brown ink)

They have all gone to bed. I want to say something and I can't think what it is. From your unworthy Mother good bye Albert

They all join with me and wish you a happy birthday –Auntie says

Benson Feb the 22, 1871

My Dear Children in Missouri if I have any there. *(mother)*

I have waited a long time with a great deal of anxiety to answer the letter from you but not any yet unless we get one yet tonight, your Father was so tired. He could not go down *(to get the mail)* He says tell Albert I have shod seven horses today and taken 25 off, he is lounging trying to rest. We are all quite well, the girls have gone down street, a Meeting of Trustees to arrange matters for the Donation next Tuesday eve, can't you come, wouldn't it be gay to have you come in about that time.

Our singing school continues yet, Isa fell down last night in the Church yard, hurt her arm badly still she is not layed bye. We have had a few inches of snow and very soon melts off and then we have plenty of ice and skating. Ebbie has been trying his since school he often says can I skate as well Albert? Isa often says you didn't think much of her letter as you would have answered sooner. I believe you haven't written but once since you were married. *(8 December 1870)* It seems a long time. I don't think of any news to write you have been gone so long. I don't suppose the everyday items would interest you, for the bell has just rung for a side walk Meeting. They have tried if two or three times they want to make a slate walk. Your Father says he don't care. He had as leave walk in the middle of the road as on a slate walk. Some are in great earnest about it.

Your Uncle Abram was here two weeks ago. He brought this little boy with him and left him till spring- seven years old- he is a very good boy. Eb thinks he is made - he's his, got someone to sleep with him. For he has given up the idea of Albert coming home to sleep with him and slide down. I promised him this morning I would go up some time and ride down I told him I did with you. Well I have been looking over my marks and I guess you will both say, well Mother couldn't write much oftener for there isn't much in this but if you were here I could think of a great many things to say that I can't to write. O how I do want to see you both when,

when will that be? Well the girls have just come home, they say the vote has gone slate stone sidewalk. The Strongs talk of selling out. What are you doing this winter. I am so glad you have some one to take care of your clothes and have company besides. So you think you will make Missouri your home, I wish it was in the order of providence that our children could all be situated nearer by. I have not heard from Chazy for a long time. Julia is at home. Elvira and family are well. Willie reads in the third reader, Edwin and Mag enjoy life first rate. I wanted to send you a box but couldn't. Laurie do you have to bake him a little pie or cake. I was to make him a cake every year till he got married and then she was to make it. Well I guess I will close and go to bed (written down the side) I had forgotten to say anything of Auntie. She is just the same. She don't worry so much as she did about your clothes. Laurie I wish you could write or do remind Albert of Mother. We had at YMCA association here last week had a very good Meeting from home. Albert don't forget to write to your Father.

Love to all my friends.

come home.

Benson   Nov 10, 1872

My dear children,   *(mother)*

While the rest are at Church I will write a few lines to you, the family are well as usual. I was very much disappointed last night for I had thought so much of you through the week. I must certainly see or hear from you but I am doomed to disappointment, a week last night we had a corn festival at our Church, I was going down with Auntie it was very dark, I stepped of one foot and sprained my right ankle very badly but still I hobbled on down there but was sorry I went for I presume it made it worse but rode back here. I have set all this last week, my foot is very badly swollen and discolored. What shall I do, it pains me so hard. The Dr says it is only a sprain but will take some time to get well. You know I have had a number of such like and always kept up good courage but now I fear it will be a long time and what shall I do. We have so much to do. Auntie has a carpet in the loom for my room that is the North East room, she is not very strong and Isa is getting ready to be married in December sometime I don't know the day yet.

After Supper

I will finish this before dark. Julia has four weeks to teach on this term then only three weeks vacation. I should think she would be tired of teaching. Elvira is pretty well. She has a splendid little boy. Mrs. Walker has another swelling on her neck very bad it makes her sick but they think it is a little better.

Seven O'clock

I wish I could see you all come in this evening as Edward, Maggie and Lilly came. They have gone to prayer meeting with Isa Maturin and Ebbie, your Auntie is taking care of baby and talking about your baby and wishing she was here to compare the little cousins but I don't never expect to see them together.

I thought last fall when your Father was sick he would never get well again but he did and works hard all the time but is wearing out. My foot pains me so I don't know (what) to do. I haven't any news to write. Have you been to meeting today. Do you see Miss Walker? Where does she live? She so often speaks of you Laurie and baby. Have you got your fall work done yet. How does your crops yield. Are you going to hire that farm another year? Write to tell me all your plans Laura. How is your health? You haven't written this long time, Ebbie is a big boy. I shall look for a letter tomorrow night. Write often my dear Children. Love from all to all. Mother *(on the side)* Kiss baby for grandma)

October 14, 1871

Dear Albert & Laurie

No doubt you are anxiously looking for a letter from home. I am very tired, but must write a few lines.

Your Father is some better, yes a good deal for he has been out in the kitchen with his crutches, he coughed some yet. His feet or ankle are badly swelled.

Sometimes I think he will never be any better but the Dr. says if the lung..., I have had fears about the quick consumption but hope for the best.

I don't know what we shall do if he can't walk and work anymore. Isa's health is very poor, still she is earning a little. Julia is going to teach in Poultney this winter. She gets forty dollars a month and board, herself, four dollars per week. You say you wish we were out there, well I wish we was but we are getting too old to change climates. We never had much ahead nor we never shall have but having food and raiment we ought to be content with the promises that we have on record for those that live uprightly. Poor little Ebbie. His Father says he would like to live a few years longer on his account, he's a little boy yet. He isn't very strong, his lungs trouble him in the winter, he coughs incessantly, he talks about you and Laurie as if he had a correct recollection of you both, he was sitting so still the night (for once, he broke out, well said he: I wish Albert and Laurie would come in just now. I spose Laurie goes home every day to see her Mother but Albert can't. Why don't Albert do like the other boys that get married, takes their wife home. Why don't Albert do so. So we had quite a conversation. He says I wish you would write and tell him so but I never expect to see you again. You are getting so removed from home, it almost makes me crazy sometimes to think how young you was and how long you have been gone and no prospects of coming home. I am glad you have found friends even those you call Father and Mother. I hope you will be to them a son. Remember me in much kindness to your Father and Mother and friends.

Mrs. Varrows and Mrs. Allison. How does your corn yield. Albert you never have told me yet whether you have sold your building lots or not. How do you get along with your sewing machine. Can you make pants? Have you been to Church today. I haven't been for four weeks. Elvira and family are well. Mags school was out last Friday. *(written across the top and side)* Your Father says he don't know what he shall do if his hip don't get well so he can work. He says tell Albert and Laurie I want to see them very much and hope to sometime. Good night. Well I must get for I am so tired being up day and night. You would hardly know me. I would not live always. Write both write, from your Father and Mother.

If he is careful he will come out of it in a few days. He was shoeing Potters horse, he threw him, he struck on his hip, he thought it was broken. He worked the next day and at night he was going up stairs. He caught his foot some way and fell on his shoulder, it struck him senseless for a few minutes. He thus had Benson

November 27, 1872 or 1873

Dear Brother, Sister and little Niece, *(from sister Isa)*

How I would like to step in and give you a call this afternoon. I want to see you all very much, especially little darling baby. I think it is pretty hard to live so far apart that we cannot ever see one another. Laura, the night before we received All's letter I dreamed you came here all alone. I thought you were dressed in black. I did not dream that Albert was dead. I thought your dress was not cut-gored and that you had no flowing sleeves to it and I was so afraid you wouldn't look fashionable. I urged you to let me take your dress all to pieces and make a basgne waist and flowing sleeves before I would consent to go out in the street with you. You very unwillingly consented. Now don't you think I have forewarning of my little niece? I had just finished repairing a dress and had such a time getting out the sleeves that I suppose it troubled me. If we had have known of it sooner we all should have tried to to have sent some little presents. I have gathered a few burs. I don't know as you can make any use of them but they were the best. Ed and I could get. Elvira says there is just about room enough for the little bureau which you bought for little Eva which now belongs to little baby, her bottle of C is in the drawer which belongs to you also. Ebbie looked out some of her things which were in the drawer for baby and put in a little box. Eb often is angry..? I wish All had plenty of money. Don't you believe he would come home? He came across your horn this morning. He never had happened to see it before. So we had to tell him when you got it and Ebbie. He never gets tired talking about you. Well I will not write any more this time. I will try and give you a good long letter one of these days. Kiss baby 10 times for m. Every day I remain you loving sister Isa.

Poultney Jan 5, 1873

Dear brother and sister,   *(from sister Julia)*

I received your short letter last week when I was at home. Of course we were glad to hear from you as always are – more than I can tell you – Mother wanted me to write to you while Maturin and Isa were gone but I told her I would surely write today. Isa said she would send you a paper with the notice of their marriage – but-neither of their names were spelled right. If you are at all like me you will want to know how the wedding passed off – and I think you are – I presume she told you they were to be married in Church – we young folks from both families rode to the Church with them at a little before ½ pat 6 left our wrappings down in the lecture room and then we went upstairs. M & Isa went up on the north side and stood in the aisle in front of the altar – the ceremony was not the longest or shortest – but very pretty. After they were married we congratulated them and placed in her hands a present of $25.00 from his friends in the Church. They passed out of the south aisle and we followed down to wrap up again. Mrs., Sister, brother and his lady, Edd and I went down to Fair Haven with them had a pleasant ride a good supper and a nice time in general and started for home nearly 12. Next morning they started for Ross's had a nice ride and a good visit, and arrived at home on Monday eve. She told me to tell you how she spent his money- She bought a half dozen teaspoons, three large spoons, a sugar spoon, all solid silver. A cake basket and pickle fork plaited. Maggie put on the tree a half dozen silver forks. Elvira a spoon holder and Mrs. Wilcox a new dress. They seem very happy indeed. I pray they may always be.

But Albert and Laura I am afraid you will be disappointed when I tell you we had so much to do while I was at home that I could not find a minute to finish up your things. Mother persuaded me not to try till next spring then I would have nothing else to do. Then I thought perhaps it would be better not to send them if you come home which I assure you I expect.

Wednesday morn. I've not had a minutes time to finish my letter but will try this morn. I left my letter Sunday night while speaking of your box. I think on some account It would be much better to wait till spring even if you do not come home.

I do hope you will and I don't believe you will go back for one while. If you do not come I will have what fun things we have made ready by the first of April. If you do come so much the better. Albert I wish you could content yourself with some other employment than farming. Now Frank Conver gets such good wages on the steamboat. He is promoted every year. Last year he was first mate. How much I would to see you all and so I want to hear from home. From that young couple. They seemed very happy indeed when I came away. I expect them down to see me sometime this winter.

The boy is waiting to take my letter to the office so I must stop today.

It seemed New Years day when we were all at home that we must have you and yours there too. I hope to next year I don't know what out folks would say if they knew what I do. Don't disappoint – for little Minnie give my best love.

Your sister Julia

(written down the side)

Will soon I am in Poultney for this winter. I told our folks when I was home that I should not teach here another year if they wanted me ..? so much. Why they said. My reply was pretty good yet the true reason was withheld for if you are at home I shall be there too. Julia.

November 21, 1873

My dear children,   *(mother)*

It has been sometime since the last I wrote you, but not a day passes without speaking of you so If I don't write often you must take this will for the deed.

How are you all this Sunday afternoon, we have all been to Church. All but Auntie. She is not very well. Isa and Maturin has just gone home. Julia is at home. She teaches out in Dewitt's School house, for 4 dollars per week, board at one place has kept one week. Elvira and family are well. Maggie has a nice little boy.

We always speak of your little ones, would be so glad to see them together, has the dear little girl got well again. It has been very healthy here this fall. Your Father is better than he was in hot weather but says he dreads the winter and so do I. I wish his shop was near this house. How do you get along with your full work? How is your corn crop? O dear, I can't write what I want to say. This is a poor way to talk to a dear boy that I haven't seen for nine years. I have thought every year you would come home and still I hope to see you again.

Ebbie talks he shall go out west when he gets a little older. Well it is getting dark and I must rest awhile. Evening the wind blows very hard. I think I will not go to prayer meeting but will … Julia for her hard cold. I don't think she can go to school tomorrow, if she don't get better.

Well I have got them all to bed just eight o'clock. Ebbie is going out to Julia's school till ours commences. I wish he could go al winter for she is the one for to teach dull boys. I hope he will take a start by and by.

The folks are all well. Willie Bascom has gone to see Joseph mother, Sadd Newton has got a little girl four weeks old. Roger Well and Dan are doing good business. Mr. Ladd looks as if this hard wind would blow him away. I heard from Chazy last week. Oscar has gone to Mass to live. Charley has grown to a big man. Well my lamp is growing dim for want of trimming so I guess I will have to send you a blank page. I shall look for a letter every day this week. Laurie what are you doing this fall. Don't sew too steady on your machine unless you are trying to get money to come out East with. Take good care of Minnie keep her warm for winter and kiss her two times every day for Grandma. Now do write. Julia said today she was going to write but she feels to bad. Write soon both of you as ever your loving Mother from all to all Mother.

Poultney Jan 5 1873

Dear brother and sister   *(from sister Julia about Isa's wedding)*

I received your short letter last week when I was at home. Of course we were glad to hear from you. Always are more than I can tell you... Mother wanted me to write to you while Maturin and Isa were gone but I told her I would surely write today. Isa said she would send you a paper with the notice of their marriage – But neither of their names were spelled right. If you are at all like me you will want to know how the wedding passed off and I think you re. I presume she told you they were to be married in Church. We the young folks from both families rode to the Church with them at a little before ½ past 6, left our wrappings down in the lecture room and then we went upstairs. M(Maggie) and Isa went up on the north side and stood in the aisle in front of the altar. The ceremony was not the longest or shortest but very pretty. After they were married we congratulated them and placed in her hands a present of $25.00 from his friends in the Church. They passed out of the south aisle and we followed down to wrap up again. Mrs' sister, Brother and his lady –Eddie and I went down to Fair Haven with them, had a pleasant ride a good supper and a nice time in general and started for home nearly 12.

The next morning they started for Rosses had a nice ride and a good visit, and arrived at home on Monday eve. She told me to tell you how she spent his money. She bought a half dozen teaspoons, three large spoons, a sugar spoon, all solid silver = a cake basket and pickle fort plaited. Maggie put on the tree a half dozen silver forks, Elvira a spoon holder and Mrs. Wilcox a new dress. They seem very happy indeed. I pray they may always be.

But Albert and Laura I am afraid you will be disappointed when I tell you we had so much to do while I was at home that I could not find a minute to finish up your things. Mother persuaded me not to try ill next spring then I would have nothing else to do. Then I thought perhaps it would be better not to send them if you come home which I assure you I expect.

Wednesday morn.

I've not had a minutes time to finish my letter but will try this noon. I left my letter Sunday night while speaking of your box – I think on some account it would be much better to wait till spring even if you do not come home. I do hope you will and I don't believe you will go back for one while. If you do not come I will have what things we have made ready by the first of April. If you do come – so much the better. Albert I wish you could content yourself with some other employment than farming. Now Frank Cowee gets such good wages on the steamboat. He is promoted every year. Last year he was first mate. How much I want to see you all and so I want to hear from home from that young couple. They seemed very happy indeed when I came away. I expect them down to see us sometime this winter.

The boy is waiting to take my letter to the office so I must stop writing. It seemed New Year's day when we were all at home that we must have you and yours there too. I hope to next year. I don't know what our folks would say if they knew what I do –don't disappoint me- to little Minnie give my best love

Your sister Julia

Write soon- I am in Poultney for this winter.

Nov 2, 1873

My dear children,   *(mother)*

It has been sometime since the last I wrote you, but not a day passes without speaking of you so If I don't write often you must take this will for the deed.

How are you all this Sunday afternoon, we have all been to Church. All but Auntie. She is not very well. Isa and Maturin has just gone home. Julia is at home. She teaches out in Dewitt's School house, for 4 dollars per week, board at one place has kept one week. Elvira and family are well. Maggie has a nice little boy.

We always speak of your little ones, would be so glad to see them together, has the dear little girl got well again. It has been very healthy here this fall. Your Father is better than he was in hot weather but says he dreads the winter and so do I. I wish his shop was near this house. How do you get along with your full work? How is your corn crop? O dear, I can't write what I want to say. This is a poor way to talk to a dear boy that I haven't seen for nine years. I have thought every year you would come home and still I hope to see you again.

Ebbie talks he shall go out west when he gets a little older. Well it is getting dark and I must rest awhile. Evening the wind blows very hard. I think I will not go to prayer meeting but will … Julia for her hard cold. I don't think she can go to school tomorrow, if she don't get better.

Well I have got them all to bed just eight o'clock. Ebbie is going out to Julia's school till ours commences. I wish he could go al winter for she is the one for to teach dull boys. I hope he will take a start by and by.

The folks are all well. Willie Bascom has gone to see Joseph mother, Saddy Newton has got a little girl four weeks old. Roger Well and Dan are doing good business. Mr. Ladd looks as if this hard wind would blow him away. I heard from Chazy last week. Oscar has gone to Mass to live. Charley has grown to big a man. Well my lamp is growing dim for want of trimming so I guess I will have to send you a blank page. I shall look for a letter every day this week. Laurie what are you doing this fall. Don't sew too steady on your machine unless you are trying to get money to come out East with. Take good care of Minnie keep her warm for winter and kiss her two times every day for Grandma. Now do write. Julia said today she was going to write but she feels to bad. Write soon both of you as ever your loving Mother from all to all Mother.

November 27, 1872 or 1873

Dear Brother, Sister and little Niece,   *(from Isa)*

How I would like to step in and give you a call this afternoon. I want to see you all very much, especially little darling baby. I think it is pretty hard to live so far apart that we cannot ever see one another. Laura, the night before we received All's letter I dreamed you came here all alone. I thought you were dressed in black. I did not dream that Albert was dead. I thought your dress was not cut-gored and that you had no flowing sleeves to it and I was so afraid you wouldn't look fashionable. I urged you to let me take your dress all to pieces and make a basgne waist and flowing sleeves before I would consent to go out in the street with you. You very unwillingly consented. Now don't you think I have forewarning of my little niece? I had just finished repairing a dress and had such a time getting out the sleeves that I suppose it troubled me. If we had have known of it sooner we all should have tried to to have sent some little presents. I have gathered a few burs. I don't know as you can make any use of them but they were the best. Ed and I could get. Elvira says there is just about room enough for the little bureau which you bought for little Eva which now belongs to little baby, her bottle of C is in the drawer which belongs to you also. Ebbie looked out some of her things which were in the drawer for baby and put in a little box. Eb often is angry..? I wish All had plenty of money. Don't you believe he would come home? He came across your horn this morning. He never had happened to see it before. So we had to tell him when you got it and Ebbie. He never gets tired talking about you. Well I will not write any more this time. I will try and give you a good long letter one of these days. Kiss baby 10 times for m. Every day I remain you loving sister Isa.

April 17, 1874

Dear brother and sister   *(from sister Julia)*

I received your very welcome letter so long ago I am ashamed to answer it now, but the longer I wait the more ashamed I shall be. We are all quite as well as usual. Auntie I think will never be well again. I was glad to hear you had got moved and was so pleasantly situated. We all said we would just like to step in and surprise you. Through the month of March we had uncommonly nice weather. The roads were so dry on the surface. They were really dusty but we have had several hard snow storms lately and O the roads! Last night it commenced snowing again and it has certainly fallen 15 inches on a level and still it snows and blew and Isa said there were drifts through which they came 3 feet deep. I don't know how lately Isa has given you one of her letters so can't tell what old news I shall write. Eugene is going to work for his father this summer for $36 per month and board. He goes Sundays as well as Mondays. His P's health is very poor. John Skeels is at home helping his father. Lorn Watts has a great tumor growing on the back of his neck (very dangerous place) Grandma Ladd is very poorly and Richardson is not expected to live. Frank Cowee has bought out Davis interest in the store and … is doing nothing now. Miss B. Walker is getting some better. Jennie Gibbs gave birth to a little boy last Friday (week) It died Saturday and poor Jennie kept growing worse and worse the result of a severe cold and pain in her side which finally killed her. She died Monday morning and was buried Wednesday. She was conscious to the last. Gave them all a parting message. Sent for the Dr. to see if he couldn't give her something so she could "live till pa comes" He was in Gardiner, Mass. He did not get here till Tuesday. I tell you there never was a household more sadly bereaved. Poor Patsey. I do feel so sorry for him. Mrs. Smith was at conference but was sent for. Got here just in time for the funeral which was held at the house which was full. The baby was buried in the same coffin – lying on her arm. She was buried in her wedding garments. Her bearers were members of the choir. They also did the singing which was the most solemn part of it. We expect our new minister this week. Of course we are anxious to know how we shall like him. Maggie's health is very poor. We are afraid sometimes that she is not going to live long. I brought Lillie home with me last Sunday night and kept her till Tuesday, when of course they had to come to see her but I tell you it was a short call, for Lillie seemed to fear they were going to leave her and she began to say "go ride, ride with papa. Lillie ride, ride with papa" would have him get her things and was so glad to see Willie boy as she calls baby. School begins tomorrow but this last has been such a week of excitement. I don't feel quite ready. By the way I am going to teach the upper school here this summer. They sent for me to go back to Poultney but there is no place like home. I will write oftener this summer and you do the same.

April 17, 1874

Dear brother and sister   *(from sister Maggie)*

I received your very welcome letter so long ago I am ashamed to answer it now, but the longer I wait the more ashamed I shall be. We are all quite as well as usual. Auntie I think will never be well again. *(Margaret's maiden sister Julia Honsinger who lives with the family)* I was glad to hear you had got moved and was so pleasantly situated. We all said we would just like to step in and surprise you. Through the month of March we had uncommonly nice weather. The roads were so dry on the surface. They were really dusty but we have had several hard snow storms lately and O the roads! Last night it commenced snowing again and it has certainly fallen 15 inches on a level and still it snows and blew and Isa said there were drifts through which they came 3 feet deep. I don't know how lately Isa has given you one of her letters so can't tell what old news I shall write. Eugene is going to work for his father this summer for $36 per month and board. He goes Sundays as well as Mondays. His P's health is very poor. John Skeels is at home helping his father. Lorn Watts has a great tumor growing on the back of his neck (very dangerous place) Grandma Ladd is very poorly and Richardson is not expected to live. Frank Cowee has bought out Davis interest in the store and … is doing nothing now. Miss B. Walker is getting some better. Jennie Gibbs gave birth to a little boy last Friday (week) It died Saturday and poor Jennie kept growing worse and worse the result of a severe cold and pain in her side which finally killed her. She died Monday morning and was buried Wednesday. She was conscious to the last. Gave them all a parting message. Sent for the Dr. to see if he couldn't give her something so she could "live till pa comes" He was in Gardiner, Mass. He did not get here till Tuesday. I tell you there never was a household more sadly bereaved. Poor Patsey. I do feel so sorry for him. Mrs. Smith was at conference but was sent for. Got here just in time for the funeral which was held at the house which was full. The baby was buried in the same coffin – lying on her arm. She was buried in her wedding garments. Her bearers were members of the choir. They also did the singing which was the most solemn part of it. We expect our new minister

About 8 o'clock Saturday afternoon **December 1874**

Dear brother and sister and niece.

We have just finished packing your box and find it weighs something- I am afraid you will begrudge the cost. The presents are from us all. Louis got the materials to work with and the rest did the work.

Albert do you remember that first patch work quilt I pieced ? I gave it to you. Well of course it has been used up. This one I pieced for you instead of the old one. If we could have sent it we would have quilted it but Laura will quilt it for you sometime. I pieced it two years ago this winter. The hair wreath is yours Laura. You will see that the flowers are mostly numbered. The numbers corresponding to the owners of the hair are on a sheet of paper. The cross is not quite complete, you will see for the frame was not quite large enough. I made one for Isa sometime ago and put a margin of white around it and this little square that I send wants to be in the middle at the bottom. The velvet is large enough. So if you care enough about the absence of it sometime you can get a larger one for it. I should have done it, if we had lived in Fair Haven Laura, I did have two pretty engravings for the little frame but they accidently got spoiled. You can take this one out and put in something else if you choose. These old book I thought perhaps would look like old times. This little dress is like Lillies – Mag mad it – so far last summer – we thought we would send them in August and she forgot all about it till tonight. Sunday night. Of course these little things are for Bertie – Ebbie wanted to send him a doll for his present but as you said Old Santa brought him one. We thought the dishes would be better. Ebbie got two diaries on the Christmas tree so he sends one of them to you. Of course Mother made the cake. It ought to be good for it is fruited, shortened, sweetened and thickened with her love. Father says tell Albert I wish I had something to send – just as if he hadn't sent anything. Auntie says tell Albert I have been too sick all the fall and winter to knit him his socks. I am sorry and ashamed that the pictures have not cords but we could not get them. The old pillow is put into keep the things tight. I don't believe they will move enough to break. I hope they will get to you safely and I guess they will. Father says the walnuts came off from the tree down in Walkers lot where our cornfield was.

Good night but by the way this is not going to be sent till Tuesday. Mother says it will get there long before your birthday but I rather have it there a week before than a day after. You must tell us how many of the glasses broke. I hope the bottom one did not for it would be some work to get another one. We shall want to know when you get it.

December 12, 1875

Dear Brother Sister and little darlings,

(from sister Julia after his first visit home in 10 years)

Do pardon us all for not writing you, only that short scrap and I will give you my excuse by and by. I know you have been as impatient as I would have been had we not heard from you. In the first place, we are all well and have been hard at work and all the rest of us. I will begin with that Saturday morning after 7 o'clock. We finished cleaning up that day. Sunday we did not attend Church but rested our tired bones and Monday went to washing. After which I went over to the store and bought Mother and myself a new dress like this and some new cotton. Tuesday I made mine. If you remember I was sadly in need of it. Wednesday I got in Mr. G carpet and the others attended the funeral of Henry Wilson. You remember, Laura, the one who went to Baltimore for his health. Thursday was Thanksgiving. I wove and got dinner while Mother went to hear the Sermon. Thursday eve we received your letter and how glad we were. You can only partly imagine. Edwin, Yuron and Isa were here to hear and read it and it was sent down to Vira's the next morning. We were busy the rest of the day. Father in the shop day and night, Ebbie blowing the bellows and laughing at the close proximity of fathers pants and the dandle. Mother in the buttery and myself in the old loom, the carpet was finally finished about dark but try all I could I could not get the old thing down that night but we just fixed up and went to mending. Mother taking her dresses in hand and I my own things. I tell you we just worked. Sunday morning Mother went to Love feast and I did the work and then to Church thinking all the time I will write when I go home but Mrs. K asked me to go out to the funeral of Mrs. Hooper. Yuron's old grandmother and I never got back till dark so it had to be give up for that day. Sunday night it snowed and Monday morning it blowed, but we took down the loom, cleaned the room and I corked the cracks. (I tell you I begrudged the rags) settled up moved my bed and mothers and cut one of my fingers most off. We finally decided not to change carpets but put down rugs enough to shield this only and if we spoil it we can make another only we shall not have Laura to help us. Monday night we all nearly froze to death. Ebbie in his old room which he is still to occupy. The plants all froze stiff although we covered them with a quilt and oil cloth. Tuesday morning I drew off father's slate and now it is full again. He charged $22.75 in four days. Yoron came for me in the afternoon and I took my dress (black) to make which by the way looks quite fine. I have it on now. Isa had cleaned and papered her kitchen and looked real nice. Mrs. Gibbs his grandmother has gone to live with her son and the little old house looks lonesome enough. Her singing class has closed but she begins again tomorrow evening. Do you believe Yuron's ill luck continues for Saturday night his little colt died with the horse distemper and something or someone helped themselves to 14 of his hens Tuesday we went down to visit Mary Perry. Wednesday we colored our old light worsted dresses brown. Thursday we cut them out and Friday we were expecting to do ever so much when about 2 who and what should come but Smith and a piano. It took all the afternoon to get it in and unboxed. It is a $600. Piano, perfectly beautiful, of course he wants them to buy it but they say no. So how long he will leave it is uncertain. Isa will go out shut the door and then come in make bows, stress and cries for joy and then says I never can let it go out of this house again and I doubt if they will. He says she can have her time and for the same price as the one he spoke of which was sold when he got home.

The spread and cover for stool are green. Yesterday Yuron's father helped him kill his pig. Isa had some work to do which she did with a very poor grade. He got it salted and they brought one home in the evening. Found Ed here. Almost my first question was to Mother, "Have you written to the children?" and she replied ,"no, for I have expected you home every day". My next was" Have you heard from them and both of your were forthcoming. Mother and Ed both watched me as I read for Ed had told Mother what I would say. We were glad you had a safe journey but how sorry we were that we had not said more against your going. Father says if he had known how much work there was going to be All (*Albert*) could have worked in the shop till he found something more to his taste. Ed said, he felt bad to have you go and didn't want to say much about your staying for fear he should be sorry for it afterwards but now wishes he had. Yuron said he should hate to raise corn for 21 cents per bushel, father said he wished he had a $100.00 bill he'd put it in this for another journey easternward and Mother says I wish I had done more to stop them going if I could and I say Laura complete your plans and put them in force as soon as you can, only don't sell your children. I can't begin to tell you what a lonesome house this is. It seemed as if I had been gone two months instead of weeks. Mother went with Y and Isa up to Mr. Potters funeral at 1 o'clock today, he died yesterday morning. I stopped writing and got dinner ready when they got back. They ate in a hurry for Yurin told Ed of the piano and he thought they would go out tonight and they wished All and Laura were here to go too and I wish you were. Isa says she now has a great attraction in her little home and she intends to stay there most of the time. Ed said last night he thought you were going to write to him and told me to tell you that he would write to you but he did not know where to direct. I expect he meant to give you a hint to write and tell him. Well I have got to the present only. Mother says tell Laura I have been doing house work and mending all the while. Yet was gone, for you know she says there wasn't a thing in or about the house that did not need mending excepting the "round baking tins" Mrs. Smith is failing. Lucy Cowes has been very sick but is better. Mrs. Walker has not returned. Walker and C. Still supply the market with coffins. Although father and mother …have a fine stock which they design to sell at prime cost. They had a tin wedding (10th anniversary) last week but very few were there. Mother is just saying I wish I had kept Lol just as if she could. Mother says will you sleep with Granny and Ebbie says no. Ebbie says they have said that a hundred times since I've been gone. Mrs. Kellogg says tell Laura that I was sick Monday night and could not come to say good by. And Tuesday night they were hindered by company.

Benson Dec 16, 1878

Dear Albert & Laura   *(from Maggie)*

I have let all these long months go by without writing a word but the news Mother brought from you today calls for a word of congratulations no more – as well as desire to let you know we are a little a head of you in having a_boy_three days older than yours.

I wish we could compare. I am sitting up a while to day for the first time – am very smart I think. The children are delighted with the baby and want to hold it all of the time. I am really tired but I will write soon – hoping to hear you are doing well Laura and have as healthy and pretty baby as ours_ Maggie

Sunday evening

My dear children,   *(Mother)*

I have just come from Edwins. Maggie is quite smart for her. I staid with her a week and wish I could go and do likewise for you, your letter came to us Friday night. And we congratulate you all and Father says three cheers for another Sherman and hopes he will be a better man than either of the former Alberts. Says he will get him his first copper toes.

Says he wishes you could express Loll *(pet name for Laura)* and send her on. I think there is prettier name than Albert, still I like the name and persons that have them. O dear what a poor way to talk with those you want to see so much.

Laura I thought you hadn't been so silent for nothing. I hope the rest of the children won't have the chicken pox. Your Father says the Lord is good to the poor in giving them larger families of first lay children, you have quite a large family and but none to spare. I wish I could step in today with you all night. I hope your darkie won't kiss the baby. I think I should have to be kept blindfolded if I had one around me. I guess you will call me a copperhead. I wish the times were better. Would like to send you a box full of things but you must take the will for the deed.

I guess the Lord nor the people won't see us go hungry. I think trouble comes fast enough.

Your Father don't have much work and if he had he couldn't do it. He has the catarrh so bad and it has gone to his lungs. He coughs like one with the consumption. Says he feel better tonight. We have always been comfortable and without borrowing any. Our family is quite small. Now Julia is teaching out in Maturin School house. The teaching wages are cut down. She gets only $4.25 and board. She will be at Maturin's a good share of the time. Isa has a singing school at the village over forty students. Their baby boy is up in the morning sings "do, ra, me, fa.." Elvira folks are all well as usual considering their years. Aunt Mary can't walk without her crutches and not much with them. Elvira still keeps her Latin club. Albert what about Mrs Walkers farm? Does she get any good from it. She don't say anything about it. Laura you guess what I found in the straw bed, it was Lolls slipper. It looks just like her. Well If you can read this I shall be glad. Ebbie says he thinks that Ebenezer Honsinger is a prettier name than Albert Sherman. From your poor old Mother, Kiss all the children for me. Good-bye. Write soon.

Benson Jan the 2, 1881

My Dear Children   *(from Mother and Isa)*

Another year has passed and gone and I hope we as a family, we are all alive. Well we have just got though with our supper. We had a splendid sermon. Maturin and Isa staid out. They want to have a rehearsal before meeting this evening. Maturin and Ebbie have gone out to do the chores.

Well did you have a Merry Christmas and Happy New Year? We had a Christmas tree and a cantata in three parts. Isa took the drilling for her part for acting, singing and playing. Susie played most of the time. The Santa Claus was Maturin. The tree was not very heavy laden. The children love Christmas and you were not forgotten. Well I have neither pencil nor pen that is fit to write with. I can't get Julia to write. It has been so long I don't know whether we have written since we got them pretty little pictures or not. They are beautiful. It is a great satisfaction to see them on paper. Much more if I could see their face. I expect Minnie will be teaching school in a few years, does Lolly learn as fast as Minnie. I don't expect I shall ever see them again. I wish it wasn't so far. We held watch meeting Friday evening. I watched the old year out and the New one in. We had nothing going on yesterday. Our union meeting commences this evening. Mr. Lion from the other church preaches. Well I guess I must go and get ready for Church. Mother

Mother is writing and as it is getting dark I will help her a little. I don't know when I have stayed out before to attend evening meeting. Maturin and Ebbie have gone out to do the night chores. Gay...? Is in mother's room with Julia, he has on her watch and I tell you it just makes him a man. How I wish I could step in where you are and have a good visit. I just turned to mother and said, I believe if I couldn't see but part of your family I should say, let me see the little folks. I can look at these pictures hours at a time. What did Santa Claus bring you? We had a splendid time here. Best Christmas ever. Yurin was Santa Claus, the tree was over loaded with presents. We are having dry cold weather. I never shall wish for winter again. Well it is nearly time for church. This is a short letter. I will finish it before many days. Good bye and write often. Isa

Your Father and Ebbie make out to get a living. Ebbie can Shoe (a horse) very well now. Love from all to all. (on the side Julia is teaching Mother)

Arkansas City   Jan 30,1881

Dear Sister,   *(from Isa)*

Your letter came to hand last week I thought I would answer it last Sunday but did not. I do not feel like doing anything since Dear Willy is gone. O how lonely it has been yesterday and today. He was a pretty child. We have not got his picture, but his face is ever before me, go where I will in the house I see him and miss him for he was after me. He suffered so much I do not think the Dr. understood Willy's sickness, we had two Dr and did all we could for ...but in vain. Johnny sings *(ripped corner of letter)* They miss <u>Dear little</u> Willy. I have enough rags cut for 15 yards but have not got them sewed yet. I sometimes feel as if I do not want to do anything more but cry. I had a letter from Anie yesterday, I wish I could get a letter every day. It has been very cold here this winter. It is now looking as if we would get some rain. We have not moved yet and do not know where we will go yet but I want to go some place where Flora can go to school. Where we live now it is too far from the school house. All can you tell me what a small tombstone will…and on what terms. They…let me have one. I want…one before we leave, please…me If I could get one …to cost. This is all to….

(Willie is Maggie's son who had gone to school in Amherst, Mass)

Nov 20, 1881

My Dear Niece,   *(from Julia)*

I cannot tell you how very glad we were to receive your little letter the other day. I thought I would not go to Church tonight but would talk with you, Minnie. Grandpa and Ma were delighted to read your letter. We think you are getting along nicely in your studies. You write well too. I saw just one mistake, shall I tell you what it was. You said "is" when you were talking of more than one thing or person. What should you have said. Auntie wishes you could be taking music lessons, and I hope you will learn with all your might till you are twelve, and if you do not begin before, Auntie will let you then if she is earning money. Lollie, *(Laura)* Grandpa says he does remember when you crawled out to the shop and how black you got, but you cared little for that. Do you remember when granny struck your little fat arm with the long comb. You cried more from grief than from pain I guess. Your little coffee can is on the what-not, where you left it. Do you know that Grandma came very near going out to see you this fall. You would have been surprised. Would you not? And little Julia, are you large enough to go to school and to write letters. Guy don't read so much as that, nor write any but he tries to play the scale on the piano. He has just got him a new relsturett..? and he does feel so manlike. It is quite amusing to watch him. He is lying on the bed in the room where Minnie and I used to sleep, fast asleep. Grandpa is on the new lounger that Grandma bought, resting. He has grown old and forgetful very much since last fall. Grandma sits in the little rocking chair near the stove by the bedroom door, a little lamp in one hand and a paper in the other reading. Guy's papa and mama and Uncle Ebbie have gone to Church and will soon be back. Cousin Willie is larger than your papa. He came home from school last week to get his cough cured. His mama has given him a lot of medicine and he is going back tomorrow. Lillie does not go to school, for there are no little girls to go to her school, so she studies at home some. Lillie Will goes. How would you like to go to school where there were only six boys and no girls. Little Roy is just as old as Bertie. You know but he don't talk much, only grunts. He knows all one says to him and will make us understand him and will talk sometime. That baby is very pretty. Susie is a large as her mama I guess. She will soon be home from school and will stay till Feb then she is going with Willie to Poultney. Rufus don't grow very fast, but he likes to go to school and come up to Grandpa's. Auntie is going up to Orwell to teach this winter and she has just decided she will not come home till school is out in the Spring. Tell Mama that Auntie has got a new nice cloak and is going to have a new dress. She has got on now the one she made for her. Tell papa that potatoes are only 50 cents here and will soon be less. Apples are dear. We have only a few this winter. We want you to write to us often. I wish we lived near enough to exchange little Christmas gifts and birthdays and sometimes Auntie is coming to see you then she will bring you something. Love to that little "Plow boy" and to all from all Auntie

Jan 15, 1882

My dear children,   *(mother Jan 24 is Albert's birthday)*

I suppose you think we are all well or I would write oftener and so we are except hard colds, your Father is almost down sick coughs very hard nights, he isn't able to do much in the shop this winter. He has failed very much in body and mind since he had that stroke last fall. Seems downcast all the time. We do all we can to keep him up. I wish you would write to him. Ebbie works in the shop all he can. They don't have much to do but I guess we shall stand it through the winter if it isn't too cold. We have had just one week of sleighing. Ebbie is cutting wood this week on the mountain, we are holding meetings this week. We have had come home, we have very interesting meetings but no seekers yet.

I thought I would spend one hour in talking with you. I suppose the little folks are all fast asleep for the clock is striking ten but if Grammie should step in I should soon have them all up even the baby boy. How I do wish I knew what you were all doing and how you look. I thought we all talk about you during the hollow says, we didn't have any tree nor home gathering this year, only Isa she has never been absent from home one Christmas and I hope she never will while we live. She is teaching singing school in the hall this winter and has a house class beside. She gave a concert on New Year evening. I hope you had a Merry Christmas and a Happy New Year. Girls and you hang up your stockings. Did old Santa serve you as he did us.

Minnie what are you studying this winter and what is music a … I wish you could begin to take music. You could sing so pretty when you were here. Do you remember us. I suppose Loll does, Alexandra said the other day, he would like to see Lollie just as she crept out to the shop one day. What book do you read in Lolly and there is little Julia and Bertie, I never shall see them. I wish I had a purse of money I would like to make you all a Christmas present and I am reminded to that the twenty-fourth day is so near and I have no cake nor box. It would be just as much pleasure to me now as it used to be when you was such a good little boy, but the times are not now as they used to be. You must take the will for the deed. There is one thing you certainly have that is my daily prayers or those little ones are not forgotten.

Albert and Laura I hope you are living Christians for you need the grace of God to help you to discharge the duties to your little family, seek first the kingdom of God and all things shall be added unto you. I have made many failures in life but the Lord is good and his mercy endures forever therefore I hope to come off conqueror.

Julia is teaching up in Orwell this winter her health is not very good. She said the last time that she was at home she was afraid she could not teach the school out. ..I expect her home Friday night. Elvira's folks are all well. That old trouble still lives Mr. W tells her she will outlive them all … yet she is old ugly troublesome and very helpless. It is wearing on Elvira very much. Mag is well. They have a large family. Her heart troubles her. She is very fleshy. Isa seems to be the Happy one.

They were up to meeting this evening. They have only one little boy. He sung his part in the concert nicely. Now girls I want you to see how many misspelled words you can find in this poor written letter and write and tell me what you are doing or studying or which of the girls mama loves best. I hope you will have as good a brother as Aunt Julia when she was a little girl Love from all to all Mother, Grandma Good night. Write soon. Laura make your mark if no more what are you doing or making nowadays big dresses or little ones. I hope you will not be tired or hungry ..you get this letter. Minnie you must make your Papa a cake and cut a piece for Gramma.

April 19, 1885

My dear Children

We received your letter in due time from Julia but I can't get Julia to write. We are all quite well but poor Father, he has been losing very fast for two weeks but seems a little better today. I think he will come up again. Julia had the chilblains last winter and I guess froze one foot it troubles her very much, can't wear her shoe it is badly swollen and discolored. I don't think she will teach this summer. The rest of the family are quite well. Meg dropped in yesterday. She has the rheumatism , you know that belongs to the family. So you must be careful this cold winter. Elvira seems the most enduring.

Willie is home on the short vacation, goes back this week on Wednesday. Susies' health is not very good, she was obliged to leave school. She was to graduate in time but she will have to stay out till her head gets better. She wants to teach but they think that will be as hard as going to school. She is a beautiful young woman. You must be careful and not let Minnie apply her mind to closely to study. I won't caution Loll (Laura) for I presume she has to stay out some times to help Ma. Lillie grows fast and learns well, but Julia says she don't know whether she could get such perfect marks in examination or not. They all think that was doing remarkable well for such a young girl. I think they are all good scholars of their age. Julia what book do you read in and what do you study. Write and tell me. Bertie do you go to school? Well I must take a new page.

Johnnie, *(born after Bert Nov.25,1881)* dear boy how have you stood this cold long winter. I never knew of your adventures till the last letter or I should have written to you sooner. I guess they didn't give you a hearty welcome or they would have written sooner, but you have begun to write so young. You will soon be able to write your own letters in your middle name.- how you got boots this winter. I suppose you or Bertie play out doors now its got so warm but if you were here with your hand sled you could slide down hill in some places but the snow is going fast now. It is raining now. Our cistern has been froze most all winter but didn't hurt the pipe, it was a good week for sugar. Eds folks have made a lot and they hope for more. Ebbie has tapt our six trees so we have had syrup. We had some this morning and wished you could have a taste with us. I have some over a boiling enough for two quarts, I guess. As you said, it was a great comfort to write. I think so to but it would be a greater one if we could see each other.

It has been a very hard winter for work. Ebbie has had but very little, not enough so he could live and pay one cent of rents he thought he had better give it, so he has he moved his things up yesterday. I guess he will work up here some. Mr. Walker has hired it out to another blacksmith, we can't spare him to go away from home while your Father is so poorly, he gets discouraged sometimes. Ebbie he can't stand up with our help, he sets here in the rocking chair an object of pity, poor man but he is very patient and talks about dying waiting for the time to come. Maturin and Isa have moved up to the village in Carters' house her scholars come to her now. Well my paper isn't large enough but since it is God's holy will we should be hurten for awhile in sweet submission. All are one, we'll say our Father's Will be done.

Albert I thought I had written about Uncle Harry's death, he lived and suffered a long time. They had to feed him for three years. He has been dead most four years. Aunt Vira and Lucy was here two years ago. Last fall. Good bye. All from your poor old Mother Margaret Sherman.

August 1885

Thursday morn. Your card of last week and letter of this week are both received. How nice to hear so often, it is only careless of us not to write oftener. I mean on my part. Father understood about your letter. I asked him in the morning about it and he was ready with a correct answer then he cried. He doesn't help himself so much as to keep the flies off. Yes, he does get himself up on the side of the bed. Sometimes he falls off. Mother is dressing him now. Sometimes he sleeps till noon. After being turned over his hip is getting sore. If he would only talk a little we would be so glad. The only word he says without being questioned is Margaret. My fingers are getting some better although a new sore on the end of one has made its appearance. I have not served an hour hardly this summer. They are a stiff but my health is getting a little better. Isa and her big classes are doing nicely. Isa let Ebbie bring up..2 yesterday. He staid 2 hours I guess. Well I never heard a better sermon on temperance than you preached by your refusal to sign. Mother as well as all of us were glad. I supposed you have heard of Grants death —what a fuss. Many thanks for you letter. Don't worry aobut us. I am glad you have work. Stand for the right. Julia

Note: Ulysses S. Grant (born Hiram Ulysses Grant ; April 27, 1822 – July 23, 1885) was the 18th president of the United States (1869–1877)

Benson   Sunday August 5, 1885

My dear children we all well as usual but your Father he has been failing for a few days, he don't talk any only, yes or no. He has a good appetite but can't help himself. He slept till three o'clock today. I had to wake him then, I fed and shaved him which I have to do.

Isa was up home last Thursday with her two babies. They are healthy and growing nicely and a great charge for Isa. The road out yesterday. How are you all this Sabbath day. I wish I could see you tonight. There the bell is singing and I must go and milk. I have all the chores to do. Ebbie went away the 4th. We have heard from him once he was in Mass working in the shoe factory then. I don't know how we can get along without him. He didn't get much work and got discouraged but I did not think he was going so far off.

Julia is at home, her health has failed so she can't teach any more till she gets better. The girls think we had better sell the cow but I don't , how are all the children. They must write. How they get along in their studies. Morning it is quite cool. It reminds me of winter which I dread. Good bye I must go and see to Father.   Mother

Sunday evening   **Benson Dec 8, 1885**

Dear children   (from mother, Father died 5 weeks ago)

Your letter today found us quite well all but Julia and Isa but so <u>lonesome</u> in thought I would drop a line to you this evening. It is five weeks all ready since poor Father lay here suffering and so continued till Tuesday …departed in June I believe. Oh Albert I miss him so much. He has been in my constant care for more than five years. And I am thankful for the patience he had and for all I done for him. Wish I had done more. He was never dissatisfied with anything. we done for him. We were going to have his bed in here this winter but I don't wish him back for I shall soon go to him. Still my health is quite good but hard work with so much care and sleepless nights has made rapid strides in my looks. It will be on Thursday forty-seven years the 14th day of February since we were married, we have worked hard, had our cares and sorrows, clouds and sunshine in common with others. I can bear afflictions but if my children should do wrong I should down the last time. I talked with him about you he said I might see you all again but he never would be remembered. The little girls and Loll crying out to the hope he felt very anxious for Bertie's wishes. He could send him something but could not. I had my picture taken last fall but your Father was not able to go down. We have one of his taken some years ago which looks very natural. There was an agent here last week trying to see grave stones. He had some beautiful designs but we did not take any. Julia likes one monument representative. It was carved out in the middle. Said he had been out in Missouri last spring in Clinton and was going again next summer and would call and see you-

Well now I have another piece of sad news to write, last Sunday evening about when you were writing home, one of Isa's dear little twin babies..one was passing away. He died a very poor spell the next day after Father died. The Dr. thought it was caused by her grief. It got better so the winter. The funeral has been as well as the others until last Friday it was taken down with the Christian Infantism . It went to Maturin he suffered intensely . We were all there. Isa was or is almost frantic with grief. She don't sit up much. They all called him the prettiest but I could see no difference. Her head has troubled her for a long time. I have great fear for her. She has the kindest husband. He has to keep calm. We all love them very much. Maturin and Susie went to Fair Haven, got a little white casket, price $15.00. The funeral was at the house. The moment the plate was our darling, they drew a little Church no one I wish I could tell you more about it but can't. Julia can't walk around any bub house he is ??? I am glad to hear that you are prospering in temporal things and hope you will not forget the spiritual things. I am glad you are going to write so often. This sheet is too small, Mother.

Arkansas City Jan

Dear Sister,   (*Maggie's son Willie died*)

Your letter came to hand last week I thought I would answer it last Sunday but did not. I do not feel like doing anything since Dear Willy is gone. O how lonely it has been yesterday and today. He was a pretty child. We have not got his picture, but his face is ever before me, go where I will in the house I see him and miss him for he was after me. He suffered so much I do not think the Dr. understood Willy's sickness, we had two Dr and did all we could for …but in vain. Johnny sings *(ripped corner of letter)*

They miss <u>Dear little</u> Willy. I have enough rags cut for 15 yards but have not got them sewed yet. I sometimes feel as if I do not want to do anything more but cry. I had a letter from Anie yesterday, I wish I could get a letter every day. It has been very cold here this winter. It is now looking as if we would get some rain. We have not moved yet and do not know where we will go yet but I want to go some place where Flora can go to school. Where we live now it is too far from the school house. All can you tell me what a small tombstone will…and on what terms. They…let me have one. I want…one before we leave, please…me If I could get one … to cost. This is all to….

APPENDIX 7

Albert Sherman's 87th Birthday

87TH BIRTHDAY

Today A. G. Sherman is celebrating his 87th birthday. A marble cake was baked for the occasion by his daughter, Miss Minnie. While Mr. Sherman is not having a family re-union at this time he has had this past fall one "Merry Go 'Round" of pleasure by having the different members of his family present. A trip to Kansas City and a few days visit with a son B. G. Sherman and family was a rare treat.

A quail dinner on Sunday November 12, was enjoyed at the home of his son Carl Sherman and family. He was also entertained at a Thanksgiving dinner prepared by a daughter Mrs. F. R. Wall and family.

Out-of-town guests were a daughter Mrs. J. H. Cowman and husband, of Manitou, Colo., and Mrs. W. G. Bassler and son Sherman, of Zelienople, Penn.

APPENDIX 8

Albert G. Sherman's Obituary p.1

OLD RESIDENT DIES

A. G. Sherman Passes from Age Infirmities

A. G. Sherman, for sixty-six years a resident of Clinton, succumbed to the infirmities of old age and passed away at his home, 411 East Green street on Wednesday night at o'clock.

So passes a man who in his active life was always identified with the growth of our city. Coming here in 1868, he found but a village in the prairies. The railroad was not built thru here until years later. He was always noted for his sympathy, courtesy and unfailing kindness. He was a monument dealer, and was an expert workman, many of the handsome monuments in Englewood cemetery bearing testimony of his skill and craftsmanship. He was a man of social instincts and this was manifested in his affiliation with fraternal organizations. He was an old time member of the Oddfellow lodge, and had passed thru all the official chairs of that order; and it is related that he even to a few days before his passing, was thorough and accurate in his memory of the ritualism of that order. A quarter of a century ago he joined the Elks order, and has long appreciated the distinction and honor accorded him of being the oldest Elk in Clinton; and his recurring birthdays were always remembered by the fraternity of Elks with a birthday bouquet which was a great joy to his heart even when his increasing infirmities kept him confined to the house so that he could not be present at sessions of the order.

A. G. Sherman was born in Cha county, New York, on January , 1847, being consequently 87 years of age at his last birthday. His boyhood days were spent in Vermont, the vicinity of Lake Champlain.

From Vermont he came west and located here on November 22, 186 For the ensuing five years he was engaged in farming, but he then engaged in the granite and marble business, which he followed actively until his increasing decline something over two years ago, forced his retirement. During his business career, his shop was at 113 East Jefferson from 1893, up to the time he had to give up his trade.

APPENDIX 8 (CONT.)

Albert G. Sherman's Obituary p.2

years afflicted with a nervous di
order that caused his hands to shak
when he had a mallet and chisel i
them, and his design to follow, h
strokes were as clear, accurate a
perfect as they were in his mo
active years in this occupation. F
was a man of notable characteristi
and to know him was to admire h
personality.

Mr. Sherman was married Dece
ber 8, 1870, to Miss Laura E. Bue
ingham, at the home of her pare
on North Main street, in what is n
known as the Dr. Douglass home. F
more than fifty years he had resi
at the Green street home, where
died.

A great shock came to him six yea
ago when his beloved wife pass
away, he never fully recovered fro
the loss. The latter part of last Ma
he had a light stroke, which led to
gradual failing of his health and b
had been confined to his bed for som
time. But his mind was clear to th
end, and he was in full possession o
his faculties, welcoming the ol
friends who dropped in to see hi
with that kindly hospitality and court
esy which had been his life-tim
characteristic.

The children left to mourn his lo
are: Mrs. W. C. Bassler, of Zelienopl
Pa.; Mrs. J. H. Cowman, of Manito
Col.; B. G. Sherman, of Kansas City
Carl Sherman, of Clinton, and Mr
F. R. Wallace and Miss Minnie,
the home address. He also leave
nine grandchildren.

The funeral service will be at th
First M. E. Church, on Friday after
noon at 2 o'clock, and interment w
follow in Englewood cemetery wit
Spore's service.

APPENDIX 9

William G. Bassler's Will

Signed 23 October 1916

I, William G. Bassler of Zelienople Boro in
the County of Butler and State of Penn'a. being of sound mind and
memory, do make publish and declare this to be my last will and
testament in manner following "to wit":

1st.   I will and direct that all my just debts, funeral
expences and charges of proving this my last will, be in the first
place fully paid and satisfied.

2nd.   I will and bequeath to my wife Julia E. Bassler
all my property both real and personal, which I may have at my death
to be hers absolutely, to dispose of as she may desire.

3rd.   I do hereby nominate and appoint my said wife
executrix of this my last will and testament.

In witness whereof, I, the said testator, have to this my last
will and testament set my hand and seal, the 23d day of October A.D. 1916

                                W. G. Bassler   (seal)

Signed, sealed, published and declared by the said testator as and for
his last will and testament, in the presence of us, who in his presence
and at his request, and in the presence of each other have subscribed
our names as witnesses thereto.

                                Harry Gross
                                Theo E. Stout

APPENDIX 10

Minnie Sherman's <u>Family Record</u>

Additions by Margaret Eloise Sherman Boyle

1870 Albert Galiton Sherman and Miss Laura E. Buckingham, both of Clinton, Missouri, were married by the Rev. J.W. Newcomb on the evening of December 8th at the residence of the bride's father in Clinton. (This information from the item in the *Daily Democrat* of Clinton.)
Albert G. was born January 23, 1847, Chazy, Clinton County, N.U. Raised, Benson, Vermont. Laura E. Buckingham was born July 14, 1850, Piqua, Miami County, Ohio.

1871 Mary Parsons Sherman (Minnie), born Clinton, Mo., Nov. 10th at J.L. Buckingham's residence in the north part of town (Property now owned by Mrs. Dr. Douglas) died December 6th, 1950.

1874 Laura Evans Sherman born in Clinton, Mo, April 21st in home on North Main Street. (Mother of Murhl Padfield) Died June 9, 1901.

1875 This year father, mother, Laura and I were at our grandparents in Benson, Vermont.

1876 Julia Elizabeth Sherman born March 10th in Clinton, Mo. At Grandpa Buckingham's home in the north part of town.
During the spring father rented a place on 411 East Green Street and moved to that address.
Died January 10,1975

1878 Albert Gilbert (Bert) born December 6th at the home, 411 E. Green Street.
A memorable day, very cold weather.

1881 John Larkin Sherman born November 25th; I, Minnie, started to school in September in what was then known as the Christian church located at the corner of 3rd and Green Street. (This place now occupied by the High School gymnasium building) Died November 23, 1902

1885 Wilber Sherman, born March 30th and died May 30, 1885. Dr. Jones conducted the services. Wilber was the second person buried in the Englewood Cemetery.

1886 Eva Bell Sherman born July 20th. Father and mother built an addition to their home during the spring and summer (411 E. Green Street). Died July 1974.

1886 I, Minnie, graduated from the public school May 18th. Exercises held during the afternoon and evening in the Opera House. This was above the buildings in the central part of the east side of the Square.

1889 Carl Buckingham Sherman born in Clinton, November 25th at 411 E. Green Street.

1893 Clara Wells Sherman born July 5th in Clinton at 411 E. Green Street. Irene Kreamer (a cousin) visited us. Father went to World's Fair in Chicago. I secured a position to teach in the city schools of Arkansas City, Kansas.

1895 Grandpa Buckingham died January 4th. (I, Minnie, home for the holidays. Very cold weather. School term (1895-1896) spent at home. Laura in the millinery business.

1896 Accepted fifth grade work in the fall. (Ark.City,Ks.)

1897 Missed school three days in the spring. Out with the "grippe".

1898 Julia went with me to Arkansas City. We kept house in rooms at Flora McDowell's home until November when mother and Clara came for a while.

1900 Laura and Corey W. Padfield April 28th. Muhrl born.

1901 Laura died June 9th. Buried at Englewood Cemetery June 10th. Services at the home conducted by our minister of the First Methodist Episcopal Church.

1902 Bert and John went to Colorado for a short trip. John took sick with typhoid fever on July 14th. Passed away November 23rd. Buried at Englewood Cemetery on the 25th (his birthday).

1903 In January I returned to my school work after an absence of four months.

1904 Grandma Buckingham died in April.

1905 I attended the World's Fair in Sr. Louis. Visited Julia in Zelienople, Pa during the summer.

1907 Sherman Bassler born November 8th, Zelienople,Pa.

1910 Margaret Eloise Sherman born in Kansas City, Mo. 13th & Euclid, April 8th. Mother visited Bert and Stella. I went back to teach in 4th ward in Arkansas City.

1912 Bert, Stella, Eloise, father and I went to Colorado Springs in August. Enjoyed the Moffat Road trip out of Denver.
C.W. Padfield went to Woodman Sanitorium in September with tuberculosis.

1913 Rented a cottage on 17th Street Colorado Springs, Colorado for summer. Eva, Muhrl, C.W. and I occupied it. Frank Walker of Vermont and Clara visited us, also Lauretta Wilcox of Vermont. (Frank and Lauretta, cousins). C.W. Eva and Muhrl moved to Platte Avenue, Colorado Springs in fall.

1914 Mother visited Eva and C.W. at Colorado springs. Father broke a rib while helping to set up a monument. Clara and Floyd Wallace were married at home (411 E. Green Street) by Rev. Gaither of the First M.E. Church, September 1st.

1916 Clara visited Eva during the summer. Herschel Lee Wallace born on November 7th.

1917 World War I was declared April 8th.

1919 Carl home from World War. Went to Colo. Spgs. And brought Eva home. I met them at Kansas City. Eva not well all summer. Operation at Kansas City, August 5th. Home until October. Mother took her back to Colo. Spgs. Carl married to Katherine Markley on November 22nd.

1920 I visited Eva and C.W. when they lived on Colo. Ave. Carl and Katherine in Colo. Spgs for an outing. All home for mother and father's Golden Wedding anniversary, December 8th. School granted me a leave of absence. C.W. Padfield visited his home folks, too.
Carl M. Sherman, Jr. born at 411 E. Green on Dec 10th

1922 C.W. Padfield died at Colo. Spgs. Remains brought to Clinton. Short services at our home (411 E. Green) by Rev. Haney. Eva home for a while. Clara returned with Eva to Colo. Spgs. For a short visit. Herschel started to Franklin School in September.

1923 Carl and Katherine built their new home at 309 E. Ohio. Moved in the fall.
Waneta Ruth Wallace born Feb 2nd at 411 E. Green.

1924 Harold Lee Sherman born Nov. 6th at 309 E. Ohio, Clinton

1925 Clara and Floyd built their new home at 406 E. Lincoln St., Clinton. Moved July 3rd.

1926 Howard Vernon Wallace born Jan. 18th at 406 E. Lincoln, Clinton.
Carl Jr. started school at Washington building in September.

1927 Mother, father and I visited with Eva in Colo. Spgs. For one month, parts of July and August. East side upstairs rented during the summer to Mr. & Mrs. Harley Hunter of Sedalia.
Mother took sick about Thanksgiving.

1928 Julia, Bert and Eva came home for a visit. All together the last Sunday in February. Uncle Will Buckingham died February 12th in Illinois (Danville-Veteran's Hospital (?) Buried February 16th, Clinton, MO. Marie Padfield (Muhrl's wife) visited us in March. Mother passed away at 1:30 May 7th. Services held May 9th at the home, 411 E. Green, conducted by Rev. Wolfe, pastor of First M.E. Church.

1929 House arranged to rent as apartments. Lillian Brown, neighbor girl, married to Clarence Kaney in August. Left for Lake Charles, LA
Waneta Ruth Wallace started to Franklin school in September.

1930 Eva and J.H. Cowman married.
Hershel graduated from grammar school.
Julia and Sherman visited in the fall. Eva and J.H. visited in December.

1931 All visited Bert and family in December, Eva and J.H. were in Kansas City and came out for dinner.

1932 Pa and I visited with Bert and Stella in June for three days. Came home with Carl through a very heavy rain storm.
Father and I went to Manitou, Colo. July 9th; visited Eva and J.H. for two weeks. Eva and J.H. visited us in November. Howard Wallace started to school. Wayne Sherman Wallace born December 9th at 406 E. Lincoln, Clinton.

1933 Bert visited us on New Year's Day. Muhrl and Marie spent the first week of the New Year with Mabel Loudermilk and Grandma Padfield. Ate supper with us on Saturday evening Jan. 7th. Howard not well. Ear trouble.

1934 Bert, Carl, Carl Jr. and Mr. Boyle went north for an outing.
Carl Jr. graduated from grammar school May 18th. Played a clarinet solo at the exercises. Father and I attended both exercises. Father had a light stroke on the 21st of May.

Uncle Ben Buckingham died June 2nd in Iola, Kansas. Burial June 3rd at Clinton.

Aunt Isa Wilcox (father's sister) died June 9th. Clara and Wayne left for Julia's in Zelienople,Pa. June 18th.

W.G.Bassler (Julia's husband-Sherman's father) died June 20th. Buried June 22nd.

Clara and Wayne returned home on the 30th.

Aunt Lelia died July 1st. Buried July 3rd.

Bert, Stella and Eloise came down on July 17th. On August 1st, Floyd, Clara and family left for Manitou, Colo. Arrived at Eva's August 3rd. Came home August 15th.

August 19th Bert came down. Eloise sick.

August 20th father passed away at 9:50 Wednesday evening. Services at the First M.E. church conducted by Rev. Olsen. Burial at Englewood Aug. 31st.

Sept. 10th Herschel's school work opened at Fayette, Mo.

Carl Jr. enters high school at Clinton.

APPENDIX 11

Minnie's Letter to Laura

Clinton Mo. Mar. 11, 1899

Dear Laura,

I received your letter Thursday and as ever was glad to hear from home.

As this is pay day and I have a number of things to see to. I can not write a lengthy letter also, this machine does not work as fast as my thoughts fly and it would take me all day to write a little.

This is a blustery day. When I wakened this morning, I heard rain falling. Not long after it began snowing and has kept it up all morning. If Ma had been here yesterday and tasted of the sand as I did she would have said, "Give me Missouri weather" I could scarcely keep my eyes open.

I think your dress colored nicely and I am sure it will pay you for the trouble in coloring.

I am glad your washing machine has come and hope you will find it to be as represented. Be sure and do not remove that piece Mr. Warren nailed on the stand.

I happened to think this morning that yesterday was Julia's birthday, but I have nothing to send but the wishes that she had a pleasant day.

It is clearing off and I must draw this not to a close.

Flora and I are going down town to look at spring goods. Don't you think we will be rushing the season? (HA! HA! Look at the mistakes I am making) So much for hurrying. Well, we have two months more of school. I am glad. Kiss Clara for me. Write often. Love to all. Minnie S

The above was typed followed by a note In handwriting.

I have been trying Mr. M & D new type writer. This has been the first since I wrote the other. I am as poor as the school children about keeping the margins, but I will learn how, I guess. I sent $15.00. Let me know if you get it and write. I am well.

APPENDIX 11A

Minnie's letter to Sherman May 1910

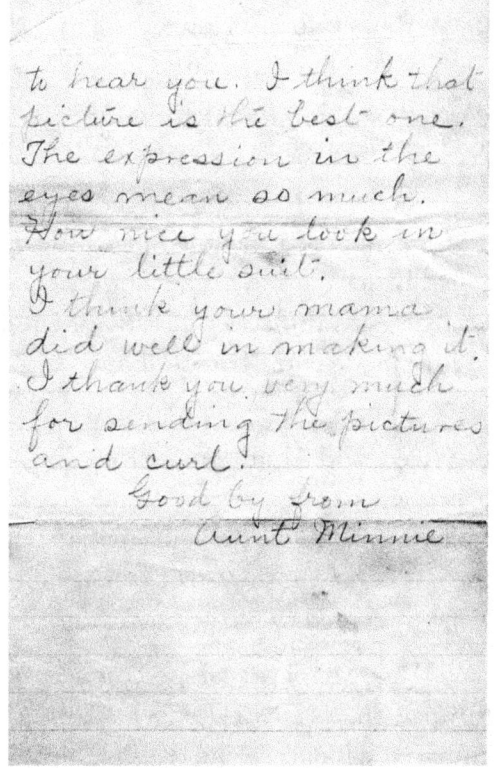

APPENDIX 12

Family Recollections

from Waneta Wallace Smith & her daughter Connie Smith

Mary Parsons Sherman (Aunt Minnie)

Aunt Minnie was the oldest of the Sherman children.

She graduated from Clinton High School and took tests and became a primary teacher in Arkansas City, Kansas. She taught 40 years there. She knew some people that knew Dr. Hollingsworth, a Clinton doctor.

When Grandma Sherman became ill, Aunt Minnie resigned her teaching position and moved back home to be with Grandma and Grandpa. Grandma died shortly after Aunt Minnie moved back. I was not quite four years old and I barely remember riding to the cemetery in a car with the curtains tied down because it was raining.

Aunt Minnie always was like a grandmother to me. She was the oldest and my mother Clara was the youngest of the Sherman family.

Aunt Minnie belonged to the Methodist Church and a club called "The Tourist Club". Another lady, Hattie Poague, also a member, was in Aunt Minnie's graduating class. Aunt Minnie loved preparing the lesson when it was her time and I'm sure the ladies had wonderful travels.

She helped me with my geometry when I was in High School. She was so patient and encouraging. She was a wonderful seamstress and I learned to sew doll clothes at an early age. She let me use her sewing machine and remarked to Uncle Bert that she was afraid I would get hurt, so at Christmas, Uncle Bert gave me a little toy machine to use! Aunt Minnie made many beautiful dresses for me through the years.

Shobe and I lived in the downstairs east side apartment of the Sherman house at 411 E. Green and Aunt Minnie lived downstairs on the West side of the Sherman home. We lived there the first 8 years of our marriage. Our two boys, Lowell and Mark were five and four years when we moved. We had built a house on East Franklin Street. Our house was the last house on the street at that time. There was no highway and no buildings beyond. Ohio Street led to the cemetery. It is hard to believe all of the changes.

Aunt Minnie developed cancer and died a year after we moved. She was a dear sweet tiny person, less than five feet tall and never reached 100 pounds. She was tiny but mighty, and lived with grace and dignity.

Laura E. Sherman

Laura E. Sherman was the second Sherman child. My mother said she was so beautiful! I don't know much about her except she was married to a man named Padfield and gave birth to a son Murhl Padfield. She died shortly afterwards from hemoragic bleeding. My mother said that would not have happened today.

Aunt Eva helped take care of Murhl and later married Mr. Padfield. He became ill with tuberculosis and they moved to Colorado for his health. That is how Aunt Eva got to Colorado.

Aunt Eva raised Murhl after Mr. Padfield died. She later married J. H. Cowman.

Julia Elizabeth Sherman

Julia Elizabeth Sherman was the third Sherman child. She looked like her mother with red hair, blue eyes and fair skin.

She was married to William Bassler and gave birth to a son Sherman Bassler. I do not know how she got to Pennsylvania. She lived on Newcastle Street in Zelienople , Pennsylvania. Her husband did photography and they developed film in their basement. Mr. Bassler was much older than Aunt Julia and he died when Sherman was a teenager. Aunt Julia continued with the business and baked angel food cakes and made beautiful hand braided rugs to sell.

Aunt Minnie said when my mother was born with red hair and blue eyes, Aunt Julia went around telling the neighbors she had a sister like her.

Aunt Julia was full of fun like my mother and Uncle Carl and I loved it when she came to visit.

One time when all of the children came home, Aunt Eva and J. H. were staying at our house, and Sherman and Aunt Julia were with Aunt Minnie. J. H. loved to listen to a radio station in Albuquerque, New Mexico, to check on his investments. Sherman worked in electronics and he and my brother, Herschel, rigged up something in the barn back of Grandpa's house that would interfere with the reception every time that program came on the air.

After two or three times the boys couldn't contain themselves any longer and confessed! Everyone had a good laugh.

Sherman married a girl named Ethel. They had two children, Bill and Susan.

Bill became a lawyer and I think Susan was a teacher. She married and had children and when I wrote to her after my mother passed away, the letter was returned.

When Aunt Julia could not live by herself any longer, she lived with Sherman and

Ethel. When she passed away, mother said a friend said Bill delivered her eulogy and it was beautiful.

Albert Gilbert Sherman (Uncle Bert)

Uncle Bert's wife was Stella and they had a daughter names Margaret Eloise. They lived on Euclid Ave. in Marlborough, a suburb of Kansas City. They had some land back of their home and Uncle Bert grew raspberries. It was beautiful. Row after row of beautiful hand pruned bushes with a lovely grass walkway between the rows!

He would have Herschel and me come and help pick sometimes. Uncle

Bert worked at Union Station and when I was little I used to go home with him after he had visited Aunt Minnie and Uncle Carl and mother. Eloise was older and would take me swimming at Unity Farm and play tennis "ha" with me. She played the piano quite well and played for her youth group at the Methodist Church she attended.

She had Herschel and me come one time and Herschel played a solo at the church.

I used to go to Union Station with Uncle Bert and spend the day. He would buy me ice cream sodas. They were 50 cents then! About 15 years ago my son Mark and his wife Gay took Shobe and me back to see the Station and bought a soda for us from the same fountain, only it cost over five dollars each!

Eloise worked at the Business Men's Insurance Company across the street from Union Station. She met her husband there. She married Elroy Boyles and had a home wedding. She bought a floor length pale green dress from Hartzfeld's for me! I was flower girl (about 8 years old)

Eloise had two boys, John and Jimmy and later the family moved to California.

Aunt Stella died and then Uncle Bert and the last time I saw Eloise was when they brought their ashes back to be buried in Englewood. Eloise and Elroy died and I lost contact with their sons.

John Larkin Sherman

Mother said their whole family was quarantined with typhoid fever.

John had been very, very ill and was getting better when he had a relapse and died at the age of 21 years.

Wilbur Sherman

Wilbur died at two months of age.

Eva Belle Sherman

Eva Sherman married Mr. Padfield and raised Murhl Padfield. After Murhl was married, she married J. H. Cowman. They lived in a big rock house by their "tourist camp". It was called Cottonwood Camp. There was a little stream that bordered the camp and it was lined with Cottonwood trees. So pretty! J. H. also had a "dime store" or two. One was located in Kansas and one time he let my mother work behind the candy counter just for fun! My mother made wonderful candy, all kinds, and she enjoyed doing that. J. H. said he couldn't afford for her to do that very long because she was very generous!

The cabins at Cottonwood Camp were adobe and had little kitchenettes.

When I graduated from grade school, Aunt Eva sent money for me to come see them.

An open tourist car came by the camp every day and picked up passengers to go to Pikes Peak, The Garden of the Gods, Cave of the Winds and Royal Gorge. If Carlos, the driver, had an empty seat, Aunt Eva would let me go along.

On Saturday evenings Aunt Eva would take me to Manitou Springs to a weekly Band Concert. I remember hearing The Whistler and his Dog for the first time. It featured the piccolo.

Aunt Eva and J. H. loved to fish and spent winters at his camp in Brownsville, Texas.

They sold the Camp and bought a home on Cascade Ave, in Colorado Springs.

After J. H. died, mother visited Aunt Eva there. They giggled like teenagers.

Shobe and Connie and I drove out and brought mother home.

Carl Buckingham Sherman

Carl and my mother were "pals". They told of some of the pranks they did. One time, Uncle Carl got a cigar which mother and he shared behind the barn. Uncle Carl got sick but mother said she didn't. She didn't say what the consequences were!

Uncle Carl had a motorcycle and mother rode on the back of it. When he was learning the plumbing trade, he let her watch.

When Uncle Carl married Aunt Katherine, they lived on the upstairs apartment on the West side of the Sherman home. My parents and Herschel lived upstairs on the East side.

My brother Herschel loved mashed potatoes. If mother didn't fix them he would go see if Aunt Katherine was having them. If she wasn't serving them he would go downstairs and Grandma Sherman would fix them!

I was born when Herschel was six years old. When I was three, mother and daddy built a house at 406 East Lincoln St. right behind the Sherman home on East Green Street. Uncle

Carl did all of the plumbing and heating.

Uncle Carl and Daddy built a miniature golf course in our back yard. Daddy did the wooden windmills etc. and Uncle Carl did some things with pipes and they used sawdust from the saw mill instead of sand. Mother planted flowers and people came at night to play.

Uncle Carl also had a cabin at the Club Lake which was adjacent to Artisian Park. He would come get Hersh and Howard and me and Carl and Harold and take us fishing. He came when my father was about to die and sat up nights with him so Wayne and mother and Shobe could get some rest. He and Aunt Katherine were dear people!

Clara Wells Sherman, the youngest Sherman child

I've been told my mother was full of vim and vigor as a child. She had auburn hair, bluish green eyes and very pale complexion.

She had a pony named Barney and a white Spitz dog named Snowball.

My Grandpa Sherman set stones at the cemetery and when he worked there, Grandma Sherman would send mother with his lunch. Mother said she would ride "properly" sidesaddle until she was out of Grandma's sight and then she would get astride her pony and ride so fast that her braids would stand out. Then when she thought Grandpa could see her she would get back in the sidesaddle.

She had a girlfriend, Susie Montgomery, who loved on the corner from her. Mother's brother Carl, Susie and Mother would play "Go Sheep Go". It was an early day version of "Hide and Seek".

Mother told me her pony broke his leg while he was tied in the pasture. Grandpa explained to her that Barney couldn't get well and they would have to shoot him. Mother said she ran to the house and put pillows over her head so she wouldn't hear the shot.

She and Uncle Carl played a prank that she told me about. They took some black long stockings and made a roll to look like a snake. They tied it with black thread and rolled it into a coil close to the sidewalk. They tied a string and ran it to the front porch. Then they waited behind the shrubbery and when this lady came along, they pulled the string to move the "snake". The lady screamed, raised her skirt and ran down the street!

When mother was in High School, she broke out a window playing baseball with some boys. Knowing her mother would be chagrinned, she ran to her daddy's monument shop. She said he told her he would take care of it and it would be their secret.

Mother played the piano very well and when she started dating my father, he wanted her to teach him to read music. After he learned to read music, he ordered a Cornet and taught himself to play.

My mother was the pianist for the North Methodist Church and after she and daddy were married, they started a Church Orchestra. Wayne King was a boy then and played in the orchestra. After he became famous he came back and played a solo at the church. My mother accompanied him. When she picked up her music she noticed the music had been upside down.

It was ironic that my son Mark was band director at Clinton High School when Wayne King was brought here to do a benefit to raise money for new band uniforms. The *Clinton Eye* took a picture of Mother and Uncle Carl and Aunt Katherine. As a young man, Wayne had stood up for Aunt Katherine and Uncle Carl when Reverend Lindsay married them in the Parsonage. The parsonage is now a Bed and Breakfast.

Mother belonged to Eastern Star and The Rebekah Lodge and was always the musician. When she was 87 years old, she wanted to go to a Halloween party in disguise. My brother Wayne and I helped her. She wore old coveralls, a horrible rubber face a stocking cap and work shoes. At that time the IOOF meeting place was upstairs on the Southwest corner of the Square. Wayne helped her up the long flight of stairs and she hid when people came up. She had forgotten the password and had to wait and listed to someone else say it!

The evening went on and no one ever guessed who she was. I don't think she had been to a meeting for years, so we didn't expect anyone would! There was much laughter and tears.

My mother made all kinds of candy. When Carl and Harold Lee would come over, mother would make taffy and let us help pull it and spread it out and cut it.

When my mother was in her eighties my brother Wayne and his wife Virginia and their children Carole and Chris, took her to Silver Dollar City at Branson, Missouri. Mother, tired of walking, needed to rest awhile, so Wayne took her to the store where they were making peanut brittle. He asked the man if she could rest and watch awhile. When Wayne and Virginia came back to get her the candy maker said, "Grandma knows what she is talking about!" The next year Wayne and Virginia went back to the shop and the man asked where is Grandma?

When I was four, Uncle Will Buckingham (Grandma Sherman's brother) came to visit Grandma Sherman. Mother invited Grandma, Grandpa and Uncle Will to supper. Mother apologized for her unmatched dishes. After Uncle Will had been gone several weeks, there was a knock at the door. The Railroad Express was delivering a large barrel. When mother unpacked the barrel, it contained a china set of dishes for twelve people! Also a small set of dishes and a beautiful dress for me!

After Grandma Sherman died, mother always fixed Sunday dinner for Grandpa and Aunt Minnie. After lunch Grandpa always wanted mother and daddy to play with Herschel and me. After his "concert" he and Aunt Minnie would go home so he could have a nap.

Mother was sixty-five when my father died. Daddy had just been retired one year. She chose to stay in their home until she was 93. She decided herself that it was time for her to go to a nursing home.

Mother was a Royals and Cardinals fan. She listened to the games and the nurses and medics would come by and ask "what is the score Clara?" She always knew! She delighted in Shobe and Wayne visiting about the games.

My son Mark sang in the Heart of America Barbershop Chorus. One time he brought a quartet and they serenaded mother on Valentine's Day. She moved her hands in time to the music. She loved it!

Aunt Katherine and Uncle Carl were eventually brought to the same care center and one of the nurses brought Uncle Carl to mother's room. It was so sweet! They just held hands and patted each other.

My mother was a wonderful mother. She was a good teacher and a good friend. I knew how to bake Angel Food cakes from scratch and iron starched shirts by the time I was 12 years old.

She always welcomed my friends and always served something. In the summer she served bottled grape juice and cookies and in the winter popcorn and apples.

Mother loved to play cards. In the winter the neighbors would come and play cards. We "kids" had fun and television was still unknown!

She was also creative. When I was in second grade I was invited to a birthday party. She thought my shoes didn't look very nice, so she painted them green to match my dress. My green shoes were the talk of the party but by the time I got home, they had started to crack!

My mother was also very brave. When I was eight my brother Howard was burned severely on both hands. The doctor had come and sedated him and Aunt Minnie sat with him while mother went right a\head and had my birthday party.

Another time when she was in her seventies, she caught her finger in the mix master and couldn't get it out. She undid the beater, wrapped her hand and the beater in a towel and walked next door for help!

It was difficult when Herschel, Howard and Wayne were in the Service, especially when Howard went overseas, but she always had a smile.

When mother was 96, Shobe and I had gone to Blue Springs to a school program. Connie's daughter Heather was in a play and she was a tight rope walker. When I went to see mother first thing the next morning, she wanted to hear all about the program. I told her that Heather kept turning her head to make sure Shobe was taking pictures. Mother laughed and laughed.

Mother died later that day. The nurse said she had just been waiting for me to come.

What a great lady!

These writings are profiles of the Sherman children. I have tried to put memories from my childhood on paper.

— *Waneta Wallace Smith   daughter of Clara Sherman Wallace*

APPENDIX 13

Susannah Gilbert Bassler's essay on the Bible

Composition *The Bible* – Susanna Bassler

Most wondrous book by which man may gain true riches; by which many are sent to heathen lands and people may worship true god and through the missionaries throw away there idols. Who gave us this book? God. Did God write it? No. Who write it then? The prophets and apostles. Now was it not good in God to send us this book? O that all people would become good and love God and such other then all would be peace and happiness. But it is not always as we would have it. But if we are good we shall have our sins forgiven and go to heaven and if all people would be good would have no need of jails and prisons but we have to exercise some laws and government. But Pollok has given us a good sketch about the bible. I will give you a few hints of it, it is, the Bible most wonderous book bright candle of the Lord star of Eternity the only Star by which the bark of man could navigate the sea of life and gain the coast of bliss securely Susanna Bassler 8 yr.s old

(William Gottlieb Bassler's sister)

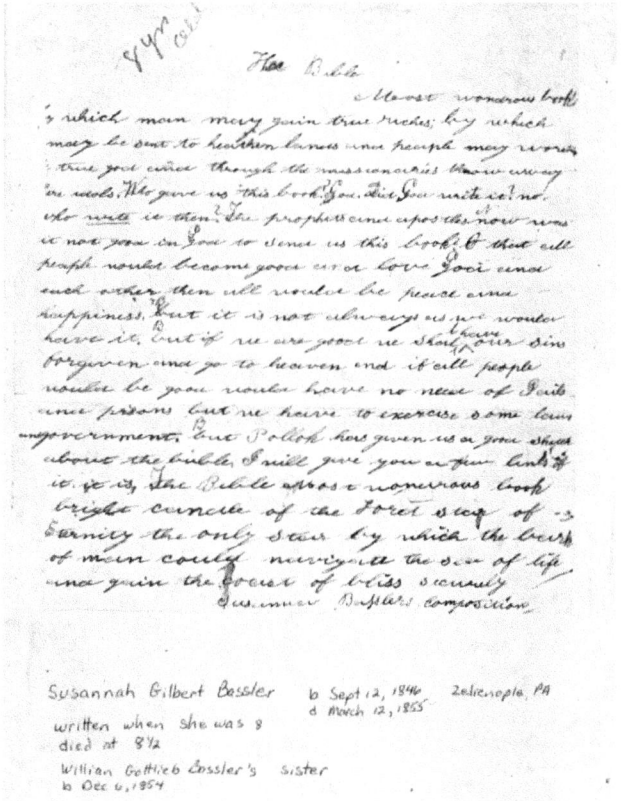

Susannah Gilbert Bassler   b Sept 12, 1846   Zelienople, PA
                           d March 12, 1855
written when she was 8
died at 8½
William Gottlieb Bassler's   sister
b Dec 6, 1854

APPENDIX 14

Elizabeth (Eliza) Gilbert Bassler's <u>Family Record</u>

Page 1

Family Record of Barnhard Gilbert and Susanah Gilbert of Adams County Penn. Barnard Gilbert my great-grandfather, a native of Germany, came to this country in about the year 1744 landed at Philadelphia, Pa and was married to Miss Catherine Bender and settled in Adams Co. Penn and he died Feb 28, 1862 aged 78yrs 2mos and 11 days. George Gilbert, my father, died April 20, 1803 aged 48 years and 11 months

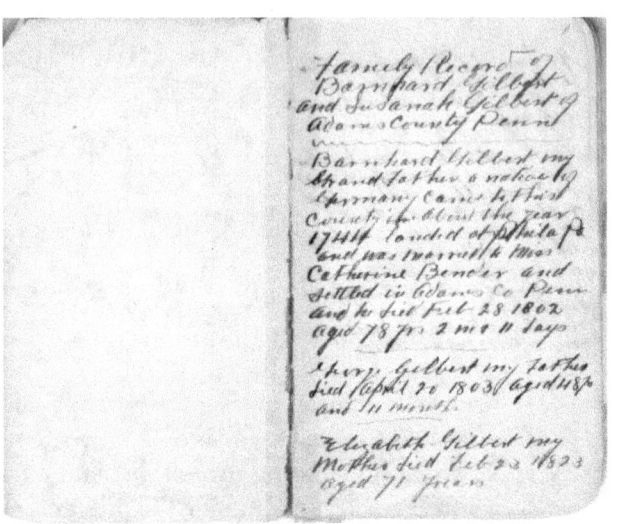

Elizabeth Gilbert my mother died Feb 23 1823 aged 71 years

Page 2-3

John Gilbert, my brother, died November 29, 1802 aged 75 yrs one month and 19 days.

George Gilbert, my brother, died Dec 17, 1809 aged 28 yrs one month and five days. Father of:

Dr. David Gilbert

John Gilbert of Gettysburg

George Gilbert of Tenn

And Sarah Gilbert who married to William Atlee who is brother of Edwin Atlee who is married to Deliliah Gilbert (my Mrs. B's mother's sister)

Barnhard Gilbert, son of George Gilbert, and grandson of Barnhert Gilbert was born March 22, 1786 was married to Susannah Gilbert daughter of Jacob Gilbert *(in paranthesis Jan 22, 1805 See page 2)*

Page 4-5

Of Adam Co. Pa Susannah Gilbert died July 21, 1863 and Barnhart Gilbert died October 1868 (82 yrs 6 mo) This Jacob, Susanah Gilbert's father, was married twice, the first wife living only about a year and left a son called Barnhard Gilbert. He was in the store business with Barnhart

Gilbert, my mother Elizabeth C's father named Barnhart, they were called Black Barny and Red Barny to distinguish them apart. My mother's father being fair and the other dark. This Jacob Gilbert was in the War of 1814.

Page 6-7

Children of Barnhart Gilbert and Susannah his wife

1. Elizabeth Gilbert born November 23, 1805 and died Nov. 30 1805

2. Jesse Gilbert born March 7, 1807 married to Jane Sloan Slang of Samuel Sloan

She died Aug 31, 1832 leaving no ? and he was married to Elizabeth Forney of Gettysburg daughter of Samul Forney Oct 14, 1834. He died Aug 28, 1838 leaving two daughters Clara Jane and Jessie Elizabeth. His wife afterward married.

Page 10-11

Married Col Buehler of Gettysburg and had two daughters

3. Delilah Gilbert born September 27, 1809 and was married to Edwin Atlee of Lancaster, Pa November 21, 1826. He died March 1869 and she died July 10,1885 (aged 75 yrs 8 mos and 14 days.

4. Sarah Ann Gilbert born Dec 7, 1811 and was married to Henry G. Dill of Gettysburg December 29, 1829. She died Aug 20, 1877 and he died May 30, 1887

Newspaper clipping glued to opposite page: *Death of Marshall Dill's father Lewisburg,Pa May 31.- Dill, father of Hon. Andrew H. Dill died yesterday aged eighty-four years. He was licensed to preach in 1831 entered the Baltimore Conference of the Methodist Spiscopal Church in 1888 and was in the active ministy for 38 years. In 1871 he retired and locted in Lewisburg. He has for many years been the superintendent of public schools.*

Page 12-13

5. George Ritter Gilbert born Sept 11, 1814 and was married to Sarah Jane Jones of Monroe Co. Tenn by the Rev E.A. Atlee

She died Aug 9, 1851 leaving two sons, Abram Barnhart and William Edwin, George was married again to Mrs. Susan Taylor of Marrietta, Ga by Rev Wm Tuckert. This wife died and he was married to... He died Dec 4, at 10:30 AM 1893. Aged 79 years 1 month and 24 days

Page 14-15

6. Jacob W Gilbert born October 8, 1815 and was married to Elizabeth Sweigart, daughter of Gary Sweigart of Adams Co., Pa Dec 13, 1836

7. Susanah Margaret Gilbert born Feb 8, 1818 and was married to John L Buckingham October 10, 1837 in Gettysburg, Pa. He died Jan 2, 1895. She died April 6, 1904 age 86 years 26 days.

Page 16-17

8. Elizabeth Catherine Gilbert born May 18, 1820 and was married to the Rev Gottlieb Bassler of Zelienople, Pa by the Rev John Kelly of Athens, Tenn. Oct 31, 1844. He died Oct 3, 1868 and she died June 11,1908 age 87 years 24 days.

(this information was written in by Julia Sherman Bassler, Eliza's daughter-in-law)

9. John Barnhart is born June 6, 1833 and died March 28, 1823

Page 18-19

10. Mary Ann Gilbert born Jan 9, 1824 and was married to the Rev George Parsons of Muncey Pa by the Reb. Wm Kelly of Athens,McMinn Co. Tenn. Oct 31, 1844 and she died January 4, 1846 leaving one son William Edwin born Oct 18, 1845.

11. Benjamin Franklin Gilbert born Jan 31, 1826 and died March 21 1826

Page 20-21

12. Edwin D. Gilbert born Jan 6, 1828 married to Nancy Jane Cox. Daughter of Col A Cox of Macon Co. Tenn by Rev Edwin A. Atlee Dec 20 1854. He died April 30 1864 aged 36 years 3 months and 24 days. His wife died Aug 30 1865 leaving three children: Sarah Susannah born April 7, 1856 married to Dr. Ziegler of Tenn. She died.... Jesie Summerfield born Feb 8, 1859 and has died from injuries received by being thrown from a horse. Ida Ceciwha born April 22, 1861

Page 26-27

Jacob Gilbert had twelve children.

One Barnhart Gilbert by his first wife and eleven by the second Mary.

Mary married to David Bescher has granddaughter living in Harrisburg.

Mrs. Weistley

Betsy Gilbert married to Michael Crowl

_____ Gilbert married to _____Saltsgiver (after her death he married a Mrs. Weaver) had two sons Henry and Daniel

Sarah A Gilbert married to Daniel Herr and had six sons and six daughters. Hon A J. Herr of Harrisburg.

Page 28-29

And Daniel B Herr Mrs. Dr Wiestling and

Mrs. George L Kunkle all of Harrisburg

Gilbert Henry,

Mrs. George Leonard and

Mrs. CA Barnart of Philadelphia

Mrs. Asni Hassler of Carlisle and Mrs. C C Lips of Los Angelos Cal.

Sophis Gilbert married to _____ Harmon

Susanah Gilbert married to Barnhart Gilbert

Barnhart Gilbert son of the first wife was in War of 1814

On the side: *See page of Susanah Gilbert was born January 15, 1786 married to Barnhart Gilbert Jan 22, 1803 and died July 20 1863 age 77 years 6 months and six days.*

Page 30-31

Was in store (business) with his cousin Barnhart in Gettysburg.

Magrie went west out to Dayton Ohio.

Jacob Gilbert

John Gilbert went to Indiana

George Gilbert moved to Dayton, Ohio

Samuel Gilbert lived and died in Gettysburg his descendents living there yet.

Page 32-33

George Gilbert father of Barnhart Gilbert married a widow Knouse (her maiden name was Elizabeth Ritter) with four children. There may have been nine but I am sure of four. The two sons Daniel and Henry lived in Missouri, one daughter married a Baltzer Snyder and lived a short distance from Gettysburg, the other married Henry Gilbert her step-father, brother and one of Barnhart Gilbert the first.

George Gilbert, father of Barnhart Gilbert had seven children by the marriage

Page 34-35

to the widow Knause. Three sons

Barnhart,

John and

George and four daughters,

Mrs.Fahl lived over 90 years has son in the ministry Bishop Fahl of Chambersburg United Brethern Church.

Mrs. Rupley 17 Green Castle has son in the ministry Rev Fred A Rupley. Another son was killed at battle of Chanclersville.

Mrs. Hoffman

Mrs Myers children living in Gettysburg

Notes on left side See page 2

Last page

In memory of John C Nietman who departs this life Sept 2, 1823 aged 32 years

Henry Neitman departed Sept 30, 1818 aged 11 years.

This is the father and brother of Mrs. Potius

In memory of John Carley who departed this life Sept 20 1932 aged 38 years.

This is the first husband of Mrs. Portius.

APPENDIX 15

Gottlieb Bassler's Lutheran Alumni Catalogue

Property of
Adams County Historical Society
Gettysburg, Penna.

Gettysburg Lutheran Theological Seminary

Volume Two

ALUMNI RECORD

Compiled and Edited
By
ABDEL ROSS WENTZ

Published by the Authority of the Directors
Printed for the Seminary by
THE EVANGELICAL PRESS
Harrisburg, Pennsylvania

ALUMNI RECORD   1840

LEHMAN, JOHN, b. Mar. 10, 1818; lic. W. Pa. Synod, 1841; ord. Mia. Syn., 1845; pastor, Zelienople, Pa., 1842-64; tutor, Gbg. Col., 1841-42; wife, Sarah Elizabeth; d. July 20, 1844; m. Louisa M. Weaver, Feb. 16, 1846; he d. May 31, 1883.

RHUDY, STEPHEN, b. Burke's Garden, Va., Oct. 23, 1814; Gettysburg Col., 1837-39; Gbg. Sem.; lic. S. W. Va. Syn., 1842; ord. same, 1846; miss. work in Tazewell and Bland Cos., Va.; engaged in teaching; m. Cynthia Mahood; d. June 9, 1894.

TRIMPER, ABRAHAM A., b. Claverack, N. Y., Feb. 17, 1816; grad. Hart. Sem., Union Col., and Gbg. Sem.; lic. Syn. of the West, 1841; ord. same, 1843; pastor, Indianapolis, Ind., 1841-44; Hillsboro, Ill., 1844-52; several chs. in N. Ill. and Ia., changing frequently; Lawrence, Kas., 1873-84; prin. Hillsboro Acad.; prin. Peru Acad., 1854; pres. Mendota Col., 1858; agt. for Carthage Col., 1869-72; m. Catherine Miller, who d. 1881; children, Mary, Katie, Lucy, Henry S., Ed. P.; m. Susan R. Rand, Sept., 1883; he d. Dec. 28, 1884.

WADSWORTH, WILLIAM A., b. Jefferson, Md., 1812; s. William and Susan W.; grad. Gbg. Col., 1839, and Sem., 1841; lic. Md. Syn., 1841; ord. E. O. Syn., 1843; pastor, Canton, O., 1841-43; prof. Washn. Sem., Perryopolis, Pa., 1843-44; d. Apr. 29, 1844.

WILLARD, PHILIP, b. Jefferson, Md., Sept. 29, 1809; s. Geo. and Susanna (Culler) W.; grad. Gbg. Col., 1839, and Sem., 1841; lic. W. Pa. Syn., 1841; ord. Md. Syn., 1842; pastor, Manchester, Md., 1841-42; Westminster, Md., 1842-45; Lovettsville, Va., 1845-48; Danville, Pa., 1850-56; Loysville, Pa., 1856-58; Mifflintown, Pa., 1858-61; Schuylkill Haven, Pa., 1861-62; agt. Gbg. Col., 1849; agt. Luth. Bd. Pub., 1863-68; supt. Loysville Orphans' Home, 1868-80; m. Margaretta Christzman, Oct. 21, 1841; children, Martin L., Geo., S. S., Ezra, H. F., T. Newton, Jennie, Nettie; she d. Feb. 2, 1891; he d. July 26, 1893.

Entered 1840

BASSLER, GOTTLIEB, b. Berne, Switzerland, 1813; A.B., Gettysburg Col., 1840; grad. Gbg. Sem., 1842; lic. W. Pa. Syn., 1842; ord. Pb. Syn., 1845; pastor, Zelienople, Pa., 1842-64; tutor, Gbg. Col., 1841-42; dir. Zelienople Orphans' Home, 1854-68; one of founders of Pb. Syn.; pres. Reading Convention, 1866; pres. G. C., 1867-68; m. Eliza Gilbert, Oct. 31, 1844; d. Oct. 3, 1868.

BERG, ANDREW, b. Mundenbein, Palatinate, Ger., Nov. 30, 1810; arrived Balto., Sept., 1832; Gbg. Col., 1837-40; grad. Gbg. Sem., 1842; lic. W. Pa. Syn., 1842; ord. same, 1844; pastor, Perry Co., Pa., 1842-43; Shrewsbury, Pa., 1843-73; Chambersburg, Pa., 1873-74; Sunbury, Pa., 1874-77; Leacock, Pa., 1877-84; m. Eliza A. Williams, 1842; 6 children; d. Feb. 6, 1884.

19

Catalogue cover   *Inside catalogue*

APPENDIX 16

Diary of a Journey to Virginia

Commenced April 14, 1841 by Rev. Gottleib Bassler

About 2 1/2 o'clock P.M. I started from Gettysburg and after a tolerably pleasant although fatiguing walk of 3 1/2 hours we arrived in Emmittsburgh. Brs. Bear and Gelweck accompanied me, (the latter of whom will stop here) I immediately went to Mr. Winter's and although I did not meet with that cordial and warm reception apparently which I had expected, my especial friend Miss Barbara having from home yet after this family recollected me again more distinctly I began to feel at home.

It happened that a bible Class was held at the house of "mine host" in this evening by Rev. Fries, pastor of the German Reformed Church. I was tolerable pleased with a few exceptions which I will not mention here.

After the dismission of the bible class I paid a short visit to old Mr. Gunnar ? who has been for some time confined to his bed by palsy. I had some religious conversation with the old gentleman in which I endeavored

Cover and first page of Gottleib's journal

to direct his mind to Jesus and then engaged in prayer with him.

I soon returned and after family worship (p.1) retired to my room when I enjoyed more of God's presence than for a week past. Glory be to his name.

April 15, 1841

Started from Emmetsburgh this morning about 8 1/2 o'clock A.M. without particularly calling on any one though I met with a few of my friends. We soon passed the sisterhood and crossed Yonis Creek and jogged as long with Mr. St. Mary's in view on our right for almost 6 or 7 miles. After going about 4 miles we had the village of Graceham in view to the SW. It looks pleasant at a distance. We had some trouble in crossing Keunt's Creek a few miles before we reached Creagerstown when we took a chum? when we arrived. We stopped better than an hour and a half here and I saw Mr. J. Williard and lady who were on their way to Jefferson. After we left C we met with no incident worthy of remark except that we fell in with an old toper? Who could scarcely walk with whom we had some talk. We arrived in Frederick City at sunset quite tired and stopped at the widow Lunian's ? After supper we went to Church and heard Mr. Kearkey preach. The sermon was on Rev. 3:20 and was very good. There is quite an interesting state of things in Br. Y C's Church about 25 or perhaps 30 persons appeared as mourners.

I have not enjoyed myself much spiritually today. But my room is cold and I must retire. God forgive me for Jesus sake. Amen (p.2)

April 16, 1841

Mr. Deavers Fred Co....? I.

This morning after enjoying the hospitality of Mrs. Luman in Frederick City and visiting Mr. Harrison's and Rev. Harkey's family we got started about 10 1/4 o'clock A.M. We walked middling briskly to Jefferson (7 miles) and stopped at Mr. Willard's where we were kindly invited to take dinner by Miss Willard. The old gentleman (71 in May next) is lying very ill and I conversed sometime with him and before I left united with him in prayer.

Left Jefferson about 2 1/2 o'clock P.M. and after a fatiguing walk of 6 miles we arrived at this place.

I passed today through Jefferson and Petersville crossed Cotorsiur ? passed by a Lutheran Church between Frederick and Jefferson and an Episcopalian and Papal between Jefferson and Petersville.

Health middling good. Spiritual health languishing.

April 19 1841

On Saturday morning left Mr. Deaver's at a reasonable hour and after a few hours walking arrived at Harper's Ferry. I was much pleased with the scenery about the place and with the public works and also with the hands in the workshops but the minions about the taverns and railroad were very impertinent and saucy. The workshops are a real curiosity. Division of labor is carried I presume to the highest pitch of perfection. The number of hands was however I thought small. The armory containing a great number of the instruments of death was also worth seeing. (p.3)

Newtown April 19th 1841

About 2 o'clock P.M. we started off in the cars for Winchester. When we were within about 7 miles of W. the train of bauxite cars was immediately before us and going at a middling rapid rate when suddenly the axle of the hindmost car which was very heavy laden with iron broke and the whole car was broken into pieces and the contents scattered on the road and down the banks which were high on both sides at this place. This accident caused a delay, (as we were not able to pass until the road was cleared, of about half an hour. We soon however got under way again and after a short time we were enabled to pass the bauxite cars and reach W at about 6 o'clock.

There we sought out Br. Stork (Stock?) who very kindly entertained us until this morning.

On Saturday evening we attended a prayer meeting in the lecture room of the Ev Lutheran Church. I was I have reason to believe benefited by the exercises.

On Sunday I went with Br. Eichelburger to a country congregation and spoke for him. I became acquainted with a few individuals here, but more especially with Stein's family where we took dinner.

In the evening I was to speak in the lecture room. After speaking some time I became very sick with a kind of fainting spell to which I am sometimes subject. I was obliged to sit down for a little while. After a short time however and after getting a drink of water I recovered and proceeded. (p.4)

Emmanuel's Church April 25th 1841

The exercises were protracted rather too long. In the evening Br. F again preached. There seemed during the day and in the evening much seriousness but Br. F layed them out completely by a talk of nearly two hours in length. When he was done nearly all seriousness had vanished and when the anxious were invited forward none appeared. I did not enjoy myself until the forepart of yesterday evening. But towards the close it nearly vanished. This morning I feel weak in body and dull and unsatisfied in soul.-

Mrs. Misers Augusta County, VA April 26

Started from father Kirch-hofs about 8 ½ or 9 o'clock A.M. and after traveling at quite a moderate gait until 1 ½ P.M. we arrived at Mr. Bear's on Jenning's Branch. There were three of us (Br and Sister Shickel and myself) in the carriage and we got along quite well. Br. Bear had not yet arrived at home and as his sister was very sick and a number of persons visited the family I did not feel myself justifiable in remaining with them, but continued with Br. Shickel's until we arrived at his mother-in-laws where we arrived about dusk. My bodily health has been quite as good as I could expect. My spiritual enjoyment has however not been so good. This morning I neglected to read my usual morning lesson as also at noon and I felt a coldness and indifference during the day. This evening however p. 10 I stole awhile away from every cumbering care I spent a few moments in solemn prayer to God and found more enjoyment in it than I found all day in other things- But on the whole I do not enjoy myself as I ought to do and might do by using the means which God places in my hands. May god of his infinite mercy help me to be more faithful for Jesus' sake-Amen-

Staunton, Va April 28th 1841

Yesterday morning I rode from Mrs. Misers to Br.Bittle's about two miles distant. Br. Bittle was not at home but as I had promised Br. Shickle to wait until he and Sister S would come to BBr. B's I was obliged to make the best of my time until about 3 o'clock P.M. when B S arrived and soon after Br. B. After some conversation we started on our return; but went almost immediately to Br. Shevey's (a short distance from Mrs. Miser's) where we spent the night. After breakfast we again made our way to Mother Lhuey's but soon started for this place. Br. L brought me on horse back. Truly he is kind to me as well as Sister S who has tried all to make me comfortable. Then I stopped at Mr. Heciskill's to whom as well as to one of his grand-daughters I had a letter of introduction from Br. C.P.Krauth. The old gentlemen is in his teens and is not very profitable company. And the old lady is in some respects reserved and seems to stand a little in her dignity. Miss Sowers called towards evening (p11) and is apparently a very fine lady. I had the pleasure to accompany her to prayer meeting at the

Presbyterian Church. The meeting was thinly attended and wanted life and action. Mr. Lowers the young lady's father led it in the absence of Mr. Stephenson the pastor. I was called upon to pray which I did or rather I made a prayer for it can be called nothing else. After seeing the young lady safe home I immediately returned to my lodging although invited to stop. My bodily health not so good; have a headache and do not feel so well on the whole. But spiritual health much worse. I seem to have lost all my religion for I feel nothing. It all seems cold calculating work. Oh! What God wants revive me for Jesus sake, Amen.

Mr. Daniel Kiser's April 30th 1841

Started from Staunton between 7 and 8 o'clock A.M. After a short time it began to rain and I stopped at the gate-house until 12 o'clock M when it ceased and I got under way and I arrived after some little trouble I found Mr. Kiser's where I had the pleasure of meeting Br. Wagner.

Staunton is a pleasant town situated in the midst of hills with some very pleasant and neat dwellings. There are three churches, Presbyterian, Methodist and Episcopalian with a large Sunday school attached to each. The Court-house is a neat building and the Lunatic Hospital is a large and beautiful edifice on a very excellent site. I did not visit it. (p.12)

There is also an asylum in a course of building for the blind and deaf and dumb. The situation I do not admire so much as that of the other. The foundation is laid and the wall in some places raised as high as the first story. I stopped at Mr. Peter Heiskill's to whom I had a letter of introduction from Mr. C.P.K. I also became acquainted with Miss Caroline L Lowers to whom I had also a letter from the same individual.

On my way hither I had a lamentable example of my cowardice and want of Christian zeal. For when I stopped at the gatehouse I could not bring myself to say a single word on the subject of personal and practical piety. It seems to me that by giving way to this mercenary spirit it has grown upon me until I have become unfit to bear the name of a Christian soldier. May God of his infinite mercy help me to become bold and fearless in his cause, for I feel that only through his blessing and grace can I do so. My spiritual enjoyment has been better since last evening than for some days I have been able to humble myself under God more lowly and I still feel that he will "never leave me nor forsake me." Bodily health is good now._____

May 1st 1841

Yesterday afternoon Br. W & myself took a ride to Mr. Aughy's a member of the Church. The gentleman was not at home himself but his lady was as also a young man who intends going to Gettysburg to study. He seems an excellent young man fully determined to give himself to God's service. The family appears to be pious and friendly. Thence we went to town (Waynesboro) It is a small town (p.13) of a few hundred inhabitants with some respectable dwelling houses in it. A very good Presbyterian church and an old dilapidated Methodist Church. There is also a small brick building for an academy. The Lutheran Church where I am to hold forth tomorrow is about 3 miles from town. I have not yet seen it. I am much pleased with Mr. Kiser's family. They are pious and very kind. On our home road yesterday we also visited Mr. Crouse's family. There was no one in the room except two daughters, one grown and the other nearly so and a small girl. The eldest daughter as also her mother is very pious-

This morning I have been making out a skeleton and studying a discourse for tomorrow. God help me to speak it in the fear of god, and give me wisdom and words to speak to his glory. Amen

Bodily health good. Have also enjoyed myself butter spiritually than for some days but do not feel <u>perfectly</u> satisfied with my attainments and condition. I feel a great and strong desire to become holier and more devoted in the cause of Christ and I feel a great assurance that God will grant me the grace. To him belongeth the work and the glory.

This morning rose rather late but had quite a solemn time in my private devotions. A little after nine o'clock I started with the family to the Church to Sunday school. The school was small but very orderly and seemed in a fair way to do good. I asked them the questions at the close of the school on Mark 6:30-44 (p.14) Some answered very well whilst others did not. Immediately after school the public services of the sanctuary commenced. The number present was rather small we did not enjoy much freedom in speaking. I addressed them from Exodus 17:12. They seemed on the whole attentive.

This afternoon Mr. Jonathan Kainer, a young man of interesting appearance and promising in every way was far as I could judge called at Mr. Kiser's and I had an opportunity of conversing with him, he has for some years been desirous of studying for the ministry. His father however being a Hunkelite? And unconverted would not give his assent. He unwilling to disobey his father, at least during his vicarage has served him faithfully and intends so to do until May 10h when he will be 21 when he will leave him and throw himself into the arms of the Ed Soc and go to Gettysburg to study.

This afternoon at 3 ½ o'clock I spoke German at the church to a small audience many of whom could not understand me. I felt bad and spoke with little or no effect. The remainder of the day I spent down in the family conversing on various subjects but non especially on religious subjects. This evening we sang some of the songs. Zion and I felt comparatively happy though I have reason to examine my own heart as I feel some uneasiness in my mind some degree of guilt. May God take it away for Jesus' sake.

My bodily health is not so very good. I felt weak on my breast today and speaking went hard (p.15) with me. This evening my throat does not feel so well and I have a little headache. My spiritual health is not so good as it might be. I feel an indescribable fear and dread of something. I know not what; a kind of a dissatisfied mind, or rather unsatisfied.

May 4th 1841

Morning. Yesterday did very little. Read Campbell's "Pleasure of Hope" Book I and studied some little at a sermon. At 10 A.M. rode in company with Miss Kiser to town and called at the post office and got no letter but the Observer which I combed over after my return. In the afternoon Br. Wagner returned and we spent the evening mostly together. A circumstance came to my knowledge which excited my sympathies very much. A colored man, who is married to one of Mr. K's colored women is owned by some man across a the mountain, who inherited him from his parent's. When they died they requested that he might be free which the son has most shamefully neglected to do. This colored man has now been hired out by his young master for a number of years and being an intelligent and smart man has earned for him about $1200. Now the master is in want of money and wishes to sell the poor slave unless he can redeem himself but to make his case desperate if possible he demands $1200 more for his release. It needs no comment, it speaks for itself.

My bodily health has been tolerably good. Spiritual enjoyment very imperfect. I cannot realize (16) I cannot realize fully that my name is written above in the Lamb's book of life. Doubts and a kind of foreboding fears seem to rest upon me. But I am determined to act honestly with myself. And not to rest until I can rest fully in Jesus. This morning I had more spiritual enjoyment than I have had for some time more nearness to God in prayer but do not feel the joys of world to come as I desire and as it is my privilege to do.

May 5th 1841

Did but little today; remained at home except that I went out fishing, during which time I thought of the Savior's words when he called Andrew and Peter "Follow me and I will make you fishers of men." I now hope however that when I go forth by the grace of God and under his guidance I shall meet with better success than I did today. Tomorrow I start to Armentrout's to assist Br. Shickle.

I felt rather languid and dull today in body. However feel more of confidence in Jesus this evening than I have for some days. My soul seems stayed on Jesus my adorable Savior. Oh! That I could rest entirely and fully on him and that continually god grant it for Jesus' sake Amen

Mr. Samuel Sheet's Rockingham County May 6th 1841

Started at about 7 A.M. and rode at a moderate gait. Passed some beautiful scenery between Mr. K's and Mt. Meridian. Crossed Middle and North rivers besides some little branches. Had my (17) horse fed at Mr. Kiblinger's Tavern. No charge. Arrived about 5 ½ O'clock. Br. Shickle came to the house at about 7 and we then went to a neighbors and had prayer meeting. About 20 were in attendance. There was much seriousness. Br. S tells me about 40 individuals are under conviction in the neighborhood. Several have found peace and pardon. This part of the country is rough in the face of its country and dark in morals and intellect. There seems however to be a stir going on among the people God seems to be stretching out his hand among these people and the slain of the Lord are many.

I feel well but tired and drowsy from m ride. This also destroys my spiritual enjoyment. May God clear up my horizon and may he, by his holy Spirit prepare me for proclaiming his truth among this people. Amen.

Mr. Lewis Kirchhof's Rockingham co. VA May 7th 1841

Rose late this morning, breakfast being nearly ready but after breakfast I enjoyed some time in reading God's blessed word. About 9 A.M. we started to church. There were a reasonable number present. Br. Shickel first spoke to the catechumens and we had several prayers after which I spoke to the congregation for about half an hour. We then dismissed them intending to have meeting in the evening. (p.18) After the people were dismissed I went home with Br.Kirchhof whose wife is serious. Then I had a practical conversation with Br. Kirchhof and his brother who lives close by and also with Mrs. Kirchhof. With the former two I conversed on prayer in general and family prayer especially and with the latter on repentance and faith.

About 5 ½ we started to the church through the rain. To secure myself I put on Br. K's overcoat. There were five at church and we concluded after having a good prayer meeting to dismiss the people in order that they might reach dome before dark.

After supper I had a conversation with Old Mother K. I tried to keep the Apostolic injunction "the old women as mothers" When we had sung several hymns the family retired and I am now alone with god

Bodily health middling good

Spiritual strength much renewed this evening. May God help. Yes

Bridgewater May 12th 1841

Arrived here with Br. Shickel yesterday evening I felt somewhat unwell and much fatigued and very drowsy but this morning I begin to feel a little better having taken a good dose of Braudreth's.

The meeting at A church was quite interesting. On Saturday morning I spoke at the church in German and Br. Sheperdson, a dicentiate of the Rev. Lynan in English. The meeting was solemn and interesting. In the evening we had meeting at Mr. H Sheets. The meeting was solemn and good. I remained at Mr. Hassler's (p.19) „„All soon, however

German and Br. Shickle followed in English. The house was much crowded and was not so quiet as it might have been. After Br. Shickle closed the Lord's supper was administered. It was a solemn time although I did not enjoy it so much as I might have done. Before preaching however about 28 persons were added by the solemn rite of confirmation to the church most of whom had already or have since expressed a hope of pardoned sin. The congregation seemed much moved and I trust impressions were made which will be matters of rejoicing though out all eternity.

In the evening there was preaching in the Church the first time a candle had ever been seen burning in the church since its erection perhaps more than twenty years ago. Although the evening was dead yet a considerable number of persons were present. Br. Shepherdson preached. I stayed at Mr. Isaac Baltirns. Monday morning we had a meeting at Church. I spoke first and Br. Shickle followed me. There were a considerable number of persons present who were very attentive although we were both lengthy in our addresses to them. In the evening there was an interesting meeting at Mr. Sheet's house where I remained all night. On Tuesday morning we had meeting at Mr. Lamil Sleuts. It was very interesting. In the back of the U.Brethren Church, who preached on Monday evening was also present and after I had spoken he gave an exhortation. The meeting was very interesting. At almost 1 ½ o'clock PM we started for this place.

I did not enjoy myself much at the meeting until yesterday morning when I was enabled to look with an humble simple faith to Jesus which I have not for a long time if ever in the same degree enjoyed. I could look to Jesus and trust to him alone. OH! That I may ever enjoy it. Thou blessed lamb of God help me ever to listen to thy voice and trust in thee.

Mr. Kiser's May 13th 1841

Arrived at about 2 ½ o'clock after a middling pleasant although lonesome road. I left Bridgewater yesterday afternoon and after wandering about considerable in consequence of having lost myself I arrived at Mr. M Bear's on Jenning's Branch where I expected to meet Br. Jacob B but was disappointed, he having gone to Br. Bittle's the day before. I however staid all night and talked with the folks. A daughter has for some time been very ill but is recovering slowly. She is a very pious and interesting young (p.21) female. I conversed with her and found her in a most delightful frame of mind. Instead of gloom and dejection being seated on her countenance she appears more like a bride ready for the happy hour. Oh what can not religion do? This is a young lady just in that period of life when she might be supposed to desire life and when death would be most unwelcome not only perfectly resigned to suffer but even happy and rejoicing under it and willing to depart and be with the Lord. When I think of Father Miller and Br. Lease and then of this young lady I must say Bless the Lord. Oh! My soul and all that is in me bless his Holy name. A serious accident happened on Monday evening in this neighborhood. A young lady Miss Ale A Crouse was riding to meeting on horseback she was thrown off. Had her right arm broken and was otherwise so severely injured that she is not expected to recover.

There was no particular excitement here at the meeting. I did not feel so well this morning but feel much better now. My faith has been somewhat clouded although I still have a good confidence yet my soul does not appear to enjoy it so much. But by the grace of God I will not rest satisfied until I am back in the smiles of my Jesus and feel like persuading all to come to him. God help me for Jesus' sake. (22)

Mr. Kiser's May 27th 1841

On Sunday morning I endeavored to preach in Zion's church. I spoke entirely too long and became exhausted before I was near done. Some of the people too seemed wearied.

About 2 ½ o'clock Br. W., Mr. Kiser and I started to synod about 22 miles distant. We met with some rain and I became damp but fortunately it was warm or it might have injured me very much. When we arrived it was almost night and we put up at Mr. Kibluzer's. There was no preaching in the evening. On Monday morning 8 ½ o'clock the Synod was organized. Mr. Eichelberger was chosen Pres. Mr. Bittle , Secretary and Mr…. treasurer. There were present 10 ministerial brethren viz: ordained ministers, Eichelbeerger, Bittle, Riemuisynder, Miller, Stork, Davis, Licentiales, Shickel, Wagner, Baker and Shepherdson. Messr. Hamilton, Schniucher, Oswald, Layford and Shaffer were absent. At 11 o'clock the Synod adjourned and Mr. Stork preached from the words" it is it well with thee." The sermon was good. The sacrament of the Lord's supper was then administered to a large number of communicants (large for the place) and truly it was delightful to surround the blessed cloister's table with so many dear brethren who seemed full of the love of Jesus. May we all walk in the strength of that food for many days. At 3 in the afternoon the Synod again met and a little after 5 adjourned to give place to preaching. Mr. Shepherdson preached. The audience was small owing principally to the fact that the weather was very bad. I staid during this night at a Widow Pence's about 2 miles from the church.

On Tuesday morning Synod met at 8 A.M. and remained in session until 11 o'clock when Mr. Baker preached. Synod again met at 2P.M. and in the course of an hour or two concluded its business. Their Education Society then held a meeting. A smart little discussion took place in this body with regard to the appropriation of monies by the Parent Society. But after almost saying some hard things the whole matter was dismissed and left as it was. After the Education Society adjourned the Missionary Society had a meeting in which nothing was done. After this the ministers withdrew to hold a ministerial session and in the mean time a very good prayer meeting was held in the church conducted by Brother Shickel.

At early candlelight Br. Rech from Indianapolis preached an excellent sermon. Then Br. Eichelberger made a number of appropriate remarks previous to the ordination of Brs. (p28) Wagner & Shickel. This ceremony was very impressive and solemn and caused many serious reflections to pass through my mind concerning my fitness and ability for the sacred office to which they were now set apart by the laying on of hands.

After this thrilling ceremony the anxious were invited to take front seats to be conversed with and prayed for. There were some went forward but I do not know the number. This night Mr. Kiser and myself went to a Mr. Parkey's a nephew of Mr. K.

Yesterday Mr. K and I started off through the rain in order to get home. In our way we visited the celebrated cave in this neighborhood called Weyer's (Grand Canyons) It is a wonderful exhibition of the works of the great Creator. And although I have the outlines of many of the rooms and yet quite distinctly in my mind yet I feel myself entirely unable to enter into a description. In some of the rooms the floor was beautifully level, in others rough and uneven, some have something of an angular figure in their outlines whilst most of them are entirely irregular. There are particular designations for almost every prominent room and rock and hole. There are Congress Hall, Senate chamber, Washinton Hall, the taveran, the steak house (a rock in which suspends from the ceiling is called a leg of mutton) Jacob's ice house. One place somewhat resembling an elevator seat is called Soloman's seat and a rock near it his pillow; a large rock in the centre of Washington Hall is called Washinton's national monument; another rock is called the "lugman's nose" One place is called the falls of Niagara. This is a beautiful sight very much resembling the tumbling of water down a beautiful cascade. Another beautiful white rock is called the snowy mountains. We were also admitted into sbar room where we saw many beautiful examples of chrystalized carlemate of lime. But I might go on describing these and various other things if time (p.29) and talent would allow it. But I must cease saying "How wonderful are thy works Oh! Lord God of Hosts" At Synod I became more or less acquainted with all the brethren of the Rev Synod and was much pleased with them all. I also became acquainted with Br. Keck and was quite delighted with him. He is an old soldier of Jesus who has been in the foremost rank, nay in advance of the whole Lutheran band in many a well fought battle. May the God of Israel continue to be with him through life for Jesus sake.

My spiritual health has been tolerable good. I have had much exercise of mind which I trust will be profitable to me. I have also been near Pisgalis' top several times. My bodily health is feeble and I feel somewhat discouraged in reference to it but I will continue to God and trust in him alone. Amen may I do so.

May 28ᵗʰ 1841

Yesterday afternoon rode to Mr. Bush's to take the horse home which I have been riding for some time. On my way thither I called at Ms Crouse to see Mary Ann (the lady who was so badly hurt a few weeks ago) I had some very edifying conversation with her. Her soul seems continually stayed upon Jesus and although she is still obliged to lie in the same position and to endure much pain she is enabled to rejoice in Jesus her Savior. She seems to enjoy a clearness of spiritual view which few do. Before I left I engaged in prayer with her after reading a few portions of scripture. And

God enabled me to pour out my soul in prayer before him not only for her but for her mother and the rest of the family.

I went immediately thence to Mr. Bush's where I (30) spent some time in conversation with the old gentleman and lady. Came home about 7 ½ o'clock PM spent the evening in conversation with the family and afterwards with Br. Wagner.

My spiritual enjoyment is not so great as I am privileged to possess. I find so much carelessness, so much favoring and fearing of man, so little energy and zeal in the cause of my Master that I am almost inclined to sit down in despair and conclude that I can do nothing. But why would I do so. Why not go forward in the strength of my Master to glorify his name and do good to the souls of my fellowmen. May God help me for Jesus' sake Amen Bodily health delicate.

Kneisley's Hotel, Shenandoah Co. June 3rd 1841

On Friday last remained all day at Mr. Kisser's having no horse to ride out. On Saturday Mr. K, Br. W and I went to Tinkling Spring Church in Augusta Co. to attend a conference meeting. There were not many present. Mr. Geyer of the Methodist and Mr. Smith of the Presbyterian Churches delivered addresses. A society was then formed on the principles of total abstinence and considerable part of those present joined. On the evening an adjourned meeting was held in Waynesboro. Few present. Br. W and I made a few remarks. Several men made a few remarks in opposition. Some also joined him (31) On Sunday I spoke at Zion's in the morning , in the afternoon I visited a poor family in the neighborhood.

On Monday morning Mr. Bush sent one of his son's to accompany me some distance on horseback and bring back the horse on which I rode. And which belonged to Mr. Keiser. Br. W started with us and accompanied us about 11 mies. Young Mr. B took me about 20 miles. I then walked a few miles to Friedens Church where I met with BR. Shickle. Br. Keck and Br. Fut? In the evening I spoke a short time at the Church. There were during the day and in the evening 3 mourners and considerable seriousness in the congregation.

On Friday morning a young Br. Lutz took me on horseback about 11 miles to Mr. Sarnel Nut's in the neighborhood of Arnesstrout's. He sent a hand with me about 10 miles further within six miles of New Market to which place I walaked and stopped at Mr. Bear's. In the evening by candle-light I spoke to considerable congregation in the Lutheran Church. I did not enjoy much freedom in speaking but was a little scared. This morning (Wednesday) I started at an early hour from Mr. Bear's walked 7 mi to Mr. Jackson for breakfast. Then to Woodstock for dinner where however I staid too long and instead of setting to Strasburgh as I had expected I remained 5 mi south of it.(32) My spiritual enjoyment during part of this time was good and during other parts not so good; but I have? Than heretofore endured whenever I might be; to carry out my Christian character. Yesterday I got in company with a man who swore I reproved him and instead of becoming angry, as I feared he would do, the man seemed grateful and we conversed considerable after that on religious matter. Today Br. Tabler met me. He seems almost distracted. He became led on by his cares and the temptations of the Devil, intoxicated in Frederick City, Maryland and was found in company and in rather a plight with a woman of ill repute of which he declared to me however he was entirely unconscious. I pitied him and directed him to go to his offended Savior for forgiveness and show by his future conduct that his repentance is sincere. He seemed completely bowed down and asked me to pray for him which I promised to do. My bodily health has been about as good as I could expect in my situation. I drank much water, walked fast in the sun and now, notwithstanding, feel quite well. Thank God for it. (33)

Gettysburgh June 6th 1841

On Thursday morning left Mr. Kneisley's. In the evening I had been very sick after I retired to my room and did not feel wo well when I started as was desirable but I trudged along until I reached Strasburgh where I stopped at Mr. Kearn's for breakfast. About 8 I left this and went on until I came near Newtown when I turned off for Br. Davis' and stopped with him about 3 hours and took dinner. Thence I made the best of my way to Winchester and stayed all night with Br. Eichelberger. Br. Davis lives with his father-in-law Mr. Hemmings.

On Friday morning I left Mr. E before the family were up and started in the cars for Frederick where we arrived between 10 to11. There I visited Br. Hearly, Mr. Harrisons and Mrs. Lunian and in the afternoon walked about 10 miles almost exhausted with the extreme heat of the sun.

Saturday morning after doctoring my feet I walked two miles to Creagerstown for breakfast then 10 miles to Emmetsburg where I took dinner and then toiled home 10 miles more before sundown sometime. I thank God that I am still in the land of the living and again here although I bear much I shall not be able to study much unless my health becomes better. May God grant it for Jesus' Thus endeth the first lesson.

For further research on Pastor Bassler:

Passavant Center (basement)
Greenville, P A
Tri-Synod Archives

Passavant Center
Thiel College, Greenville Pa 46125
Sally Roth
Lutheran Church

Greenville Church Archives
Tue and Thurs 9-noon
724-589-2131
home: 724-588-8883

Pastor Journals 1839 1842 1848 1868
Folder 1837-1842 Henry Muntz
5 Small book of Church minutes
Synod Histories 1905 1925 1959 p.83   Pittsburgh

APPENDIX 17

Taken from

The History of the Pittsburgh Synod of the General Synod of the Evangelical Lutheran Church: 1748, 1845, 1904

by Ellis Beaver Burgess

During this same period, the West Pennsylvania Synod had nineteen representatives on the field, while the MInisiterium of Pennsylvania had but twelve. A number of our General Synod churches were served for many years by the devoted pioneers of the Ohio Synod. We owe them much. When the Pittsburgh Synod was organized there were twenty-nine Lutheran pastors (serving about one hundred churches) in this section of the State. Of these twenty-nine pastors, seventeen were members of the Ohio Synod. The Allegheny Synod men numbered but seven. Under such circumstances, we cannot but express regret that the Ohio Synod had such a small part in the organization and development of the Pittsburgh Synod whose missionary energies have made the Evangelical Lutheran Church one of the commanding religious forces of western Pennsylvania. (P.48)

Chapter II the Organization 1845 "Other foundation can no man lay than that is laid, which is Jesus Christ"

For many years before the Pittsburgh Synod was organized the need of such an organization was most keenly felt. The pastors felt their need of it in order that they might enjoy a closer fellowship with each other, and carry on their home mission work more effectively. The people felt their need of it, in order that they might be supplied more readily with suitable pastors. It was this need that led seven of the Lutheran pastors of Ohio and western Pennsylvania to hold a "special conference in the old Mount ion church of Baidland, Pa on the 17th day of October, 1812. When this "special conference" was reported to the MInisterium of Pennsylvania, in June, 1813 that body officially expressed its gratification that their brethren on the frontier were "so active in the spread of the kingdom of God;" but when this first conference was followed by another in 1813, and another in 1814 and the members of the conference began to ask for themselves certain privileges which had always been regarded as the special privileges of the Synod, the leaders of the Synodical body began to show a decided disapproval. In 1816 the conference requested permission of the "Mother Synod" to organize themselves into a separate Ministerium, but their request was not granted. It was not the policy of the Ministerium of Pennsylvania to encourage the formation of new Synods, and the Evangelical Lutheran Synod of Ohio was therefore organized under protest, in the year 1818. The Ministerium also protested against the organization of the West Pennsylvania Synod in 1825; and the West Pennsylvania Synod protested against the organization of the Alleghany Synod in 1842. And there was more or (p.49) the Synod in 1845, it was under very different conditions. The organization of the Alleghany Synod had taken up the eastern half of the proposed territory and the now thoroughly organized Eastern District of the Ohio Synod was opposed to it. This opposition was partly due to the fact that the Eastern District regarded the movement as an intrusion, but it was also due to doctrinal difference. Four of the men most interested in the proposed organization, namely, Rev. W.A. Passavant, **Rev. Gottlieb Bassler,** Rev. G.F. Ehrenfeld and Rev. Samuel D. Witt were Gettysburg men, and the Ohio Synod had already begun to show quite a decided aversion toward the Gettysburg theology. In a sermon delivered before the Eastern District, in 1843, Rev. J.G.C. Schweizerbarth said: " *Those who come from Gettysburg are, with few exceptions, anti-Lutheran. They neither believe the entire catechism nor the entire Augsburg Confession. Can those who tear down the foundations of the Church build up the same? In short, the ministry for the church, under the assistance of Almighty God must come from Columbus." These men were especially averse to the "new measure" spirit of Rev. W.A. Passavant. It was a type of religion with which none of them had any sympathy. The movement for the organization of the new Synod began shortly after Rev. W.A. Passavant took charge of the First English Evangelical Lutheran church of Pittsburgh. The preliminary meeting was held, August 27-28. 1844 in Butler, Pennsylvania and was attended by Rev. W.A. Passavant, **Rev. Gottlieb Bassler**, Rev. Elihu Rathbun, Rev. John Esensee and Rev. Gottlieb Kranz. Fifteen years later, **Rev. Bassler** spoke of this meeting as the meeting of "a few brethren who wept and prayed over the desolations of our Zion." All of these men expressed themselves as being heartily in favor of the organization of a new Synod, but Rev. John Esensee and Rev. Gottlieb Kranz never entered it. It was decided to hold the next meeting in Pittsburgh in the following January. Full notice of this meeting and its object was given to all the Lutheran pastors of

*Schmidt and Peters"'Geschicthe Der Allgemeinen Ev. Luth.Synode von Ohio" p. 87 As a further evidence of this opposition of the Ohio Synod to the Gettysburg Theology, see letter of **Rev. Bassler** to the President of the West Pennsylvania Synod in 1843. (p.51)

Less opposition to the organization of the Pittsburgh Synod in 1845, especially on the part of the Synod of Ohio. These facts do not all appear upon the Synodical records, but they are none the less true. In the year 1831 a special conference of the Lutheran pastors of western Pennsylvania was held in Greensburg, Pa to discuss the advisability of organizing a new Synod on the territory now occupied by the Alleghany and Pittsburgh Synods. This conference was attended by the following pastors

Rev. Jacob Krigler, Berlin Pa of the West Pennsylvania Synod
Rev J.G.C. Schweizerbarth, Zelienople Pa of the Ohio Synod
Rev. Michael J. Steck Greensburg Pa of the Ohio synod
Rev. Jonas Mechling, Westmoreland Co.,Pa of the Ohio Synod
Rev. Gabriel A. Reichart, Kittanning, Pa of the West Pennsylvania Synod
Rev. J.C.F. Heyer, Somerset, Pa of the West Pennsylvania Synod
Rev. N.G. Scharretts, Indiana,Pa of the West Pennsylvania Synod
Rev. John Brown, Washington Co., Pa of the West Pennsylvania Synod
Rev. Henry David Keyl, Clarion Co. Pa of the West Pennsylvania synod
Rev. Daniel Heilig, Erie, Pa of the West Pennsylvania Synod.

The opinion of these ten men was that the formation of a new Synod was greatly desirable and a resolution to this effect was unanimously adopted. Rev. Schweizerbarth was instructed to lay the matter before the Ohio Synod at its next meeting but when he presented the petition it was met with manifest disapproval * A play waws then adopted by which the Synod was divided into conference districts to each of which such special privileges were granted that the Pennsylvania pastors of the Synod were satisfied, *and the first attempt to organize a Pittsburgh Synod resulted in failure.*

When the second and successful attempt was made to organize (p.50) western Pennsylvania; but when the brethren assembled in the First English Lutheran Church of Pittsburgh on the evening of January 14, 1845, only eight of the twenty-nine men laboring on the territory were present. These eight men were:

Bishop Michael J. Steck, Greensburg Pa, representing 7 churches with 1,005 members

Bishop William A. Passavant, Pittsburgh, Pa representing 1 church with 175 members

Bishop Gottlieb Bassler, Zelienople, Pa representing 5 churches with 208 members

Bishop George F. Ehrenfeld, Clarion, Pa representing 2 churches with 100 members

Bishop Samuel David Witt, Shippenville, Pa representing 2 churches with 201 members

Bishop David Earhart, Leechburg, Pa representing 4 churches with 181 members

Bishop Abraham Weills, Ginger Hill, Pa representing 2 churches with 275 members

Bishop Elihu rathbun, Mercer, Pa representing 3 churches with 110 members.

Accompanying and co-operating with them were six laymen, representing the principal parishes: Jacob S. Steck of Greensburg; George Weyman of Pittsburgh; C.S. Passavant of Zelienople; James Griffin of Mercer county; Frederick Carstens, of Washington county and Joseph Shoop of Freeport. All of these founders of our Synod have been called to their reward. These eight pastors exerted a larger influence in the Lutheran life of western Pennsylvania than their members would seem to indicate. While they reported but twenty-six churches under their care, there were more than a score of others that were looking to them for the bread of life. The people expected great things from them, and they were not disappointed. The founders believed that they were call of God to a great work, and of this we have the clearest evidence in the Minutes of their Pittsburgh Convention. "Several hours were spent in friendly discussion" of the question of the advisability of the proposed organization. Finally a committee was appointed, consisting of Rev. W.A. Passavant, Rev. M. J. Steck, Rev. G.F. Ehrenfeld, (p.52)

Frederick A. Carstens and James Griffin, who prepared and submitted the following "plan of Union:"

"we the undersigned ministers and delegates of the Evangelical Lutheran Churches in the western counties of Pennsylvania being painfully sensible of the great destitution of the preached word and the ordinances of the gospel in our midst, and fully persuaded of the necessity of uniting our efforts for their supply, hereby form ourselves into a synodical body, with the express understanding that each minister and church or churches shall be at perfect liberty to support such literary, theological or benevolent institutions, without the limits of our Synod, as may best accord with their own views of duty; and also that as a Synodical body, we recognize no such distinctions among us as those commonly known by the terms of *old and new measures* the Synod to be known by the name of *The Pittsburgh Synod of the Evangelical Lutheran Church.*"

This "plan of union" was unanimously and heartily adopted...

2. **Rev. Gottlieb Bassler** was born in the Canton of Berne, Switzerland, in the year 1813. His parents emigrated to Butler county, Pennsylvania when he was but a child. He was brought up in a humble home and

THE ORGANIZATION. **53**

FOUNDERS OF THE PITTSBURGH SYNOD.

DAVID EARHART.		GOTTLIEB HASSLER.
MICHAEL J. STECK.	ABRAHAM WEILLS.	WILLIAM A. PASSAVANT.
G. F. EHRENFELD.	S. D. WITT.	ELIHU RATHBUN.

learned the printer's trade, working in Greensburg, Pa and Washington, D.C. In 1836 he began to study for the ministry and received his classical and theological training in the institutions of the General Synod at Gettysburg. He was naturally of a sincere and pious disposition and was much beloved by his classmates. Receiving a pastor's license from the West Pennsylvania synod, in 1842, he returned to his Butler county home and began the work of building up the English Lutheran church. In a short time, he organized churches at Zelienople, Butler, Riders, Prospect and Middle Lancaster, all of which are now in a thriving condition. His salary was so small, at first, that he was subjected to not a little hardship, but he toiled on, like the true, brave servant of the Lord that he was and wrought a splendid work. In addition to his pastoral work, he had to bear the heaviest burden of th synodical Academy, and his health was not strong enough to endure it. His love for the Synod was a passion; all her interests were his. Among the last words that he spoke on earth were: "God bless the Pittsburgh Synod." He took a deep interest in the organization of the General Council and was elected President of the Reading Convention. The men of the General Synod, very generally recognized and respected the sincerity of his Lutheran convictions, and admired even while they opposed him. He died (57) October 3, 1868, mourned by all those who knew him. As an evidence of the high esteem in which he was held, the Pittsburgh Synod of the General Synod adopted the following memorial:

"Inasmuch as our Heavenly Father has been pleased to remove from this scene of toil and care to the realms of glory our dearly beloved brother, **Rev Gottlieb Bassler**; and.

"Whereas, He has so long, so earnestly, and so successfully been laboring in the Master's cause in our midst; and, as the righteous are ever to be held in reverent remembrance, therefore;

"Resolved 1. That our departed brother, by his unassuming piety, Christian courtesy, conscientious devotion to principle and self-denying labors for Christ, has endeared himself to us all.

"Resolved 2. That 'he was a faithful man and feared God above many; that we feel thankful to God for his example, and will ever hold in grateful remembrance his virtues, and will strive to profit by them.

"Resolved 3 That by his death we are again admonished to renewed diligence and faithfulness in our holy work.

"Resolved 4. That we tender our sincere sympathies to the afflicted family, and pray that our kind Father may, by his comforting grace, sustain them in their heavy bereavement." (58)

...This missionary constitution was the battle flag of the Pittsburgh Synod. Under it her grandest victories have been achieved....

...In 1850, at the earnest request of Mr. Adam Keffer, Rev. Gottlieb Bassler was sent on a missionary tour to Canada. He found the Lutherans of the Province in great spiritual destitution. After spending several weeks with them, journeying from settlement to settlement, baptizing the children and conducting divine services in their churches and school-houses, he returned to Pennsylvania and published a full account of his journey in *The Missionary*. A large interest was created at once. The Pittsburgh Synod determined to send them missionaries; and by the liberal help of the Ministerium of Pennsylvania, accomplished such a good work that on July 18, 1861 The Evangelical Lutheran Synod of Canada was organized...(p.78)

...**Rev. Gottlieb Bassler**, good man as he was, served four years as a licensed candidate. The committees appointed by the Synod to examine candidates for the ministry treated each case on its merits and reported accordingly. They had no words of flattery to waste on any applicant, believing that the publication of a critical report was a good thing for the intellectual and moral improvement of the candidate... (81)

...the average salary received by Pittsburgh Synod pastors, from 1845 to 1867 was about $300.00. in addition to the usual perquisites from marriages, baptisms, etc.

It was during this period of synodical history that the Civil War occurred. Naturally, it had a very depressing effect upon the life and progress of the Church. It could not have been otherwise. The Lutherans of western Pennsylvania, as a class were loyal in their support of the government. When the Pittsburgh Synod met at Canton, Ohio, in 1861, the following action was taken unanimously:

Resolved 1. That the unanimous conviction of this synod is that it is the duty of the Church to bring to the aid of the Government, not only her effectual, fervent prayers to Him who appointed the powers that be, but also the moral force of an outspoken declaration

Resolved 2. That we recognize in the policy of the General government toward those in rebellion, a just and righteous war. ... (p.84)

The convention proposed in the "Fraternal Address" of the Synod of Pennsylvania , met in Reading, Pa on the evening of December11, 1866. Rev. Gottlieb Bassler, of the Pittsburgh Synod delegation was elected chairman of the convention before he had arrived at the place of meeting...The friends of the General synod in the Pittsburgh Synod for the sake of unity were willing to endure the"independency" thrust upon them by the action of the previous year; but they could not endure the "General Councilism," which was thrust upon them by the Reading Convention. The majority party offered no compromises. Indeed, if the principles of Professor Loy's sermon at Reading were to be carried out, and every Lutheran compelled to "hold the same faith in the same truth, having the same confession of the same faith, and the same judgment under the same confession," it was impossible to offer any compromise. Long before the first delegate arrived in Greenville, it had been decided by the leaders to carry the Synod into the proposed General Council at any cost. (p.100)

Uncompromising Lutheran particularity and General Synod Lutheran catholicity could no longer dwell in the same house, and rupture was inevitable. The "Fundamental Principles of Faith and Church Polity," as adopted by the Synod at Greenville, are herewith presented:

Article IX In thus formally accepting and acknowledging the Unaltered Augsburg Confession, we declare our conviction that the other Confessions of the Evangelical Lutheran Church, inasmuch as they set forth none other than its system of doctrine, and articles of faith, are of necessity pure and Scriptural. Preeminent among such accord and, pure and Scriptural statements of doctrine, by their intrinsic excellence, by the great and necessary ends for which they were prepared by their historical position and by the general judgment of the Church, are these: the Apology of the Augsburg Confession, the Smalcald Articles, the Catechism of Luther and the Formula of Concord, all of which are with the Unaltered Augsburg Confession, in the perfect harmony of one and the same Scriptural faith.

On the adoption of Article IX the yea and nay vote stood as follows:

Yeas. Pastors Rev. M. Kughler, Rev. G.A. Wentzel, Rev. W.A. Passavant, ,(p.102) Rev. David Earhart, plus 58 more. Nays totaled 21. (p.103)

The minority party thereupon prepared and presented to the Syod the following solemn protest and request….the request was ot granted and the petitioners…withdrew from the convention.

And thus the curtain falls upon one of the saddest scenes in the history of the Pittsburgh Synod. A breach was made in the Evangelical Luttheran Church of western Pennsylvania that has not been healed even to the present day…(105)

APPENDIX 18

Thiel College Catalogue 1877-78

William G. Bassler

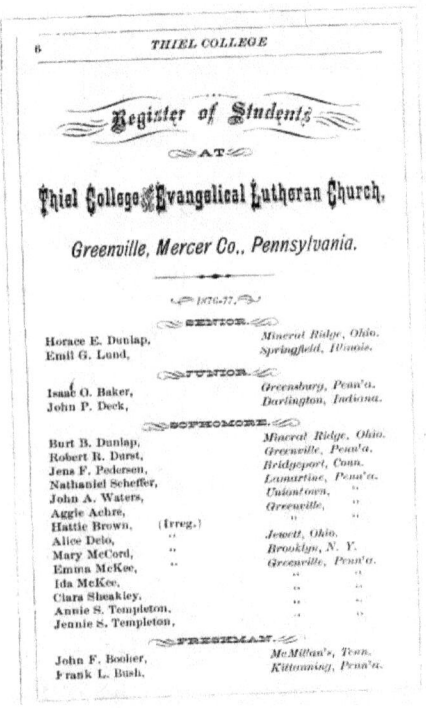

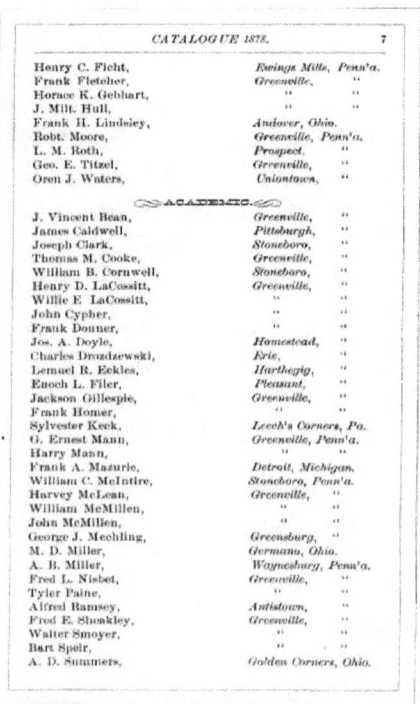

THIEL COLLEGE (page 8)

William Swingle,	Prospect, Penn'a.
John Templeton,	Greenville, "
Walter R. Titzel,	Bridgewater, Nova Scotia.
Rufus Wile,	Greenville, Penn'a.
Olive Bean,	" "
Laura Campbell,	" "
Sadie Cooke,	" "
Sadie LaCossitt,	" "
Nettie Dunn,	Mercer, Penn'a.
Della Garber,	Pittsburgh, Penn'a.
Kate Kennedy,	Greenville, "
Sadie Leech,	" "
Melisan McLean,	Lamartine, "
Clara Scheffer,	Greenville, "
Annie Smith,	Prospect, "
Emma Swingle,	Greenville, "
Annie Titzel,	" "

1872-78.

SENIOR.

Isaac O. Baker,	Greensburg, Penn'a.
John P. Deck,	Darlington, Indiana.

JUNIOR.

Burt B. Dunlap,	Mineral Ridge, Ohio.
Robert R. Durst,	Greenville, Penn'a.
Dettmar L. Passavant,	Pittsburgh, "
John A. Waters,	Uniontown, "
Aggie Achre,	Greenville, "
Hattie Brown, (Irreg.)	Jewett, Ohio.
Alice Delo,	Greenville, Penn'a.
Ida McKee,	" "
Clara Sheakley,	" "
Annie S. Templeton,	" "
Jennie S. Templeton,	" "

SOPHOMORE.

John F. Booher,	McMillan's, Tenn.
Henry C. Fieht,	Ewings Mills, Penn'a.
Frank Fletcher,	Greenville, "
Horace K. Gebhart,	" "
J. Milt. Hall,	" "
Frank H. Lindsley,	Andover, Ohio.

CATALOGUE 1878. (page 9)

Robt. Moore,	(Irreg.)	Greenville, Penn'a.
L. M. Roth,		Prospect, "
Geo. E. Titzel,		Greenville, "
Oren J. Waters,		Uniontown, "

FRESHMAN.

Albert J. Graepp,	Neustadt, Canada.
G. Ernest Mann,	Greenville, Penn'a.
George J. Mechling,	Greensburg, "
M. D. Miller,	Germano, Ohio.
Alfred Ramsey,	Antistown, Penn'a.
David Snodgrass,	Jamestown, "
Emma Bond,	Greenville, "
Sadie Brown,	" "
Sadie Leech,	" "
Evelyn Miller,	" "
Clara Packard,	" "
Effie Reznor,	" "
Annie Smith,	" "
Mary West,	" "

ACADEMIC.

James T. Armstrong,	Greenville, Penn'a.
T. Merrill Austin,	" "
Edward Baker,	Greensburg, "
William G. Bassler,	Zelienople, "
Norman Bean,	Greenville, "
J. Vincent Bean,	" "
Franklin H. Bortz,	" "
Alvin O. Burnett,	Coalburg, Ohio.
James Caldwell,	Pittsburgh, Penn'a.
Charles Caldwell,	" "
William Campbell,	Greenville, "
Thomas M. Cooke,	" "
William B. Cornwell,	Stoneboro, "
Henry D. LaCossitt,	Greenville, "
Willie E. LaCossitt,	" "
John Cypher,	Jewett, Ohio.
Alonzo Delo,	Homestead, "
Jos. A. Doyle,	Pleasant, "
William G. Emery,	" "
Enoch L. Filer,	" "
Thomas Filer,	" "
Jackson Gillespie,	Greenville, "
Uriah O. Heilman,	Rosston, "

THIEL COLLEGE (page 12)

MATHEMATICS—Arithmetic, Algebra through Quadratics.

GERMAN—Whitney's German Grammar, Erzaehlung.

GREEK—Harkness' or White's First Lessons, Goodwin's Grammar, Anabasis, or their equivalents.

LATIN—Bingham's Grammar, including translations from English into Latin: Cæsar, Virgil, or their equivalents.

Candidates for a more advanced class must stand satisfactory examinations in all studies through which the class has already passed which they propose to enter.

CLASSES AND STUDIES.

Four years are required to complete the course of study in the Collegiate Department. Classes attend three recitations or lectures daily, except on Wednesday and Saturday, when they usually have but two.

The studies pursued by each class are as follows:

FRESHMAN CLASS.

GREEK—Selections from Greek Authors (Boise and Freeman's), or Xenophon's Anabasis, Memorabilia, Greek Prose Composition (Jones'), Goodwin's Greek Grammar.

LATIN—Cicero's Orations, Ovid, Livy, (Chase & Stuart's), Prose Composition (Arnold's), Baird's Classical Manual, Ancient Geography.

GERMAN—Whitney's Grammar, Whitney's Reader, Schriftliche Uebersetzungen ins Deutsche.

ENGLISH—Rhetoric (Hart's), Trench on the Study of Words, Fowler's English Grammar, Smith's Old Testament History, Rhetorical Praxis (Day's), Composition and Declamation throughout the year, Bible Recitation.

MATHEMATICS—Algebra (Ray's Higher), Geometry completed (Loomis').

SOPHOMORE CLASS.

GREEK—Felton's Greek Historians, Plato's Apology and Crito, Smith's History of Greece.

LATIN—Horace (Chase & Stuart's), Augustini Confessiones Cicero De Officiis, De Amicitia, Tusculan Disputations, Prose Composition (Arnold's), Allen & Greenough's Latin Grammar.

CATALOGUE 1878. (page 13)

GERMAN—Whitney's Grammar, Gustavus Adolphus (Heydenreich), oder Cornelius Nepos ins Deutsche uebersetzt, auch schriftlich, Schiller's Tell oder die Geschichte des dreissigjaehrigen Krieges, Deutsche Aufsaetze.

ENGLISH—Fowler's English Grammar completed, English and American Literature (Shaw's & Hart's), Day's Praxis, Natural History (Hooker's), New Testament History (Smith's), Composition, Declamation, Bible Recitation.

MATHEMATICS—Conic Sections (Loomis'), Plane and Spherical Trigonometry (Loomis'), Surveying, Navigation and Analytical Geometry (Loomis').

JUNIOR CLASS.

GREEK—Homer's Iliad or Odyssey, Aeschylus' Prometheus or Agamemnon, Euripides' Alcestis.

LATIN—Horace's Satires, Epistles, Ars Poetica (Chase & Stuart's), Augustine's Confessions, Latin Hymns (March's), Latin Composition.

GERMAN—Heyse's Leitfaden, Goethe's Hermann und Dorothea, oder Goetz von Berlichingen, Phaedri Fabeln ins Deutsche uebersetzt, schriftliche Aufsaetze.

ENGLISH—Mental Philosophy (Haven's), Natural Theology (Paley's), Ancient History (Thalheimer's), Botany (Gray's), Physiology (Hooker's), Moral Philosophy (Wayland's), Church History, Essay, Original Oration and Discussion, Bible recitation.

MATHEMATICS—Calculus, Physics, Chemistry.

SENIOR CLASS.

HEBREW—Deutsch's Grammar and Chrestomathy.

GREEK—Demosthenes or Aeschines on The Crown, Sophocles' Antigone or Ajax, Eusebius' Historia Ecclesia.

LATIN—Tacitus' Histories, Agricola and Germania, Original Composition, Latin Hymns, Augsburg Confession.

GERMAN—Heyse's Leitfaden, Goethe's Faust, Tacitus' Germania oder eine Schrift Cicero's ins Deutsche uebersetzt, schriftliche Aufsaetze, Deutsche Litteraturgeschichte.

FRENCH—Otto's Conversation Grammar, Bocher's Reader.

ENGLISH—Church History, Modern History (Thalheimer's), Evidences of Christianity (Paley's), Aesthetics, Art of Criticism (Samson's), Logic (Atwater's), Political Econo-

> 14   *THIEL COLLEGE*
>
> my (Bowen's), Original Oration, Declamation and Debate, Butler's Analogy, Constitution of the United States (Andrew's).
>
> MATHEMATICS—Astronomy (Loomis') Mineralogy, Geology (Hitchcock's), Keith on Globes.
>
> *LADIES' COURSE OF INSTRUCTION.*
>
> The Ladies' Course, which has been established by the Board of Trustees, embraces the studies of the Collegiate Department, except that Greek is optional, and French may be taken in place of German.
>
> A Diploma *ad gradum Artium Baccolaureæ* is awarded to those who complete this course.
>
> *THE GERMAN LANGUAGE.*
>
> A special Professorship has been established for instruction in the German Language and Literature. The German is part of the regular Collegiate course. Superior opportunity is thus offered for the study of this most rich and useful of modern languages.
>
> *Academic Department.*
>
> This department is under the direct supervision of the Principal. During study hours, all pupils will be in charge of the Instructors.
>
> Any student having completed his academic course, and who passes a satisfactory examination, will, on application, receive a Certificate of Scholarship.
>
> *ADMISSION.*
>
> All applicants must present satisfactory evidence of good character; if from other schools or academies, they must bring regular certificates of dismissal.
>
> Every applicant will be examined and assigned to that class for which he is found to be fitted by previous study.
>
> Every pupil will pursue the regular studies of his class, unless parents or guardians make special arrangements for a different course.

> *CATALOGUE 1873.*   15
>
> *CLASSES AND STUDIES.*
>
> Three years are required to complete the course of study in the Academic Department. This course has been arranged so as to embrace such studies as will furnish the faithful student with a substantial business education, or thoroughly fit him for college. Pupils in this Department will have from three to four recitations daily except on Wednesday and Saturday, when they usually have but two.
>
> The studies pursued by each class are the following:
>
> *SUB-JUNIOR ACADEMIC.*
>
> Spelling and defining (Scholar's Companion), Reading (Osgood's 5th Reader), Modern Geography (Guyot's Grammar School), Arithmetic (Ray's IIId part), English Grammar (Harvey's), Composition (Hart's First Lessons), Declamation, Penmanship, Luther's Small Catechism, Bible Recitation.
>
> *JUNIOR ACADEMIC.*
>
> Spelling and Defining (Scholar's Companion), Reading (Osgood's 5th Reader), Modern Geography (Guyot's), English Grammar (Harvey's), Arithmetic (Ray's Higher), U. S. History (Barnes'), Elements of Natural Philosophy (Martindale's), Latin Grammar and Reader (Bingham's), Viri Romæ, Rhetoric, Composition, Declamation, Penmanship, Catechism, Good Morals and Gentle Manners (Gow's), Bible Recitations.
>
> *SENIOR ACADEMIC.*
>
> Latin Grammar, Caesar and Virgil (Chase & Stuart's), Harkness' First Lessons in Greek, or Goodwin's Greek Grammar, White's First Lessons and Xenophon's Anabasis, Whitney's German Grammar and Reader, English Grammar, Analysis of English Sentences (Welch's), Watts on on the Mind (Emerson's Ed.), Book-keeping (Ellsworth's), Physiology (Brown's), Physical Geography (Warren's), Algebra (Ray's Elementary), Geometry (Loomis'), Rhetoric (Hart's), Composition, Declamation, Bible Recitation, Luther's Catechism.
>
> *SPECIAL STUDIES.*
>
> Should any pupil desire to pursue special studies, arrangements will be made for his accommodation in either Department.
>
> *TERMS AND VACATIONS.*
>
> Each Session will open on the First Thursday in Septem-

APPENDIX 19

Julia Sherman Bassler's <u>Diary</u>

24 December 1902 - 8 June 1904

Transcribed by granddaughter, Susan Bassler Pickford 2002-2012

Introduction

Julia was born in Clinton, Missouri 10 March 1877 to Laura and Albert Sherman, Jr. Her oldest sister Minnie became a school teacher. Her second sister Laura married but died shortly after giving birth to her first son. Julia at 26 was still at home seemingly destined to become an old maid until a distant cousin came to court her. William G. Bassler's mother Eliza had an older sister Susannah Margaret (called Margaret) who had married a Buckingham and moved west. Her daughter Laura married Albert Sherman. Her story is told more fully in the Family Genealogy. William G. visited his Missouri family, when he was a young man and Julia was a toddler. In 1901 he visited again to propose marriage and bring her to Zelienople. He was now forty-seven years old and Julia was twenty-seven. His mother also living in the family home was eighty-three. Julia accepted his proposal. She traveled east in February and the couple were married in Pittsburgh, Pennsylvania,16 July 1902. From there they traveled to Zelienople. And Julia began her diary five months later.

Dec. 24, 1902 Wednesday

Got up at 6 o'clock, had breakfast by seven. Will went to the office. I then cleaned our room and brought Mother over. I then made her bed, then dressed and went down town, went to office first, left my bundles, then went over to Mrs. Iffts to see about getting my waists made and took the little bread girl a cream pitcher for her Xmas gift. I then went and ordered our groceries and chicken, went back to the office and waited till the mail came – it was late but I stayed until it was delivered. Will got a letter from Minnie. I came home and went down to the office again. It commenced snowing. Will went with me to Dindingers and got me a nice pair of shoes. We went to office and tried them on. They fit OK Then we came home and rested and talked of the past, by that time our supper was ready. Sophie is going to the exercises. Mrs. Bloom just brought a mince pie. I am going to set our table in the sitting room tonight. I am feeling real well, but somewhat lonesome, from thinking of last year. Mother does not feel the best today.

Dec. 25 Thursday

Arose at usual time, had breakfast, buck wheat cakes. I straightened the house fixed my chicken for dinner, then put on my black dress and went over to Stoutts to see what Lillian got. I then came home and went down to the office and kept Will company until train came in. I got a pck of maple sugar nuts from Aunt Maggie. After the mail was distributed we came home and opened some of our packages. Cora Linnenbrinckenbrink gave us a lovely vase, Anna Debendarfor gave me a box of candy and a hat brush, Mrs. Stoutt gave me a stand for my coffee pot, Will gave me a pair of nice shoes and a dresser set, Sophie Young a lovely little vase, Will also got me some perfume. Miss Bentle gave me a white apron. Mother got a table, candy, han- kies from Cora L. and Sophie and Miss Bentle , Mrs. Krebbs sent in a nice chicken and cookies, 2 little ice wool shawls. We ate dinner at 12-30. Mother ate hers up stairs. We had stewed chicken and gravy, mashed potatoes, peas slaw, cranberries, mince pie, cookies, celery, coffee and bread and butter. After dinner Sophie went away. Will lay down and took a sleep while I wrote a letter home. We sent a box of things home. I took a nap and read a little in the Y-C by that time it was supper time. Will went back to the office. I washed the dishes and straightened the house then got ready to go to church. Will came by 7-30 and we went, the house was crowded. The ex were good, we got our candy and came home, read our bibles and went to bed. Wishing one another many more happy Xmases. *(Under the line signed* Julia Dec 8 AM)

Dec.26 Friday

Has been snowing all day, this AM we sewed a little, S & I made me a light calico apron. Will fixed the pump, it was frozen, after dinner I went out calling, called on Mrs. Gelbach but she was not at home, I then went to see Mrs. Bastian, had a very pleasant time, I then went down to Mrs. Phas Goering's came by Mrs. B then came home and helped get supper, finished my letter to Murhl, I got a nice cushion cover from Stella and Bert, sent Will a tie, Mrs. A. Goering and daughters called while I was gone.

Dec 27 Saturday

Snowing all day, In AM I done nothing much, I took a black waist apart of Mother's and sewed up the lining. In the PM I ended some stockings, got out Will's heavy clothes and dusted them, and then I read awhile until I got sleepy, lay down on the cot and fell asleep. I did not sleep long. Mrs. Stoutt and Lillian came over, then Miss Young came and brought Sophie a new waist. We had supper. Then Will went back to office. I had a nice letter from Bert.

Dec 28 Sunday

We had breakfast after 8, were out to the fire and slept late. We were awakened about 12-30 by the cry of fire. Will dressed and went down. I soon followed, it was Loutons meat market. Mrs. Kline's house, Bastians store and the hotel. It was an awful fire, long to be remembered, men had hard work to keep the PO from burning and also Dindingers store and Wright's. The glass in the office were all broken and in Wrights store. We came home at 2 and went to bed. Sophie went to church in AM I got dinner, stewed chicken. In PM Will and I went to look at the ruins. We are going to church this evening.   Written as the clock strikes.

Dec.29 Monday

Snowing - 20° below zero. We got up late. Will went to office after 8. I made an elderberry pie and got my dinner ready, at 8 Will came home for the mail sacks. I sewed all day on Mother's black waist, had a letter from Stella, to be Mrs. Sherman tomorrow afternoon. Mr.Sleatore (?) will marry them. Will gave me a nice pair of black kid gloves today. Sophie and I melted enough snow to wash with tomorrow, we want to get up early tomorrow and get through. Will had to go away out to Lockwood's with a registered letter and he was very tired.

Dec. 30 Tuesday

Bert & Stella married. Weather clear most of the day. We washed. I went up town and bought some lining and thread I then went to Mrs. Iffts to see about getting my waists made, she could not make them until next week. I then came by the office, waited there until Will went for some meat and then came home and got dinner, after dinner I worked around until 3 then I got my crazy quilt and worked some on it, I then got supper. Will is not feeling well. I feel very well only lonesome and sleepy none of us feeling good.

Dec 31 Wednesday

Weather very cold, 4 below zero. We ironed all morning, I baked a blackberry pie for dinner. Will came home at 10-30 and stewed some oysters for his Mother, Mrs. D and Anna called in PM I sewed a little, was not very well, looked for a letter from home but did not get it. Snow still on the ground.

Jan 1, 1903 Thursday

New Years day. Weather very frosty cloudy in AM but clear in PM I ironed some this morning, went up town to buy some meat for dinner, went in the office awhile. The train was late so I did not get my letter until 4PM The folks box had not come, when they wrote. I worked all PM cleaning corners and the front room. After supper Miss Bentle and Miss Steudebaker came, we had a fine time.

Jan 2 Friday

Weather more mild, 14 above zero. In the AM I swept my bed room. I sewed about 10 min then commenced to get dinner, we had beaus boiled potatoes, stewed onions and biscuits. Will came by once before with a short letter from home saying they received their box the 31 and would all write Wed night. After supper I took my work up in Mother's room and sewed awhile then came down and finished my letter to Clara and sewed some on my log cabin quilt. I worked some on that square of Indian head muslin. Will came by 3 and read some out of the Y until 4. I went down and got supper, then went up town, I read some in "Esther" Will came at 8. Rained all PM.

Jan 3 Saturday

Weather cloudy and dismal. In the AM I baked two pumpkin pies, next down street. Went in the office. Will handed me a letter from Bert. I was looking for one from home and felt some what disappointed. I came home read a little in my book "Esther" then I got dinner, pork steak and potatoes and pie.

In PM I read some. I began to feel tired and sleepy so I lay down and slept 1 hr. I wakened at 2-30 feeling better. Helen Wright came over bringing me such a pretty calendar. Will came home at 4 he held his hands behind him and then asked which hand I would have. I took the right one but got nothing, he then gave me a letter from home, which I enjoyed very much. We sat on the sofa and read it. After supper Miss Studebaker called. I first read my letter out loud to Mother then went down and finished my book. This is our long evening.

Jan 4 Sunday

Weather cloudy, we went to church in AM came home helped get dinner, after dinner I read some and Will went to sleep so I went up on our bed and went to sleep too slept from 15 of 2 until 4-30 sent in Mother's room awhile. I then got supper, helped Sophie wash dishes then S and I went to church.

Jan 5 Monday

Weather cloudy and damp in AM In PM snowed. I did not feel well this AM I sewed a little then got dinner. Sophie went up town. After dinner I went down to Mrs. Debendarfors and got a pattern of a cap then I went to Dindingers got a waist for Mother and some goods to make Minnie a night cap. I stayed in office till Cora came then I came home and made the cap, Sophie got supper. After supper Mrs. Reid called. She wanted me to a 6 o'clock dinner she was to have this week.

Jan. 6 Tuesday

Weather cloudy in AM snowed a little and cleared off. In the AM I went down to Miss B and got some mince meat came by the store got some groceries. Will asked me if I would go down and get some cookies so I did. I came home and made a frame for my log cabin quilt, mashed my finger in making it, I sewed some on my lining, got dinner after dinner I tacked it and finished it by 4 o'clock and helped get supper. After supper Mrs. Bloom came over, I wrote some in my letter, Cavanaugh's baby took morphine pills for candy and died.

Jan 7 Wednesday

Weather cloudy, snowed most of the day, Sophie washed, I baked pumpkin pie and mince then I made a shelf in the cellar way under steps, Got dinner and washed the dishes, read some home papers Pa sent, then wrote to Bert. Will came home a little early and fixed the doorbell, after supper I ironed some then went down town and got some meat and some muslin for pillowcase.

Jan 8 Thursday

Clear and cold. Snowing now at 8PM this AM I ironed. In PM I went over to Mrs. Iffts to try on my waists. We had two callers, Mrs. Kirker and Metz. Will worked all PM first he put the tin under my gas hot plate then painted it. He then went down in the cellar and emptied the two vinegar barrels and got them ready for use. Sophie went out in the country, don't know how long she will stay. I got through my supper work at 20 of 6. I wrote on my letter then I went upstairs and read awhile then talked, put M to bed. I feel miserable but hope to soon feel better.

Jan 9 Friday

Cold all day, in AM I dressed M and cleaned her room, was all done my work by 9. I read awhile then Will came, brought me a letter from home. All was well. In PM Will came home early and took a sleep. I finished my pillowcase in evening. Will wrote to Minnie and sent her a cap, about nine I went to bed. Will was late this evening.

Jan 10 Saturday

Clear and cold but very nice out this AM. I got Will off in plenty of time, I was all through my work by 9. I commenced to get sick and had quite a time, could scarcely move for a while but by 1 I felt better. Mrs. Ifft sent my waists, they are very nice, the red one was too small in the neck. In PM Mrs and Miss Passavant called. Will got a gas jet put in Mother's room. Minnie sent me my nice photo frame.

Jan 11 Sunday

Weather very changeable, first snow then rain and sleet. We were home all day. We read most of the day. Miss Mary Goehring called in the PM I read in my book until my eyes commenced to hurt.

Jan 12 Monday

Zero most of the day, dreadful cold and icy. I was in bed until 3 PM with sick headache. Will got dinner and supper, by the evening, I felt better and washed the dishes. Hope to feel better tomorrow. Had a letter from Anna Loran in Deepwater, MO.

Jan 13 Tuesday

Weather very cold but clear most of the day. In AM I finished my book and then sewed awhile, fixed the collar of my red dressing sacque then it was dinnertime. Will brought me a letter Mabel and Murhl which I enjoyed very much. In PM I worked awhile on my square. I wrote some on my letter and read some. After supper I read in my book "Alice of Old Vaucluse" and my bible.

Jan 14 Wednesday

Got up at 5:30 had all my work done by 7-30. I washed and had it all done when Will came at 15 of 11. In PM I swept the hall and my room, Will came home and put Mother's gaslight in her room. Weather little warmer, snowed part of the day. Mrs. Stout to see Miss Bentle then I came by the store got some muslin and ribbon and apples, yeast, came home and got supper, after supper I wrote on my letter, Miss Studebaker called awhile.

Jan 16 Friday

Weather warm and pleasant the snow melted very fast. This AM I finished my square and read awhile and wrote home. In PM I made Carl a cap and darned Will a pair of stockings. Helen Wright came over about 5. After supper I made me a collar out of some white ribbon then I read some in "Alice of Old V" Will came home on time, gave me 25 cents for my bank, while getting his slippers out he upset the buckwheat batter on the floor but nothing was hurt. I stirred up some more.

Jan 18 Sunday

Got up at 8 had breakfast by 8-30 I cleaned the house and went to Church, I got the dinner ready before I went and Will put it on. We had dinner by 12-30 baked chicken, potatoes and gravy. After dinner I finished my book and dressed and went to see the Dambach girls.

Jan 19 Monday

In AM I did not feel extra lively so just did my work up and sat down and pulled some threads in a pillow case, mended my black sateen skirt. Then got dinner. After dinner I put up a shelf for my flowers at the South window, then I combed my hair and changed my dress, by that time Will came, he scrubbed the cat, we had a great deal of fun with it. In evening I wrote some, put his Mother to bed, then locked the house and went down to the office and waited till Will came.

Got up at 6 had my work done by 7-30 commenced washing. I got Lillian Gloss to help me, we were through by 10-30. In PM I went down town, bought Pa some handkerchiefs for his birthday, went down to Miss B to see called in evening. Will came home and said he had such a hard bump on his nose it made him very sick for a while.

Jan 15 Thursday

I got up first this AM as Will did not feel well. I ironed all AM and until 2 PM I made 2 pies for dinner. In PM Will came home and I went downtown. Called

how her brother was, then called on Mrs. Debendarfor. Came home got supper, ironed some and went out to hunt my cat, found her at Mrs. Georges. Going to bed soon 8-30.

Jan 21 Wednesday

In bed all day with sick headache. Will got his own meals. I had a letter from Clara saying Minnie was going to Kansas Thursday.

Jan 22 Thursday

Ironed some this morning and mended some, watered my flowers, after dinner I cleaned Sophie's room and changed things around some. Will came home at 2 we hunted some pictures up in the attic. We found them and were just ready to hang them when Mrs. Kirker and daughter came. I got supper and after supper Mrs. Teeple came, had a jolly time

Jan 23 Friday Papa's Birthday 56 yr.

Weather gloomy in AM but cleared off in PM In AM I was busy cleaning and washing off flowers. I then baked an apple pie and made a dumpling for dinner. After dinner I swept his Mother's room, hung some pictures up in her room, finished my letter home, then Mrs. Wright came over. I went upstairs and sewed some on a pillow case. Will went to the funeral of a Zeigler boy, after he came home he put some hooks in our new brooms, got supper I wrote to Miss Cornish, Miss Studebaker called. I put his M to bed then I read some.

Jan 24 Saturday

Snowed most of the day, in the PM Will and I went to Church, in the evening the Gelbach girls came down. I had a long letter from home, it made me feel so lonely and sad for a while.

Jan 25 Sunday

Got up and had breakfast, done up the work with Will's help. We then got ready for Church at first I did not think I would go but finally decided I would, so I got ready. Lillian Gloss came over and stayed with Mother. In PM we all took a sleep, later on, Will read a piece, I finished my, "In His Name" read some in my Bible and retired.

Jan 26 Monday

Weather mild bright in PM. In AM I did my house work was all through by 8. I sat down and finished a letter home and one to Minnie. Will came home early. I had dinner early, biscuits and cold meat and gravy. In PM we went sleighing intended going to Lancaster but our old horse was so pokey we turned around and went out South to home at 3-30, very much disgusted with the horse. In evening I sat up stairs not feeling in a very good humor, intended going to bed but Will would not let me so I came down and sat here til 9-30 then I retired.

Jan 27 Tuesday

In AM Lillian Gloss and I washed, the sun came out so pretty and warm and our clothes did look so pretty and white, we were all through by 10-30, everything put away. In PM I dressed and went out calling. Went to see Mrs. Linnenbrinckenbrick about an apron pattern, went in office and chatted with Cora. Then called on Mrs. Kirker, had a very nice time, came home and got supper. Will helped me wash the dishes then I ironed until nearly 7. It commences raining about 6-30. Mr. Rape commences his work shop and had some tiling haul Ed for his foundation.

Jan 28 Wednesday

Cloudy and dismal all day. I had the headache until 3 PM Then I got up washed the dishes ironed a few pieces and rested until suppertime. After supper Sophie came and stayed quite awhile. Then I got ready to go to the musical at the P Church (Presbyterian) The concert was grand, came home and went to bed.

Jan 29 Thursday

Still cloudy in AM I ironed the rest of my clothes, darned a few pieces then baked two pies for dinner. After dinner I went to the sewing society, got a pattern for a large apron, got some gingham, came home and got supper. Miss Bentle came before we were through, she went upstairs and talked until we were done. When she went I cut out my apron and basted it up. I had a letter from Anna Loran today. 9 PM my wrist pains me.

Jan 30 Friday

Weather cloudy, snow and cold winds. In the AM I done up my work then went over to Mrs. Blooms and got her apron to go by. Came home and went over to Stoutt's to stitch my apron, came home and helped his Mother down stairs then got dinner. Train was late. Will never came till early 12. In PM I sewed on my apron and nearly finished it, got supper. After supper Mrs. Bloom came over and stayed until nearly 8. The walls of Bastian's ruins tumbled down. I am going down to meet William .

Jan 31 Saturday

In AM I got Lillian Gloss to come over and help me sweep, we swept the sitting room hall and kitchen, we were . All through by noon. I had dinner ready on time. Will brought me a letter from Eva. In PM I dressed and went down to office, got Will to take a walk away out the plank road, we went along looking at the flowers. I then went down to see Mrs. Debendarfer and Mrs. Goering, came home and got supper, after supper I wrote on my letter home and then put Mother to bed. Then I came down and washed out a pair of stockings and then cut off my big apron pattern. Will came and we read until 10 and went to bed.

Feb 1 Sunday

Got up, had breakfast at 9, Will helped me wash the dishes. We neither one felt like going to Church. I did not anyway for I had taken 3 pills. We had dinner by 1, dishes, afternoon we read. Miss Studebaker came over a while. We intend to go to Church tonight.

Feb 2 Monday

In AM I cleaned the house and mended Will's overcoat. Will brought me a letter from Minnie. After dinner he came home early and we went down to Mrs. Teeple's, she was not at home so we came back. We read some. Got supper. After supper I read until he came. Weather lovely, just like spring, so I guess Mr. Groundhog saw his tail.

Feb 3 Tuesday

Weather cloudy, rain in evening. Lillie and I washed our clothes, got nearly dry. Will brought them in while I was downtown. I bought some blue velvet to put on my dotted waist , also some black velvet for a belt. Went down for some cookies, came by Miss B went in Mr. Goehring was there, came home and cut out Eva's apron and got supper, after supper I ironed most of my clothes, then put M to bed. *(Eva was the 7th child and the 4th daughter in the Sherman family. She was 10 years younger than Julia)*

Feb 4 Wednesday

Windy all day. In AM I ironed some and sewed on Eva's apron, went over to Mrs. S and stitched some, came home awhile then went over to Mrs. Blooms and finished sewing. After supper I wrote to Minnie and went to bed early, have been lonely all day.

Feb 5 Thursday

Windy most of the day. I sewed some on Eva's cap and apron then sent it off. This was a funny day. In evening I went down to meet Will. I had a letter from home and Mrs. Biggs.

Feb 6 Friday

In the morning I cleaned the house up a little, brought down the cot and put it in Mother's room. First at noon I went down town for some corn, I went in office got a letter from Minnie. In PM I finished my work and finished my letter to Ma and Murhl. Then I commenced darning stockings when Will came and said it was too pretty to stay in the house so we went over to Mrs. Kirkers. She gave us such nice apples and some books to read. We came home and were first ready to eat supper when Anna Debendarfer came. Will ate his and went on to office. After supper I went down town stayed in Office awhile then went over to see Sadie Young. Then I went over to see Sadie Young. Then I stopped to see the Gelbach girls and came home.

Feb 7 Saturday

Weather warm and pleasant. I worked hard all day. In AM I washed my flowers and arranged them nicely at the window, our lily is in bloom, my flowers look read well. I swept the hall and steps, scrubbed the porch and fixed my dinner, then went upstairs and straightened things, combed my hair and changed my waist, came down and finished my dinner. After dinner Will and I scrubbed the walk and I finished the porch and closet.   *(A waist was the top part of a woman's dress. Today it might be called a blouse except it lay fitted on top of the skirt and was not tucked into the skirt.)* Then I washed my dishes and baked 2 pies for Sunday. By the time I was dressed it was 8 o'clock. I went down to the office then came home and went over to see Mrs. Weigel. Will came home, he wakened me. I was not well so I went to bed.

Feb 8 Sunday   *(in margin G.M. Birthday)*

Weather some colder rain in AM and colder in PM. We had breakfast at 15 min of 9. I then went to bed, was sick, I got up at 1PM Will got dinner, in PM we were upstairs most of the afternoon. I commenced a letter to Minnie then I crawled up on the cot and listened to Will read an old Catholic piece. We neither one went to Church.

Feb 9 Monday

Weather dismal. In AM I worked some on a handkerchief, did not feel very well. Mr. and Mrs. Winters, Mrs. Rape and Ketterer called after supper.

Feb 10 Tuesday

Lillian Gloss washed, did it all by herself. Will came home early in PM and we fixed a box for our flower seed. We went to the entertainment in the evening.

Feb 11 Wednesday

In AM I ironed, done by noon. I did not feel good, my head ached some, had a letter from home which made me feel very

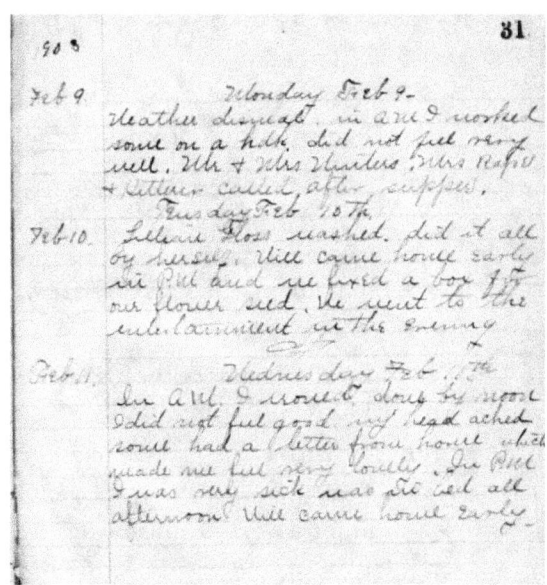

Diary entry Monday Feb 9, 1903

lonely. In PM I was very sick, was in bed all afternoon. Will came home early.

Feb 12 Thursday

Weather very pleasant. In AM I did not feel well, in PM I sewed some on my quilt. Mrs. Kirker and daughter called, were here quite a while. After supper went down to see Miss B but did not stay long did not feel well, came home and went to bed. Lillie G stayed while I was gone.

Feb 13 Friday   (in margin: 1 year since I left home)

Weather cloudy and damp. In AM Lillie Gloss and I swept and dusted. I put my flowers in at the North window. In PM Will fixed our rain barrel. After supper I watched the people go by to Steinbergers party, about 8 I went down to meet Will, the office was full of men so I went in to Mrs. Linnenbrinckenbricks and waited awhile, I had a letter from Cory and a paper from Pa.

Feb 14 Saturday

Weather cloudy most of the day. I did not work much today sewed some on my quilt in AM, at 11 I went down street for some bread came home with Will. In PM I worked on Helen Wright's doll bed and Clara's handkerchief. Mrs. Zehner called about 4-30. After supper I wrote home.

Feb 15 Sunday

Rained all day long, we went to Church in AM Came home and got a very light dinner. We both took a sleep, in PM I read some in David Harum. *(David Harum: A Story of American Life was the best selling novel of 1899)*

Feb 16 Monday

Cloudy and cold. I worked on Helen's bed. In AM I went up town for the blue goods. After supper I went over to Stoutts awhile.

Feb 17 Tuesday

Snowed very deep in AM I sewed some, Baked a cake , after dinner. Then went over to Mrs. Wrights to stitch some. All alone in evening.

Feb 18 Wednesday Blizzard

A regular blizzard, very cold. I sewed all day on Helen's bed. In evening Mrs. Stoutt came over awhile. Will fixed a shelf in the corner of the pantry for a can of soft water. No letter today.

Feb 19 Thursday

In bed all day with sick headache. Will had it too. In evening Mrs. Bloom and Stoutt came over.

Feb 20 Friday

Clear and cold in AM I swept and dusted, went down town before dinner to get some meat. Saw Miss B had a little talk. In PM I finished my work and Helen's doll bed. In evening Anderson's house was blown up by a gas explosion. Mrs. A and sister were badly burned. I was just getting ready to go to an entertainment at the UP Church. *(United Presbyterian)* We went anyway.

Feb 21 Saturday

Cloudy most of this day, but warmer in AM I finished my work and went over to see Mrs. Anderson. In PM I was home, worked some on my quilt and wrote home. In evening I went over to them than came home and sewed from 8 to 10 of 9 then I went down to office to meet Will.

Feb 22 Sunday

Slept late but got ready for Church. In PM we both took a sleep, about 5 we went down to see Mrs. Teeple's. Came home and sat upstairs until Helen and Brandon came over with Sport and such fun as we had watching Frisky and Sport play.

Feb 23 Monday

Weather clear and pretty. Lillie Gloss and I washed, were through by 10, I then got dinner, after dinner Mrs. D and Anna called. Later Miss Bentle and her niece. After supper I went down town, the Gelbach girl called me in, I stayed a little while then went on down, got some gingham for an underskirt, got some cookies and came home ironed some and commenced a letter to Mrs. Biggs, 15 of 9 Will not here.

Feb 24 Tuesday

Weather cloudy in AM but pleasant in PM. In AM I ironed, was done by 11. In PM Will and I went down to Hoffman's to look for wallpaper, we were gone all afternoon. After supper I went over to Stoutts a few minutes, came home and cut out my underskirt and a lining and ruffle to a cushion cover, about 8 Miss Gelbach and Mary Shaffer came, they stayed till 10. Will went to bed.

Feb 25 Wednesday

Weather fine, just like spring. In AM I went over and sewed on my skirt. Will came home early about 4-30, Mrs. Kribbs called. I am going down to meet Will. I don't feel extra well.

Feb 26 Thursday

Weather very warm and nice. In AM I went down town and got some groceries, talked to Mrs. B's niece and came home, got dinner, Will never came until nearly 1. After dinner I finished my underskirt and went over to Stout's to sew it. Mrs. Goering was there and came over here. I came home and after supper went back and finished it. Mrs. Weigel came over with her baby and stayed quite a while. After supper I wrote to Minnie and sewed some on my quilt.

Feb 27 Friday

Sent for my bank. Cloudy and rainy. I went downtown in AM and Will and I selected our wallpaper. I came home and swept Mothers room, got dinner and after dinner I straightened my pantry and storeroom. Mrs. Wright called. Will is home, reading 3PM.

Feb 28 Saturday

Got our bank. Weather cloudy, rained most of the day. In AM I went downtown took Mrs. D books and dish home, also Miss B's, came home baked two pies. Mrs. S gave me some pumpkin. In PM I sewed on my quilt patches and finished two rows. I had a good letter from home. Mad dog in town.

March 1 Sunday

Weather colder, some sunshine. Will went to Church. I had the headache. In PM we took a sleep, then I wrote three letters. Mrs. Teeples came over. I lay down and slept from 6-7 then we went up and I sung some but X_____   Will is reading David Harum.

March 2 Monday

We washed and took up Sophie's carpet and cleaned that room. Mrs. Stoutt came over in the evening. I went down and came home with Will.

March 3 Tuesday

Clear and pretty, ironed and then put down his Mother's carpet, worked hard all day. Miss Bentle was here in the evening.

March 4 Wednesday (in margin:Bryan spoke in P Church, saw 1st robin)

Cloudy part of the day. I put down the carpet in the spare room. Lillie swept down stairs and washed windows. Wright's Killed Sport today, he was bitten by a mad dog Saturday. I am very tired.

March 5 Thursday

Rained most of the day. Mr. Hoffman papered our front room. I planted some flower seeds and my cleodendron (*bleeding heart*). Then wrote to Minnie. I commenced a" husher" for Mrs. Stoutt's birthday. I sung a lot of songs for Will last night. It was ten o'clock before we went to bed.

March 6 Friday

Lovely spring day. Mr. Hoffman papered the north room upstairs. I scrubbed the porches, cleaned my pantry and finished my letter home. After supper I went over to Mrs. Wrights and sewed some.

March 7 Saturday (Found Frisky, Mrs. Stout's birthday, Edna Johnson's birthday)

Cloudy and rain. Will found Frisky at Linnenbrincks. In AM I worked on a cushion for his Mother's commode. In PM I drew some threads in Lillian's dress and darned some stockings after supper Mrs. Stout and Lillian came over.

March 8 Sunday

Rained most all day. Will went to Church but I did not feel like it. In PM Mr. Goehring called, later on it cleared off real pretty.

March 9 Monday

Cloudy part of the day. I washed by myself. Got my clothes out early, sewed some in PM Toward evening Will went up in attic to hunt for something and found I had sent it to Minnie. He was very angry. I was very sorry. I sent for them and got them back again.

March 10 Tuesday

My birthday. Will gave me a pretty pocket book with a dollar in it. Mrs. Stoutt gave me a hair receiver. Minnie sent me some music. I had a letter from Minnie and Mrs. Cornish. Pa sent me the <u>Clinton Eye</u> for one year. *(Julia is 26 yrs. old)*

March 11 Wednesday

Cloudy all day. I was very sick all day inn bed most of the time. Mrs. Harper, Miss Weeder and Stoutt called in PM After supper Mrs. Bloom called. I had a good long letter from home.

March 12 Thursday

In AM I worked awhile then went down town for some silk floss and ribbon for Eva's hair receiver. In PM Will went over to Harmony, came by Mrs. Kirkers and she gave him two jars of fruit cherries and peaches and dried apples.

March 13 Friday

Lovely weather, I worked out doors most of the PM, finished Eva's hair receiver in AM wrote home and went down to Debendarfers in evening. *(Hair receivers were small receptacles that sat on a dressing table to "receive" hair from a lady's comb or brush)*

March 14 Saturday

Lovely day. Helped Mrs. Stoutt bake a cake, in AM washed and ironed a little dress for Lillian, came home and got dinner. After dinner, I baked some doughnuts. Mrs. Hoffman was here from 1-30 to 4. Mrs. Stout, old lady, called after supper. Mrs. S gave me some cake and pineapple ice.

March 15 Sunday

Weather lovely, we went to Church in AM, In PM walked out to the cemetery then around by Passavants, saw Mrs. Wiegel and talked to her and home. Very tired, was home all evening.

March 16 Monday

Cloudy most of the day, Lillian and I washed, were through by 10, she then took up the tacks in kitchen carpet and after dinner we washed it, quite a job. In evening, I went down to office to meet Will. I had a letter from Stella. *(Stella is married to Bert, Julia's brother Albert)*

March 17 Tuesday

Sick all AM after dinner I straightened around some. In evening I ironed some, Miss Bentle was here awhile, I had a letter from home.

March 18 Wednesday (in margin: Rapes commenced their house)

In AM finished my ironing, went down town for meat. In PM I put down the carpet in kitchen and worked hard. Will hauled manure on the garden. Mrs. Stout was over in evening.

March 19 Thursday

Weather beautiful, warm and spring like. In AM I cleaned my kitchen good. My cupboard aired, shined my stove, sewed on a sash curtain for the kitchen windows. IN PM I finished them and put them up. Mrs. Kirker called. After supper I went down town. Will and I went to an entertainment at P Church.

March 20 Friday

Weather pleasant but heavy rain in evening. In AM I sewed on my curtains also in PM. After supper I went down to office to mail a letter home, came home and went over to Stouts.

March 21 Saturday

Cloudy in AM I baked two pies, went down town. In PM I made Stella a hair receiver and wrote a letter to her, also finished a doily commenced 1 year ago. Rained all PM.

March 22 Sunday

Some cooler but pleasant most of the day. We went to Church in AM, after dinner I wrote some home and read some in my Bible. Will went to sleep. He did not feel well, has a cold. About 3 we went to see Miss Bentle, came home and undressed and got supper. It is now nearly 9 and I am going to bed.

March 23 Monday

Cloudy, I did not wash. In AM I sewed some on my curtains, in PM I went over to Mrs. Weigel's and stitched them.

March 24 Tuesday

Cloudy part of the day, Lillie and I washed then she swept his M-room, our room and hall. In PM I sewed some on my curtains and put one up in hall. After supper I ironed most all my clothes.

March 25 Wednesday

Some colder in AM I just fooled around. In PM we went to a meeting at the Church. In evening I went over to Mrs. Goehring's for some dirt. Went to a musical in the evening which was fine.

March 26 Thursday

In AM I did not do much, worked with my flowers. After dinner I baked some doughnuts, then I took down all my curtains and washed them, in evening we went to a Bible lecture in the P Church.

March 27 Friday

I worked with my flowers in doors and out. Will came home soon after dinner and said Mr. Swain was dead. We worked some out in yard. In AM I cleaned all my windows and put up my curtains.

March 28 Saturday

Weather cloudy and cold most of the day. In AM I made some candy, in PM I made a box for my dust rags. Emma Passavant called in PM

March 29 Sunday

In AM we went to Sunday School and marched with the school over to look at Mr. Swain for the last time on earth. Came back and had short services, came home got dinner. In PM Will rested some then we went out to the cemetery. There were quite a number out there. We did not go anywhere in the evening. Lovely day.

March 30 Monday   Wilbur's birthday *(He was Julia's little brother who died in 1885 at three months of age)*

Weather cloudy and gloomy all day, had quite a rain in AM I worked on my curtains. In PM I did not do much. I had a letter from Stella, a card from Minnie and a letter from home. In evening I went over to see Mrs. Bloom.

March 31 Tuesday (in margin: Frisky died)

Cloudy half of the day. In AM I finished my work. Went down town and bought some white goods for ruffles to some sash curtains. Came home and got dinner. Then went over to Mrs. Stoutts to sew, came home and popped some corn. Will came home with an express package from home. Ma sent me some bulbs and slips. I planted them while he buried Frisky. We then went over to Mrs. Goehrings and got a lilac bush and planted over her grave. In evening I kept Mrs.

Will's mother, Eliza Gilbert Bassler circa 1900's in her upstairs sitting/bedroom. Photo by her son WGBassler

Weigel's baby while she went uptown. After supper I worked on a collar for Eva then put his M to bed and went down street, came by Mrs. Allens and called awhile and came home. I don't feel well, my back hurts me.

April 1 Wednesday

Lovely day. I finished my work then washed some, got them out at 12 then I mowed the back yard. Will came home not feeling well. But he would mow the front yard some after supper. I went downtown and waited for him. I was fooled in AM by him calling me to see a pretty cat. I fooled him at noon by putting an empty dish on the table and covering it. *(April Fool's Day was celebrated.)*

April 2 Thursday

Cloudy in AM but cleared off. I ironed was done by 9-20 Then I put away my clothes then pressed Will's pants. He got him a new pair. In PM I planted my bulbs and wrote to Minnie. I had a letter from her. I then finished Eva's collar, put M to bed, then hemmed my tea towels and wrote some to Murhl.

April 3 Friday

In AM did not feel well so I just fooled around, cleaned my pantry and cleaned the silverware. In PM I dug out some dandelions and finished my letter home. In evening Anna Debendarfer came. After supper I went down street, it was pouring down rain. I too Anna the pattern of my hair receiver then I went for some meat and groceries. Came home and was reading when Lillian Gloss came over. Mother fell off her chair and don't feel well. None of us do.

April 4 Saturday

Cold and snowed all day but melted as fast as it fell. I done my work in AM washed some and baked two pies. Then copied some in my diary.

April 5 Sunday

Clear and somewhat cooler. We went to Church in AM there were 8 or 9 confirmed, very nice services. Came home and got dinner, after dinner we both took such a long sleep. I was lonesome and not well all day.

April 6 Monday

Clear and windy. I never washed, did not feel well. Copied some in this book, wrote some to Stella. In AM I ironed some that I washed Saturday. Sick all night.

April 7 Tuesday

April showers in AM but lovely in PM I rested most all morning, in PM Will and I were working outdoors, planting some trees and digging dandelions up neither one feeling well. I suffered later on.

April 8 Wednesday

Weather cloudy in AM and rain. I finished my work downstairs and then went up made Mother's bed, then went in our room and took up our carpet and turned it and put it down, after dinner I took up the hall carpet and Will helped me dust it. I got supper and done up the work. Then I went down in cellar and washed all the white clothes and boiled them, came up and put his Mother to bed and dressed up and went down town, came home with Will.

April 9 Thursday

Weather cloudy in early part of AM but cleared off. I hung out my washing then mopped the hall, made the beds then got dinner. After dinner I put down the papers upstairs in the hall and the carpet, then put down the under carpet on the steps. Will came and put down the top carpet. I helped some but got sick so I rested awhile. Will did not feel well either. After supper I got Lillie to come and finish putting it down. I felt better then and scrubbed my porch and pantry. Went down to meet Will.

April 10 Friday

Lovely day. In AM I took things easy , went to Church. Will got dinner, I had an awful headache, after dinner I dug out some dandelions, wrote some home, after supper I dampened my clothes, went over to Stouts a second, came home. Mrs. Bloom came over. I worked some on a collar for Ula. I am tired and will go to bed early.

April 11 Saturday

Cloudy and rainy most of the day. In AM I washed my dishes then commenced ironing was all done by 10. I then put them all away and made the beds etc. then got dinner. After dinner I colored some eggs then covered some pots with white paper. Then got ready to go to Church. Will helped me carry some of the flowers. We came home. He read and I worked on a collar for Ula. Finished it and done it up by 4. Then got supper. I feel lonely tonight.

April 12 Easter Sunday

Weather very warm and nice. In AM we went to Church. It was communion Sunday. Came home, I had quite a time, was sick. In PM we just sat around on porch and upstairs some. Did not go to Church in evening.

April 13 Monday

Weather cloudy and rainy all day. In AM I felt very well. Baked a pie but first at noon I took quite a sick spell. Mrs. Wright came over and stayed until Will came. After dinner Will went for the Dr. but he never came until 6 o'clock he gave me some medicine and I went to bed and was in bed till Thursday A> Will got me a new oven.

April 14 Tuesday

Rained most all day. I was in bed all day. Mrs. Wright came in and Mrs. Stoutt felt some better. Lillian Gloss done the work.

April 15 Wednesday

Cloudy and rained most all day. I still stayed in bed. Lillie did the work. Will came home about 8 to see how I was. Miss S gave me some noodles. Will got my flowers from Church.

Thursday

Got up in AM was up all day, felt real well. Sewed some in AM. In PM I sewed some on my pillow cases. I went over to see Mrs. Studebaker and Will scolded me good.

April 16 Friday (in margin: 9 mo. Married)

First pretty day this week. In AM I done my work and baked dumplings and pie, in PM I sewed some and dug dandelions. Will's roses came and we planted them.

April 17 Saturday

Lovely day. I never got up until 8. Lillie done up my work. In evening I went down to Dr. office, came home and went to bed early.

April 19 Sunday

Lovely day. I was in bed all day, got up about 6 but lay on cot. Felt real well by 8PM Will was home all day. Lillie washed the dishes.

April 20 Monday

Lovely day. Lillie washed a big washing. I got dinner, baked biscuit, fried meat and mashed potatoes. Will came home early in PM and dug dandelions but would not let me. I ironed from 5 til after 8.

April 21 Tuesday (In margin: Laura's birthday, would have been 29)

Lovely day. I ironed until 9. Then put away my clothes, cleaned up the house. Mr. Goehring put up our new clothes line in AM, Will came home about 10-30 and dug dandelions. I got dinner, after dinner I went over to see Miss Ella Swain, went by the store and got some curtain goods, came by Mrs. Kirker's on my way home. She asked me to stay for supper, so I did have such a jolly good time, came home and found 3K (?) waiting for me. I am going to bed early. *(Laura was the second child and second daughter and two years older than Julia)*

April 22 Wednesday (in margin: Snowed Sent for machine)

Cold, snowed some. In AM I sewed some and done the house work. In PM I fixed the hall carpet and sewed on Mother's curtains. Will went over to Stoutts to look at her machine, he sent for one for me. In evening, I went down and got some curtain poles and called on Mrs. D and A.

April 23 Thursday

Cloudy and cold. In AM I sewed on Mother's curtains. I finished them soon after dinner. Then I swept her room and put them up. Hunted around in attic for some things. Then I combed and dressed, got supper. Then went over to Harmony for some lace and fringe for rug, came home and washed my dishes, put her to bed. Then put one of those little baskets together and found I had not enough ribbon, we went down town for some, came by office but was full, came home and washed, now I am ready to retire as soon as Will comes.

April 24 Friday (in margin: Ma took Gma to B)

Clear most of the day until evening then it rained. In AM I swept and dusted my sitting room, washed off my flowers. Mrs. S and Lillian were over awhile. I got dinner then dug a few dandelions. Will came and made me stop so I dressed and called on Mrs. Zehner. Came home and got supper, after supper I went downstreet for some eggs came home and commenced one of those collar fixings for Minnie.

April 25 Saturday

Cloudy and cold. In AM I baked cookies, pie and biscuit for dinner and cleaned my pantry. After dinner I swept my kitchen and painted my sink and stool. Then I washed off my clothes line. Dewed a little while and got supper after supper I went down street called on Miss B and came home. Finished my collar and will go to bed.

April 26 Sunday (in margin: Cory cut Murhl's hair off. Bert and Stella were home)

Cloudy and rainy until about 3-30. We went to Church in AM In PM Will took a sleep and I read the Companion, then I commenced a letter but got so lonesome I quit. Will and I then took a walk. We went down to see Mrs. Teeple and she took us through her new house. Then we went down to the extension and home. I was lonely all day.

April 27 Monday (in margin: Used my new line)

Lovely day. Lillie and I washed, I washed 3 quilts, used my new line. Which was fine. After Lillie was through she cleaned my cupboard down in cellar and shelves. After dinner she came over and we cleaned the cellar and took the sprouts off of the potatoes.

April 28 Tuesday

Lovely warm day. In AM I ironed some, did not finish. Will came home and dug some in the garden. I straightened the house some. In PM we worked out doors some but got tired and quit. In evening Mrs. Bloom and Miss B came. Will came home out of humor, had a letter from Sallie Hunt.

April 29 Wednesday

Another pretty day. In AM Will came home and fixed the walk outside. I finished my ironing and swept some, made the beds and baked a pie for dinner. In PM I cut some potatoes, then dug dandelions. Will came and we planted them. I came in and fixed the wires on my pictures. After supper I went down, took my hat to get trimmed. We are somewhat tired.

April 30 Thursday

Windy all day & rained in AM I dug dandelions & Will trimmed grass and mowed some. I painted the big iron kettle and broke some clods in my rose bed. In PM Will hung my pictures and read some. I hunted some pictures upstairs. I had a letter from home and one from Stella & Bert. After supper Mrs. Stoutt and Lillian called.

May 1 Friday

Clear but wind was a little cool.
AM I just did my housework then went downtown for some groceries, came home and made soup for dinner. Will did not feel well. After dinner I dug out some dandelions, then Mrs. Stoutt and I went over to Harmony. I got some percale for a waist and a jardinière, also some onions to plant. After dark I went over to Wright's, came home and Will had me locked out.

May 2 Saturday (In margin: Rape commences his house)

Lovely day. In AM I washed all downstairs, windows on the outside, swept my kitchen and scrubbed my walks and porch. Will brought my roses home, so after dinner I went over to Mrs. Goehring and got some good soil, she gave me some slips. I came home and planted them very carefully, then went back and got some more dirt and lilies of the valley, by that time it was supper time. After supper I went down town got some meat, apples and my hat. Went down to see Anna D then came home the G children were over til 9.

May 3 Sunday

Cloudy in morning Will and I went to Church, came home and were getting dinner when it commenced raining and rained hard for a few minutes then it cleared off. We read some then we both took a sleep, about 5 we took a walk, after supper I was so lonesome. I could not keep from crying.

May 4 Monday

Cloudy part of the day by AM I was sick so did not do much. In PM I dug dandelions. Will came home about 3. In evening Flora Gloss came over and I helped her with her lesson.

May 5 Tuesday

Lovely day. I was sick most of the day with headache. In PM I lay around but after supper I felt
 better and went over to Harmony with Anna Debendarfer, we took Lillian Stoutt with us.

May 6 Wednesday

Cloudy in AM awhile but cleared off. Lillie and I washed, were through by 9-30, then Lillie swept the kitchen, then owed the grass. I washed my dishes then done the upstairs work, dampened my clothes. Will came and brought me some ice cream.

May 7 Thursday

Lovely day. In AM I ironed until 10 then I got dinner baked an elderberry pie and biscuit fried beefsteak and mashed potatoes. Will came home about 8 and worked in the garden some.

May 8 Friday

Lovely day only a little cool wind in AM. In AM I was done my work early then I dug dandelions and went down to office and waited for my letter. Then I went down to Mrs. Debendarfers to see about getting Anna to make my waists. She said she would try, so I came home and got an early dinner and then took my goods to her. Then came by the store and got some flower seeds, went in office awhile, then came home and changed my dress and planted my seeds and bulbs etc. Will soon came and we worked until nearly 5, after supper I watered them all good then dug the dirt away from my sweet peas and got some manure and other dirt and put around them.

May 9 Saturday

Pretty day. In AM I finished my work and went to try on my waist. It fit OK. I came home and finished some shelves on the back porch for my flowers and got dinner. After dinner I cut some silk for ruffles and some fringe for my underskirt. Will came home about 4 and worked some on my shelves for my flowers. I went down street and got some oranges. Saw Miss B awhile. Will brought some cream.

May 10 Sunday

Lovely day in AM we got up and took a look all round at our flowers and trees. We went to Church, came home and got dinner then both took a sleep. I slept until 4-30 then we took a walk. Went out along railroad to see if there were any ferns. We climbed up the hill and found a fine seat by a tree. We sat down and ate an orange, waited till a train passed then came home. Will came home about 4 and worked some on my shelves for my flowers. I went down street and got some oranges, saw Miss Bentle awhile. Neither one went anywhere in the evening.

May 11 Monday

Another pretty day but very dry and dusty. In AM I washed, was done by 9-30 Then I came up and got dinner El pie, biscuit, asparagus and fried potatoes. After dinner I cleaned the cellar and Will's den. Then went up and put away my winter hat and jacket. Got supper and went down street bought Will a shirt and collar, went by Anna D and got my waist.

May 12 Tuesday

Dry and hot. I ironed but never commenced until 9. I planted some geraniums out and my oleanders. I got dinner and finished ironing, after dinner made the beds and fooled around. Will planted some beans. After supper I went down town and got some eggs and coconut came home and baked a cake. Will brought some cream, he was fine.

May 13 Wednesday (in margin: M down and in pencil: machine came)

Lovely day no rain in AM I worked around in the house, watered my flowers. Will came home and said he heard from my machine. Anna D came up to fit my lining for my waist. In PM he came home and we worked out doors some. He brought his Mother down. I cut out his shirt. About 6 the machine came. Will came home and unboxed it. I sewed some on it. Mrs. Teeples called.   .

May 14 Thursday

Dry and hot will put the posts in for my sweet peas. I sewed on his shirt and had quite a time but finally got it. In evening I sewed on my underskirt. Mrs. Stoutt called.

May 15 Friday

Still dry and hot, In AM I watered my flowers and wrote some home and swept some. Will came and we put the wire up for my peas. After dinner I went over to A D' to fit my waist. I then bought me a new gingham dress. Came home and finished my letter and sewed the sleeves into Will's shirt.

May 16 Saturday

Still no rain. In AM I finished my work then fixed my shirt waists over. After dinner I then washed and dressed and went up town. I met WG coming home. I got some buttons for my waist, after supper I went over and made some cream for Mrs. Stoutt. Later on I made me a collar for my waist.

May 17 Sunday

Warm and no rain. In AM we fooled around then got breakfast and dressed for Church. In PM we read and slept. We neither feel very well.

May 18 Monday

Still no rain. Lillie helped me wash. She ironed for me, finished about 8. In PM I sewed some, Emma Passavant brought a cake to Will's Mother. After supper I went down town to get my dress shirt and later I went to meet Will

May 19 Tuesday

Got up with the headache but managed to clean his M room. Mrs. Brandon called just as I had finished it. I got so sick about noon that I threw up but fell asleep and felt better. Had a fine letter from home.

May 20 Wednesday

In After dinner I worked on my skirt. I finished it. Mrs. Bloom was over in the evening.

May 22 Friday (in margin: rained)

Cloudy and hot in AM I watered my flowers and worked on my waist. Will said we would go after ferns but it clouded up so we gave it up and he fixed the poles for my sweet pea vine, after supper I cut out a shirt waist

May 23 Saturday

I swept and dusted the whole house. I was done by 2-30 then I took a bath and went down town. Came home and got supper. After supper I went over to see Mrs. Weigel, came home and went over to Mrs. Blooms. Helen Wright brought us some ice cream. I put his Mother to bed, then went down to Gelbachs awhile, came home and sat on the porch till Will came home. Had a hard storm.

May 24 Sunday

Cloudy in AM and cool most of the day, had a hard thunder storm, In AM we went to Church, in PM we slept. Will was not well. I was very nervous.

May 25 Monday

Cloudy in AM but cleared off. I done the washing myself and Lillie ironed after supper I went down town to mail a letter to Mrs. Beggs. Rained at night.

May 26 Tuesday

Bright but cool day, in AM I worked out doors some. Then came in and sewed some on Clara's bonnet. In PM Mrs. Stoutt, Sr. and I went out for ferns, we went over to P farm and got some lovely ferns. We stayed for supper had such a fine time. I came home and planted mine. I am a little tired.

AM I finished my work and commenced working outdoors and it commenced to rain but did not last long. I went over to Miss S to get her to baste up my linen skirt but she was baking cookies so I came home. She came over after a while and did it for me. I sewed some in the morning. Then baked Will a rhubarb pie, in PM I sewed some, Will helped me to cut the flounce to my dress. After supper I ironed my linen skirt and went down to meet Will.

May 21 Thursday

Cloudy but no rain. In AM I commenced
to fix the vines on our porch. Will came and finished then we worked around until 9. I straightened the house.

May 27 Wednesday

Cloudy and cool. In AM I worked some out doors. Will came home and worked some. In PM we went out for some ferns had such a fine ride. Will took picture. After supper I fixed some ferns in a box and sent them home. I took them down to the office then came home and finished my work and set out my ferns. Rained in the night.

May 28 Thursday

Another fine day. I did not feel very well in the AM so after dinner I lay down and slept 1 ½ hours got up and made 6 calls, came home and got supper and then went over to Mrs. Kirkers, stayed awhile, had a fine time, she gave me a can of raspberries and apples. I stopped to see Mrs. Rape, then came home and went down for some oatmeal. Came home and put Mother to bed. Then Mrs. Jackson and daughter called so it was 11 before we got to sleep.

May 29 Friday

A perfect day. In AM early, Will and I took some flowers out to his Father's and Mary's grave. *(burial grounds at Lutheran Orphanage)* I came on home and mowed some of the front yard. After dinner Will came home and we worked out doors all afternoon. I planted some popcorn. I finished my letter home. Then got supper, after supper I cleaned my pantry and cupboard and planted some tomatoes. Will came home and brought my letter from home.

May 30 Saturday Decoration Day

Cloudy and cool most of the day. In AM I cleaned my house got some meat and lettuce for dinner. Then Brandon put up my flag and I put out the little flags. Then I came in and set my table in the sitting room. Then froze some cream and got dinner by 12. Will closed the office from 12 to 4. In afternoon we looked at our flowers. Mrs. Brandon came over, then Mrs. Kline came in. We had a nice visit, I gave her some cream, after she left I sat out on the porch until Will came.

Then we ate supper. Mrs. Bloom came over and I gave her a dish of cream, then Brandon came over and wanted me to take a drive so Mrs. Bloom stayed with his Mother. After I came home I gave Mrs. Stoutt a dish of cream.

May 31 Sunday

Pretty day but still cool. Will went to Church in AM I did not feel like going. We had breakfast late so we ate dinner at 2. I slept some then we went for a walk East of our place up on the hills then came home and sat up in Mother's room and sung some.

June 1 Monday

Cloudy and rained most of the day. Lillie washed but I finally dried them in the laundry. In PM I sewed on my quilt. After supper I popped some corn for Will and ironed some.

June 2 Tuesday

Clear and some warmer in AM I canned a pint of strawberries and made a glass of jelly. Ironed some and got dinner. I made a strawberry shortcake and put soda in for baking powder.

June 3 Wednesday

Cloudy and cool. In AM I just worked around. Lillie ironed in PM After dinner I worked some on my strawberry doily before Mrs. Graham and Miller called. After I put M to bed I went over to Mrs. Blooms.

June 4 Thursday

Lovely day In AM I worked around out doors. Will came home and cut grass, after dinner I went down town and got some grey cardboard and a center piece. Will came home with me. He took a picture of the house and developed the one he took in the woods.

June 5 Friday

Cloudy and rainy. In AM I worked around out doors in PM Will came home, worked at the door bell. I worked on my doily.

June 6 Saturday

Very nice day. In AM I finished my dish work. Then I washed all that was dirty, then scrubbed my front walk and got dinner, after dinner I swept his Mother's room and went down town. I commenced working on my center piece. It clouded up and I came home. Just got home in time, for it commenced raining. I worked some on my strawberry doily and then got supper, after supper I read some and slept some. Will came at 9 and brought some cream and strawberries.

June 7 Sunday

Cloudy and rainy most of the day. We went to Sunday School and church, came home and got dinner then took a sleep. Will brought his Mother down awhile 4-30. We had quite a heavy shower.

June 8 Monday

Cloudy part of the day. We had a heavy shower in the evening. In AM

I mended some, set out some carnation pinks and verbena. In PM I worked on Ma's cover then went down to meet Will

June 9 Tuesday

(In margin: 2 yrs since Lollie died) *Nickname for Julia's sister Laura who died June 9,1901*

Cloudy part of the day, threatened rain but did not. I helped Will out doors some and Brandon Lorne worked on my table cover and got dinner, in PM I worked and lay down some. Will hoed the potatoes. I went down town to meet W.G.

June 10 Wednesday

Cloudy most of the day. In AM after my work was done I went down town for some embroidery for Clara's skirt, came home and cut it out and tucked some on it. Then I made a rhubarb pie after dinner. Mrs. Stoutt and I went over to Mrs. Harper's, came home and found Will eating supper. After supper I worked on Clara's skirt. Mrs. Teeples came by and wanted me to go with her over to see Rape's house so I went. Then came home and dewed some more. Put his Mother to bed and went myself.

June 11 Thursday

Clear awhile in AM but soon clouded over and rained most all afternoon. I worked on skirt some and weeded some then got dinner. Will came home about 6-30 with some peas. After dinner I finished Clara's skirt. Bro Lettell called to see Will on business. After supper I cleaned the front room, sitting room, kitchen and my bed room.

June 12 Friday

Cloudy and rainy most of the day, in AM I swept Mother B's room and hall up stairs. Will came home and finished the hall and steps. After dinner then I went down in cellar and cleaned it all up nice. In PM we framed some pictures, after supper I washed all my clothes. Sadie Young called, also Mrs. Harper and Bloom soliciting for Donation Day.

June 13 Saturday

Rained the whole day long. In AM I finished my washing and hung them in the laundry, some got dry and I ironed some curtains, after dinner I ironed some and fooled around. Framed one little picture. After supper I baked some ginger bread. Going to commence saving one dollar a week. Will brought me some nice oranges.

June 14 Sunday

Cloudy all day. In AM we went over to the M.E. Church in Harmony (Methodist Episcopal) His text was Ecclesiastes 12 Chap. It raining before we came home and kept it up til 6 o'clock. I slept quite awhile then got up with an awful headache. We had new beans for dinner.

June 15 Monday

Clear and much warmer. In AM I finished my work and cleaned my pantry, set out some geraniums and ironed a few pieces and mended a few, got dinner then went upstairs and finished my work. Then downtown. I paid Anna Defendarfer for Eva's doily, then came home, found Will sleeping, he has not been well all day. I went down after supper. Mrs. Stoutt came over awhile.

June 16 Tuesday (11 months married)

Clear part of the day. In AM straightened my house good. In PM I framed some pictures and worked on my centerpiece. Will slept some. After supper I took my music over to Mrs. Kirker's and played them over.

June 17 Wednesday

Cloudy until about 9 then cleared off and was a fine day. Mr. Kirker came over for me to go with Mrs. Katie Fanchester. I went and had a fine time. We got home about 2:30. I walked from Harmony over and was good and tired.

June 18 Thursday

Cloudy and rainy and cool. I did not do much in AM I fooled around. Will came up and we took a look around then planted some pear. In PM I worked on my table cover. I went upstairs awhile. Then came down awhile. Will was sleeping. He had headache. At 3 I mixed up some ginger cookies. After supper I worked at my flowers then went down to Mrs. Teeples. We went through her new house. It is fine.

June 19 Friday

Lovely day. Lillie and I did a big washing and ironing. Will painted the back porch floor and steps. I finished my letter and sent Ma those aprons. After supper I commenced a letter to Bert and Stella. *(Bert was the eldest boy but two years younger than Julia)*

June 20 Saturday

Cloudy and rainy all day. In AM I ironed a few pieces and mended some then I fixed Will's wash bench and etc. after dinner I went down to the office and took some quilt pieces to cut, tried to get something to eat but could not, I got some cream. We lost our good umbrella some way. We don't know how. After supper Mrs. Weigle called, then I put his M to bed. Then Mrs. Stoutt came over, then Mrs. Goehring. After they left I sewed some on my quilt.

June 21 Sunday

We went to Sunday School and Church, came home and got dinner then read some, then we took a walk out to the cemetery. It was a lovely day. We went through Mrs. Teeples house.

June 22 Monday (a Mr. Bolton called to see W's Mother)

Clear and pretty until nearly 5 PM then it rained hard and most of the night. In AM I fooled around and then washed some doilies and center piece. Then I sewed some on the Flounce quilt. In Pm I sewed until 3 then I went out where Will was working and helped him pull weeds out. After supper I worked on Ma's table scarf.

June 23 Tuesday

Cloudy and dismal until afternoon then the sun came out nice and warm. We got up early and I baked three cakes for Donation Day and swept my dining room. I had very good luck with my cakes. After dinner I scrubbed the back porch and swept the stair steps and hall and kitchen then made the beds etc. cleaned up and picked some flowers. I will work some on Ma's fancy piece. Will is up on the bed asleep.

June 24 Wednesday Donation Day

Lovely AM I got up a little earlier and had breakfast early, then I iced a cake. Will came home and helped me some by sweeping the porches then after I finished my work I got ready and went down town with him. I stayed until nearly 11. Then we came home and had a piece. I did not wash my dishes but got ready and went down to office. We took a hack about 1 and went out to the Home. There were quite a crowd. We met several strangers. We had 2 good dishes of cream. We came home about 5. A Mr. Ulery was here for supper. I was very tired at night. In evening it rained some.

June 25 Thursday

Lovely day, but I was sick so I did not do much. I cut out some quilt pieces in AM In PM corpse was brought home I dressed up and sat around thinking we would have callers. I wrote home. After supper Mrs. Bloom and Miss Bentle called. They stayed quite late. I was just putting M to bed when Mrs. Durst and Linnenbrinck called. They were here till 9-30. We were worn out. I went to bed.

June 26 Friday

he helped me, then took a picture of the rose bush. At supper time Mrs. Roth called. I left my supper on and it burned. After supper I went down town to mail a letter. Came home and studied my Sunday School lesson.

June 27 Saturday

Lovely day. 8-10 Will home cutting grass. I fooled around with my flowers etc in AM. In PM I sewed on that quilt until I got such a headache I quit and went to sleep. I had a letter from home saying Carl was hurt so bad. *(Carl was Julia's youngest brother and youngest of the family.)*

June 28 Sunday (last Sunday in old Church hall. Gloss girl found)

We went to Sunday School and Church morning and evening. In PM we slept and read and looked at our flowers. Rained in PM Mr. and Mrs. Wright called in evening.

June 29 Monday

Lovely day. I washed by myself. Will came home and turned the wringer for me. I was all done by noon. In PM I sewed some. Will came home bringing our Church cushion, he wanted me to go over to the Church so I went. The women were cleaning and tearing things up. I came home and finished that quilt. They brought the organ for us to keep.

June 30 Tuesday

Lovely day only quite warm. In AM ironed. Will came home and mowed the yard some. After dinner I made beds and put away the clothes. Then went down in cellar and made me a little stand. About 3 we had a heavy shower. After it was over we finished my stand. After supper I went down town for some muslin for Clara's skirt. Came home and cut it out and partly made it.

Another pretty day. Mrs. Millemen's corpse was brought home and will be buried Saturday. In AM I sewed some, Will came home and worked on his yard. Sowing grass seed. In PM he came home I was making a little stand and

We sat out on the porch for quite a while.

July 1 Wednesday

Pretty but warm. In AM I swept the front some, sitting room and kitchen, washed some windows. Will came home about 10-30 and helped me after dinner. I finished. Then fixed his Mother and then took a bath. Then I finished Clara's skirt. After supper Mrs. Bloom came over. After she went I dug around in my flower bed then I went over to Mrs. Wright's awhile.

July 2 Thursday

Warm. I was in bed all AM with an awful headache. By PM I wrote home. Will is not well either.

July 3 Friday

Very warm. In AM I got through my work and went downtown for something to eat. Will had bought some peas so I came home. I got some ribbon at Mrs. Linnenbrincks. In PM I slept from 1 till 2. I finished my letter Clara. Will came and we sat upstairs awhile then I came down and played some on the organ. After supper I went down town to help Will get a hat. Later on Mrs. Wright and Helen came over and sat on the porch until Will came then we sat out there until 10.

July 4 Saturday

Warm, a little shower in AM I worked around. Will never came home until 12. In PM he slept some and so did I. About 3-30 we went down to office. I stayed until 5 then came home and picked Mrs. Teeples a bouquet of sweet peas. I came home and got his M supper. Will came about 7 then we went down and got some fine ice cream. We sat on the front porch and watched Br. Andon shoot off his fireworks.

July 5 Sunday (In margin: Clara's birthday) *(she was 10)*

Rained off and on all day long. We neither one went any place. I was not feeling well nor Will either. In PM we sat upstairs and wrote some on the life of his father.

July 6 Monday

Lovely day. I washed. Will came home and helped me. I was through early. Sophie called awhile in AM After dinner I ironed and mended some then went down town after supper. We had an invitation to Clara's party.

July 7 Tuesday

Pretty Day. In AM I canned 1 qt of raspberries and made 2 pts of red raspberry jam. Then I got dinner. In PM I had nothing to do. Helen came over. After supper I went down town and bought M a grey calico dress. Came home and cut out the lining. I went down to meet Will but stopped at Mrs. Gelbachs. Then I came home and Will was not home yet.

July 8 Wednesday

Hot all day. In AM I finished my work down stairs and then went out and dug around in my flower beds. Trained up my nasturtiums and grape vines then I discovered Gloss's dog on my front porch so I had that to scrub. I never got through until nearly 11. I then baisted up a lining for a waist of his Mother's. After dinner I made her waist almost finished it after supper. I sewed until dark then put her to bed and wrote in my diary. Will came home and had some work to do so we worked until 10 PM In the midst of our work Mr.Wruter's called but never came in.

July 9 Thursday

Lovely day, in AM I straightened my kitchen and pantry, took down the pipe and pushed the stove back, got some paper and covered the pipe hole, then I scrubbed my back porch, then went upstairs and cleaned up some 10 AM. Will bought some ice cream in the evening. Sadie Gloss was over to show us the baby.

July 10 Friday

Cloudy and a few showers and somewhat cooler. In AM I did not feel well so did not do much. I wrote some home to Carl. In PM Will came home and we lay around awhile. I slept from 1-2. He developed a picture of the Old Church. Mrs. Steudebaker called on Will's Mother. After supper Mrs. Teeples and Stoutt were her

July 11 Saturday

A very nice day. We had a shower in the morning. I cut some of the grass around the trees. Then repotted some flowers and fixed my shelves in my pantry with oil cloth. Will brought me a good letter from Minnie. Carl is not getting along so very well, his sore is not healing very fast. I hope it will though.

July 12 Sunday

Clear in AM. We went to Sunday School and stayed for Church. After Church it commenced to rain but did not rain very much. I was lonely all day, in PM I slept and Will went up to the cemetery. We did not go to Church in the evening.

July 13 Monday

Cloudy, I washed. It commenced raining but cleared off real nice about 9. In PM Will took my picture and we fooled around all PM I was good and tired.

July 14 Tuesday (In margin: Ma's birthday Bengie was here) *Laura was 53.*

Lovely in AM I ironed until 10 then I baked biscuits, fried meat and cooked potatoes. After dinner I went over to Mrs. Kirkers and practiced some. After supper I went down to office and waited for Will to come. Very cool. I wore my grey suit.

July 15 Wednesday

Nice day but cool in AM I finished my ironing and mended some. Will brought me a picture of Eva and Murhl. After dinner I went out in the year and mowed some. Mrs. Hoffman came and stayed all afternoon. After supper I went over to Wrights and practiced some. *(After Laura died her husband Cory W Padfield married her younger sister Eva and they raised Murhl together.)*

July 16 Thursday (In margin: Wedding anniversary)

Cloudy and cool most of the day. In AM I hurried and got my dish work done and then went out doors and worked all AM Will came home and helped me fix up tomatoes. Then he got dirt ready for his prime roses

Will gave me a $10 gold piece, he wrapped it up in 17 pieces of paper then put it in a box. And then in my stocking. We had fun all day, teasing each other. In PM we both worked hard out doors fixing the yard. In PM I went down to Mrs. Zehners and took napkins home. Will and I looked at some furniture but never got anything. I came home and sat on Mrs. Wrights porch a long time.

July 17 Friday

Clear and some warmer. In AM I worked out doors some. In PM I slept some so did Will. We neither felt well. In evening we had callers. Mrs. Pedamendsess and two nieces. After they went I dressed and when Will came we went to a social on Harmony Hill given by the ladies of the Macabees. *(a fraternal organization with women's auxiliary begun in Canada in 1878 provided burial and widow benefits)*

July 18 Saturday

Fine day. In AM I finished my work and washed Eva's doily and got it ready to send off then I finished hemming my table cloth. In PM I slept most of the PM After supper I went down to office.

July 19 Sunday

Clear and nice in AM but heavy rain about 6. We did not do much in AM Will studied his Sunday School lesson. I got dinner about 2. We went to SS had a good lesson. About 3-20 we went up to the cemetery. Came home and ate supper. I wrote some to Ma, Mrs. And Mrs. Gloss, Florence and Leslie all went to Alleghany today.

July 20   Monday (In margin: Eva's birthday 17 yrs.)

Clear in early part of the AM but about 9-30 we had an awful hard shower, I washed but did not hang them out until after it was over. After dinner I finished hanging them out. Then I swept 4 rooms and hall. Lillie Gloss ironed all the white clothes. Mrs. Gelbach called in evening.

July 21   Tuesday

Lovely day. In AM I ironed 2 or 3 pieces then Will came and we dug out weeds. I got dinner, after dinner Will and I went over to Harmony to get some jardinières but we could not see any we liked so we came home. I went down street for a box to send some primroses home so I bought Will a jardinière. He thought it was pretty. I sat over in Wright's yard awhile in evening. I am not feeling very well. The top of my head hurts me. 8-25 Will not home yet.

July 22   Wednesday

In AM I was sick all morning but managed to get my work done. In PM Will cut the grass around and I sat around and watched him. In evening Mrs. Passavant and Emma called. Will brought me a good letter from home. We heard such bad news about my Mr. Welsh.

July 23   Thursday

A fine day . In AM Will came home and we cut grass. I baked 2 pies and cooked beans for dinner. After dinner Will took some pictures. I made my little stand for my begonia.

July 24   Friday

Fine day but I was in bed all morning. In PM I felt better. Will came home and took a picture of Brandon Wright and Helen. Then we took one of Lillian Stoutt and a crowd 2, Mrs. Stoutt, Melisa Meeder and myself. After supper I made prints of them then went down to Mrs. Teeples, came home and got a bucket and went for some cream, came home and found Brandon and Helen here, we each had a dish.

July 25   Saturday (Junior Gloss came home sick)

Very warm day. In AM I baked two pies and got dinner ready. Will was home awhile. I got a long letter from home. They had quite a storm. In PM I slept from 1-30 to 3. Mrs. Knibbs called awhile then Will came and we had supper. About 8 Mrs. Kirker and Miss Wertz called. It was 11 before I got to sleep.

July 26   Sunday

Lovely day. In AM Will and I went up to the cemetery, came home and got dinner. We went to SS, I did not feel like going so I slept. I have neuralgia in my left arm. This has been a lonesome day.

July 27   Monday

Fine day. I washed a small washing then cleaned up my house. After dinner I ironed all but three pieces done by 2 PM Will mowed some after supper, Mrs. Bloom came over, I went over to the neissengans (?) to send to town for some indian head muslin and doily.

July 28   Tuesday

Fine day in morning, I fooled around with my flowers, scrubbed porches etc. then I made dumplings and sent June Gloss one. After dinner I finished ironing. Will finished mowing the yard. I watched and then I sewed some on my quilt. After supper Mrs. Allen and sister called. Then I went downtown, called on Mrs. Debendarfer. Came home found Mrs. Teeples here. I was very tired and nervous.

July 29   Wednesday

Fine day. I worked around all morning. In PM I worked some on my neck tie. It rained some in PM then cleared off. I bought 10 qts of black berries about 5 PM, Miss Bentle called after supper. After she left I washed my dishes.

July 30   Thursday

Fine day. In AM I canned my berries. Cooked dinner, was tired. Then in PM I took a picture but it was not good. Will came and we fooled all PM taking pictures, after supper I went downtown, got a waist and calico for quilt.

July 31   Friday

Lovely day. In AM I sewed on my shirt waist nearly finished it, in PM I set my quilt together. All done by 6 PM Mrs. Wright and Mrs....*left blank*, left for a trip to Canada. Sent a letter home.

August 1   Saturday

Fine day. In AM I finished my work down stairs then washed two lace curtains in sitting room and ironed them and cleaned the house up. After dinner I baked two pies and scrubbed and picked flowers, through by 3.

August 2   Sunday

Fine day. After breakfast we went out to the cemetery. Took some flowers and put them on Mrs. Swains grave. We stopped at Mrs. Teeples awhile. In PM we went to Sunday School and Church.

August 3   Monday

Cloudy in AM but I washed. Mrs. Stoutt Sr. washed some of her clothes with mine. We were done by 9-30, in PM I slept some and hem stitched my tie,, then after supper I ironed nearly all my clothes.

August 4   Tuesday

In AM after Will left I cut the grass but it commenced to rain so I came in to my dis work. Will came and trimmed the trees some and dug out some weeds. After dinner I finished my tie and commenced my linen square. Will did not come until 3-30. After supper I cut the grass in the back yard and dug out weeds. Don't feel so good either 8:35.

August 5 Wednesday

Pretty day. In AM I finished my work. Will came home and fixed the vines on the front porch and dug out weeds. I went downtown with him. Got some oil cloth and a can of corn. The mail was late so I came on home and fixed my cupboard. After dinner I finished my cupboard and cleaned around. It was 3 before I was done, then I tried to work some but felt so dizzy I lay down until 4 then got up and got supper. After supper I dressed and went down street. Went to see Mrs. Hoffman. Came home about 9. Will went down and got some ice cream. It was fine.

August 6 Thursday (Hailed)

Cloudy and some showers in AM I worked out in garden nearly all morning, after dinner I wrote to Murhl and went to the society. I hemmed two sides to a quilt. I brought home 6 gingham aprons to make. I made 1 ½ after supper. About 5 it rained and hailed but not long. I sewed some and then went to bed. I had a card from Mrs. Wright.

August 7 Friday

Fine day. In AM I swept 3 rooms upstairs and the hall steps and hall and kitchen downstairs. In PM I did not do much of anything. I went down to Mrs. Teeples awhile, came home and printed some pictures. I sewed on Minnie's tie. Mrs. Teeples and Zehner called after supper. I went down to meet Will

August 8, 1903 Saturday (Murhl's birthday 3 years)

Weather very nice. In AM I washed all that was dirty. Will came home and helped me so much. I was all done by 10. After dinner I ironed them all. Washed windows and hung my clean curtains up. I never got done until 6 PM I was very tired then, I went down to see Will and got some things for Sunday.

August 9 Sunday

Fine but was sick all day, never went anywhere.

August 10 Monday

Cloudy in AM but cleared off and was very pretty. I worked all morning changing the dining room table etc. In PM I finished a tie for Minnie and made an apron.

August 11 Tuesday

Fine day. In AM I mowed all the yard. Miss Bentle came up the back way and we sat and talked quite awhile. After dinner I worked on my linen square and made an apron. After supper I went down street, came home and went over to Mrs. Cavanaughs.

August 12 Wednesday

Fine Picnic Day

August 13 Thursday

Lovely in AM I went down and got some flower pots to put some young plants in. In PM Will came home and we took a boat ride. We went about 3 miles up the creek, had a fine time, came home good and hungry.

August 14 Friday

Nice day. In AM I printed some pictures for Will. Then finished my center piece, stamped of a laundry bag pattern and leaf. After dinner I put my ferns back in the front room. Will came and worked on the pictures. I made an apron. After supper I went down street awhile then came home and commenced Bert's laundry bag.

August 15 Saturday

Fine day. In AM Will came home to finish some pictures. I worked around baked a pie for Sunday. In PM I worked some on Bert's laundry bag. Then I dressed and went down to office, intended going over across the street for ice cream but after Will closed, I felt so badly thinking of last year that we came home. *(in the summer of 1902 John and Bert contracted typhoid fever while on a camping trip. Eva, Carl, Clara and Minnie also became sick but John died)*

August 16 Sunday

Nice day. Will went to Church, I did not feel much like it so I read and slept. I had dinner ready when he came. In PM we read and slept toward evening. I got lonely and had a good cry.
Incorrect date which eventually gets corrected

August 18 Monday

Nice day. I washed a very large wash. Then put up 7 quarts of elder berries. After supper I went down street, sat and talked to Mrs. Linnenbrinck, Mrs. Teeples came by and I went home with her.

August 19 Tuesday (Rapes's moved in their new house)

Fine day. I ironed all morning. Will came home and worked awhile after dinner. I put up plums and ironed. Will bought some more plums so I was busy till 8-20. Mrs. Linnenbrinck called too. Had a letter from home.

August 20 Wednesday (in margin: Mary Laferer died)

Nice and warm, rained about 8. In AM I finished ironing. In PM I finished Bert's laundry bag. Will developed some negatives. I was very tired all day. I sent a letter and some pictures to Stella today.

August 21 Thursday

I was down street in AM got me some shoes and linen for a doily, came home and got dinner. Was sick all afternoon. Will dug potatoes, I went over to see Jennie Gloss. She was doing very poorly.

August 22 Friday

Lovely Day. In AM I just worked around and scrubbed my front porch after Glosses dog. In PM I went to a party at Passavants. There was a large crowd. We ate in the yard and on the porch. Mrs. Stoutt, Gelbach, Harper, Dumbart and myself went. All took their fancy work. Came home about 7-30 with an awful headache, about 2AM I wakened in such misery. I threw up some and went to sleep but wakened in the morning with it.

August 22 Saturday

Lovely day but dreadful warm. I got up about 8-30 washed the dishes and canned 7 quarts of elderberries and got dinner. I was pretty well worn out. Will came home early and helped me, the dear boy is such good help. In PM I lay around. Minnie sent me a gook of songs from home. I tried some of them and found they were pretty.

August 23 Sunday (in margin: Laying of the cornerstone of the L church)

I was sick Saturday night so did not get up until 10 o'clock Sunday morning. Then I lay around until 2 PM then I dressed and went with WG to the services. Came home and sat around not feeling good.

August 24 Monday (in margin: M downstairs in PM)

A very warm day in morning, I straightened the house. In PM Will came home in afternoon and pulled out weeds I worked on my leaf doily. After supper I went over to see Mrs. Kirker and had a fine time.

August 25 Tuesday

Warm but had a heavy shower about 5. In AM I dug out weeds. First I baked a huckleberry pie and then made the beds. Then worked out doors till 11. In PM Will worked some and I too but we both lay down and took a sleep. After the rain I sat on the front porch and worked and talked to Mrs. Bloom, then went down town.

August 26 Wednesday

I worked out in the yard, pulling out grass all morning. In PM I made my last apron for the society. After supper I pulled out more grass. Then went downtown. Mrs. Bloom was over awhile.
(Julia's maternal grandmother Susannah Margaret Gilbert Buckingham was 86 yrs old in 1903. She died April 6, 1904 at age 87.)

August 27 Thursday

Very warm, rained all PM and night. In morning I went down and got some gingham for 2 aprons. Came home and got dinner. After dinner I made one and went over to Mrs. B she wanted some silk pieces so I came home and got some. After supper I made another apron and went down to meet Will. It was raining.

August 28 Friday

Very warm, rained till 8, cleared off warm. I swept and dusted and cleaned around in AM In PM I sewed some I had a letter from home. GMa has been sick.

Aug 29 Saturday

Cloudy in AM but cleared off about noon. Very warm in PM In AM I helped Will pull weeds until 9 then came in and baked a pie and got dinner. Mrs. Kirker's company called to see if I would come over in the evening. So I hurried and got through my work, cleaned everything, then started for Harmony. On my way I called on Mrs. Ketterer and Mrs. Dumbart, Mrs. Kirker and company were ouit calling so I sat down on the front porch and worked on my fancy work. Then I went over to Winter's store and got some machine oil. I met them coming home. We had a fine evening. One lady played some pretty pieces. I got home by 7-30, was tired and not feeling very well in my stomach.

Aug 30 Sunday

Rainy and cloudy most of the day. I had a lonesome cry all AM. In evening we took a walk over to see the new Church and houses. Came home and sat on the porch till Church time. Then we went to the Presbyterian Church. I had such pain in my lung I could hardly enjoy the sermon.

Aug 31 Monday

Nice wash day. Had a big one, got through about 2. I ironed some in the evening. Jennie Gloss had such a sinking spell. So I went over and never ironed any more.

Sept 1 Tuesday

Rained nearly all day. I ironed until 3. I put up 3 pints of tomatoes after dinner. After supper I went over to Mrs. Weigle's awhile. Came home and went down and stayed with Will.

Sept 2 Wednesday (in margin: Jennie Gloss died 25 of 5)

Lovely day. I ironed 2 shirts and swept my front room, setting room and kitchen. Got dinner and canned 2 pts. of tomatoes. After dinner Will raked the grass up and I sat out and I worked on my doily and watched him. After supper I went down street got some gingham for Stella's apron. Then went over to look at Jennie, poor soul is resting and how soon we will be I cannot tell.

Sept 3 Thursday

Cloudy in AM I worked hard all morning, baked pies, then apples for Glosses, cooked beans and corn and meat, baked biscuits for dinner, then I got the headache so after dinner I lay down and slept 2 hours and got up and dressed and made beds. Then went to the society but my head still ached. I came home about 4-30 and found Will lying on the cot with the sick headache.

Sept 4 Friday

In AM I worked around and then made 2 wreaths for Jennie Glosses funeral. In PM I rested and then sewed some on Stella's apron. Will felt some better. I also swept and dusted my bedroom.

Sept 5 Saturday   (very cool in evening)

Fine day. In AM after I was done my work I went down to the office. Will got Eva's picture and a letter. I got some silkaline for a shelf, In PM I fixed it, then sewed on Stella's apron. After supper Brandon gave me a young chicken and killed it for me. I was just dressing it when Miss Bentle called. She did not stay long. Then put Will's Mother to bed. Then I dressed and went down to office.

Sept 6 Sunday

A fine day. Will and I went to Church in AM. After dinner we went over to Wrights and sung. Mrs. Weigle came over too. In PM we went to the Reformed Church in Harmony. They had Harvest Home services.

Sept 7 Monday

Fine day. I washed, not a large one. I cooked a pie all pumpkin too. Will's M is sick today. I ironed all my clothes after supper. Then went down town and got some tape to finish my hair receiver.

Sept 8 Tuesday

In AM I baked my pumpkin pie, finished my hair receiver. In PM Will fixed the light in the front room. I cut out a muslin (?) box and made it. Ella Swain called. After supper I went down town and got some gingham for Mrs. Rape. I am going to make her 2 aprons. I cut out one and almost made it

Sept 9 Wednesday

Fine day but hot. All AM I worked down stairs cleaned all the shelves in pantry and cupboard and swept both rooms, scrubbed porch and closet. In PM I swept upstairs and hall. After supper I sewed on Mrs. Rape's aprons until 9PM then I went to bed but did not sleep well. I was too nervous.

Sept 10 Thursday   (Fire at E works)

Fine morning but warm. I finished those aprons. Then canned some tomatoes, then made two pies and got dinner. After dinner I went to the society and took my quilt, came home just as it commences to blow and rain terrible. I had a letter from Ma. She has been to Kansas City. (Laura, Julia's mother, went to visit her sister, Mrs. Kreamer, in Kansas City)

Sept 11 Friday   (Cascade Park)

Cloudy part of the day. We left about 9-15 arrived in New Castle 10-30 then we took the car for the park. After we landed we went and got 2 sandwiches and a cup of coffee a piece. From there we went to the tintype gallery and had our pictures taken but they were hideous and it made us angry. We went and watched the merry-go-round then took a stroll down the cascade and around, then we climbed up ever so many steps to the top of the hill and came out to the fairgrounds, watched the ferris wheel then went and took a ride on the roller coaster. Then down to the dancing hall. There we looked at the displays and watched them dance awhile. Then we took another round and a little boat ride on the electric launch. In PM we listened to a play and saw a dog performance which was fine. Then we went up on the dancing floor and saw the balloon go up. Then we came back to town and looked around, got some fruit and a salt and pepper stand and came home. All went well Gena Linnenbrinck stayed and Mrs. Stoutt got dinner.

(A year after the park opened, its owners added a carousel, baseball park, theater, and dance pavilion, of which the pavilion is still standing. At the time, the dance pavilion was the largest in the state of Pennsylvania. The park's first roller coaster, the *Toboggan*, was also installed at this time. The year 1899 saw the addition of a zoo, picnic grove, and lake, the latter being created by damming the Big Run Creek which ran through the park. In 1922, the park's original carousel was replaced. A new roller coaster, *The Gorge*, was also added at around this same time, and by 1925, the park's area had been expanded to 138 acres (0.56 km^2) and its midway had 17 rides.)

Sept 12 Saturday (In margin: Dagoes digging the sewer)

Very warm all day. In AM Will came home and cut the grass and propped up his boards. The dagoes were working. I baked two pies and got dinner. After dinner I crocheted on my shawl. In evening Sophie was here. After supper I scrubbed all the walks and porch. Then dressed and went down town but could not stay until 9 so came home and sat on Mrs. Rape's porch awhile. Will did not come until nearly 10.

Sept 13 Sunday

Very warm day, we went to Sunday School and Church but came home sick. Will does not feel well yet.

Sept 14 Monday (in margin: commenced shawl)

Nice day. I thought I would wash but got things ready and gave it up, so I cleaned the house then I commenced my shawl. I sat out on the front porch all morning and watched the Italians dig. Will was home sick all day.

Sept 15 Tuesday

Lillie and I washed, then I straightened the house. In PM I worked on my shawl. Will brought his Mother down. Mrs. Meekley was down.

Sept 16 Wednesday

I ironed steady all morning, had a letter from Stella, sewed some on my aprons and worked on my shawl.

Sept 17 Thursday

Worked some on the aprons but I got <u>sick</u> and quit. I could not go to the society but took a sleep. Later on Mrs. Grant came over in evening. I felt good. Mrs. Stoutt came over and brought some cotton that was left of my quilt.

Sept 18 Friday

Nice day but very cool. In morning I finished 2 pieces, I did not iron. Then I worked around in my flowers. In PM Will and I cleaned up the back yard some. Trimmed the peach tree etc. Mrs. Endress called. After supper I went down to the office.

Sept 19 Saturday

In AM I fooled around, got down on gas store. Washed off some flower pots, baked 2 pumpkin pies and 1 apple. After dinner I went up to see Mrs. Teeples, worked on my shawl. Mrs. Debendarfer called and brought a pie. I planted my fall bulbs After supper Mrs. Teeples and Stoutt came in a while. I worked on some lace for a skirt.

Sept 20 Sunday

Clear day. Will went to SS in PM I did not feel well all day.

Sept 21 Monday

I washed, got done early. After dinner I went down and got some white goods for an apron for Minnie. Came home and commenced it. I finished it by 8 PM I had a letter from home and Minnie and some from CW.

Sept 22 Tuesday

Fine day. I ironed and put up some tomatoes, went down town for ceiling wzx and meat. Went over to Mrs. Blooms and worked on my shawl. Sent M apron.

Sept 23 Wednesday

Nice warm day. In AM I went down town for a roast of meat. First I washed my large window off and my pantry window. At noon Will brought me a letter from home. GMa is sick in bed. Carl was no better and all were blue. It made me feel very lonely and blue.

Sept 24 Thursday

Very cloudy and cold. I baked two pies then went down town and waited until Will came home. Then we had an early dinner. He went down to look for a flower stand for me.

Sept 25 Friday

Nice day. In AM I worked with my flowers and swept. After dinner I swept our room and dusted. Will came and commenced to put the boards away. The Italians were shoveling away the ground but were very slow we got tired. After supper I cleaned away some, Will came home and helped some. I then got ready and went down town with him.

Sept 26 Saturday

Lovely day. I went to Pittsburgh with the society. I went to Harmony and got on. Wlla Swain and Mrs. Sitler and Steiners went from there. Mrs. Wrath, Ralston, Byers and daughters Neby, Eyles, Partridge were in the crowd also. We 4 went shopping in the AM Mrs. Sitler got her suit then we went to dinner. Had a fine dinner. After dinner we went to Soloman & Ruebens and Ella got her suit there. Then to the 5 & 10 store. I got a glass dish and a cream pitcher. From there to the Opera House. We met most of them there. After the play, Mrs. Sitler, Ella and I went to a friend's house for supper. I was very sick with head-ache. Mrs. Ralston gave me some tablets and they made me vomit but I soon got over it and we went to the Expo in the evening. All met again at 10:25, we went to the depot and all got home safely. All had a nice day.

Sept 27 Sunday

Rained from about 1 hr in AM then cleared off. Will sent to SS. I did not feel like it.

Sept 28 Monday

Cool I did not feel like washing. I was downtown early. I wrote a let-ter to Minnie in the office. I got a short one from her. I bought me a red dressing sacque and some outing flannel for Clara's skirt. In PM I cut it out but could not get it to fit so I put it away. Over to Stoutt's in evening.

Sept 29 Tuesday

Still cool. In AM I worked with my flowers all morning, putting up shelves etc. in PM Will and I went out for some milk weeds. Came by Mrs. Teeples and chatted her awhile. Will planted a rose bush for her. In evening Miss Bentle called.

Sept 30 Wednesday

Nice and warm again. I washed. I first straightened the house, made one bed. Then I commenced washing. Will helped me at noon so I had them out by 12, then I baked bread too, scrubbed my walk and porch. Passavants were here, Lillian and Emma. After supper I cooked pumpkin and ironed most of my clothes then went down to office. I was tired enough to go to bed. One year ago today I bid John good by for the last time.

> (John's obituary appeared in the *Clinton Democrat:-*
> The shadows of death darkened the beautiful home of A. G. Sherman on East Green Street Sunday, November 23, 1902, at 6:25 p.m., when the death angel claimed John, fifth child of A. G. Sherman and wife, as his own. He was born in Clin-ton in 1881 and if his life had been spared until Tuesday, the 25th, he would have been 21. He was a sufferer from typhoid fever for four long months but all that loving hands could do was in vain. He leaves his parents, four sisters and two broth-ers. The funeral was conducted at the house Tuesday, after which the remains were tenderly laid to rest in Englewood Cemetery.(This was not in the diary.)

Oct 1 Thursday

Cloudy and rainy most of the day. I ironed some and baked two pies. In PM Ella Swain came by and we went to the sewing society. Had such a nice time till 10, quilted on my quilt.

Oct 2 Friday

Nice day. In AM I swept the 2 rooms and hall, upstairs hall and 2 rooms downstairs then I washed the curtains in the North room and got dinner. After dinner I ironed them and washed the windows and put them up, scrubbed etc. then finished my letter home and got supper. After supper, Mrs. Newberg and George called. After I put M to bed, I went down to Mrs. Teeple's had a nice evening.

Oct 3 Saturday

No letter from home this week. In AM I worked on those milk weed balls. Herbert Beakley brought me some nice apples up. After dinner I made some more balls and fixed the bag, themn I made Clara's skirt and crocheted on the lace for it. When Will came I showed him the milkweed work thing I took it down and gave it to Mrs. Teeples. She thought it fine. I came home and got supper. After supper I made 2 balls, washed his Mother, then dressed up, came down and finished Clara's lace. Then went down to office. Will gave me some money to buy some grapes. When I came back I stopped in Mrs. Linnenbrinck to look at some hats. We talked till 9, I went in office and said: "Why you waiting on me?" Will said; "Who else would I be waiting for." He was very angry but I was innocent.

Oct 4 Sunday

Nice day but warm. We got up late. After our work was done, we gathered some flowers and went out to the home to put them on Mr. Bassler's and Mary's graves. We came back and sat down under one large pine tree and ate some grapes and apples. After dinner we both took a nap. After supper I played and sung some. Then Will read some out of my Bible.

Oct 5 Monday

Cloudy and rainy most all day. I worked all AM making milk-weed balls. Will went out and got me some. In PM I finished one sack and sold it to Mrs. Rape for 30 cents. I finished the others about 8. I went down and got stuff and ribbon.

Oct 6 Tuesday

Rainy most all day. I worked on balls all AM finished another sack. But have not sold it yet. In evening I went over to Rapes. Mary and I went out for more pods then about 7, I went over and helped her make some.

Oct 7 Wednesday

Nice day but dreadful windy. In AM I swept then went down to office. I got a letter from Ma, Carl is better. In PM I fixed over my old white waist and blue one. Will was lying down, did not feel well.

Oct 8 Thursday

Made some balls, then cleaned the house up some. In PM I went to Sewing Society. After supper I wrote home and went down to office. I did not feel well.

Oct 9 Friday

Cloudy and windy but I washed. Was done so early. Then I cleaned up the house. In PM I went over to Harmony and got me a new table cloth, 2 sheets, 2 tea towels and some white goods. Came by Mrs. Kirkers, stayed awhile then came home , got supper. Then I ironed most all of my clothes and hemmed my apron and towels.

Oct 10 Saturday

Finished my ironing, baked 3 pies, swept. After dinner I cleaned up and went down to office, stayed till Will came home.

Oct 11 Sunday

We were home all day. I had roast port and baked sweet potatoes for dinner. Will did ot feel well all day. We read. Mrs. Teeples came up in AM.

Oct 12 Monday

In AM I took all my flowers upstairs, then cut out Minnie's white apron and almost made it before dinner, as the time was late after dinner, Mrs. Rape and I went downtown and got new hats. Came home and finished Minnie's apron. Then I went down again with Will and got goods for Jennie's apron.

Oct 13 Tuesday

Cloudy. I cut my tomatoes for chow-chow then crocheted some, then cut out the waist for Clara's underskirt. After dinner Will and I worked in the garden pulling up beets etc. After supper I helped Mrs. Rape peel apples, came home at 8, went down to office and came home with him.

Oct 14 Wednesday

Fine day. In AM I made my chow-chow and watched my bread. At noon I stirred apple butter for Mrs. Rape. In PM I helped her some and worked outdoors some. In evening I went down street.

Oct 15 Thursday

Will and I went to Pittsburgh. Our train was over 2 hrs. late so it was nearly dinner time before we got there. We first went to the bank to deposit my money, then we hunted Miller's Restaurant for our dinner. After dinner we went to Horn's Campbell's and Rosenbaum Kaufmans. We had hard work finding anything to suit both of us. About half of Zelienople went. Mrs. D and Anna, Miss Bentle, Gelbach's, Mrs. Ifft, Stokey.

Oct 16 Friday

I worked hard all AM sweeping and dusting and watering my flowers. Inn PM I trimmed my old hat over. After supper I went down own, came home and made a sheet and faced an old skirt. Mrs. Dumbart called. Mrs. D (Debendarfor) came by for her and stayed quite a while.

Oct 17 Saturday

Rained nearly all morning. After I finished my work I painted my porch chair. Then cut out Jennie's apron. After dinner Mrs. Teeples called. We planned to go to Pittsburgh Monday if I am well enough. After she left I went downtown, Will got me a nice underskirt.

Oct 18 Sunday

A very nice day. Yet cool and windy. We were home all AM after dinner we went to SS came home and read. After supper Mrs. Teeples came up to see about going to Pitts. Monday. We had a jolly time. I was sick Sunday night and was awake a great deal.

Oct 19 Monday

A nice day. Mrs. Teeples and Herbert came by for me. The bus came for us, train on time. We had a nice day. We first went to Rosenbaum and exchanged my suit or had it fitted. Then we went to Norm and Steiner's' and got Herbert a suit and Mrs. T a silk waist. Then we went to Miller and got dinner. After dinner we went to the 5 & 10 cent store. I got some picture frames and jardinière, knife, potato brush, some hose for Clara. I also got Will some goods for 2 shirts and Carl 2 for Xmas. We got home on time.

Oct 20 Tuesday

Nice day but I was sick all day with a awful headache. Mrs.Passavant and Titzel were here but I never felt like going up and Will got angry at me.

Oct 21 Wednesday

In AM I straightened my house. Then went downtown. Will gave me a letter from Ma and Minnie and Eva all well but poor G.Ma. In PM washed all my white clothes. Mrs. Stoutt and Lillian came over awhile. Will came home and helped me after I was through Mrs. Teeple came up awhile. I got Will's supper early. After jour supper I fixed him some and took it down to him. Trains were late. I worked on lace.

Oct 22 Thursday

In AM I ironed and cleaned up the house. After dinner I went to the society. Mrs. Brandon came over and stayed all PM I went down to Mrs. Teeples after supper and finished my lace.

Oct 23 Friday

In AM I hemmed my quilt then cut out a shirt for Will. In PM I sewed on it and got so nervous for I got the sleeves too short. Then I worked on an apron for Jennie's Xmas. After supper I worked on shirt and nearly finished it. Then went down to office awhile.

Oct 24 Saturday

Nice day. In AM I washed my dishes then baked a pie. In PM I sewed on Jennie's apron. Mrs. Kirker and niece came and stayed until 4. Then I got supper, after supper I finished the apron and commenced a pair of drawers for Clara. Froze ice.

Oct 25 Sunday

A very nice day but cool in AM. We got up late and I had a surprise dinner for Will. I had roast chicken and dressing, celery mashed potatoes, slaw etc. He was very much surprised. We went to Sunday School in PM. I taught my first class – Mrs. Stoutt's. Went with Mrs. Wright in evening.

Oct 26 Monday (snowed nearly all day)

Snowed nearly all day. I commenced washing but did not hang them out. I came up and finished Clara's pair of drawers. Then I took all the books out of the book case and when Will came he and I moved it to the front room. After dinner I helped him put in the books, then cleaned up the sitting room. After super I went down to see a man develop films at Mr. Seller's store. Will came by for me and we came home.

Oct 27 Tuesday (Gloss's baby died) (Will found a cat)

Glosses baby died 2:20 this AM I hung out my clothes, baked a pie, got dinner. After dinner I sewed awhile on Clara's skirt. Then I went down to Mrs. Geisinheimers to see about getting a waist made. Came by Mrs. Byers and stopped awhile. Came home then went over to Glosses, came home and made some apple dumplings, got my supper, then dampened my clothes and sat down.es Then over to Stoutts,

Oct 28 Wednesday (in margin: M downstairs)

In AM I ironed then made a wreath and took it over to Mrs. Gloss. Came home and got dinner, then I swept the three rooms upstairs. I had an awful headache but I kept on. Will helped me some. Mrs. Goering and Zehner called. Will brought his Mother down to see them. Miss B (Bentle) called in PM

Oct 29 Thursday

In AM I crocheted on some wheels for my piano cover. In PM I went to the society then went over to Kirkers. Came home and baked a cake then went to bed.

Oct 30 Friday

In AM I iced my cake and cleaned around some, cut some honeysuckle to take over to K (Kirkers) in the afternoon. Kate came after me. I took my fern over. We had a real nice time. I came home with the Gelbach girls. Will came early and put his Mother to bed. I had 3 letters. Pa, Stella and Minnie.

Oct 31 Saturday

Nice day in AM I worked around and crocheted. IN PM I went calling. After supper I went down to office and stayed until I broke Will's glasses. Then he got mad and I came home. I will not go down again. I will go other places first.

Nov 1 Sunday

Fine day. We slept until 8 o'clock then got up had breakfast and got ready for Church. In PM we read and sat around.

Nov 2 Monday

Very foggy early but cleared off. I finished my work then I crocheted 8 wheels. In PM I went down to Mrs. Geisinheimer's to get my measures taken for my waist. Then I came by Mrs. Bentles but she was not at home. Then I came by Mrs. Teeples. I had my work along and made one wheel. After supper I sewed on an apron for the society. Mrs. Gloss came over.

Nov 3 Tuesday

In AM I crocheted on my wheels. In PM I took up the sitting room carpet and cleaned that room good. Will came home and helped me. I got done about 7. Then I cleaned up and went down to Mrs. Linnenbrinck. I had my work along and made one wheel. The weather was lovely. Cleaned my pantry too.

Nov 4 Wednesday

Nice day but cloudy. In AM I cleaned the front room and hall. In PM I helped Will take up the bulbs, by evening I made some wheels. It rained some at night.

Nov 5 Thursday

Rainy most of the day. In AM I worked on my wheel's and society aprons. After dinner I went down to Geisinheimers to try on my waist. Then over to Wraths. I was worn out when I got there. Then Mrs. Byers made me mad and I did not enjoy the PM much. I came home and after supper I made 3 wheels and cut out 2 calico aprons for Ma's Xmas.

Nov 6 Friday

Clear and cold. This AM I made my 3 wheels and commenced an apron. After dinner I finished one apron and worked on the other one. Mrs. Kribbs called and I had to go upstairs. We were eating supper and Benze came. After he went I washed my dishes and made 3 wheels and finished my other apron. A good days work. 8-30 and Willie not here but think he is coming soon.

Nov 7 Saturday

I worked on my wheels some in the morning, then made apple dumplings for dinner. In PM I finished the aprons. Then I stamped another laundry bag, after supper I finished Clara's waist to her skirt and made a rosette for a hair receiver.

Nov 8 Sunday

Fine day. Will and I loafed around all morning. In PM we went to SS and stayed for an after meeting then we went walking. Came home and went down to Mrs. Teeples. Came home and got supper then read some.

Nov 9 Monday

Nice day. Lillian glass and I washed a big washing , after dinner she ironed. I worked on my wheels until 3 then I went down in cellar to make me a flower stand. When Will came he helped me. We finished it. It is nice. After supper I worked some then went down street, stayed until Will came.

Nov 10 Tuesday   (in margin: Minnie's birthday 32 yrs old)

Nice day but windy. In AM I finished ironing, cleaned up the house and made 1 wheel. After dinner was working on my wheels when Mrs. Kolcher called. Then Mrs. Hoffman but I finished my 5 wheels but along I have the headache. I am taking cold, I think. Will does not feel well either.

Nov 11 Wednesday

In AM I worked awhile then went down to Geisinheimer's to see if my waist was made but it was not done yet. In PM I took my laundry bag and wheels down to Mrs. Goehring and spent the afternoon. We had a fine time. She showed me all through her house.

Nov 12 Thursday

Pretty but wind was cool. In AM I made 4 wheels. Will came home and I got ready and went downtown, got my linen for Eva's piano cover. Came home and got dinner. Fixed liver, mashed potatoes. In evening I went on to Mrs. Grant's to measure my cover. Then came by Mrs. Wrights and stayed till 3. Made 3 wheels. Will fixed his rose bush. After supper I went down street. Alfretta Grant was here for supper. We had a fine time. I went over to Mrs. Bloom's. She is sick. Came home and put Mrs. B to bed. Then went over to Mrs. Stoutts awhile, then home. (going some)
(It is interesting to note that this is the first time Julia calls her mother-in-law Mrs. B rather than M or Mother.)

Nov 13 Friday

Lovely day. Swept and worked with my flowers all AM In PM I went to see Mrs. Dumbart, took my work. We had a nice time. Came home and got supper over, then went to call on Mrs. Debendarfer but she was not at home. Then I went to Mrs. Linnenbrinck and came home about 8.

Nov 14 Saturday (sick x)

Fine day. I got up with sick headache. Was in bed all day. Mrs. Rape and Stoutt called.

Nov 15 Sunday

Nice day but neither one of us were away from the house. I was not feeling very well.

Nov 16 Monday

Rainy all day. In AM I worked on my piano cover. In PM I made wheels and pressed out some gingham and calico pieces to make a comfort top for the Home. After supper I cut them out and commenced sewing them.

Nov 17 Tuesday

Cloudy and rainy all day. In AM I made 1 wheel and sewed on my patches, baked 2 pies. After dinner I went to Geisinheimer to try on my waist. Then went to Debendarfer's, came home and got supper. Then worked awhile then went down to Mrs. Teeple's made 2 wheels. Came home and worked some then quit.

(Wheels were crocheted individually and then sewn together for tablecloths or runners etc.

When women went calling on each other they brought their "work" they never sat and talked without doing something useful.)

Nov 18 Wednesday

Cloudy and cold. In AM I worked on my comfort top and finished it. Brought down my flowers. When Will came home after dinner, he said Mrs. Geisinheimer wanted me, so I went down. Mrs. Stoutt was over just after dinner. After she left I ripped all my wheels apart and commenced sewing them on. I had them on wrong, after supper I worked steady on them.

Nov 19 Thursday

In AM I straightened the downstairs. Then I went up and commenced sweeping about 8-30. Will came. I took a notion to wash so I got Lillian Gloss and Will carried the water. I helped her some and we were done by noon. After dinner I swept the kitchen and dusted good. Then I went upstairs and cleaned good. I got through by 2:00 then I worked on my cover. After supper Mrs. Geisinheimer and Gish brought my waist up. They stayed until 8.

Nov 20 Friday (in margin: finished piano cover)

Clear day. Some warmer. In AM I ironed, got done by dinner also cleaned the upstairs, after dinner I watered my flowers, then I worked on my cover steady. After supper I was at Miss Rapes, a little while then came home, she sent me a dish of apples, and put W Mother to bed, then finished the cover and pressed it. Then went down and showed it to Mrs. Linnenbrinck, came by for Will then home. Cut out an apron for his Mother, now to bed.

Nov 21 Saturday

In AM early I commenced a shawl for Minnie after I had my work done. I went down to the meat shop and ordered some hamburg steak. Then went to Mrs. Iffts to see about getting her to cut out W Mother a house jacket. Then I went over to the office. I crocheted some. When the mail came it brought my wrapper. I came on home and got dinner. I then tried on my wrapper. It fit fine. After dinner I washed off some of my flowers. Then commenced his Mother's apron but Mrs. Dumbart came and was here most all PM. Then in the evening I wrote home and took it down. Mrs. Wright and children came over and were here until 8-30. She had her work.

Nov 22 Sunday

Cloudy, snowed some. We ate breakfast at 9 o'clock. Then I fixed my beef loaf for dinner. Fooled around. After dinner Will and I took a walk away out the railroad track. We gathered some fern leaves and cattails. We came home and got supper. Then I got ready and we went to Church.

Nov 23 Monday (in margin: I yr today 6:20 since Johnny died)

Very dismal day. In AM I finished M's apron and made a fixing for the neck for Ma. In PM I worked on a leaf doily. Mrs. Stoutt was here. Came to learn how to make those wheels. Just at 4 Mrs. Kirker came and when she left Mrs. Gloss and Foley came but we ate and Will went after supper. I finished the doily and worked some on Minnie's shawl. *(Pressed in this page 168 of the diary is a cutout from a newspaper. It says*

GEMS OF THOUGHT
A sad bride makes a glad wife
Happy is the bride the sun shines on,
And the corpse the rain rains on
The weeping bride makes a laughing wife
There's no handsome woman on the wedding day except the bride

Nov 24 Tuesday

Dismal day. In AM I put the border on my quilt or comfort top. Then went down town and got the comfort lining and cotton. Came home and got dinner. Then I took the frames up in Mother B's room and put the comfort in. Will came home and helped me some. After supper I took it in our bedroom and worked on it until nearly 9.

Nov 25 Wednesday (*in margin: Carl's , John's birthday*)

In AM I swept and worked with my flowers. Then on the comfort awhile. After dinner I finished it and Will took it down to the office to send out to the Home. After supper I went down town and got some bread and silkateen, came home and commenced a silk hood. Mrs. Stoutt and Nellie Meeder were here.

Nov 26 Thursday

Snowed most of the day. In AM I baked 2 pies and cleaned up around. Then I worked on that silkhood for Mary Rape. Will came home at 12. We were getting dinner ready when the door bell rung and there was a Home boy with a bucket of turkey and dressing so we ate right away. After dinner I worked steady on the hood and after supper, was over to Rapes awhile. Flora Gelbach was here and wanted us to come up but Will did not feel well so we did not go. Another Thanksgiving day. Where will we be next year. I hope all here and well. God willing, 20 of 9 Will eating Sam bo apple.

Nov 27 Friday

I worked in AM on Mary Rape's hood. In PM I went to see Anna Debendarfer and took my work. Came home and got supper. Then worked on the hood. Mrs. Rape and Mary were over. I finished it. Mrs. Had to go home so Mary stayed and I finished it.

Nov 28 Saturday

In AM I worked on Minnie's shawl, also in PM Mrs. D and Anna were here just at supper time. I was home all evening. Mary came over awhile.

Nov 29 Sunday

Cloudy dismal day. Will not I either were well, so we were home all day. I had a headache. Brandon Wright was over in PM.

Nov 30 Monday

Cold day, snow on ground. I was sick in bed most of the day. A Mr. Wiley was here to find out about a Mr. Switzer Iart (?) After supper I worked some on Clara's hood.

Dec 1 Tuesday

I worked on Clara's hood most of the day. After supper I went over to Mrs. Wrights and worked on Minnie's shawl. Mrs. Dumbart was here while I was away.

Dec 2 Wednesday   (in margin: Harper's Tea Party)

Fine day. In AM I worked on the hood. In PM I swept some then Mrs. Dumbart came for me to stamp off some leaves and laundry bag pattern for her. After dinner I went down town to get the silk for Clara's ties. Came home went over to Stoutts but they were busy so I came home. About 5 I commenced to dress for the tea party. Mrs. Teeples came by for me. Mrs. Stoutt and Dumbart also. Then we went by for Mrs. Linnenbrinck, Mrs. Benze came there. So all 6 went together. We had a jolly good time and plenty to eat. We had a guessing game and Mrs. Ralston got the prize.

Dec 3 Thursday

Clear and cold. I washed a large washing all by myself. After dinner I baked a pie. Then put on my new wrapper and went to the Sewing Society. Mrs. Eyless brought some cinnamon bread and Mrs. Rath made coffee and we all ate heartily. I came home and took in my clothes. Then got supper and put M to bed. Then went up and helped tack a comforter.

Dec 4 Friday

In AM I ironed, was nearly through by dinner. Mrs. Stoutt came over and brought some milk weed pods and wanted to make some balls to put on a bag for Lillian's Xmas tree.

After dinner I was downtown. Took Mrs. Zehners dishes back. Then I went to the office awhile. I got some silk and a handkerchief to make a pin cushion. After supper I commenced it. Mrs. Stoutt came over to see if I had made any balls. I had 4 done. I then sewed up the bag and we stuffed it. Lillian Gloss brought me over some panhas and sausage. I finished my cushion, all but some ribbon. *(panhaus is another word for scrapple which is made from pork scraps)*

Dec 5 Saturday

In AM it was real warm but the wind soon changed and it got cold. I took all my flowers out in the pantry and swept the sitting room, then I washed off my flowers and put them back. Then I made one bed. Then got dinner. After dinner I sewed some on Will's Mother's jacket but run out of thread so I commenced Will's shirt. Mrs. Rape came over but did not get to stay long for she had company. I almost finished WG's shirt. After supper I went over to Mrs. Bloom's then downtown. I got Will a neck tie. I came home and worked on his shirt.

Dec 6 Sunday

(in margin: Sherman's first bouquet to Mama.)
On page 175 is a small pressed dried bouquet tied with a string.
Sherman was born in 1907. So Julia used her diary to press flowers.
Windy and cold. In AM after I finished the work, I commenced a letter to Bert. After dinner I read and wrote some for Will. Then we dressed up and went over to Dumbart's, came home and got supper, then we went to Church.

Dec 7 Monday

Very nice day. In AM I finished Will's shirt and went down town. Came home and got dinner. After dinner I cut out Will's outing flannel night shirt. Will came home with a box to send the Xmas things home. Then we went up in the attic and gathered up some books.
Mrs. Mickley was here. After supper I went down with Will. I got Pa 3 handkerchiefs and a tie. Came home and was working on Will's gown when Mrs. Stoutt came over with an apron to cut out so I helped her. Then I made his gown. Finished it for him to sleep in. They were my first but were OK.

Dec   8   Tuesday

(in margin: Ma's wedding day)
Cloudy part of the day. In the AM early I worked on a dressing sacque I had commenced so long ago and I finished it soon after dinner. Then I cut out Will another gown. I worked on that little music box. Then made me a neck tie. Mr. Sesson came for the box, after supper I made Will's gown. Then went downtown and waited for him to come home. It was snowing then.

Dec 9 Wednesday

Snowed some but was warmer. In AM I hurried with my work and went to the attic to clean it. I took up some nails and I made some shelves for some papers. Then I straightened the books out and cleaned up. I did not finish in AM so after dinner I went back up. Will had told me at noon he would take the big stove down in the cellar and bring that little coal stove down from the attic so after dinner I hurried, baked an apple pie then I cleaned out the big stove and took it all apart and carried some of the pieces in the cellar and some in the attic. I then went up to the attic again and was working when he came. He seemed pleased with what I had done so we finished up there and then we brought down the stove and got Frank Gloss to help us carry the big one down, then we set the other one up and made a fire. Then we had supper. After supper I changed our table cloth and cleaned out my cupboard, then I cut out a pair of drawers, then went over to Stoutts and crocheted 2 wheels. Came home and soon went to bed.

Dec 10 Thursday

Snowed most of the day. In AM after my usual work I went up in the store room and took up the matting and swept the floor. Came down and popped some corn it popped fine. Then I got dinner. After dinner I sewed on a pair of drawers. Will came and I went down town and got some curtain goods for hall door, 2 new aprons and the stuff to make some stove polish. Came home tired and almost sick. I sewed some then I lay down on the cot and fell asleep. And when I wakened it was 4-30 I got up cross and sleepy. After supper I finished my drawers. Hemmed my curtain, made a wheel and read some. Will came with a basket of meat and sausage and panhass from Kolaf's (?)

Dec 11 Friday

Still cold. I was sick in AM so after I was through my work I lay down. I had not been there long when Anna Debendarfer came to learn how to make those wheels. While she was here Mrs. Stoutt came to borrow my recipe book. She brought me some popcorn. I felt real sick when Will came but felt better by 1 PM Will brought me a letter from home. In PM I made an apron out of my big one. I spoiled them, I made a pair of drawers. After supper Mrs. Stoutt came to borrow the hotwater bottle. We went to Old Folks concert in the Presbyterian Church. It was very good. They also had a bazaar.

Dec 12 Saturday

In A.M. I made two apple pies then I went down town and got some yarn for Will's slippers. Came home and got dinner then about 1:30 I took my work down to office and stayed with Will
After supper I went down to Anna D. to see her work. Then over to McKiness then to the office and waited for Will

Dec 13 Sunday

Clear and cold. We were both not well so we were home all day. We ate breakfast at 9:30 dinner at 2. In P.M. We were upstairs some I wrote a letter to Minnie after supper we read.

Dec 14 Monday

Very cold. I finished my work then went down to Miss Bentles after my apron pattern. Came by the office. Will gave me a letter from Jennie. At dinner I took a notion to wash so after Will left I put the water on and was just emptying the flat bucket of water when he came at three. Then I cut out a kitchen apron and after supper I made it. Also made a wheel and a half. Mrs. Stoutt came over to see if I would help her make some wheels.

Dec 15 Tuesday

Cloudy and cold. In A.M. I finished my dish work then I took up the stair carpet and the kitchen carpet and after dinner I put them down. Will came and helped me. After supper Mrs. Bloom came over then after I put M to bed I made two wheels. Will came prompt at 8 P.M.

Dec 16 Wednesday

In A.M. I ironed, was all done by dinner. After dinner I cleaned out my pantry good, watered my flowers then went upstairs and put away the clothes then I dusted our room and cleaned it up good. Came down and Will and I made some stove polish.
Mrs. Stoutt came over awhile after supper.

Dec 17 Thursday

In A.M. I hurried with my dish work then I got out that little basket and glued it together after while I heard Will come and I went in to see and here was Det Passavant. They were hunting a book. Will could not find it. So he went on down to office and I thought D had too. So I went to making his M bed when he called up to see if I had found it. Will's M said she had given it to Glosss'. So while I went over to see, he poked in her room. I was so mad. I could of told him so. After he went I went down town for some ribbon for the basket went in office and waited until the mail was distributed and got a letter from Minnie saying she would leave for home Fri. night. After dinner Will and I went down and got Cora, Anna D, Retla Ifft all presents. Came home and got supper. After super I went down and got calico for Aunt Julia an apron also pocket book for WG. Came home and made the aprons all but strings.

Dec 18 Friday

In A.M. we got up so late that Will went to office first then dame home. I got M breakfast then I baked two apple pies and fried some potatoes and at 15 of nine we ate out breakfast then I washed out a few pieces, got dinner. Then watered my flowers then darned WG a pr of socks.

Dec 19 Saturday (in margin: Xmas boxes came)

Cloudy in P.M. but clear in A.M. First I finished all my work then I washed all my doilies. Then I ironed some pieces I had washed Fri. Then my doilies then I washed out my sash curtains and the lace curtain to the S window. Then got dinner. After dinner I brought in my clothes. Then I hurried and went down to office. I took some blacking and Will and I blacked his stoves then I cleaned the back room some. Came home and ironed my curtains and put them up then I fixed some tissue paper around a shelf for in M room for Xmas. And got supper. After supper I was over to Mr. Stoutt awhile. Came home and made 2 wheels. Will came and brought a package for him from Minnie. I got our box from home. I had a cry. Then went to bed.

Dec. 20 Sunday

Gloomy. I was sick all day and night with an awful headache, so was Will but the dear boy read to me and we tried to enjoy ourselves.

Dec 21 Monday

Clear part of the day and very windy. In A.M. I rested until 8 then I done my house work and watered my flowers. After dinner I dressed a little doll for Alberta Gloss. Then I hemmed two towels for M room. Mrs. Stoutt Sr. was over awhile and I finished Lillian's little box. Then I cut out some stars. Will cut me a pattern for a large one and I covered them with tinfoil. Then I popped some corn and took it upstairs and M and I strung some. I got Anna Lorquis' Wedding announcement today.

Dec 22 Tuesday

In A.M. I finished my work down here then I went upstairs finished our room then took W M in then while I put up her shelf and made her bed. Got dinner. After dinner I was working on some towels hemming them when Mrs. Stoutt Sr. came over I finished my towels then I worked on a little music box for Lillian Stoutt. Will was down in cellar working. After supper Mrs. Stoutt came over and we dressed Lillian's doll.

Dec 23 Wednesday

In A.M. I was through early then I went down to office. Took 2 napkins and hemmed them. No letter. Came home and got dinner. Then I went down again took my work and made wheels. Came home and commenced to get supper and Mrs. Ifft came over, then Mrs. Wright. Mrs. Stoutt brought a cinnamon cake over. It was fine. After supper I got so nervous I went down town Will had told me of a mistake he had made and oh I was so blue but the inspector did not come. I went in Mrs. Linnenbrinck's awhile. Then went by for Will.

Dec 24 Thursday

Cloudy and rainy most of the day. In A.M. I finished my work down stairs then I went up and made the beds and cleaned out the closet in M room then I came down Brandon brought 8 eggs over for my Xmas. I went downtown to see when Will would come home then I bought a head of cabbage and a pork roast. Then Will and I came home. The train soon came and Will hurried and ate and went back. I washed my dishes then went upstairs and brought his Mother down. Then I popped some corn 2 dishpan fulls. Herbert Beakley brought a basket full of doughnuts, sausage, apple butter and a piece of pork. Will came home a brought a letter from Minnie no box yet. Raining. I went with Mrs. S to Lutheran exercises.

Dec 25 Friday

Cloudy and dismal most of the day. In A.M. about 6 we wakened and got up to open our box and see what Santa brought us. So Will made the fire and we opened Minnie's pck first. Then I found a lovely tea gown all made grand and fit me to a T. Will got two fruit pictures and his M one. Then we opened the box from home. There we found ½ doz knives and forks from all including Bert and Stella, Corry and M and the home folks. Quite a surprise to me. Then I found Laura's and C picture in a lovely frame. Then Carl sent us a paper with the ME Church under it and our nuts and corn which were very nice. After my A.M. work I ran in to Wrights a few minutes then to Rape's, Stoutts and Weigles. Then I came back to Rape's and helped Mary make some popcorn balls. Then home and down to the office. Cora gave us a lovely burnt wood scenery picture and Jennie sent me some sachet bag and hearts. Anna D came by and said she was coming up so came on with her. She gave me a pretty work box very nice. The Gelbach girl brought Will's Mother a box of candy. Will came to dinner and brought a basket of cookies, candy and a chicken from the Home also a pretty grey shawl from Mrs. Knibbs.

Will gave me two lovely pictures: one a yard of white and purple violets and one a tug of war cats and dogs. Both framed in white, ½ doz handkerchiefs. His M a blue calico dress. Will and I went down to Mrs. Teeples' in P.M. Mrs. Stoutt gave me a pretty plate. Mrs. Gloss sent me some candy and some fine apples. After supper I finished writing home I went over to Mrs. Grant's and Wrights to show them my dress. I brought Freitia home. Helen came too then Mrs. Wright and Grant came in. Mrs. W went home but Mrs. Grant went upstairs until I changed my dress. Then we went down to the office. Came home and was sitting upstairs when Mrs. Wright came over. She wanted me to go see Mrs. Allen for Mrs. A thought she was keeping her away. 8 P.M. I feel lonely after the busy day. We had a roast pork and mashed potatoes for dinner. I hope and pray we may be well and happy 1 year from today and our present worry and trouble be over.

Dec 26 Saturday

Snowed last night and this A.M. is much colder. In A.M. I straightened my house good and cleaned our room some. Watered my flowers just got done and was writing to Anna Loran when Will came so I got dinner. After dinner I cleaned up some. Put on my green wrapper and was crocheting when Mrs. Rape came over. She stayed all P.M. We cracked nuts and had a nice time. In P.M. I went over to Stoutts and bought a spool of silkateen then came home and made a couple of wheels. Mary Rape came over and was with me an hour. After that I read until Will came home. Then we sat here and talked until 10:10 and we went to bed.

Dec 27   Sunday

We slept late after my work was done I commenced reading *Bondman Free*. We had dinner at 1. After diner I read some then cracked some nuts and we went upstairs and ate them. Brandon came over and came up. Then Helen came and gave us a history of a book she had read. After tea. Will and I read a long time then went to bed.

Dec 28   Monday

In A.M. I finished all my work then I made 4 wheels. After dinner I put on water and when I got done my dishes I went down and washed a big washing. Was through by 4. then came in and got supper. Mary Goehring came but I sent her upstairs while I finished my supper. Then I went up. She staid till 5:30 Then I came down and washed my dishes then put M to bed. Then I went over to Rapes. Mrs. And M were gone but I stayed with Mrs. Wikely. I made 2 wheels. Came home and made 1 more, 7 today. Will came. We ate an orange and read some then went to bed.

Dec 29   Tuesday *(Letter from home. Box got there Sat. 26)*

In A.M. I brought in my clothes and hung them around at the stove today as it had snowed and they were wet yet. About 9 I commenced ironing some but was not done by dinner. So I put them away.
Will came home and we sat upstairs awhile. I hemmed an old napkin. After supper I went down to Gelbachs. Mrs. Learned how to make a wheel.
Dec 30   Wednesday
Heavy snow. In A.M. I finished my ironing and put things away then I took a notion to cut carpet rags and went over to Mrs. Stoutts. She gave me some and in P.M. I sat upstairs and cut some also after super. Will came home with some good news pertaining to the Post Office. In P.M. I pasted a story in a book.

Dec 31   Thursday

In A.M. we got up very late. Will went to the office first then came home. After breakfast I put on my dinner. We had noodles.
After dinner I went to the SS and Mrs. Wraths gave me so many carpet rags. After supper Mrs. Bloom came over and brought some apples and cookies.
Will read to me until late. I cut carpet rags. Nearly 11 when we went to bed hoping the next year would be a happy one, full of pleasures and no sorrows.

January 1, 1904   Friday

Clear and very cold zero. In A.M. I colored some rags red for my carpet rugs (braided rugs) and cut some besides my other work. In P.M. I sat right down and sewed on them and made over two pounds. After Will came I quit and got supper. We had oysters. After supper I went down to call on Miss Bentle but she was not at home. Then I went to see Anna Debendarfer. She was not at home either. Then I went to office and stayed until Will came home almost 9 o'clock.

January 2 Saturday (terrible snow storm)

Very stormy all day. A terrible snow storm . Was sick all day with an awful headache. I managed to do my morning work. Then I lay down most of the A.M. what time I was not throwing up. I slept until 2 P.M. then I got up and cleaned the house and got some potatoes ready to cook for Will was to bring home some meat. So we had a good supper. After supper I commenced sewing on my carpet rags. I made 1 lb then I went up and gave M a bath then came down and sewed another pound. I now have 5 lbs and only commenced Friday Jan 1, 1904. Will came home at 9 and we read until 10:10 and I retired. Will soon followed.

January 3 Sunday

Almost 10 below zero and snow very deep. We got up late had breakfast about 9. I finished my work. Will brought out the organ so I could play some. I read and played then got dinner. We went upstairs about 4 and Will read some out loud. He put his Mother to bed then came down and we ate a lunch. Then we read in our bibles. Now we are going to bed soon. We were home all day.

January 4 Monday

Too cold to wash so I sewed on my carpet rags. In P.M. I went down to see Miss Bentle and Mrs. Teeple. Came home and after supper made 2 lbs.

January 5 Tuesday

Lillie and I washed in A.M. and I colored some rags green. Then in P.M. I sewed some and cut some. Mrs. T sent me such a nice basket of rags so I cut and after supper I sewed 2 lbs.

January 6 Wednesday

I did not get much done. I swept some upstairs then went down and got some things for dinner. In P.M. I went down to see Mrs. Goering then she and I went out to the Home. Had a nice time. I only sewed 1 lb last night. Mrs. Stoutt was over awhile. Letter from Ma.

January 7 Thursday

Cloudy but warmer. In A.M. I ironed and baked 2 pies and cleaned up. After dinner I went to the society had a fine time. After supper Helen and Brandon came over and studied and I sewed 1 lb rags. Then we played Flinch till 9:30.

January 8 Friday

In A.M. I finished my work early then went down town to get some meat to cook with my kraut. Went by Miss Bentle's and she gave me some carpet rags. Then I came home and put on my kraut. Then I took Mrs. Eyliss's bucket home. She gave me some nice rags. I came home and cut some then got dinner. It was fine: biscuit, mashed potatoes and kraut. Then Lillie G brought some rags over for me. In PM. I sewed a pound. Then I went down in the cellar and washed Lillie's pieces and hung them in the attic. After supper I went over to Wrights and played Flinch. Mrs. Wright's niece died today.

January 9 Saturday

Snowed most of the day. In A.M. I cleaned my pantry and put away the kraut and then I cut a few rags and got dinner. After dinner I sewed a pound. Will came home and emptied my barrels and washed them out. The little Goehring boy brought me more nice carpet rags. I cut most of them then I sewed my wheels together and whipped them on linen for a doily for a center table. Now I am going to bed nearly 10.

January 10 Sunday

Clear but cold. We were home all day. I was not well. We read and slept.

Mrs. Wright brought some flowers over for me to keep while she went to Butler to her niece's funeral.

January 11 Monday

A nice day. The snow melted a great deal. I sewed on rags in A.M. After I baked a pie. I took Freitia Grant a little pie over. Mrs. Grant brought me some carpet rags over. In P.M. I finished my center piece then cut out quilt pieces after supper. I took a hot bath and went to bed. Mrs. Wraths and Louella were here in P.M.

January 12 Tuesday (sick x)

Very much colder. In A.M. I finished my work and then I sewed quilt patches. Then got dinner after dinner I felt miserable so did not do much. Mrs. Harper was here awhile. After supper Mrs. Stoutt came over to see if I would go out to her brother's tomorrow if they went I a sled.

January 13 Wednesday

Snowed most of the day. About 9 Mrs. Stoutt and Lillian came by for me and we were up to her Mother's and waited for Mrs. Harper and another Mrs. Meeder. We all got in and away we went. We got out there about 12:30. I commenced to get the headache soon after landing and it staid with me until about 4 when I threw up all my dinner. Then I commenced to feel better. We started home about 6:30 I guess. Got home before Will but soon went to bed for my head still ached. Will got along all right.

January 14 Thursday

A regular snow storm nearly all day. I did not feel well so I sewed on my carpet rags and made 1 lb. Then I got dinner. After dinner I commenced to plat rags for my rug. I made quite a circle. Mrs. Stoutt came over to see why I was not out to the SS. They did not elect officers. Not enough there. In evening I sewed on my rags until Will came.

January 15   Friday

Nice clear day. We did not get up until nearly 7. Will went without his breakfast and never came home until dinner time. I washed and got them out by 12. Then I colored a blanket green. Then I washed my dishes and swept my sitting room hall, steps and kitchen. Then brought in my clothes and got supper. Then finished my letter and got ready and went down to office with it. Mrs. Wright wants me to go to Church with her tonight.

January 16   Saturday

Sleeted and snowed some but got colder in evening. In A.M. I finished my work and sewed some rags. In P.M. Will and I went to Church. After Church they held a meeting but we did not stay until it was out. After supper I went up in M room and sewed until 7 then I came down and went over to Rapes and stayed until 9 o'clock. When I came in Will was here.

January 17   Sunday

Clear but very cold. We got up very late so never had dinner till 1. Then we went to Church. In evening we sat up stairs some then came down and read. I was very tired and went to bed.

January 18   Monday

Weather and cold. We got up some earlier so I got through my work and sewed 1 11/2 lb of carpet rags.
After diner I dressed up and went over to harmony to see Mrs. Kirker. From there I went over to Ulla Swain's then home. I stopped to see Mrs. Sitler but she was not home. I came home and Will came soon and said she had been here.
After supper I sewed on rags and made 1 lb. Then I sewed on my rug until 8:30 Will came and we ate apple and oranges.

January 19   Tuesday (in margin:Benze here)

I was sick all day but not in bed. My throat and head bothered me. I cut a few rags in A.M. After dinner I cleaned up. Mr. Benze came. I felt miserable all the time. Mrs. Rape came over soon after dinner to get me to show her on her rug. I made quite a lot for her. She came over after supper and we both worked on it. I was so sick after she left. I went to bed.

January 20   Wednesday

Rained nearly all day, very cloudy.
In A.M. I commenced a new rug and baked a pie. But I felt miserable. After dinner I worked some then I slept some. Will came home with headache too. After supper I commenced a letter to Pa then sewed some. I ran over to see Mrs. Rapes rug then home. Will came home

real sick.

January 21 Thursday (rained all day)

Did not feel well. I sewed some on my rugs. Then took care of my flowers got dinner. Then cut some rugs. Then cleaned my house up, straightened my front room and put my ferns in there. Then swept my kitchen and got ready to go to the Society.

Will came and brought me 2 letters. One from Cory and Minnie. I read them then went but I felt so badly and never sewed much. Mrs. Stoutt, Teeple and myself and Eyless were all that were there. Mrs. Teeples brought doughnuts and we had a fine time. I came home and got supper. Mrs. Wright came over then a boy from the Home brought me so many carpet rags. I cut so many before bedtime.

January 22 Friday

Cloudy and warm all day. In A.M. I cut some rags then about 10 I went down town to get some onions. I met him coming , no trains he said. Then I made him go back with me and then we came up together and got dinner. After dinner I finished my carpet rags then I put the rest away and was just cleaning my machine when Mrs. Goering called. I showed her how to make those wheels and gave her 6 but she lost them and don't know if she found them or not. After 7 I went over to Wright's and played *Pit* then came home and was reading in my diary book when Mrs. Raths and Louella came. They said Mrs. Nelby had lost her baby. Will soon came and we ate supper.

January 23 Saturday (Papa's birthday 57 yrs.)

In A.M. I hurried and finished my work then I went down to the office and Will and I went to see the high water. I was good and tired when I got home. I sat down and rested after dinner I sewed some on my rug. Then I lay down and took a nap. Slept nearly on hour then got up feeling so good that I sewed on my rugs again. Mrs. Stoutt came over and brought me a dozen wheels very nice ones. After supper I went over to her house and we played *Flynch* and had so much fun. I beat 2 games . Very warm today.

January 24 Sunday

Very cold again. A very sudden change. We got up late and just sat around. In P.M. we went over to Grants awhile then came home. I was very tired so went to bed early.

January 25 Monday

Clear part of the day but very cold. Snowed in P.J. some. In A.M. I sewed some on a quilt then crocheted 1 1/2 wheels and fooled around. Then I colored a blanket red. After dinner I cleaned the kitchen good and washed off the woodwork. Mrs. Teeples came by on her way to Mrs. Blooms. I washed and dressed. Finished a letter to Corry and went over to Helen's to see how she was. Came home and got supper. After supper I sewed on my rug.

January 26 Tuesday

A heavy snow storm cleared off about 3 and turned colder. In A.M. I washed. Got through at 11. I hung them in the attic. I was worn out by the time I was done too. After dinner I took a notion to have my teeth fixed so I went down but he could not fix them until tomorrow. Then I went up to the carpet weavers to see about my carpet. Came by office and Will and I came home. I sewed one round on my rug. Got supper. Then I run over to see Mrs. Rapes rug then home and finished mine before 8. I had a letter from Papa.

January 27 Wednesday.

In A.M. it was very cold. I ironed most all my clothes then I went down and had my teeth filled came home tired and cross. Will was home with headache after supper I went upstairs and cut some rags until dark then came down and cut some. Mrs. Wright came over awhile. Then I went down for some figs. Went in to see Mrs. Linnenbrinck. Came by for Will but the train was so late I came on home and soon went to bed.

January 28 Thursday

Cold in A.M. but warmer in P.M. I baked two pies. Sewed some on a quilt and got dinner. Then I went to the Society. I was the first one there. We had election of officers. I am President. Mrs. Rath Vice. Mrs. Stoutt Secretary and Ella Swain Treasurer. Mrs. Rath treated us with cake and coffee. Mrs. Linnenbrinck brought some New Wrinkle, popcorn, peanuts etc. Mr. Benze came just at the close of the meeting. After supper I sewed some on a comfort top.

Jan 29 Friday

Warming up some. In A.M. I finished my work, watered my flowers and sewed almost 2 lbs of rags for Ma's carpet. Went to Gelbachs. In P.M. I sewed rugs . In P.M. I sewed rugs and at night I played *Flinch* well.

January 30 Saturday

In A.M. sewed on the quilt but felt mean. After dinner I slept some. Mary Rape came over awhile then I gathered up my quilt patches and went over awhile. Came home about 3. After supper Stoutts came over and we went over to Wrights to play *Flinch* but did not stay long. Then they came home with me and we played until 11 *(Flinch* is a 1901 card game invented by A.J. Patterson. The deck has 150 cards and 2-8 may play)

January 31 Sunday (lonely day)

Slept until nearly 9 o'clock. Worked nearly all day. In P.M. we went to Church. Came home and sat upstairs and talked and sung. Then we came down and ate supper.

February 1 Monday

Very cold in A.M. it snowed some but cleared off after dinner and got so cld. I sewed on my quilt patches and cleaned up a little. In P.M. I went over to Mrs. Weigles and sewed on my quilt. Came home and was upstairs when Emma Passavant came . Then at 4 I came down and got supper 4:25 and Will not here yet - just coming.

February 2   Tuesday

Cold and disagreeable nearly all day. The ground hog saw his shadow and immediately our bad weather commenced. In A.M. I commenced my apron a large gingham one. About 10 I went down town and got some meat. Some   muslin for gowns and bolster covers. Then I worked on my apron. By 3 I had it done. Just finished when Mrs. Setler came. She stayed until after 4. Then Will and I hurried and got supper over. After supper I made a bolster case and put lace on it. Then I finished my letter to Jennie.

February 3   Wednesday (weather cold)

In A.M. I commenced sewing on my quilt setting it together for the Home. In P.M. I put it in the frames and commenced to knot it but in evening I did not feel like doing anything so I read and wrote some.

February 4   Thursday

In A.M. I worked all morning. Just cleaning around and baked two pies. In P.M. I went to the sewing society. Quite a number there. I did not feel very well. In evening Stoutt's all came over and played *Flinch*.

February 5   Friday

In A.M. I had the headache until nearly noon. Then I went up to Mrs. Raths to tell her I would not go over to Harmony. Then I came home and got dinner fried kraut. After dinner Mrs. Byers came to see about taking a quilt to quilt them. Mrs. Rath came by. We got our goods and then went down to Nebie's. Came home and I got supper. After supper Stoutts came over and played.

February 6   Saturday

Weather some warmer. I got up with an awful headache did not do much all day. I never got better until about 4. Then I finished my work. After supper Mrs. Wright wanted me to go over to Nelshes and play *Flinch*. So I did awhile.

February 7   Sunday

Weather much warmer, rained some and wind blew hard all day. In evening it turned cooler. We got up about 7 ate breakfast. Will helped me wash the dishes. I felt very weak all day. I was so nervous I could not read much. I got dinner. Hamburg steak, baked potatoes and gravy and bread and butter. After dinner Will took a nap. Then we ate nuts, oranges and apples (upstairs) After supper we read. I felt lonely and blue.

February 8   Monday

Still cold and gloomy. It tried to snow some but turned too cold. I felt some better so I thought I would sew some. I made a pair of drawers. All but facing back the ruffles. In P.M. Mrs. Rape and I went to see the carpet weavers then we came by the store and I got some blue chambray for a sun bonnet. Came home and started to cut it out when Mrs. Alf Goering came. Then it was time to get supper when she left. After supper I worked on my bonnet and almost finished it.

February 9   Tuesday (Sick x)

In A.M. I hurried and cleaned my down stairs for I knew Mrs. Kirker and Elizabeth were coming by dinner time. I felt bad so I never got my dishes washed until after 2. After super Miss Bentle came. Then Mrs. Debendarfer and about 7:30 the others came. It was after 10 before I got to bed.

February 10   Wednesday

In A.M. I finished my bonnet then took it up to show Mrs. Rath but she was gone so I came home. Then downtown for meat. After dinner I helped Mrs. Wright bake a cake and cut out some hearts. After supper I went up to Rath to see about getting some goods for some bonnets. Then down to Hursels with my bank. Then to town then home and up to Raths, then home.

February 11   Thursday

Clear day. I had headache this A.M. but got some better and went to the sewing society in P>M. We had quite a crowd some sewed on sun bonnets and some quilted. I made one sunbonnet. In evening I went up a little and helped put in the quilt. Mrs. Teeple was there and quilted.

February 12   Friday

Snowed some in morning. I got up with a headache but wore off. I made 47 popcorn balls for Helen and Brandon's party. I took them over in A.M. and helped them string hearts. Came home and got dinner. After dinner I went over but could do nothing. I gave a dozen plates and 3 chains. I came home and got my crocheting and went over to Mrs. Blooms. I made 1 wheel and came home after supper. I had to take my letter down. Will forgot it then I came home and put his M to bed. Then went over Lillian Gelbach and Mrs. Grant were helping but I helped entertain them. They had a good time. They left around 9:30.

February 13   Saturday

Clear but right cool. I felt some better so after I got done my upstairs work I commenced washing and was almost done by noon. After dinner I finished then cleaned up the washroom. Then came up here and swept the stair hall and kitchen and cleaned the pantry. Then porch. Then went up in my (own) room and swept and dusted it and the hall upstairs. Then it was supper time so after supper I was tired and lay down and slept from 5:30 to 6:10. Got up and put Mrs. B to bed. Then came down and read some and commenced a table cover. Will came by 9 and we were up until after 10 then went to bed.

February 14   Sunday

Dark and gloomy all day. We ate breakfast by 8 then Will helped me do up the work and watered my flowers. Then I got my dinner on. I read some but by the time I got the upstairs cleaned up it was dinner time. Then we got ready and went to Sunday school and Church. Came home and was just undressing when Mrs. Linnenbrinck and sister came. After they were gone it was super time. So the day was most spent. We read after super till 8:30 or 9. Then went to bed.

February 15   Monday

Gloomy and cold, snowed some then cleared off in evening. I ironed in the morning and baked doughnuts, after dinner I went up to Rath's to see about cutting out some aprons but they were going down street. So I got the pattern and came home. I was cutting them out when Sophie came, then Mrs. Zehner, then Mrs. Rath and Louella, after supper I went up and we cut out 9 more and 2 sun bonnets. I came home and went to bed.

February 16   Tuesday

In AM I sewed on a comfort top, then after dinner I cut out my green apron and worked on it. After supper I went down and bought 2 towels for tea towels and some linen for tray clothes and muslin and embroidery and a spread for the table. I came home and sewed on them, finished the tray clothes and towels, then went to bed (very cold & no gas) M unwell all PM

February 17   Wednesday

Still very cold, no gas. Inn AM I finished my green apron then commenced my table spread and got dinner, kraut, biscuit and mashed potatoes. After dinner I made my drawers and patched 4 prs and put a new yoke to my old white skirt. Brandon and Helen came over and we played *Flinch*.

February 18   Thursday

Cold & snowed, In AM after I finished my work I went up to Rath's to sew awhile, then Mrs. Teeples and Ella Swain came. I only stayed until 10-30 then came home and got dinner, went down to office, got a letter from home. After dinner I cleaned away then went back up and made 2 aprons. Some quilted and got out Mrs. Teeple's quilt and finished 8 aprons, all had a good time. I came home and rushed the dishes and made Mrs. B's bed then wrote a letter home and some in my diary.

February 19   Friday

In AM I swept and cleaned up the house then cut out a shirt waist and got dinner, after dinner I sewed on it and went down town to try on my blue calico dress Mrs. Ifft was making, came home and finished my shirt waist. After supper I went over to Mrs. Stoutt's awhile and took my table cover but did not stay long, came home and worked some on it.

February 20 Saturday

Clear, not so cold, snow melted in PM In AM it was really cold. I worked on my table cover, then after dinner I cleaned up some and went up to Rath's to learn how to made a pattern, did not stay long, came home and went down to office, stayed until Will came home. After supper I took it over to Mrs. Rapes and showed her., then came home and worked on it awhile but I got tired and quit and soon went to bed.

February 21 Sunday

Warmer and rainy. We were home all day, read and acted a dunce most all day, raining out. In evening we went to Church.

February 22 Monday

I got up feeling tired but was going to wash but found out I had no gas so mended some stockings and worked on my table cover, in PM Will came home and made me lie down and rest so I did, he went up on our bed and took a sleep, after supper I went over to Rapes and showed them my cover then came home and worked on it.

February 23 Tuesday

Still cold and snowy in PM, In AM I did not do much but in Pm I brought my quilt out and told Mrs. Bloom and Stoutt came over and we marked some and Mrs. Stoutt quilted some. Then Mrs. Bloom had company and went home, but she came back after supper and e quilted until 8-30.

February 24 Wednesday

Snowed and blowed all day. Mrs. Bloom came over in AM and we quilted, then after dinner she came back and we worked until supper time. After supper we quilted until 8 then we took it out.

February 25 Thursday

Still cold, in AM I swept and cleaned my pantry and after dinner I went to the society , we quilted and finished some aprons and started one sun bonnet. Mrs. Rath served coffee and fruit cake. I came home and found Will sick, could not eat anything, after I got through my work I went down to the office and found him working with the gas, so he asked me to go over to the hardware store and get a wick so I did and we fixed it, I came home and made him some tea, he drank some and went to bed.

February 26 Friday

Some warmer but gas low. I washed a big washing. After dinner Mrs. Dumbarton came and brought her work. I bound my quilt, after supper I sewed 1 ¼ lbs of carpet rags and made a wheel, then I read some in the Youth Companion. Will came then.

February 27 Saturday

Clear and much warmer, In AM I sewed some carpet rags for Ula then made a wheel and got dinner, after dinner I sewed some on a comforter top and made a wheel. Anna Debendarfer called just as I was lying down to take a sleep. After supper I went down town and got some peanuts, came home and made some candy, then went over to Stoutt's and made some & played *Flinch* till 9.

February 28 Sunday

Cloudy and rainy all day. We were home all day. I did not feel very well. We both slept some. Will's Mother was in bed all day. After supper we read and talked, rained hard in the night.

February 29 Monday

Cloudy & very dismal. In AM I ironed, then went down and got some meat for dinner. In PM I cut some carpet rags. After supper I baked some doughnuts.

March 1 Tuesday (in margin: Got my new carpet)

I sewed carpet rags all AM Mr. Ketzel brought mine, in Pm I sewed some, We found we were 3 yrds short so after supper I went down to see him about it. Mrs. Debendarfer was here in evening. I stayed down quite awhile. Came home and wrote in my diary.

March 2 Wednesday

Got up early, it was a lovely spring day. I was up to Eyless all day quilting and making aprons. Mrs. Rath and I sewed on a rug. We had a fine day, nearly all were out. After supper Mrs. Ralston and I went up and put her quilt in and marked some.

March 3 Thursday (in margin: Flood, 1st robin)

Rained all night, best night and lightening and thundering and everything was over in AM I commenced sewing but Will came and wanted me to go down Main Street and see the water, it was terrible. We came back and went over to Harmony, there we saw water a plenty. We were in a hard shower all the way home and I was as wet as I ever will be when I got home.

After dinner I sat down and made a wheel then went up to the society, there were only a few there. We quilted on Mrs. Wilson's quilt. After supper I was cutting rags and Mrs. Stoutt came over to get a spool of silk then Mrs. Wright came over, she wanted Will and I over for supper Friday evening.

March 4 Friday

Lovely day in AM I swept up stairs and hall and kitchen down then got dinner. (no gas) after dinner I commenced sewing Ma's carpet rags. I sewed about 4 lbs. Will could not go over to Wright's so I went. The trains came in and he could not leave. Mr. & Mrs. Luther Welsh & Gelbach and Grant and I. We had a fine supper. After supper we played Flinch. Mr. Luther and I beat all 4 games it was 11 PM when I got in bed. Had a letter from Eva and Carl & Minnie.

March 5 Saturday

Clear but cooler. I sewed on rags most of the day, made 4 lbs or more.

I made 3 wheels. No regular trains today. Will took some mail over to Harmony. Will's Mother has been sick all day, had La grippe.

March 6 Sunday

Cloudy and rainy most all day. We were home all day. Mrs. Teeple was up and Mrs. Wright and Helen were over in AM I felt midlin all day, in evening I got sick X

March 7 Monday

Still cloudy and more rain by AM I felt so bad, so after breakfast I lay down until 9 then got up and done up my work went over to Mrs. Stoutt awhile, then came home and got dinner, after dinner I sewed on carpet rags, after supper I made wheels, 5 during the day. Went to bed but did not sleep well.

March 8 Tuesday

Cloudy and more rain but cleared off in evening. This AM I finished my work and commenced sewing rags. I made 1 lb then went down for meat for dinner. Will then bought an umbrella, I came home and baked biscuit for dinner after dinner I swept the front room and watered my flowers, carried some letters up in the attic there I finished sewing my rags and mended a shirt for Will and made a wheel. After supper I baked some ginger cookies over at Rape's we had no gas later on I played some then read some and wrote in my diary. No mail yet. Having an awful time. Got Minnie's picture and 2 dust caps also Miss Cornish's picture.

March 9 Wednesday

A lovely day. Lillie and I washed a large wash were through by dinner time. After dinner I swept and cleaned the porch etc. then brought in my clothes. Mrs. Wrath and Louella were here and said Mrs. Linnenbrinck had another order for a bib apron to be done by Sat. so I went up after supper and cut out one then came home and put W. Mother to bed and went back and cut another one.

March 10 Thursday (in margin: My birthday 28 yrs.)

Very nice day in AM I commenced ironing, ironed a few when Lillian Stoutt came over and brought me a toothpick holder, then Harry Rape and Elmer came, then Mrs. Stoutt, Lillian had a crying spell because Harry burned some papers of hers. Then they went home. I put away my ironing and sewed some on the aprons then got dinner. Will gave me a $5 gold piece. I got some fancy hair pins from home. After dinner I sewed on the apron then dressed and went up to the society and finished it.

Mrs. Bloom came over after supper, then we went over to Mrs. Allens.

March 11 Friday

In AM I ironed the rest of my clothes and put them away and after dinner I went downtown and I got some ribbon for a collar and some blue silk. Will and I went up to Kitzels and paid for our carpet then came back and paid Zehner and priced the side brands. After supper I went over to Stoutts and got her to show me how to make those collars, then I came home and finished mine and worked on another one very…

March 12 Saturday

Clear part of the day but colder. Sophie came in AM was here for dinner. I crocheted on my blue wheels in AM After dinner I finished my blue collar, after supper Mrs. Wright and kids came over and Mary and Harry we played *Flinch*. Helen was so loud and rude her Mother scolded her until she went home balling.

March 13 Sunday

Sick with a headache all day but went to church in PM came home feeling worse. I took a tablet and soon felt better. After supper Will read to me then about 9 I went to bed.

March 14 Monday

Cold and sleet and ? and sun shine all day. In AM I brushed up the upstairs then came down and went down town and got some chiffon for my collar and some starch then came home and made my collar. In PM I cut out a shirt and shirt waist.

March 15 Tuesday

In AM I cleaned my flowers and swept the two rooms downstairs made biscuit for dinner and had kraut. After dinner Elmer Rape helped me carry my machine upstairs and I commenced sewing soon after 12. I made my shirt waist and commenced on Will's shirt. After supper I went over to Rape's then came home and about 9 went to bed. The weather is cold and snowy.

March 16 Wednesday

No warmer. In AM I finished Will's shirt and my waist, after dinner I went up to Rath's and cut out 3 aprons. She cut sun bonnets and came home and got supper, then went down and got some goods and embroidery for a skirt, then came home and put W Mother to bed, then went up and she (Rath) cut out skirt.

March 17 Thursday

Partly clear and some warmer, in AM I ironed 3 shirts and finished my work and commenced a collar, about 10 I went up and to see how the Ladies were getting along. I brought home a bonnet to stitch then I got dinner, after dinner I finished stitching then I worked on my collar, about 2 I went up and helped them. Came home and found it was 5 and no gas for supper but Will never scolded me, he drank some tea and went. I went along and took some sun bonnets to Lucy Frishkorn. Came home and washed my dishes and worked some on my collar then went down for some groceries.

March 18 Friday

Still gloomy in AM I finished my work and put on beans for dinner then I commenced sewing on my skirt after dinner, I sewed some then Mammie Rath came to learn how to make wheels so I taught her how, after supper I worked some on some blue ones for Mrs. Rape a collar. Mrs. Stoutt and Mary Rape were here. When Will came we read out of an old book he had, *Travels Through America.*

March 19 Saturday

Rain nearly all day, off and on. In AM I baked 2 pies worked around and then cut out my skirt again and tucked some on it, in Pm I worked steady at it. After supper I went downstreet for some groceries and meat. I called on Miss Bentle awhile then waited for Will

March 20 Sunday

Lovely day but real cool. We went to the Presbyterian in AM After dinner we went over to Rape's then came home. Will went upstairs and I went over to Wright's awhile, came home and had supper then we went to church.

March 21 Monday (in margin: Mrs. Weigle's boy was born 11PM)

Still gloomy. I did not work until after supper then I rubbed out one tub full and boiled them I worked on my skirt and finished it. Mrs. Wright came over a while. Miss Shontz was here about 4 to see M-

March 22 Tuesday

Cloudy till noon then the sun came out hot, my clothes were dry by 12 and then I hung out all my bed clothes and then cleaned the attic some and the store room, dampened my clothes after supper I wrote to Ula. I had a letter from her today. I am tired.

March 23 Wednesday

Cloudy in AM but cleared off and after dinner I took up the carpet in Will's M room and put it down, worked until 8-30

March 24 Thursday

Lovely day but windy. I took up our carpet and the spare room did not get either down for we took a notion to paper so I went down to look but it got dark and I gave it up until AM Was over to Rapes and played 1 game of Flinch.

March 25 Friday

Cloudy and very warm when we first got up and about 8 it commenced raining. I started down town to get our wall paper and met Mr. Reung (?) coming up so I hurried and brought the heavy paper up and then he never came until 9 o'clock and I had to make the paste. He commenced about 10. I finished up the other room and got dinner. After dinner I washed out all the dresser scars and curtains and ironed them then helped Will tack down some old carpet on our back walk and he planted my sweet peas about 5 he got through papering and I hurried to put down the carpet. Lillie Gloss helped me. I then brought in everything and then came down and finished ironing. I got done by about 8-30 very tired and went to bed.

March 26 Saturday

Colder and rained some. I finished up stairs and swept halls and 2 rooms downstairs. I then scrubbed the front porch. I had the headache some. I went down for some meat for dinner. Will came while I was gone, he scrubbed off the back porch nice for me. After dinner I lay down and took a short nap as Brandon came over and bought a fosset he found. Then I went upstairs and hung some pictures up in our room and I heard another knock and down I came, found Brandon with some horse raddish. After that I went over to Mrs. Weigle's to see her boy. Came home and got Ula's & Minnie's letter ready. Then after supper I went up to Rath's to get a skirt pattern, came home and cut it off and took it over to Wright's then I went over to Stoutts about 9 to play *Flinch*. Mrs. S beat I and Helen once.

March 27 Sunday

Got up and found the ground white with snow. Will had breakfast when I came down. He slept about 2 hrs in AM while I read and wrote in my diary.

March 28 Monday

Clear part of the day then snowed quite a storm but soon melted. I sewed some on a skirt. I first made a corset cover then after dinner I cut out my skirt and sewed some on it. Will came home and then went out to see how Mr. Kribbs was. After supper Mrs. Stoutt and Lillian came over. I made candy before they came and when I came down from upstairs I found them sitting eating some. After they left I went over to Rapes and we played *Flinch* until 9-30 Will had gone to bed.

March 29 Tuesday (got Thomas the Cat)

In AM I fixed my carpet some upstairs then I sewed some and then went down town to get some meat to try to find a pair of shoes. Came home and got dinner, after supper I took my shoes back and got a nicer pair and went to Kaufman's and got a good 95¢ pair for every day. Came home and finished my skirt. After supper I made me a new harness. Miss Bentle called after she left Mrs. Grant and I went to Miss B and bought her cat house. We sat up awhile and played with it.

March 30 Wednesday

Washed and baked pies, made noodles for dinner. After dinner went up to Raths to cut out 2 sun bonnets, after supper dampened my clothes and sat down awhile and read.

March 31 Thursday

I ironed till noon and got dinner after dinner I lay down and slept until 1 I got up and washed my dishes and sewed some on my carpet, after supper Miss Wood and Stoutt came in then when I was putting Mrs. B to bed I saw Mrs. Debendarfer leaving. Mrs. Rape, Elmer, Mary and Miss Rape came over and we played Flinch till 9-30. Rained in night.

April 1 Good Friday

Rained all night heavy and stormed. In AM I made an apron for Mrs. Rape and baked 3 pies and got dinner, after dinner I worked on some collars, Will came home then went back and worked on his reports. I had a letter from Minnie.

Will fooled me by giving me a box. I thought it was an April Fool but it was not, he had a dollar wrapped up in it.

April 2 Saturday

Dismal and cold. Tried to rain but was too cold so it sleeted. I sewed some at my carpet found I needed 3 ½ yds more. I got dinner and after dinner I hunted up some more rags and cut them put button and 2 holes in my corset cover, then Mary and Harry Rape came over and we cracked nuts and made some candy, after supper I went over and played *Flinch* till nearly 9, Mr and Mrs. Stoutt were there. The room was full.

April 3 Sunday (in margin: Easter snow on ground and very cold)

Cloudy and cold most of the day. We went to church in afternoon were late. Came home and read some and got supper. After we read some.

April 4 Monday

Clear and some warmer. I did not wash as I did not have enough to 'ool with so I sewed on some carpet rags in AM after dinner slept some and crocheted some after supper I went over to Mrs. Weigles, came home and got ready and went out to Ketzels and took some carpet rags I sewed. I soon went to bed. No I didn't for Will brought some work home.

April 5 Tuesday

Lovely day, in AM I swept a little and commenced sewing rags. I sewed over a pound. Then at noon Will said Benze was coming and Mrs. Rape said a crowd was coming. So I swept the downstairs took out some of my flowers. After Benze left. Will said he wanted me to copy some names for him so I commenced on them and finished later Mrs. Rape, Adie, Harry, Mary and the two Ketterer girls were here and we had a nice evening. 10 when they left. I pushed my table back and set it again so it was 1 before I slept. Will was worn out.

April 6 Wednesday (in margin: G. Ma died 86 3 mos. 6 days)

Cloudy most all day and rain in evening. Will and I both got up sick. I had the sick headache. Mrs. Rath was here telling me Mrs. Linnnenbrinck had orders, Mrs. Rape came over in AM awhile. We both felt better along in evening I got me some of Lydia Pinkhams medicine and will try one bottle.

(From the internet: Lydia Pinkhams is made up of pleurisy root, life root, fenugreek, unicorn root and black cohosh plus alcohol 40% proof)

April 7 Thursday

Lovely day. In AM straightened my house. Carried most of my flowers upstairs, was done by dinner time, after dinner I wrote some home and lay down awhile my headached, then I finished the ties for a bouquet. Will came and we wrote a letter or sketched it out to Cong. Huff and I copied all the names again for him. After supper I fixed Helen and Mary Rape a boquet also Lizzie Dumbach, then I went down to PO and in to see Mrs. Linnenbrinck, then I waited for Will. Olive Dindinger had a party. Pa sent me $5 for Ma's comforter.

April 8 Friday

Windy all day with a few showers in AM I scrubbed my cupboard and all the dishes, got a good dinner then after dinner I fixed a commode for Will's Mother's room and sewed some on my carpet rags for Ma. Then we planned another letter, Mrs. Mickley was here this PM I still have the headache. After supper I finished sewing the rags, have 16 lbs.

April 9 Saturday

Clear half a day. I straightened my house then scrubbed off the front porch then Will came and I copied some names for him. After dinner I copied some more then I trimmed my summer hat, went down town and got and play *Flinch* so I went over awhile.

April 10 Sunday

Cold and rained most my new one, met W G and came home with him, after supper Sophie came to help me clean house next week, after dark Mrs. Rape and (?) came over, then they wanted me to come over all day. All went to the Presbyterian this morning, came home and got dinner, then I wrote some to Bert and Stella. In evening Will read some to me. I <u>felt lonely</u> and not well, my stomach hurt me.

April 11 Monday

I ironed some, cloudy part of time but windy so our clothes dried Sophie and I washed. After dinner we cleaned the front room and she took up the tacks in the hall. Up and down stairs and steps, after supper I went down street and came home with W.

April 12 Tuesday

Cloudy cold, some snow and everything else. Sophie ironed some while I cleaned the pantry. I felt so blue at noon but after diner we cleaned the west room and got the carpet down. Will came and helped me. Sophie and I carried the stove up in the attic. After supper she went down street and I sewed the piece on my carpet. Will brought it home, I have plenty.

April 13 Wednesday (in margin: snow)

Some brighter but cold and snow. In AM we washed the kitchen paper. I did most of it for she would not do it right so I sent her to cleaning wood work upstairs while I finished and got dinner, after dinner I washed some carpet and then put down the hall and stair carpet. Will came and helped me. He broke a window glass up in the hall trying to get the window down.

April 14 Thursday

Still cold but the sun shown some. In AM I put down the pantry carpet, Sophie finished the woodwork and then I commenced putting down my kitchen carpet, after dinner I finished it all but one corner rear where the gap stone was. After dinner Sophie washed the west room windows. Mrs. Hoofman called. After supper I lay down and slept from 5 to 6 then got up and went down to office and waited for Will. I felt so tired and sleepy so I went to bed early.

April 15 Friday

Somewhat brighter but nothing to brag about, in AM I finished an under skirt and sewed some on a rug for the porch. Sophie washed the attic windows. After dinner I hurried and washed my lace curtains and stretched them. I put Sophie at cleaning the cellar way and Will at the curtains then the gas man came and worked till dark, then humed (?) and put down the carpet and (?) the table and pictures. Rained in evening later.

April 16 Saturday

Clear but very cold. In AM we straightened around. I went down town and Sophie got ready to begin after dinner. I fixed my curtains and washed 2 windows. After supper I gave W Mother a bath, then went over to Rapes a little while. We played 2 games of *Flinch*. Came home and found Will here and we went up and talked awhile.

April 17 Sunday

Sorely day, house all AM Church in PM

April 18 Monday

A lovely day for once. I washed was done by 10-30 after dinner I papered the closet and ceiled it over head. Then came in and ironed some. Will came and cleaned the yard some and burned the trash. After supper I ironed nearly all, then put Will's M to bed. I went over to Mrs. Stoutts awhile came home and finished crocheting a wheel. Will came home and said he thought he would buy some more ground back of us but I guess it will fall through with.

April 19 Tuesday

Cold and snowy all day. I finished my ironing then worked on a rug, Will came home early and we had dinner early, after dinner I sewed on my rug. After supper I went up to Mrs. Rath's and cut our 2 sun bonnets. Mrs. Beyers was along. Mrs. Rath gave us coffee and doughnuts before we came away.

April 20 Wednesday (in margin: Mr. Rape made his fence around his lot)

Cold and cloudy, In AM the gas got on and I went up in our bed room and sewed on some bonnets, had hard work to get dinner. After dinner I finished one and made a little one. After supper I went down street to meet Will. Came home with him.

April 21 Thursday (in margin: Laura's birthday would have been 30 yrs.)

Lovely day, in AM I baked my pies then I spaded my long flower bed. Will came and would not let me do anything so I just sat around and felt miserable, after supper I cleaned up and crocheted a wheel then went down to see Mrs. Teeples, came home and went down to meat shop and got some meat. Will brought some work home and we were up till 10 o'clock.

April 24

Came home and said he had given up buying this lot back of us. After dinner I sewed some on a little bonnet then Will came and I went up to the sewing. After supper I went down street. I stopped in to see Miss Bentle then went up to Ketzels and then by the office and home with my hubby.

April 23 Saturday

Raining, I done the work scrubbed the front porch etc. then after dinner I baked a nut cake, had good luck then I took a bath and went over to Mrs. Wright's and worked on a collar. Came home and went over to Mrs. Rapes to show her, they were having their dining room papered. After supper Mrs. R and I went down to Millinery Shop and she got a hat.

April 24 Sunday

Bright and very warm in the morning but rained in PM and evening. We went over to the M E Church *(Methodist Episcopal)* in AM. In PM we tried to sleep but Will's Mother called him just as we got asleep. We were home all evening.

April 25   Monday

I washed a very small washing, went downtown for some meat, got a letter from Jennie Titus. Monmouth Ill. After dinner I ironed some then helped Mrs. Rape with her curtains. We are going down to get some curtain stretchers after while. No letter from home for so long.

April 26 Tuesday

Cloudy and rain nearly all day. I finished my work ironed my wash. Then cut out a sun bonnet for Clara and after dinner I made it, after supper I went over to Rapes to try it on Mary. We played *Flinch* awhile.

April 27 Wednesday

Still rain in AM I swept some then I crocheted some did not do much, after dinner in evening I went up and got Mrs. Ralston's bonnet and came home, got supper in PM I baked a nut cake for Mrs. Rape

April 28 Thursday (in margin: Got my sideboard)

Still rainy nearly all day, in AM I finished my work and sewed on that bonnet till dinner time, after dinner I finished it, then I went up and sewed some, not many out. Came home and found my side board here. Then I hurried and got supper over and put things in it. Then I fixed a curtain for my pantry window, then I commenced on my cover for my side board. I sewed all the wheels together and baisted it on. Will came and had some work to do so I quit.

April 29 Friday (in margin: Laura's wedding day, 4 yrs dead. M downstairs.)

Still raining nearly all day in AM I finished my work and then finished my side board cover, after dinner I hemstitched some. Mrs. Rape, Apr and Harry were here.

April 30 Saturday

Cloudy but not raining. Will went to Butler to see Cong Huff about Post Office. I baked a nut cake and scrubbed etc. in AM He came about 2-30 bought me some oranges and peanuts. I took such a cold that I went to bed early.

May 1 Sunday

We were both feeling badly so were not off of the place all day.

May 2 Monday

Lovely day. I washed all my blankets and quilt spread etc. then cleaned around some. Mrs. Passavant called in PM I begun to feel bad toward evening was sick so went to bed early. (*x placed in margin may indicate Julia's monthly period*)

May 3 Tuesday

Was sick nearly all day so did not iron. I felt better about 6 so went down town for my meat for Wed. evening. The surprise on Mrs. Steiner came home and went over to Mrs. Stoutts to see her new rug. I had a letter from home from Clara and one from Minnie, her school will close the 13th of May. Sprinkling some 8 PM.

May 4 Wednesday

Lovely day but I felt weary again but I ironed all of my clothes but 1 shirt after dinner I went down to Mrs. Teeples to tell her I was not going but she said I must. I baked my veal loaf in PM then I helped Will with my flower bed. Mrs. Bloom was over and we sat on the front steps awhile. After supper Mrs. Teeple came by and we went up to Raths. All were there but Old Mrs. Passavant. We sure surprised Mrs. Steiner and such fun as we had. I got home about 11-30.

May 5 Thursday

Lovely day. I worked out doors all morning then soon after dinner I went up to Raths and I made a little sun bonnet for Dorothy Ralston. After supper I went down street and out to Kitzels came home very tired.

May 6 Friday (in margin:made some garden)

Still nice out. In AM I swept nearly all the house and got all cleaned by 2. Will came home and we made some nice garden. Mr. Roguer was to spade it but he growled so Will done it hisself. After supper I went down street for some more seeds and some gingham for Mrs. Mickley's bonnet.

May 7 Saturday

In AM I baked two pies before breakfast then I cut out Mrs. Stoutt's bonnet and made it and stitched Mrs. Mickleys after supper, Mrs. Stoutt paid me 15¢ I went over to Mrs. Weigels, she had the sick headache came home and went down to office. Will came home mad.

May 8 Sunday

Long lonely day. Will was out of humor most of the day. We took a walk in PM Then went to Church.

May 9 Monday

I washed it was awful windy after dinner dug out dandelions after that I went down to Mrs. Teeples after supper I was over to Mrs. Grants I ironed some before I went then I went down to Mrs. Teeples to see about my bank. Will came and we thought we could carry it but it was too heavy so we left it till next AM.

May 10 Tuesday

In AM I ironed twas real cool all day. Will came home and said Eva L was to be married and Corick wanted to get off, I   because he did not like its because I told her some girls had been after her place. In PM Will and I worked hard in the garden. In evening Cora came and I told her we decided on Virgina Klingenswulk. I went down to meet Will.

May 11 Wednesday (in margin: "got" Verna Klingenwulk in office.)

Lovely day. Mrs. Rape made soap. I went down town and got my curtains for dining room also some good for a nice waist. Mrs Grant and I are going to make it. I finished our curtain and put it up looks fine.

May 12 Thursday

In A.M. I sewed on my curtain and finished Mrs. Mickley's bonnet. Then about 2 I went up to the society and worked on a sun bonnet. Came home and went over to Mrs. Grant's to see if she would go down street. Then I came home and washed my dishes and dug some dandelions. Then we went down town. Got some ice cream. Came home and I went over to Stoutts and made some candy for her. Came home then went over to see how Mrs. Rape was. She was sick.

May 13 Friday (In margin: Minnie's school was out)

In A.M. I swept the whole house. After dinner I slept 1 hr. Then washed my dishes and then I took the machine in Will's M room and finished my other curtain and put them up. Will dug and mowed some. After supper I pulled some of the honeysuckle down. Then I went down town for some groceries. Came home and went over to see how Mrs. Rape was (better) Went to bed but could not sleep well.

May 14   Saturday

A nice slow rain in A.M. I finished my work and Will and I pulled the rest of the honeysuckle down. Then I finished the border to my Center piece. After dinner I papered the trunk and put some things in it. After supper Mary Rape and I went down street awhile.

May 15   Sunday

I had the headache all day and slept most of the day. Will went to Church in the P.M. in evening I felt better and Will and I read.

May 16   Monday

I felt miserable all day. Was in bed part of the A.M. Then I went down and got some goods for Mrs. Mickley's cap. In PM. I made it. I was down at the office awhile.

After supper I went down to see Mrs. Debendarfer came by office and waited for WG.

May 17   Tuesday (Will planted roses. Thomas got hurt)

Cloudy with a few light showers. I worked out doors all day. Planting my flowers and making flower beds. Mrs. Brandon was over a long time.

May 18   Wednesday

Rained all day long. I went over to Grant's to help Mrs. G cut out a waist for me. I sewed all day and after super went back.

May 19   Thursday

Was over all day. Still rained. We finished my waist about 4. I went home and got supper then I sewed some and then Mrs. Grant and I went down town.

May 20   Friday

In A.M. I cleaned up some swept my kitchen then cut some back ruffles for underneath my black skirt and gathered it on. After dinner I finished it and made a tie and Mrs. Mickley's bonnet.

Later on Will and I went to the entertainment The District School which was a silly affair.

May 21   Saturday

Lovely day. Mr. Hartman plowed our garden. In A.M. I swept my kitchen and cut grass. Then scrubbed. Will came home and worked around I forgot my parasol and left it at the hall. Will went for it.

After dinner I made 5 calls, Mrs. Zeigler, Danbart, Sitler, Fredericks and Koecher. After supper went down and got my meat etc. Came home and gave Mrs. B Sr. a bath then I sat on Mrs. Wright's porch awhile.

May 22   Sunday (in margin: Found Tom. He came home.)

Lovely day. In A.M. we went to the U.P. Church. After dinner we slept most of the afternoon. Then went to Church in P.M.

May 23   Monday (in margin:Planted taters)

I commenced washing then went and planted our potatoes. Then finished by noon. After dinner Will put in all the screens – a good job.
I have felt so weak all day. My stomach troubles me. After dinner I cut out a white apron.

May 24   Tuesday

I got up feeling badly but I finished my ironing then I lay down and slept most all P.M. Will came and cut the grass. Will brought me some cream.

May 25   Wednesday

In A.M. I baked two pies and put on some new screen. Will came and put up the shade on the west end of back porch.
After supper Mrs. Debendarfer was here. After she left I went up to Mrs. Rath's and helped quilt some. They came on down to meet Will. He brought me some more cream.

May 26   Thursday

Rained some in A.M. then cleared off.
After I baked my pies. I went up to Rath' and got some goods then came home and cut out 4 aprons and sent them up after dinner. I put in the P.M. printing my name on some paste board for my trunk. In evening I went over to Mrs. Bloom's then down street. and was caught in a storm. I got as far as Dindinger's and left my hat. She gave me an umbrella and I came on home.

May 27   Friday

Lovely day but so cold. Mrs. Rape cooked soap. I swept and cleaned my house up good. Then went down to office after dinner. Stayed awhile then came home and was helping Will when Miss Gross, Mrs. Linnenbrinck's sister came.
After supper I trimmed some grass and then went down to Kaufman's and got a slip of begonia and took a fern to him. Came home and then went down to see Mrs. Teeple. Came home and Will and I tied Thomas's leg up. We tried to put him to sleep but could not.

May 28   Saturday

Lovely day. In A.M. I straightened my house and went down town for some meat for dinner. I wrote some in my diary. After dinner I got done early so I lay down to sleep but never slept long. I got up and next over to see Mrs. Stoutt awhile and Mrs. Rape. After supper Mrs. Bloom came over. Mr. Rape put in our window. Will and I took out the glass in AM. About dark I dressed and went down for my meat. I felt bad so came home. We dressed Tommy's leg again. Will never came to bed until 11 o'clock but it was 1:30 before I got to sleep. I was sick.X I came down stairs at 12 and lighted the gas and toasted myself and then lay on the cot until 4! And went up again. I never put over such a night. I got a letter from Minnie.

May 29   Sunday

I lay around all day. Will went to Church. In P.M. we both went to the

P Church to Memorial services. Mr. Litell preached. It was 11 P.M. before we got to bed.

May 30 Monday (D-day)

Rainy of course all day long. After I finished my work. I went down to office about 10 and waited for Will. He closed at 11:30. We ate diner then sat around. Then we both took a sleep. We sat out on the front porch awhile. I worked on my Mount Wellick center piece. Mary and Harry Rape were over awhile. Will went down about 6 and came home at 7:30. We sat on the porch a long time then came in and soon went to bed.

May 31 Tuesday

Rained most all day and now 7:30 is still raining. I have put in a long day doing nothing all morning. I wandered around and after dinner worked on my doily and then took a sleep so did Will. He wanted me to go to the graduating entertainment but I did not care to. He is not feeling well today.

June 1 Wednesday

A nice day until after supper. It came up quite a storm and rained hard a long time. I washed a large washing this morning. We got up early and I was all done by dinner time. My house work and everything. After dinner I was over to see Mrs. Stoutt awhile then I came home and dressed up and went down street.

Cashed my draft for $45 then bought some embroidery for a collar and a waist and came home not feeling good. My head aches so badly. I read some in my bible and waited patiently for Will to come home and 1 week from today I would like to start.

June 2 Thursday

Cloudy and more rain. We both got up with an awful headache. I lay down all morning. After dinner I threw up some and commenced to feel better. Will came home and went to bed. Lillie Gloss ironed in P.M. for me. Mrs. Teeple's stopped on her way to the society. Rained hard about 2:30. In evening I went downstreet. Came home and set on Wrights porch till dark.

June 8 Friday

In A.M. I got up with an awful headache again. So I took some soda and it felt better but about 9 it commenced again and I had it very hard until after 1. Then I got up and washed my dishes. I stayed home all evening. I cut Will out a shirt but got it wrong someway. I trimmed grass till dark.

June 4 Saturday

Lovely day I baked two pies in A.M. then I finished up the room some and got dinner. I was looking for Sophie but she never came till evening. After dinner I slept some then Mrs. Rape and I went down and got Ham a hat. I got Will some underwear and hose. After supper

Anna Debendarfer came and Mrs. Teeple. After they left I went down
street and waited for Will. We got some ice cream and came home and
ate it. Sophie came and I gave her some of mine.
June 5   Sunday
Lovely day. We first sat around all day until evening. We went to the
Presbyterian Church. Came home and sat on the porch till nearly 10
then went to bed. We had a little shower in P.M.

June 6   Monday

Lovely day. Sophie and I washed. I went down town and helped Will
select a suit and a shirt. Got some meat and came home feeling so
weak. Mrs. Goering called in P.M. I took a sleep after dinner I ironed
underskirt after supper. Mrs. Sitler came and I showed her how to
crochet those wheels.

June 7   Tuesday

Cloudy part of the day. In A.M. I transplanted some beets and then
came in and made two pies. Will had a man to fix our drain. Will came
home at 8:30 and brought my veal loaf, for my lunch. I then fixed it.
I went over to see Mrs. Stoutt awhile. Came home and lay down for
I did not feel the best. Then I got dinner. Will got the man to fix his
grape posts and my sweet pea vine. Sophie ironed. Then after dinner
she went down street. Mrs. Bloom and Wright were here.
Getting ready to go home. I packed my trunk this morning and fooled
around getting things ready and doctoring my sore throat. I leave tomorrow at 5:55 Elmer Rape will meet me.

June 8   Wednesday (started Home)

Got up at 5 looked around at our flowers and I got my lunch ready.
We had breakfast at 5:30. I am all ready and feeling pretty good.

*The diary ends with Julia's first visit home since she left February,1902.*When Julia Sherman
Bassler passed away in 1975 in New Jersey her body was returned to Zelienople, Penn-
sylvania for burial in the English Evangelical Lutheran Cemetery. She was waked at the
Ziegler Funeral Parlor where the friends and children of friends signed her Memorial
Book. Many of the surnames mentioned in Julia's diary can be found in her Memorial
Book 60 years later.

APPENDIX 20

Julia Sherman Bassler's death certificate 1975

APPENDIX 21

Julia Sherman Bassler's Funeral Memorial Book

Relatives and Friends

Howard C. Ifft
Mrs. W. R. Eygbo Sr.
Beach Z. Wieck
Mr. & Mrs. Russell Schweingruber
Mr. Mrs. A. Schramm
Mrs. Laura Miller
Mrs. Helen Trimble
Jane Bloom
Beany & Thyra Schiffer
Mr & Mrs. Harry Thomas
Mrs. Jesse M. Clelland
Mr. & Mrs. Howell R. Snyder
Mr. & Mrs. Mark McBartol
Mrs. Gertrude Ford
Mrs. Robert Blum
Mr. & Mrs. Elmer Rodgers
Mrs. James Hogan
Mr. & Mrs. A. C. Kennedy (Irene Mohr)
Mr. & Mrs. Clifford F. Albert
Mrs. James Hogan
Alice M. Shotesker

Relatives and Friends

Anna Wright
Mary Lintz Wark
Esther Lintz
Elmer Reed
Mr. & Mrs. Russell Schiekmantel
Mary Kay Stunkard
Raymond E. Kaufman
Adam H. Rape
Mary E. Rape
Mr. & Mrs. Chas. S. Passavant Jr.
Elmer & Sara Gross
Kenneth F. Gross
William L. Kerr
Mr. & Mrs. Ned P. Grandin & Addie Dee
Rev. & Mrs. Douglas J. Joepel
Mr. & Mrs. Carl E. Hartman
Thomas R. Kerr
Mrs. Mildred Bowman
Robert E. Herr
Maude S. Hopper
Mr. & Mrs. Blair Zeigler
Lois Peffer

APPENDIX 22

William G. Bassler's <u>Diary</u>

Oct.1, 1909 - 16 Jan. 1912

Zelienople, Pennsylvania Transcribed by granddaughter Susan Bassler Pickford

Oct 1, 1909 Friday

I made some postcards for Elmer and others

Oct 2 Saturday

Went to Harmony to see about birth certificate & took some cards to Barnhart came home on trolley put some cards on squeegee board scrubbed porch, in P about home attending to various household duties and looking after S (Sherman), was down at office awhile, home all evening weather pleasant a little cool.

Oct 3 Sunday

We were all at Church in AM. Sherman good boy (new)Rev Rex of preached good sermon in the PM. Julia Sherman and I walked out past the Catholic church and gather S little basket of acorns stop to see Adam Endress in evening we all went to Church again but S was restless and Julia brought him home. Weather pleasant

Oct 4 Monday

Julia washed. I was down at a number of times helped a little developed a film for Schullers, looked after S who was fairly good. I felt quite well most all day in evening down St awhile at Dr. office Weather pleasant. Commenced laying brick on our street.

Oct 5 Tuesday

I went over to Henry Bisphly in Harmony to photo some children, came home …made some prints for Rape & Lockhort about 21 prints went up…did Passavant with camera but did not make the…trim did not suit me…did not feel good today, did not get much done. Weather pleasant.

Oct 7 Thursday

In PM I was down at the Irwin City Enamel works and made a number of exposures of the buildings and interiors   very tired   weather warm (S climbed up on cot by himself)

Oct 9 Saturday

Julia very sick all day in PM went down to Samest & med photo of Mavd V 1 of house then went to Monroe Rice on Mill St. but he was not home. A Mrs Bighty of Harmony was over and I made ex of her baby, then about 4:30 went to Rice and made ex of house and group, this was an exceeding hard day on Julia so many annoyances and inter-ruptions..door bell, telephone, peddlers and one thing and another till we were both most distracted and wild

Oct 10 Sunday

I went up to cemetery, rode down with Zehmer & Fogel who took a bottle up for Hunky baby, after awhile Zehner came up and wanted me to made photo of baby so I went down, but they wanted it done at 2:30 so came up again, in PM went down again with Harry R we rode down in cab made a couple of ex of the crowd, came home out of humor and disgusted, this is the first time I ever made on Sunday and I hope it will be the last. None of us were at Church, at the Congrega-tional meeting to vote to call a pastor they failed to elect Longenocker of Dubois got the votes Weather pleasant

Oct 11 Monday

A good soaking rain fell today began in the night and rained most of the day. I put out tubs and c....water and carried it in cellar. Julia washed big washing and hung up in attic. I developed ten plates, in PM I was down street on several times on business errands

Oct 12 Tuesday

I was working in the den making post cards about all day in evening down street short time, weather cold, windy. Sherman good boy

Oct 13 Wednesday

Made a few cards Mrs. Hofman work and I could not do much, and her head ache; took proof of postcards to Rice. Weather cold and windy

Oct 14 Thursday

Working at postcards but did not accomplish much was sick most all day, lay down awhile after dinner,

weather a little warmer. S very good all day

Oct 15 Friday

I was working in den about all day but in AM did not accomplish much in PM made postcards and help Julia a little clean house. Julia cleaned the sitting room and dining room had the rug and carpet out of bathroom and a strip of hall carpet. Sherman was a sweet dear good boy all day weather cloudy

Oct 16 Saturday

Duncan came up with bill of $12.00 for water meter and putting it in, it riled me, I went down Street with some cards to deliver and try and collect some money, saw McMichael and we figured that he owed us nearly that much so we hunted him up and had a settlement and the balance due Duncan was $4.69 which I gave him a check for in PM went to Harmony to deliver some cards, for evening Julia and I were down street.

Miss Venie Bentel died this PM about 1 after a long illness, weather cool and windy.

Oct 17 Sunday

Julia and I went up to cemetery, I at Rapes in PM Julia went to Harmony about home rest of day. All at Church in evening. Sherman right good. Weather pleasant. Rev Waters preached.

Oct 18 Monday

In PM attended Venie Bentel funeral. Rev Koibbst conducted the services. She looked very nice and natural. I rode up to the cemetery after the funeral. I was down at the office wrote up some insurance. Weather damp and raw

Oct 19 Tuesday

Julia washed this AM I looked after Sherman and helped a little in PM down at office wrote up some insurance. Sherman opened a door turned the knob for the first time – the door to hall from dining room. I was hot all day. Old Stoutt took up flag stone in side walk and dug it down   Weather pleasant

Oct 20 Wednesday

About 10 I went to Harmony and …for Ulrich Prints of Barne Store and 1 of group of Ulrich, his mother, sister and Henry Milhmes. Came home develop them in PM went to Harmony and made a couple of ex for Mrs. Beighby. About 1:30 Julia and I went to Presbyterian Church to the wedding of Miss Lockwood and Peansol quiet and fine affair, about 9 telephones me to come down and make some fresh light photos of wedding party. So down I went. Weather fine.

Oct 21 Thursday

Sick nearly all day upstairs in bed.

Oct 22 Friday

Down at office most all day writing up insurance. Home all evening playing with Sherman who has been a good boy all day. Julia cleaned off the garden. Weather warm

Oct 23 Saturday

Made some print from the Lockwood negatives and prep from the winter ones. Then was down at office down at office again in PM weather rainy

Oct 24 Sunday

About home all day none of us at church. Sherman has bad cough Weather cloudy raw and camp

Oct 25 Monday

I took S down to Dr. and got some medicine for him. Julia washed and I took care of S. Went down for mail and bank then made another trip down with some mail I forgot to take to office. In PM made ex of the People's Bank and Sid Passavant horse came home develop some of them wrong with Sid's went up and made it over. OK this time, down Street awhile in evening weather pleasant.

Oct 26 Tuesday

Everybody sick today. Julia had dreadfull sick headache all day long and I was not much better and S has a dreadfull cough. All most strangles sometime neither of us got anything done. I took S down Street for mail and in PM gave him big long ride up Mile Street Almost Spring Home again, weather fine warm beautifull. I ought to have made exp but nothing done another day wasted

Oct 27 Wednesday

Another day gone and little or nothing accomplished. Sherman was unwell and it took a great deal of time to amuse and wheel him around and Julia is still not well. I was down at office awhile in PM and in evening took S up to the Dr. but he was not in. Weather pleasant, slightly cooler than yesterday.

Oct 28 Thursday

Everybody sick today. Julia was very sick all day and I was not much better off, neither of us got a stroke of work done. S was better than yesterday and I gave him a couple of rides. I hope to get something done tomorrow but we never know what a day will bring forth. Weather raw

Oct 29 Friday

Everybody feeling better today I was working in den most all day felt tough for awhile, in fact I was weak and tired all day about 4 or 5 PM gave S a long ride down WC Street to Railroad then up home on other street in evening Julia and I took S up to Dr. R who said he has whooping cough. Weather pleasant.

Oct 30 Saturday

Made some print for Ulrich….gave S ride in PM took S along down to Bastians and got bottles for sending sample of water to Philadelphia for examination then I took some post cards to Harmony rode home on trolley went to Goehring tin shop and got zink for under the hot plate, brought it home and we were fitting in under when Mr. Halstiens came wanted his picture taken so I made two ex, in evening Julia and Sherman were down street and after they came home I was down a few minutes. Weather pleasant

Oct 31 Sunday

I was up at cemetery, then at Church. Rev. Lonager of Detroit preached and excellent Reformation Sermon, good attendance, after dinner…& slept. S was a good boy had some bad spells of coughing. Weather fine.

Nov 1 Monday

Had to be in office most all day. McMichael was at Brighter, his son got shot on Saturday. I wrote up some insurance and made out reports. Weather good, warm and pleasant. Julia started to wash but had to give it up. S would not be quiet.

Nov 2 Tuesday

Julia washed. I took care of S in PM I was at the office wrote up some insurance felt tough this PM took a good while to wear off. Election day voted for constitutional Tukonal amendment. In evening gave S a good long ride. Was down street done some work of office. Weather warm rained a little

Nov 3 Wednesday

Working in den made some photo for Lockwort then and invitation and some post cards at office awhile then went up to Poseo & Frishkorns and….for sample of water to send to Philadelphia to be analyzed. Came home and went to Killdors for sample then took them to Bastian and went down to City works for sample. Came home by Bastian and left the bottle there, in evening was down street awhile. Weather pleasant

Nov 6   Saturday

Julia washed some this AM I went down and mailed photo to Ulrich Winter, in PM about 3 made several ex of Tobi Meeder and children at his golden wedding in evening we were all down street awhile. I was sick about all day. Weather warm and pleasant

Nov 7 Sunday

I was at Church, Rev. White preached, had Congregational meeting, unanimous vote to call Rev Lonager of Detroit, Michigan a pastor.

We had chicken for dinner in honor of Sherman's birthday which occurs tomorrow. In PM we took a walk down New Castle Street and to the trolly station to meet Miss Kuatz but she did not come, home rest of day. Sherman is getting over his whopping cough. Weather quite pleasant 65 degrees at noon.

Nov 8 Monday

Sherman's birthday –2 yrs old. Julia washed I looked after S in PM I mixed upvelot fixing and velot developer. Developed Saturday ex –fair- Then made about 5 post cards and got them on the boards. Down street awhile in evening weather raining in AM cooler in evening.

Nov 9 Tuesday

No entry

Nov 10 Wednesday

Miss K paid $10 paid till to Dec.

Nov 11 Thursday

Julie and I went to Kinker spent the day I helped them over, came back the viewers were around inspecting the street. I was about home, At PM made exposure

 of peoples bank, Schubos baby, I and Sherman came home about 4, weather quite pleasant 74 in afternoon.

Nov 12 Friday

Mrs. Keck and men began grading down our side walk and taking the trees down. I was busy with making some copies of pictures and enlargement

Hair cut down street at office awhile in evening, weather quite pleasant 76 in afternoon.

Nov 13 Saturday

Worked in den awhile in AM in Pm down at office

Nov 14 Sunday

At church in a Rev Kohler preached, read letter of acceptance of call of Rev Lonager, in PM we took a walk down New Castle St. home rest of day, weather very pleasant 80

Nov 15 Monday

Everybody sick about all day. Julia started to wash but had to give up. My but it goes hard when we are both sick at one time. Weather pleasant

Nov 16 Tuesday

Everybody better. Julia washed. I took care of Sherman and done some house work, in PM was down street wrote up some insurance, home in evening. Felt weak and done out. Weather cloudy, rained last night quit hard and now tonight it is raining. Sherman was just the sweetest best boy all day.

Nov 17 Wednesday

Working in den at post cards and in PM from 1 to 3:30 The Board of Health was about the town looking after the drains in and out houses, of must froze found some dirty places, after I got home I resumed the work in den, and got something done but not much, but if I don't get sick from exposure I will be very thankful. Weather strong and snow flurries. Sherman good boy

Nov 18 Thursday

I was working in den about all day but did not accomplish much put in a lot of time fussing with making a print for Myers, then I made some for Kaufman, weather a little milder than yesterday, S a goodie boy day

Nov 19 Friday

Working aat photos most all day in office a little while in AM down Street a couple of times had Sherman down two trips, weather warmer

Nov 20 Saturday

Julia washed this AM I looked after S in Pm cleaned the pavement and scrubbed porch cleaned away the stones and rubbish from the next yard

Made a couple of ex of a little boy at Youngs, Julia down street and I cared for S gave him a ride down toward the trolly station and up to Millers Church, in evening we were all down street awhile. Weather warm and pleasant

Nov 21 Sunday

About home all day, none of us at Church and I felt tired used up- and tough…all day weather warm with very slight rain

Nov 22 Monday

In PM went to Harmony to attend to various business matters in evening we all were down street short time. Weather very warm

Nov 23 Tuesday

I was very busy all day done some work at home awhile then was down at office wrote some insurance in PM was working out in front of house sloping down the cut at side walk and dug the heavy clay out from between the side walk and curb and filled it in with good soil so the grass will grow in evening down at office doing some work

Nov 24 Wednesday

Lovely day. Julia washed in the AM and I watched Sherman who was very good. In PM I graded down the lawn and filled in the space between the walk and curb with good ground. I worked most too hard for I was worn out in evening.

Nov 25 Thanksgiving Thursday

Fine day. In AM after a late breakfast I cleaned up and went up to find Zieglers and took a picture of Mrs and the baby. I then went down for the mail, got only papers (Julia ironed all AM. We had dinner at 11:30 Chicken and mashed potatoes and gravy. I slept some after dinner. Mrs. Alf Goehring was here awhile. Mrs. Rape was over also. In evening we were home all evening. In evening I rocked in Shermans fingers ? weather quite pleasant 30° at 8AM warmed up in middle of day.

Nov 26 Friday

Weather pleasant. Sherman wakened up in a good humor and was good all day, so full of fun. In AM made prints for Lambertons and some proof for Duncan. In PM I was down street then came home and sowed some timothy seed in front yard. After super was down street awhile. Julia ironed some in AM and swept some. 10 PM going to get stove. Put up stove in dining room.

Nov 27 Saturday

I was working some in den, went down for mail with S was gone a good while, attended to some insurance business with title, and was detained by this business, in PM was working at post cards but did not accomplish much, made a couple of exposures of Fred Zieglers baby and one of Sherman Julia and S down street in PM got a set of springs for Julia bed in evening Julia and I and Mary Rape and others went to basket ball game the first we ever saw. Weather quite pleasant.

Nov 28 Sunday

Weather Lovely like Spring. I went to Church in Am and was home all day with headache, very sick. Julia and Sherman were out walking in AM

Nov 29 Monday

Lovely day. I was sick all day in bed most all day, felt better in the evening. Mrs. Schuler and Julia were down street after supper.

Nov 30 Tuesday

Nice day. In AM I helped Julia wash, in PM I went up to Harmony Junction to take a picture of Zinkhaus Farm. After supper I developed them most were good.

Dec 1 Wednesday

Fine day. I printed some of the pictures and made cards. Also some for Mrs. Duncan. In evening I made a negative of Ethel Schuber.

Dec 2 Thursday

Nice day. Julia swept. I made postals and prints for Guiklam and prints for Ethel Schruber. Julia finished ironing (Tom is sick)

Dec 3 Friday

Cloudy, I was down street in AM and in PM I was at office making out reports was down after supper.

Dec 4 Saturday

Got up late made velox developer, then began on the photos of the day. He was poisoned and was suffering dreadfully. Gave him chloroform. Dug hole in yard and buried him planting a box alder tree on the grave. Made 21 photo of the day down street a little while in evening.

Dec 5 Sunday

Julia and Sherman went to church I had head ache and did not go, in PM Julia Sherman and Mary Rape took walk . I lay down, feeling better in evening. Weather warm and pleasant.

Dec 6 1909 Birthday Monday

(William was born in 1855 so he was 53 years old)

Julia washed. I took care of Sherman and we went down street for the mail brought back a letter and me a reply from my application as census enumerator – stating that I would receive **careful** consideration. In PM I went out to the Home intending to make photos of school house but it did not please me so gave it up and came home. On the way out I made ex of telephone…raising a pole, mixed up fixing bath, down street in evening. Weather quite pleasant, colder than for some time previous

Dec 7 Tuesday

After attending to some household duties I went down street. Took insurance policies up to Mrs. Wolf and went to see Mrs. Schaffer in regard to her insurance, then came home in PM went to Harmony for the birth certificate and took insurance policy to Millenn… Then made four postcards and was down street awhile in evening. Julia ironed some and cleaned up the front room. Took the bed out and put it up in our room. I took the cot up in the attic. Weather rained in AM but colder in PM and evening.

Dec 8 Wednesday

After I came up from the mail brought card from Minnie and letter from Rev. Chas Read who ordered …photos made of his grandmoth-

er, Mrs. Myers. Then I went up and made exposure of Cliff Blooms home and all most perished with cold, then Julia and I got at the .....
..... in PM several Flinew girls came and I made them ....Felt unwell all day blue weather quite cold

Sherman can say all of Baby bunting, he was sitting on my lap and....

Dec 9 Thursday

I touched up the photo for Mrs. Myers wrapped stuff up and took down for mailing at the office and wrote up policy for Mrss. Schaffer, attended to some errands and came home in PM we were making some prints for Klievfellin and made sample caard of the girls. About four PM took Mrs. Schaffer's baby pix to her, in evening down street awhile weather very cold all day. Sherman very good boy today.

Dec 10 Friday

Went down at office a few minutes. At Bank and paid gas bill $3.00 At Hardware store paid bill. at office again and worked till 12 m came home in Pm Julia was down street and Sherman and I stayed home. About 3 PM went down to office again but did not stay. A number of people in. Came home and about 4 got at making...photos for 2 Zinkhaus and some postcards of Sid Passavant house and was down before 7 in evening Julia was down street again. Weather milder

Dec 11 Sat.

Weather some warmer, In AM I was down street and attended to some business came home and commenced making some cards. In PM finished cards and made 6 prints for Zinkham. He came for 6 and paid me for them. Some girls came for their cards and a lady came to have her children's pictures taken but it was too dark so she will come again. I was home all evening. Julia, Harny and Sherman were down Street.

Dec 12 Sunday

I went to Church Rev. Koher preached about home all rest of day. Weather good, mild rainy a little in evening.

Dec 13 Monday

Julia worked on card for Sherman did not feel very well all day, got worse and sent for Dr. in evening had dreadfull pains in my bowels. Julia worked and dosed me a long time and got some relief after supper.

Dec 14 Tuesday

In bed all day very weak and exhausted

Dec 15 Wednesday

Up again and about the house feeling weak and shaky. Weather stormy

Dec 16 Thursday

About the house. Julia weak took a nap helped me a little. Weather showing Julia down street in PM

Dec 19 Sunday

About house all day. None of us at Church. Weather cold

Dec 20 Monday

Julia washed, hung them in attic. Mrs. Rape kept Sherman . In PM I was down at office awhile and again in evening. Weather very cold

Dec 21 Tuesday

Went down street, mailed some packages, went to Harmony saw Dr. Ralston. Got Sherman birth reports from him, went down to new house Ralston is building to see Geo Kleinfelter to collect some money then went to see Milburners and had a settlement with him, then was at Swains Store and home and down for mail but got nothing in PM some mail and a package from Bert. Julia and I fixed up our 1 Christmas tree in front rooms and put some of the trimmings on. Sherman was over at Rapes a good while and was a good boy, Julia went up to Rogers and got two holly wreaths, I was down at office in evening, weather warm, snowing this evening.

Dec 22 Wednesday

Snowy and cold, in AM I made 6 pictures for Mrs. Lusk. I then developed a film, and sat around the rest of the day. Julia ironed some and trimmed some on Sherman's Xmas tree. Sherman was pretty good today. Julia was down street in evening and got some mail and a package from Bert

Dec 23 Thursday

About home all AM went for mail, got book for Sherman from Mrs. Summer of St. Louis, in PM went to Harmony, took some photos to Mrs. Luck, saw Millermas on insurance business and got some dry goods at Swains, came home in evening down street got letter from Mrs. Myers and card for Sherman from Ruhers. Weather milder

Dec 24 Friday

About home most all day down street a few times, made exposure of Sherman in yard with sled but it was not good. Several packages came for Sherman, cleaned out the stove in evening. Mrs. Goehring brought some cookies in evening, Julia and Mrs. Devine down street. Weather milder, clear and cold in evening. Have our tree all trimmed and ready for Sherman and have a stocking filled for him. God bless the dear boy. He is the sweetest affectionate boy

Dec 25 Saturday

A perfect Xmas day, snowed most all day and covered all the trees and houses. Just lovely. In AM we both got up about 7AM. We could not get Sherman up so we went down and were eating breakfast when he called Mamuu. We both went up stairs and Julia got him to hunt for his stocking. He got it and then came down stairs and opened it. Then we dressed him and took him in the front room to see his tree and how he did enjoy everything. He went from one place to another. All day, and enjoyed his playthings, his train and bug etc. Elmer Adam and Mary Rape came over to see his tree and play things. Here is a list of his presents. I took a wreath of holly up to Mothers grave

Train & track (Papa)
Drum (Mama)
Little Doll (Harry Rape)
Little stuffed dog (Mrs. Setler)
Crawling bug (Ethel Schuber)
Mother Goose book (Miss Kuhur)
Baby Relm book (Mrs. Summer)
Music Tattle (Lillian Stout)
Fire wagon (Mrs. Diner)
Bell harness (Murhl Padfield)
Large orange ball (Elmer Rape)

Carol Setler was here awhile and played with Sherman's train. In PM Sherman & Mama were over to Stouts and Schulers. Then Miss Rosensteil and Oliver Andrew and Grace were over here. After they left Sherman went to sleep. Mama went over to Geisenhumers, Papa took a picture of Almina Bastain and the Allen girl. Sherman got awake and cried so they came for me. We all went to Church in evening. Schuler were over before we went and so was Mrs. Rape. We took Sherman in a little box for as sled of Yoder Lethis we had quite a time getting him there. After Church we rested awhile. Sherman was a dear good boy in Church. We All went to bed happy and feeling so thankful that we were all well and permitted to enjoy a nice Xmas day.

Dec 26 Sunday

I was at church. Home all rest of day, over at Schullers short time in PM, package from Missouri came this AM Weather slightly colder than yesterday.

Dec 27 Monday

Snowed most all day. Julia washed for herself and Mrs. Diren got done by 4PM. I was home all day. In evening I was down to office. Sherman was fussy all day but I guess he did not feel well.

Dec 28 Tuesday

Cloudy and snowy most all day. I was home until mail time then went down to office in PM out oat old folk's home made exposure of Christmas tree, five of them. Down street in evening.

Dec 29 Wednesday

Made a few cards for AJliner in PM out at Old peoples Home and made the exposure over again yesterday were not good. Got sled ride home. Developed exposures OK, mended plate holder and done some other tinkering, home all evening. Weather cold, snowed. Julia ironed washed spare room curtains, made night gown, shortened my nightgown, shortened a apron for Sherman, lengthened the sleeves of Sherman's nightie, put away the Christmas tree trimmings in the attic, swept dining room

Dec 30 Thursday

Making post cards of Old People's Home. Had sick headache. Julia finished up the cards and I went to bed. Very sick, threw up

Dec 31 Friday

Made a few more cards felt weak and unwell all day. Julia down at Gruchering Weather much milder then was a watch meeting at our Church and at midnight the Church bells rang and whistles blew.

Jan 1 1910 Saturday

Got up late after breakfast, read paper and was down street for mail then gave Sherman a sled ride around the square and up and down the street a few times he enjoyed it. After down street a couple of times and home developed a few plates, weather quite mixed and rained in PM and evening. I was somewhat blue and out of sorts today as on Monday my assessment for paving the street must be paid and I will have to borrow the money and there are many other uses I could put it to that I need more than paved street 10 PM 43

Jan 2 Sunday

About home all day not well lying down a good part of the day. Mrs. Kuntz came back this evening. Weather quite mild, snow melting fast. Sherman was a very good boy today.

Jan 3 Monday

Jan 4 Tuesday

Went down to the bank and borrowed a hundred dollars to pay for my paving, at office a few minutes then came home and made some proofs, in PM went up to Klingfellers and Ketters to let them see the proofs, then went to Harmony to gather up the birth certificates and some other business, came home and got the death certificates ready for mailing and done some other work, reading in evening. Weather quite cold all day

Jan 5 Wednesday

Weather icy and rainy. Dreadful walking. In Am I made post cards of Kinefellers and Ketters baby, in PM I finished them. Was home all evening reading. To Have and to Hold, ...while Julia and Mrs. Dinen cut out quilt patches. Sherman not well.

Jan 6 Thursday

Snowed all night and all day today but not cold. This AM I was down to office and in PM some too. Julia swept in PM, some. Sherman some better this evening

Jan 7   Friday

Woke up in night Sherman sick. Got Dr. about 9AM and got medicine dose, got nothing else done was both of us

Jan 8 Saturday

Sherman still sick but better than yesterday. I was at Church in PM Weather milder

Jan 9 Sunday

I was at Church had communion, home rest of day, had headache, lay down awhile. Weather cold

Jan 10 Monday

Julia washed, in evening I was down street wrote up policy, weather very cold below zero in AM I was down street awhile up at Ralston's office awhile for birth reports. Down at office in evening wrote up policy. Weather cold

Jan 11 Tuesday

Down at office awhile, but it was too cold to stay, brought work up home, then was writing up Board of Health minutes from sarops hat of had them on, weather milder in evening.

Jan 12 Wednesday

Down street in AM at office and attending to some insurance, in PM Julia, Sherman and Mrs. Devin took a sleigh ride to Middle Lancaster. I went as far as Harmony and got some more insurance from Sister Swain and Meyer, came home, took nap and lounged about home, did not feel well, folks got back at 5 OK had nice ride and pleasant visit, Julia was down street awhile in evening, weather quite mild, wet snow all most rain

Jan 13 Thursday

Before breakfast I took a letter to Charlie Beighley to mail at Harmony, after breakfast went to office was there all AM at office again in PM and down an hour or so in evening. Weather snowing all day almost rain.

Jan 14 Friday

A heavy wet snow fell last night I had walks to shovel out was quite a job, down street for meat, Julia washed, weather quite soft. Mrs. Mickly very poorly

Jan 15 Saturday

I went down street and got Yat Kicher of Bally news to endorse my application for census enumerator, then went to Bank and asked Klepperuster to also endorse my application. They both willingly endorsed for me, after mail was opened came home and made some postcards.

Jan 16 Sunday

I was at church in AM about home reading and sleeping most of day. Weather cooler did not thaw much

Jan 17 Monday

Julia washed and I cared for Sherman in PM made a few prints and packed away some negatives down street . In evening weather raining.

Jan 18 Tuesday

Down street in a …Dindinger note at bank at office in afternoon , at office wrote up some insurance then home. Weather terrible rained all last night and today till evening it is growing colder. Very, very, icey. Dreadfull walkin

Jan 19 Wednesday

Made a bunch of postcards in PM. made exposure of Edgar Shaffer children, then tried a couple of Sherman developed them, one covered the roses old carpet, weather clear and warm

Jan 20 Thursday

Was down at office writing up insurance in PM fixed the rocking chair, Mrs. Swain called, and was at office all afternoon and down again in evening. Weather mild.

Jan 21 Friday

Down at office most of day not well, grew worse toward evening, headache and was sick. Went to bed early, weather raining and snow and melting at it fell forming slush, then got a little colder and snowed

Jan 22 Saturday

About home all day in the house felt quite unwell for a while in AM but gradually wore off and felt right good. Weather snowed all last night and all day today is quite deep and drifter is still snowing and storming tonight. The worst snow we have had this winter.

Jan 23 Sunday

The first thing this AM was to shovel out walk. Snowed all night and snow was deep and drifed. Cyrus Hooper drove all around with a snow plow. About house all day, none of us at church. Weather quite mild and pleasant, clear and bright. Miss Kuntz went to New Wilmington Friday evening and is not back yet 9:30 PM. Harvey Seaton died this morning.

Jan 24 Monday

Julia washed. I took care of Sherman. Miss Kuntz got him about 10 AM was snowbound. I was about home all day, took Sherman down Street about. About ex PM the UP Church was found on fire and was almost a total wreck. Weather mild. (United Presbyterian Church)

Jan 25 Tuesday

After doing some house hold duties I went down and took a look at the U Church then went to office and wrote up insurance plicy, in PM I was down to Al Householders and made a couple of exposures of their children, then at Charlie Kioker and took their baby, came home. Julia and Sherman went down street, in evening Julia and Sherman were up to see Ellie Swain and Mrs. Sither, I developed exposures. Weather quite pleasant

Jan 26 Wednesday

I was down at office all day. Mc Michael at Butler. Weather very cold and damp this AM but warmed up and rained in evening.

Jan 27 Thursday

Went down street was down all AM waiting to hear from the insurance adjuster, but heard nothing from him, in PM made a few postcards and proofs of the Householder and Kirker babies, down street in evening. Weather mild snowed some

Jan 28 Friday

Took some post cards Friday up to..AM went down to office and then to Householders and Kirkers with the proofs and came home. Mrs. Albert Miller telephoned for me to come up. Went up to see what she wanted, wanted a picture made of her five generations, went up in PM and tried it. Weather mild made some prints for Roy D.

Jan 29 Saturday

Down street most of AM made some postcards for Householder and Kinker, made some exposures of Keftuser girls down street in evening. Weather colder.

Jan 30 Sunday

Everybody at Church this AM took Sherman in sled. He was just as good as it was possible to be. Condiust 100 home all rest of day, at Rapes a little while Mary and Henry over here. Weather snowing most all day

Jan 31 Monday

Was down awhile attending to various errands at bank and elsewhere, at Harmony went down about 4PM over some errands, the insurance adjuster for the UP fire was here and reported for the fire amount of loss $1,500.00 was very nice gentleman, the German Mutual Fire Insurance of Zelienople had $2,000 on Church. (In margin: Sherman can cut paper with scissors)

Feb 1 Tuesday

Feb 2 Wednesday

Fine bright sunshine all day. Ground Hog or any other kind of a hog could see his shadow. I made exposure of Irvin Gelback in PM in evening was at Church. Rev Lonager was installed. Rev Pseuss of Kittanney preached athe sermon and conducted the installation services

Feb 3 Thursday

Julia sick I was at office making out reports and wrote up policy down a little in PM, then made a few careds and prints. Weather rain then turned to snow.

Feb 4 Friday

In PM down at Drushers on Arthur Street made exposure of baby. On way home Mrs. Luuke (nee Sadie Young) delayed me went in and made a couple of her baby, came home and made a couple of Sherman in front room by west window, developed them.

Feb 5 Saturday

In PM went to Evans City to take examination for Census enumerator, but made an awful botch of it, got badly rattled and felt miserable and sick, have not been well for some days. Weather cold and stormy

Feb 6 Sunday

At church in AM home rest of day, weather cold and stormy

Feb 7 Monday

Very, very cold this AM down at office awhile and down again in PM, I am feeling better but Julia has a bad cold

Feb 8 Tuesday

About home all AM Keeping Sherman, Julia sick has very bad cold, in PM went to Harmony to collect birth reports and took policy to Millerman, got ride home with Doushel of Middle Lancaster, gave Sherman a good long sled ride, then fire bell rang and I went out to fire at Softethallers in exdivision, did not amount to much, home rest of day. Weather quite mild and pleasant.

Feb 9 Wednesday

About home all day. Julia sick and I was not much better. Got some medicine for her from Dr. gave Sherman a good sled ride. Weather mild then rain in evening colder and snow a little

Feb 10 Thursday

About home down street couple times. Julia sick a little better in evening, in evening made flash light of Lee Cunningham in baseball suit, made it in front room. Weather cold all day.

Feb 11 Friday

Did exposure OK went for mail took cards to Luke got $2.00 in PM made picture for Cunnngham. Church stove out. Weather quite cold in AM slowly moderated and began to snow and then it did snow and now at 8 PM it is still snowing fast and furiously.

Feb 12 (Lincoln's birthday)**Saturday**

Julia not very well this AM took her some toast and coffee up, I went down for insurance and at office, went down in extension to see Fran Stauffer about insurance in PM made exposure of Bastians log cabin, Sherman can carry dishes out from the table and has been helping that way for several days – weather everything covered with about a foot of snow, snowed all last night and off and on all day. Weather colder this evening. Sherman can say all his prayers.

Feb 13 Sunday

Papa was sick all day with headache, We were home all day Weather clear and cold (Grandma B's handwriting)

Feb 14 Monday

Julia washed and I cared for Sherman. Down developed a cold. Weather mild and pleasant

Feb 15 Tuesday

Julia finished washing and looked after Sherman who was very good, then Sherman and I went for mail, got card from Minnie gave Sherman a good sled ride up main St. as far as Schaffers. In PM was working in den made some print for Young and Lambestian, weather mild, warm getting slushie

Julia washed, swept two rooms cut out two suits for Sherman, washed out a piece of carpet

Feb 16 Wednesday

Made a few cards, went for mail in PM took some cards down to

Dumbahs was at Farmers Institute a little while at prayer meeting in evening, Julia unwell all day has bad cold in head. Weather raining in AM then turned to snow again. Snow, snow Julia made Sherman a pair of rompers

Feb 17 Thursday

Snowed about all day and night about a foot full, growing colder at night

Feb 18 Friday

Weather very cold. In the AM down street doing various errands in PM went over to Mill St. to make a couple of exposures for Pa Zeigler and waiting on him to get ready, went in to Mrs. Goehring to get warm, developed exposure. Julia and I and Mrs. Dibes at church in evening.

Feb 19 Saturday

I was sick all day. Was not away from the house. Julia went down street in AM paid Latchaw $5.00 on..but I went to bed early dreadful headache.

Feb 20 Sunday

Julia brought me breakfast up, then got up AM much better and thankful that I did not get a dose of pneumonia from my…Weather much…

Feb 21 Monday

Julia washed this AM I looked after Sherman. Weather mild

Feb 22 Tuesday

Everything covered with snow looked beautiful. Made exposure of our house in AM then went down street and made a couple of Maine St. developed them OK in PM down street at office awhile, at Pa Ziegler's to show him sample photo, he ordered a dozen, down street in evening. Sherman has been a good boy all day, feeling so good and well. He was just boiling over, screaming and laughing and romping with me in evening.

Feb 23 Wednesday

Down at office in…and about LeParent to Barnhart in Harmny to photo the flowers at the funeral in evening everybody at church

Feb 24 Thursday

About home all day. In AM developed plates, one is OK in PM made prints for Pa Ziegler. Weather quite bright, cold in AM and evening at Rape's a little while in evening Julia and Sherman down at Goehring

Feb 25 Friday

Very cold this AM I made a couple of prints of the flowers Barn-harts and one of Ziegler, down for mail, filled up place holders, in PM Mrs. Walter Rogner came with baby to have photos made, exposed a number of plates on it in front room while I was doing so Mr. N Myers wife and baby came to have theirs taken, made eight exposures in all, then developed them, very tired not very well today, had bowel trouble. Julia and Mrs. Diben at Church in evening Sherman and I stayed home. Keelers at Fireman's entertainment

Feb 26 Saturday

Made proof of Zerlenty exposures. Weather quite mild rained a little in evening, to photo around to pa Ziegler in PM down street, got board at Patusen lumberyard down street in evening.

Feb 27 Sunday

I was at church in AM home all rest of day. Weather raining

Feb 28 Monday

Julia washed. I took care of Sherman. Down at office in PM McMi-chael sick. Weather mild, raining a little in AM

Mar 1   **Tuesday**

Make a few proofs again then went to office making out reports, in PM down at office again and went to Harmony to see Mohyer & Millerman in regard to insurance, took sample photos to Barnhardts, in evening down at office again. Weather quite mild in PM was quite bright and pleasant

Mar 2   **Wednesday**

Down at office off and on most of day in PM ripped up a board into strips intend to stretch muslum on them for a background at Church, in evening weather mild and pleasant (in margin: Saw first robin this mor

Mar 3 Thursday

Was down at office all AM got my vouchers from Harrisburg for Birth and death reports, Births in Jackson Lancaster township and Zeli-enople Births, were 110; deaths, 54 for Harmony Borough, Births 25, deaths 13 Amounting in all to $50.00 in PM I was working in den made Barnhart photos, some for Lamberton & postcards for Myers. Julia and Sherman were down at the dentist and had a tooth filled for Sherman. He was a perfect little man about it, just cried a little bit, in evening was down street. Weather damp and raw in AM but cleared up nice and pleasant in PM

(in margin: Vouchers   Red)

Mar 4 Friday

Down street and at the office a little while only cleaning up about the yard a little, about 4 PM I went to Harmony by way of Lambertons took Barnhart photos, was first at Millermans store in evening we were all at Church Sherman good. Weather quite pleasant, I was feeling quite unwell most of the day.

Mar 5 Saturday

Weather quite warm and pleasant. Julia washed. Sherman and I were down street a number of times, in PM working at hot bed making a new frame. Down street in evening.

Mar 6   Sunday

I was at Church in AM in PM I gave Sherman a long ride down to the Railroad and after which gave him another up New Castle Street to Division St. to Spring St. to High to Beaver, Main St. to Spring, High to New Castle and home. Weather was wonderfully warm and pleasant: 70 about 3PM but now 8:30 PM it is raining

Mar 7 Monday

Julia sick, got better by afternoon and ironed in PM. I was down street awhile, wrote up some insurance down street again in evening. Sherman a very good boy all day. Weather cold, stormy and snow flurries a wonderfull change from yesterday

Mar 8 Tuesday

Playing with Sherman and running to the door to look for the paper which did not come till about 1 PM down street for mail but got nothing, in PM made a few postcards and made several exposures of Mrs. Devens mother, sister and baby in front room, we were all down street in evening. Weather pleasant, also went to new school building with camera but there is so much rubbish around that I did not make exposure.

Mar 9 Wednesday

Julia, Sherman and I went to Pittsburg this AM on the 8:34 train, got off car at Horns Store and Julia bought a black suit then wandered around the city in some other stores In children's store bought Sherman a little hoe,…and spade all for 10 cents, got dinner at Kaufmans. Went back to Horns waiting on car, owing to misunderstanding we missed a car and came near missing another, but finally got home OK. Sherman was just the best clever boy that could be. Weather pleasant, had…at prayer meeting in evening. *(Julia's birthday & she was 34 years old. Sherman was 3 years old)*

Mar 10 Thursday

I was sick all day, caught cold going in to Pittsburg, car was cold and draughty

Mar 11 Friday

I was making some postcards in PM, in AM was down street awhile had Sherman along and was a good boy in office doing some work and he made no trouble, he walked down and back, weather pleasant

Mar 12 Saturday

I filled up the plate holders and went over to Barbers in Swamp Poodle made four exposures of some homemade rustic chairs, stopped at Kirkers a short time, made some postcards for Kr… in PM made exposure of new school house and of Freida Gravet, cleaned off our crossing, carried water for Julia to scrub porch and walk, developed exposures , down street in evening, weather quite pleasant.

Mar 13 Sunday

Julia, Sherman and I at church in AM Sherman slept all the time, in PM we all went up to cemetery, home all rest of day. Harry McKim died this PM Weather quite windy

Mar 14 Monday

Julia washed, Sherman and I were down in laundry, Sherman sat on stool and high chair and played and was a good boy, while I made some prints and postcards, in PM made some prints for Luke, in evening down at Rape a little while and down street, Weather quite stormy and cold, snow flurries

Mar 15 Tuesday

Home most all day, Julia down street awhile, then I was down and done some work, had letter from Department of Health notifying me to bring suit against OW Ziegler of Harmony for b….without a permit, in PM made exposure of High Street Church, then went to Harry McKim's funeral. After which developed plates OK down street again, in evening down street another time. Weather much milder but air was cold.

Mar 16 Wednesday

Down at office awhile looking up the law in regard to undertakers etc and made information against Ziegler, in PM was doing some fitting and repairing at a sash for a hot bed and down at office in evening, at office ag… Ziegler was over and we are trying to get the matter fixed up. Weather pleasant.

Mar 17 Thursday

Down at office awhile in AM and in PM McMichael, Ziegler and I went to Butler, went to see Attorney Wilson who will try and get a license for Ziegler, then went over to court, then was about town awhile, came home on the …car. I enjoyed the trip very much. Weather quite pleasant.

Mar 18 Friday

Went down for mail and to office, made exposure of Bumgardners horse at Wilson livery stable down at office in PM wrote up some insurance about 3 PM Sherman and I went to new school house with camera but did mothering as grading is being done will wait a day or two, clean the street in front of house and put the dirt between pavement and curb. All at church in evening Sherman was good, only bumped his head and cried a little. Weather pleasant.

Mar 19 Saturday

Raked up the yard and garden, tinkered a little at hot bed, developed plate in PM, Martin Durst came and I was running around town with him, he took supper with us, and then we were down street attain, he left in evening. I bought new pair of shoes weather quite warm and pleasant.

Mar 20 Sunday

All at Church in AM Sherman good boy, slept all the time, in PM Sherman and I were up at Ralstons. Doris gave Sherman a fresh egg which he carried safely home in evening Julia and Rose Harman were at Church and Miss Devin kept Sherman and their baby. Weather quite warm and pleasant. I have been cross…and out of sorts all day

Mar 21 Monday

Julia washed, I helped a little, Sherman was very good, sat on the table down in laundry and played. Then Sherman and I went down to the office and sat in big arm chair by a little table and wrote and played with rubber stamps, after dinner made several exposures of a baby and a child, then made some garden and planted onions and lettuce, before making garden Julia and I were down at Zehmerz..and bought a carpet for the hall, in evening down street. Caroline Peffer died yesterday. Weather quite pleasant. Mrs. And Mrs. Kribbs here in evening.

Mar 22 Tuesday

I made exposure of Bumgardner's horse at Wilson's stable then Bumgardner drove me over to Harmony, took some insurance policies to Millerman, was at the store quite a while he was busy, saw Allie Ziegler and George Millerman came home on in PM made exposure of High School, made a little garden put ground in hot bed carried a pile of stones away from the corner of the street and lane, developed the plates, down street awhile, mad and out of sorts, a blacksmith shop is to be built below us. Weather rained a little in AM but cleared up and was quite warm and pleasant. Asked Mrs. Wright to pen her chickens up.

Mar 23 Wednesday

Sherman and I were down street, saw Schaftner, made some prints and postcards of the high school, down street and at Church in evening. Weather pleasant

Mar 24 Thursday

Julia boiled two kettles of soap today, Sherman and I were down for mail and I made a few more high school cards, did not feel very well, fixed a window shade for Debendorfer, all at church in evening, weather very warm 83 about 1:30

Mar 25 Friday

We all went to church this AM in PM Sherman and I were down street awhile, Julia went to Harr see Mrs. Kirker and bought a hat at Mrs. Cholfould. I made exposure of little boy for Ripper from Evans City in evening Julia and I were at Church. Rapes kept Sherman, a large number were…in church. Weather quite pleasant. *(Good Friday)*

March 26 Saturday

Julia washed. I took Sherman down street ..down through the extension and home by way of Beaver St. in PM made some postcards developed film for Elmer Rape and made him some prints, in evening Julia was down street and I kept Sherman who cried and fussed. Weather quite pleasant, Mrs. Debin sister left this AM

Mar 27 Sunday (Easter)

I took a couple of hyacinths up to the cemetery when I came home Sherman came to meet me, came almost two blocks, Julia and I went to Church had communion, large attendance, after dinner we went over to Kirkers, when we came home I took a sleep, felt tired and tough, home all rest of day. Weather quite warm and spring like.

Mar 28 Monday

Sherman and I went down street and got some meat then we went to the office and made up some insurance. Sherman sat in chair and played with rubber stamps etc. and was as good as could be, in PM I dug some garden and Sherman played around the yard, so nice, after supper Sherman and I went down street with his wheelbarrow, he was just the best, sweetest dearest boy all day long, Julia ironed, cleaned attic and took up hall carpet, had Duncan put in sink in cellar, weather warm and pleasant. At Board of Health meeting.

Mar 29 Tuesday

Julia cleaned house washed five blankets, Sherman and I were down street awhile, then I was down on some errands, fixing up the front yard, some grass seed, beating carpet, had the rubbish hauled away, in PM a nice little rain fell, the street sweeper was up our street, in evening I was at Harmony on business, Weather pleasant.

Mar 30 Wednesday

House cleaning still going on. I was down street a little while, but was sick most all day, lay down awhile. Sherman right good boy. Weather pleasant

Mar 31 Thursday

I was sodding the terrace in front of the house, wheeled the sod from the back end of lot. Sherman had his little wheel barrow and helped to wheel sod, weather pleasant, cooler than yesterday, Julia still cleaning house

April 1 Friday

Sodded along the lane. Sherman helped wheel sod. Then I cleaned, I cleared bins and shelves away in the cellar so to dig for the sewer pipe, dug a little but was tired out and quit. Weather pleasant

April 2 Saturday

Made some postcards in AM in PM was at Harmony made exposure of children of Charles Buickly and Shoots, over in Harmony awhile. Julia washed. Weather pleasant

April 3 Sunday

I went up to cemetery. Sherman and Julia came to meet me. Julia did not feel well. I stayed home to care for Sherman so she could rest, in PM

I attended the Brotherhood meeting, home all rest of day. Sherman a very good boy all day. Weather quite pleasant.

April 4 Monday

Developed a film for Lamberton and some plates and then was helping at the house cleaning, taking the paper off the dining room. Weather pleasant had several delightful showers

April 5 Tuesday

Cleaning paper from wall worked hard all day, tired. Mrs. Dan Stauffer helping at Board of Health meetin in evening. Weather pleasant Sherman good boy

April 6 Wednesday

Both sick all day, did not do much, took supper with Mrs. Diben. Weather

Cooler

April 7 Thursday

Working down in den made some postcards. In evening was at Harmony to see Jacob Ziegler and Milleman settled up with Mr. to date .

At office in evening, weather quite cold, a wonderful change from a few days ago. Sherman a good boy all day.

April 9   Saturday

Julia washed. I made some post cards in evening. I took them to Harmony. Weather cooler.

April 10   Sunday

All at Church. Sherman could not have been better, a dear good boy all day. Home all rest of day, sent a few flowers up to cemetery, Weather pleasant, cool wind.

April 11   Monday

Down Street with Sherman. Attended to business at home afterwards, down again for mail, filled up plate holders, packed up camera, in PM got rig from Wilson, and we all went up to the Schiver school house, made a number of exposures and went to Lancaster and was there quite a while, came home in evening, down street, had letter from Clinton. Mrs. Bert Sherman had daughter 8 ½ lbs. Arrived April 8. Weather pleasant. (In margin:beat Sherman ie.weighed more than he did at birth)

April 12   Tuesday

Developed plates. OK, beat a little carpet, trimed honeysuckle vine, Julia and I planted a few onions, some beets. Felt unwell and blue most of day. Weather cool.

April 13   Wednesday

Made sample prints and cards from negatives of Monday is right good. In PM worked in garden, got quite a piece dug, Julia cleaning house, weather pleasant day.

April 14   Thursday

Felt used up, caught a little cold yesterday, did not sleep well. Sherman and I were down street and down at Bastians, B wants to resign from Board of Health, he and Sib Passavant, President of Council had a disagreement, in PM mowed the grass, planted beans and tinkered about the place, watered the front grass, down street in evening. Weather cool and dry.

April 17   Sunday

I went to cemetery, all at church. In AM Sherman was very good, after dinner I slept, inevening Julia, Sherman, Mrs. Devin went with Rapes to their church to hear Rev. Doyer. Weather cool. Sherman was a good boy in church in evening

April 18   Monday

Julia washed, down at office in evening. Work civil.

April 19   Tuesday

Snowed last night, went to John Iffts before breakfast and made exposure of his house, then made one of Muntz house, went out to the Old People Home but done nothing, came home and went down street to office. I saw Bert Knox about insurance, wrote up policy came home, got camera ready and in PM went to Harmony and made photo of school at bridge and the Schiver house, Julia and Mrs. D went to Harmony, I kept Sherman, covered the roses, was down street with him, developed photos. Weather cold

April 20   Wednesday

I was sick in bed most all day, weather snowing in AM

April 21   Thursday

Down street a couple of times in AM and at trolley station at office in PM made some sample postcards from Tuesdays exposures , mixed up velox developer, Hoffman painted ceiling , down street in evening, weather wet and cold

April 22, 1910   Friday

Cloudy in AM but cleared off in PM In AM I went down to the station and got some card's and plates. Came home and made some card's, in PM we were at Miss Tuiths sale then home and made some more cards of Shearer school house. Julia, Miss Dubin and Sherman were over to Harmony, Julia called on Ohner's and Goerhing's and Brown's. After supper, was down street. Hoffman painted the ceiling in dining room. (Mark Twain died) *(Samuel Clemens was a favorite author of both William and his son Sherman. The family owns an early edition of Huckleberry Finn belonging to William)*

April 23   Saturday

I was down at office wrote some insurance, down street in PM at Harmony, down street in evening. Wet and cold.

April 24   Sunday

Cloudy and dismal. We went to church in the AM was home all PM in evening telephone and door bell

April 25   Monday

Put water in boiler, while eating breakfast heard Sherman brought him down, washed dishes while Julia went down in the cellar and washed. Then when she was through I went up to Holtens and fumigated one room, they had diptheria, and put up a sign on home, then after dinner I went down and made postal cards of the Shointz school house.

Dr. Ralston was here in the AM to talk board of health matters after I made my cards I went up to Mrs. Titzell's for some potatoes she promised to give us. After supper I went down to see Bastain, then home, Julia called on Mrs. Reed after supper.

April 26   Tuesday

Julia did some papering then I packed up the camera and after AM early dinner we started for the corner school in Lancaster. Trip we arrived after 1PM and after their exercises were over I made photos of the school got home about 5:30 PM weather very disagreeable, cold, wet and mud.

April 27   Wednesday

Julia finished papering the dining room. I helped a little in PM went down to office, then to see Bert Knox about insurance, then went to Harmony, took some postals and photo saw Weigel and called to see Elmer Shortz about insurance and Milleman came home, down street a couple of times. Weather clearer and bright but still cold.

April 28   Thursday

Weather warmer and bright. In AM I made prints for Mr. Iffts and post cards for Teeple. Then went down to New Castle St. and made a picture of concrete mixing machine, after dinner I developed 11 plates and cleaned the cellar, was down street after supper.

April 29   Friday

I made sample pictures from the Corner School negatives, took sample of John Iffts to him, he ordered a dozen, to photo Heberling's, after dinner took nap, then went to Harmony got my money for Shortz . I …after supper, Sherman and I were down street. Weather rain in AM and warmer. Julia and I are both unwell a day and used up

April 30   Saturday

Cut the grass, trimmed some bushes, took Sherman to barber's shop and had his curls cut off, in PM went up to Mrs. Aitken's on South Maine St. made exposure of baby, then was making postcards for Young, weather warm til evening grew colder (*Sherman's curls cut off. They were saved in an envelope which was saved in Grandma B's box which we have*)

May 1   Sunday

We all went up to cemetery before breakfast. Took Sherman in cart part way and walked, then we carried him some, I was tough and we were all tired, did not go to church, about home all day, in evening I was at church. Weather warm, rained in evening.

May 2   Monday

Julia washed in AM I looked after Sherman, cut some grass with sickle in front of house dug out some weeds in PM made prints for John Iffts and others, Weather quite warm, at office in evening making out schools, rained.

May 3 Tuesday

Burglars prowling about the place last night. Mrs. Deben and Lorn saw them. I was at office awhile in AM then working in den on school photos and cards for contractor Young busy all day. Weather wet and cooler.

May 4 Wednesday

Took some photo to Swains store for people up church country, then working on postcards, made exposures of Lutz girl, then dug garden finished, down street in evening. Weather quite cool, danger of frost tonight, had haircut.

May 5 Thursday

Down street at office and went to see Dr. Ralston for Julia's throat, made some postcards for Roy and others, felt miserable most all day and Julia not much better. Mrs. Oliver in evening. Weather quite cold and unseasonable, frost last night.

May 6 Friday

Frost last night or rather a freeze…ice. Sherman and I down street at office, made information against OW Ziegler for burying two brothers without burial permits, went up to see Mrs. Aiken's with prop, wrote up insurance came home for dinner, in PM Julia and Mrs. Devin rode out to MicKleye, I worked in garden, straightening up edges, planted some potatoes and a few hills of popcorn, mowed the grass, down street in evening. Weather cool all day.

May 7 Saturday

King of England died last night (Edward VII) I made some postcards. Worked a little in garden, took the cards to Mrs. Aiken, made exposures of Freda and Fern Grant and Mrs. Brown's baby, all down street in evening, Weather warm and pleasant.

May 8 Sunday

All at church, in PM Sherman and I went up to Dr. Ralston then he took us out to the Home in the Auto, home rest of day. Weather pleasant, shower in evening.

May 9 Monday

Last night after we had gone to bed Tom Devin was brought home hurt, we dressed and helped him to bed. Dr. Ralston came examined him, no bones broke, ankle sprained, side of head and body bruised, was struck by pole while getting on car, I made some cards worked some in garden, planted beets in evening went to Harmony, very tired. Weather cool.

May 10 Tuesday

Julia washed, Sherman and I were down street away from New Castle Street all most to RR, worked a little in garden, made a few cards. Sherman and I down street in evening. Weather quite cool.

May 11 Wednesday

Both of us sick all day. Weather cool.

May 12 Thursday

About home, down street several times. Julia out calling in PM. At Board of Health meeting, at Dr. office in evening. Sherman a very good boy all day. Weather quite cool and this evening it is cold. Will be a freeze tonight.

May 13 Friday

Tinkered about home, planted some more beet seeds, trimmed grass, in PM at Harmony made photo of some baskets for Milleman, Sherman and I went over to High school intending to make photo of class but did not do it, made a couple of dog postcards, down street in evening, weather very cold all day, no frost but clouded over, if it clears up tonight will freeze. In margin: chicken pox put notice up at Gibson.

May 14 Saturday

Made a few prints, weather cold, not well.

May 15 Sunday

All of us at church. Sherman good boy, class confirmed in PM evening all went out to see Det Passavant and then to the Old Peoples Home to see Charlotte Douglas, home rest of day. Weather slightly warmer.

May 16 Monday

Julia washed in AM, in PM I made exposures of the John Struft Sr. house, developed it, took Millermans photo over, down street in evening, weather a little warmer, we were all p and down stairs last night from 2 to 6:30 AM and down stairs last night, looking for the comet but could see nothing of it.

May 17 Tuesday

Worked a little in the garden, planted some more beans, dug the flower bed along walk, in PM went down to William Eicholtz and he and I drove out to Iffts island at old creek to inspect a road way that Knoff had made across the old creek to the dumping ground, after coming home I developed film for Lyde Bentsel and made a print from yesterday's exposure. Weather quite pleasant and warm, the first nice day we have had this month, had warm rain in evening.

May 18   Wednesday

Sherman and I went up to the cemetery, took some flowers up to Mother, Afternoons we mowed the grass and I made a few prints for Lida Bentle, took nap, Miss Kate Kirkeohan for dinner, down street in evening, this is the day the earth is to pass through the tail of the comet, but so far 10:20 PM cannot see or known anything of it. Weather has been pleasant all day.

May 19   Thursday

Sherman and I went down to Struts and got a horse and buggy and we all went up to Middle Lancaster, it was Miss Mitzi's 91st birthday, in the PM I made some photo of the family, had good chicken dinner and a pleasant time, got home safely about 6PM. Weather quite pleasant, no harm whatever came from the earth passing through the tail of the comet last night.

May 20   Friday

Developed yesterday exposures made some postcards, set out tomato plants, weather warm, gentle rain most all day.

May 21   Saturday

Sherman and I walked over to Harmony on some business but did not have any success. Sherman walked over and back as far as Milleman's shoe shop, he done fine.

May 22   Sunday

At Church had communion, Miss Ruhus kept Sherman home rest of day. Had fine showers in PM weather warm.

May 23   Monday

I made up sample photos from the Metz negatives, made some cards put grass worked the garden. Julia washed in PM, Sherman and I were down street in evening, Weather quite windy.

May 24   Tuesday

Down at office awhile, wrote up insurance for Sheridan's put new wire on window screens, over at Harmony at Kirker's. Home rest of day. Weather showers.

May 25   Wednesday

Down at office and down street, made some post cards, weather cool, in evening I saw the comet, had Gisenheimer's glass and saw the long looked for comet at last.

May 26   Thursday

Sunshine and showers in AM we had quite a rain, After dinner we all went up to the cemetery and planted some flowers and cut the grass,

Sherman helped us carry the grass away. After supper I was down street, weather cold.

The young men are having a surprise on Clarence Newberry tonight at the hotel.

May 27   Friday

Went to Harmony to see Ziegler, then went out to Home cemetery to plant a couple of Geraniums on our graves, down at office all PM and up to Dr. Ralston to get death certificate for Mrs. Catherine Stauffer, in evening at Harmony to get some death certificates that Ziegler never turned in.

Weather cold and windy all day. Comet quite bright this evening.

May 28   Saturday

All up at cemetery in AM in PM straightened up edge of grass along lane, trimmed grass, put up chicken pox sign on Weigel's house, down street in evening. Weather pleasant

Comet bright this evening, Sherman and all of us were looking at it Hope Sherman will live to see it when it comes again. (Hally's Comet 20 April 1910 and 9 February 1986 *Sherman died in 1973 and did not live to see it again.*)

May 29   Sunday

About home all day we had 120 church, our minutes being a synod at Erie, Theo Stout is delegate. Weather cloudy and threatening rain, warm but cooler in evening.

May 30   Monday

Clouds and very cool all day, rained from 5 PM on till 7 or so

In AM after breakfast I took a bouquet up to Mothers grave, then came by Dr. Ralston's office and read awhile, then Dr. took me for a ride in his automobile. Then I came home and we had dinner early, Julia and Sherman dressed up and went over to Stouts. Lillian had a surprise party, After supper we went up to Swains and spent the evening. We then went down to Mrs. Titzel but she had company so we came home. A lonely, cold lonesome day. Drew's are at Young's Town this PM

May 31   Tuesday

Julia washing through by 10. It rained all PM. I was home all evening.

June 1   Wednesday

Rainy and cold. I went to Harmony wore an overcoat in AM, in PM I developed a film for Joe Gelbach and some plates of Sherman. Then I went down street to the office.

June 2   Thursday

Weather some warmer, but we had showers in PM and evening. This AM I was sick and after dinner I was down to the office. Julia swept the house and transplanted some beets, Julia and Sherman were down street after supper.

June 3   Friday

I was down to office writing insurance, was home all PM making post cards for Clarence Newberry and Gelbach's, was down street with Sherman in evening. Weather cloudy and cool.

June 4   Saturday

Put 1 measles sign on Crawford's house, down street took chicken pox sign from Weigle house, in PM down at office, wrote insurance policy, up street as far as Dr's office, came home planted some lima beans, down street in evening made flash light exposure of kids at Schuler's party, weather warm and pleasant, but grew colder in evening and rained.

June 5   Sunday

Julia sick headache all day. Sherman good boy, weather drizzle nearly all day. About home all day. Rev. Lewis Reiter, pastor of Grace Reformed church, Harmony preached sermon to the graduating class in the auditorium.

June 6   Monday

Worked in garden all day, planted some potatoes, lima beans, lettuce. Was down street a little while in evening, weather fine and warm till about 5 PM when a heavy rain came up and then it was much colder

June 7   Tuesday

Julia washed, after she was done I went down to see Bastian on some B H business (*Board of Health*) then went to Harmony on some insurance business, down at office awhile in PM weather windy, cloudy with occasional streaks of sunshine and cold. Almost cold enough for frost tonight. Blue, despondent, discouraged. Mrs. Tuple here in evening, could have fire. Put glass in front door.

June 8   Wednesday

About 10 AM Sherman and I started out with camera, made exposure of Sam Ziegler .... Then made 5 exposures on Milton Street, got home about noon, in PM I made exposures of Eichholtz on Mill St., developed them OK in the evening we all went to the auditorium to the graduating extension of the High School as Class of 14, Mary Rape among them. The weather is warm, one lovely day.

June 9   Thursday

Made some sample card made prints of Schulber's party and made 5, down street several times, took yesterday proofs around and got some orders. Weather, cold, rain disagreeable, unpleasant. Oliver's over in evening.

June 10   Friday

Developed a film for Rev *blank*

In PM went to Harmony, made several exposures of puppies, rabbits and a corn for a miller, weather cloudy and cool had fire in house.

June 11   Saturday

Went to Harmony to mail Kate Keeper's photos and took a couple to Cookers, took some flowers up to cemetery, made postcards, weather, rain in AM showers warmer.

June 12   Sunday

A nice day. We were all to church in AM afternoon we went out to the Orphans Home and came by Old Peoples Home and went to see Miss Douglas, then came home for the rest of the day.

June 13   Monday

No entry

June 14   Tuesday

In AM out at Home made four exposures

June 15   Wednesday

Went to Harmony to photo to Kisked and some postals to Miller but he was not home, went down to Formbell, made six exposures, came home about 5, developed OK Weather quite warm.

June 16   Thursday

Working at post cards all day, in evening we both were digging out some weeds from the grass. Weather pleasant.

June 17   Friday

Repaired lock for Mrs. Debendorfer, making postcards took some weeds out of backyard, weather fine, worked in garden before breakfast, made exposure of some children in PM.

June 18   Saturday

Down street, wrote up insurance policy, went to Harmony in PM was making post cards. Sherman and I were down street in evening, Julia and Ella Swain went to Kirker's in Harmony. I am dreadfully tired. Weather very warm.

June 19   Sunday

Sherman and I went to Church, he was just the best little boy. Julia not feeling well, her eyes are sore, went home rest of day, Sherman and I took walk around the square then we all went to the Dr. to see about Julia's eyes, weather very warm.

June 20   Monday

Julia washed and I mowed the grass. Sherman and I went down street, brought Sherman up and I went down to office and wrote up some insurance, in PM developed film and mixed up developer for Velox and plates and exposed postcards, down street in AM short time, weather quite warm

June 21   Tuesday

Worked in garden awhile before breakfast, afterwards cut some grass, trimmed around with shears, Sherman and I went down Street, he had his hair cut, planted some bush lima beans in PM, developed two films, made developed a host of post cards, dug a few weeds, weather very hot.

June 22   Wednesday

Worked in garden and yard til about 9AM Sherman and I went down for mail, made exposure of medicine wagon, working at post cards, Julia sick all day. Sherman a good boy all day.

June 23   Thursday

Worked in yard a little while, Sherman and I down street. I had my hair cut. Sherman waited in barbershop like a little man, he is the grandest, manliest sensible little boy, work in on post cards for Donation Day. Sherman and I down street in evening. Julia better, Weather very hot.

June 24   Friday

Tinkered a little about the yard, then Sherman and I went up to the cemetery and cut the grass, coming home I put a big bunch of grass on the lawn mower and set Sherman on and rode him all the way home, in PM Julia and I were making postcards for donation day, watered the flowers and garden, Sherman and I down street in evening. Weather quite hot but cooler in evening.

June 25   Saturday

After trimming grass about yard went to Harmony, back about 9AM got Rape's hose, wet down the front yard, porch washed out the gutter and street. Sherman and I went for mail and bread, About home all PM made exposure of some kids for Mrs. Duncan, Julia and I down street in evening, weather pleasant not so hot.

June 26, 1910   Sunday

Sherman and I were at Church, he was a very good boy, made no trouble, home all rest of day. Harvey Rape and bride are home on a visit. Julia not well. Weather very warm.

June 27, 1910   Monday

Julia washed, I worked in garden set out beets til about 11AM Then Sherman and I went down street. Sherman got letter from GrandPa, (*Albert Sherman in Clinton,MO*) in PM I developed the films for Ed Young and was making postcards, dug a few weeds then we all went up to cemetery, took flowers up, began to rain before we got up, all got wet, had to change when we got home, had fine gentle rain.

June 28   Tuesday

No entry

June 29   Wednesday

Dug weeds out of the terrace before breakfast, after cut grass, went down street, bought parts to fix lawn mower, went out to the Home, made exposure of children in schoolhouse, after dinner went to Harmony, got some groceries at Millemans. Came home, developed exposures, no good, all undertime, made a number of prints for Lamberton made exposure of Geisinhiemer and brother, filled plate holders. Weather quite pleasant.

June 20   Thursday   Donation Day

Got up early, trimmed a little of front grass, after breakfast went down street on errands, the lined up the camera and plate holder and post cards in basket, Julia not well but baked a couple of cherry pies for the home. Harry and Andrew and I started for the Home. I sold post cards all day but did not sell enough to pay expenses, weather perfect, mad a couple of exposures, developed film for Rape when I came home.

July 1   Friday

Made some cards and prints for Rapes and was working in developing at postcards, prints for Lamberton and Geisenhiemer, down street a couple of times. Sherman and I down in evening. Weather very hot and sultry.

July 2   Saturday

Very busy all day making prints, postcards, developing film for Roger and developed Thursday's exposures, made exposure of Dorothy Reed in PM at Harmony, in evening down street, made out reports. Weather very hot.

July 3   Sunday

All at church this AM Sherman good boy, Miss Shade, missionary from India, spoke, took bit of sleep in PM. Slight shower, weather quite pleasant.

July 4   Monday

Went up to McConnell's Mill with Schuller and some kids that they invited, had pleasant day. Sherman was the best, dearest, sweetest boy, did not make a bit of trouble all day. Weather quite pleasant.

July 5 Tuesday

I was taken sick in the night and was sick about all day, went down to Lockwood's to make view of horse but could not

July 6 Wednesday

Working some in developing made exposures of Lockwood's horse, developed Schuller's films down street in evening, feeling some better. Weather pleasant, little shower in evening.

July 9 Saturday

Did not do much good today. Weather extremely hot, go in PM an…. was in town I took Sherman down street to see the parade, about home, Sherman and I down street in evening, not feeling well, exhausted and used up. The heat was dreadfull

July 10 Sunday

None of us at Church did not feel equal to the exertion, did not sleep well last night, was so oppressively warm, not so hot today, a little breeze in giving and slight shower in PM, in PM had call from Miss Stanford of Allegheny. We were all up at cemetery. Sherman was a dear good boy all day.

July 11 Monday

Julia washed, I gathered potato bugs and worked in garden, down street work up some insurance, down street again in PM, then made out birth reports, came home made some postcards for Schneiders and about 5 PM went to Harmony to collect $1.00 from a Miller, did not find him. At 6:30 went to see a Schmith, corner of Burr and Clay street to collect $7.20 but got nothing, home rest of evening. Weather quite warm in middle of day but pleasant in evening.

July 12 Tuesday

Worked in garden quite a while

July 13 Wednesday

Worked some in the front terrace, went to Harmony by way of Henry Rape and gave him sample of his photo, down street and delivered photos to Rev White, done some work in developing in PM made some postcards for Miss Peters and some prints , Sherman and I down street in evening, took some beans to Mrs. Debendarfer. Weather quite pleasant. Nice rain last night.

July 14 Thursday

Worked a little in garden. Sherman and I went up to cemetery and mowed the grass. Sherman rode home on mower, down street, wrote up policy, in PM made photos for Henry Rape made some postcards, cut grass, down street in evening. Weather warm and pleasant.

July 15 Friday

Made a few postcards, cut grass in front yard, made exposure of Miss Bastian and Dambach's house, not well sick headache, in evening Julia at Harmony with Mrs. Holl and others. Weather very warm. I was lying on cot this evening when Sherman came up to me and said "I like you papa." God bless the dear boy.

July 16 Saturday

Down at office all PM writing up insurance, went to Harmony in evening to see Miss Beiber about insurance, stopped at Kirkers, Weather looked for rain in PM but went around only got a sprinkle, blue discouraged.

July 17 Sunday

Sherman and I started early to Church went around by Dambach and Sitlers, then Julia came after dinner, had a sleep and we all went out to see Det Passavant. Weather quite cool and pleasant. Depressed, discouraged.

July 18 Monday

Was at the office writing insurance, came home got camera and went down to Bastians to make photo, stood around waiting on him for an hour and then came home, in PM done a little work in den, then went to Harmony delivered policy to Miss Beiber at Milleman's and other business, down street with Sherman and afterward developed 2 films for Endres. Weather pleasant, cool in evening.

July 19 Tuesday

Julia washed, I made postcards for Endres in PM we were over at a sale of household goods, then developed some postcards street scenes, watered the roses. Sherman and I down street in evening. Sherman who has been cranky for several days is feeling much better. I am feeling better this evening but Julia is not well.

July 20 Wednesday

In PM Rev White came for me and I went out to the Home made exposure of his residence and of the Farm house.

July 21 Thursday

Busy all day, made exposure of baby Smith of Youngstown, Ohio who is visiting Mrs. Devin and all of Mrs. Devin. Weather very hot and dry

July 22 Friday

Working in den, busy in PM Devin and Smith took drive to Portersville and Julia and Sherman went as far as Middle Lancaster and stayed till they came back. I made a number of photos of them. Weather hot and dry.

July 23   Saturday

Made Monday postcards for Smith, got them ready for them to take with them about 10:30. All of us at Church in PM down street a little while in evening. Weather hot.

July 24   Sunday

I took some flowers to cemetery, I went to church alone. Julia not feeling well, has trouble with her throat, had communion, Some Catholic Society had a parade up our street just as church was out, about home rest of day, took sleep in PM, Sherman a real good boy all day. Weather very hot and dry, looked for rain but none came. Nice breeze blowing.

July 25   Monday

Made a few cards for Devin, Julia washed, was down street all PM at office and again down on numerous business in the evening. Weather hot and dry, looked for rain but none came. Sherman a dear best good sweet boy all day. Julia not well, throat trouble.

July 26   Tuesday

Was sick in night had to get up six or eight times and lay around the house and tried to sleep most of the day, developed four films for Roy. Sherman and I down street in evening, was trying to collect a bill but failed, Weather hot, breeze giving most of day. Sherman a good boy all day.

July 27   Wednesday

About home most all day, slept some feeling better. Julia some better too, made a trip to trolley station for package. Mrs. Ralph Heiger and children visiting at Stouts. Weather hot and dry. Looked for rain but none came. Sherman good boy.

July 28   Thursday

Working at print for Gelbach and Roy Dindinger , made a couple of exposures for Mrs. Wilson, Julia a little better. Sherman and I down street in evening Weather warm and dry.

July 29   Friday

Finished up some odds and ends of work. Sherman and I down for mail, mixed up developers. Phillis of Turnbill called. Took sleep in PM, not feeling very well, down at office. Sherman and I down street in evening. Weather very warm and dry. Everything burning up. Sherman good boy. Mrs. Rosenstein gave Sherman some marbles (his first).

July 30 Saturday

After attending to some household duties I cleaned up and Sherman and I went down street attended to some errands got the bread etc. in PM about home, took nap, not well. Julia some better, in evening Sherman and I down street, Rained a little last night.

July 31 Sunday

Home all day, no one at church, in PM all went up to cemetery, weather cool. Sherman hauled Lois Gelbach in little wagon, hauled her home, first girl he took home.

August 1 Monday

Julia washed, Sherman and I down street. I made information against undertaker Zeigler for removing the remains of Mrs. Wright of Eidenau (*Harmony Junction*) to East McKeesport without a removal permit, in PM down street at office wrote up policy, and tried to collect some money from Bert Knox but failed, went to Harmony for birth certificates, Sherman and I down street in evening. Sherman a dear good boy all day, he is now singing out of his little book. Weather hot and dry. Julia slowly improving.

August 2 Tuesday

Developed a couple of films Sherman and I down street , in PM Julia and I went over to Harmony to see Dr. Ralston, printed some cards, Stuart Schuller, Rev Lonaker are playing croquet at Stout's. Weather hot and dry. Sherman a good boy all day. Mrs. Rape not well. Julia feeling much better this evening. Mrs. Devin at Youngstown.

August 3 Wednesday

Sherman not well this AM when Julia brought him down he was sweating and was quite unwell but after taking some peppermint and sleeping awhile felt better but we have kept him in the house all day as the heat is terrible today, numerous persons called to see Sherman today. Mrs. Rape and Harry, Mrs. Stout, Grandpa Stout, Grace. Weather very hot and dry looks for rain but none comes

August 4 Thursday 6:40AM

I slept in west room by myself, got up took a letter to Charles Beighley (living in Coony King's house) to take up 1 on his Rural Delivery Route, to Peffers they want us to come up on Friday, Developed film for Bastians made some print from it and made some cards, went over to Harmony to see Dr. but he was not home, Mrs. Sitler called in evening. Weather cooler but no rain yet.

August 5 Friday

I got a horse and buggy from street drove up to William Peffer made a number of photos of the family reunion, coming home stopped at

Mrs. Myers. Weather cool, pleasant and very dry.

August 6   Saturday

Developed plates, made prints from them in AM exposures of Halls house, down street in evening. Weather dry

August 7   Sunday

All at church Sherman right good, took nap in PM home all rest of day. Weather pleasant but very dry. Julia feeling better.

August 8   Monday

Julia washed, after she was through I went down to Harpers to see him about insurance on Church in PM down at office awhile, then came home and made some prints and post cards, down at office again in evening.

August 9   Tuesday

Down at office writing up insurance etc about all day, down again in evening, Earnest Moiser was buried this PM. He was killed on Sunday while walking on trolley line track. Tried to rain this evening but only a few drops fell. Julia improving. Sherman good boy.

August 10   Wednesday

I was down at the office all AM and in PM was making postcards for Meisel Pythian, Home picnic today and the Merchants Outing at Cascade Park, had nice little shower last night and another this PM sown street in evening awhile.

August 14   Sunday

All at Church, Sherman was a good boy, good all day. I was up at cemetery in AM, home all rest of day, Julia slowly getting better. Weather very hot and dry, looked for rain but none came.

August 15   Monday

Julia washed. I was down street short time and about home most all the day, not well, did not sleep well last night. Weather very hot 89 about 4 PM Julia slowly improving. No rain, blue discouraged.

August 16   Tuesday

Watered the flowers and down street for mail, came home and Julia went down to Dr. Reid's office. She is slowly improving. I then went to Harmony on the Health Department. Did not get back till after 12AM at 2:30 went to Eicholtz Hotel to take photo found it was a girl had her come to the house made exposure and developed it, about home rest of day, down street in evening down street, Ed Winks house in evening. Weather very, very hot and dry. Ground was broken for a new home above Purdunes. Sherman was a very good boy.

August 17   Wednesday

Made some post cards developed a couple of films, down street awhile. Weather very hot, very dry, no rain yet. Julia getting better, Sherman the best sweetest most interesting dearest boy all day. Julia went to bed first and Sherman and I were playing on the floor, directly he said "I am going to bed" and starts off. I said "Put your playthings away" so he came back and put some in the box and said "You put them away" and started off again and I said: "Aren't you going to give me a hug and kiss?"

So he came back and hugged and kissed me and said: "Good Night"

August 18   Thursday

About home most all day, not doing much, not feeling well, German Lutheran Sunday School picnic at Eckarts grove, pipe line picnic at Conneaught Lake, had several fine showers this PM and evening. Sherman good boy all day.

August 19   Friday

Weeded the garden which took about all AM in PM was down in extension st and at Charlie Stokes made a number of exposures, in evening at Board of Health meeting. Weather pleasant

Aug 20   Saturday

Working at postcards and developed a couple of films, about 4 PM made exposure of Stokey's spring, Sherman and I down street in evening. Weather quite pleasant.

August 21   Sunday

All at Church, Olivers went with us. Sherman good boy, home all rest of day. Julia not feeling very well. Weather pleasant.

August 22   Monday

Julia washed for herself and Mrs. Diben, I did not do much good today, put in considerable time with Sherman who was somewhat cranky and I out of sorts, and I was not much better, worked and fussed trying to letter a negative. Sherman and I down street in evening. Weather warm.

August 23   Tuesday

In PM was down in extension with camera delivered some postals, got stuck in some of them, down street in evening. Weather very hot.

August 24   Wednesday

All of us with Sitlers and Ella Swain, Stouts and some friends of Sitler went down to Pine sun and had a little picnic, had a very pleasant time. Weather very hot.

August 25   Thursday

Made some prints and postals for Peffer in PM down at office Weather very warm but considerable wind blowing. Sherman a good boy all day so sweet and loving, he had been a little cranky for several days but our good little boy has come back to us.

August 26   Friday

Was making the form for a concrete sidewalk at our back porch, then made another Peffer print. Sherman and I down street in evening. Weather quite cool, had a nice rain last night.

August 27   Saturday

Made several exposures of some of the Jungs across the street, developed them and made some wet proofs, was served with notice to appear at Butler on Sept 6 in case against OW Ziegler, made another Peffer print, lounged about the house some, did not feel well, Julia over at Kirkers in evening, and about 8PM Julia, Sherman and I went to the trolley station to meet Miss Kuntz, who is going to room at our house again. Weather pleasant, cool in evening.

August 28   Sunday

All at home all day, Julia had sick headache and sick otherwise with her throat and stomach, went to see the Dr. in evening. Weather cool and pleasant.

August 29   Monday

Made some post card and done a lot of fussing and running about trying to get some ink and get some lettering done on negative. Weather quite pleasant. Julia feeling right good today.

August 30   Tuesday

Julia washed after she was through I went to Bastians got the water bottles for collecting samples of the water, got a sample in the extension where a Zinkhaus had lived, then at Buhlers where there is a case of typhoid fever, another sample at Kildoors, went to Pa Ziegler for sample, he was not home, in PM was down at office awhile and then over at Ziegler's got sample of his cistern water and of the milk he is using, down street on errand, then got in and packed around the bottles and took them to the station and shipped the case to Philadelphia. Sherman was a good boy all day. Julia and Mrs. Diven made jelly. Weather pleasant.

Sept 1   Thursday

Went down to the office intending to move to when Dr. Reid made some preparations reading up, in PM made a couple of prints and fussing around the den. Sherman and I down street in evening. Had nice shower this PM.

Sept 2 Friday (in margin: moved office)

Went to office to help move, but McMichael was not ready, came home. Sherman and I took his bank to the bank and deposited it, had $4.65 in them. I went to office and helped

move, down again after dinner, cleaned out the old room, came home and Julia and I went down to Ed Young's camp and made three exposures went to another camp near Philps but made no exposure, came home, developed plates OK, developed these films for Ziegler. Weather quite pleasant.

Sept 3 Saturday

Made some prints for Ziegler, Julia washed had sick headache and was lying down when Abe Moyer sent for me to make photo of some friends and relatives at his house, went down and made two exposures, came home and lay down again, in evening when better developed them OK. Sherman and I down street in evening. Had heavy rain last night and several showers during day.

Sept 4 Sunday

All at church in AM in PM all walked up to cemetery, home rest of day. Weather warm and pleasant

Sept 5 Monday

Labor day- copied the death certificates, down street gathering up the birth certificates, made a few postcards, prints and rested awhile in evening down street and had a settlement with Dindingers, borrowed $47.00 from the Peoples Bank for four months

Sept 6 Tuesday

Sherman woke up sick this AM, we intended going to Butler this AM but Julia gave it up and I had to go alone, took the 7:55 car, went to court house, found that nothing was …in my case of Undertaker Ziegler, as Dr. Batt of Harrisburg was expected at about 10:30, so I went off and looked about town, came back about that time, Dist Atty Troutman had read a letter from Batt that he was in Milwaukee and could not be present, Batt had not arrived yet and then was no other train till 1:17 so I went off again, got some dinner at about 1 PM I turned up at the court house and found that Dist Atty Troutman had read a letter from Batt in Milwaukee stating he could not be present. About 2:30 I was call in to the Grand Jury room and questioned in regard to Ziegler burying without a burial permit, after I was through I took a car ride about town and to the park, the park don't amount to much, about town some more, west to see Mrs. Wegley but she could not be found, started for home at 4:15 got home OK found Sherman better. Weather showers in AM, cleared up in PM

Sept 7 Wednesday

Sick in night and sick all day with bowel trouble. Weather pleasant , a little neighbor boy Joseph Anstin was drowned in the creek today.

Sept 8 Thursday

Sick most all day, again with headache

Sept 9 Friday

Went to Harmony for birth certificate and took sample photos to Mrs.Fred Weigle

Sept 10   Saturday

Working in den made Moyer photos in PM attended funeral for Austin boy, down street awhile in evening. Weather pleasant.

Sept 11,1910   Sunday

All at church in AM but Sherman had to come out in PM we took a walk to Stokey's pond to see the fishes then went to Geisinheimer's. Weather pleasant.

Sept 12   Monday

Cut the grass and trimmed around in front, Julia helping, went to Casper Knauff to make photo of house, but they had the wash hanging out so I could not do it, in PM went to Harmony delivered photos to Weigle, down at office awhile, in evening at Board of Health meeting. Weather warmer.

Sept 13   Tuesday

We all went to Butler, arrived about 10:00 went to Willard Hotel then I went to court house found out that Ziegler case would not come up, has been continued to Dec. time, we then started out to see Butler, took a car ride and on car met Mrs. Hoffman – who lived in our house a month – looked around town some more, got Sherman a pair of shoes $1.00 in the five and ten cent store, came home about 1PM, Julia got dinner for Mr. and Mrs. Devin as she was in bed sick. I was down to office.

Sept 14   Wednesday

Julia washed in AM I cut some grass, then Julia got ½ bushel peaches and Mrs. Rape helped her peal them. She made 4 quarts of butter, in PM I made the cement walk at the front of the steps, A man who lives across the lane helped me finish off the last of it. I am very tired and so is Julia.

Sept 15   Thursday

Man working at walk this AM and awhile in evening got from the steps to the lane made. Sherman and I went to Heberlings to make photo of him and his dogs, came home went to Gotlieb Ziegler, made a couple of exposures, made one on way home of some men working on street, got home at dinner time, in PM developed photos, made a print of Knauff's house and post cards, piled up, some of the old plank from the walk, Donation Day of the Old Folk's Home. Weather pleasant.

Sept 16   Friday

While we were eating breakfast, Gisson brought four crates of peaches for Devin and Julia with Mrs. Rape help put up 31 quarts and made some peach butter, was very busy and worked hard all day. I made some postcards for Heberling, made another exposure of the man working on the Harmony road, developed it and got some cards made from it, at office a while in evening did not feel well all day, work was a drag, Weather pleasant. Sherman a good boy.

Sept 17   Saturday

Julia made a lot of fine peach butter, I helped her stir for some time. Sherman and I went down for the bread and some other errands, in PM made some prints of Casper Knauff and Ziegler house, made an exposure of a dead Hungarian baby, and then made some of children and other folks in that neighborhood, developed exposure took photo to Knauff, Sherman and I down street in evening. Weather pleasant. Sherman good boy all day.

Sept 18   Sunday

I took some flowers to cemetery, Julia and I were at Church in AM, after dinner I slept awhile. About home rest of day. Weather cool.

Sept 19   Monday

Julia washed, I helped a little and cleaned up about the yard, piled the old plank up, Sherman and I down for mail, got letter from Mrs. Griggs for Julia, in PM I was making some photos from Saturday exposures and helping at the walk (but the first thing this AM I went down to Patterson's lumberyard and borrowed several stringers and had them brought up) Julia went to see Dr. Ralston about her throat who gave her some nitrate of silver to burn it out with. Sherman played in sand pile all PM. Weather pleasant.

Sept 20   Tuesday

Took photo and postal to Ziegler in Harmony, got an order amounting to 4.50 from her, to post cards to Extension got $6.60 Cobel brought a load of coal 60 bushels, finished the walk, made some post cards down street a little in PM. Weather pleasant.

Sept 21, 1910   Wednesday

Carried some sand in cellar, made a place for the rain barrel to stand. Sherman and I down street, made some prints for Geisenheimer and

Ziegler, made an exposure of Teeple's home and tried Sherman on the sand pile but failed in his case, down street in evening weather pleasant, Mrs. Rape and Julia making Sherman a suit out of blue cloth, Julia feeling right good today.

Sept 22   Thursday

Worked out in the yard cleaning up and filling along the edge of sidewalk, about 10 AM went to Harmony to make photo High School class, came home, developed exposures OK, in PM went out to Det Passavant made exposures of old map, came home developed, developed film made some post cards, Julia went to see Dr. Ralston about her throat, he pronounced it better, Sown street a little while in evening weather pleasant. Sherman a good boy, played in sand pile a long time

Oct 10   Monday

I have given up keeping a diary, will only write occasionally, yesterday was a pleasant day had a heavy frost the night before (Friday night) but nothing was hurt, yesterday we were both sick. I had a dreadful attack of sick headache. I have not been so sick for a long time, was in bed most of the day and today I was sick, it was most evening before it wore off, but in the PM I managed to develop some plates, Sherman was just the best little boy all day yesterday. Today he is not quite so good, got cranky and stubborn when I had him down street this AM and had had several stubborn spells through the day, Julia is not well her throat and stomach still give her trouble.

Oct 10   Monday

I have given up keeping a diary, will only write occasionally, yesterday was a pleasant day had a heavy frost the night before (Friday night) but nothing was hurt, yesterday we were both sick. I had a dreadful attack of sick headache. I have not been so sick for a long time, was in bed most of the day and today I was sick, it was most evening before it wore off, but in the PM I managed to develop some plates, Sherman was just the best little boy all day yesterday. Today he is not quite so good, got cranky and stubborn when I had him down street this AM and had had several stubborn spells through the day, Julia is not well her throat and stomach still give her trouble

Oct 11   Tuesday

This PM we made a pit size 10 by 14 and set out 50 rose cuttings in it. Julia also put a number of cuttings into jars and she has quite a number growing nicely that she has started this summer, Mrs. Kirker was over this PM Weather fine. Both of us dreadfully blue and discouraged.

Oct 13   Thursday

This PM we went to cemetery took up the geraniums we had planted, cut the grass, Weather quite pleasant, Sherman a sweet dear good boy all day.

Oct 14   Friday

Making postals this AM in PM Julia, Mrs. Diven, Sherman and I went up to Harmony Junction. Julia and Mrs. Diven made a visit to Mrs. Laughin and I made several exposures in the power house. Weather quite pleasant Sherman a good boy

Oct 16   Sunday

All at church in AM in PM we all walked over to Kirkers but no one was at home. Weather fine, grand, delightful.

Oct 19   Wednesday

Sherman and I went to Harmony junction to deliver some photos, delivered some at the power house, Sherman was afraid to go in so he stayed at the door, then we went to the car barn, but could not find the men we wanted, was told they were working on other side of Luntz bridge, I took Sherman up to (Laughin a family we know) and he stayed there awhile, I went up and beyond but could not find the men, came back got Sherman and left photos with Winter and came home. Sherman was a good boy and made no trouble, in PM at office writing up insurance, made exposure of a couple of girls, weather perfectly delightful, perfect, grand.

Oct 20   Thursday

I was down at office, wrote up some insurance. There was a collision on the trolley line between a freight and a passenger car (at Harmony Junction and quite a number were hurt, some girls seriously, made some prints and post cards, weather fine, grand 86° at 1:30 PM

Oct 21 Friday

Julia cleaned the sitting and dining room. I went down to Biebers with photos for Kirkers in AM in PM at office awhile. Weather warm but hazy look for rain

Oct 23   Sunday

All at church, sent a nice bouquet of roses to church.

Oct 26   Wednesday

Julia and I went to Pittsburgh at 8, 217 and went to Hornes store, looked at some suits for Julia but was not pleasant, went to Rosenbaums with no better success, then we strayed into McCresney and bought a blue suit for $25.00 and was well pleased with it, looked at silk shirt waist but did not buy, went to Kaufmans, got dinner and bought yard of silk for waist, went about the city in stores 5 and 10 cent, then I went up to Starfords and had a pleasant little visit, got home about 7:00. Let Sherman with Mary Rape and he was a good boy all day. Weather quite pleasant.

Oct 29 Saturday

Snow flurries and blizzard today, the ground was quite white with snow, the sun came out and melt it, then clouded over and another snow flurrie

Oct 30 Sunday

No one at Church, none of us felt well. Weather rough and cold

Oct 31 Monday (*Halloween*)

I took some flowers up to cemetery, down street with Sherman for mail, after dinner at office a short time and came home and put some beet6s in cellar and burned buried some in garden, in evening we all were down street awhile, the kids and young folks are having great time. We had a pumpkin face for Sherman and lit it up with a candle and how he did enjoy it. He got a wonderful amount of pleasure with it, Weather quite mild and pleasant

Nov 4 Friday

When Julia came downstairs this AM she found the back door open and the window from the porch open, the side board drawer open, she called up to me and I hurried down and found the house had been ransacked by burglers, but nothing missing But Sherman's bank and that only had a few cents in as we had taken it to the bank last week, they were also in Seaton's, Iffts, Patersons and Ed Jennys.

Nov 6 Sunday

All at church Sherman was restless, after dinner I took a nap, reading All at church again in evening Sherman was good boy, Weather cool.

Nov 7 Monday

In evening Rev. Lonaker called to see Miss Kuhrs as she was not here he spent sometime with us. I made a flash light of some girls at Lydia Bentle's.

Nov 8, 1910 Tuesday

Went down and voted, first developed last night's exposures, after voting came up home, got several cars for Sherman, we gave him a silver spoon. (*Sherman's birthday, he was three*)

In the afternoon I made several photos of him and in the evening I measured him, he is 2 ft 10 ½ inches in height around the head 20 in, chest 22 in, he weighed- In the PM I was over at Harmony. Weather rained a little in AM cleared up and was cooler.

Nov 10 Thursday

I was sick about all day yesterday and got little or nothing done. Today I am some better a with Julia help I got some cards made, I lay down a couple of times, weather raining in AM, cleared up and grew colder. Sherman, a dear good boy, how much I love him and how I sometimes worry for his future, what will become of he and Julia when I am gone, how they will get along. God bless them both and keep them.

Nov 11   Friday

This AM I went up to Harmony got and canvased the town for fire insurance not much success, got home about dinner time, tired did not do much in PM down street in evening. Weather quite cold and strong. Sherman a good sweet boy all day

Nov 12   Saturday

In PM made a few prints of the flashlight down street in evening not feeling very well. Weather cold and strong

Nov 13   Sunday

None of us at church about home all day, weather right wintry

Nov 17   Thursday

In PM put up shelf in the laundry to put negative on, made several exposures of Mrs. Devin –Tom's mother) then of Tom, Mrs. Tom and his mother, sorted out a lot of negatives and arranged them in better order, in evening was at Harmony took policy to J. W. Adams. Weather warmer but cloudy and disagreeable as it has been all week. Miss Florence Newton cut her throat this evening.

Nov 18   Friday

Mr. PC Frederick died of pneumonia Nov 19 after an illness of a few days

Nov 20   Sunday

All at Church, Sherman was just the best grandest boy that could be, in PM we all went out to the Old People's Home. Sherman wanted to go, was so eager and insisted on giving, Weather was bright and sunny. The first nice day we have had for almost two weeks.

Nov 21   Monday

Julia washed, from PM I was at Harmony. Weather cloudy, dismal with a few sparks of sunshine. Wrote up some insurers at office

Nov 22   Tuesday

Down at office most all day over at Harmony in PM down street a little while in evening weather dismal, cloudy

Nov 23   Wednesday

In PM out at Orphans Home, made exposure of all the children standing in line, came home and developed, fussing around, mixed velox developer. Weather is a quite bright but grew cloudy and in evening rained

Nov 24   Thursday Thanksgiving

I went down to PO, then we all went to Church. Sherman was good as usual about 1PM had dinner, stewed chicken and potatoes, cranberry etc. Mrs. Passavant sent it.

After dinner we took a few flowers and vines up to Mother, it is the anniversary of her coming here a bride, 66 years ago, come home we stopped so see Mrs. Schaffer, it started to rain while we were there, borrowed an umbrella, and came home. Home all rest of day, reading some and playing with Sherman who is a wonderful boy for his age, Weather was

fine and bright sunshine in AM I hoped that it would clear up and have nice weather but it gradually clouded over and rained.

Nov 25   Saturday

Developed film, Sherman and I went down street, in PM went to Harmony on various business matters, got suit of clothes, tried the pants on, the were too large, took them back, We were all down street at Drug store awhile, in evening weather cloudy.

Nov 26   Sunday

All at Church in AM in PM I attended a lecture in our church was not very well pleased with it, Julia was over at Rapes, Mary is sick, home all rest of day, not feeling very well, Weather quite bright and pleasant in Am, but clouded up and rained in evening.

Nov 28   Monday

Had severe sick headache all day long, began yesterday even and head ached all night and today I was in bed most of day, and today I was in bed most of day, and at times even threw up some green bitter gall after which I began to get better. Weather rained all day

Nov 29   Tuesday

Slept good last night and felt better but somewhat weak in PM put a new sucker rod in the pump which got broke on Sunday, made a couple of prints, had a lot of trouble the developer would not work, weather unpleasant, snow melting as it fell

Nov 30   Wednesday

Julia washed I looked after Sherman then we went down for mail, in PM at office a while. Weather snow flurries and in evening snowing right fast, Sherman talking all day. Julia no better.

Dec 1   Thursday

Swept the walks, snowed in night made some post cards started for mail with Sherman on sled but he did not like it and hung sled on telephone pole and walked down, in PM was at the office making out reports, till nearly 4 PM when I went to Harmony to some post cards to Miss Cooper and was at Kirkers got some butchering at K that Kate Kirker sent down, after supper Julia and I were down to the Dr. to see about Julia's tongue. She feels better now. Weather cold, snow and strong all day.

Dec 2   Friday

Bess Reed here in evening

Dec 3   Saturday

Sherman and I went down for mail, then I was down at office a little while, in PM copying the death certificates, then down street went to Dr. Ralstons office about a certificate was then quite a while then was at office, in evening Julia, Sherman and I were down street and up at Passavant's had pleasant evening. Weather a little milder, sun out bright and nice for a while in PM the first for many weeks, snowing in evening.

Dec 4   Sunday

All at church, Mrs. Diver to, took Sherman on sled when we came home I gave Sherman a ride up to Dambach corner, back he enjoyed it very much, in PM I gave him another sled ride up to Dambach corner then across to Spring St. then to Clay St. to New Castle St. and down to the B & O station, then home. He likes it and holds on like a fine boy, played with him some and al. All most got off patience with the dear boy for he done so much talking and asked so many questions, but he is a dear good boy and bright. Julia not very well, Weather right pleasant. Sun out some

Dec 5   Monday

Julia washed. I was at office awhile in PM at office Mrs. W. G. Goehring. brought Julia some cookies for her lunch. Weather snowing. Sherman a wonderful good boy all day just boiling over feeling good

Dec 6   Tuesday *WGB's birthday. He is 56.*

Went into office let fine got some rope at the hardware store for the trunk, then Sherman in PM on sled went to office and I wrote up insurance policy for Klinersmith. Then Sherman and I went to PO I stopped at the office and Mary Rape took Sherman on home. In PM I went to Harmony for birth certificate and settled with Milleman bill was $12.00 came home Julia and I went down street and I went out to Det Passavant to see Miss Gross about insurance, in evening all of us were at the Dr. office in regard to Julia's mouth – took Sherman on sled. He enjoys the ride so very much and can stick on without any trouble. Weather cloudy and I am blue, despondent, discouraged

Dec 7 Wednesday

(Julia's 2nd visit home to Clinton,MO but first trip with Sherman who is three in 1910)

The morning was spent in final preparation for Julia's trip. Julia, Sherman, Debin and I left in the 127 car for Pittsburg arrived safely, stopped at several stores on way to Hahns got to station, found we could get train at 6PM bought ticket through to Clinton, Mo cost $20.85 got trunk checked and sat down to wait, I walked and carried Sherman about a good deal, at last the train was announced and we went out through the gate I carried Sherman, Mrs. D helped Julia with the suitcase. I carried Sherman up in the car and had a last hug and kiss and then left them, hoping and praying that everyone would all safely be together again, waited in the train shed a long time to see them go by but had to give it up and run for my car. Got home O.K.

Dec 9 Friday

Had sick headache all day

Dec 11 Sunday

Slept till 10AM about home reading all day

Dec 12 Monday

Got up before 7AM got breakfast started at 8:10 for Buster McMichael also saw District Attorney Troutman who informed me the case *vis* which I was interested Commonwealth vs OW Ziegler had to be settled. Ziegler pleading guilty afterward. I saw Dr. Batt, State Registrar of Vital Statistics of Harrisburg, PA and secretary of the state board of Undertakers. Neither of them liked it that I had been issuing burial permits to Ziegler. Dr. Batt was a perfect gentleman and was very sincere about it but Haultz is a big overbearing bulldozing hog, I stayed about Butler till PM then came home tired. Weather strong snow flurries.

Dec 13 Friday

Down at office, considered wrote up several insurance policies, began to get sick headache.

Dec 14 Wednesday

I had sick headache all day, lay on cot most all day, sick all night. Weather bright and pleasant

Dec 15 Thursday

I was sick all night got up about 8 AM lay on cot awhile but it wasn't warm, went back to bed till 10AM got up ate a little breakfast, felt better, went for mail got letter from Julia.

She is feeling nigh well, at office awhile in PM then home rest of day. Weather snowing and stormy.

Dec 16 Friday

After I got mail a card from Julia I went out to see Miss Gross, she paid her insurance after dinner made exposure of Charlie Young, of Sadi's baby, then went to the school house to see the Christmas entertainment and exercises, came home developed plates, split some wood, down street in evening, weather bright and clear today but cold blue.

Dec 17 Saturday

Busy calls this AM was at office awhile in PM made some exposure of Clarence Iffts children, developed film and plates made some post cards for Frank Lockwood, down street awhile in evening.

Dec 18 Sunday

Mrs Devin and I at church, Mrs. J gave me some dinner, reading, wrote to Dr. Bennet and Julia. Weather quite cold in AM but moderated and rained in PM

Dec 19 Monday

About the house at post office at office a few minutes, in PM working in den, in evening at home reading and writing, weather turned cold in night and this AM everything is ice, cold all day and now at 10:50 PM it is snowing and storming dreadfully

Dec 20 Tuesday

After breakfast and the work done up I went to post office then took sample photos to Youngs got good order, came home went to office with samples got 2nd order had letter from Julia both well, fine pleasant Weather out, working in the den all day till PM Weather cold and stormy.

Dec 21 Wednesday

Took card and photos to Iffts and Young, got my pay, at office till noon and about all afternoon. Weather clear cold.

Dec 22 Thursday

After doing up work went down street, was working in den most all day, made exposures of interior of Jewelry store. Weather bitter cold this AM moderated during day.

Dec 23 Friday

Went up to see Mrs. Titzel about insurance, then wrote her up a policy. I took it to her, in PM developed the exposure of the Jewelry store

OK, then was at office making out reports. Weather quite mild, raining.

Dec 24 Saturday

Done some work at the office, got life insurance policy from the bank filled out an application for a loan of $250.00 had it witnessed before McMichael notary public and mailed application and policy to the Equitable Insurance Company at NY, took a holly wreath up to Mother , down street till after 9PM waiting for letter from Julia but it did not come.

Dec 25 Sunday

Went to church in AM took dinner with Divers upstairs, had headache and laid down on cot and slept all afternoon till evening, then Mrs. Diver and I went to the Christmas exercises. They were nice. Weather cold, snow and ice.

Dec 26,1910 Monday

After I got the mail which brought two letters from Julia and several cards, I went out to the Old Folks home and made exposure of their Christmas tree, a lot of the orphan girls were there and Sister Katherine treated them to some music of the graphophone, I then went in to see Miss Douglas, came home read my letters and after dinner was reading and went down to Eicholtz Hotel and made exposure of girl in boys clothing, home rest of day, on down street in evening to mail letter to Julia. Weather much milder, thawed some

Dec 27 Tuesday

After the mail, I went out to the Old People Home made another exposure of tree, in PM developed it. OK and was working in den all PM had trouble and no success, something is wrong with the paper or the developer, Kate Kirker and Mrs. Metz sent me box of sausage apple cookies and a handkerchief. Weather milder, tired this evening going to bed early.

Dec 28 Wednesday

I was working the AM all day made post cards for Old People's Home and some others, developed 2 films for Frank Lockwood. Weather raining in AM quite warm all day. crabby in evening, tired and lonesome. Hope all are well

Dec 29 Thursday

Working in den most all day made cards for Old People and Frank Lockwood. Weather warm, rained all day. Mrs. Eli Hoffman died.

Dec 30 Friday

Had letter from Julia, Sherman not very well . I was working in den awhile had no success, can't get the velox paper to work right, home and down street, in evening at funeral of Mrs. Hoffman. Weather colder and snowing

Dec 31 Saturday

After breakfast etc, went for mail, got postal from Julia, Sherman is better, went to Bert Knox on Clay St. to collect $15.50 for insurance but no one would come to door, afterwards I met Bert at his shop, who promised to come to the office and pay at 5PM Then I was at the office till noon, after dinner I made some postals for Old People Home, then was down street, after 5 waiting on Bert Knox who did not come, wrote to Julia, Mrs. William Iffts died this PM, she has baked bread for us for many years, in evening I was home reading, read the evening paper, then the death of Iffts, old dear, The nine years we, and in the prayer book for nine years, some hymns in the Church book, very quiet and lonesome. Weather quite cold last night, moderated and was pleasant during day, Julia and Sherman far away.

Jan 1,1911 Sunday

Went to Church in morning did not feel like going was tired and head-ache, it grew worse, lay down on cot with hot water bottle at my feet and slept all PM did not read anything but the devotional exercises for the day, weather rained more or less all day. Kuntz came back in evening.

Jan 2 Monday

About house and over at Rapes till time for the mail, went for mail, got letter from Julia, to Rapes took dinner with Rape, good dinner chicken at Pm went to funeral of Mrs. Ifft, then came home wrote to Julia, made copies death certificates, down street little while in evening at drug store, home reading. Weather quite warm

Jan 3 Tuesday

After breakfast and done up work, went down street for mail, got nothing was at the office doing some work till noon, was down again in PM awhile, settled with Burr and Rogers, then was home working in den but had no success, sent the paper to the Eastman Kodak Co to find out what the trouble is. Weather snowing all day

Jan 4 Wednesday

Went to Post Office got letter from Julia and one from the Equitable Insurance Co with check for loan of $250.00 less 6 months interest, came home out of sorts, after dinner shaved and cleaned up, went down and settled with bank, went to Harmony to Kirker's and numer-ous other places, home all rest of day. Weather very cold last night, but moderated during day, blue out of sorts

Jan 5 Thursday

About home most of day, done a little of indexing the insurance register, Weather cold, had card from Julia and letter from Minnie

Jan 7   Saturday

Cleaned up the house, down street, had haircut, took both about home, Weather warm

Jan 8   Sunday

Mrs D and I went to church. In PM I went to men's meeting at church, over at Rapes little while, had headache, went to bed early Weather raining, thunder and lightning

Jan 9   Monday

Got up late, had headache all night, wore off after getting up, about home all day only down street a few minutes early in evening, weather cold, turned cold last night high winds

Jan 10   Tuesday

Down at office awhile in PM washed some underclothes and about town awhile in evening went to see Al Goehring about insurance, Bastian here in evening about board of health, B and I at Ralston awhile, Weather pleasant

Jan 11   Wednesday

Down at office greater part of day, writing up policies. Weather moderate.

Jan 13, 1911   Friday

Went down to the office in PM got no mail, about town, settled with Frishkorn got him to take a bill of measles on at about town attending to various other matters, went down in the extension to see Ed Knauff about insurance, came home, Dibie said Winter wanted me to call him up, down street, he wanted me to meet him at the bank at 12, got some dinner and hurried down, he wanted me to canvass the county along the trolley line to see who wanted some boarders, I jumped at the offer, was home all PM working in den at Church in evening. Weather raining

Jan 14   Saturday

Down at office, went up Street to see Osterling, he was not home, went down in extension to see him and most stuck in mud, in PM at church and wrote up some insurance in evening down street for provisions for Sunday. Weather rainy and drizzling, colder in evening.

Jan 15   Communion Sunday

At church in evening, home rest of day at Rapes awhile in evening, D gave me some dinner. A Sitler's wife and 2 sons and 4 others joined our church. Weather cooler, Kirkers have company.

Jan 16 Monday

Went to PO got letter and card from Julia, good news she is coming home soon, at insurance office in PM made exposures for John Ifft of some patented trolley line he is getting up, developed 2 of them OK home rest of day. Weather quite cold, blue, despondent and sad.

Jan 17 Tuesday

After I got mail, letter from Julia saying she could not start today as her mother is sick. I then went down to the RR station to see when trains came in from St. Louis, then was at insurance office and after dinner was working in den all rest, had fine success, in evening down street and drug store a little while. Weather cold.

Jan 18 Wednesday

Down at office in AM in PM working in den not much success. Weather pleasant. Blue despondent, very lightheaded, all got better in PM

Jan 19 Thursday

Down at office and looking of the some insurance, in PM in den little while but quit and went to office could not stand had to sit down, and wasted all PM home, in evening weather cold, blue through evening

Jan 20 Friday

Down office about all AM and down again in PM and up street on Board of Health business, was done at trolley station three times looking for Julia but she did not come. Weather quite warm and pleasant

Jan 11 Saturday

At insurance office and PO got no letter was about town and down at station about all day, quit going at 7 PM was tired and had headache, lay on cot till bed time, waiting perhaps they will come and call me up from station.

Jan 22 Sunday

Had not got up till after 11AM was not at church at all, about home all day worrying for fear Ma *(Julia's mother)* is worse, weather quite pleasant.

Jan 23 Monday

Hurried down to PO before breakfast to get letter from Julia, Ma is better, after breakfast and the work done I went down street, got another letter, home working in den and Ifffts photos had great success. Weather fine pleasant.

Jan 24 Tuesday

While I was eating breakfast, Winter phoned me to come up, so I went up at 8:25 and saw Ethend g ? and we made a bargain, I am to see all

farmers along the trolly line and find boarding places for some boarders, came home, went to see Clappor about insurance, got mail, card
from Julia. She will start home today, in PM. I was up at Harmony, I
try again to make photo of Laughlin's baby, came home made some
prints for Iffts, down at office and down street in evening. Weather
quite sharp and cold in AM but moderated and was a beautiful day.
*Julia visited family in Clinton, Mo from Dec 7,1910 to Jan 24,1911 There is a
large gap in the diary – the whole of February. One can presume there was much
catching up to do when the family reunited.*

March 5 Sunday

Julia went to Church this AM Sherman and I stayed home. We played
with blocks and looked at pictures, he was just the best boy could not
have been better, in PM Mrs. Geisinheimer, Rebecka and George were
here.

March 6 Monday

About home till 10 then went down street and was at the office til
noon, in PM put up some wire from the grape arbor to the house for
the grape vine, gave Sherman a ride, was down street with Sherman
for a couple of books, went to Harmony and was down street at office in evening, Weather pleasant, Julia washed. Sherman was a good
boy

Mar 7 Tuesday

Went down to office at 9:55 AM I went up to Ebberhart stores on the
trolley, I wanted to see the dog that had bit me about a month ago, I
worried about it sometimes and I wanted to see if the dog was well or
had developed hydrophobia.*(rabies)* It was OK and ready to bite me
again if it could have got at me, got home at dinner time after Surgery
was at office and went down to see McMichael who is sick in bed,
then was at office all PM and down awhile in evening.

March 8

March 9, 1911 Julia Bassler's birthday. She is 35 yrs.old.

Mar 12 Sunday

During the last week I have been down at the office a good deal of the
time, McMichael has been sick

This AM Sherman went to Sunday School with Miss Kuhns he was
anxious to go and was a good boy, Julia and I went at Church Miss K
brought Sherman home from SS and kept him, we were all at Church
in the evening Sherman not very good and Julia whipped him when
she came home. Weather warm and rainy. I am blue, blue

Mar 13 Monday

Julia washed, Sherman and I was at office a little while then came home to trim grape vines, then down at office and went down in extension, at office in evening,

Mar 14   Tuesday

Made a number of prints for Dr. Wilson, then Sherman and I went down for mail. Julia got letter from home, I was at office awhile in PM I was back and forwards from the office down street over at Harmony, down street and at office again, mailed prints to Dr. Wilson, in evening developed the plates I had exposed of Sherman on Saturday OK, down street in evening a little while, weather colder and snow and rain.

Mar 15   Wednesday

Julia baked today, I was down at office most all day, weather all kinds snowing blowing storming and occasional streaks of sunshine

Mar 16   Thursday

About the office most all day fixed the dresser for Julia, weather very cold last night, water froze in pantry, cold all day. Sherman a good boy all day.

Mar 17   Friday

At the office a little while, then to PO and home by way of Mill and High Street stopped at Mrs. For package, then went to work experimenting trying to make green postcards, had some success after numerous failures, in PM was at Harmony, down at office in evening and then we all went to Church. Sherman was good, fell asleep and I carried him home. He was a sweet good boy all day. Weather much milder than yesterday.

Mar 18   Saturday

Down at office most all day

March 19   Sunday

None of us were at church, I was sick all day long til night. Weather damp, dismal

March 20   Monday

I still feel weak and shaky was down at office off and on most of day, down street awhile in evening. Weather pleasant but high wind blowing

March 21   Tuesday

Made a porch box for Julia, weather warm and pleasant and spring like, very tired and blue

March 22   Wednesday

Down at office and about town in PM made some green post cards, in evening at Church. Weather cloudy, gloomy and air much colder

March 23   Thursday

Down at office off and on most all day, blue discouraged, Hoffman hounding the life oiut of me for his bill, in evening was up at Charlie Goehring to borrow some from him but Mrs. Goehring has four hundred and did not want to break it wants to loan it all, all in one lump so I went to see Jake Gelbach, who loaned it to me without any hesitation for one year, feel a little better now. Weather cold, stormy, snowing

March 25   Saturday

In Pm Sherman and I went to Stokey's Spring for a bottle of water, then I was fixing the hotbed sash (*for vegetables*) in evening we were all down at Reeds. Weather warm I was dreadfully tired and worn out.

March 26   Sunday

Julia went to church, Sherman and I stayed home, in PM we all were out at Old People Home, began to rain just as we started home and has been rainy ever since, over at Rapes in evening.

March 27   Monday

Julia washed and I helped a little and trimmed and tied up crimson rambler rose bush. Sherman and I went for mail and got mama a lot of clothes pins, in PM we both cleaned the paper in the big upstairs room which was a job, we dreaded getting at, in evening at Board of Health meeting, Mary Goehring here and Rapes over. Weather quite warm in AM but had a heavy rain and grew colder and stormed very big wind blew in windows in high school building and done other damage, tonight it is blowing and snowing quite a storm.

March 28   Tuesday

About home went for mail at office a few minutes in PM at Harmony to see Milleman down street at Dr's in evening, weather cold and snow flurries

March 29, 1911   Wednesday

Weather still storming snow flurries, not feeling well all day

March 30   Thursday

Down street for mail, brought up box from bank and looked over something in it and put a lot of stamp in, in PM was down street and at office, Ella Swain and Mrs. Setter here in evening, Weather freakish, bright sunshine for a few minutes then a blinding snow storm, snow would fall so thick and fast that I could not see, a very strange day

March 31   Friday

Julia and I cleaned the paper in the sitting room, I was down at office in PM and evening. Weather cold

April 1 Saturday

Julia had sick headache all day

April 21 Sunday

Joseph Pollack's store (beside Reeds drug store) burned last night about 1:30 I did not hear anything of it, Julia was up looking at it, after breakfast Sherman and I went up looking at it, I had headache nearly all day. None of us over at church

April 3 Monday

Down at office all day very busy, the lock on front door got out of order and had great time getting in office

April 4 Tuesday

Down at office about all day

April 5

April 6 Thursday

In PM at Harmony

April 7 Friday

About home and at office

April 8, 1911 Saturday

Julia washed I was about home and helped some, scrubbed porch, tacked up crimson ramble rose bush, down for mail, at office short time, in PM over at Harmony but done no good. Weather quite pleasant in AM but clouded up and drizzly rain fell which later turned to snow, making very unpleasant and disheartening weather, Miss K was in PM

April 9 Sunday

Julia and I were both at church, Mary Rape kept Sherman, in PM Julia and Sherman went to Kirkers, Mrs. K is at Middle Lancaster but Lizzie was there. I was home reading and up in the attic looking over old diaries of Father's,(Rev.Gottlieb Bassler) in evening we were both at Church,

Rev Lonaker preached on " Why I am a Lutheran", very good sermon. Weather quite pleasant.

April 10 Monday

Down street and at office awhile about 10:30 went up to the Schiever school to make photo of school, made exposure of school and after dinner…then made exposure of whole crowd, after which we came down to the Harmony road and drove up to Middle Lancaster, was there a while, got good supper, came home getting safe home about dusk, roads are bad, the hills were dry, but from Fra Stauffers they were horrible, weather quite pleasant.

April 11   Tuesday *Olive Dindinger married*

Julia washed, Sherman and I made a trip down street then home, Julia and Sherman went to Evans City in PM I was sick about all day til evening, Weather warm and windy

April 12   Wednesday *Edith Gelbach married*

Developed Monday's exposures OK down street awhile, made a few prints from old negatives of snow scenes in May1, 1908 at Harmony, at office wrote up insurance policy for Scheidemantle, down street in evening Julia ironed, Sherman right well, we were alarmed about him last night thought he was going to be sick, Weather rained all day

April 13   Thursday

Made some postcards of Scheiver school, then down for mail, got some pieces of crate for Zehners and made a platform to sit the stove on and roll it out in the hall, put pipe a way made some prints of snow scene for Sisson down street, Julia at Church in evening. Weather warm, rain in PM and evening

April 14   Friday

I was at church in AM, in PM was at Harmony took insurance policy to Milleman and had hopes of getting a settlement with him but was disappointed.

April 15   Saturday

After attending to various household duties Sherman and I went for mail, Sherman got a postcard and a box and Julia got a post card, I was then sown at office attending to some business in PM I was down again, then we all went over to the Church to help decorate, but there was nothing doing so we came home that is Sherman and I came, Julia stopped down street awhile, in evening we were all down street and it rained and snowed fast and furiously, I carried Sherman home, this morning it looked so bright and warm I thought it was going to be a fine day but what a change before the day was over.

April 16   Sunday

I took some flowers up to cemetery, we all were at Church, a Measel girl took Sherman and looked after him while we went up to communion, a very large attendance, home in PM and all at church again in evening, the Sunday school children had exercises in evening consisting of drills and recitations, when we came home found Kuhns and Will Fogel here, weather ground white with snow in the AM but warmed up some and was bright and fair, but wind was cold.

April 17, 1911   Monday

Julia washed I ripped up some old cloths for her, after noon I was making Schiever School pictures, down street awhile in evening. Weather clear and cool

April 18 Tuesday

Made a few more Schiever school pictures, uncovered the roses and trimmed them, found my scissors I lost last summer, Lizzie Kirker was here for afternoon and supper, made exposure of Rev Lonaker, was very tired. Weather quite warm and pleasant.

April 19 Wednesday

Got up with headache, to photo Charly Beighley to take to Harmony but he had gone, I went to Harmony took Sherman and the cart took a package of photos to Snows Store for the Schiver School, was down at Zeiglers and Mrs. Chalfaut, got home just in time began to rain and rained steady all day, in PM I took a sleep, down street in evening, made a couple of prints for Rev Lonaker. Weather warm, rain.

April 20 Thursday

Julia doing some house cleaning and I helped a little and worked about the yard and garden raking and picking off stones and rubbish, getting ready to make garden tomorrow. Weather pleasant.

April 21 Friday

Julia washed curtains, spread and a tick, also bought two pair at Ed Meeders for $3.00 per pair, she then hemmed them, I was about home most all day till in the PM I went to Harmony for the bread and to see Milleman, we were all down street in evening, up at the fire sale store and the plumbing shop to see about having bath tub put in, the weather was terrible cold damp and gloomy and depressing early in the AM, after while it started to rain and rained steady all day

April 22 Saturday

About home all day, till in the evening I was down street, at Dr. Ralstons til about 6 PM, this has been one of the most disagreeable days we have had for a long time, the weather was rain then turned to snow and slush all the day long, Mrs. Rape and Harry over in evening.

April 23 Sunday

In the AM it was bright and clear, I had hoped it would be a fine glorious day but it clouded up some and a little rain fell only a triffle, none of us were at church as our church is under-going repairs, and we all felt to sick, used up to go anywhere else, in PM we went up to see Mrs. Titzle and then up to Heberling, Sherman has been restless and fussy today, wanted out and the weather would not permit of his running around. Miss Kuhns uncle was visiting her today.

April 24 Monday

Julia washed the starched curtains she had washed several days ago and in the PM she cleaned the big front room, put up a gas light she got from Rape in the PM Sherman and I were up at Reed's tying up and trimming these crimson and rambler rose bush it was quite a job but we got it fixed up fine, in evening was down at office awhile. Weather warm and pleasant.

April 25   Tuesday

After the mail came in Sherman and I went up to Passavant and trimmed rose bushes worked till dinner time, after dinner we went up again till about 3 PM, got a dollar, came home trimmed and tied up a climbing rose of our own and puttered about several other things, down street awhile in evening, weather quite pleasant and warm.

April 26,1911   Wednesday

In the night we were awakened by the fire bell and whistle – that is Julia heard them and awakened me we found out it was Harpers mill, in the AM Julia and I cleaned the cellar took everything out of the cupboard and the shelves, getting ready to paint. In the bathroom Julia took up the carpet in store room and stairs and cleaned it. I dug some garden, was over at the constable sale of Flugers goods seized for rent by Wright, they brought $30.00 First garden down street in evening. Weather warm and pleasant, dug some garden.

April 27   Thursday

Julia and I and Sherman all working in the garden, got some onions, lettuce, radishes, and some cosmos planted, put the porch box in place and filled it with ground, painted the hot bed sash, very tired, weather quite warm, Sherman took a couple of letters to post office all by his self, the first time he has gone alone *(Sherman was 3 ½)*

April 28   Friday

I made a post card, then made another porch box, dug some garden and we planted beets, bush lima beans and string beans, Julia not very well. Sherman was the sweetest best boy all day. Weather quite warm

April 29   Saturday

Had a delightful warm rain last night and weather stayed nice and warm all day, a perfect growing day, it was too hot to work in the garden, in the PM the plumber was here and made a start of putting in a bath room. We were all down street in evening, Julia not well

April 30   Sunday

About home all day, neither of us felt well. Mrs. Diver here a little while, in evening we went to the station with her. Weather quite warm, fine growing weather

May 1 Monday

I was down at office awhile making out reports, then home helping Julia clean house, in PM Sherman and I went to Harmony, Julia cleaned the big front room upstairs, she was down street and bought linoleum for the bath room, I was down in evening. Weather warm showers all day, in the evening it is now crowing colder.

May 2   Tuesday

Julia washed, I looked after Sherman then Sherman and I were at the office awhile, In PM I was at office, then home, the plumbers were at work this PM Weather quite cold with a little snow at times. Sherman was the sweetest dearest best boy all day, he went to the Post Office today again but could not get the door open and started back but met Rape who opened it for him.

May 3   Wednesday

I went up on Endres Hill where Swain and Marin are starting to dig out a reservoir for the Borough water works, I made a couple of exposures, came home and Sherman and I went down to Geisenheimer's and made a couple of exposures of him, after dinner I developed them, fair to middling, down at Dr.'s awhile in PM, carried some ground out of cellar, about the house huddled over the stove, took Sherman down street in evening to hear band. Weather quite cool

May 4   Thursday

I was sick this AM did not get up till after breakfast and did not get anything done for quite a while, Julia made a couple of prints from Geisenheimer and took them down to him but he did not like them and came up in the afternoon and I tried again, we laid the

linoleum up in the bath room and I mowed the grass, Sherman was crabby and out of sorts today, wants to be out all the time. Weather cool

May 5   Friday

Lovely day – got up about 7 made some prints for Geisenheimer, then went down to PO Sherman and I trimmed the grass around. After dinner Sherman Mama and I went down to the run to please Sherman. He wanted to play, Julia cleaned the pantry was all day at it, but she was not well. I spaded a flower bed and planted phlox, painted the porch boxes and I filled one with ground, was home after supper. Sherman was a good boy today, a heavy frost last night ice in the basin on the porch

May 6   Saturday

We pasted white oil cloth on the walls of the bath room (and put a little more linoleum on the floor) it was quite a job but we succeeded and it looks fine, we were all down street in the evening. Weather quite warm and pleasant, frost last night not quite as severe as the night before

May 7   Sunday

I went out to Catholic Church this AM in PM we all went up to the cemetery and we were over to see Householders pups and then over at Teeples, Sherman was the best sweetest dearest boy today. Weather fine, beautiful day perfect.

May 8   Monday

Lovely day, got up 6 AM after breakfast went down street for while paint for bathroom came home and mixed it up and cleaned a brush and Julia painted the word work in bathroom and I spaded garden. I went down for mail and got the Alabastine *(gypsum wall finish)* for the walls and after dinner Julia put 2 coats on the wall, I worked in the garden awhile then went to Harmony to collect some money from Milleman, after supper went down and had my hair cut. Sherman was a good boy.

May 9   Tuesday

I painted the wood work of the bath room, Julia cleaned the hall, Weather quite pleasant.

May 10   Wednesday

Rained a little shower, I painted the bath tub a coat a paint, Julia cleaned the sitting room. And took up the carpet in dining room, Was down to Board of Health meeting

May 11   Thursday

Warm day. I painted the tub again then cut the grass, Julia washed then cleaned the cellar way and washed all the dishes in the cupboard. Sherman and I were down street , in the evening – we heard from Mrs. Metz, she is quite poorly

May 12   Friday

May 17   Wednesday

Fixed up grape vines, dug a little garden, down at office started to go up to the reservoir but gave it up, in PM at office and went up to see Lew Welsh who lives in the* poor house

May 18   Thursday

Julia washed I helped a little, then I took a veal loaf to the Church for the Lutheran league which met there, quite a number were there from out of town, then was down street and home in PM was at the church awhile but was so hot that I did not stay log, took some flowers up to the cemetery, it is Mother's birthday – Sherman came to meet me beyond Poffenbach's – Julia and set out some tomato plants and cosmos. We thought it would rain but only a few drops fell. Weather very hot and dry.

May 21 Friday

We all went to church this AM several addresses were made in the interest of Thiel College $100.00 fund which is what they are trying to secure, Julia was sick all the rest of the day. Rev. Lonaker delivered the baccalaureate sermon this evening but we did not go, several young ladies are visiting Miss Kuhner. Weather very warm.

May 22 Saturday

Julia did not wash, I made a few cards for Miss Kuhns and her friends then went to Post Office. I worked on screens, taking off old ones and putting on new.

May 23 Tuesday

Julia washed, I made garden, Julia scrubbed the front porch, cleaned the rails, I watched the plumbers work in the PM, Sherman has been a good boy

May 24 Wednesday

Nice day cool and pleasant, I finished the garden, the plumbers finished the bathroom, all but changing the gas pipe

May 25 Thursday

Miss Kuhns left for home this PM I was down at the office most all AM in the PM was helping about the house and at about 3:30 went up to the reservoir with the camera and made a couple of exposures then made exposure of the men working in the water line, came home and developed them OK Weather very warm

May 26 Friday

Working at Postcards most all day did not have very good success. Weather hot and dry

May 27 Saturday

Weather very warm. In AM I went up to the cemetery, took Sherman along and mowed the grass and fixed the flower bed ready to put the flowers in

May 28 Sunday

Warm day we were both sick all day, were home all day in PM A Mr. Ben *(left blank)* and son came to see Will. *(in Julia's handwriting)*

May 29 Monday

Still warm Julia ironed what clothes she washed Saturday and in evening I went up and planted red geraniums in the lot

May 30, 1911   Tuesday Decoration Day

A lovely day, we got up about 7 and Sherman wanted to decorate so we put up our flags, before breakfast, Sherman seemed so delighted all day, in evening he and his papa went down and got some ice cream for supper

A man and wife came to look at our rooms but did not take them, I guess they found rooms at Walkers. I was up at cemetery in AM took some flowers up and mowed the lot and raked the grass from Stanfords lot, in the PM I was up again and made exposure of the Old Soldiers

Weather quite pleasant, not so hot as it has been. Sherman was a good boy.

May 31   Wednesday

Julia and Sherman over at Kirker's all day, I helped them over part of the way, I was developing and printing, down in the extension about fire insurance and up at the reservoir, got some orders for photos, in evening went over to Kirker's to help Julia and Sherman home and later was down street, Weather blew quite hard awhile in PM and then we had a delightful soaking rain.

June 1   Thursday

Developed some plates and was at the office making out reports etc. most of the day, Julia and Sherman at Geisenheimers , in PM at Board of Health meeting, in evening weather pleasant and cool.

June 2   Friday (in margin: rented room)

Fine day, partly cloudy with a little shower in evening, In AM was down to office, in PM made cards and prints, in evening was down to office again, Sherman worked with me in the cellar all PM and was a good boy all day. In evening Sherman and I were over to Mrs. Hulls, Mrs. Diver was there, we later went down to the station with her

June 3   Saturday

I was not feeling well all day, cough/cold yesterday, down at office a little, went to Harmony on insurance business and other errands, almost noon when I got back about home most all PM and tested and fixed camera for …Frederick down street in evening weather cloudy

June 4   Sunday

Julia and I at church, I was too tired and unwell about home all day. Weather cloudy with shower in early evening. Sherman a very good boy all day

June 5   Monday

About the office and home, had Sherman's hair cut, down in the extension about insurance. Sherman a good sweet boy all day

June 6   Tuesday

Went down in the extension to see about insurance at office about home, planted some beets and beans cut the grass, in the evening a terrible rain storm, the water was clear across the street and main street was flooded. Sherman was the best dearest boy today

June 7   Wednesday

Dug out weeds and trimmed the grass between the walk and the curb, after breakfast made some prints, was down street in PM Julia and Sherman went to Evans City, I went as far as Harmony, attended to some business and came home and wrote up some insurance, got some supper, went down to meet Julia but did not come, dame home and at 7 PM went again and they arrived. Sherman and I down street on some errands, weather cooler

June 8   Thursday

Trimming the grass down street on errands, then made up velox fixing bath, a package of roses came by mail that we had sent for a long time ago, Julia and I planted them out and worked some in the garden, made some post cards, down street a number of times, was busy all day. Weather quite pleasant

June 9   Friday

Did not feel very well all day. Weather warm

June 10   Saturday

Julia sick most all day, after attending to some house hold duties I went to Harmony on insurance business, took some onions and lettuce to Kirker, came home and had to go right back as I forgot our bread, made a couple of prints, down street in evening delivering some pictures. Weather very hot 92° in PM.

June 11   Sunday

Took some flowers to the cemetery, at church, home all rest of day. Weather very warm expected to get a rain but it all went around up to the north. Sherman a good boy.

June 12   Monday

Trimmed the maple tree, put new wire on window screens, made some prints and a few postcards, made several exposures of Sherman and Julia, cupboard and emptied out a number of old elderberries, put the fruit back. All of us were up to see the Dr and over to see Passavant roses, Weather quite pleasant, rained last night. Sherman was a very good dear sweet boy today

June 13   Tuesday

Dug the ground out and hauled it away and replaced it with good soil from the garden in a place in the front yard, the grass wouldn't grow, Lizzie Kirker and children were over, down street and attended to some business Weather cool, threatening rain several times but only a few drops fell

June 14   Wednesday

Developed plates and making post cards Weather cool

June 15   Thursday

After 10AM I went up to the reservoir, came home got caught in shower, stopped at Rices store, made a few post cards, for Kirkers worked the garden and rose beds we have some beautiful roses in bloom, Julia and Sherman over at Kirkers in evening. Weather cool.

June 18   Sunday

All at Church, Sherman a good boy, in PM Sherman and I were up at cemetery, I got a bad fall on the way up, my foot caught in a piece of wire, home all rest of day, in evening a couple were here looking at the rooms, promised to let us know tomorrow, weather quite pleasant, no rain.

June 19   Monday

Julia washed had Rape's machine run by water motor, about noon

I went to Harmony for some meat and groceries, in PM developed film was down street at office.

Weather pleasant. *One of many early washing machines can be found at http://www.oldewash.com/articles/lives.htm*

June 20,1911   Tuesday

Made some post cards before breakfast and was working in den, about 10AM Sherman and I went up to Mrs. Walkers and made exposure of her house and then one of Mrs. McKim, came home and developed them OK then was down at office and about town, after noon made a couple of the Walker, McKim negatives went to Harmony, Mrs. Diver was down and spent afternoon and supper with us, in evening Sherman and I took walk to trolley station. Weather cool and pleasant.

June 21   Wednesday

Took sample of postcard to McKim and Walker, down street at office then home making cards, Julia and Sherman at Kirkers in PM, Sherman a very good boy all day. Weather pleasant.

June 25   Sunday

About home all day, no one at church, sat around and seen David Harun in PM, Sherman and I were up at cemetery, Weather quite warm till about 2:30 PM it rained and had showers off and on for the rest of day. Sherman was restless and cranky today.

June 26 Monday

Julia washed, I helped a little, then was at the office wrote up some insurance and was down again in PM, then home and made some post cards. Weather warm, shower in evening.

June 27 Tuesday

Weeded the garden then working at postcards for Donation Day, in evening was down street at Miss Titzel awhile and up at Wm Moors about insurance. Weather quite warm

June 28 Wednesday

Working at postcards all day

June 29 Thursday

Out at Donation Day, Rev White said he would want a photo of the school, so I came home and got camera and then we all went out, we sold some cards and photos, 8 or 10 dollars worth had a pleasant time and nice weather.

June 30 Friday

Mixed up fixing for plates and developer for plates, developed yesterday exposures (9) most of them were good, in PM had sick headache, lay down awhile, made some exposures of folks on Halls porch, weather hot

July 1 Saturday

Julia and Sherman in the morning went out in the country with Adam Mickley to stay a week, I made out some check and paid some bills at the bank and down street till noon, in PM down at office made out reports wrote up some insurance, was down again in the evening, after 8 PM I painted the bath tub out in the yard. Weather very hot.

July 2 Sunday

About home all by myself. Weather very hot 90°

July 3 Monday

Developed some plates and a film for Julia down at office in PM made some cards from Julia film and down at office again in evening down street, had a letter from Julia and Sherman

Weather was terrible hot, the hottest I know of 95° on the porch this PM

July 4, 1911 Tuesday

About 8 AM I walked out to Adam Mickleys to spend the fourth,

Sherman came running to meet me when he saw me coming, picked some cherries and loafed around in evening had quite an enjoyable time, sack races, clothes pin races, fire works, singing etc. I started home after 9 PM and arrived home about 10 PM had a very pleasant day. I don't know when I enjoyed a day more. Weather very hot.

July 5 Wednesday

Developed a couple of plates made some sample prints and cards and worked with my hand camera trying to get in shape and find out what the trouble with it is, made exposures of a Vance brother to the man living in the Gloss house, was not very well, felt languid and tired, did not feel like doing much. Weather very hot.

July 6 Thursday

Went to Harmony at Kirkers and Biebers then down in the town, came home and was at work developing plates film made prints and postcards working at my Primo camera but did not have much success in evening at Board of Health meeting, weather hot looks for a shower to night. (Internet picture of Primo Camera 1900's)

July 7

all day in PM went to Harmony and made several exposures of children down street a little while in evening weather not quite so hot, had a very slight shower in late afternoon which cooled off and made it much pleasanter

July 8 Saturday

I was working at the pump repairing it, it broke last night and it took all morning to fish out the sucker and repair it, in the PM I made some proofs of the Harmony exposures and took them over, I than packed up the camera and at 4:28 took the trolley car for Franklin road and made several exposures for Mr. Hoehn, got home a little of the 8PM Weather very hot

July 9 Sunday

About home all day, no one at church, had headache, Weather dreadfully hot

July 10 Monday

Julia done a big wash, I went to Charles Stokey for a bottle of water, down street and at trolley station for package, helped Julia a little, in PM developed plate for Rev. Reed and my Saturday exposures which were OK made some cards from Julia film which I developed through AM, weather very hot till a very slight shower came which cooled it very much

July 11 Tuesday

Weeded some in the garden then was working in the den at postcards and some prints

July 12   Wednesday

Cut off the weeds in the backyard with the sickle, then was down street at office wrote up insurance policy and attended to some other business, in PM working in den, in evening

July 15   Saturday

Sherman and I were down street. Weather not so hot, pleasanter.

July 13 & 14   Thursday & Friday

Busy in the den all day at Harmony and made some exposures

Working in the den got all most caught up with my orders, in the evening we were all down street, Mrs. Wm Peffer was buried this PM at Middle Lancaster

July 16   Sunday

We were all at Church this AM Sherman was a good boy, in PM we took walk down past Stokey Spring and out to Det Passavant and the Old People Home. Weather warm, much cooler in evening. Some one has been at my book

July 17   Monday

Weather much cooler. A little rain last evening. I made cards today in AM I cut grass in the back yard. Julia did not feel like washing today. Sherman was a good boy

July 23   Sunday

We all went up to cemetery early in AM about home rest of day, no one at church. Weather pleasant

July 24   Monday

Made some postals for Birch and others was down street at office, in PM at office and down street, Sherman and I were up at Mrs. Titzel in evening. Weather quite cool.

July 25   Tuesday

Julia went to dentist, I entertained Sherman, went for mail got a couple of letters for Julia, down at office a good deal today, made 1 exposure, Sherman and I were up at cemetery and cut the grass, down street at Dr's office en evening, Weather quite cool 56 at 7:30 AM

July 26   Wednesday

I made a few cards down street some did not do much good. I thought of going to Harmony with camera but it was so gloomy and looked for rain that gave it up, down street in evening. Weather cool and cloudy

July 27   Thursday

I got a horse and buggy from Wilson's and we loaded up with the camera and 14 plates and started on a wild goose chase to hunt up some work, we went out to Beaver Co, toiled up Mullen hill picking blackberries by the way, we tried all along the way for work but with no success, went to the Oak Grove Church and made exposure, then went to the Douglas house and made an exposure, went back to Christ Leitz store but couldn't do any good then we went to Union Hill and I canvased the whole town N.G. then we came home (on our way out in the AM we stopped at John Teets and picked a bushel of apples) got home at 2PM tired, then Julia took some apples out to Charlot Douglas at the Old People's Home. Weather pleasant

July 28   Friday

Done some photo work at Harmony in PM made a couple of exposures Lizzie Kirker and family over in PM, Julia was going over then but met them coming over and came back with them. Weather somewhat cloudy and cooler.

July 29   Saturday

Made a couple of prints in PM took some samples to Harmony, all down street in evening

July 30   Sunday

All at Church in late PM we all were out at the Old Folks Home. Weather pleasant.

July 31   Monday

Sherman and I took up the onions, Julia was up very early washed, went to dentist and was at Geisenheimers about dress, then home, got dinner then baked ginger cookies and ironed some, moved the office over to the room occupied by Dr. Reed, he took over room as he had moved into the house

Aug 1   Tuesday

In AM Julia baked 3 apple pies, I fixed Julia's cosmos, then I went out to the Old People's Home and got Miss Douglas and brought her home, she stayed all day, had Dindingers horse and buggy, weather quite warm had light shower in evening at office a good while making out reports

Aug 2   Wednesday

Cut weeds out of the backyard at office a good deal developed a few plates, down street in evening weather pleasant a little shower in evening.

Aug 3   Thursday

We all took the trolley to Ellwood and then the steam cars to Rock

Point, where we spent the day. Sherman rode the merry-go-round and the roller coaster, had quite a shower in the PM but we got under shelter and kept dry, took dinner with the Vance's and their folks from near Rochester, got back safe and tired

Aug 4   Friday

Weeded the garden in PM Julia took Miss Charlot Douglass out to John Teet's got back in evening, I was working at postcards and at office awhile.

Aug 5   Saturday

Sherman and I took some letters to Charlie Beighly to take to Harmony, then we took a policy to Mrs Titzel and came home, I went back to office and was there til noon.

down again in PM, Julia went to Harmony and after Sherman woke up we went as far as Sitlers to meet him, stopped at Swains awhile, Julia and Sherman down street in evening. Weather hot

Aug 6   Sunday

I was at church, all took nap in PM, about home all day. Weather hot

Aug 7   Monday

I cut the grass in front yard and trimmed the border took grass out of pavement and Julia was up quite early about 5 AM and washed, I went down street, collected the birth certificates, went down to Fred Zehners with Dr. Ralston in his auto, in PM developed film for Ad Rape and Lockwood, went to Harmony in evening had a fine refreshing shower which was very much needed

Aug 8   Tuesday

Weeded the garden in the AM in PM was making postcards for Edith Reed, Rape and Mickleys, Julia to dentist in AM. Sherman a dear good boy all day. Weather pleasant

At the bottom of the page Sherman's feet are traced with the date Aug 10, 1911. He would be 4 in November.

Aug 9   Wednesday

This AM we went down to Pflughs with a big crowd of ladies. Mrs Sitler, Mrs. Swain etc spent the day with a lot of couples from town had a very pleasant day. I made a number of exposures in evening I developed many plates, Weather quite pleasant Sherman pulled a slide out of a plate holder and spoiled one of my exposures.

Aug 10   Thursday

Made some sample cards and prints down at office, weather quite hot, feel considerable used up. Sherman sitting up on the desk upset the bottle of ink, he has been a good boy all day.

Aug 11   Friday

Made some prints and cards from yesterday, exposures, down at office some

Aug 12   Saturday

Taking out weeds from backyard, down street some not feeling very well, several very

Slight showers, Julia had ride in auto with Mrs. Pettigrew. Weather pleasant.

Aug 13   Sunday

I was at church in AM text was from the Epistle for the day 1Cor 10-6-13. Hymns *Am I a*

Soldier of the Cross and *A Pilgrim and a Stranger*. A very good sermon, in PM I was up at cemetery and later we all took a walk, in evening Julia went to Church with Rapes, all well today. Weather delightfully pleasant, had showers in night and again in morning about 6AM.

Aug 14   Monday

Julia got up early and washed this AM after which I made some prints everybody seems to feel out of sorts today, had nice shower, Weather pleasant

Aug 13   Tuesday

This AM I went over to Harmony and made exposure of Rapp's Seat but did not succeed very well was so dark and cloudy, shower came up , came home developed plate, in PM was making postcards til evening, then Sherman took some butter bears up to Swains and at 8PM Sherman and I went down to PO. Weather showers

Aug 19   Saturday

Julia washed bed clothes and some others with Vance's machine, in PM I was at Harmony made a couple of exposures and later I made some exposures of the Vance family and her sister and her children. Weather pleasant.

Aug 20   Sunday

We all went up to the cemetery , the office after resting a while, we kept on up to the reservoir, it was dinner time when we got back. All took sleep in PM, in evening Julia and Mrs. Oliver went out to Old Peoples Home. I gave Sherman a long ride in his cart, then came home and we went up to Old Mrs. Sitlers house where Dr. Ralston's Auto was and rode down to his house with him. Weather cool Rev. Peters – Rape's pastor was installed this PM

Aug 21   Monday

Julia washed I worked the machine, then developed some plates and made some sample cards for Vance's and others, at office a little while, Julia picked a bushel of plums, in evening I was at Harmony with proofs. All down street in evening, got Sherman a pair of shoes. Weather pleasant.

Aug 22   Tuesday

I was busy at various duties in AM and in Pm about 2:30 went out to the Wagner reunion, through a misunderstanding I got off the cars at Kaufman Station in place of Kiser so I had quite a walk, made several exposures, coming home I missed my car, but rode down to the car barn and waited there for the next car and got home OK

Aug 23   Wednesday

Developed plates made a number of cards and developed 4 films in evening was very busy all day

Aug 24   Thursday

I did not succeed in doing much good today, was trying to make some prints but had very poor success, mixed up some developer but it would not work right and I have all I made to throw away. Weather raining most all day

Aug 25   Friday

Down at office, connected up the radiator in the bath room, had considerable trouble in getting it tight, done several other jobs about the house. Weather rain all day. Sherman got up and came downstairs by his self this morning for the first time. *(Sherman is 2 yrs & 9 mos.)*

Aug 26   Saturday

Working at prints about all day was not well had headache. Mrs Kuhns at house.

Aug 27   Sunday

About home all day in evening we all went up to Rape's church - had harvest home, Sherman a good boy all day feeling his oats. Weather warm and pleasant

Aug 28   Monday

Weeded some in the front yard and Sherman had a fine time sailing a boat in the gutter. I made a few prints and cards down street on various errands Weather rain most all day, steady. School open.

Aug 29   Tuesday

Julia washed I looked after Sherman then I cut grass in front yard, down street in afternoon and at Harmony in evening, felt tired weak and languid all day. Weather quite cool almost, wonderful grand sunset this evening, beautiful, beyond description.

Aug 31   Thursday

Picnic by way of the car, up there about an hour and came home, Julia went over to Kirkers in the AM intending to go up to the picnic but Lizzie's baby was sick. Man struck by B & O train and killed near Harmony Junction. Weather quite pleasant.

Sept 1   Friday

Made some prints of the Wagner's reunion and a few cards

Sept 2   Saturday

About 8 AM we all got started for McConnells Mill, stopped at Middle Lancaster a few minutes, got to the Mill about 11AM…and went at making some photos, which I found very hard to do on account of this dense trees which shut out the light, on way home stopped for supper at Mitz's got here OK about 8:30 down street in evening, got Sherman his ice cream. Weather pleasant

Sept 3   Sunday

All at church this AM, Julia and Sherman out at Old People's Home in PM I slept. Weather pleasant.

Sept 4   Monday

Julia washed, ironed, swept the street, made catsup, and in evening was out at Old People's Home, I was at office and down street awhile in PM developed plates and took sleep. Sherman and I were down street in evening. Town very quiet, all closed up Labor day. Weather pleasant.

Sept 8   Friday

Julia and Sherman took Miss Douglas out in the country this AM and were gone all day and had a very pleasant time but got caught in a shower on way home and got wet, I was about home and copied the birth certificates about 3 PM went over to Ollie Zeigler at Harmony and made some exposures of the children. Weather very warm.

Sept 9   Saturday

I developed yesterday's exposures then I went out to Old Peoples Home and made exposure of main building, about noon and a man came and wanted our room and we moved downstairs in front room which made a lot of work and moved Miss Kuhns into her old room again. I was down street a number of times for one thing and another, in the evening Mrs. Marston (the woman who rented our room came) and Julia went down street with her, Weather quite warm

Sept 10   Sunday

Julia had headache all day. I went to church in AM Sherman was cross and fussy most of Day

Sept 11   Monday

Julia went down street and ordered a motor washer and then went to Latshaw's and looked at a gas range, after which I went over and looked at it and thought it would be OK and then saw Latshaw and told him I would take it at $8.00. I had it brought over and then we were both sorry that we got it. We then phoned Latshaw and he promised he'd take it back, then Julia ordered a new one from the Hardware store and at about noon they brought it up and we are well pleased with it, in PM Julia was putting Sherman to sleep when Lizzie Kirker came with her three young ones. I made some prints, started out to the Old People's Home to make photo when I got to Muntz's corner I saw the light was too high, left camera and came home, went out about 5 but was too cloudy, brought camera home. Julia brought Mothers little bed down from the attic for me to sleep on.

Robbers in town last night broke windows in Lockwood's store and were in other places, several were caught. Weather pleasant, heavy rain last night.

Sept 12   Tuesday

Julia got up early this AM I started washing but the machine was not a success would not work, we got some plums from Mr. Siegler and started to make plum butter, I was at office awhile in AM weather cool. Sherman a good boy.

Sept 13   Wednesday

I was at office awhile then made a few postcards and prints, down street awhile in evening. Weather quite cool have fire in room this evening. Sherman a right good boy.

Sept 14   Thursday

In PM Julia and Mrs. Morton out at Old People Home, I was mending leaks in camera. Weather warmer, at Harmony in evening.

Sept 15   Friday

Very heavy rain last night, South Main Street flooded, creek quite high, Evans City flooded. No mail today, no trains or B&O or on trolley line, I was down at the creek in the AM and again in PM with Sherman, I did not get any work done. Weather gloom and rainy a little sunshine in PM.

Sept 16   Saturday

Repairing some leaks in camera then was at harmony made some exposure up at Enslines of boy and pony, Julia was at the church helping to decorate for Harvest Home. Weather warm, not feeling well.

Sept 17   Sunday

All at church Harvest Home services in PM, Julia went to Kirker's,

Sherman and I stayed home and went to Teeples, the Miss Edna and Emma Boggs were there, then we took

walk around the back and came home, then went up around by Sitler, down Miles Street. Sherman played in sand awhile. Weather warm. Not very well.

Sept 18   Monday

I made a number of trips to the church for jardinière and plants, cut the grass in front yard, in PM developed plates and made some post-cards of Old People Home, Julia Sherman and Mrs. Morton down street in evening. Weather quite pleasant. Sherman undressed himself for the first time this evening.

Sept 19   Tuesday

Busy making prints all day

Sept 20   Wednesday

Down at office for awhile, came home, went to Harmony to Ensline cottage, dinner time til I got home, in PM Julia and I repairing camera, then after resting awhile I went to Reed house intended to make exposure of house but too many trees, made exposure of Roger's grains store, Julia made some candy for the Old Folks home and took it out in evening, Sherman went along – Mr. Carpenter at the OPH had a stroke today

Rapes are boiling apple butter today. Sherman was a dear sweet loving boy all day. Mr. Fred Weigle of Harmony died. Weather pleasant.

Sept 23   Saturday

Tinkered with one thing and another. Julia tried to wash with the machine and it wasn't working, In PM Harry Rape and I went to the Ensline cottage and made some exposures, Julia and Mrs. Morton down street in evening, weather very warm. I have not been well for some days and can hardly drag myself around, my bowels hurt me so dreadfully.

Sept 24   Sunday

None of us at church , in PM we walked around the square to see how Mill Street is getting along, Lizzie Misner and kids over, Oh my, feel better this evening. Weather warmer, shower in evening

Oct 1   Sunday

All at church Sherman right good boy rained as church was out. I came home and got umbrella, rained all day, much warmer than yesterday

Oct 3   Tuesday

Bess Reed married today

Oct 4   Wednesday

Weather quite warm in AM down street and at harmony, in PM at office and about town, not well. Julia not well either. Sherman good boy.

Oct 8   Sunday

Beautiful bright sunshine today. All at Church, Rev. White preached. Rev Lonaker away from home, Sherman was a very good boy, a dear sweet boy. I wonder what is in store for him, what the future holds for him? I wish I could do more for him and Julia, times are hard now and it requires planning and scheming to get along, but how are they to get along after I am gone. Julia and Sherman have gone over to Kirker's this PM.

Oct 9   Monday

In PM out at Old People's Home made eight exposures, down street awhile in evening and took some insurance policies to Mrs. Nixon, Weather pleasant.

Oct 10   Tuesday

Julia, Sherman and Mrs. Morton went to Pittsburgh this AM I fixed a print board for the camera, repaired a plate holder, developed eight plates and one film, copied the birthcertificates in the early evening, the folks got home Julia had sick headache, Julia got a long coat and an overcoat and hat for Sherman. Weather rain all PM.

Oct 11   Wednesday

Julia Sherman and Mrs. Oliver went down to Wurtemberg I made some prints of the Home and had sick headache about all day

Oct 12   Thursday

Julia and Sherman home today. They intended going up the country to Mrs. Myers but some of the old ladies at the Old Peoples Home who were going along were not able. I made some cards the hardware men put new motor on the wash machine and it worked all right today. Rev White here in evening. Weather cloudy and cool

Oct 15   Sunday

I was at church, Julia and Sherman at home not feeling very well, had communion in PM made photo of Hungarian funeral, came home to take flowers up to Mother, Julia and Sherman out at Old Peoples Home in evening and Julia and church, Sherman and I stayed home. Weather delightful, pleasant warm

Oct 16 Monday

Julia washed, machine worked fine. I went down to Latshaws store to get reserved seat for lecture, made some cards and a couple of prints, in PM Sherman and I made several exposures of Trixie – Teeple's dog and got one good negative. Weather quite pleasant

Oct 17 Tuesday

I was down street awhile in AM made some postals and a couple of prints, rained all day steady. Sherman was a very good boy today.

Oct 20 Wednesday

I made some prints of Hungarian funeral down street on various errands, at office had headache all day til evening, in evening over at Rapes church to attend the Bible class examination.

Oct 22 Sunday

None of us were at church in the morning I had sick headache, Julia had several of the old ladies from the Old Folks Home for dinner and they enjoyed it very much rained in PM and Julia sent them home in a buggy. Julia at church in evening, Sherman and I stayed home. Sherman was a good boy all day

Oct 23 Monday

Julia washed, Sherman and I were down street awhile I made a couple of prints in PM was at Harmony. Weather much cooler. Sherman was the sweetest dearest best boy all day.

Oct 24 Tuesday

Julia and Sherman got a horse and buggie and took Miss Douglas out to Branch Creek and were gone all day had a pleasant time, I made a batch of postals and photos up, was bushed, down street a number of times. Weather pleasan.t

Oct 25 Wednesday

Made a few postal in PM Julia and Sherman went up to Middle Lancaster with Miss Metz. Weather pleasant, heavy frost last night.Water froze in basin. Sherman a good boy

Oct 26 Thursday

Down at office and about town on various business, in PM at Harmony took some postcards over and attended to some insurance business, in evening made some more exposures of Wisers pony. Weather quite pleasant, brought in a bunch of lovely roses

Had sick headache about all day, put in a good deal of time in bed, down street a few times. Weather cold and raining

Oct 30 Tuesday Halloween party *(this section is in Julia's hand)*

I did iron today, but made candy and popped corn to make balls for Sherman's "Halloween Party" as he called it. I made 2 kinds of candy for him. I then made 4 pumpkin faces, and one beet face and in the evening we turned out the lights and just left the Jack O'Lanterns. I put the large round rug in the room and the children sat down on it. Sherman passed the candy and balls around to them. Harry Rape, Ray and Hershel Purdium, and Lillian Stout, then a little Meeder boy came in. Sherman was so excited. I made a Dutch Doll for him and how they laughed. Mrs. Rape and Mary and Lizzie Dumbaugh were here awhile. After while we went upstairs and Mrs. Montrose (the lady who lives upstairs) played her phonograph for the children. Miss Kuhns and Mrs. Stout dressed up and went out for fun. There was a crowd of children came in and showed Sherman their false faces.

Oct 31 Wednesday

I ironed all AM then Sherman and I went out and we tied all the roses up and scooped the ground out of porch boxes.

Nov 1   Thursday *(returns to W.G's handwriting)*

Sherman and I put leaves on our rose bed

Nov 3   Friday

I took some cards over to Ensline's cottage, home by way of Mrs. Fredelrich, got package, in PM made over 3 doz 5x7 prints for Snauffer of his hunting trip in Adironacks of deer etc. also made exposure of Lutz' boys mounted a few, very, very tired.

Nov 4   Saturday

Finished mounting prints, developed film for Lockwood and made cards for Lutz and Lockwood. Julia and Sherman down street in evening. Weather pleasant

Nov 5,1911   Sunday

All at church in AM Sherman good boy in PM Julia and Sherman and I at Old People Home, in evening, Julia and Sherman at church. Sherman not so good. Weather pleasant.

Nov 6   Monday

Julia washed I helped a little then was down street and down street several times in PM Weather rained all day.

Nov 7   Tuesday

I went down street to see Dowds about photographing his house, then it clouded up so that I put it off, voted, went to Dr. Kerr and Ralston for birth certificates came home in PM made a few cards took enlarged pictures of Teeple dog to them, much pleased with it, down street at office awhile and home all evening, Julia baked cakes and made candy for Sherman's birthday. Weather colder

November 8, 1911 Wednesday   *Sherman's Birthday-he is 4*

Julia had a sick headache all day long, Sherman and I made several trips down street to give her a quiet rest. This was Sherman's birthday, he had a number of postcards and letters and cake and candy, he was a good boy all day

He is 3 ft 3 in tall and increase in height of 4 3/8 inches

Weights 33 ½ thigh 13 ¾ foot 5 ½ Is 20 in around head, chest is 22 inches, arms 6 1/2

In PM was out at the Home, Charlie Goehring was removing the remains of Father and Sister Mary to the cemetery above town. Weather quite pleasant

Sherman had a letter from Aunt Minnie with a dollar in and one from Grandpa with a dollar. We gave him a silver spoon and a box of paints, Harry R, Miss Kirker, Lillian Stout, Aunt Clara

Nov 10   Friday

Repaired a latch on upstairs door, put up piece of asbestos over the lamp in hall upstairs and both rooms. Sherman and I were down street, in PM Sherman and I were at Harmony on various errands, then down street, made a couple of exposure of Sherman, in evening Julia and Sherman, Mrs. Swain and Ella, Mrs. Sittler and Mrs. Stoutt and Lillian went up to call on Rev Lonaker. Weather pleasant and warm.

Nov 11   Saturday

I went down to the extension to see if I could get a photo of the Hungarian parade which was to take place, but after waiting and trying to get a chance at them I gave it up as it began to rain and came home. Sherman has been sick all day, I went up and asked the Dr. about him and he asked if he had been eating pork – came from indigestion. Weather quite warm

Nov 12   Sunday

Sherman much better this AM I went to church, home all rest of day, a great drop in temperature this AM at 8:00 it was 59 at the PM it is 22

Nov 13   Monday

Julia washed I helped a little, developed the plates for Miss Reid and 2 of Sherman and 1 film for Young went to Harmony to see what damage had been done by a fire at Weigels, home rest of day, Weather very cold all day

Nov 18   Saturday

I went to Harmony did not get back til noon, about home til about 2:30 went to office and wrote up policy for Machtrick. Came home rest of day, in evening Julia and Sherman down street short time. Weather cold and stormy

Nov 19   Sunday

All at church this AM, Mr. Stout took Sherman over to their house and he stayed for dinner. Julia at church in evening. Sherman and I over at Rapes. Sherman a good boy all day. Weather moderate

Nov 22   Wednesday

Sherman and I went to trolley station and made exposure came back and we went to PO got letter for Julia and Sherman went home and I stayed at office, in PM Julia and Sherman went to serving society ,and I went up to the reservoir and made exposure. Weather moderate, sun out at times then dull and gloomy.

Nov 30   Thursday Thanksgiving

We all went to church I came home by Post office, Sherman received card from Dibie, Bogart, the Miesner children, we had a chicken for dinner, mashed potatoes and rice cooked in chicken gravy it was very good, about home all rest of day in evening got a package from Minnie with some fancy work and pictures and cards for Sherman, Julia had sick headache in PM Sherman was right good boy might have been a little better. Weather clear cold and stormy. I am blue.

Dec 1   Friday

Sherman and I went down street mailed a letter for mama. I borrowed 15 dollars from The People's Bank sent Alexander a check for $17.00 came home and Sherman and I went to trolley station and made exposure, developed it, in PM I went up to reservoir hill and made a couple of exposures, inn evening I was at Harmony settled up with Milleman. Weather mild, pleasant.

Dec 2   Saturday

I was down street short time for mail, about home rest of day, with sick headache

Dec 3   Sunday

Sherman went to Sunday School, Julia and I to church, I was home rest of day, I also went to Lutheran League and church in evening. Miss Kirker came back this evening had been home over Thanksgiving. Weather snowing all day. Sherman a good boy all day

Dec 4   Monday

Julia washed. Sherman on sled and I went down to trolley station and made exposure of car and station, developed it, made a few prints, down at office wrote some policies and reports, had to go to Harmony to exchange insurance policies with Milleman as the Humbolt ..to carry insurance on his store. Weather pleasant, some sleighs and sleds running. Sherman good boy

Dec 5   Tuesday

Made some prints for Burns

Dec 6 Wednesday

Sherman and I went to trolley station made exposure in PM I made exposure of Sisons house, made some prints for Mrs. OW Ziegler, Julia and Sherman at Serving Society had a hot time, in evening Julia and Sherman were down at Goehring, I was at Harmony. Weather pleasant

Dec 9 Saturday

I went to Harmony then for mail in PM made some prints for the Mill Street men, Julia and Sherman at the serving class and at the food and handwork sale at Sitlers store held by the Ladies Aid Society. All of us down street in evening. Sherman pumped a bucket of water today, the first. Weather was rain, foggy and dreary

Dec 10 Sunday

Sherman at Sunday School. All of us at church, home rest of day. Mrs. Rape, Julia and Sherman up at Swains in PM. Weather very mild 12 noon 53 8:30 63

Dec 13 Wednesday

Down street a little and went down to Railroad to see a car from the St. Paul Milwaukee RR fitted up with the products of Montana, Dakota, Idaho and Washington. It was quite interesting and instructive, in the evening we all attended a subsequent exhibition in the Auditorium showing the products and scenes of that country. Weather wet.

Dec 14 Thursday

About home most all day. Rain.

Dec 15 Friday

About home most all day, in evening Miss Lette Metz was here, I made flash light of householder store front. Wet weather all day

Dec 16 Saturday

Down street a while in AM, in PM about home dug out iron post at grape arbor, Julia and Sherman and her sewing class, in evening Morton brought their graphophone down in the hall, we had the telephone open so that Kate Kirker and Middle Lancaster could hear the music, not feeling very well. Weather wet.

Dec 17 Sunday

No one at Sunday School or church, Julia and I were both sick all day. I got a little better at 4PM but Julia is still sick. Weather a little colder

Dec 18 Monday

About home about all day not feeling well. Weather cloudy and gloomy, growing colder ..evening

Dec 19   Tuesday

Julia washed in PM we were all down at photo gallery and had two exposures of Sherman made and two of us all together, I had Sherman up at the Doctors in the AM he has a skin eruption. Weather cloudy

Dec 20   Wednesday

Made a few postcards from our negative, don't like them at all, dreadfull looking thing, made exposure of Latchaws store and looked at Blooms but made no exposure, in PM made a couple of exposures of Harper's children on New Castle and at Mrs. Grant's baby, the Householders storefront. Came home a developed all OK but Latchaws, Julia out at Old Peoples Home. Sherman and I down street short times in evening. Weather pleasant and bright, the first nice bright day we have had for some time.

Dec 21   Thursday

Working in den most of day, but did not accomplish much, down street awhile in evening, headache

Took some holly wreaths up to the cemetery, delivered postcard to Harpers, at office awhile.

nearly all day, weather drizzling and murky all day

Dec 22   Friday

Julia cleaned the dining room and sitting room took the big rug out washed windows, I took couple of postcards to Harpers and Grants in PM made down street a couple of times. Weather dreary bloomy

Dec 23   Saturday

Dec 24   Sunday

All in Church in AM Mrs. P C Frederick gave Sherman a dollar. Weather mild in evening, After Sherman had gone to bed we brought down Sherman's tree and with Mrs. Morton's help we trimmed it and filled Sherman's big stocking.

Dec 25   Monday Christmas

Julia got up first and found a pair of kid gloves in her stocking when Sherman woke up he looked about the big room and found his big stocking, when he came out in the room and saw the tree and his engine, he said I don't see any horn. Julia told him to look on the tree so he found it and ...one had the tree on a board platform the set on a table and had a little fence made out of card board and had a little gate standing open with a Santa inside, then in one corner there was a low round soup dish with water in and two swans floating in and standing by the pond were three little sheep, the tree was very nicely trimmed with balls and bells and other ornaments, Julia received a fine quilt from Eva, I gave Julia some heavy flannel good for a bath robe,

Page from William G. Bassler's Diary December 25, 1911

Mrs. Morton gave her 6 linen handkerchiefs, Kate Kirker 1 hankie and a gingham apron, I made a flash light exposure of the tree and Sherman, Morton gave Sherman indian suit with feather headdress, in PM took picture of him in it, other presents to Sherman were checkers, dominos, story book. We had chicken for dinner, in PM Mary and Nellie Goehring were up and after while I and Sherman went down there, we were at Stouts a few minutes and I and Sherman at Oliver's and I at Allen's, Mary Rape got a piano, in the evening we were all at church exercises, Sherman got a lot of candy, after we were home

Morton's I made flashlight exposure of our tree, Weather quite nice and bright at times but mostly cloudy

Sherman was the best sweetest happiest dearest boy that could possibly be, he played so nice all day with his toys mostly the engine and now the dear loving boy is asleep, God bless him and keep him.

Dec 26, 1911   Tuesday

I was sick most all day

Dec 30   Saturday

Developed film for Mickley, got horse and buggy at Strutt and went out to Campion Church to made photo of John Scotts Sunday School class. They had congregation at meeting and annual Sunday School, the folks brought baskets of grub and all had dinner in church, after all the services I made exposure of class after a lot of trouble from rowdies, got home at 5 PM roads are very rough, can't drive faster than a walk, in evening at Board of Health meeting. Weather dull, murky in evening, rain.

Dec 31   Sunday

I was sick most all day, none of us at church, Sherman was at Sunday School, he took up the collection in his class, I done some reading in PM, Sherman was a good sweet boy all day. Weather quite warm 58 in AM, but down now it is growing colder 10:30 PM

Jan 1 1912   Monday

Got up before six this morning, Julia washed I developed plates, right good in PM I made exposure of Sherman developed OK went to Harmony in evening we took the trimmings off the Christmas tree and took the tree out, down street awhile. Weather pleasant

Men are digging a drain along our lane to drain the water from New Castle Street where it has been leaking for some time, Sherman was a good happy boy all day and all the next, had a pleasant day.

Jan 2   Tuesday

Working in the den about all day made print from each negative for Scott and made postals for him and Emma Geisenheimer, made exposure of Christopher Walker and wife (Mrs. Vances parents) weather cool and pleasant. Sherman good boy

The page and entries from Jan 3 to Jan 7 are written over with the notation that the entries are Transfered to new book Jan 17,1912 which has been lost.

Jan 3   Wednesday

I went to Harmony the first thing to mail photos to Scott. Came home and Sherman and I went to Geisenheimers took some post cards for Emma, then went down to Lusk's for a piece of drain tile to fix up my cellar drain that was dug up by the men working in the lane, in PM made some postcards for Howard Mickley. Made exposure of Klouse' store and baby of Thomas Carver, developed them, Rapes are entertaining the two bible classes this evening and Julia and Sherman are over helping. Weather pleasant

Jan 4 Thursday

I was working in den most of day, Julia out at Old People Home, in PM Sherman took a long sleep PM, I was down street short time in evening. Weather growing colder

Jan 5 Friday

Made out death certificates, down street awhile got my voucher for salary as Secretary of Board of Health, cashed at Peoples Bank and deposited it in the First National Bank ($10.00) up at Valley News a few minutes, and at our office wrote up policy, Came home and was home all rest of day, Julia down street in PM Weather very cold

Jan 6 Saturday

Down street awhile in AM about home in PM at Sam Zeigler made exposure of Christmas tree, Julia at church at sewing class. Weather very cold

Jan 7 Sunday

Sherman at Sunday School, I was at church, Julia not well, home all rest of day. Sherman a good sweet boy. He can repeat the *Lords Prayer*.

Jan 8 Monday

Developed the Zeigler exposures not much good, down street, read paper at office up at Dr. Ralston's office for birth certificates in PM attended to some Board of Health business, made some prints for Scott, down street in evening at Reed's, weather much milder raining in evening.

Jan 9 Tuesday

I was down street at Dr. Reed for birth certificates , then at Dr. Kerr quite awhile in PM I was making photo for Scott, Julia with Mrs. Rapes help tacked a comforter. Weather very cold and stormy. Sherman can say the Lord's Prayer all by himself. He was a very good boy all day.

Jan 10 Wednesday

Mounted pictures for Scott, down street in PM at Harmony, in evening Julia and I are at Rapes staying with Gross Muller. Weather milder

Jan 11 Thursday

Done some work in den, Julia washed, I had sick headache and went to bed early

Jan 12   Friday

Working some in den and about home, Julia went to church in evening. Weather quite brighter and cold snowed last night.

Jan 13   Saturday

Weather very cold 16 below this AM, in PM gave Sherman a little sled ride and was at church

Jan 14   Sunday

Sherman at Sunday School, Julia and I at church had communion. Weather cold

Jan 15   Monday

Ed Heberling and I collected samples of water at Knauffs and other places about home rest of day. Weather cold, Julia and Mrs. Rape are quilting

Jan 16   Tuesday

About home most all day, Julia and Mrs. Rape finished the quilt. Weather cold. Sherman good boy.

March 24, 1914   *In Julia's handwriting*

Miss Douglas's birthday and Bula Holly's we were out to OP Home and surprised them.

Transcriber's note: Every effort has been made to correctly spell the surnames in this diary which included using the 1927 Zelie-Ann Yearbook, the 1900 U.S. Census and the 1950 Butler County Sesquicentennial book and cross-reference to Julia Bassler's Diary.

APPENDIX 23

Julia's humorous letter from Clinton, MO

1 Oct., 1909 - 16 Jan. 191

Circa 1910 on her dad's stationary to her husband on her first trip home.

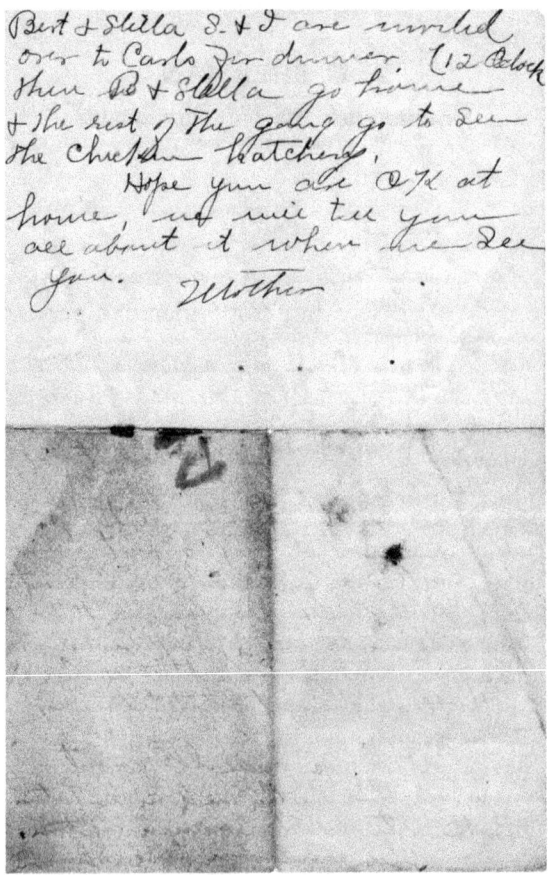

APPENDIX 24

Sherman Bassler's report cards
from Zelienople High School

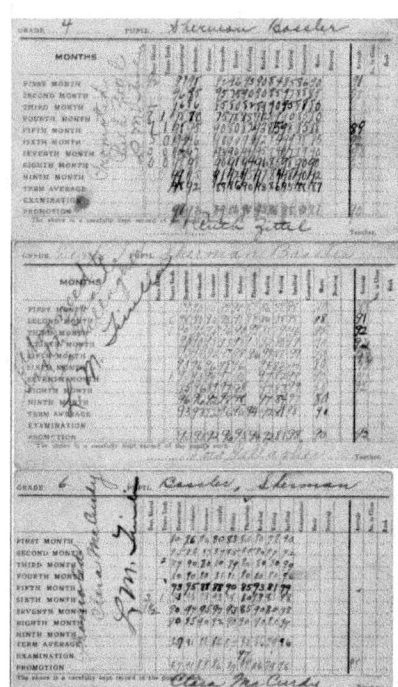

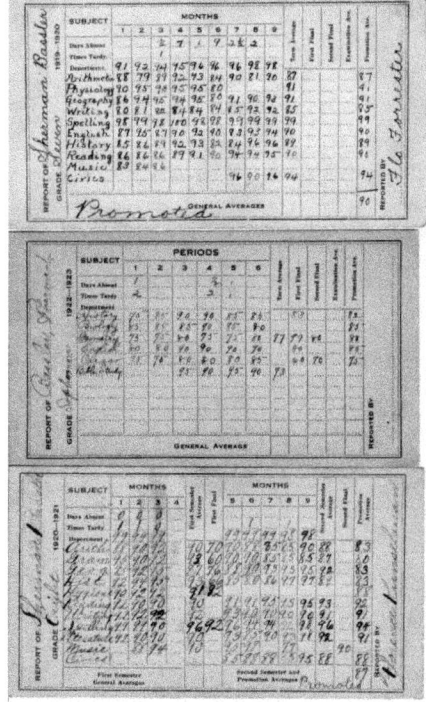

APPENDIX 25

Sherman's Halloween essay at Age 9

31 Oct 1917

Sherman   Room 5 -
Age 9.

5th grade.

Sherman Bassler   Oct. 31, 1917

A long long time ago the Queen of Scotland was going to please her subjects by celebrating All-hallow eve. So she orderd her coach to be brought to the castle door where she and her Princesses stepped in the coach.

They all carried torches. Around the estate they drove with a long procession following the coach. And when they came to the castle a big bonfire was burning. They danced around the fire til after a while troop of fairies came, bringing with them a cross looking elf. He looked so cross and ugly that

the Princesses began to weep. The fairy Queen came up and asked her not to weep, because the old elf was only an wooden image made to represent all the evil things the fairies had done. They were going to burn him.

After a while the fire died out and the fairies left. So they went into the castle and had nuts to crack and apples to eat and they had a jolly evening.

APPENDIX 26

Sherman's letters to Ethel Kerr 1931

Dear Ethel:

Eight thirty AM And full of vim and vigor and so on. Very much different than last night for I sure did have the tummy ache. Due to the hamburgs down at the Hotdog Shop I guess.

Talk about walking. H and I walked more yesterday than the whole weeks walking put together. Dan stopped for me Saturday night and we waltzed all through the dime stores buying radio parts. Then picked up H and went up to his room. Dan had to go home with his parents so nothing to do but "hit the hay" or retire or got to bed in other words. Up bright and early Sunday morning (11AM) had dinner and walked up the hill to see Dan. Their little house had just burned down. That's one fire that H and I missed. Dan had just brought in his radio stuff to Mooreheads in the morning so that was saved. He also left his suit over at the other house. Dan said his dad called him in the morning and he got up and went in with his mother and dad then his father came out later and made a fire in the coal stove and then returned to Dan's Grandfather's. About ten thirty Hannah called Dan and told him to be ready to come home with Mr. Lardin when he came past the Station for the little house was on fire. By the time they got there it was too far gone to do any good. The township fire department came but thought they could do nothing and that they had better save their chemicals in case the other house would catch. They sure do have tough luck. You know I just thought that you probably know all this stuff for Hannah would probably call you up. Oh well its down now and it does fill up this sheet so beautifully that I haven't the heart to tear it up. So guess you will have to endure it. That's the only exciting thing there is in the news for yesterday.

After loading at the Filling Station all afternoon we walked up to the Lindseys in the evening. Taking a big breath I went up and pushed the bell. Mrs. Lindsey came out of the living room and went upstairs. She was smoking a cig in a long holder. Did she look hot. I think she thought it was the telephone and she must have had guests or at least one guest for she was answering it from upstairs. Then I gave the bell another of my determined pushes and got results. Isabelle wasn't in but I explained about the gloves and Finally got them. You should have seen her try to hold the dog and that cig and hand me my gloves at the same time. She missed her calling. Ringling Bros is looking for an act like that. I thought plenty after seeing that woman. Well, I got my gloves and that was that. Went back to H's and listened to the radio then back up the hill again. In bed by 11 with an extra blanket and my overcoat on the bed. Was I cold. Had the chills and sure thought I was in for the Hoof and Mouth disease or something.

But feel fine today. Not nutty though. Maybe that will come later on.

I'll bet you thought that was a terrible date Friday night. I don't often feel like that so cheer up. It may not happen for a long time. But when I gets the blues I has em. Stand by for lunch. The Finger Print Operator just gave me a drop cake so if there are any crumbs in this letter you will know where they came from. It was pretty good and now I'll have to go and get a drink of water. You know me....Be seeing you. SB

Appendix 27

Typed Letter to Ethel Kerr

May 5 with drawn horse

```
                    BUTLER PA

                    MAY 5


   Lo Hon;
              How do you feel by now? I'm just a bit stiff.Harold is just
   beginning to feel his fall.We went to Zelie last evening about 4 30
   He had some signs to paint and I wanted to put up an aerial at home.
   Sure was a lovely day.Gee don't you wish we were out this afternoon.
   H has to finish painting signs tonight but cant get off until 5 30
   and it takes some time to get down driving so slowly.Oh say! Our
   pictures were just fine.Of course I was up to my old tricks and left
   the feet off . Hi. Never could get peoples feet in pictures. The
   pictures will probably be done tonight.+ was just looking at the
   negatives.You remember the one I said you turned your head just as
   I snapped it.Talk about a profile.Its the berries.Can even see your
   tongue sticking out.Boop Boop da etc.If I ever get on to the trick
   of leaving enough space at the bottom of the view finder to allow
   for the bottom of the picture I'll give myself a medal.It seems
   I always do that.The one of you was ok feet and all.You see I wouldn't
   want to miss even a tiny ekle bit of Ethel.
   Felt just fine yesterday.Think it does me good to get up early.
   Only three cig today.That leaves me one for after supper.Never miss
   em after the first day or so.
   Aint we got fun.This must be Dans day off as I didn't see him at the
   station.Poor Hannah and Otey.Do they have my sympathy.
   Say before I forget.I won't be able to meet you Thursday night.
   Woe is me.Made an appointment with the Dentist for Thurs evening so
   will have to leave here right after work.Will I miss meeting my honey
   I'll say.Probably be it the old chair with my mouth open like Joe Browns
   and grunting.I always grunt wehher it hurts or not.Do I know it will
   hurt . My o My from preliminary examination and poking around myself
   it don't feel so hot.Well I'll just imagine you are holding my hand and
   I'll enjoy it.Sounds like a serious operation to hear me rave.He would
   have to make it Thurs but thats the only evening he had open.
   This weather has got me down.Birds bees and what have you.Me for the
   woods.Lets have another frolic Sunday and I'll make it earlier.Can
   stay up Sat night so will not get sidetracked again.
   Must stop now so I can get this in the mail.

                           Your   (x)?,,,...........

       88                        Sherman
```

This is a horse

Thank you

Appendix 28

Sherman & Ethel's letter to Grandma B on Honeymoon

Oct 28, 1934

Appendix 29

Dear E B & S Sherman's letter home from Sperry Plant

1944

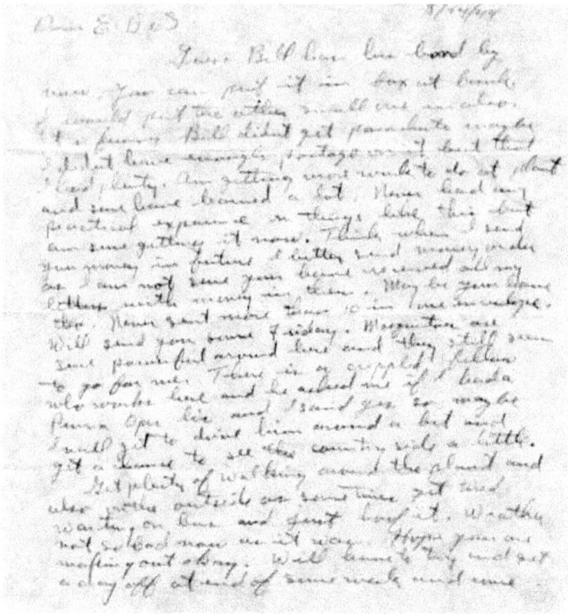

Dear E B & S [illegible]

Guess Bill has been bored by now. You can put it in box at bank. I [illegible] put the other small one in also. It's funny Bill didn't get parachute maybe I didn't have enough postage on it but that I [illegible] plenty. Am getting more work to do at plant and sure have learned a lot. Never had any practical experience in things like this but am sure getting it now. Think when I send you money in future I better send money order [illegible] as I am not sure you [illegible] letters with money in them. Maybe you [illegible] [illegible]. Never sent more than 10 in one envelope. Will send you some Friday. Mosquitoes are sure powerful around here and they still seem to go for me. There is a crippled fellow who works here and he asked me if I had a [illegible] and I said yes so maybe [illegible] and I will get to see the country side a little. Get plenty of walking around the plant and get tired [illegible] outside as some times waiting on line and just [illegible] it. Weather not so bad now as it was. Hope you are making out okay. Will [illegible] and get a day off at end of some week and come.

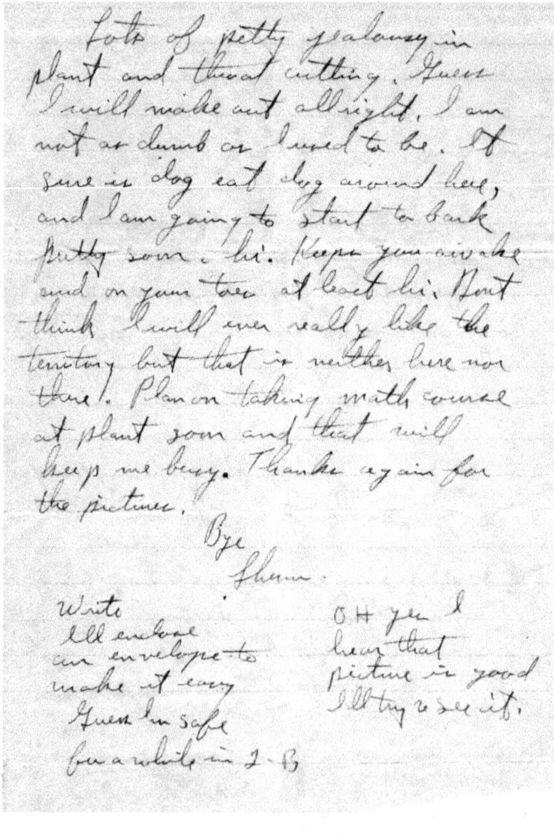

Lots of petty jealousy in plant and throat cutting. Guess I will make out allright. I am not as dumb as I used to be. It sure is dog eat dog around here, and I am going to start to bark pretty soon. hi. Keeps you awake and on your toes at least hi. Don't think I will ever really like the territory but that is neither here nor there. Plan on taking math course at plant soon and that will keep me busy. Thanks again for the pictures.

Bye

Sherm.

Write
Ill enclose
an envelope to
make it easy
Guess Im safe
for a while in 2-B

OH yes I
hear that
picture is good
Ill try to see it.

Appendix 30

Sherman's letter to family from San Juan, Puerto Rico

Jan 5,1947

```
        1                   Hotel Normandie
                            San Juan      Max
                            P.R.          Jan 5 1947
                                          9 PM
     Dear E and all
          I can hardly believe this is the same day that
     I phoned you. Plane was delayed and we didnt leave
     until 1.36 PM. Arrived in San Juan 7.30 PM.
     I was so glad to hear your voice and to know every
     one was well and happy. made my trip so much more
     enjoyable.I am certainly glad that I never had one
     of those little hops in a plane as this flight was
     and experience I never will forget. The weather was
     perfect and it couldnt have been a more enjoyable
     flight for my first one. I am writing now before
     I forget the experience. The time went very fast
     for me and the latter part of the trip as the
     sun went down is something I never will forget.
     We were above the clouds and you could look down and
     see them just like a fluffy white blanket. Then when
     the sun went down below them they were illuminated
     with a red glow. Later as it grew dark just before
     we got in to San Juan the moon came out and was that
     beautiful. Made the planes wings all silver and with
     the stars up above it was indescribable. I certainly
     am sold on travel by air. And I had some distinguished
     company Anthony Eden was on board and I went back and
     got his autograph. They said Lord Beaverbrook and
     his wife were also on board but I recognized Mr.
     Eden after he had been pointed out. He was very
     gracious about signing his name. That will be some-
     thing to keep. I had company coming down as a Mr.
     Mead and his wife and boy age 4½ years is also
     going to be here with me at the radio station.
          It was all so sudden that I can hardly realize I
     am here at all. I had a very interesting chat with
     a young couple who were coming home from their
     honeymoon in Miami. He was helping me with my Spanish.
     Its surprizing how much of my High School spanish
     comes back to me. I think I will go along all right.
          This fellow Mead and his wife are here at the
     Hotel also. He attended school with me. Seems like
     a pretty good hearted fellow but hasnt been around
     too much so I give him a hand and its nice to have
     xxxxxxx  another recruit with you on a new venture.
          It will be a relief to get away from Jim for a
     while. We were just about ready to bite one another
     anyway. Of course I knew how it would be and cant
     complain too much but you can imagine what I went
     through with him.
```

2

I cant begin to tell you and it would make pretty
dull reading anyway. I certainly had one time with
him Xmas eve.

Today it was funny. I really think he is jealous of
me in a certain way. MAYBE He only thinks of himself.
It was funny when I told him I was leaving.He said
why didn't you tell me sooner.I just learned myself.
Right away he said what am I going to do I cant pay
for this double room myself. He wasnt worried abit
about me but just himself. Saturday night instead of
trying to cheer me up a bit he got miffed at something
and wouldnt talk.Guess because he wasnt the whole
show. If it hadnt been that I wanted him to take me
to the airport I would have told him off. Also after
getting along for that length of time I wanted to
leave as friends. Today he wouldnt wait to see me
off at the airport as he wasnt the center of attraction
and that was too much for him. I I was really in
pretty good spirits and didnt let him think I felt
badly about leaving.Was kind of lonesome thinking of
being so far from home but talking to you was such a
help. He sure is a funny character. But I believe
we both make people envious of us for some reason I
dont know.He has lots of good qualities and took me
over to the beach on Saturdays and Sundays but a person
pays an exhorbitant price in self esteem .

I am glad to get out of the second place we moved to
as it was a good place to get out of. The people there
were drunk continiously from Xmas eve until after
New Years. They were ok when sober but that was seldom.
They didnt cause any particular trouble when drunk but
it just wasnt the place to be as some kind of trouble
is bound to happen in a place like that.One of the
women there had to have the Dr. I thot sure she was
going to pass out. There were two sisters one was
married. They were about 50 I guess. You just have to
be in Miami to appreciate some of the activities.

After Xmas eve with all the drunken driving etc I
stayed in the room over new years. J went down town
to see the parade. Came back sober too. But I wouldnt
go out on the streets.

4

anything as I dont know if I can handle my own job yet or not but I just wanted taxkasw you to know what he did.

You know he has more coming in from the pension than I do and he can splurge around more even tho he gets less than I do from Pan Am. I am on salary and he is an hourly worker and I suppose some of those things rankle a little bit. He probably will talk himself into a big job h yet or out of the one he has who knows. When he gets into one of those spells I jut let him rave on. He couldnt buy a house in Fla now if he wanted to. All real estate too high. Certainly it will come down but when.

I couldnt have a minute to myself and study was impossible as he never shuts up a minute unless he was peeved at something.

Well thats enough of that. I have other worries. I have either passed out a 20 for a one dollar bill or I have it mixed into my own money and spent it for my pants and things. I like to think the latter. We were in such a muddle coming over here from the airport with all the baggagg and all and the taxi jamed full with myself and Mr. and Mrs Mead and their little boy that it could have happened but I dont believe it did. It was confusing enough as the taxi driver swooped in to the hotel tooting his horn 15 bus boys all around jabbering in Spanish and poor ol Mead and myself all in a dither with our ears still ringing from coming down in the plane. Well Ill make it up somehow. We only had a few bumps in the air when coming down and of course your ears ring a little from the change in altitude.I always get mixed up when I have over a couple bucks.Well I will be on my toes from now on. I hope I can handle the job all right. I am going to try and not worry about it. At least they need me badly enough to send me down and that plane trip was worth everything even if they send me right back. Mead's little lad sure was a good boy and stood the trip wonderfully even the long wait in the station when the plane was late. Was thinking how Bill would have taken everything in. I believe you would enjoy a plane trip all but the going up and coming down thats about the only unpleasant part of it but it doésnt bother mee too much.

Well I have some sox in the washbowl soaking so must get them out then go down and mail this and take a shower and head for the bed.

Address. XMdtMMMX Hotel Normandie
Escambron
San Juan
Puerto Rico

Appendix 31

Sherman's letter to Billy

25 Dec. 1944

SAT:- (1944)

Dear Billy :-

Here is a War Bond for you. When you are a big boy and ready to go to college it will help you out. Mama will put it away in the bank for you.

Daddy will send you all the little Bonds he gets. This is a big one but the little ones will help too.

How did you like the Boats Greenwalt J. Gremlin built for you. I hope you liked them. Don't know what the old gremlin is up to now but I'll bet he is making something because I hear him knocking around under the bench so I suppose he is building something.

Bye Bill

Sherm

Appendix 32

Sherman's letter to Billy

25 Dec. 1946

 **PAN AMERICAN AIRWAYS SYSTEM**
EASTERN DIVISION, P.O. BOX 3311, MIAMI, FLORIDA

Dec 25 1946

Dear Billy;

Well this has been a long day for me, and very lonesome
being away from all of you.

I hope you had a nice Xmas and that Santa was very good
to everyone. It has been very warm here today and down here
the boys shoot off firecrackers just like it was the 4th of
July. I have heard a few crack but not too many. I went to
church today and it was a very beautiful church. The altar
was all decorated with beautiful red flowers called poinsettas.
They had a beautiful crib all decorated with palms. I suppose
you have some snow there. Little boys down here dont even know
what snow looks like as it never snows here. Tell Susan I have
picked up a few colored sea shells. I always look for the
colored ones but they are hard to find. I'll bet you and
Susan and Mama and your Grandmas and Grandpa had a big dinner
today. I had turkey too but it was by myself out at the cafeteria
at the base. Today I was through one of the big planes and saw
where the Pilot sits and all the instruments he has to watch.
It was a big four engine plane with 53 seats in it. They bring
them in to be overhauled and made shipshape for another flight.

My Christmas presents were very nice and I got all dressed up
in my new shirt and tie and the new socks that Grandma B gave me
and took the bus and went to church. I was wondering what you
were doing. I'll bet you had quite a time getting the cocoanuts
open .

You are doing fine in school and you are trapping right up to
first place Your grades are coming up very nicely and I think
you are writing much better. Tell Mama it was xxxx cool enough
to wear my new grey suit and my blue tie and blue socks looked
very nice.

Write and tell me what Santa brought everyone. Santa travels by
airplane down here as there is no snow. He must park his reindeer
someplace after he has been around to all the little boys and girls
up north and then hops in a plane to deliver his presents down
here.

      Well I'll be looking for a letter from you.

I have a new address so dont forget it.

      Your loving Pop

          1861 N W 39 th. Street

          XIXXX   x Miami Fla.

    I sure liked the pyjamas shirt and tie.

      Thank you again.

Appendix 33

Pan American assigned to San Juan

9 Jan. 1947

MEMORANDUM

FOR USE BY ADDRESSEE

SEND ORIGINAL BY

TO   J. G. Beeler

FROM   Section Communications
          Supervisor

DEPT OR DIV.   Communications

DEPT OR DIV.   Miami Center

LOCATION Miami

LOCATION Miami

FORM 9-29 D

DATE: January 9, 1947.

In reply refer to

SUBJECT: ASSIGNMENT - SAN JUAN

REFERENCE:

This is to advise that you have been assigned duty as Airport Radio Operator at San Juan, Puerto Rico, for which point transportation has been arranged on trip 248, January 9, 1947. Upon arrival in San Juan, you will report to the Station Manager and, in turn, to the Operator in Charge for details in connection with your assignment.

In accordance with present company policy, your assignment to foreign duty is for a period of three years. During this period, you will be allowed two weeks of vacation each year to be taken locally and at the termination of the tour of foreign duty, a sixty-day home vacation will be allowed.

On this assignment, you will be classified as Airport Radio Operator with a base salary of $225.00 per month. Effective on the date of your arrival at San Juan, you will also receive the foreign allowance for that station which is presently established at $140.00 per month. It is to be understood that this allowance applies to San Juan only and is subject to change in the event unforeseen circumstances might force a transfer. This, however, is not anticipated.

You will be allowed legitimate actual expenses for a seven-day period as relocation compensation to assist you in becoming permanently located. In this connection, you are being provided with funds in the amount of $200.00 which are to be accounted for by the submittal of expense reports in quadruplicate and supported by all receipts possible to obtain.

With your past experience in radio work, we believe you will have no difficulty in performing your new duties and trust you will enjoy duty on this assignment.

C. A. Chase

jt

cc: Division Communications Supvt., Miami
    Industrial Relations Department, Miami

SHOW COPIES IN LOWER LEFT CORNER, GIVING NAME OR TITLE, LOCATION, AND MAILING INSTRUCTIONS

Appendix 34

Sherman's letter to his mother
on Sherman's 50th birthday

1957

8 Nov 1957

Dear Mom:

Well another birthday has rolled around for ole S. J. B..

I always think of you in particular on my birthdays. Sometimes its easier to write some things than to say them. Just want you to know how much I love you and appreciate all the things you have done for me while growing up. I remember all the things we used to do like building radio sets & winding coils on oat meal boxes. Taking your table board and using it for a panel. Wasn't that a job though; and hundreds of other things.

Many times when it is snowing I think of you singing 'Snow Flakes are falling so Silently down. Well I better stop enumerating because I couldn't possibly list them all.

But it all adds up to what you mean to me and that I will always remember.

It seems as a person grows
older it becomes harder to find
common interests to talk about as
I get engrossed in my own problems.
Today I have a little time and am
alone at a desk at the Signal Corps
West Coast Office in Pasadena Calif.
so this is the result.

Tomorrow I start back east with a
stop over in San Francisco then to New York.
The weather has been wonderful but will
be glad to get back to the folks in New Jersey
                                88 Sherman

Appendix 35

Oratory Program Inside Pages 1959

BRIGADIER GENERAL DAVID SARNOFF
Chairman of Awards Committee

FREEDOM ▽ OF SPEECH

Freedom of Speech

AWARDS	COMMITTEE

DR. SAMUEL BELKIN *President of Yeshiva University*

ADMIRAL RICHARD L. CONNLEY, USN (Ret.)
President of Long Island University

DR. PAUL DAWSON EDDY *President of Adelphi College*

DR. MICHAEL B. GILLIGAN
President, N. J. State Teachers College

PAUL GREEN *Playwright and Pulitzer Prize Winner*

BRIGADIER GENERAL FRANK L. HOWLEY
Vice-Chancellor of New York University

RT. REVEREND MSGR. JOHN L. McNULTY
President of Seton Hall University

REVEREND BROTHER AUGUSTINE PHILIP, F.S.C.
President of Manhattan College

DR. PETER SAMMARTINO
President of Fairleigh Dickinson College

DR. KENNETH D. WELLS
President of The Freedoms Foundation

The Candidates

WILLIAM BASSLER, RED BANK CATHOLIC HIGH SCHOOL, RED BANK, N. J.
REGINALD O'BRIEN, BISHOP DUBOIS HIGH SCHOOL, MANHATTAN
BARBARA SHEPPARD, SACRED HEART ACADEMY, HEMPSTEAD, LONG ISLAND
WILLIAM WHELAN, MT. ST. MICHAEL ACADEMY, THE BRONX, NEW YORK

★

JACOB HELLER, YESHIVA UNIVERSITY OF NEW YORK
MIDSHIPMAN PAUL SIDDHARTH, UNITED STATES MERCHANT MARINE ACADEMY
CADET RONALD WEISS, THE CITADEL AT CHARLESTON, SOUTH CAROLINA
SIDNEY WOLINSKY, PRINCETON UNIVERSITY

THE PROGRAMME

PRODUCED AND DIRECTED BY JIM MORTON
ASSOCIATE PRODUCER RICHARD ARDOIN

OVERTURE . . . . . . THE CARDINAL HAYES HIGH SCHOOL ORCHESTRA
REVEREND JOHN W. ZIEMAK, *Conductor*
"BUNKER HILL" MEDLEY . . . . THE SONS OF LIBERTY
NATIONAL ANTHEM . . . . LUCY MONROE
WELCOME . . . . JIM MORTON
"THE LOST COLONY"
Selected scenes from Paul Green's outdoor symphonic drama
concerning the first English settlement in the New World.
Choral background by the combined Chorus of the Mozart Society
(Turn page for scenes and characters)
EPILOGUE . . . . ANNE SEYMOUR
TRIBUTE TO A PATRIOT . . . . THE HIGH SCHOOL ORATORS
"BOSTON HARBOR" . . . . . A Folk Fantasy of the Revolutionary Period

THE ST. JOHN'S COLLEGE GLEE CLUB . REVEREND JOSEPH I. DIRVIN, *Director*
featuring
ELAINE MALBIN — STUART FOSTER
THE MARVIN GORDON DANCE COMPANY

INTERMISSION

CELESTIAL STRINGS . . . . THE ANGELAIRES
Harp Ensemble *comprised of* CAROL BAUM, MARIAN HARDING,
KATHLEEN HADEN, DIANE WILLIAMS *and* MARJO BRUESING.
GRAND PAS DE DEUX FROM "DON QUIXOTE" . MARINA SVETLOVA AND JACK BEABER
THE MAN WHO WORE THE MANTLE OF WASHINGTON . THE COLLEGE ORATORS
PAUL LAVALLE AND THE BAND OF AMERICA
Flag finale by The Regiment of Midshipmen of the U. S. Merchant Marine Academy
In observance of the establishment of Kings Point as a permanent federal academy
INTRODUCTION OF THE AWARDS COMMITTEE . . . . JIM MORTON
PRESENTATION OF FREEDOM OF SPEECH AWARDS
VICE PRESIDENT RICHARD M. NIXON
BRIGADIER GENERAL DAVID SARNOFF

WRITTEN BY JIM MORTON MUSICAL CONTINUITY, FATHER DIRVIN
CHOREOGRAPHY BY MARVIN GORDON LEONARD TEMME
MAKEUP BY ZAUDER BROTHERS FATHER ZIEMAK
HOSTESSES: MOTHER CABRINI HIGH SCHOOL — BAY RIDGE HIGH SCHOOL
MASTER OF CEREMONIES KENNETH BANGHART

Program Art: M. B. ROBINSON AND AL MANDELL

Appendix 36

Sherman's letter to his mother
after Bill and Eileen's wedding

1966

Sunday morning we all had breakfast and
later played records for awhile. After Fr Baurenfiend
left we took   Sue back to Conn. We went up one
way and ~~xxxba~~ came back another. ~~Sue~~ They
served us a nice hot lunch at the Convent. It really
hit the spot. Sue showed us the school and her class
room. A nice new school and a very homey convent only
9 Sisters there. It isnt much farther than Howard Beach
and not bad driving. In the school there is a little
kitchen where they can fix their lunch without going
out of the school. Great for bad weather even if it
isnt far th the convent from the school.

Back to the wedding. E says she cant name all
the gifts but among them.   elec. skillet 6 place
settings 4 from Mrs Bejour   Elec mixer   vacuum
elec slicing knife ...   elec food warmer... two bible
the law firm gave a complete set of sterling silver

for 12. Judge Labrecque gave sterling carving knive
& fork to match the set. Wedding cake knife..

They decided not to display the gifts so we havnt
seen or learned of them all yet. Mrs Held sent dishes
from Maine. The neighbors sent gifts Mrs Johnson
Mrs Grayzell Mrs Vacarelli and some ~~xx~~ more we dont
know yet. Silver coffee service from sone one.

5

That covers about all we can think of this time.
We may think of more later on.

Yxxtxrxx   Ethel got hat shoes and bag to
match the blue dress she showed you. E looked just
great with a white orchid oxx that Eileen sent.
She pinned it on the blue satin bag. White kid gloves
etc. Mrs S wore an aqua dress with feathered hat to
match. I was laid out like an undertaker in striped
trousers tail coat etc.

E & I went sailing yesterday . Was a nice
day. Today was nice. Took a little ride over to
Princeton.

Thats all for now

88   sgb

Appendix 37

Julia Sherman Bassler Notes on Family Heirlooms
Wednesday July 15, 1953

<u>DINING ROOM</u>

Large Willow Ware Tureen (blue) was Grandmother Bassler.(Billy's great -grandmother) *Elizabeth Catherine Gilbert Bassler*

Teapot (white with birds) also cup and sugar bowl was great-great grand-mother Buckingham's good dishes. Married name-Sherman *Susannah Margaret Gilbert Buckingham*

Little glass vase (pineapple design) was grandpa Bassler's vase *William Gottlieb Bassler*

The little tin box was great-grandfather Sherman's bank. He lived in Benson, Vermont *Albert Galliton Sherman*

Large silver spoons were great-grandmother's Eliza Gilbert Sherman. Grandfather Pastor Bassler had teaspoons made out of silver dollars to match the big ones.

Big silver spoons buried at Gettysburg during Civil war. Gilberts lived there at the time.

<u>LIVING ROOM</u>

Tilt top Cherry table was my (Bill's) great grandmother Eliza Bassler's table. She brought it with her from Gettysburg when she came to Zelienople after her wedding to Gottlieb Bassler (Eliza Gilbert married Gottlieb Bassler. He was studying at Seminary in Gettysburg. She also lived in Gettysburg.) *Eliza married in Athens, Tenneesee so perhaps the table went to Tenneesee and then to Zelienople.*

<u>BEDROOM</u>

Big chest cedar – came across the Atlantic Ocean from Switzerland. My (Bill's) great-great grandfather Franz Bosler (Bassler)

Cherry piece with deep drawer was Bill's great-grandmother Eliza Bassler

Appendix 38

Sherman G. Bassler's Desk Diary
1973

Introduction: A small black book titled "Desk Diary" was kept by my father for the last eight months of his life in 1973. In late December his mother Julia (Grandma B) contracted pneumonia and after a hospital stay went to King James' Nursing Home in Middletown, NJ. During this time Ethel, my mother,was also hospitalized. My infant son Richie went to the hospital to repair a cleft lip. Sherman had been diagnosed with multiple myeloma, a bone marrow cancer, in 1969 the year after I left the convent. It is an incurable disease and at that time the life expectancy from diagnosis was four years. Sherman wrote in his own shorthand but for the sake of readability I have typed out the abbreviated words and added information in italics for clarity.

1973 Desk Diary

Property of S.G.Bassler 5 William Red Bank, NJ 07701 741-1188

Monday January 1

Sick in bed, Dr. Movelle Sue & Dick party MBC (Monmouth Boat club) Mama kept Richie, Grandma"B" still in hospital. PRED PRED Prednisone. Movelle prescribed same medicine as for Grandma B.

Tuesday January 2

Dr. Heffernan 10.00 cancelled will make new appointment. Call from Dr. Movelle concerning Grandma B discharged from hospital

Bill to see Representative of Social Sec. Papers signed

Wednesday Jan 3 Grandma B went to King James in the evening

Thursday January 4

Weather Rain Sue over. SGB *(refers to himself by his initials)* still have cough Out of bed in room

Ltr fm England will ship storm jib their quote # 9 67/2

Friday January 5

Bill stopped for supper

Saturday January 6

Xmas tree down. Ethel and SGB all packed away

Sunday January 7

Sauerkraut for supper very good Cough a little better Mama (Ethel) went church brought Times home weather cold

Weather cold, someone called concerning Grandma B social security, state she had parts A & B and number ended in S-1

Called Dr. Heffernan's office, girl will send me Medicare claim form. Unable reach Social Security office by phone, line always busy. Sent checks for local bills. All this above is under Jan.9

Monday January 8 Ethel kept Richie while Sue went Doctor

Tuesday January 9

See Monday

Weather cold no wind, sent to Holland America for cruise information

Wednesday January 10

Sent to Dr. Heffernan bill $110.00 back with Medicare form filled in. Ethel and I got groceries at Acme $67.00 First day out of house.

Thursday January 11

Bill stopped in in evening. William had stitches at Hospital, cut his face.

Friday January 12

3:45 P Dr. Heffernon appointment. I'm down 3 lbs from normal (not bad) Dr. H prescribed cough medicine it seems to help. See her in two wks. She gave me alternate Dr. when they are not available. Still a quarantine at King James Nursing Home. Dr. Heffernon said I had London flu.

Sautrday January 13

Cough medicine helping Weather warmer. Grandma B's bill from Dr. Movelle $124. House call Sept. $20.

Monday January 15

Bill stopped by. Sold his house in Apple Brook to Skip Rice. Sue stopped by had visited Grandma at King James.

Tuesday January 16

Called travel about cruise. Read brochure. Left eye still sore. Good supper, chicken and potato pancakes, cake and jello

Wednesday January 17

Eye better, cough loosened up, better. Monmouth World Travel called. Room 321 A deck 17 Feb 73 total $1,150. Leave New York. on Saturday. Feb 17 to be on board after 3 P.M. Bill stopped by in the evening. Good steak for supper

Thursday January 18

Paid Monmouth World Travel

Friday January 19

Sue stopped. Brought good clam chowder. Helped Bill with car.

Saturday January 20

Ethel and I to King James. Got groceries.

Sunday January 21

Bill stopped in P.M. will go to King James. Good dinner stuffed pork chops. Sue stopped at King James said they are changing Grandma B's room at King James.

Monday January 22

Go to Hospital for blood count. Ethel in bed with cold. Received Monmouth Boat Club bill for dues.

Tuesday January 23

Bill picked up music stand. also taking care of medicare action. Some news expected by Friday. Sue and Ritchie stopped for supper. Ritchie's operation week of 12 Feb. Ethel got up and taught piano and got supper. Vietnam War; peace agreement.

Wednesday January 24

Called Federal Communication Commission, New York City about Amateur (ham) radio license renewal. Girl said they had forwarded it to Gettysburg. I had sent to FCC N.Y. by mistake on Dec.27. Ethel in bed sick. Ham for supper.

Thursday January 25

Called Dr. Movelle prescribed antibiotic for Ethel. Ethel very sick. Got groceries.

Dr. Heffernan appt. 1: 45. Hemaglobin low. Gave me prescribtion for tetricicycline, to try get rid of cold. Beef stew for me, chicken pie for Ethel.

Friday January 26

Ethel in bed. Bill phoned - good news. Medicaid approved. Bill stopped in evening. Pizza for supper, Ethel came down stairs.

Saturday January 27

Cough worse stuff. Ethel very sick. Down for supper.

Viet Nam cease fire at 7:00 EST

Sunday January 28

Shoulder glands still enlarged. Ethel and I stayed in house all day. Weather: drizzle. Ethel got supper, chicken legs. Bill stopped in evening.

Monday January 29

up 0530 5:30 AM

Bill phoned said no need to detail income tax. Sue phoned. Ethel received Sue and Dick's Valentine present. Egg poachers. SGB and Ethel in house all day. some snow flurries. Mr. Shirley tuned piano.

Tuesday January 30

9:00 At Riverview Hospital for blood count. Reviewed Home Owners Policy with Redden Agency and Boat Insurance. and N.J. Workmen comp. Phoned FCC Gettysburg, PA OK on Ham License renewal. Got groceries at Acme. Fell going down stairs with laundry.

Wednesday January 31

Neck still swollen. Sue stopped. Ethel and Susan downtown short time. Called travel Agent. Cruise tickets O.K. I was home all day. Cough much improved. Next appointment is Thursday February 1

Dr. H 1:30 P.M.

Swollen neck from coughing. Blood transfusion at Hospital, Friday. Picked up cruise tickets.

Friday February 2

Transfusion 1 pint at Hospital. Drug bill sent Aetna total $51.30 Bill stopped in eve. I called Gramdma B's room 66. Heavy rain all day. Ate good spaghetti dinner 2:30 P.M.

Saturday February 3

Bill borrowed small step ladder. Received Social Security checks. Visit to Grandma B Room 66. Check to WGB. Ethel to Bamberger's 4:30 P.M.

Sunday February 4

Went to Church 12:00 with Ethel. Back rib sore from fall. Sue and Dick visited Grandma B. Dick phoned Monday. February 5 next Blood transfusion at hospital O.K. Blood sample to be taken later. O.K. Sue took Ethel to Asbury Park and return.

Tuesday February 6

To Doctor for Bone marrow sample 9:30 DISCONTINUE CYTOXAN Spent 3 hours at Sue's.

Wednesday February 7

Stayed in house

Thursday February 8

Hair cut. Ethel to Dr. Starke for sinus. Was trouble with ear. Got prescription. Next Visit. Cartrier cruise. Gave girl at Starke's office medicare form for his visit to Hospital $35.00 She also filled in Aetna $20.00 for Ethel's visit. Big T.V. nite Specials

Friday February 9

Dr. Heffernan called had me have a and blood sample for test of iron retention. Also to get "MOL-IRON" 3 capsules daily and have (cbc) Complete Blood Count taken Tuesday and see her Thursday. Ethel and I at Sue's in P.M. Bill stopped with ValPak

Saturday February 10 cold

Visited Grandma B, stopped to see grandchildren. Took Grandma B's Social Security check to King James. Bill visited also with guitar.

Sunday February 11

Ethel and I 12:00 mass. Stopped at Bills. Bill stopped in for a lunch 3:00 P.M.

Monday February 12

Hospital blood sample cancelled. Stayed in house all day.

Tuesday February 13

Tuxedo. Sue took car to inspection. It didn't pass.

Wednesday February 14

Take car to Tinton Falls, Esso 8:00 for lights, wheel alignment. Bill picked me up. Sue took car to inspection O.K. Sue visited Grandma B.

Thursday February 15

See Doctor 9:15 O.K. Doc supplied an injection of deca-durobelin to be given on shipboard. Ethel to see Dr. Starke. Sue took Richie to Hospital. Operation 7:30 A.M. 16 Feb. Sail for the Susan Ann came from Rockall.

Friday February 16

Pickup tux 7:30 A.M. Richie's operation

11:30 Sue and Dick stopped. Richie's operation 1 1/2 hours. Received 27 Aetna 1972 drugs

Saturday February 17

EMBARKATION 3 p.m. cruise

Sunday February 18

Rough WEATHER

Monday February 19

At sea

Tuesday February 20

At sea

Wednesday February 21

St. Maarten took tour in bus. Stopped at nice hotel for drinks. View. Someone took our pix by pool

Thursday February 22

St. Lucia Sanfere and Cartrier went ashore by tender (SGB) waterfront and store and duty and not very attractive. Left Cartrier midnight for Barbados at Midnight.

Friday February 23

Arrive Bridgetown, Barbados 8:00A.M. Bought shoes, looked at camera, Ethel bought a blouse. Ship left at midnite

Saturday February 24

Arrive Fort de France 8:00A.M. No purchases Leave 4:00P.M. for Charlotte Amalie

Sunday February 25

Arrive St. Thomas 10:00A.M. went Mass on board. Took very nice trip to St. John. Bus to Red Hook Ferry to St. John. Bus to Trunk Bay. Beautiful- Fun with bus driver, dancing and informal music

Monday February 26

Shop St. Thomas could not get camera I wanted, Bought Sony cassette recorder. Toys for William, Julia and Rosann. Liquor for gifts. Left 1:00 for N.Y.C.

Tuesday February 27

At sea

Wednesday February 28

At sea   About 2 hours from Ambrose to dock

Thursday March 1

Bill met me at Pier 40- we were last thru customs. Sue had hot chowder waiting for us. Got home about 6 P.M. Ritchie looks great after operation. Good to be <u>home.</u>

Friday March 2

Visit to Doctor. Shot of Deka--- see her in 2 weeks. Endorsed medicare check gave to girl $88.00 New balance owed is $20.00 Visit with Sue- left 5th of Scotch, 5th gin. Returned tuxedo

Saturday March 3

Gave Grandma B's Social Security check to King James. Groceries. Visit to Grandma "B" Bill stopped, I gave 2 fifths scotch. Returned Val Pak. New battery in Grandma B's radio. Loaned Bill cassette with recordng on it. (returned ok) Read home owners policy from Redden Agency. Good steak for supper.

Sunday March 4

12:00 Mass Visit Bill's with gifts for kiddies.

Monday March 5

Sue visit with Richie. Sent Medicare claim to Dr. Movelle (believe (GMB) second time) Checked with KingJames to see if they had received anything for Medicare. NO

Paid GMB Hosp balance

Paid Dr. Stake $30 in full (Ethel)

Paid Redden for workman comp insurance.

Paid Steinbach in full.

Wrote Hinebaugh's recommendation (he was a friend from Fort Monmouth)

Julia visiting. Homeowners Policy in safe deposit box in bank.

Tuesday March 6

Bill's birthday —he's 36. Julia had early breakfast with me. Fixed roller on shower glass. Bought speaker card for Bill.

Wednesday March 7

Took Sue to Dr. Robertson. Very sick, sore throat etc. Keeping Ritchie at 5 Williamm St. Bought Prednisone and mal-iron at Pathmark

Thursday March 8

Keeping Ritchie. Sue is a little better. Rain, cloudy

Friday March 9

Weather is little warmer and sun

Saturday March 10

Grandma B's birthday. *(She is 97 years old)* Sue, Dick and Ritchie, we took pictures. Slippers, cookies. Bill played guitar. Read cards to Grandma B, Grinders *(friends from Zelienople)* sent little wind-up bird that sings. Took card to answer, slippers, were too small

King James Nursing Home: Sherman, Ethel, Susan holding Richie, Bill,Grandma B sitting.

Sunday March 11

Drizzle. Went 12:00 Mass. Sue and Dick and Ritchie in P.M. Sue left a carriage and high chair for Ritchie when he visits. Showed cruise slides.

Monday March 12

Weather: rain early, clearing and sun 10:00 AM, Dick going pick up camera in New York City

Tuesday March 13

Weather like spring 60 F, Took trailer wheel put in 65 lb air. Will do right wheel next. Sue called on phone. We are going to lunch tomorrow at her place. Had lunch with Fitzgerald *(another friend from work)* at McDonald's. Sewed in Brummel hook at clew of new storm sail.

Wednesday March 14

 Got blood count at hospital. OK

Lunch at Sue's. Good. Took off starboard wheel on trailer. Borrowed photo book and "Admiral"

Thursday March 15

Ethel & I went to Bill's to keep Rosann, Julia & Elizabeth from 9:00-11:30 A.M. Put air in trailer tire. Weather is overcast and cool. Visited Sue and picked up camera at Sue's. Olympus 35 RC

Friday March 16

See Doctor at 10:15, Change to 6 Predisone daily 2 - 2 & 2, Got Mal-Iron tablets 3 per day. Visited Grandma B, Got groceries. Bill stopped.

Saturday March 17

Rain, cleared, windy. Kept Ritchie. Dick gave me strap for camera

Sunday March 18

12:15 Mass. Snow flurries. Colder Weather.

Monday March 19

In house all day. Worked on rudder. New shock cord attached to rudder.

Tuesday March 20

Wind NW -15 Sawed off nut on swing rudder. Couldn't tighten.

Wednesday March 21

Hospital O.K. Coffee with Miss Paterna

Make appointment with Dr. Littman call 22 March.

Bought bolt and wing nut for boat rudder at Boatman's shop. got reel

IX listed. Bought 3 cassettes. Ethel looked at wall paper. Ordered check book at Bank Thursday March 22, Finished job on rudder bolt. epoxy on top of mast to stop water going down inside. Scraped window sill in the East bedroom Soaked in neatfoot soap and fixed strap binocular case. Sue left Ritchie while at hairdressers in P.M.

Friday March 23

I phoned Dr. Littman Thurs. does not have Deca-- Bought 2cc DEcadaroblin at Katskin's Pharmacy on Shrewsbury Ave. 2cc for $22.00 Dr. Brodsky -too many to wait. Will try Dr. Littman on Sat. Visit at King James Fixed shock cord on rudder.

Saturday March 24

8:30 AM Dr. Littman Gave me 0.5 cc DEka charge $3.00 paid cash. Raked leaves. Mr. Stone came will estimate fix porch ceiling. East bedroom ceiling and fix 2 shingles o house siding. Took trailer off clocks. Sun and warm.

Sunday March 25

O'cart went 100:00

Bill and I took off cover and plywood from boat. Loaned him T.V. stand (Sue's) William and Julia stayed while Bill visited BMB Sawed few inches off boat hook to make it fit cuddy caban. Sue et al dinner. some muniformations ? from KingJames via Bill. Spent bad night worrying.

Monday March 26

9:10 called King James everything all right, still on program. Went out to Grants new store. Not much. Weather: drizzle. Dr. Starke 's office called Bill the time he came to hospital at night. She said to pay no attention. to bills as they came in. Medicare & Aetna will take care $60.00 Wow! Books at library.

Tuesday March 27

Good night's sleep. Monday night much refreshed. Sue and Ritchie lunch and dinner. Fixed table for Sue. Old counter top. Took picture of Ritchie's new shoes on porch. Color slides ASA 64 Automatic 125 and 60 speed and one at 15 in front room

Redden agency boat insurance check write,   Red notice (late) re Dolphin Book Club

Wednesday March 28

Bill stopped by. Got trash and leaves out. Sent in check for boat insurance. Boat moved forward in driveway. Mr. Stone called - we decided not to do ceiling in bedroom. $35 for porch ceiling and 2 siding shingles.

Thursday March 29

Ethel sanding in east bedroom Weather: overcast Sue taking Ritchie to Dr. Jacitis will stop. *(Dr. Jacitis the surgeon doing the cleft lip repair)*

Friday March 30

Early drizzle. Sue and Ritchie and Dick dug up locust trees for transplanting. Dick brought photo images. Transfered some of Julia's tape from reel to cassette. Received new check book. Gave Sue trellis from basement. Ethel looking at wallpaper. Think mimosa is there.

Saturday March 31

Boat club 125 speed auto 60 speed auto kodachrome x painted rustoleum inside cart. Ethel looked at carpet. Bill stopped in afternoon with Julia, Rosann and William

Sunday April 11

1:00 in auditorium Got paper and rolls 7:00 Am. Bill stopped took out cans We kept Ritchie while S & D went movies "Macbeth"

Monday April 2

Weather drizzle. Ethel painted ceiling (1 qt) East bedroom Kemtone white - used brush. Received some $ for Grandma B anything better than 0.

Tuesday April 3

Paper hanger: 10 single rolls front room 10 single rolls east room

recommends 2 coats paint ceiling front room white sand just take off loose paper feather edge with spackle for crack in door (linseed wood filler) Books (3) arrived. Sue had fire. Rosann caught in door at A & P grocery story in Fairhaven.

Wednesday April 4

Visit Sue and got groceries Little Silver. Sanded in East room base board removed most of 1/4 round front room sanded. Sanded off top of closet door so it would close. Read "Sail Magazine" Roth's "Two on a Big Ocean" very good.

Thursday April 5

Overcast cleared in P.M. bought 1 gal sand/whiter paint. Looked at w/paper Took off rest of 1/4 round front room. Sue stopped for Dr.'s with Ritchie. He had shots. lunch. Took pix some at speed 15 some at 30 and 1 at 2.8 stop on floor. Read boat Insurance policy. Visit GMB in P.M. Deposited her medicare check in bank 11.68   35.92 Ethel spackled. Tried to get linseed wood filler. No luck.

Friday April 6

10:15 Doctor OK predisone 2 every 6 hours. 1 cytoxan daily pred 8 tabs/day Took walk with Sue and Ritchie. Sue got us some fish for supper. Bought wide brush at LB also lantern battery. Bought water putty and took pix of terns and mallards at Sue's.

Saturday April 7

clear-sunshine

Sent income tax form - no tax to pay. Sent sheet giving interest received. Did not have to list C-S pension just State-Police

Visit Bob Geisler. *(friend from work)* Stopped K port Y club

Sunday April 8

Weather: rain windy. 10:30 church

Bill stopped left Graham Green's autobiography. Took out cans.

Monday April 9

2 pix Ritchie speed 15 auto front bedroom. handheld. Sue and Dick at dinner at Held's (Gladys was visiting)) Ethel fell on street. SGB kept Ritchie. Sanded door sill East R. Ethel left 1st roll of slide film at Dorn's Photography store, Water putty in crack. Bedroom door seems very good. Gave Sue two drilled wood strips to brace the hibachi table.

Tuesday April 10

Hospital O.K.

Ethel patched and sanded East bedroom.

Wednesday April 11

Windy -some sunshine.

Sue painted texture paint on ceiling front room. stippled with sponge. Fine job. Had to buy another gal to finish job but didn't come in Quarts. Ritchie was so good. Mrs. Held stopped (Sue) Sue suggested putting magnetic latches on closet doors. Good idea.

Thursday April 12

Sunshine

Received medicare check, Dr. Stake bill, called Bards Doctor 14.15 sent prednisone order for $16.15

Knife engraving loaded camera kodacolor X ASA 80. Ethel worked on east room. Bought magnetic door latches, they work fine. Lunch at Sue's, Platelet count up Take 6 prednisone.

Friday April 13

Sunny   6 prednisone daily, 3 iron, 1 cytoxan

Got groceries. Bought wallpaper and rug samples home. Took cookies and visited Grama B. Got slides from Dorn's Photo shop. All good.

Bill stopped, his foot sore where Doctor removed wart. Made copies of Time article for Doctor. (at library)

Saturday April 14

Weather: sunshine

Mr. Stone fixed siding (2 shingles) fixed ceiling on porch. Lunch E and SGB at Sue. Took (6am) pix Oceanic Bridge. Bought flotation at Blaisdell lumber 60 ($15.00) Helped Sue and Dick work on dock. (at their apartment) Bought new sabre saw at Red Bank Hardware $21.00 Closed hole where gas pipe came thru in front bedroom. Left tools at Sue's.

Manual stop 2.8 exposure 15 and 30 into sun. Sun was up too much should go over about 05:30.

Sunday April 15

Sunshine:Palm Sunday, 9:00 AM Mass. Good roast beef dinner. Quiet day. Phoned Aunt Clara. Thanked her for cookies she sent to Gr. B for birthday. *(Aunt Clara is Grandma B's youngest sister)*

Monday April 16

Sunshine, Nauseous all day. Sanded front room. Ethel painted east room, spackled. Kept Ritchie. Paid Movelle's bill Grandma.B $182, called Karen White (welfare board about the $17.)) the KingJames keeps from the Social Security check. She said King James kept it separate. Asked if it couldn't be put toward Dr. bills. She said I should not pay **any more** Dr. bills that if Medicare stopped, Medicaid picked up and that Dr. Movelle was completely familiar with procedure. I said never mind about past ($182) as some was 1972 some 1973 and the deductibles were involved but I was concerned about future bills. She was quite cooperative.

Tuesday April 17

Partly cloudy

Hospital 9:00 , Electron placement CBC samples. Bought turpentine, nailed squeaky boards front room Ethel enameled doors white in the front room. I sanded storage room door (R) east room. Phone call from Bill Weintraub.(friend at work and sailing friend) Good braised steak for supper. Mailed check to Dr. Movelle for Grandma B.

Wednesday April 18

Sunshine warm 70 degrees. More enamel. Ethel painted in front room. Was up early. Bought aluminum tubing (6 ft) for jib boom to make it self tending.(so he could sail by himself) Good spaghetti with pork for supper. Sue cut more board ends with sabre saw. Bought DiGel tablets, 1/2 gal Gallo chianti no good. Sue and Dick also 99 brunch at Bill's Easter.

Thursday April 19

Saw the Doctor at 9:45 (Gave Dr. Ethel's copy of Time Medical article) temp 75 degrees. Ethel to opera at NYC Don Giovanni. SGB at Sue's saw pix very good. 06:30 Mass. Sue brought back tools; hacksaw?

Friday April 20 (*Good Friday*)

Fair about 60 degrees

Bill got ? at Sue's. Got and fixed rake from Sue's. Bill brought up mower from basement. Drilled holes in jib boom for self tending rig. Went to Good Friday services at 2:30. Had to leave after 1 hour, no air.

Saturday April 21

Sunshine warm 65 degrees.

Mowed yard front and back. Bill stopped with tulips for Ethel. Ethel worked in back yard. I got too tired. Took carpet samples down. Decided on dark green for both front and east room. Sue phoned - dock with flotation works fine. Sue asked us for Easter dinner. Brunch at Bill's 12:00, Ethel bought baskets and bunnies for kids. Bill returned w's cart to Sue.

Sunday April 22 Easter

Hot 75 degrees 09: Bill's for brunch and Sue and D and Ritchie. Up early took pix at highlands 2 @ 10 sec some at 15 auto

Took 2 at Oceanic bridge

Sue's for dinner. Very good.

Visit Grandm B with Sue and Dick and Ritchie. Gave front office King James $7.00 Bill for Medicare. Told girl I was not responsible for doctor bills. Ethel got chewing gum on pants from kids.

Monday April 23

Hot 75 degrees rain 1700 5:00

Hospital for blood sample. Electrophoresis and CBC, RETIC

Coffee with Nedaz?

Took Ethel's pants to cleaners get off chewing gum. Went to paper store but didn't stay- got scrap carpet for car trunk. Bought prednisone at Pathmark and some groceries. Looked around Rickles Hardware. Ethel and I both very tired so came home for nap and just rested. Read *Sail Magazine*.

Tuesday April 24

65 degrees Warm nice day Ethel went to paint store for wall paper samples. Bought 100 ft. wiring #12 + outlet $ 17.98

Over to Sue's for 1 hr 1/2 tea. Pix Ritchie one at 30 other at 60.

Brought back cart and shovel and hacksaw. Left drill bit. Cut hole for outlet Ethel's room . Aperture straight shot to basement near phone line. Sue coming tomorrow help with wiring.

Wednesday April 25

Sue & Ritchie over early. Sue paid for flotations. We put in electrical outlet in front room. Dropped wire from attic and connect to outlet north wall. Put in outlet in Mama's room ran from box in basement up wall to south wall. Ran T.V. wire down and out electrical box north wall front room. Dropped a phone line along side electectrical on south wall and real's days work. Sue wonderful help. Will finish with mounting outlets tomorrow Must get circuit breaker and connect to switch box in basement (tired)

Thursday april 26

doctor O.K. 4 pred daily - 1 cytoxen - 3 iron up 6 A.M. worked on outlets mix up in ground will have to change in attic. Ethel enameled in front room. Very tired both of us. Called Radio Shack - black wire is HOT wire. They have rebuilt phone about $8.00 See Dr. next Thursday. Hospital on Monday.

Friday April 27

Rain: high wind, Gale warning. Up 0300 eat worked on plugging outlet hole in the front room. O.K. now. Polarity reversed on both outlets will change in attic. Cut new hole east room to lower outlet. Bought telephone 11.95. and TJ.V. wire and parts at Radio Shack. Ethel to Steinbachs bought nice dresses. Ethel tired. Bill stopped. Sent in medicare form with Doctors bill toDr. Heffernan $198.00 Asked them to make me a copy of what they send in so can try get additional from Aetna. Picked up Ethel's pants at cleaner's.

Saturday April 28

Rain cleared in P.M. Ethel and I very tired. Plugged old outlet hole east room. Ran T.V. & [phone and new 110 line down from attic. will get junction box and converted east room outlet to new wiring in attic. Will be better for ximots amd airconditioning Also ran antenae wire for receiver from attic. Took off cover on service box got circuit breaker works. Cooper electric has G. E. breakers. Dick borrowed cart and shovel. Going to do more garden. Sue studying for her oral exam for MA, Sent Aetna form and hospital bills to Riverview. Got groceries at A&P, Little Silver, prices very high.

Sunday April 29

Time change to EDST

11:00 Mass in the Auditorium, Mixed sun and cloudy. Visit King-James in P.M. Listened to tapes - good. turkey with dressing for dinner.

Monday April 30

Hospital blood O.K./ Boughtt circuit breaker. 15 amps. Sue helped install. Had short in south room fixed ok. Put in junction box in attic, connected to direct line to basement for wall outlet in east room. Working on light for attic. Outlets front room O.K. south room outlet by window direct to box in basement. Sue borrowed cart. Ethel and I went to Rosann's birthday 1900(7PM). Gus and wife there. *(Gus and Agnes Schilling, Eileen's parents)* Phone line from attic down too short. Girl at Dr's said they had submitted 1972 bills Medicare. I'll check.

Tuesday May 1

Sunny, sprinkle at 2000(8:00). Ethel ordered paper for East rooms. Returned item to Steinbachs. Ethel had piano pupils. Ethel going to measure for carpet tomorrow. No electrical work today rested. Left film at Dorn's will be ready on Tuesday, color prints.

Wednesday May 2

Warm partly sunny. Returned wallpaper book. Nailed cable in attic, finished installing light in attic. I was right about the $35.00 due Riverview. So Riverview can pay me back. Will try get straightened out at Dr. Heffernan's tomorrow about medicare and Aetna. Ethel sanded around ceiling in evening. I will have to start over in mounting box in front room closet and fit the cover plate properly. Ethel measured rooms and we ordered green carpet. Ethel to go over keep Ritchie tomorrow. Sue's exam for Masters at Monmouth College in P.M.

Thursday May 3

Heavy rain showers in P.M. cleared

0915 Doctor 4 Predisone daily 1 cytoxin 3 iron. Paid all 1972 Dr. bill by check. Receivedd medicare paymet $-- Sue passed her MA exam. Deo Gratias. We stayed with Ritchie. Ethel and I very tired. Ethel ordered 20 rolls of paper for front room. Explained to the Doctor. about payments and asked if we couldn't have check up every 2 wks. Next visit to Dr. in 8 days. Same medication.Daily 1 cytoxan, 4 Prednisosne, 3 Mol-Iron. Cashed Medicare check $ and State Police check, 10X shower in P.M.

Friday May 4

Took Medicare statement to Dr. Heffernan's office $, they took Aetna form to sign and send to Aetna. Stopped look for foam at J Ross ND. Sue stopped with Ritchie did a washing. Ethel painted hot air registers in both rooms. Think I have wall outlet hole O.K. now in front room. Sue brought good pea soup had for supper. Linseed oil on cuddy cabin doors. Package from West wrong name on knife.

Saturday May 5

Boat down to Monmouth Boat club, Weather, chilly, partly cloudy 50° F

Over to Sue's early. Back and got tail light fixed on car. Sue and Dick helped get boat down to Monmouth Boat Club. #135 was occupied so put in #136. Trouble with terminals on battery, good thing they were discovered, bolts eaten thru. Repaired with two new bolts. Ethel got used books. I kept Ritchie for a short time while Sue and Dick went to Steinbachs. Called Chev but they were closed. Call Monday ie. free motor mount check up.

Sunday May 6

Sunny. Over to Asbury Park board walk in P.M. Fresh air and sunshine. Good roast beef at 6 P.M. Tired. GE TV blew circuit breaker. Think filter cap went. Smelled like it. Good sleep after 12:00 P.M.

Monday May 7

Sunshine, warm. Mowed back yard (E & I) Bought new double outlet. Mailed back knife to WEST air mail cost $1.00. Bought barbecue briquettes and starter fluid. We are to keep Elizabeth this week starting Thurs. while Bill and Eileen makes trip to Bedford, PA. Ethel painted 2nd coat on hot air registers, got car fixed at Chev Motor cable retaining mounts. Ethel did double washing. I took sun sights in backyard.(with sextant) Picked up film at Dorn's. No pix at all, must have loaded camera wrong. Cashed Social \Security ck. deposited $50.00 in joint savings acct.

Tuesday May 8

Cloudy. Bill and I stepped mast.*(put mast into sailboat)* Bill mowed front yard and brought up picnic table and benches. I gave him T.V. set that quit. He returned T.V. stand for T.V. Borrowed sleeping bag. Sue stopped by on her way to visit Fr. Bishoff. Bill on vacation this week going to Bedford. Ethel and I went to Howard Johnson's for shrimp, enjoyed very much.

Wednesday May 9

Rain squalls in P.M. Hospital O.K. $105. Picked up wall paper. Ethel phoned paper hanger. Bought Azalea food and rye grass. Ethel sowed grass seed. Ethel finished enamel baseboard in the front room. Bill brought Elizabeth's gear. Bought new chart 824-sc ,Ethel and I cleaned out downspout on front porch between rains. Must clean out one by pine tree. It seems full of leaves also. Bill paid back loan in full.

Thursday May 10

Warm -humid. Keeping Elizabeth. SGB got groceries. Receivedd $336 rebate from KingJames. Put Bills check and this in checking acct. Bill's loan paid in full. Bill, Eileen, William, Julia and Rosann left about 09:15 for Bedford. Loaned Buick blanket and sleeping bag. Took sun sights back yard with sextant.

Friday May 11

Doctor's No Cytoxan, rest same 4 prednisone, 3 Mol iron daily.

Keeping Elizabeth. Ethel very tired. Good spaghetti with pork. Paper hanger will be here Monday. Weather variable cloudy warm. Paid C.A. Stone, Steinbachs. Got Tow bar from Sanders. Read 2 statements from Hospital. Filled out Aetna form and <u>returned to hospital.</u>

Saturday May 12

Cloudy/showers. Pumped the bilge in the boat early. Put in hanger for cuddy doors. Put up hammocks and straightened things out. Read notice from Aetna. They want more details from Dr. Heffernan. I had told girls at office but N.D. Sent Heffernan new forms and notice from Aetna and stamped addressed letter to Aetna. Plywood in trunk. Will finish job again too tired today. Paid gas and Exxon bills.

Sunday May 13

Visit King James 2:00 P.M. Stopped at Sue's with Elizabeth. They picked up Elizabeth before dinner. Took up girdle for Grandma B to King James.

Monday May 14

Wallpaper hung. good job in East room. Some mistakes in front room. Paid $120. To hospital for samples. Thought if I went Monday may get going on trip Friday if I can see Dr. Heffernan on Thursday.

Called Red Bank tax office. Sent in tax, it was due May 1.

Tuesday May 15

Some poor workmanship in front room. Ethel called paperhanger he was supposed to stop by but he didn't show. Bill stopped right at dinnertime. Fixed telephone jack in the front room. Got car greased and oil changed 7:00A.M.

Wednesday May 16

Ethel very sick. Called Sue and Bill. Bill called ambulance. Took to Riverview 11:30 A.M. 4 P.M. seems some better. Dr.Movelle will visit at hospital. Phone connected but must tack wires down in attic. 9:30 P.M. back from Hospital. Dr. Movelle never showed. Bill was there. Ate supper at Sue's. Read Dolphins' selections. very poor did not take any, Sent form to Dolphin.

Thursday May 17

Sue and I visited Ethel in hospital. Took turns keeping Ritchie in lobby. Ethel feeling some better. Enjoying food more. They took x-rays. Dr. Movelle visited but did not say what the trouble was. Sue came and did double washing and ran vacuum and straightened up Ethel's room. I made pea soup. Sue had ham. Up to Bill's for dinner. He also helped take down second batch of clothes from line. I bought 100 ea 5 mg tablets of predisone at Pathmark $2.98. I got some kind of form letter from Aetna. I don't understand re bill at Neptune Hospital. I visited Ethel for a short time before going to Bill's. Weather rain for tonite. Received receipt for taxes.

Friday May 18

Went to Doctor 10-15 but appointment was for 24 May. She told me though to take 1 cytoxan, 3 irons and 4 prednisone. I still can't get thru to girls about medicare and insurance. Have cold and fever tonight. Ethel better. Dr. Movelle saw her. Sue walked her in hospital hall. Was over to Sue's for fish supper very good. I felt too lousy to go back to the hospital at 8:00 P.M. so Sue went and took magazines. Bill to Bar Association meeting at Atlantic City. 8:45 Weintraub phoned and Fitz phoned (friends) 9:15 Said Osche died.(Oshe was an old friend from Butler,Pa who had encouraged him to take the job at Fort Monmouth)

Saturday May 19

Anthony mowed grass. I visited Ethel about 1:00P.M. Sue visited and stopped by. I have a fever 100.6 Mama phoned I can get her in morning. Good News. I talked to Harry French on phone today.(friend from work) In sack at 6:00 P.M. very tired and short of breath. Had 2 Horn-Hardot's macroni and cheese for supper. Sure lonesome here without Ethel. Read notice from Aetna. They payed Riverview $35.00. Now try get that back for myself. (Note Riverview Hospital put it on my acct.)

Sunday May 20

SGB picked up Ethel at Hospital about 9:00A.M. both of us spent day in bed after I got medicine and paper. Sue and Dick stopped. Sue brought a casserole (very thoughtful) They are on their way to Brigantine and visit Frank Rosetti's parents. Slight drizzle about 4. I had slight fever and sinus running. bought cytoxan at Profesional Pharmacy.

Monday May 21

Drizzle 60F. Brought Ethel breakfast up. Sue brought us groceries so I didn't have to go to store. Ethel and I had good sleep in P.M. Bill stopped by around 6P.M. He looked very tired. He had visited Grandma B Sunday. Ethel and I had T.V. dinners. Sinuses bad again today. Sue said visit to Brigantine Bird Refuge very interesting. Carpet in, will lay it Thursday.. My temp 99.6

Tuesday May 22

Hospital CBC platelet retic O.K.

Cashier said they credited my acct with the $35. from Aetna. down to

MBC until noon. Got Ethel her lunch. Went to Dr. Jamison 2:30 for sinus flush. Got antibiotic pills. Eileen brought a <u>good</u> stew and strawberries for our supper. Ethel and I in sack 7pm. I have fever 100F. Bought flash. Paid for wall paper $105. Ethel called paperhanger.

Wednesday May 23

Rain. Both rested.

Thursday May 24

Drizzle. Carpet down looks great. Wallpaper hanger came. No satisfaction from him. Spaghetti for supper. Phoned Sue; some hassle with Monmouth College over one (1) credit but they will let her get her diploma. Hope we can make it Sat.*(graduation)* Will try rest up tomorrow. Will have to take a little off some doors so they swing over carpet. No fever today. *(they could not go to graduation)*

1930 hours slight fever 99F

Friday May 25

1015 Doctor. Went to hospital for transfusion. Took long time. then had bad time 2nd bag of blood. Had heart attack. Could not call nurse no buzzer. Bad time. Put me in Hospital. Heffernan not available. Dr. Bradskzy covering. *(he was left alone during the transfusion and another patient called for help)*

Saturday May 26 to Thursday June 7 in Riverview Hospital

Friday June 8

Released from hospital. Bill brought me home. Air conditioner put in dining room. Roll-away bed set up.

Saturday June 9

Food tasting better Ethel feeding me goodies.

Sunday June 10

<u>Hot weather</u> 94 F

Sunday June 11

<u>Hot weather</u> 93F

Tuesday June 12

Hot weather showers Stayed in too hot to go in yard.

Stay on roll-away except one trip up stairs to go to bed. Bill stopped in evening on way home. Advised to have power of attorney given to Ethel in case I ever have another heart attack. He didn't discourage me from seeing Atty O'Hearn about heart attack & negligance at Hospital. This belongs under 14 June 73 *(he didn't sue)*

Wednesday June 13

Weather some cooler

Thursday June 14

Weather in 80's nice breeze. Sat in backyard. Kept Ritchie while Ethel and Sue got groceries. Eileen took dresses to Grandma B. See rest under June 12. taking 1 cytoxan 4 predisone 1 heart pill

Friday June 15

[Loaded KX-135 Asa 64 colored slide]

Johnson's cut hedges $15.00 E kept Richie while Sue and Joan sailed Joan's Lightning. Weather nice, stayed inside. Anthony will cut grass tomorrow.

Called Medicare at Millvale,N.J. about error in check. Taped phone conversations for record. 3 or 4 weeks to correct but OK to cash checks.

Called Dr. Heffernan's office changed date to 21 June. Go to hospital on Monday 18 June blood sample.

Saturday June 16

Bill started lawn mower. Anthony mowed lawn. Hard rain in P.M. slept thru it. Slept downstairs.

Sunday June 17

Bill brought newspaper. Took Mama to church. Mailed letters. He will pick me up early and take to hospital. Bill fixed loose connection in attic. Now have bed lamp working. He had company. His friend Tom Lennon and Family. I walked around house early in A.M. Sat out in yard. Mama baked me an apple pie and whipped cream and good roast. Dick, Sue and Ritchie brought me ice cream. Ethel gave them some pie. Sleeping upstiars. Ethel seemed pretty good today. Ruff nite.

Monday June 18

Go to hospital early. Fast from midnite. Bill took me 8:45 A.M. to hospital for blood samples. Rainy day cool, had furnace on. Good nap in P.M. Gave Bill medicare checks to be reproduced. Good supper "Shepherds Pie" Watched Hippos on Jacques Costeau TV show.

Tuesday June 19

Weather very.good, Arnone's back(next door neighbor's).They stopped in on front porch. We got local bills paid, also phoned Karen White Medicaid who said send Dr. Movelle's bill (Julia) to her which I did. Bill returned checks with copies.

Wednesday June 20

Weather: humid, drizzle, air conditioner on. Sue stopped; took Mama to bank and Drug store. Had lunch. Got suitcase and white hat. Fixed center fixture in bedroom. Bought fish which we had for supper. Tasted good. Found $40.00 which I had placed in desk, also a check for $27.00 found in bureau from Aetna Ins. Sue said she would run me over to Dr's if I didn't feel up to driving.

Thursday June 21

Doctor 1:30 A.M. good sleep but believe I will have Sue take me to doctors. Dr. says <u>no stairs,</u> EKG.

Friday June 22

No entry

Saturday June 23

Sue and Dick left for California

Sunday June 24

Weather hot

Monday June 25

Weather hot

Tuesday June 26

Staying on cot in dining room. Rainy

Wednesday June 27

Anthony cut grass. Rain

Thursday June 28

Listening to Watergate

Had to fast 12:00 on

Friday June 29

Bill took me to the hospital for blood samples.

Saturday June 30

No entry

Sunday July 1

Bill brought Times. Bad night

Monday July 2

Eileen and Ethel took me to Dr. Heffernan at 2:15 P.M. EKG Can come up stairs one trip per day. Told her how heart felt early this morning. Said it was fibrillating. She changed medication. 3 teaspoons potassium in juice, 4 prednisone daily 1 1/2 Lytoxin daily. NO cytoxan. See her 10 July. Received State-Police check

Tuesday July 3

Overcast part sunshine, no rain. Ethel down town got wallplates. Out 1/2 hr back yard. Took potassium O.K. NO cytoxan. e got leaf rake walked down and back. Received Social Security checks. Good supper schnitzels. Bill stopped in had bite, scratched out...Mitchell before Watergate committee. He seems very evasive to me.

Wednesday July 4

Good sleep. all to 9:00A.M. Some sun outside. 1 hr. Grandma B called on phone. Ethel had excellent dinner and my stomach was ok all day felt great to enjoy food. Rested some in bed. Fireworks going on at Park 9:30P.M. 1 trip upstairs to go to bed. No heart fibrillations today.

Thursday July

good day. Slept downstairs, stomach ok

Friday July 6

Beautiful day 85 sun, low humidity

Hospital for samples. 3 test tubes blood. Bill took me down. Was faint from fasting. Got some sun in backyard. Grass was cut. Ethel had good supper. Got bill for stay at Riverview. Owe $90 after Medicare. Will send the $90 bill to Aetna. Paper hanger to come after lunch. (did not come)

Saturday July 7

Sue and Dick should be home this weekend. Sue arrived 2 A.M. they got Ritchie in P.M.

Sunday July 8

Weather hot humid ate inside. Dick brought crabs. Had dinner. Cold turkey Potato salad and watermelon. Good.

They had a great trip. Got to visit San Simeon, San. Francisco, Yosemite, Sequoia, San. Diego Tia Juana. Ritchie looked good. Sue said she would take me to Doctor's Tuesday 9:00A.M.

Monday July 9

Hot humid, stayed on cot in dining room

Tuesday July 10

Weather not quite as hot as 9th

Dr. Heffernan at 9:00 Sue took me Dr. Heffernan EKG O.K. See her on 17th. Hospital 13th for blood samples, no fast. NO CYTOXAN. Ethel and Sue got big grocery order while I kept Ritchie. Gave Heffernan girls Medicare and Aetna forms. One set for Dr.'s hospital bill other set for office visits. Ethel cashed Aetna check for drugs and State Police. check and deposited savings account. Ham and fresh corn and tomatoes and strawberries. <u>Very good.</u>

Wednesday July 11

Cooler, breakfast ham-egg.Stayed in. Rain in P.M. windy. Listened to Watergate hearings. Took bath 9:00 Supper veal good and corn/cob

Mitchell before Watergate investigators. He seems very evasive to me.

Thursday July 12

Weather wonderful 85 low humidity.

Drove car downtown got haircut. Took Ethel to Sherwin William paint. Bought card to send to Mr Hoffman my hospital roommate. Ethel bought paint. Bought card for garbage can and window blinds at Prawns. E walked down and bought fern at Prawn's. Out in back-yard short time. found box in cellar. Aired out cellar. Can't find some tools but sander, sabre saw, drill O.K. Read bill from Starke $80.00 said they hadn't heard from Medicare. I never received any either so sent forms (Medicare) to Starke to resubmit. Good supper, schnitzels, fresh peaches.

Friday July 13

Due at hospital for blood samples. No fasting. Drove down with E. Ethel did some shopping.

Saturday July 14

Hot. Anthony mowed yard. Sue asked us over for Sunday supper.

Sunday July 15

Weather o"cast. Ethel bought Times. Had sleep in P.M. Went over to Sue's for supper 4:12 They fooled me and had lamb shiskebob cooked on grill. Didn't tell me. It was very good. Dick showed slides of trip and we had our desert and coffee at intermission. wonderful slides of trip 2 1/2 roto trays beautiful scenes. Got home about 10:20 Very enjoyable time. Ritchie sure some boy.

Monday July 16

Nice day. Went down MBC in P.M. Aired boat but couldn't find my good life jacket. Ethel worked in back yard and painted hinges on door. Had ham for supper. Good sleep straight through until 5 A.M.

Tuesday July 17

Paid checks to Heffernan office, Weather nice. At the doctors 9:15 (no fibrillations) potassium 4 table once day. moliron 3 tab, Lexian 1 1/2 tab Cytoxan one per day, prednisone 4 per day. Blood at hospital Friday.

Ethel bought rake, fruit at Sickles market. We hung fern over sink. Ethel played Chopin for me in evening. Chicken for supper. Bed 10:30 P.M.

Wednesday July 18

Weather very good 85 sun. Went to the Monmouth Boat Club. Sue dropped me off and picked me up. She and Joan were going sailing in Held's lightening but some one had taken boat. Went to Sue's. Mama, Sue and Ritchie in pool. I took some pix. Phoned Fitzgerald from Sue's. Little pain around ticker. In sack 7 P.M. will probably feel ok tomorrow. Riverview returned an Aetna form, forgot to sign one place. Good T.V. supper

Thursday July 19

Hot weather. Fast 12 midnite on. Drove Ethel downtown and picked her up. Stayed in. Good supper. Stew.

Friday July 20

Very hot humid. Blood samples. Down hospital early with E. Ethel gave me good breakfast over to Sue's. Ethel and Sue in pool. I rested. Got flounder at fish market, had it for supper. Bowels on run today. Anthony cut grass back yard. Reading "The Making of a Surgeon" Received notice Aetna had paid Riverview $13.50

Saturday July 21

Bill, Julia, William, Rosann came early. Bill trimmed pine and locust tree and cleared downspout. Took down cable and put up along rear of house. Gave William ...old x star radio. Bill took T.V. set to be repaired. He borrowed saw, ladder and hedge shears (manual) Ethel fixed meatloaf. We watched T.V. Burns and Schreiber. Overcast A.M. Hard rain in P.M. Harry French phoned.

Sunday July 22

Weather warm Air conditioner on. Got paper early. Did not feel very good today. Ethel walked down and back to church. Read paper and rested on cot most of day. Good roast for dinner. Stomach not good and had trots. Bed by 9:30. Bill Weintraub *(friend)* phoned but I was sleeping so Ethel told him I wasn't feeling so good.

Monday July 23

Nice Weather. Sue put up curtain rods. Tried to fix connector on cable no luck. Did temp job and worked a station Washington, D.C.on the ham radio. Sue, Ethel and Ritchie visited Fr. Bishoff. They had swim and Ethel and I had steak supper. Bought "Wake of the Sea Wild" at A&P.

Tuesday July 24

Weather warm but nice Doctor 9:15 No fibrillation. Same medications. Hospital on Friday. Out to Conrad's Nursery and bought for rose garden. Ethel took me for a walk in the evening. Dr. said I could walk some on level.

Wednesday July 25

Weather warm nice. Went to Sue's She got her master's diploma by going over to college. Ethel & Sue and Ritchie in pool. Ethel had good chicken. I worked ham radio at 10:20 A.M. Herb and Bus

Took some pix of Ritchie, one at 250 one at 500. May see splashes of water.

Thursday July 26

Hot. Went down to the Monmouth Boat Club for short while but too hot and humid. More comfortable at home with air conditioner. Fast

Friday July 27

Very hot humid. Hospital blood work. Ethel to get hair fixed. Ethel to N. Country club gave Julia dress for birthday. Ethel & Sue looked at pianos. Ritchie stayed with me. Anthony mowed backyard. Bill stopped by. They will be at Sue's tomorrow if it doesn't rain. Didn't feel so good today. Hot dog and watermelon for supper.

Saturday July 28

No rain hot and humid. Stayed in. Ethel washed sofa cushions. I fixed connections on microphone. Rerecorded Rubenstein from 7 1/2 tape to Sony. Steak for supper. Had drug store send up KC and Kaopectate. Watched Burns & Schieber on T.V.

Sunday July 29

Very warm humid. Ethel walked to 10:30 church –got the paper. I called Grossie in Fla (2 calls) Not much satisfaction re inquiries. Stayed in house all day. Not feeling so good. in bed by 8P.M. Ethel had good schnitzels for supper but appetite lousy. Chest hurt all day. *(the Grosses were old friends from Zelienople, they had moved to Florida and Sherman was asking them about places to rent for next winter but they suspected he was asking to stay with them and they were evasive. Sherman was hurt by this)*

Monday July 30

Hot humid. Drove to library. Sickles Market, Acme. Felt better. Ethel made me ginger bread mit schlag. (with cream)Very good. Ha for supper. Grandma B phoned. Ethel talked to Sue. May swim (E) tomorrow. Listened to tapes in evening.

Tuesday July 31

Doctor 9:15 A.M. Endorsed Aetna check to Dr. Asked pharmacy for receipts. Sent Dr. Brodsky Medicare form her bill $55.00

Ethel & Sue in pool. See Dr. next Tuesday. Hospital on Fri. Phoned B. Weintraub at his home. Gave girls@ Heffernans Medicare and Aetna forms.

Wednesday August 1

Hot and humid. Ethel & Sue to Freehold to buy piano. *(Sue bought a Kimbal)* To Kinkles for jacket for Ethel. Ritchie stayed here while they went Kinkles. Veal for supper Chest hurt from noon on.

Thursday August 2

Hot very humid. Sick all day, nausea. Ethel and Sue to Lakewood to Asbury Park (Piano) Pizza at Asbury Park. Bill stopped in. He will take me to hospital 8:30 blood sample. I don't feel like driving.

Friday August 3

Hospital blood. Hot humid. Bill took me to hospital. Had coffee with him. Ethel & Sue to sidewalk sale. Sue ordered piano from Freehold to deliver 4 P.M. Felt much better today not sick stomach. Stayed in all day. Very humid. Ethel had good chicken for supper. Talked to Fitzgerald on phone. up in bed 6:30 reading *YachtingMagazine.*

Saturday August 4

Anthony cut backyard grass. SS (Social Security) checks SP (State Police)check -CS (Civil Service) pension up 6.1%

Hot humid. In house all day. Bill brought Ethel a Bach record last eve. Ethel did washing dried on line. Had good spaghetti for supper. *Sail Magazine* came. Wrote check for Prof Pharmacy drugs. Something - paid to Riverview by Aetna.

Sunday August 5

Hot humid. Slept thru till 4:00A.M. Got rolls and Times at Peres 7:00A.M. E to 10:30. Good lunch ham and ice cream. Felt tired, stomach fair. Stayed in. Roast beef supper. In bed 8:30. Sent Book club- <u>No book.</u>

Monday August 6

Hot humid. Library, music store. Sue's. Was <u>sick</u> nausea, diarrhea. Left car at Sue's. She drove us home. Took to Dr's Tuesday. Ethel slept on sofa. I was on cot.

Tuesday August 7

Hot humid. Dr. Heffernan. Saw Dr. John. Increased prednisone to 6 a day 2-2-2

Sue and Ethel went to Sickles and Acme. I drove my car home. Dr. says stay out of heat. Stayed in all day. Felt much better. Good supper corn/cob and chipped beef sandwich and ice cream. Bill stopped by. Ethel played Chopin for me in evening.

Wednesday August 8

Hot humid. Savings Certificate came from Mainstay. Ethel got hair fixed. Sue came over and picked her up. Had lunch. Sue visited friend at Hospital while Ethel kept Ritchie. I was not out of house. Felt pretty good - meds fine. Ritchie has 3 teeth. Talked to Danny on Phone. Workd radio sked. Herb says Ralph's (Osche) wife may return to Butler.

Thursday August 9

Hot humid. Stayed in. Watched T.V. had good sleep until after 6:30 A.M. Read some check from SS for Gr B don't understand it as regular check came on the 3rd.

Friday August 10

Hot 90 Humid Hospital for blood specimens. Had coffee at Hospital. Came home too hot to be out. Read letter from Gross's yesterday about motels etc. Weather has been bad. Hot humid. Anthony cut back yard and swept front walk. Chicken for supper. Peaches with Ethel's home made cookies. Aetna wants Dr. Jamison's charge for ear exam. Ethel called his office. Radio Sked talked Ed Malecki at Fort Monmouth. Fitzgerald's mother died.

Saturday August 11

Hot humid. Inside all day. Ethel & I slept late. Fair today. Stomach not up to par. Bill phoned to see if we needed anything.

Explanation of extra check came today. It's to pay Grandma B's medical expenses without deducting them from regular Social Security check. Will call welfare to see who gets check. Bill Weintraub phoned.

Sunday August 12

Hot humid. Stomach not so good - felt better later on. Dick and Sue took Ethel to Grandma B in afternoon. Bill was there also. Sue, Dick and Ritchie stayed for supper. Very nice. I was inside all day. Too hot on porch except early morning. I talked to Harry while Ethel visited Grandma B. Ethel mailed tax check.

Monday August 13

Warm less humid. E and I to Acme and Sickles and A&P Meat scarce. Bought ham. Deposited State Police check in Savings. Felt pretty good. rested stayed in rest of day. Received check from Medicare for Dr. Heffernan will take over tomorrow with Aetna form. Bill stopped in at suppertime. Ethel and I on porch in evening.

Tuesday August 14

Not so hot but humid. Dr. Heffernan 9:15 Paid Dr. H medicare check. Gave Aetna form. Ethel & I went Sue's. Ethel and Sue shopping -Ritchie slept good. Had fondue supper. Eileen stopped short time. Bill returned raincoat. Sick today.

Wednesday August 15

Not so hot and humid. Slept in. Ethel and I had breakfast together. Ethel to church. I had phone talk with Bob Geisler. SOS (chipped beef)for supper with fresh peaches. Medicare check (doctors) for Grandma B Will call welfare tomorrow. Felt better today. Radio sked. W3FK lout but jib rest weak. Nixon to talk 9:02 P.M.

Called tax accessor no reduction in taxes if over 65yrs. if income above $5,000.

Thursday August 16

Tangs for lunch. Ethel enjoyed chicken. Looked for light fixture -bought chain. Little too much activity for me.

Friday August 17

Warm. To hospital for blood sample. Went to Monmouth Boat Club for an hour but not comfortable. Stomach off today. Sue and Ritchie came over had lunch together. Sue bought me a roto tray for projector. Had sleep in late P.M. Sue to fix Ethel's jacket. Talked to Fitzgerald. *(friend)*

Saturday August 18

Warm Over to Sue's for lobster dinner. Very enjoyable. Dick and Sue danced. Watched Burn & Schrieber (T.V.) Seemed good to have a little fun, made a good change for Ethel and me. Played Irish records.

Sunday August 19

Warm not so humid. E to 12:00 Later to watch children swim by Bill. Sick today. Bill and Eileen leaving for Nantucket tomorrow.

Monday August 20

Nice day. 75 Not so humid. Ethel drove car by herself. Ate very lightly today. Stomach fair. Ethel and I went MBC on porch after supper. Finished roll of film. "Susan Ann" seems ok.

Tuesday August 21

Warm. Dr. 10:15 EKG and chest x-ray. Told her I've been short of breath.1 1/2 cytoxan, 1 1/2 lamoxin, 2-2-2 prednisone, 4 tbls KCl 3 Mol Iron

Sue's for lunch. Ethel and Sue shopping. Ethel bought 2 bathing suits.

Wednesday August 22

75 warm, breeze not humid. Down street. waited while Ethel got my medicine and left film on Broad St. bought new roll. Had baked ham supper. Stomach's fair.

Thursday August 23

Nice day low humidity. To Sears - Ethel bought some clothes. Visited Grandma.B. Sue visited Muriel Hull today at Yardley, Pa.*(teacher friend from RBCH)* Stomach better today. Fast for blood samples.

Friday August 24

Nice cool day. Hosp. blood samples. Ethel drove car over to Sue's with me. They did some shopping. Had hot dogs grilled for lunch. Sue and I went crabbing, 6 crabs, 1 1/2 hrs. Ethel and Sue took Ritchie and had dip in pool. Home by 6:00P.M. Quite a day. Had flounder for supper. Was tired but feel good.

Saturday August 25

Weather nice. Went Pouior to fix car. Jim in Spain. They put in fuse. Ethel had crab cakes supper. Good but stomach not so hot. Bill back safely from Nantucket. Brought record of sea shanties, good record. Ethel and I watched Burns and Schieber. Ethel tired tonite. Baked ginger cookies.

Sunday August 26

Humid had air conditioner on. Sick 4:00A.M. Short breath. Mama stayed home. Was upstairs all day. chest hurt. Bill took Anthony, Michael and their mother ,Roseann, sailing. Piece of hardware from trailer came off but didn't lose it. Bill got stung by wasps now under trailer. They had 2 hr. sail. Bill brought Ethel a big crenshaw melon. Bill put sails and gear in Chev.

Monday August 27

Very hot 90+ humid

Stayed in. Bill got sleeping bag. 2 air mattresses. Portable stove going to Slaine State Park. We slept in Tues and I cancelled Dr's appt for Tuesday. too hot and humid. Showed some slides.

Tuesday August 28

Hot 93+ humidity. Stayed in house. Sue called about pool but too hot to leave house. Tomorrow supposed to be the same. Talked to Fitzgerald and Harry on phone. Harry took down a tree on his property and got hurt.

Doctor said keep same medication.

Wednesday August 29

95 Humid

Stayed in. Bill phoned -back from state park. Kiddies caught fish. Stomach fair, very weak. Ethel wrote checks deposited 1K savings. Paid book of months. Renewed *Modern Maturity* 3 yrs. Sent Riverview Aetna forms and paid $16 cash hospital phone bill.

Thursday August 30

90 and humid 9:15 Dr. Went to Sue's afterward. Sue and Ethel swim. Paid bills. Bill stopped and returned clippers, bag -air mattress. Said he fixed traveler on boat. Bill brought TV set back. Ethel gave him a

check. I slept downstairs.

Friday August 31

Humid 93 Both stayed in all day. Weather supposed to continue hot until Tuesday. Stomach fair. Received notice Medicare paid. Dr. Brodsky 8:20. State Police check came.

Saturday September 1

Hot humid. Cashed SP check after long stand at bank. Hair cut, picked up slides- stayed in rest of day. Sue and Dick left Ritchie in P.M. while they went to Love Lane's for dinner jacket. Came back had drink. Social Security checks came today. Chicken salad supper. Felt better today. Slides good, 2 good sunset shots at Boat club

Sunday September 2

Very hot humid. I got paper and coffee ring. Ethel drove to church. 4:30 Bill picked us up. Very hot on patio. Dick and Sue brought us home 9:00P.M.

Monday September 3

Hot. In all day. Good sleep in P.M. E kept Ritchie -Sue and Dick to movie in evening. Stomach good today. Gave Sue rest of coffee ring. Weather to be hot rest of week.

Tuesday September 4

Very hot humid. Fast -hospital 8:30A.M. Blood samples (3) Stayed in all day. This hot weather supposed to last all week. Received $35 from Aetna for Dr. Sue has my roll of film. Staying in all day with air-conditioner running getting tedious but we're grateful they are working. Wykoff checked furnace. Got in some beer from Sanders. Stomach fair. Trots.

Wednesday September 5

Very hot -humid. In all day. Ethel walked down town. Stomach fair. Receivedd *Yachting mag.*

Talked to Al Bramble on phone. I said he could sail "Susan Ann" if he wished. He has been out about 3 times in his Comet. Ethel cashed our Social Security check.

Thursday September 6

Hot humid shower. Doctor 10:30 Dr. said potassium should be Tablespoon (4) daily. I checked bottle and it said <u>Teaspoons.</u> Got her to stretch next visit 10 days. Went to Sue's. She and Ethel got groceries. Good fresh corn and flounder for supper. Weather to break tomorrow. Stomach seems O.K. tonite.

Friday September 7

Pleasant nice breeze - not so hot or humid. Ethel-Sue-Ritchie and I went to Bass river. Took lunch and stove. Very nice day. Ethel and Sue did all the lugging. Ritchie had real good time. Very good. Ethel and I had fresh corn for supper & tomatoes. In bed 7:30P.M. I'm tired but feel good. I drove down. Sue drove back. Ethel and Sue had a nice swim.

Saturday September 8

Tired slept downstairs. Visited Grandma B 3:00P.M.

Sunday September 9

Cool Nice day was supposed to sail but no one showed. Ethel and I had a good turkey dinner.5 P.M. down boat club nice sunset. Bill Weintraub called.

Monday September 10

Cool nice day. Down bank-inventory of safety deposit box. Took out Mature Savings certificate. Take to Monmouth Savings and Loan on 27th. Put in box Mainstay certificate. Sue brought over more of Ritchie's clothes. Stayed for lunch. E bought me sox. Had more good turkey for supper.

Tuesday September 11

Nice day warmer than yesterday. Dentist 1:30 fillings (poor job) Took slide to photo 5x7 matte. Sue and Dick brought Ritchie. They are leaving for Bahamas early in morning. Bill stopped by also. ...4 words can't read.. Down MBC

Wednesday September 12

Weather nice. Slept down stairs. Ritchie good

Thursday September 13

Weather nice   ?

Friday September 14

Weather mild. Sick nauseous did not go to hospital for blood samples. Ritchie good. I slept in P.M. had very bad nite could not sleep

Saturday September 15

Weather o'cast, some sun mild. Sick but better than Fri. Hospital wouldn't take blood on Sat. Ritchie sure good baby. Fixed T.V. hearing card.

Sunday September 16

Weather nice, some clouds. Sue and Dick picked up Ritchie. Dick took Ethel to church and brought her back. Gave Ethel very lovely jewelry. Bill had boat out for short time. Sue going to take me to Dr's. Very weak today. Had bath then sound sleep 1:00A.M. not sleepy. Watched T.V. movie.

Monday September 17

Doctor. Gave me prescription for nausea. See her Thurs. told her how weak. Sue took me to get pills. Average myeloma patient life span from discovery 1 to 4 years.

Sue, Joan - sailed 3:00 P.M. was so considerate of Joan. lst time in boat.

Tues.September 18

Rain.

Wednesday September 19

Cool Weather. Very weak today. Bowels and nausea

Thursday September 20

Nice Weather 1:00 Doctor. Sue took me. EKG, Haemoglobin up. Return to 1 1/2 cytoxin and rest of pills. Increase nausea to 3 per day. Sue stayed around relaxing. Took us to library and Exxon see about fix turn signals in morning. Very tired.

This is the last entry by Sherman. The following entries were made by his daughter after he died and this diary was discovered.

Friday September 21

Bad night couldn't breathe

Saturday September 22

Sherman wanted to go to the hospital. Bill took Daddy to hospital. Talked to Sue on phone in the afternoon 2 or so.

Sunday September 23

Seemed very different, hardly talked, wanted to come home

Monday September 24

Mother talked to Dr. E Heffernan - said heart was bad, could call priest.

Tuesday September 25

SGB called Mother. He wanted to come home. Bill talked to Dr. who said Dad was too sick to come home.

Wednesday September 26

Thursday September 27

Friday September 28

Dad died about 4:30 P.M. Ethel was with him.

APPENDIX 39

DAR 859335   Susan Bassler Pickford for Thomas Sherman

1776   *1890*

THE NATIONAL SOCIETY OF THE

Daughters of the American Revolution

This certifies that

SUSAN BASSLER PICKFORD

is a regularly approved member of the National Society of the Daughters of the American Revolution, having been admitted by the National Board of Management by virtue of her descent from a patriot who with unfailing loyalty served as a sailor, soldier, civil officer, or rendered material aid to the cause of American Independence during the Revolutionary War

this second day of February 2008

National No.	859335
Admitted	*February 2, 2008*
Ancestor	THOMAS SHERMAN
State	*Massachusetts*

Linda Gist Calvin
President General

Joya Harrell Cardinal
Recording Secretary General

Donna Kaye Santillan
Registrar General

APPENDIX 40

Following 3 pages of DAR documents for Thomas Sherman

APPLICATION FOR MEMBERSHIP TO THE NATIONAL SOCIETY
OF THE
DAUGHTERS OF THE AMERICAN REVOLUTION
WASHINGTON, D.C.

State Portland

City Maine

Name of Chapter Elizabeth Wadsworth

National Number 8 5 9 3 3 5   Computer Code Number 1-008ME

Susan   Bassler   Pickford
(First Name)   (Middle and Maiden Name)   (Last Name)

Single ( ) Wife (X) Widow ( ) Divorced ( ) Richard S. Pickford
                                                        (Husband)

Residence 204 Wadleigh Pond Rd   Lyman   ME   04002
          (Number and Street)   (City)   (State) (Zip Code + 4)

Applicant's E-mail address sbpworks@securespeed.us

Registrar's E-mail address RWJOHNSON129@aol.com

Name as you wish it to appear on DAR Certificate Susan Bassler Pickford

Revolutionary Ancestor Thomas Sherman

ELIGIBILITY CLAUSE

"Any woman is eligible for membership in the National Society of the Daughters of the American Revolution who is not less than eighteen years of age, and who is lineally descended from a man or woman who, with unfailing loyalty to the cause of American Independence, served as a sailor, or as a soldier or civil officer in one of the several Colonies or States, or in the United Colonies or States, or as a recognized patriot, or rendered material aid thereto; provided the applicant is personally acceptable to the Society." (Constitution, Article III, Section 1.)

Date of marriage may be substituted for dates of birth and death where such date proves the soldier to have been living during the Revolution and of a suitable age for service. Applicant must provide documentation proving lineal descent for each statement of birth, marriage and death. This shall include a birth certificate naming her parents. Data submitted as proof is subject to DAR standards and interpretation. This applies to "new ancestors" and previously accepted lineage for which documentation was not required at the time of acceptance.

Applicant further says that the said Thomas Sherman (name of ancestor) is her ancestor and that the statements set forth are true to the best of her knowledge and belief.

The applicant also pledges allegiance to the United States of America and agrees to support its Constitution. This applies to applicants for membership within the United States of America and its territories.

Signature of Applicant _____

The following chapter officer attests the signature of the applicant in lieu of a notary.

_____   _____, 20 _____
(Name)   (Chapter Office)

Notarization of applicant's signature, if necessary, may be provided below.

Subscribed and sworn to before me at _____
                                                    (City)   (State)

this _____ day of _____ A.D. _____

Signature of Notary _____

My Commission Expires _____

As chapter officers, the undersigned have examined the completed application of the above applicant and attest her signature.

                                        Chapter Regent _____

App Rec'd By Registrar General _____ Chapter Registrar _____

Endorsement for membership at large by the State Regent _____

Endorsement of member for member by Rebecca C. Johnson _____   National Number 422949

Nominated and recommended by the two undersigned members of the Society in good standing, to whom the applicant is personally known. Endorsers must be of same Chapter; if joining At Large, of the same State.

ENDORSED IN HANDWRITING BY

DAR National Number _____   DAR National Number _____

Name _____   Name _____

Residence _____   Residence _____

Chapter _____   Chapter _____

When filled out and properly endorsed, the application should be sent to the Registrar General, NSDAR, 1776 D Street, NW, Washington, DC 20006–5303, with the necessary fee and dues. When approved by the National Board, a copy will be returned to the Registrar of the Chapter or to the individual, (If Joining At Large. The application, information thereon, and supplemental data become the property of the National Society.

DARAPP 3.1.2 Proof code: (EMP)

LINEAGE

1. (applicant's name) Susan Bassler Pickford _____ declare

I was born on 18 Oct 1941 _____ at Butler, PA _____
(1) married on 10 June 1972 _____ at Red Bank, NJ, Monmouth Cty _____
to Richard S. Pickford _____ born on 07 March 1938 _____
at New York, NY _____ died or divorced _____
(2) married on _____ at _____
to _____ born on _____
at _____ died or divorced _____
(3) married on _____ at _____
to _____ born on _____
at _____ died or divorced _____

I am the daughter of

2. Sherman G. Bassler _____ born 08 Nov 1907 _____ at Zelienople, PA, Butler Cty _____
died at Red Bank, NJ, Monmouth Cty _____ on 28 Sept 1973 _____ and his (1st) wife
Ethel Kerr _____ born 22 Dec 1908 _____ at Greenville, PA
died at Middletown, NJ _____ on 19 Oct 1997 _____ Married - Date 22 Oct1934
                                                                          at Butler, PA

3. The said Sherman G. Bassler _____ was the child of
William G. Bassler _____ born 06 Dec 1854 _____ at Zelienople PA, Butler Cty _____
died at Zelienople PA, Butler Cty _____ on 20 June 1934 _____ and his (1st) wife
Julia E. Sherman _____ born 10 March 1876 _____ at Clinton, MO, Henry Cty
died at Middletown, NJ _____ on 10 Jan 1975 _____ Married - Date 16 July 1902
                                                                          at Pittsburgh, PA

4. The said Julia E. Sherman _____ was the child of
Albert Gallatin Sherman _____ born 23 Jan 1847 _____ at Chazy, NY _____
died at Clinton, MO, Henry Cty _____ on 29 Aug 1934 _____ and his (1st) wife
Laura E. Buckingham _____ born 14 July 1850 _____ at Piqua, OH
died at Clinton, MO, Henry Cty _____ on 11 May 1928 (Obit), 01 May 1928 Married - Date 08 Dec 1870
                                                                          at Clinton, MO, Henry Cty

5. The said Albert Gallatin Sherman _____ was the child of
Albert Gallatin Sherman _____ born 24 May 1814 _____ at Chazy, NY _____
died at Benson, VT, Rutland Cty _____ on 07 Nov 1885 _____ and his (1st) wife
Margaret Honsinger _____ born 11 May 1814 _____ at Alburgh, VT, Franklin Cty
died at Benson, VT, Rutland Cty _____ on 16 Oct 1899 _____ Married - Date 14 Feb 1839
                                                                          at Alburgh, VT, Franklin Cty

6. The said Albert Gallatin Sherman _____ was the child of
Ebenezer Sherman _____ born 04 July 1782 _____ at Brimfield, MA _____
died at Chazy, NY _____ on 04 Oct 1867 _____ and his (1st) wife
Betsey Belding/ Beldon _____ born 1780 _____ at
died at Chazy, NY _____ on 11 Sept 1850 _____ Married - Date 1811
                                                                          at

7. The said Ebenezer Sherman _____ was the child of
Thomas Sherman _____ born 10 Aug 1745 _____ at Brimfield, MA _____
died at Weybridge, VT _____ on 01 April 1828 _____ and his (1st) wife
Zerriah Lumbard _____ born 16 July 1749 _____ at Brimfield, MA
died at Brimfield, MA _____ on 1837 _____ Married - Date 07 March 1771
                                                                          at Brimfield, MA

8. The said _____ was the child of
_____ born _____ at _____
died at _____ on _____ and his (   ) wife
_____ born _____ at _____
died at _____ on _____ Married - Date _____
                                                        at _____

9. The said _____ was the child of
_____ born _____ at _____
died at _____ on _____ and his (   ) wife
_____ born _____ at _____
died at _____ on _____ Married - Date _____
                                                        at _____

10. The said _____ was the child of
_____ born _____ at _____
died at _____ on _____ and his (   ) wife
_____ born _____ at _____
died at _____ on _____ Married - Date _____
                                                        at _____

11. The said _____ was the child of
_____ born _____ at _____
died at _____ on _____ and his (   ) wife
_____ born _____ at _____
died at _____ on _____ Married - Date _____
                                                        at _____

12. The said _____ was the child of
_____ born _____ at _____
died at _____ on _____ and his (   ) wife
_____ born _____ at _____
died at _____ on _____ Married - Date _____
                                                        at _____

13. The said _____ was the child of
_____ born _____ at _____
died at _____ on _____ and his (   ) wife
_____ born _____ at _____
died at _____ on _____ Married - Date _____
                                                        at _____

424   Appendix

REFERENCES FOR LINEAGE

Give below proof for EACH statement of Birth, marriage, Death dates and places and connections between generations from the applicant through the generation of the Revolutionary ancestor. Published authorities should be cited by title, author, date of publication, volume and page. Send ONE certified, attested copy OR photocopy of unpublished data. Give *National Numbers* and relationships of any *close relatives* credited with this ancestor.

1st Gen.   BC for applicant and husband; MC

2nd Gen.   BC for Sherman Bassler and Ethel Kerr
                ML - Sherman Bassler and Ethel Kerr
                Obituary for Sherman Bassler

3rd Gen.   MC Julia E. Sherman and William Bassler; DC Julia E. Bassler;
                 1920 Census - Zelienople, PA; 1880 Census Record - Clinton, MO

4th Gen.   Early Birth Records 1883-1890 Henry Co, MO; DC - Albert G. Sherman, DC (obit) Laura Sherman - Henry County
                Scrapbook, 'The Wars Between the Wars' Vol 1 Daily Democrat 1976; Englewood Cemetary SB-SK Clinton Twp,
                Henry County, Missouri

5th Gen.   1850 census - Chazy, NY; 1880 census - Benson, VT; Obit of Margaret Honsinger-Sherman, 'Annals of Henry County'
                Vol 1 1885-1900, compiled by Kathleen White Miles; Cemetery Inscriptions - Benson Vermont by Margaret R Jenks

6th Gen.   The New England Shermans, by Roy V. Sherman, 1974, p 62; 1880 Census; Burial records for Rural Cemetary West
                Chazy, NY; NSDAR # 200465

7th Gen.   The New England Shermans, p 62
                NSDAR #200465; NSDAR #246062 A338

8th Gen.

9th Gen.

10th Gen.

11th Gen.

12th Gen.

13th Gen.

FAMILY TREES

KERR

1 Patrick Kerr b: Armagh, Armagh, Northern Ireland, d: 1865 New York City
  + Ann Hallagan b: Tyrone, Ireland, d: Ireland
    2 James Kerr b: 01 Aug 1839 County Tyrone, Ireland
      + Mary O'Riley b: County Cavin, Ireland, m: 1863 PA, d: 1902
        3 James Chauncy Kerr b: 14 Jul 1873 Greenville, PA, d: 1961
        Butler PA
          + Roxanna Jaxtheimer b.18 Aug 1877 West Salem Township, PA d. June 1965 Butler, PA
            m. 15 Oct 1902
            4 Robert E. Kerr b: 15 Mar 1906 Greenville, PA, d: 10 Jul 1987 Butler, PA
              + Frieda Cubbeson b: 16 Dec. 1903, d: 4 Sept. 1970, m: Dec. 1925
                5 Robert James Kerr b: 03 Dec 1926 Butler, PA, d: 15 May 1996
                  + Catherine George b: 11 Apr 1924, d: 04 Feb 2002 Butler, PA
                    6 Dennis Richard Kerr b: 10 Mar 1948
                    6 Linda Kerr b: 2 Aug. 1950, m: 21 Aug. 1971
                      + George A Patten II m 21 Aug. 1971
                        7 Kimberly A Patten Popa b: 29 Mar. 1968, m: 25 May 2002
                          + Michael C. Popa b: 30 Dec. 1968
                            8 Cardellina K. Popa b: 7 Sept. 2004
                            8 Gabriel A. Popa b: 15 Jan. 2010
                        7 Kate E. Patten Reynolds b: 4 Jan. 1976, m: 5 Mar. 2005
                          + Jeffrey L. Reynolds b: 4 June 1968
                            8 Maximus Patten Reynolds b: 22 July 2006
                            8 Samson J. Reynolds b: 12 July 2008
                    6 Bruce Kerr b: 10 Feb 1953, m: 17 Sept. 1976
                      + Charlene M. Andre b: 1 March 1955
                        7 Ryan T. Kerr b: 16 July 1982
                        7 Justin R. Kerr b: 18 Sept. 1984
                        7 Jaime E. McGann Kerr b: 22 Nov. 1982, m: 6 Sept. 2014
                            8 Rory P. Kerr b: 15 Aug. 2013
                            8 Henley M. Kerr b: 19 Aug. 2015
                5 William Leroy Kerr b: 28 May 1930 Butler, PA, d: 12 May 1989
                Butler, PA
                5 Patricia Ann Kathleen Kerr b: 06 Apr 1937 m: 13 July 1959
                  + Frank Eugene Pavlic b: 29 Aug 1933

6 Eugene Francis Paul Pavlic b: 15 July 1958, m: 29 June 1984,
d: 16 Oct. 2013

+ Lorna Lee McEwan b: 29 Oct. 1957

7 Angela Thoune Pavlic b: 08 Feb 1975, adopted

8 Tianna b: 06 Jan. 1998

7 Danielle Nicole Pavlic b: 25 Jun 1985

7 Amanda Jean Pavlic b: 20 Aug 1990

8 Mya Nevaeh Jones b: 15 Aug. 2008

5 Thomas Richard Kerr b: 16 Jun 1944, d: 24 Feb. 1994

+ Eileen Young b: 26 Oct. 1944

6 Timothy Kerr adopted

6 Kevin Kerr b: 06 Jul 1976 adopted

6 Mark Kerr b: 21 Mar 1982

4 Ethel Marion Kerr b: 23 Dec 1908   Greenville, PA,
d: 19 Oct 1997   Middletown, NJ

+ Sherman Gilbert Bassler b: 08 Nov 1907   Zelienople, PA, m: 23 Oct
1934   Butler, PA, USA, d: 28 Sep 1973   Red Bank, NJ

5 William Gilbert Bassler b: 06 Mar 1938   Butler, Adams, PA, USA

+ Eileen Schilling b. 23 Jan 1939   Plainfield, NJ m. 10 Sept 1966
Atlantic Highlands,NJ

6 Julia Elizabeth Bassler b: 28 Jul 1967, d: 13 Jun 1997

6 William Gilbert Bassler b: 22 Sep 1968, d: 10 Aug 1990

6 Roseann Bassler b: 30 Apr 1972

+ Del DalPra m: 02 Aug 2000   HI

7 William Del DalPra b: 12 Feb 2002

7 August Del DalPra b: 22 Jul 2004

7 Henry Del DalPra b: 30 Jul 2005

6 Elizabeth Bassler b: 23 Jun 1972

+ Christopher Jannuzzi m: 19 Oct 2001

7 Michael Jannuzzi b: 18 Aug 2003

7 Raymond Jannuzzi b: 19 Oct 2005

7 Julia Jannuzzi b: 22 Feb 2008

5 Susan Bassler b: 18 Oct 1941   Butler, PA

+ Richard S. Pickford b: 07 Mar 1938   New York City, NY, d: 24 Nov 2015
m: 10 Jun 1972   Red Bank, NJ

6 Richard Pickford III b: 05 Nov 1972   Red Bank, NJ

6 John Sherman Pickford b: 02 Nov 1974   Beverly, MA

+ Lisa M. Menard b: 23 Nov 1976   Brunswick, ME, m. 29 Aug 2009
Lyman, ME

7 Lucy Jane Pickford b: 21 Apr 2011   Portland, ME

7 Charles Christopher Pickford b: 17 Jan 2013   Portland, ME

4 Marvin J. Kerr b. 05 Oct 1909 Butler, PA d.3 June 1970 + Henrietta Fogel
b.10 May 1913 d. 25 Sept 1989 m.19 May 1942 Winchester,VA

5 Baby boy died preterm

5 Lawrence James infant death notice Butler Eagle

5 Doreen b. 19 Nov 1951 + Raymond Heitzer b. 24 Jan 1950 m. 11 Aug 1978

    6 Julie b. 9 May 1982 + Christopher Hertz b. 11 Jan 1975 m. 7 Aug 2010

        7 Catie Hertz b. 16 Feb 2014

3 John Kerr

3 Patrick Kerr

3 Harry Kerr

3 Charles E. Kerr

3 Annie Kerr

2 Patrick Kerr

2 son Kerr

2 daughter Kerr

2 daughter Kerr

2 daughter Kerr

2 daughter Kerr

Mary Pavlic, Robert Kerr   (standing)
Eugene Pavlic, Gene, Patricia   (sitting)
Graduation Jan 1976

FAMILY TREES

JAXTHEIMER

1 Amos Jaxtheimer b. 1806 d. 1871 + Uta Christman

    2 William Jaxtheimer b. 1831 d. 1922 + Hannah Fell b. 31 May 1823 West Salem Twnship, PA d. 02 Dec 1900

        3 William F. Jaxtheimer b. 15 Jul 1856 West Salem Twnship,PA d.1932
        m.Katherine Wiand b. 1857 Mercer Co.,PA m. 27 Dec 1876 d.1930

            4 Roxanna Jaxtheimer b. 18 Aug 1877 West Salem Twnship, PA d. June 1965 Butler, PA + James C. Kerr b. 14 July 1873 Greenville, PA d. 1961 Butler,PA m.15 Oct 1902 Greenville,Pa

                5 Robert E. Kerr b: 15 Mar 1906 Greenville, PA, d: 10 Jul 1987 Butler, PA + Frieda Cubbeson b.16 Dec d. 4 Sept 1970 m. Dec 1925

                        7 Linda Kerr b. 2 Aug1950 m. 21 Aug 1971

                        7 Bruce Kerr b. 10 Feb 1953 + Charlene M. Andre b. 1 March 1955 m. 17 Sept.1976

              6 Robert Janes Kerr b: 03 Dec 1926 Butler, PA, d: 15 May 1996 + Catherine George b: 11 Apr 1924, d: 04 Feb 2002 Butler, PA

                        7 Dennis Kerr b: 10 Mar 1948

                        7 Linda Kerr

                        7 Bruce Kerr

              6 William Leroy Kerr b: 28 May 1930 Butler, PA, d: 12 May 1989 Butler, PA

              6 Patricia Ann Kathleen Kerr b. 06 Apr 1937 +Frank Eugene Pavlic b. 29 Aug 1933 m 13 July 1959

                        7 Frank Eugene Pavlic b.15 July 1958 d. 16 Oct 2013 + Lorna Lee McEwan b. 29 Oct 1957

                                8 Angela Thoune Pavlic b.08 Feb 1975

                                8 Danielle Nicole Pavlic b. 25 Jun 1985

                                8 Amanda Jean Pavlic b. 20 Aug 1990

              6 Thomas Richard Kerr b. 16 June 1944 d.24 Feb. 1994 + Eileen Young b. 26 Oct 1944

                        7 Timothy Kerr

                        7 Kevin Kerr b. 06 Jul 1976

                        7 Mark Kerr b. 21 Mar 1982

                5 Ethel Marion Kerr b: 23 Dec 1908 Greenville, PA, d: 19 Oct 1997 Middletown, NJ

                + Sherman Gilbert Bassler b: 08 Nov 1907 Zelienople, PA, m: 23 Oct 1934 Butler, Adams, PA, USA, d: 28 Sep 1973

Red Bank, NJ

    6 William Gilbert Bassler b. 06 Mar 1938 Butler, PA

       + Eileen Schilling b. 23 Jan 1939 Plainfield, NJ m. 10 Sept 1966
Atlantic Highlands, NJ

          7 Julia Elizabeth Bassler b: 28 Jul 1967, d: 13 Jun 1997

          7 William Gilbert Bassler b: 22 Sep 1968, d: 10 Aug 1990

          7 Roseann Bassler b: 30 Apr 1972

             + Del DalPra m: 02 Aug 2000 HI

                8 William Del DalPra b: 12 Feb 2002

                8 August Del DalPra b: 22 Jul 2004

                8 Henry Del DalPra b: 30 Jul 2005

          7 Elizabeth Bassler b: 23 Jun 1972

             + Christopher Jannuzzi m: 19 Oct 2001

                8 Michael Jannuzzi b: 18 Aug 2003

                8 Raymond Jannuzzi b: 19 Oct 2005

                8 Julia Jannuzzi b: 22 Feb 2008

    6 Susan Bassler b.18 Oct 1941 Butler,PA

      + Richard Pickford, Jr. b. 07 Mar 1938 New York, NY d. 24 Nov. 2015
m. 10 Jun 1972

          7 Richard Pickford III b: 05 Nov 1972 Red Bank, NJ

          7 John Sherman Pickford b: 02 Nov 1974 Beverly, MA

             + Lisa M. Menard b. 23 Nov 1976 Brunswick, ME m. 29 Aug 2009
Lyman, ME

                8 Lucy Jane Pickford b: 21 Apr 2011 Portland, ME

                8 Charles Christopher Pickford b: 17 Jan 2013 Portland, ME

  5 Marvin J. Kerr b. 05 Oct 1909 Butler, PA d.3 June 1970

   + Henrietta Fogel b.10 May 1913 d. 25 Sept 1989 m.19 May 1942
Winchester, VA

    6 Baby boy died preterm

    6 Lawrence James infant death notice Butler Eagle

    6 Doreen b.19 Nov 1951 + Raymond Heitzer b.24 Jan 1950 m. 11 Aug 1978

         7 Julie b.9 May 1982 + Christopher Hertz b. 11 Jan 1975 m. 7 Aug 2010

            8 Catie Hertz b. 16 Feb 2014

4 John M b: 1875, d: 1944

4 William R

4 Mary (Mame)

4 Hannah

4 Katherine

4 Elvira F

FAMILY TREES

HONSINGER

Johannes Honsinger arrived on *Robert and Alice* 11 Sept 1733

1 Johannes Michael Honsinger
  + Maria Christine Hilfenstein
  2 Johann Frederick Honsinger
    + Rachel Walker
      3 Philip Honsinger b: Dartmouth, MA, d: 12 Jan 1830 Alburg, VT
        + Lucretia Deuel Honsinger b: 23 Aug 1779 Alburg, VT, d: 11 Dec 1867 Benson, VT
          4 Margaret Dueul Honsinger b: 1814 Alburg, VT, d: 16 Oct 1899 Benson, VT
            + Albert Galiton Sherman Sr. b: 1814 Chazy, NY, m: 14 Feb 1839, d: 1885 Benson, VT
              5 Albert G. Sherman, Jr b: 23 Jan 1847 Chazy, NY, d: 20 Aug 1934 Clinton, MO
                + Laura E. Buckingham b: 14 Jul 1850 Piqua, OH, m: 08 Dec 1879 Clinton, MO, d: 07 May 1928 Clinton, MO
                  6 Julia E. Sherman b: 09 Mar 1876 Clinton, MO, d: 10 Jan 1975 Middletown, NJ
                    + William Gottlieb Bassler b: 06 Dec 1855 Zelienople, PA, m: 16 Jul 1902 Pittsburg, PA, d: 29 Jun 1934 Zelienople, PA
                      7 Sherman Gilbert Bassler b: 08 Nov 1907 Zelienople, PA, d: 28 Sep 1973 Red Bank, NJ
                        + Ethel Marion Kerr b: 23 Dec 1908 Greenville, PA, m: 23 Oct 1934 Butler, PA, d: 19 Oct 1997 Middletown, NJ
                          8 William Gilbert Bassler b: 06 Mar 1938 Butler, Adams, PA, USA
                            + Eileen Schilling b. 23 Jan 1939 Plainfield, NJ m. 10 Sept 1966 Atlantic Highlands, NJ
                              9 Julia Elizabeth Bassler b: 28 Jul 1967, d: 13 Jun 1997
                              9 William Gilbert Bassler b: 22 Sep 1968, d: 10 Aug 1990
                              9 Roseann Bassler b: 30 Apr 1972
                                + Del DalPra m: 02 Aug 2000 HI
                                  10 William Del DalPra b: 12 Feb 2002
                                  10 August Del DalPra b: 22 Jul 2004
                                  10 Henry Del DalPra b: 30 Jul 2005
                              9 Elizabeth Bassler b: 23 Jun 1972
                                + Christopher Jannuzzi m: 19 Oct 2001
                                  10 Michael Jannuzzi b: 18 Aug 2003

10 Raymond Jannuzzi b: 19 Oct 2005

10 Julia Jannuzzi b: 22 Feb 2008

8 Susan Bassler b: 18 Oct 1941 Butler, PA
+ Richard S. Pickford b: 07 Mar 1938 New York City, NY,
d: 24 Nov. 2015 m: 10 Jun 1972 Red Bank, NJ

9 Richard Pickford III b: 05 Nov 1972 Red Bank, NJ

9 John Sherman Pickford b: 02 Nov 1974 Beverly, MA
+ Lisa M. Menard b: 23 Nov 1976 Brunswick, ME,
m. 29 Aug 2009 Lyman, ME

10 Lucy Jane Pickford b: 21 Apr 2011 Portland, ME

10 Charles Christopher Pickford b: 17 Jan 2013 in
Portland, ME

6 Mary Parsons Sherman b.10 Nov 1872 Clinton, MO d. 16 Dec. 1950
Clinton, MO

6 Albert[3] Gilbert Sherman b.1878 Clinton, MO d. 1934 Clinton, MO

6 John Larkin Sherman b. 1871 Clinton, MO d. 23 Nov 1902

6 Wilbur Sherman b.1885 Clinton, MO d. 4 May 1885 Clinton, MO

6 Eva Bell Sherman b. 20 July 1886 d. July 1974 m. Padfield
m. Cowman no children

6 Carl[1] Buckingham Sherman b: 25 Nov 1889 Clinton, MO d.18 Jan 1988
+ Katherine Markley b.7 Nov 1893 d.11 Oct 1988 m. 22 Nov 1919
Clinton, MO

7 Carl[2] Markley b. 10 Dec 1920 Clinton, MO d. 30 Dec 2014
+ Hazel Lucille Minor b 7 Sept 1921 d 3 March 2002 m 19 April 1941

8 Don b 2 Dec 1947 + Nancy Hodina b 25 Feb 1949
m 24 Jan 1970

9 Laura Eliza b 13 Dec 1973 + Paul McGeary 2 Aug 1969
m 24 April 2004

10 Charlotte Lucille b 23 May 2006

10 William Sherman b 19 Sept 2011

9 Mary Katherine b 28 March 1978 + Christopher D. Wilson
m 24 July 2004

10 Chase Christopher b 22 April 2008

10 Cora Lucille b 6 Sept 2014

8 Sharon b

6 Clara Wells Sherman b: 05 Jul 1889 Chazy, NY
+ Floyd Wallace m: 01 Sep 1914

7 Hershel Lee Wallace Wallace

7 Waneta Ruth Wallace b: 02 Feb 1923
+ Shobe Smith

8 Mark

8 Connie

8 Lowell

      6 Laura Evans Sherman b:21 April 1874 d: 09 Jun 1901
        + Corey W. Padfield

         7 Muhrl Padfield b. 28 Apr 1900

    5 Elvira Sherman b: 1840 Chazy, NY
     + Franklin Walker

    5 Julia Sherman b: 1842 Chazy, NY

    5 Margaret Sherman b: 1844 Chazy, NY, d: 1917 Benson,VT
     + Edwin Walker

    5 Sophia Sherman b: 1850

    5 Eva Bell Sherman b: 1860, d: 1864

    5 Ellen Sherman

    5 Ebenezer Sherman + Maude

4 Julia

4 Adaline Deuel + Asa Clark

FAMILY TREES

GEORGE SOULE
Mayflower passenger

1 George Soule b: 09 Feb 1593 Worcestershire, England, d: 22 Jan 1680 Duxbury, MA

  2 George Soule Jr b: 1639, d: 12 May 1704 Dartmouth, MA

    3 Mary Soule b: 1673 Dartmouth, MA, d: 17 Jun 1729
      + Capt.Joseph Devol b: 15 Dec 1703, d: 1782

      4 Joseph Deuel,Jr. b: 15 Dec 1703, d: 1782
        + Elizabeth Sherman

        5 Philip Deuel b: 1727, d: 1812
          + Elizabeth Sherman

          6 Michael Deuel b: 1750 Dartmouth, MA, d: 12 Jan 1830 Alburg,VT
            + Elce Slocum b: 1753, d: 12 Jan 1830 Alburg,VT

            7 Lucretia Deuel b: 23 Aug 1779 Alburg,VT, d: 11 Dec 1867 Benson,VT
              + Philip Honsinger b: Dartmouth, MA, d: 12 Jan 1830 Alburg,VT

              8 Margaret Deuel Honsinger b: 1814 Alburg,VT, d: 16 Oct 1899 Benson,VT
                + Albert Galiiton Sherman Sr. b: 1814 Chazy, NY, m: 14 Feb 1839, d: 1885 Benson,VT

                9 Albert G. Sherman,Jr. b: 23 Jan 1847 Chazy, NY, d: 20 Aug 1934 Clinton, MO
                  + Laura E. Buckingham b: 14 Jul 1850 Piqua,OH, m: 08 Dec 1879 Clinton, MO, d: 07 May 1928 Clinton, MO

                  10 Julia E. Sherman b: 09 Mar 1876 Clinton, MO, d: 10 Jan 1975 Middletown, NJ
                    + William Gottlieb Bassler b: 06 Dec 1855 Zelienople, PA, m: 16 Jul 1902 Pittsburg, PA, d: 29 Jun 1934 Zelienople, PA

                    11 Sherman Gilbert Bassler b: 08 Nov 1907 Zelienople, PA, d: 28 Sep 1973 Red Bank, NJ
                      + Ethel Marion Kerr b: 23 Dec 1908 Greenville, PA, m: 23 Oct 1934 Butler, Adams, PA, USA, d: 19 Oct 1997 Middletown, NJ

                      12 William Gilbert Bassler b: 06 Mar 1938 Butler, Adams, PA, USA
                        + Eileen Schilling

        13 Julia Elizabeth Bassler b: 28 Jul 1967, d: 13 Jun 1997

        13 William Gilbert Bassler b: 22 Sep 1968, d: 10 Aug 1990

        13 Roseann Bassler b: 30 Apr 1972
        + Del DalPra m: 02 Aug 2000 HI

          14 William Del DalPra b: 12 Feb 2002

          14 August Del DalPra b: 22 Jul 2004

          14 Henry Del DalPra b: 30 Jul 2005

        13 Elizabeth Bassler b: 23 Jun 1972
        + Christopher Jannuzzi m: 19 Oct 2001

          14 Michael Jannuzzi b: 18 Aug 2003

        13 Raymond Jannuzzi b: 19 Oct 2005

        13 Julia Jannuzzi b: 22 Feb 2008

      12 Susan Bassler b: 18 Oct 1941 Butler, PA
      + Richard S. Pickford b: 07 Mar 1938 New York City, NY, m: 10 Jun 1972 Red Bank, NJ, d: 24 Nov 2015

        13 Richard Pickford III b: 05 Nov 1972 Red Bank, NJ

        13 John Sherman Pickford b: 02 Nov 1974 Beverly, MA
        + Lisa M. Menard b: 23 Nov 1976 Brunswick, ME, m. 29 Aug 2009 Lyman, ME

          14 Lucy Jane Pickford b: 21 Apr 2011 Portland, ME

          14 Charles Christopher Pickford b: 17 Jan 2013 Portland, ME

    10 Mary Parsons Sherman

    10 Albert Gilbert Sherman

    10 John Larkin Sherman

    10 Wilbur Sherman

    10 Eva Belle Sherman
    + Corey W.Padfield

9 Murhl Padfield b: 28 Apr 1900

    10 Carl Buckingham Sherman b: 25 Nov 1889 Clinton, MO
    + Katherine Markley m: 22 Nov 1919 in Clinton, MO

    10 Clara Wells Sherman b: 05 Jul 1889 Chazy, NY
    + Floyd Wallace m: 01 Sep 1914

9 Hershel Lee Wallace Wallace

9 Waneta Ruth Wallace b: 02 Feb 1923
+ Shobe Smith

> **10** Laura Sherman d: 09 Jun 1901
>   + Corey W. Padfield

9 Elvira Sherman b: 1840 Chazy, NY
   + Franklin Walker

9 Julia Sherman b: 1842 Chazy, NY

9 Margaret Sherman b: 1844 Chazy, NY, d: 1917
   Benson, VT
   + Edwin Walker

9 Sophia Sherman b: 1850

9 Eva Bell Sherman b: 1860, d: 1864

9 Ellen Sherman

9 Ebenezer Sherman + Maude

8 Julia

8 Adaline Deuel + Asa Clark

FAMILY TREES

BUCKINGHAM

1 John L. Buckingham b: 23 Jul 1815 Baltimore, Maryland, d: 04 Jan 1895 Clinton, MO
+ Susannah Margaret Gilbert b: Gettysburg, PA, m: 10 Oct 1837 Gettysburg, PA,
d: 06 Apr 1904 Clinton, MO

　　2 Jesse Buckingham b: Abt. 1838

　　　+ Eliza A. Clark m: 1847

　　2 Anna E. Buckingham

　　　+ Zenus E. Condit

　　2 Thomas Benton Buckingham b: 24 Jun 1844, d: 02 Jun 1934 Iola, Kansas

　　2 William R. Buckingham b: 04 Aug 1846, d: 12 Feb 1928 Danville, Illinois

　　2 Clara Jane Buckingham b: Jun 1848

　　　+ William D. Kreamer

　　2 Laura E. Buckingham b: 14 Jul 1850 Piqua,OH, d: 07 May 1928 Clinton, MO

　　　+ Albert G. Sherman, Jr b: 23 Jan 1847 Chazy, NY, m: 08 Dec 1879 Clinton, MO,
　　　d: 20 Aug. 1934 Clinton, MO

　　　　3 Julia E. Sherman b: 09 Mar 1876 Clinton, MO, d: Jan 10 1975
　　　　Middletown, NJ

　　　　　+ William Gottlieb Bassler b: 06 Dec 1855 Zelienople, PA, m: 16 Jul 1902
　　　　　Pittsburg, PA, d: 29 Jun 1934 Zelienople, PA

　　　　　　4 Sherman Gilbert Bassler b: 08 Nov 1907 Zelienople, PA, d: 28 Sep 1973
　　　　　　Red Bank, NJ
　　　　　　+ Ethel Marion Kerr b: 23 Dec 1908 Greenville, PA,
　　　　　　m: 23 Oct 1934 Butler, Adams, PA, USA, d: 19 Oct 1997
　　　　　　Middletown, NJ

　　　　　　　5 William Gilbert Bassler b: 06 Mar 1938 Butler, Adams,
　　　　　　　PA, USA
　　　　　　　+ Eileen Schilling

　　　　　　　　6 Julia Elizabeth Bassler b: 28 Jul 1967, d: 13 Jun 1997

　　　　　　　　6 William Gilbert Bassler b: 22 Sep 1968, d: 10 Aug 1990

　　　　　　　　6 Roseann Bassler b: 30 Apr 1972
　　　　　　　　　+ Del DalPra m: 02 Aug 2000 HI

　　　　　　　　　　7 William Del DalPra b: 12 Feb 2002

　　　　　　　　　　7 August Del DalPra b: 22 Jul 2004

　　　　　　　　　　7 Henry Del DalPra b: 30 Jul 2005

　　　　　　　　6 Elizabeth Bassler b: 23 Jun 1972
　　　　　　　　　+ Christopher Jannuzzi m: 19 Oct 2001

　　　　　　　　　　7 Michael Jannuzzi b: 18 Aug 2003

　　　　　　　　　　7 Raymond Jannuzzi b: 19 Oct 2005

　　　　　　　　　　7 Julia Jannuzzi b: 22 Feb 2008

    5 Susan Bassler b: 18 Oct 1941 Butler, PA
     + Richard S. Pickford b: 07 Mar 1938 New York City, NY,
     m: 10 Jun 1972 Red Bank, NJ, d: 24 Nov 2015

      6 Richard Pickford III b: 05 Nov 1972 Red Bank, NJ

      6 John Sherman Pickford b: 02 Nov 1974 Beverly, MA
       + Lisa M. Menard b: 23 Nov 1976 Brunswick, ME, m. 29 Aug 2009
       Lyman, ME

        7 Lucy Jane Pickford b: 21 Apr 2011 Portland, ME

        7 Charles Christopher Pickford b: 17 Jan 2013 Portland, ME

3 Mary Parsons Sherman b: 10 Nov. 1871 d 16 Dec.1950 Clinton, MO
maiden schoolteacher

3 Laura^2 Evans b: 21 April 1874-9 d: June 1901+ Cory W. Padfield m: 28 April 1900

  4 Murhl Padfield b.28 Apr 1900

3 Albert 3(Bert) Gilbert b: 6 Dec.1968 d.16 Jun 1969+ Stella b.1881 d. 11 Sept 1969

  4 Margaret Eloise b.8 Apr 1910

3 John Larkin b. 25 Nov 1881 d. 23 Nov 1902 of typhoid fever

3 Wilbur Sherman b. 30 March 1885 d. 30 May 1885

3 Eva Belle Sherman b. 20 July 1886 d.July 1974 + Corey w. Padfield d.1922
+ J.Cowman m.1930

3 Carl 1 Buckingham Sherman b. 25 Nov 1889 Clinton,MO d.18 Jan. 1988 Clinton, MO
+ Katherine Markley b.7 Nov. 1893 d. 11 Oct 1988 m 22 Nov. 1919

  4 Carl^2 Markley. Sherman b.10 Dec 19204.d.30 Dec 2014
  + Hazel Lucille Minor b. 7 Sept 1921 m. 19 April 1941

    5 Don Sherman b. 2 Dec 1947 + Nancy Hodina b. 25 Feb 1949 m. 24 Jan 1970

    5 Sharon

  4 Harold Lee Sherman b.6 Nov 1924 d.26 Oct. 1973 + Peggy Lee Gover b. 29 Oct 1925

    5 Jana Lee b. 5 June 1950 + Tom Correll 23 Dec 1948 m. 24 June 1972

      6 Kimberlee Correll 5 May 1977 + Christopher Scripsick b. 26 Jan 1972
      m. 11 June 1999

        7 Ali Lyn b. 2 Nov 2004

        7 Ava Marie Scripsick 16 June 2006

        7 Aubrey Lee Scripsick 28 Sept 2010

      6 Kelly Lynn Correll b. 2 De. 1979

    5 Keith b. 1 Sept 1953+ Lupe Marquez Pollard b. 1 July 1952 m. 20 June 1981

3 Clara Wells Sherman b. 05 Jul 1889 Clinton MO d. 1985 + Floyd Wallace m.01 Sept 1914

  4 Hershel Lee Wallace 07 Nov 1916

  4 Howard

  4 Waneta Ruth Wallace b. 2 Feb 1923 + Shobe Smith

    5 Connie

    5 Mark

    5 Lowell

  4 Wayne Sherman Wallace 9 Dec 1932

FAMILY TREES

GILBERT

1 Wendel Gilbert b: 22 Dec 1677   Hoffenheim, Germany, d:27 Jul 1742   Hoffenheim, Germany
+ Eva Margaretha Greyas b: 1698   Hoffenheim, Germany, d: 18 Feb 1735   Hoffenheim, Germany

  2 Barnhard Gilbert b: 05 Sep 1724   Hoffenheim, Germany, d: 30 Nov 1802   Straban, Adams, PA
  + Catherine Bender b: 1728   Palatinate,Germany, m: 1752

    3 George b: 1786, d: 1868 + Elizabeth

      4 Barnhard Gilbert + Susannah Gilbert b: 1756, d: 1831

        5 Elizabeth Catherine Gilbert b: 18 May 1820   Gettysburg, PA, d: 11 Jun 1908 Zelienople, PA
        + Gottlieb W Bassler b: 10 Dec 1813   Loganthal,Switzerland, d: 03 Oct 1868   Pittsburg, PA m: 31 Oct 1844   Athens,Tennesee

          6 William Gottlieb Bassler b: 06 Dec 1855   Zelienople, PA, d: 29 Jun 1934   Zelienople, PA
          + Julia E. Sherman b: 09 Mar 1876   Clinton, MO d: Jan 10 1975 Middletown, NJ m: 16 Jul 1902   Pittsburg, PA,

            7 Sherman Gilbert Bassler b: 08 Nov 1907   Zelienople, PA, d: 28 Sep 1973   Red Bank, NJ
            + Ethel Marion Kerr b: 23 Dec 1908   Greenville, PA, m: 23 Oct 1934   Butler, PA, USA, d: 19 Oct 1997 Middletown, NJ

              8 William Gilbert Bassler b: 06 Mar 1938   Butler, Adams, PA, USA
              + Eileen Schilling

                9 Julia Elizabeth Bassler b: 28 Jul 1967, d: 13 Jun 1997

                9 William Gilbert Bassler b: 22 Sep 1968, d: 10 Aug 1990

                9 Roseann Bassler b: 30 Apr 1972
                + Del DalPra m: 02 Aug 2000   HI

                  10 William Del DalPra b: 12 Feb 2002

                  10 August Del DalPra b: 22 Jul 2004

                  10 Henry Del DalPra b: 30 Jul 2005

                9 Elizabeth Bassler b: 23 Jun 1972
                + Christopher Jannuzzi m: 19 Oct 2001

                  10 Michael Jannuzzi b: 18 Aug 2003

                  10 Raymond Jannuzzi b: 19 Oct 2005

                  10 Julia Jannuzzi b: 22 Feb 2008

              8 Susan Bassler b: 18 Oct 1941   Butler, PA
              + Richard S. Pickford b: 07 Mar 1938   New York City,

NY, m: 10 Jun 1972   Red Bank, NJ, d: 24 Nov 2015

   9 Richard Pickford III b: 05 Nov 1972   Red Bank, NJ

   9 John Sherman Pickford b: 02 Nov 1974   Beverly, MA
+ Lisa M. Menard b: 23 Nov 1976   Brunswick, ME,
m. 29 Aug 2009 Lyman, ME

     10 Lucy Jane Pickford b: 21 Apr 2011   Portland, ME

     10 Charles Christopher Pickford b: 17 Jan 2013
Portland, ME

6 Susanah Bassler

6 Louisa Dill Bassler b: 09 Apr 1848   Zelienople, PA, d: 21 Mar
1859   Zelienople, PA

6 Francis Bassler b: Zelienople, PA, d: 25 Mar 1854   Zelienople,
Butler, PA,

6 Mary Atlee Bassler b: 24 Nov 1852   Zelienople, PA, d: 05 Dec
1868   Zelienople, PA

6 Augustus Herman Bassler b: 28 Sep 1858   Zelienople, PA,
d: 11 Apr 1859   Zelienople, PA

6 Anna Elizabeth Bassler b: 16 Apr 1861   Zelienople, PA, d: 26 Feb
1862   Zelienople, PA

5 Delilah

5 Susannah Margaret Gilbert b: Gettysburg, PA, d: 06 Apr 1904
Clinton, MO
+ John L. Buckingham b: 23 Jul 1815   Baltimore, MD,
m: 10 Oct 1837   Gettysburg, PA, d: 04 Jan 1895   Clinton, MO

  6 Jesse Buckingham b: Abt. 1838
+ Eliza A. Clark m: 1847

  6 Anna E. Buckingham
+ Zenus E. Condit

  6 Thomas Benton Buckingham b: 24 Jun 1844, d: 02 Jun 1934
Iola, KS

  6 William R. Buckingham b: 04 Aug 1846, d: 12 Feb 1928
Danville, IL

  6 Clara Jane Buckingham b: Jun 1848
+ William D. Kreamer

  6 Laura E. Buckingham b: 14 Jul 1850   Piqua,OH, d: 07 May 1928
Clinton, MO
+ Jr Albert G. Sherman b: 23 Jan 1847   Chazy, NY, m: 08 Dec
1879   Clinton, MO, d: 20 Aug 1934   Clinton, MO

    7 Julia E. Sherman b: 09 Mar 1876   Clinton, MO,
d: 10 Jan 1975   Middletown, NJ
+ William Gottlieb Bassler b: 06 Dec 1855   Zelienople, PA,
m: 16 Jul 1902   Pittsburg, PA, d: 29 Jun 1934   Zelienople, PA

      8 Sherman Gilbert Bassler b: 08 Nov 1907   Zelienople, PA,
d: 28 Sep 1973   Red Bank, NJ

+ Ethel Marion Kerr b: 23 Dec 1908   Greenville, PA,
m: 23 Oct 1934   Butler, Adams, PA, USA, d: 19 Oct 1997
Middletown, NJ

  9 William Gilbert Bassler b: 06 Mar 1938   Butler,
Adams, PA, USA
+ Eileen Schilling b. 23 Jan 1939 Plainfield, NJ
m. 10 Sept 1966 Atlantic Highlands,NJ

    10 Julia Elizabeth Bassler b: 28 Jul 1967, d: 13 Jun 1997

    10 William Gilbert Bassler b: 22 Sep 1968,
d: 10 Aug 1990

    10 Roseann Bassler b: 30 Apr 1972
+ Del DalPra m: 02 Aug 2000   HI

      11 William Del DalPra b: 12 Feb 2002

      11 August Del DalPra b: 22 Jul 2004

      11 Henry Del DalPra b: 30 Jul 2005

    10 Elizabeth Bassler b: 23 Jun 1972
+ Christopher Jannuzzi m: 19 Oct 2001

      11 Michael Jannuzzi b: 18 Aug 2003

      11 Raymond Jannuzzi b: 19 Oct 2005

      11 Julia Jannuzzi b: 22 Feb 2008

  9 Susan Bassler b: 18 Oct 1941   Butler, PA
+ Richard S. Pickford b: 07 Mar 1938   New York City, NY,
m: 10 Jun 1972   Red Bank, NJ, d: 24 Nov 2015

    10 Richard Pickford III b: 05 Nov 1972   Red Bank, NJ

    10 John Sherman Pickford b: 02 Nov 1974
Beverly, MA
+ Lisa M. Menard b: 23 Nov 1976   Brunswick, ME,
m. 29 Aug 2009 Lyman, ME

      11 Lucy Jane Pickford b: 21 Apr 2011
Portland, ME

      11 Charles Christopher Pickford b: 17 Jan 2013
Portland, ME

7 Mary Parsons Sherman

7 Albert Gilbert Sherman

7 John Larkin Sherman

7 Wilbut Sherman

7 Eva Belle Sherman + Corey W. Padfield

  8 Murhl Padfield b: 28 Apr 1900

7 Carl Buckingham Sherman b: 25 Nov 1889   Clinton, MO
+ Katherine Markley m: 22 Nov 1919   Clinton, MO

7 Clara Wells Sherman b: 05 Jul 1889   Chazy, NY
+ Floyd Wallace m: 01 Sep 1914

  8 Hershel Lee Wallace Wallace

8 Waneta Ruth Wallace b: 02 Feb 1923
+ Shobe Smith

7 Laura Sherman d: 09 Jun 1901
+ Corey W. Padfield

8 Muhrl Padfield

5 Elizabeth Catherine Gilbert b: Gettysburg, PA
+ Rev. Gottlieb W. Bassler

5 John Bernard Gilbert

5 MaryAnn Gilbert
+ Rev. George Parson

5 Benjamin Franklin Gilbert

5 Edwin D. Gilber
+ Nancy Jane Cox

3 Sophia Barnhard

3 Catherine

3 Jacob

3 John Barnhard

3 Christine

3 Barnhard

3 Leonhardt

3 Henry

3 Elizabeth

FAMILY TREES

SHERMAN

1 Rev. John Sherman b: 26 Dec 1613 Dedham, Essex, England, d: 08 Aug 1685
Watertown, MA
  + Mary Launce d: 09 Mar 1709
    2 James b: 1651 Watertown
      + Mary Walker m: 13 May 1680 Sudbury
        3 John b: 20 Nov 1683 Sudbury, MA, d: 28 Nov 1774 Brimfield
          + Abigail Stone
            4 Beriah b: 15 Sep 1705, d: 01 Aug 1792 Brimfield, MA
              + Mary Burch
                5 Thomas b: 10 Aug 1745, d: 01 Apr 1829 Weybridge, VT
                  + Zerriah Lumbard m: 07 Mar 1771
                    6 Ebenezer b: 04 Jul 1782
                      + Betsey Belding
                        7 Albert Galliton Sr. b: 24 May 1814 Chazy, NY, d: Benson, VT
                          + Margaret Honsinger d: 16 Oct 1899 Benson, VT m. 14 Feb 1839
                            8 Albert G. Sherman b: 23 Jan 1847 Chazy, NY, d: 20 Aug
                              1934 Clinton, MO
                              + Laura E. Buckingham b: 14 Jul 1850 Piqua, OH,
                              d: 07 May 1928 Clinton, MO m: 08 Dec 1879 Clinton, MO
                                9 Julia E. Sherman b: 09 Mar 1876 Clinton, MO,
                                  d: 10 Jan 1975 Middletown, NJ
                                  + William Gottlieb Bassler b: 06 Dec 1855
                                  Zelienople, PA, d: 29 Jun 1934 Zelienople, PA m: 16 Jul 1902
                                  Pittsburg, PA,
                                    10 Sherman Gilbert Bassler b: 08 Nov 1907
                                      Zelienople, PA, d: 28 Sep 1973 Red Bank, NJ
                                      + Ethel Marion Kerr b: 23 Dec 1908
                                      Greenville, PA, d: 19 Oct 1997 Middletown,
                                      NJ m: 23 Oct 1934 Butler, Adams, PA
                                        11 William Gilbert Bassler b: 06 Mar 1938
                                          Butler, Adams, PA
                                          + Eileen Schilling
                                            12 Julia Elizabeth Bassler b: 28 Jul 1967,
                                              d: 13 Jun 1997
                                            12 William Gilbert Bassler b: 22 Sep 1968,
                                              d: 10 Aug 1990
                                            12 Roseann Bassler b: 30 Apr 1972

+ Del DalPra m: 02 Aug 2000 HI

    13 William Del DalPra b: 12 Feb 2002

    13 August Del DalPra b: 22 Jul 2004

    13 Henry Del DalPra b: 30 Jul 2005

12 Elizabeth Bassler b: 23 Jun 1972

  + Christopher Jannuzzi m: 19 Oct 2001

    13 Michael Jannuzzi b: 18 Aug 2003

    13 Raymond Jannuzzi b: 19 Oct 2005

    13 Julia Jannuzzi b: 22 Feb 2008

11 Susan Bassler b: 18 Oct 1941 Butler, PA
+ Richard S. Pickford b: 07 Mar 1938
New York City, NY, d: 24 Nov 2015
m: 10 Jun 1972 Red Bank, NJ

  12 Richard Pickford III b: 05 Nov 1972
  Red Bank, NJ

  12 John Sherman Pickford b: 02 Nov 1974 in
  Beverly, MA
  + Lisa M. Menard b: 23 Nov 1976
  Brunswick, ME, m. 29 Aug 2009 Lyman, ME

    13 Lucy Jane Pickford b: 21 Apr 2011
    Portland, ME

    13 Charles Christopher Pickford
    b: 17 Jan 2013 Portland, ME

9 Mary Parsons Sherman b: 10 Nov. 1871, maiden schoolteacher

9 Laura[2] Evans b: 21 April 1874-9 d: June 1901
+ Padfield m: 28 April 1900

9 Albert[3] (Bert) Gilbert b: 6 Dec. 1868
+ Stella m: Margaret Eloise

9 John Larkin b: 25 Nov. 1881, d: 23 Nov 1902 died of typhoid

9 Wilbur Sherman b: 30 March 1885, d: 30 May 1885,
2nd person buried Englewood Cemetery

9 Eva Belle Sherman b.20 July 1886- m: Corey Padfield
then m J.H. Cowman 1930; no children

9 Carl[1] Buckingham Sherman b.25 Nov.1889- d:18 Jan 1988)
+ Katherine Markley b: 7 Nov 1893, d: 11 Oct 1988
m: 22 Nov 1919

  10 Carl[2] Markley b: 10 Dec 1920, d: 30 Dec 2014
  + Hazel Lucille Minor b: 7 Sept 1921, d: 3 March
2002, m: 19 April 1941

    11 Don Minor b: 2 Dec 1947
    + Nancy Hodina b: 25 Feb 1949 m: 24 Jan 1970
    12 Laura Elizabeth b: 13 Dec 1973
    + Paul McGeary b: 2 Aug 1969, m: 24 April 2004

        13 Charlotte Lucille b: 23 May 2006

        13 William Sherman b:19 Sept 2011

     12 Mary Katherine Sherman b: 28 March 1978

       + Christopher D. Wilson b: 30 Nov 1972

       m: 24 July 2004

        13 Chase Christopher b: 22 April 2008

        13 Cora Lucille b: 6 Sept 2014

   11 Sharon Lynn b: 4 Nov 1951

     + Robert Joseph Mayer b: 15 Aug 1941

     m: 15 Sept 1981

     12 Kyle Sherman b: 30 April 1987

       + Lindsey Herrington b: 22 Feb 1987

       m: 1 Oct 2012

10 Harold Lee b: 6 Nov 1924, d: 26 Oct 1973

   + Peggy Lee Gover b: 29 Oct 1925 m: 21 Nov 1943

   div 4 March 1963. He remarried.

   11 Jana (Jan) Lee b: 5 June 1950

     + Thomas Lynn Correll b 23 Dec 1948

     m: 24 June 1972, div., m Thomas 13 Mar 2010

     12 Kimberly Correll b 5 May 1977

       + Christopher Scripsick b. 26 Jan 1972

       m.11 June 1999

       Scripsick 26 Jan 1972 m 11 June 1999

        13 Ali Lynn Scripsick b. 2 Nov 2004

        13 Ava Marie Scripsick b.16 June 2006

        13 Audrey Lee Scripsick b.28 Sept 2010

     12 Kelly Lynn b. 2 Dec 1979

   11 Robert Keith b 1 Sept 1953 + Lupe Marie

     Marquez Pollard b: 1 July 1952 m 20 June 1981

9 Waneta Ruth Wallace + Shobe Smith 11 Oct 1942

  10 Lowell Douglas Smith b. 17 March 1945 d.

  +lst Peggy Ann Mills m. 29 Aug1965

    11 Tracy Alison Smith b. 26 March 1968 m. Shawn Morris

      12 Meredith Ann Morris

      12 Kristin b.18 Sept 1970 + Huntley Wade

        13 Morgan Huntley

        13 Ethan Huntley

    11 Kristin Wyn Smith b. 18 Sept 1970 + Huntley Wade

      12 Morgan Huntley

      + 2nd Virginia Lewis m. 30 April 1977

    11 Lowell D. Smith II 17 b. Oct 1978 + lst Jenny Thomas

      12 Hayden Parker Smith

      12 Rachel E. Smith b. 9 Oct 1987

             13 Rainy Smith
                + 3rd Barbara Huntley m. 21 March ?
             (raised Doug)

10 Mark A. Smith b. 21 Nov 1946
  + Gay Evelyn Jones m. 28 Aug 1966
     11 Kelly Anne Smith + Todd Johnson
     11 Elizabeth Elaine Smith + Tim Aubuchon
        12 Evan
        12 Esme
        12 Eric

10 Connie Lyn Smith b. 15 Feb 1956 d.
  + James R. Mize 16 m. Aug 1976
     11 Marcianna Lyn Mize b. 20 June 1978
       + K Faudricle
        12 Nathan
        12 Noah
        12 Nickolas
     11 Heather Janelle Mize b. 22 March 1982
       + Chris Moore

FAMILY TREES

BASSLER

1 Franz Bassler
+ Barbra Kafer
  2 Gottlieb W Bassler b: 10 Dec 1813 Loganthal, Switzerland, d: 03 Oct 1868 Pittsburg, PA
  + Elizabeth Catherine Gilbert b: 18 May 1820 Gettysburg, PA, d: 11 Jun 1908 Zelienople, PA, m: 31 Oct 1844 Athens,TN
    3 William Gottlieb Bassler b: 06 Dec 1855 Zelienople, PA, d: 29 Jun 1934 Zelienople, PA
    + Julia E. Sherman b: 09 Mar 1876 Clinton, MO, d: 10 Jan 1975 Middletown, NJ, m: 16 Jul 1902 Pittsburg, PA
      4 Sherman Gilbert Bassler b: 08 Nov 1907 Zelienople, PA, d: 28 Sep 1973 Red Bank, NJ
      + Ethel Marion Kerr b: 23 Dec 1908 Greenville, PA, d: 19 Oct 1997 Middletown, NJ m: 23 Oct 1934 Butler, Adams, PA, USA
        5 William Gilbert Bassler b: 06 Mar 1938 Butler, Adams, PA, USA
        + Eileen Schilling b. 23 Jan 1939 Plainfield, NJ m. 10 Sept 1966 Atlantic Highlands, NJ
          6 Julia Elizabeth Bassler b: 28 Jul 1967, d: 13 Jun 1997
          6 William Gilbert Bassler b: 22 Sep 1968, d: 10 Aug 1990
          6 Roseann Bassler b: 30 Apr 1972
          + Del DalPra m: 02 Aug 2000 HI
            7 William Del DalPra b: 12 Feb 2002
            7 August Del DalPra b: 22 Jul 2004
            7 Henry Del DalPra b: 30 Jul 2005
          6 Elizabeth Bassler b: 23 Jun 1972
          + Christopher Jannuzzi m: 19 Oct 2001
            7 Michael Jannuzzi b: 18 Aug 2003
            7 Raymond Jannuzzi b: 19 Oct 2005
            7 Julia Jannuzzi b: 22 Feb 2008
        5 Susan Bassler b: 18 Oct 1941 Butler, PA
        + Richard S. Pickford b: 07 Mar 1938 New York City, NY, d: 24 Nov 2015, m: 10 Jun 1972 Red Bank, NJ
          6 Richard Pickford III b: 05 Nov 1972 Red Bank, NJ
          6 John Sherman Pickford b: 02 Nov 1974 Beverly, MA
          + Lisa M. Menard b: 23 Nov 1976 Brunswick,E, m. 29 Aug 2009 Lyman, ME

       7 Lucy Jane Pickford b: 21 Apr 2011 Portland, ME

       7 Charles Christopher Pickford b: 17 Jan 2013 Portland, ME

3 Susanah Bassler

3 Louisa Dill Bassler b: 09 Apr 1848 Zelienople, PA, d: 21 Mar 1859 Zelienople, PA

3 Francis Bassler b: Zelienople, PA, d: 25 Mar 1854 Zelienople, Butler, PA

3 Mary Atlee Bassler b: 24 Nov 1852 Zelienople, PA, d: 05 Dec 1868 Zelienople, PA

3 Augustus Herman Bassler b: 28 Sep 1858 Zelienople, PA, d: 11 Apr 1859 Zelienople, PA

3 Anna Elizabeth Bassler b: 16 Apr 1861 Zelienople, PA, d: 26 Feb 1862 Zelienople, PA

INDEX

www.ingramcontent.com/pod-product-compliance
Lightning Source LLC
Chambersburg PA
CBHW080338290526
45790CB00010B/3743